COMPACT ATLAS
Britain

Contents

II **Route planning maps** with key to map pages

VIII **Key to road map symbols**

2 **Road maps at 3.3 miles to 1 inch**

289 **Index** to road maps of Great Britain

www.philips-maps.co.uk

First published in 2006 by Philip's
a division of Octopus Publishing Group Ltd
www.octopusbooks.co.uk
2–4 Heron Quays, London E14 4JP
An Hachette UK Company
www.hachettelivre.co.uk

Third edition 2009
First impression 2009

ISBN 978-0-540-09313-7

Cartography by Philip's
Copyright © 2009 Philip's

Ordnance Survey®

This product includes mapping data licensed from Ordnance
Survey®, with the permission of the Controller of
Her Majesty's Stationery Office. © Crown copyright 2009.
All rights reserved. Licence number 100011710

Data for the speed cameras provided by
PocketGPSWorld.com Ltd.

Information for National Parks, Areas of Outstanding Natural
Beauty, National Trails and Country Parks in Wales supplied by
the Countryside Council for Wales.

Information for National Parks, Areas of Outstanding Natural
Beauty, National Trails and Country Parks in England supplied
by Natural England.

Data for Regional Parks, Long Distance Footpaths and Country
Parks in Scotland provided by Scottish Natural Heritage.

Gaelic name forms used in the Western Isles provided by
Comhairle nan Eilean.

Data for the National Nature Reserves in England provided by
Natural England.

Data for the National Nature Reserves in Wales provided by
Countryside Council for Wales. Darparwyd data'n ymwneud â
Gwarchodfeydd Natur Cenedlaethol Cymru gan Gyngor Cefn
Gwlad Cymru.

Information on the location of National Nature Reserves in
Scotland was provided by Scottish Natural Heritage.

Data for National Scenic Areas in Scotland provided by the
Scottish Executive Office. Crown copyright material is
reproduced with the permission of the Controller of HMSO
and the Queen's Printer for Scotland. Licence number
C02W0003960.

Printed in China

*Independent research survey, from research carried out by
Outlook Research Limited, 2005/06.

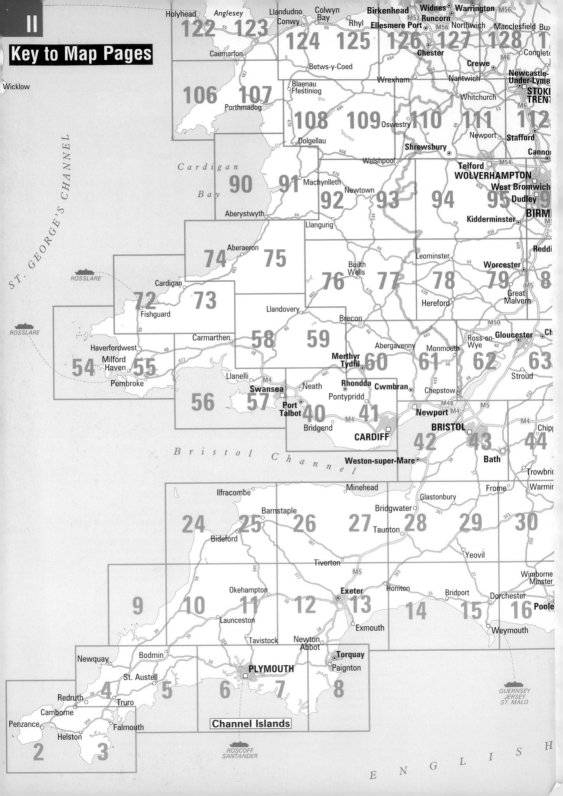

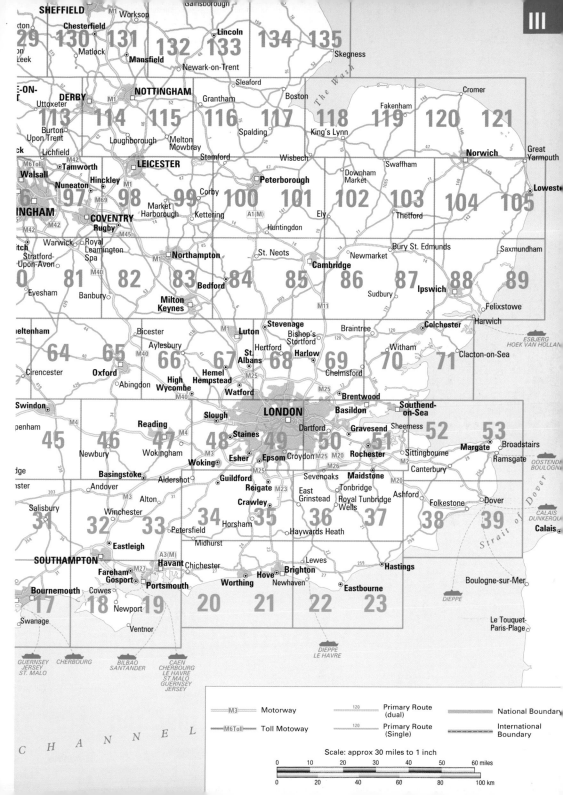

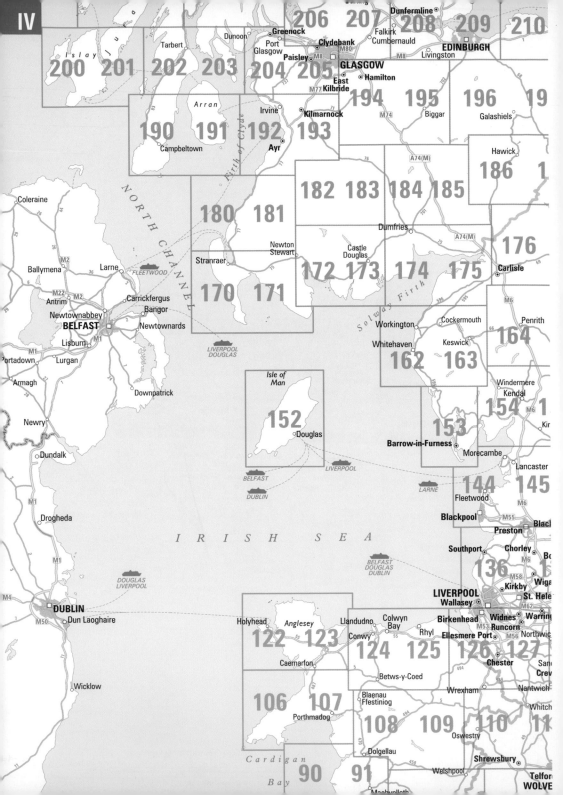

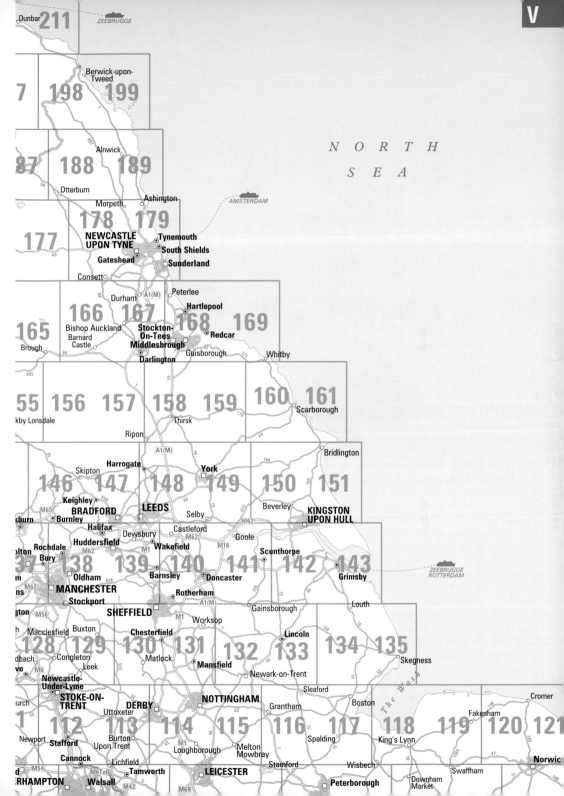

Dunbar **211**

ZEEBRUGGE

7 Berwick-upon-Tweed **198** **199**

N O R T H

S E A

87 Alnwick **188** **189**

Otterburn

Morpeth○ Ashington

AMSTERDAM

178 **179**

177 **NEWCASTLE UPON TYNE** Tynemouth

South Shields

Gateshead □Sunderland

Consett○

166 Durham **167** A1(M) Peterlee

Hartlepool

168 **169**

165 Bishop Auckland Stockton-On-Tees ○Redcar

Barnard Castle **Middlesbrough**

Brough○ **Darlington**

Guisborough Whitby

55 **156** **157** **158** **159** **160** **161**

Thirsk Scarborough

kby Lonsdale

Ripon

A1(M) Bridlington

146 Skipton Harrogate **147** **148** York **149** **150** **151**

Keighley **BRADFORD** **LEEDS** Beverley **KINGSTON UPON HULL**

kburn Burnley Halifax Selby

○Rochdale Huddersfield Dewsbury Castleford Goole

Bury M62 **Wakefield** M62

37 **138** **139** **140** **141** **142** **143**

Oldham Barnsley Scunthorpe

MANCHESTER ○Doncaster Grimsby

ZEEBRUGGE ROTTERDAM

Stockport Rotherham

ton M56 **SHEFFIELD** A1(M) Louth

Macclesfield Buxton Worksop Gainsborough

128 **129** **130** Chesterfield **131** Lincoln **132** **133** **134** **135**

Congleton Matlock Skegness

Leek **Mansfield** Newark-on-Trent

Newcastle-Under-Lyme Sleaford *The Wash* Cromer

STOKE-ON-TRENT **DERBY** **NOTTINGHAM** Grantham Boston Fakenham

Uttoxeter

1 **112** **113** **114** **115** **116** **117** **118** **119** **120** **121**

Newport **Stafford** Burton Upon Trent Loughborough Spalding King's Lynn

Cannock Lichfield Melton Mowbray Stamford Wisbech Swaffham **Norwic**

d M54 **Tamworth** Downham Market

RHAMPTON **Walsall** **LEICESTER** Peterborough

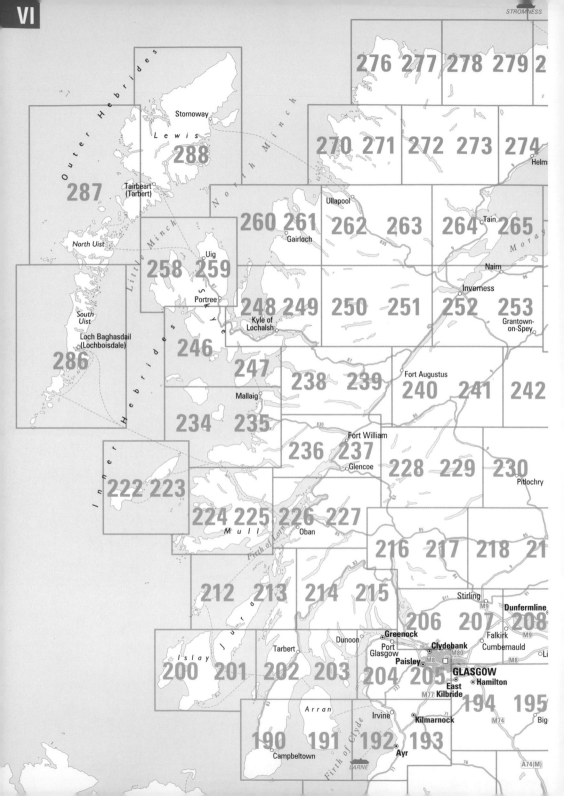

STROMNESS

Outer Hebrides

Lewis
Stornoway

276 277 278 279 2

270 271 272 273 274
Helm

287

Tairbeart
(Tarbert)

North Minch

288

Little Minch

North Uist

260 261
Gairloch

Ullapool

262 263 264 265
Tain

Moray

258 259
Uig

Portree

Skye

248 249 250 251 252 253
Grantown-
on-Spey

Nairn

Inverness

South Uist

Loch Baghasdail
(Lochboisdale)

246

Kyle of
Lochalsh

286

247

Mallaig

238 239

Fort Augustus

240 241 242

Inner Hebrides

234 235

830

236 237
Glencoe

Fort William

228 229 230
Pitlochry

222 223

224 225 226 227
Mull   Oban

216 217 218 21

212 213 214 215

Stirling

206 207 208
Falkirk   Dunfermline
Cumbernauld   Li

Islay

Dunoon

Greenock
Port
Glasgow   Clydebank
Paisley   M8

GLASGOW

200 201 202 203
Tarbert

204 205
East
Kilbride   Hamilton

M77

Arran

194 195
Big

Irvine   Kilmarnock

M74

190 191 192 193
Campbeltown   Ayr

LARNE

A74(M)

Firth of Clyde

Jura

Firth of Lorn

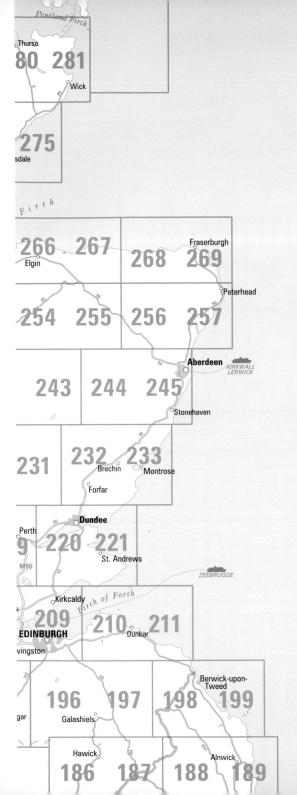

Pentland Firth

Thurso

80 **281**

Wick

275

sdale

Firth

266 **267**

Elgin

Fraserburgh

268 **269**

Peterhead

254 **255** **256** **257**

Aberdeen

KIRKWALL
LERWICK

243 **244** **245**

Stonehaven

231 **232** **233**

Brechin

Montrose

Forfar

Dundee

Perth

9 **220** **221**

St. Andrews

ZEEBRUGGE

Kirkcaldy

Firth of Forth

209 **210** **211**

EDINBURGH

Dunbar

vingston

Berwick-upon-Tweed

196 **197** **198** **199**

Galashiels

ar

Hawick

Alnwick

186 **187** **188** **189**

Shetland

284

M a i n l a n d

Lerwick

285

ABERDEEN
KIRKWALL

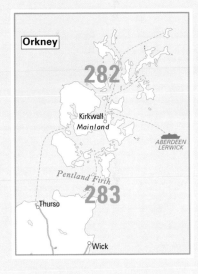

Orkney

282

Kirkwall
Mainland

ABERDEEN
LERWICK

Pentland Firth

283

Thurso

Wick

N O R T H

S E A

Road map symbols

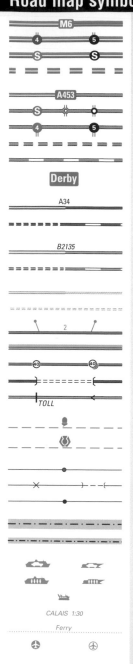

Motorway, toll motorway

Motorway junction – full, restricted access

Motorway service area – full, restricted access

Motorway under construction

Primary route – dual, single carriageway

Service area, roundabout, multi-level junction

Numbered junction – full, restricted access

Primary route under construction

Narrow primary route

Primary destination

A road – dual, single carriageway

A road under construction, narrow A road

B road – dual, single carriageway

B road under construction, narrow B road

Minor road – over 4 metres, under 4 metres wide

Minor road with restricted access

Distance in miles

Scenic route

Speed camera – single, multiple

Tunnel

Toll, steep gradient – arrow points downhill

National trail – England and Wales

Long distance footpath – Scotland

Railway with station

Level crossing, tunnel

Preserved railway with station

National boundary

County / unitary authority boundary

Car ferry, catamaran

Passenger ferry, catamaran

Hovercraft

Ferry destination, journey time – hrs : mins

Car ferry – river crossing

Principal airport, other airport

Relief

Feet	metres
3000	914
2600	792
2200	671
1800	549
1400	427
1000	305
0	0

Speed Cameras

Fixed camera locations are shown using the ⓸ symbol.

In congested areas the ⓸ symbol is used to show that there are two or more cameras on the road indicated.

Due to the restrictions of scale the camera locations are only approximate and cannot indicate the operating direction of the camera. Mobile camera sites, and cameras located on roads not included on the mapping are not shown. Where two or more cameras are shown on the same road, drivers are warned that this may indicate that a SPEC system is in operation. These cameras use the time taken to drive between the two camera positions to calculate the speed of the vehicle.

Road map symbols

National park

Area of Outstanding Natural Beauty – England and Wales
National Scenic Area – Scotland
forest park / regional park / national forest

Woodland

Beach

Linear antiquity

Roman road

Hillfort, battlefield – with date

Viewpoint, nature reserve, spot height – in metres

Golf course, youth hostel, sporting venue

Camp site, caravan site, camping and caravan site

Shopping village, park and ride

29 Adjoining page number – road maps

Road map scale 1: 212 857 or 3·36 miles to 1 inch

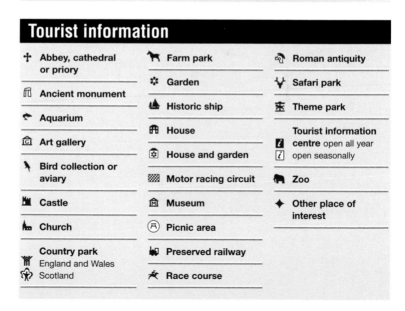

Tourist information

✝ Abbey, cathedral or priory

🏛 Ancient monument

🐟 Aquarium

🖼 Art gallery

🐦 Bird collection or aviary

🏰 Castle

⛪ Church

🎪 Country park
England and Wales
Scotland

🐴 Farm park

❋ Garden

⚓ Historic ship

🏠 House

🏡 House and garden

🏁 Motor racing circuit

🏛 Museum

Ⓐ Picnic area

🚂 Preserved railway

🏃 Race course

🐎 Roman antiquity

Safari park

🎢 Theme park

Tourist information
ℹ centre open all year
ℹ open seasonally

🐘 Zoo

✦ Other place of interest

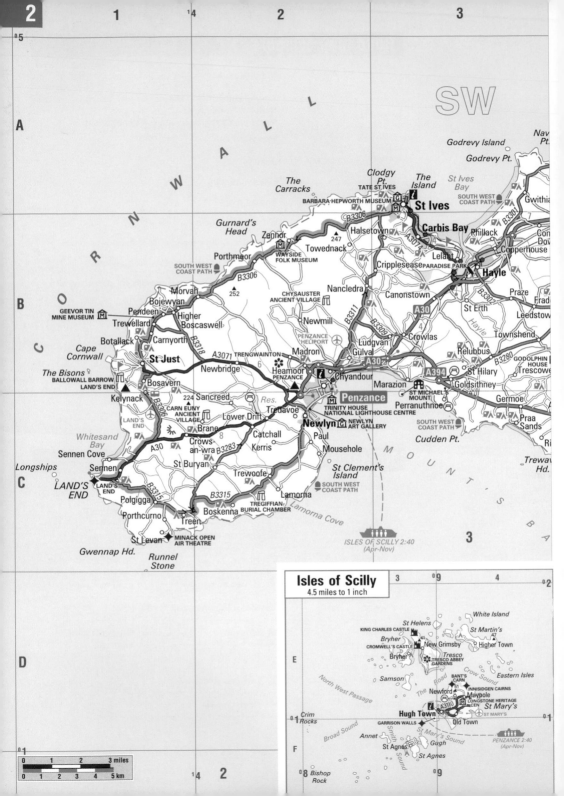

2

SW

CORNWALL

A

Godrevy Island
Godrevy Pt.
Nav
Pt.

The Carracks
Clodgy Pt.
TATE ST IVES
The Island
St Ives Bay
SOUTH WEST COAST PATH
Gwithia

BARBARA HEPWORTH MUSEUM
St Ives
Carbis Bay
Rhillack
Con
Dov

B3306

Halsetown
Copperhouse

Gurnard's Head
Zennor
247
Towednack
Lelant
PARADISE PARK
CRIPPLESEASE
Hayle

Porthmeor
WAYSIDE FOLK MUSEUM
Canonstown
Praze

B

SOUTH WEST COAST PATH
B3306
252
Morvah
Bojewyan
CHYSAUSTER ANCIENT VILLAGE
Nancledra
St Erth
Frad

GEEVOR TIN MINE MUSEUM
Pendeen
Higher Boscaswell
Newmill
B3311
Leedstow

Trewellard
B3318
PENZANCE HELIPORT
Ludgvan
Townshend

Botallack
Carnyorth
TRENGWAINTON
Madron
Gulval
A30
Relubbus
B3280
GODOLPHIN HOUSE
Trescowe

Cape Cornwall
St Just
A3071
6
Heamoor
PENZANCE
Chyandour
St Hilary
Goldsithney

The Bisons
BALLOWALL BARROW
LAND'S END
Bosavern
Newbridge
Penzance
Marazion
ST MICHAEL'S MOUNT
Germoe

Kelynack
224
Sancreed
CARN EUNY ANCIENT VILLAGE
Res.
TRINITY HOUSE NATIONAL LIGHTHOUSE CENTRE
Perranuthnoe
Praa Sands

LAND'S END
Lower Drift
Tredavoe
Newlyn
NEWLYN ART GALLERY
SOUTH WEST COAST PATH

C

Whitesand Bay
Brane
Catchall
Paul
Cudden Pt.
Trewa
Hd.

Sennen Cove
A30
Crows-an-wra
B3283
Kerris
Mousehole

Longships
Sennen
St Buryan
St Clement's Island

LAND'S END
LAND'S END
B3315
B3315
Trewoofe
Lamorna
SOUTH WEST COAST PATH

Polgigga
TREGIFFIAN BURIAL CHAMBER
Boskenna
Lamorna Cove

Porthcurno
Treen

St Levan
MINACK OPEN AIR THEATRE

Gwennap Hd.
Runnel Stone

MOUNT'S BA

ISLES OF SCILLY 2:40
(Apr-Nov)

3

Isles of Scilly
4.5 miles to 1 inch

White Island

St Helens
St Martin's
47

KING CHARLES CASTLE
Bryher
New Grimsby
Higher Town

E

CROMWELL'S CASTLE
Bryher
TRESCO ABBEY GARDENS
Tresco
Eastern Isles

North West Passage
Samson
BANT'S CARN
INNISIDGEN CAIRNS
LONGSTONE HERITAGE CEN.
Crow Sound

Newford
Maypole
St Mary's

Crim Rocks
Hugh Town
Old Town

GARRISON WALLS
St Mary's Sound

F

Broad Sound
Annet
St Agnes
Gugh
Smith Sound
St Mary's Sound
PENZANCE 2:40
(Apr-Nov)

Bishop Rock
St Agnes

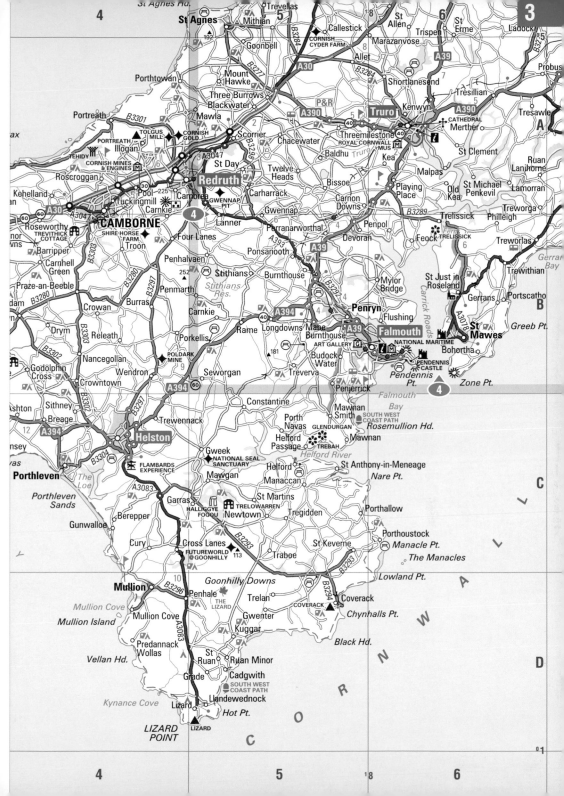

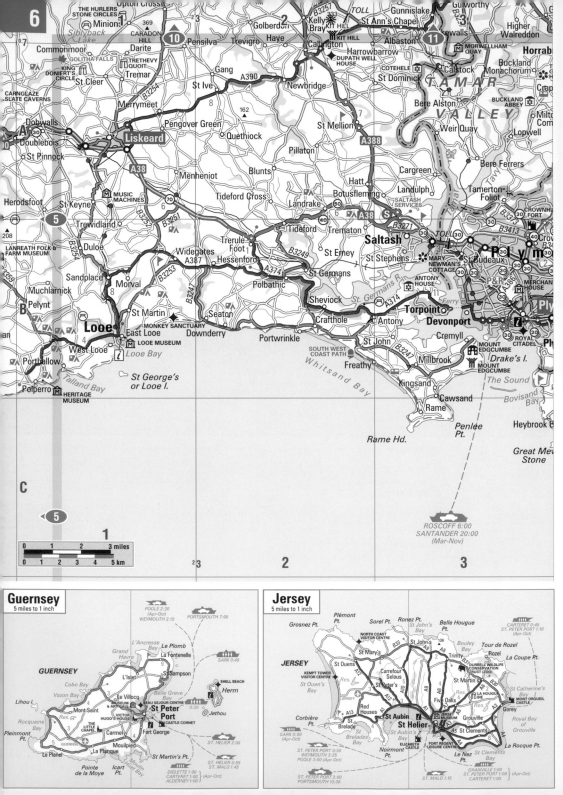

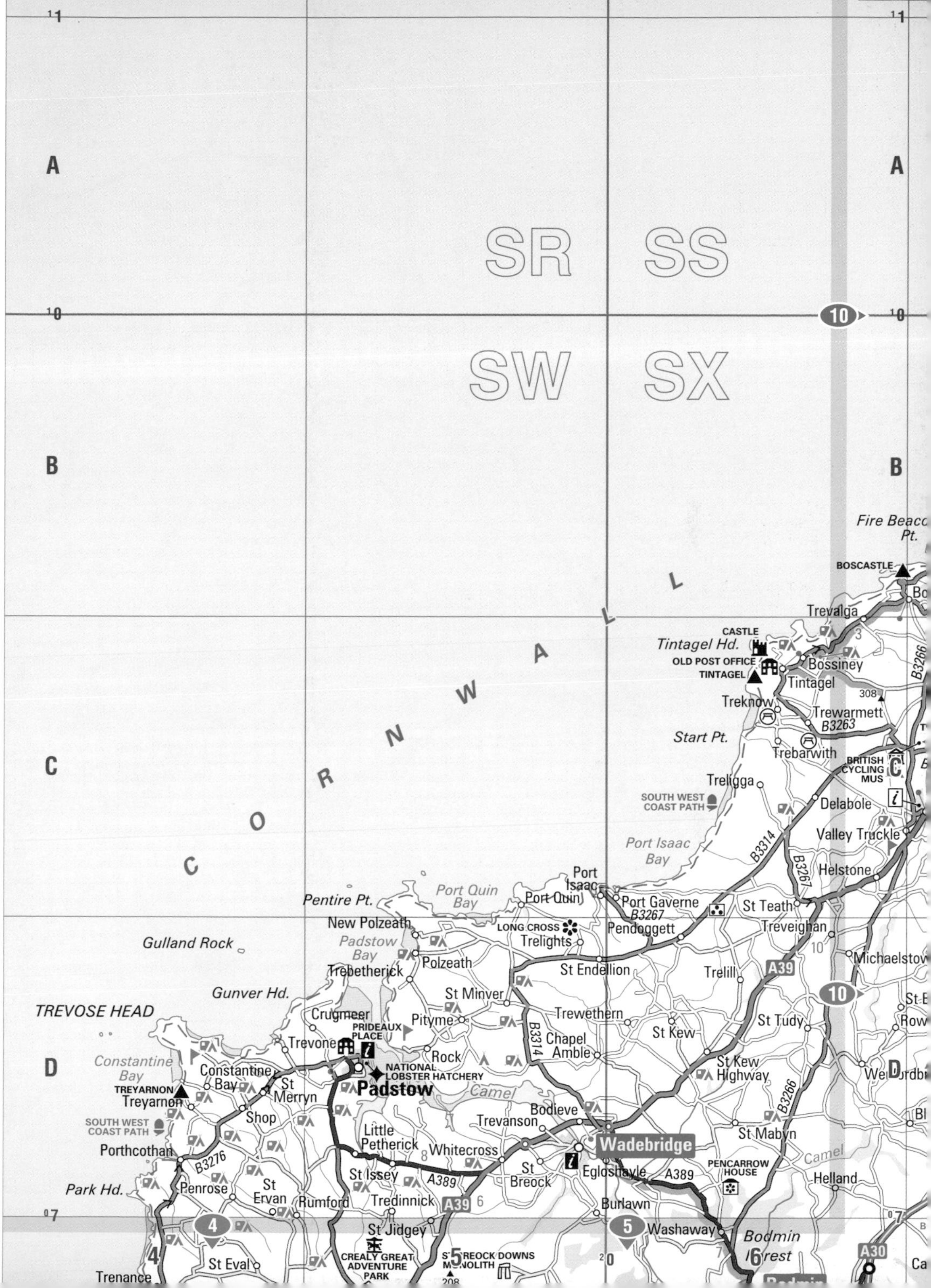

4 **5** 20 **6**

A **A**

SR SS

10 10

SW SX

B **B**

Fire Beaco
Pt.

BOSCASTLE

Trevalga Bo

CASTLE
Tintagel Hd.
OLD POST OFFICE
TINTAGEL Bossiney
Tintagel

Treknow B3263

Start Pt. Trewarmett
308 B3263
Trebarwith

BRITISH
CYLING
MUS **C**
C R
SOUTH WEST
COAST PATH Treligga Delabole
N
Valley Truckle

A
Port Isaac B3314 Helstone
Bay
C Pentire Pt. W Port B3267
O Port Quin Isaac Michaelstov
Gulland Rock Bay Port Quin Port Gaverne St Teath
New Polzeath B3267 Treveighan
Padstow LONG CROSS Pendoggett
Bay Trelights A39 10 St E
Polzeath Trelill Row
Trebetherick St Endellion A39
TREVOSE HEAD Gunver Hd. Trewethern St Tudy 10
Crugmeer St Minver Michaelstov
PRIDEAUX Pityme Trewethern St Kew St E
D PLACE Chapel Row
Constantine Trevone Rock Amble St Kew
Bay Camel Highway Weldrb **D**
TREYARNON NATIONAL Camel St Kew B3266
Treyarnon Constantine LOBSTER HATCHERY Highway
Bay St **Padstow** Bodieve St Mabyn
Merryn Trevanson
SOUTH WEST Shop
COAST PATH Trevanson B
Porthcothan Little **Wadebridge**
B3276 Petherick Eglosheyle A389 Helland
St Whitecross St PENCARROW
Park Hd. Ervan St Issey A389 Breock HOUSE
Penrose 8 6 Burlawn Camel
Rumford Tredinnick A39 Bodmin
4 St Jidgey 5 Washaway 6 orest A30 Ca
Trenance St Eval CREALY GREAT REOCK DOWNS 5
ADVENTURE MONOLITH
PARK 2 208

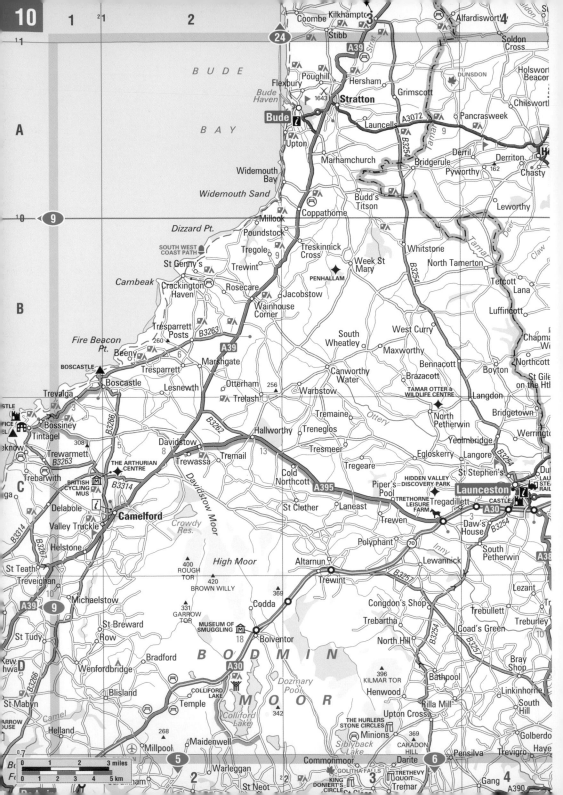

BUDE BAY

Kilkhampton
Coombe
Alfardisworthy
Stibb
Poughill
Flexbury
Hersham
Grimscott
Chilsworthy
Bude Haven
Stratton
Launcells
Pancrasweek
Bude
Upton
Marhamchurch
Bridgerule
Derril
Derriton
Chasty
Widemouth Bay
Widemouth Sand
Budd's Titson
Pyworthy
Leworthy
Dizzard Pt.
Millook
Coppathorne
Poundstock
SOUTH WEST COAST PATH
Tregole
Treskinnick Cross
Whitstone
North Tamerton
Tetcott
Lana
St Genny's
Trewint
Week St Mary
Luffincott
Cambeak
PENHALLAM
Crackington Haven
Rosecare
Jacobstow
Chapman
Wainhouse Corner
South Wheatley
West Curry
Maxworthy
Northcott
Tresparrett Posts
Fire Beacon Pt.
Beeny
Marshgate
Canworthy Water
Bennacott
Brazacott
Boyton
St Giles on the Htl
BOSCASTLE
Trevalga
Boscastle
Tresparrett
Lesnewth
Otterham
Trelash
Warbstow
TAMAR OTTER & WILDLIFE CENTRE
Langdon
Bridgetown
Werrington
Bossiney
Tintagel
Trewarmett
Trebarwith
Davidstow
Hallworthy
Tremaine
Treneglos
Tresmeer
Tregeare
North Petherwin
Yeolmbridge
Langore
St Stephen's
THE ARTHURIAN CENTRE
BRITISH CYCLING MUS
Trewassa
Tremail
Cold Northcott
HIDDEN VALLEY DISCOVERY PARK
Launceston
Delabole
Camelford
St Clether
Laneast
Piper's Pool
TRETHORNE LEISURE FARM
Tregadillett
CASTLE
Valley Truckle
Helstone
Crowdy Res.
Trewen
Daw's House
South Petherwin
St Teath
Treveighan
Michaelstow
High Moor
ROUGH TOR
BROWN WILLY
Altarnun
Trewint
Lewannick
Lezant
Trebullett
Treburley
St Breward
Row
GARROW TOR
MUSEUM OF SMUGGLING
Codda
Congdon's Shop
Trebartha
Coad's Green
St Tudy
Bolventor
North Hill
Bray Shop
Wenfordbridge
Bradford
Blisland
Temple
COLLIFORD LAKE
KILMAR TOR
Henwood
Bathpool
Linkinhorne
South Hill
St Mabyn
BODMIN MOOR
Dozmary Pool
Colliford Lake
Rilla Mill
Upton Cross
Golberdo
Helland
Maidenwell
Millpool
THE HURLERS STONE CIRCLES
Minions
CARADON HILL
Pensilva
Trevigro
Haye
Warleggan
Commonmoor
GOLITHA FALLS
Darite
TRETHEVY QUOIT
St Neot
KING DONIERT'S CICLES
Gang

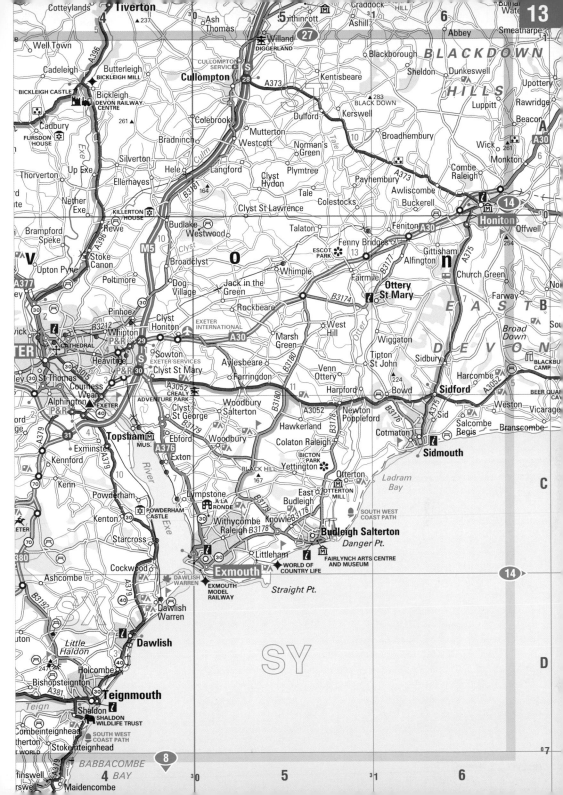

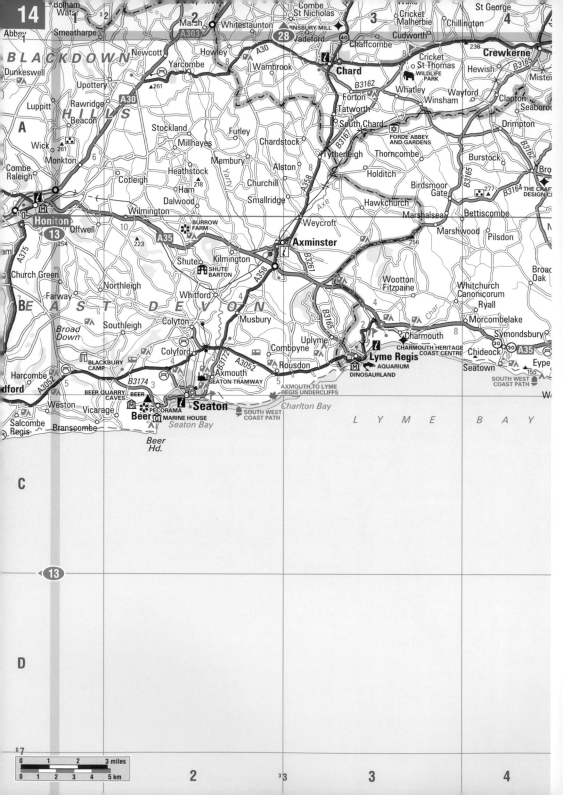

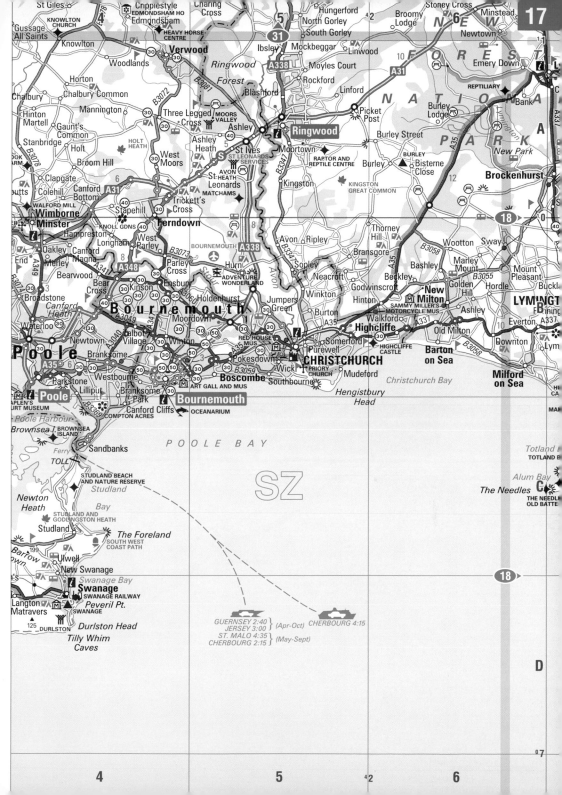

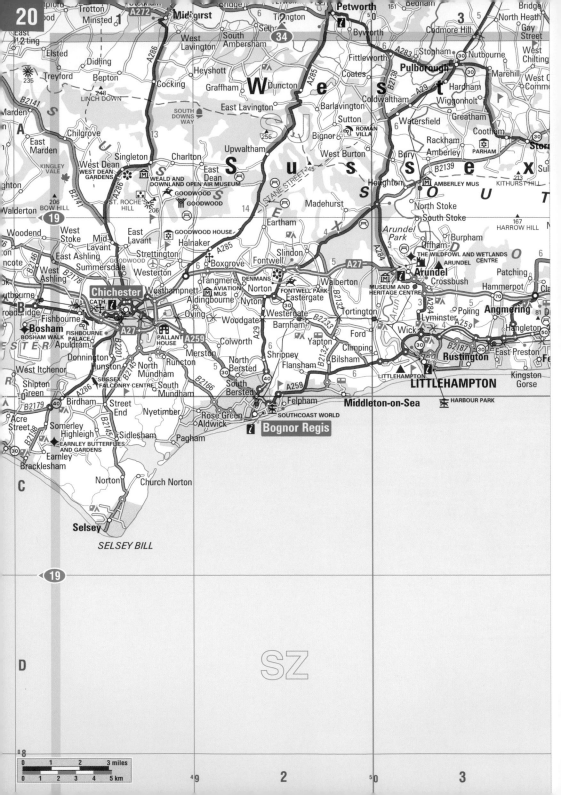

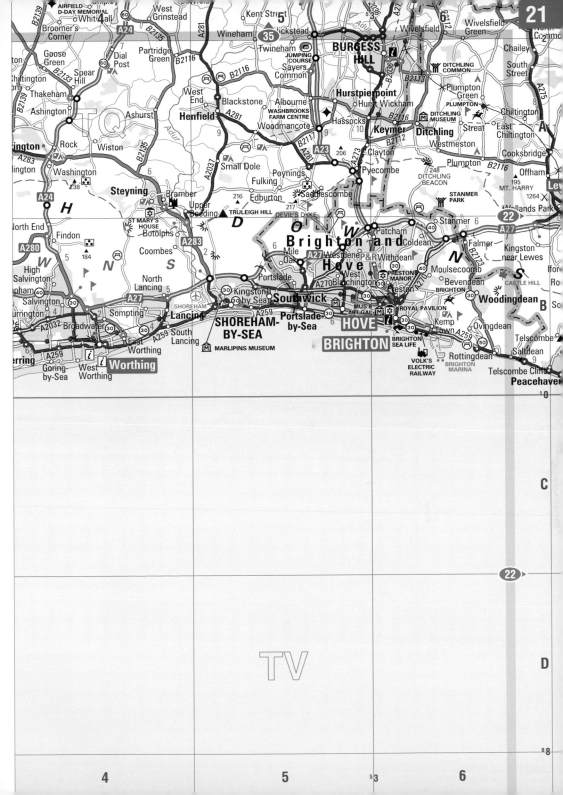

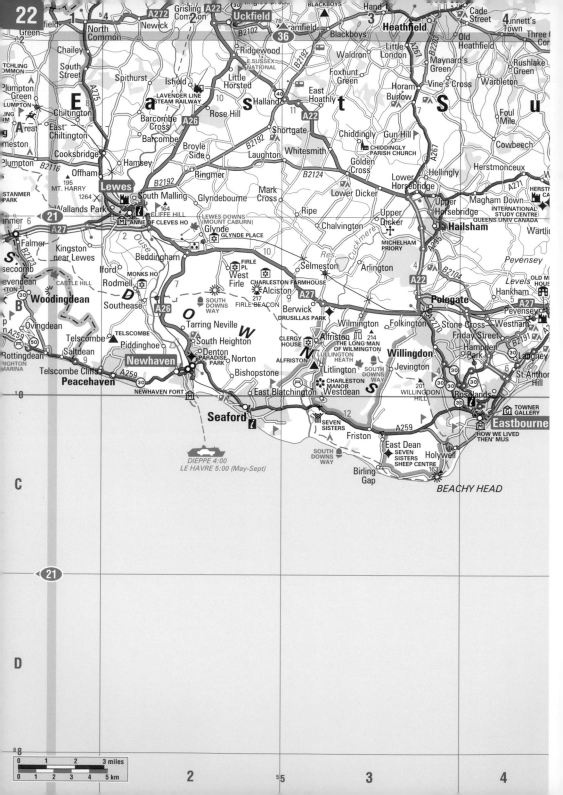

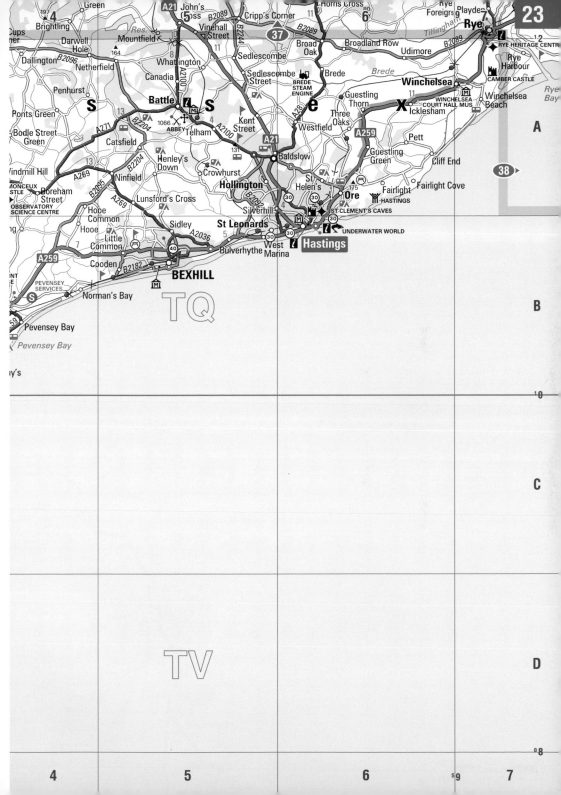

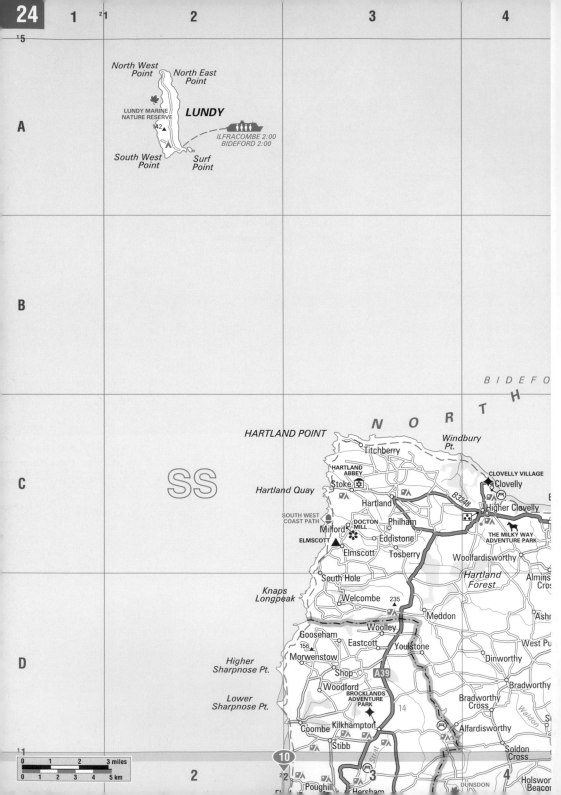

1 21 2 3 4

15

A

North West Point
North East Point

LUNDY MARINE
NATURE RESERVE

LUNDY

142

ILFRACOMBE 2:00
BIDEFORD 2:00

South West Point

Surf Point

B

BIDEFO

NORTH

C

HARTLAND POINT

Titchberry

Windbury Pt.

HARTLAND ABBEY

CLOVELLY VILLAGE

Clovelly

SS

Hartland Quay

Stoke

Hartland

B3248

Higher Clovelly

SOUTH WEST COAST PATH

Milford

DOCTON MILL

Philham

THE MILKY WAY ADVENTURE PARK

ELMSCOTT

Eddistone

Elmscott

Tosberry

Woolfardisworthy

South Hole

Hartland Forest

Almins Cross

Knaps Longpeak

Welcombe 235

Meddon

Ashr

D

156

Woolley

Gooseham

Eastcott

Youlstone

West Pu

Morwenstow

Dinworthy

Higher Sharpnose Pt.

Shop

A39

Woodford

BROCKLANDS ADVENTURE PARK

14

Bradworthy

Lower Sharpnose Pt.

Bradworthy Cross

Coombe

Kilkhampton

Alfardisworthy

Soldon

Stibb

Cross

11

Waldon

10

0 1 2 3 miles
0 1 2 3 4 5 km

2

22

Poughill

3

4

Holswor

DUNSDON

Beacon

2

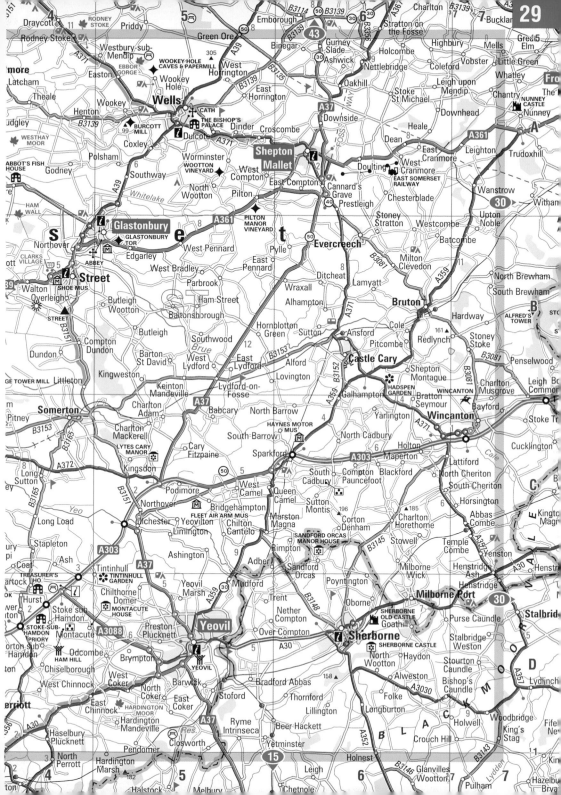

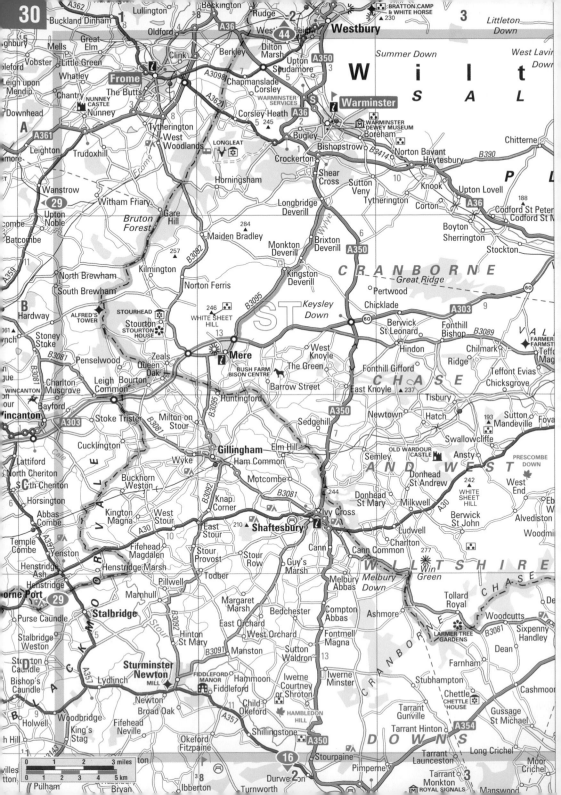

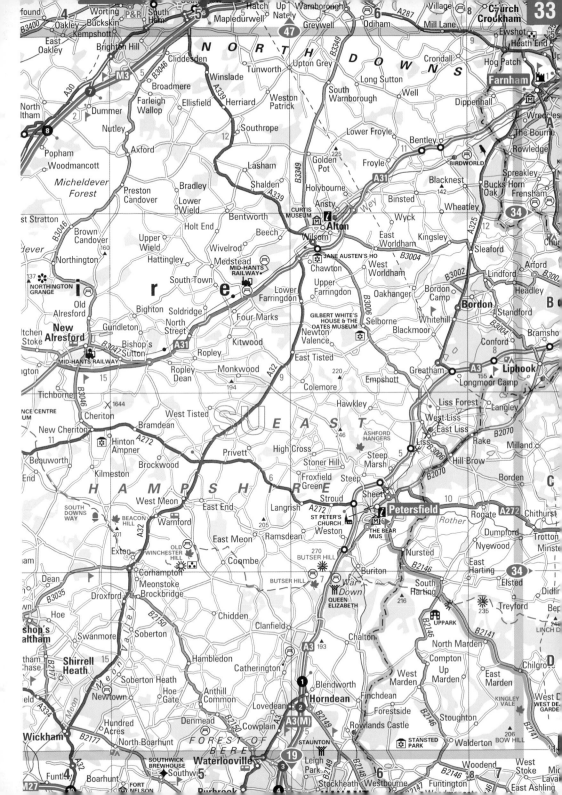

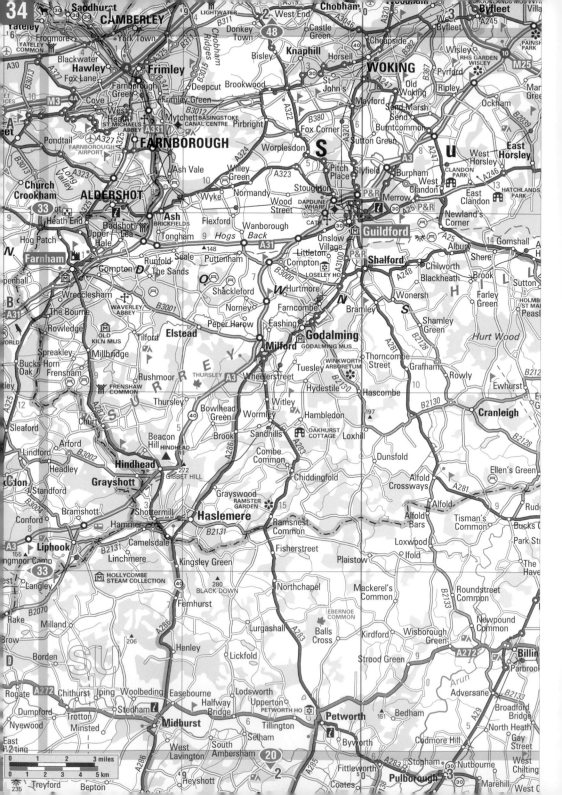

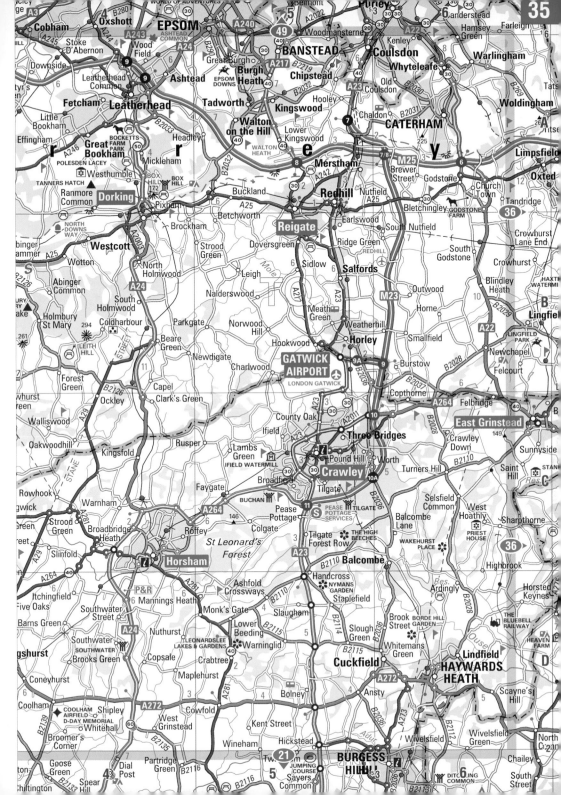

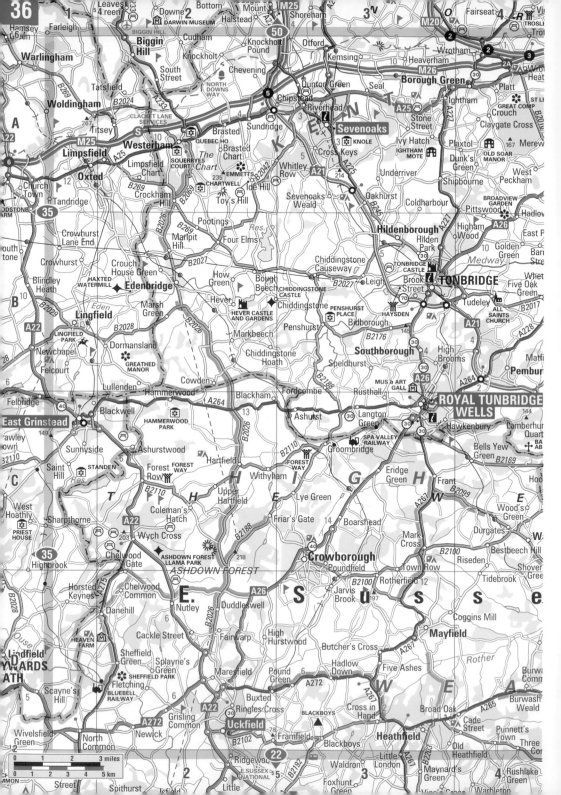

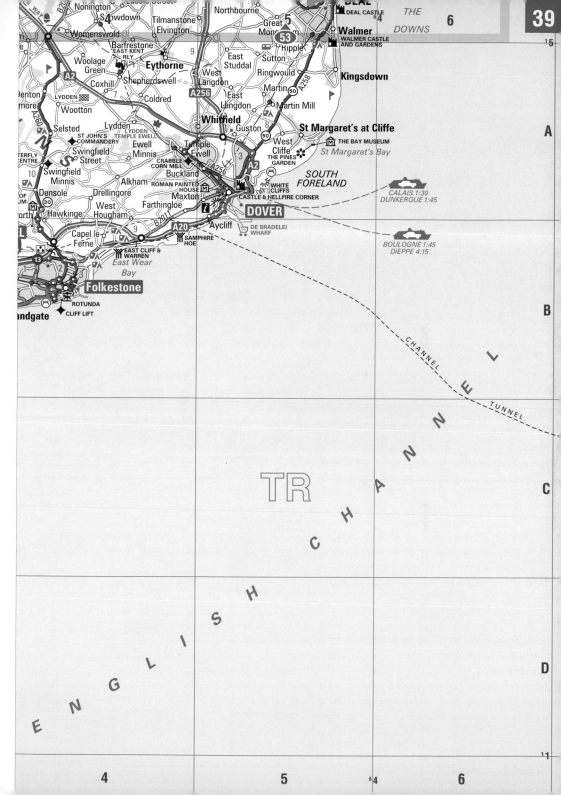

THE DOWNS

6

15

Nonington
Snowdown
Womenswold
Tilmanstone
Elvington
Northbourne
Great Mongeham
53
DEAL CASTLE
Walmer
WALMER CASTLE AND GARDENS

Woolage Green
Barfrestone
EAST KENT RLY
Eythorne
Shepherdswell
Coxhill
A2
LYDDEN
Coldred
Wootton
East Studdal
Sutton
Ripple
West Langdon
Ringwould
Martin
50
A258
Kingsdown

Selsted
ST JOHN'S COMMANDERY
Lydden
LYDDEN TEMPLE EWELL
Ewell Minnis
Temple Ewell
East Langdon
Martin Mill
Whitfield
Guston
50
St Margaret's at Cliffe
West Cliffe
THE PINES GARDEN
THE BAY MUSEUM
St Margaret's Bay

A

Swingfield Street
Swingfield Minnis
Alkham
CRABBLE CORN MILL
Buckland
Temple Ewell
A256
A2
SOUTH FORELAND

Densole
Drellingore
ROMAN PAINTED HOUSE
Maxton
Farthingloe
WHITE CLIFFS
CASTLE & HELLFIRE CORNER
DOVER

Hawkinge
West Hougham
Capel le Ferne
9
Aycliff
DE BRADELEI WHARF
A20

CALAIS 1:30
DUNKERQUE 1:45

BOULOGNE 1:45
DIEPPE 4:15

13
EAST CLIFF & WARREN
East Wear Bay
SAMPHIRE HOE

Folkestone
ROTUNDA
CLIFF LIFT
andgate

B

CHANNEL

TUNNEL

C

TR

C H A N N E L

C

E N G L I S H

D

11

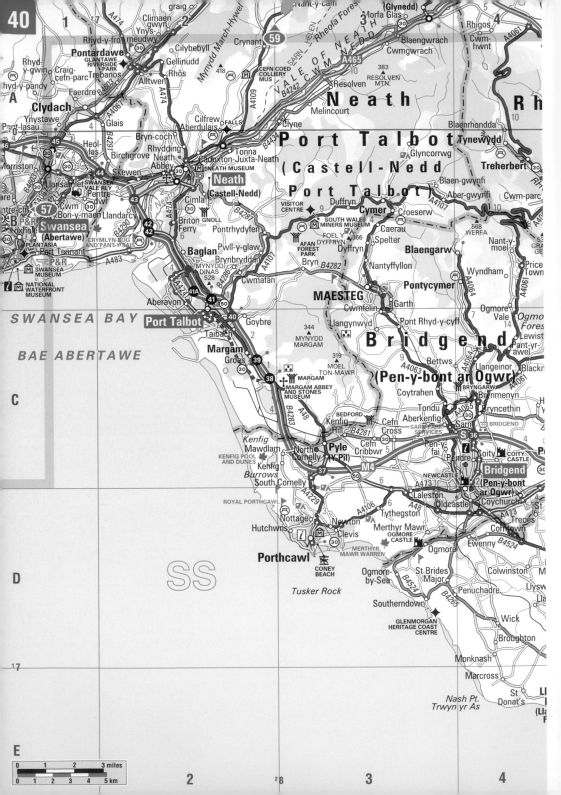

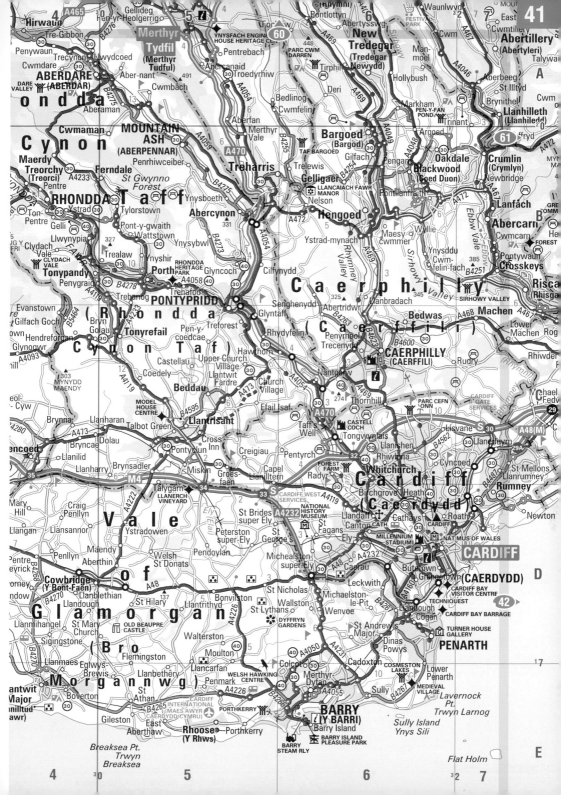

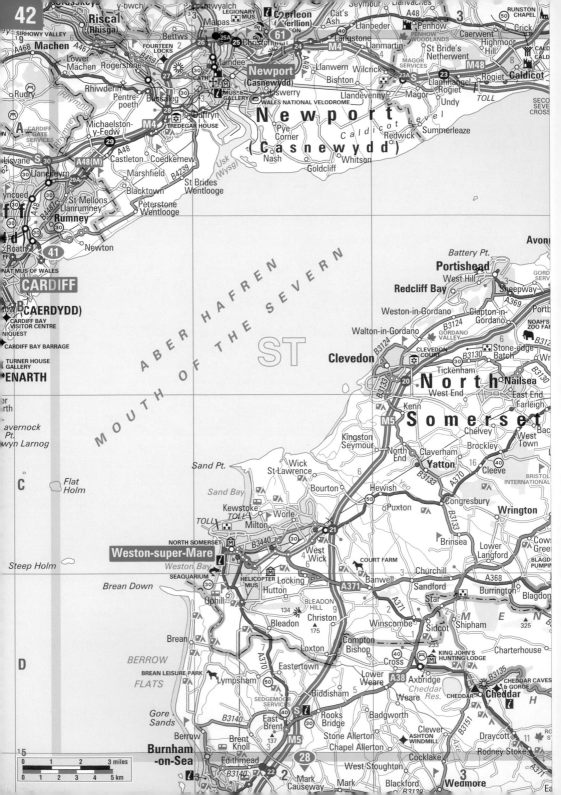

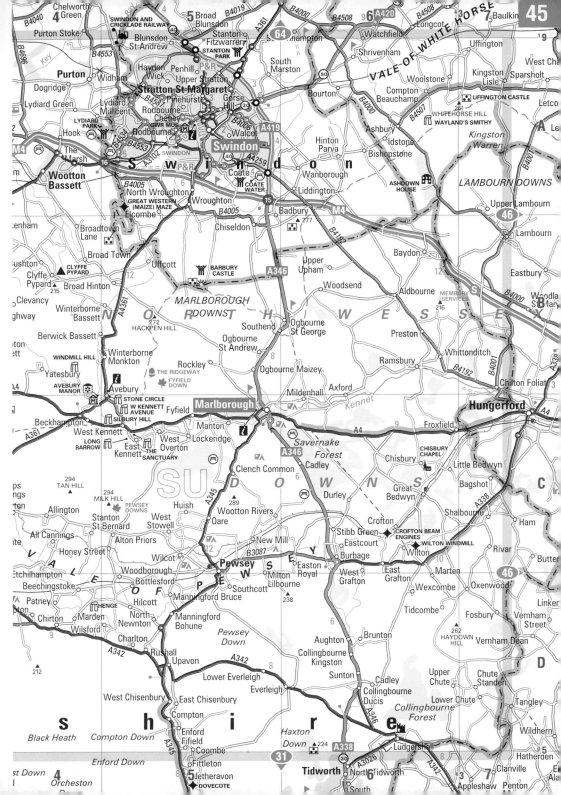

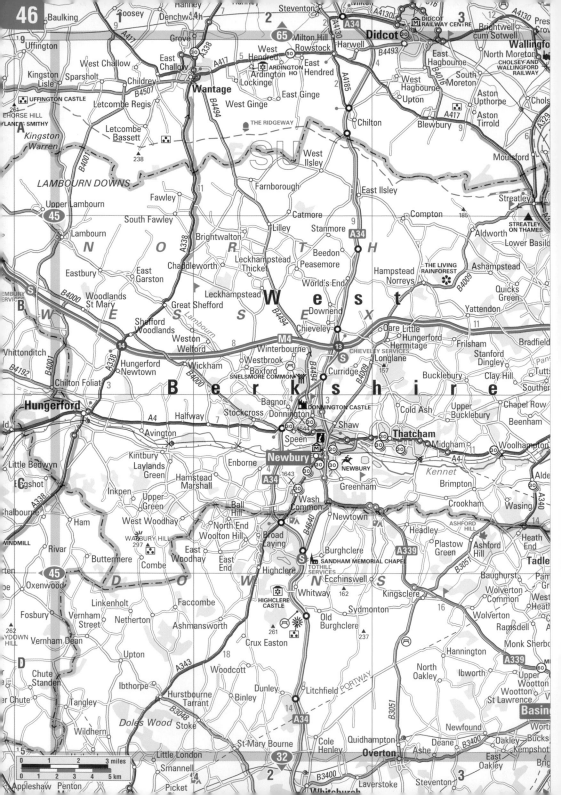

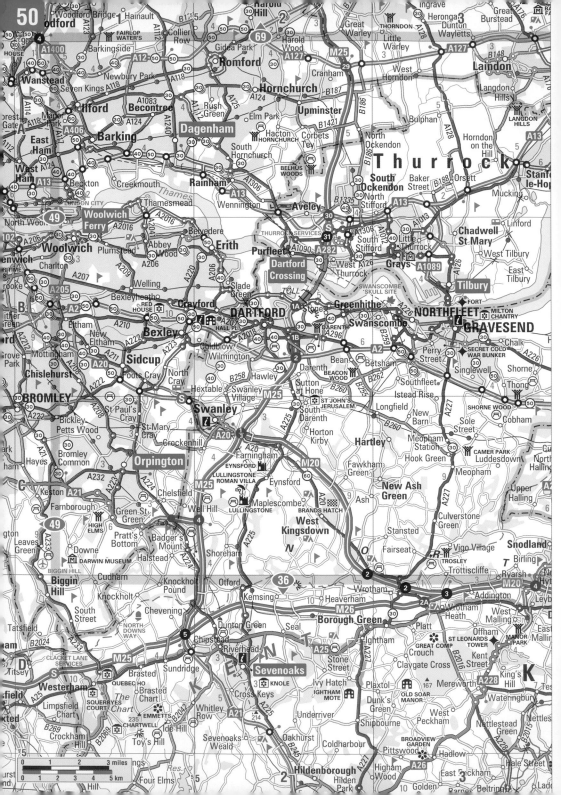

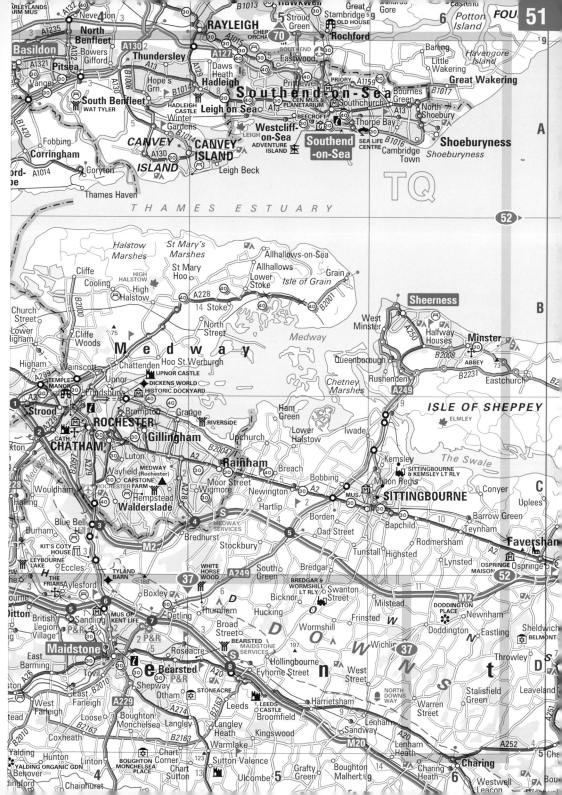

71

¹9

A

TR

B

THE SHELL GROTTO
Cliftonville   Foreness Pt.
Margate   Kingsgate
MARGATE
Westgate on Sea   B2052   NORTH
RECULVER   Minnis Bay   Northdown   FORELAND
RECULVER TOWERS   LIGHTHOUSE
AND ROMAN FORT   Birchington   St Peter's
Reculver   A255
Hillborough   QUEX HOUSE   **BROADSTAIRS**
A299   Isle of Thanet   Northwood   BLEAK HOUSE
Broomfield   St Nicholas   Acol   SPITFIRE AND   DICKENS HOUSE MUSEUM
at Wade   A28   HURRICANE MEM   A256   Dumpton
Boyden   A299   B2190   A254   Newington
Hoath   Sarre   WINDMILL   KENT   Manston   A256   **Ramsgate**
Chislet   Monkton   A253   INTERNATIONAL   Way   MARITIME MUSEUM   C
Upstreet   West Stourmouth   Minster   Cliffsend   Pegwell   OOSTENDE 4:00
A28   Stour   PEGWELL   SANDWICH &   BOULOGNE 1:15
Grove   East Stourmouth   BAY   PEGWELL BAY
STODMARSH   ST. AUGUSTINE'S   Pegwell
bere   Preston   Westmarsh   CROSS   Bay
Stodmarsh   Elmstone   Ware   RICHBOROUGH
ckhambreux   Hoaden   CASTLE
WINGHAM   AMPHITHEATRE   Great Stonar
BIRD PARK   A257   Sandwich
Ickham   Sandwich   Bay
OWLETTS WILD   Littlebourne   11   Wingham   Stone Cross   ROYAL ST. GEORGE'S
ANIMAL PARK   Guilton   **Ash**
kesbourne   Bramling   Marshborough   TOLL
Staple   Woodnesborough   Worth
xbourne   Gore   A258
Goodnestone   Ham   D
Adisham   GOODNESTONE PARK   **Eastry**   Finglesham
Chillenden   Knowlton   MARITIME AND
Aylesham   Bettshanger   Sholden   LOCAL HISTORY MUSEUM
B2046   Easole Street   Northbourne   **DEAL**
Nonington   Snowdown   Tilmanstone   THE
Womenswold   Elvington   Great   DEAL CASTLE
WAY   Mongeham   DOWNS
¹5
Barfreston   39   **Walmer**
Woolage   EAST KENT   East   Sutton   WALMER CASTLE
Green   4   RLY   **Eythorne**   Studdal   Ringwould   AND GARDENS
A2   West   6 4   6
Kingsdown

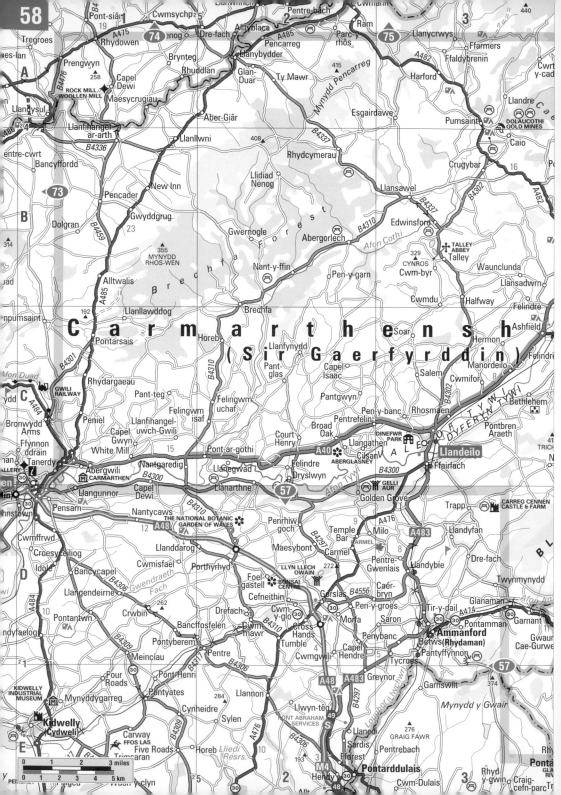

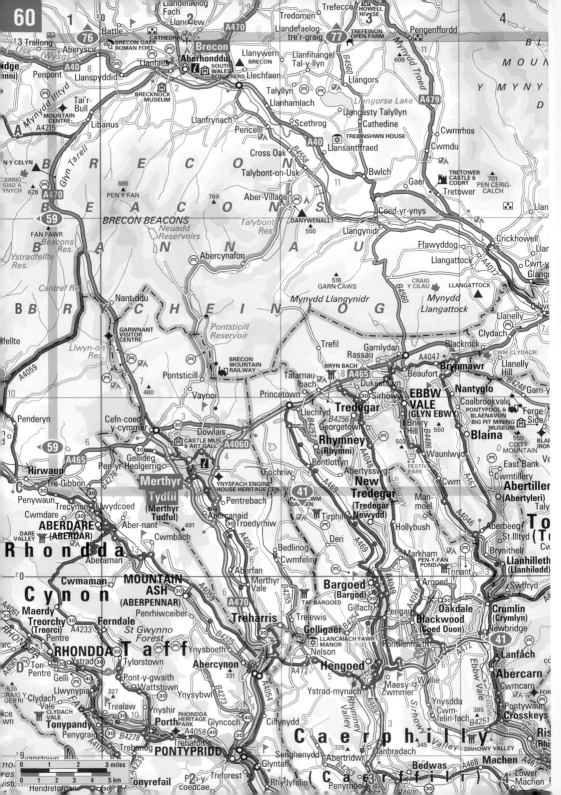

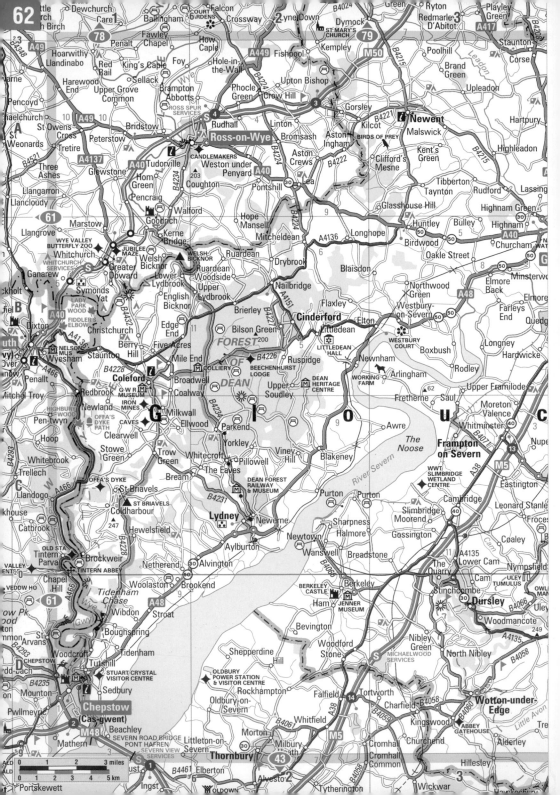

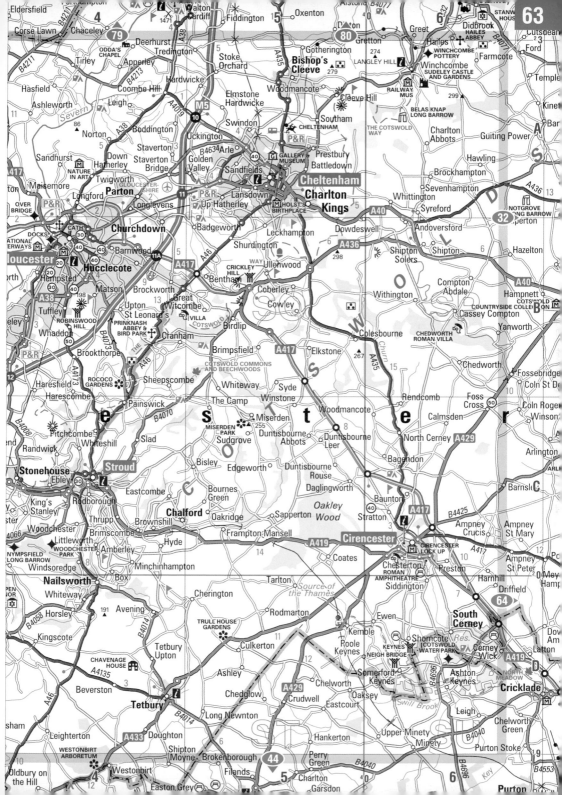

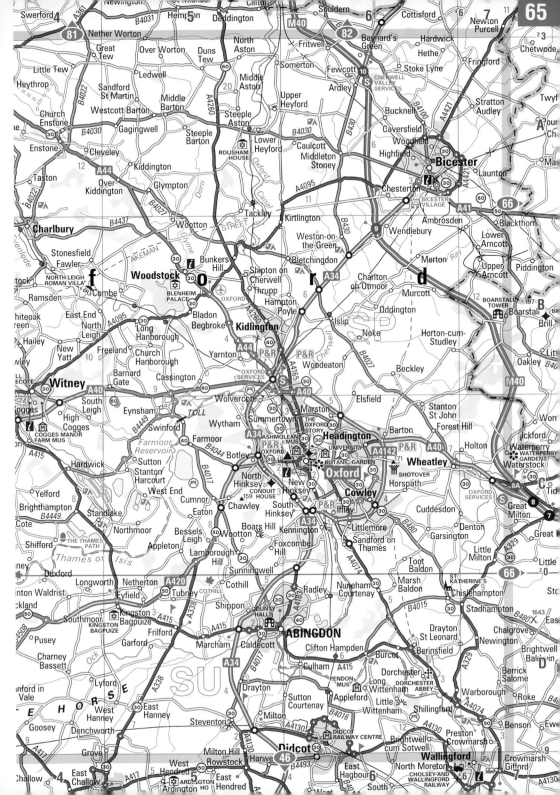

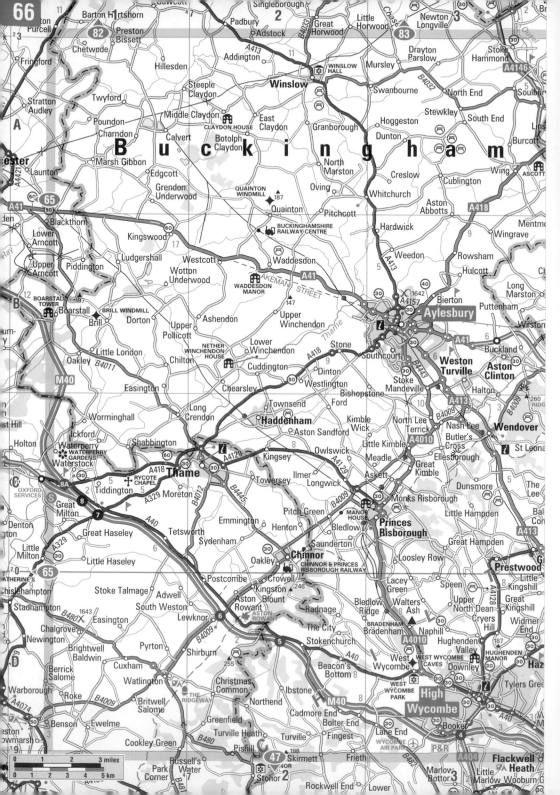

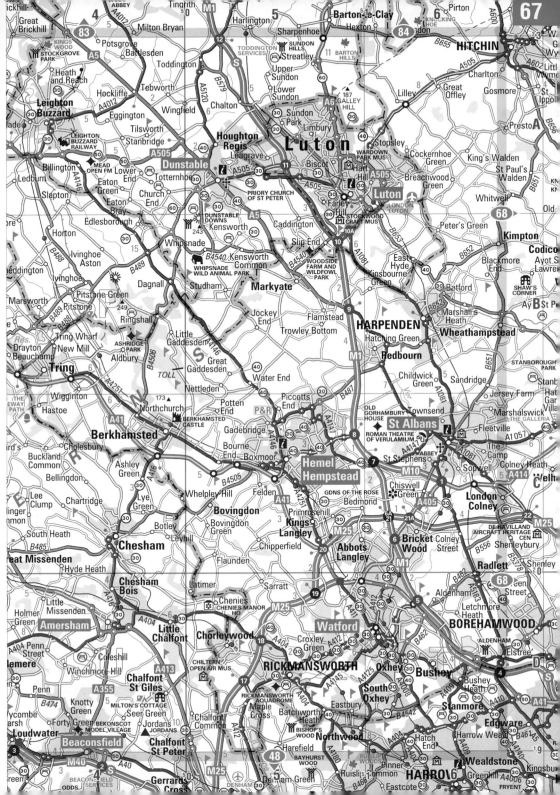

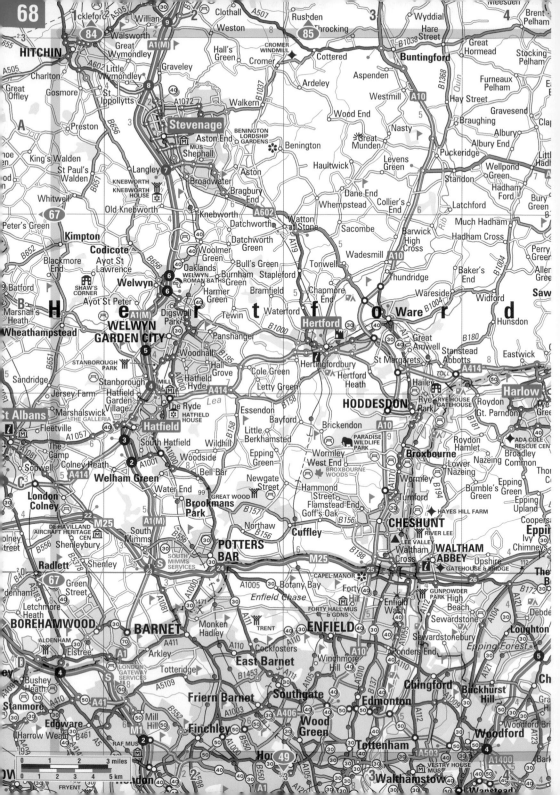

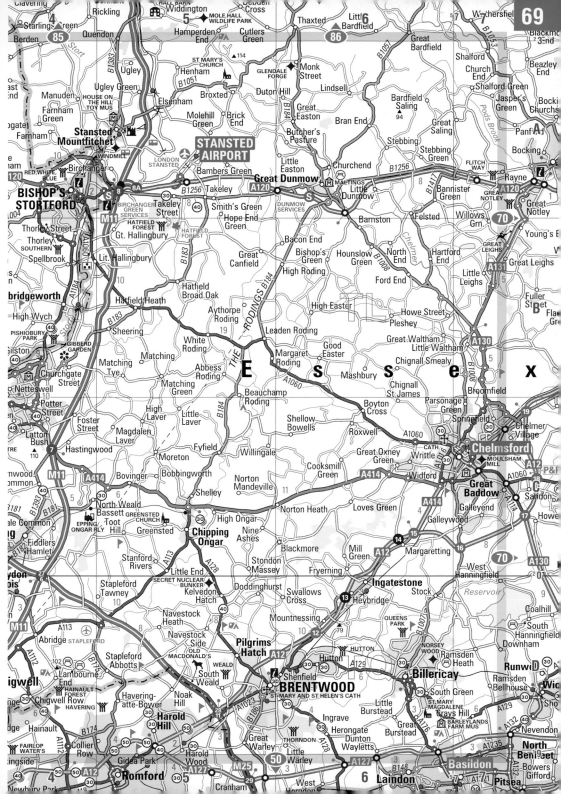

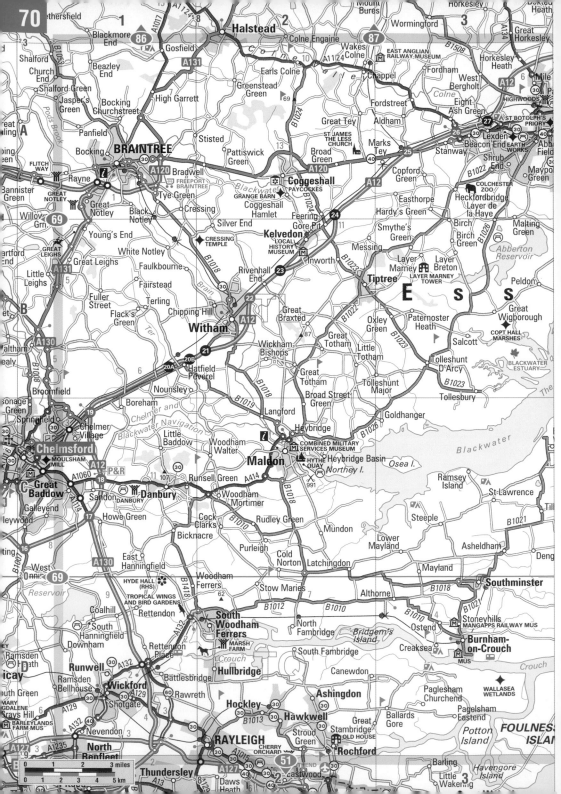

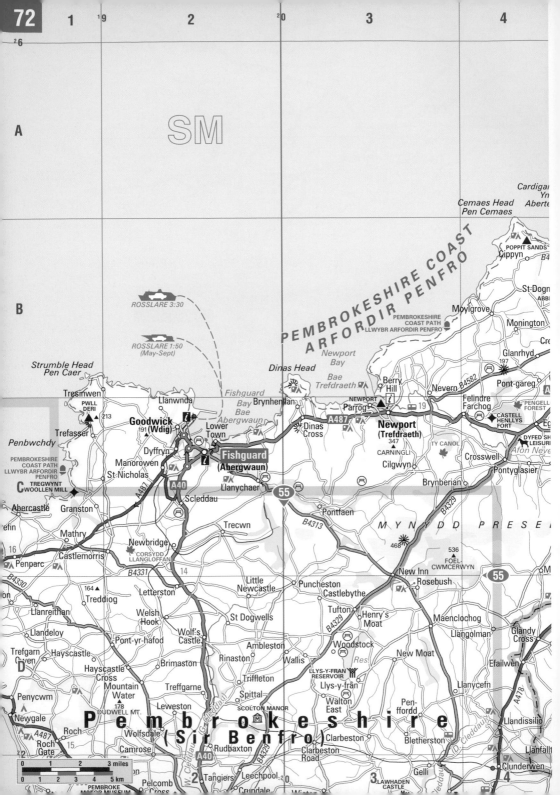

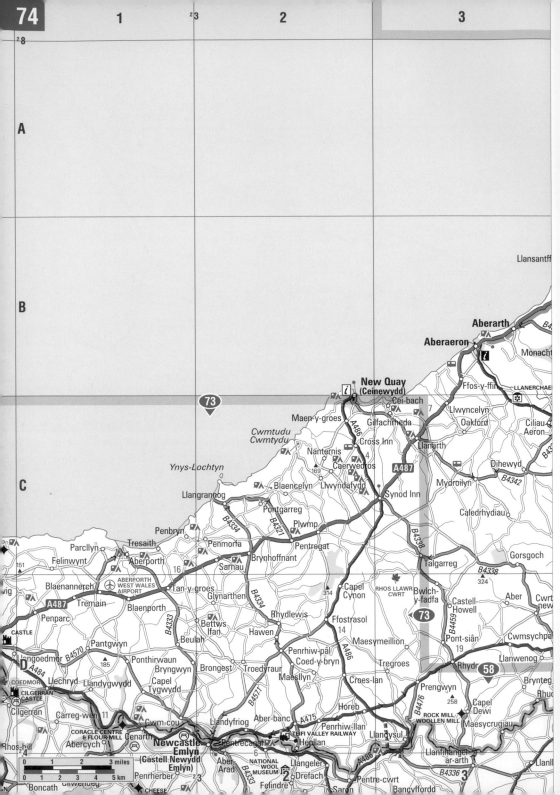

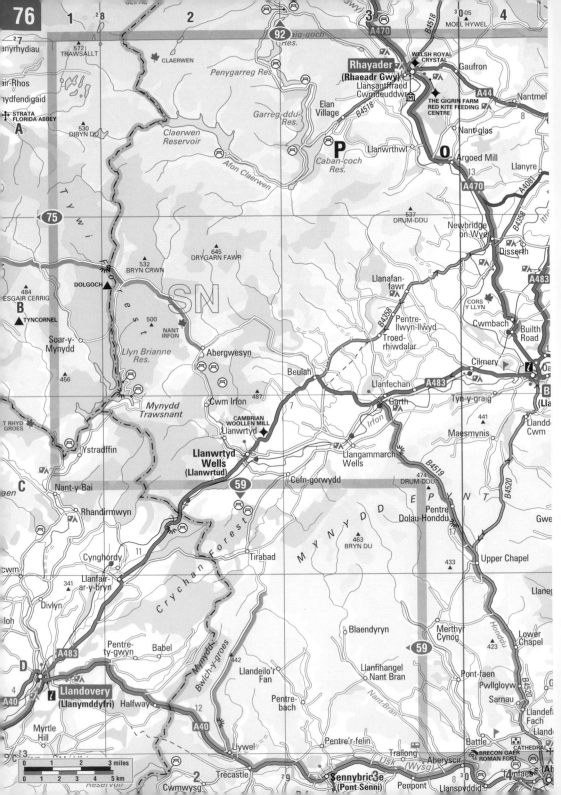

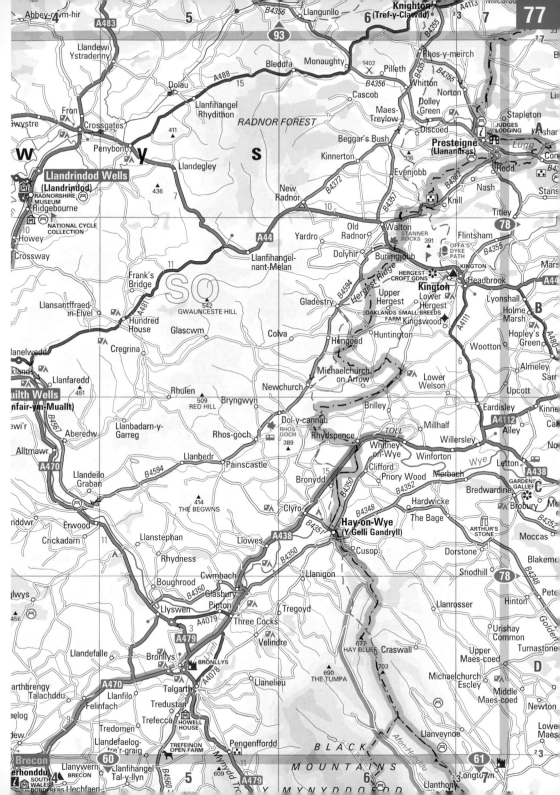

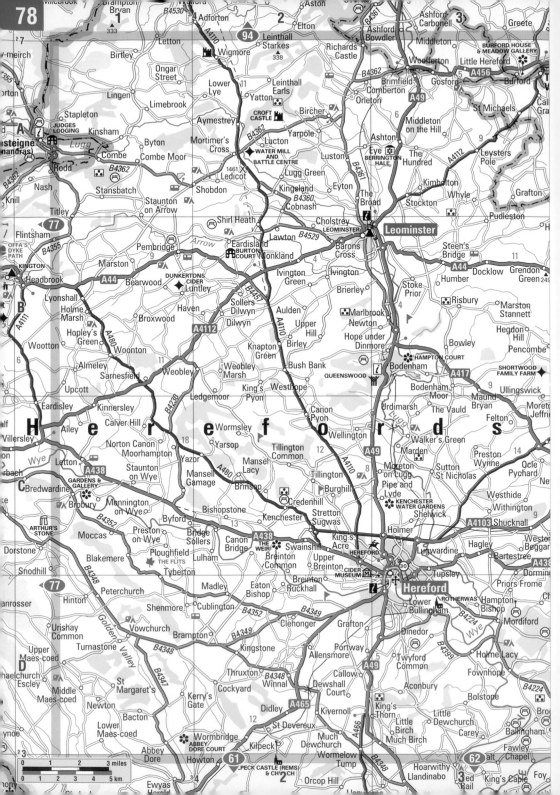

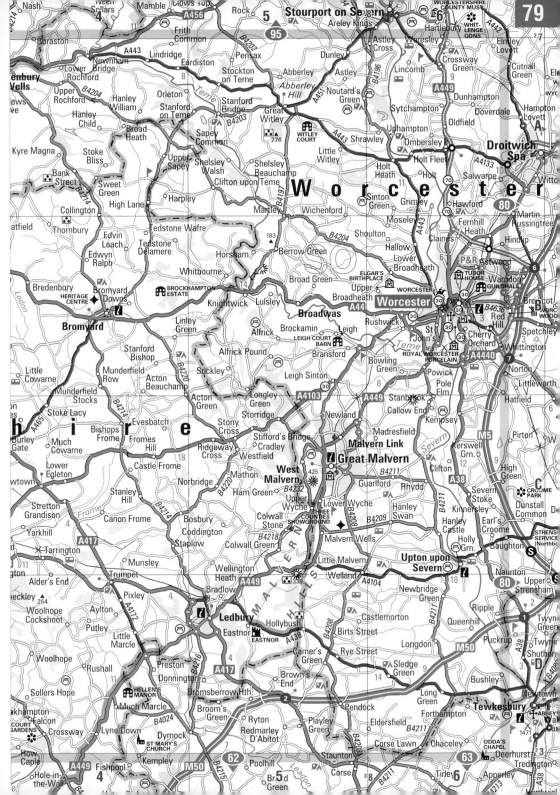

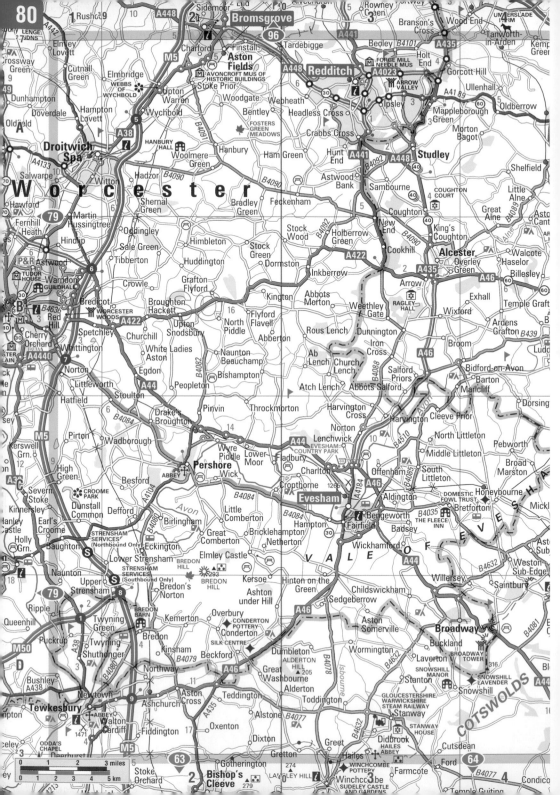

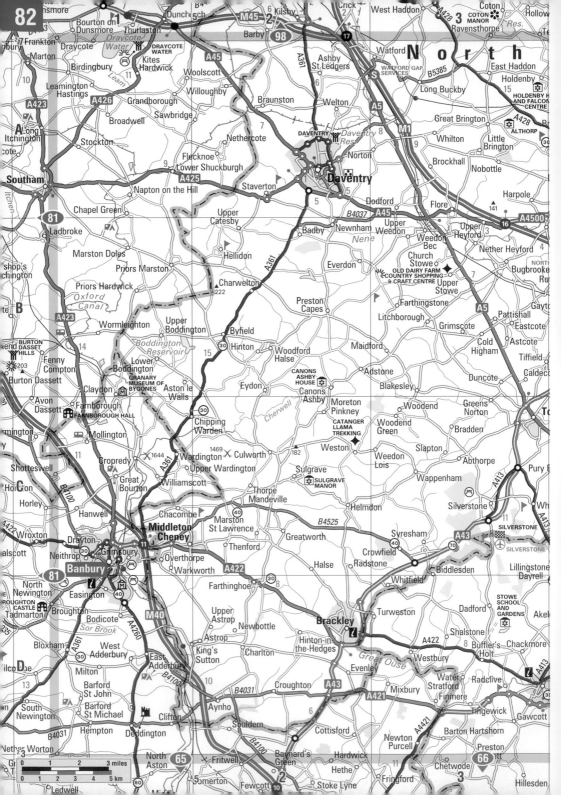

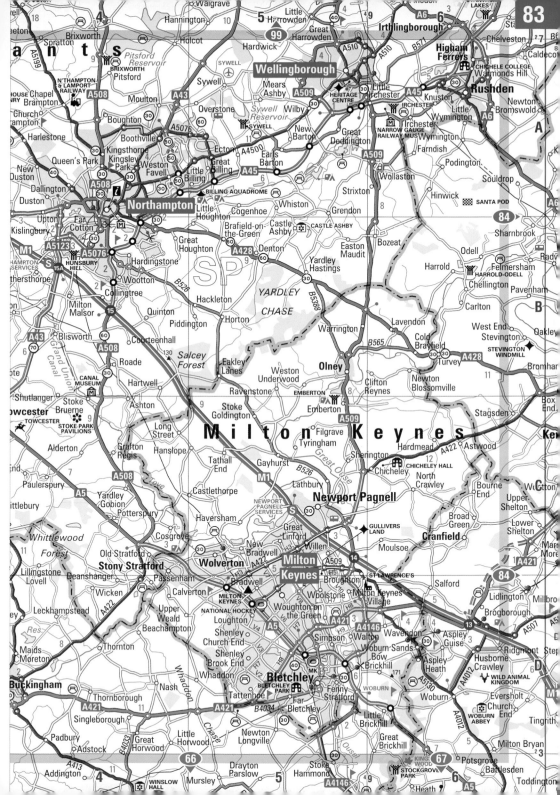

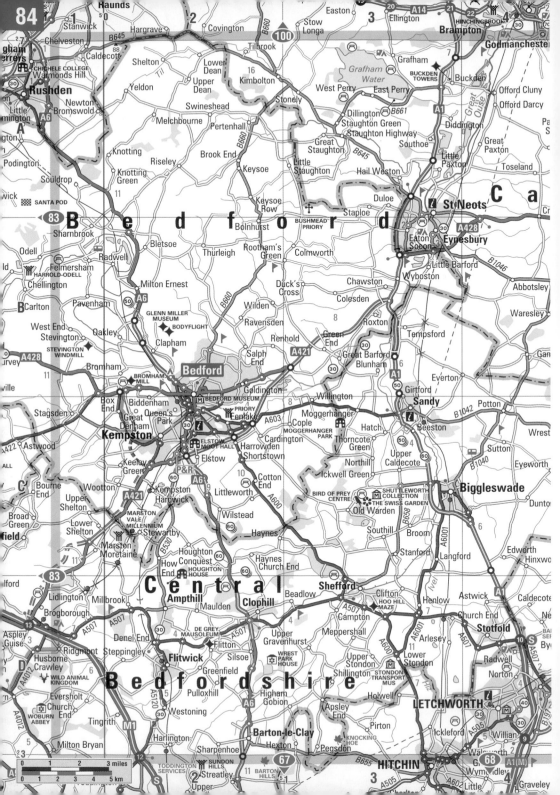

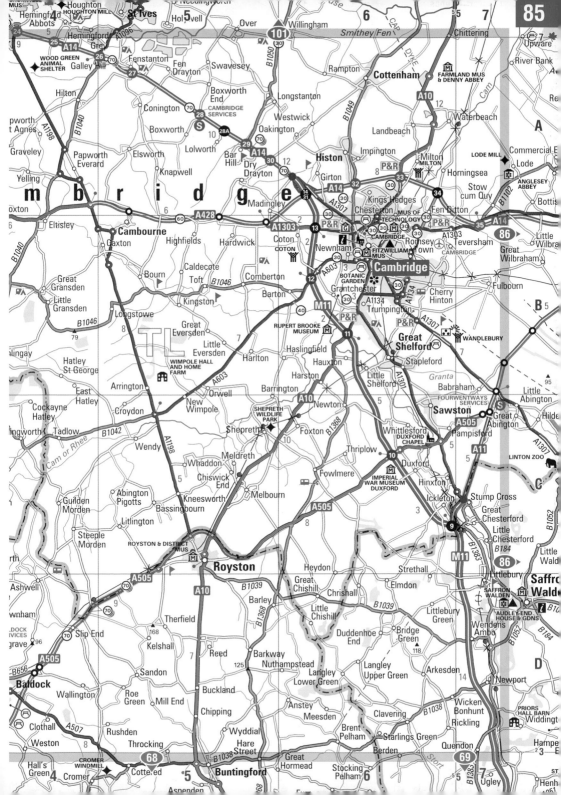

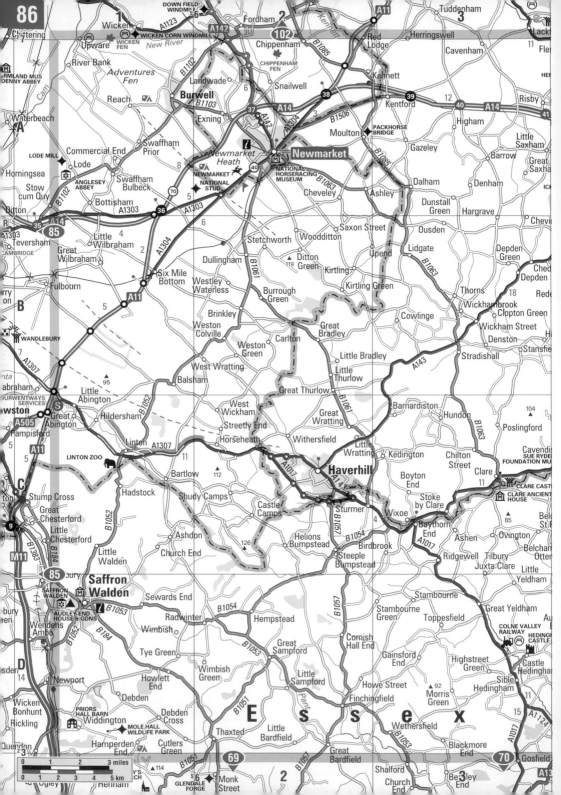

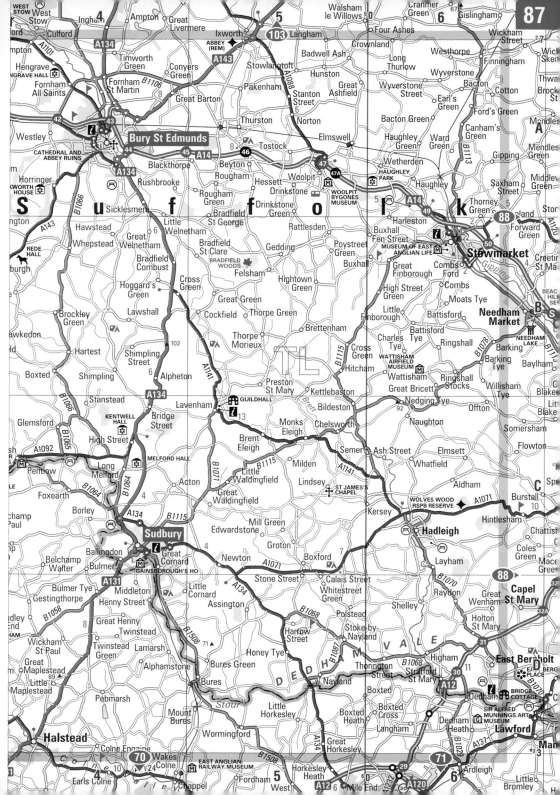

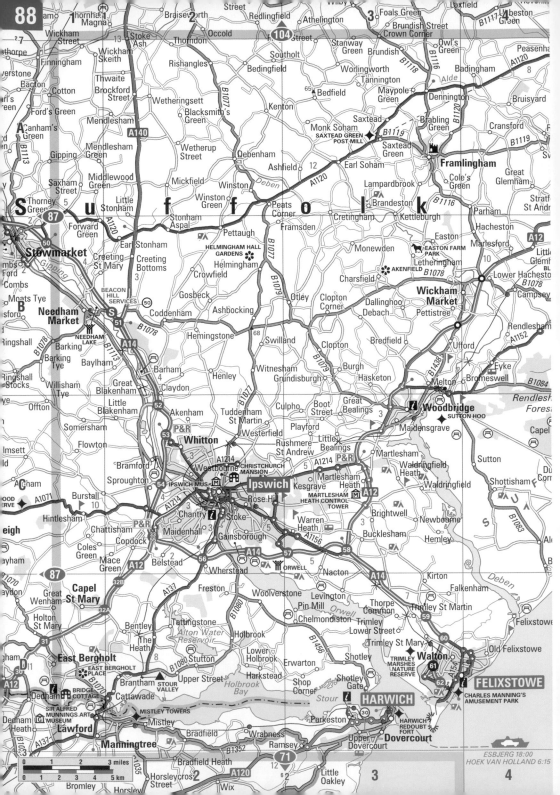

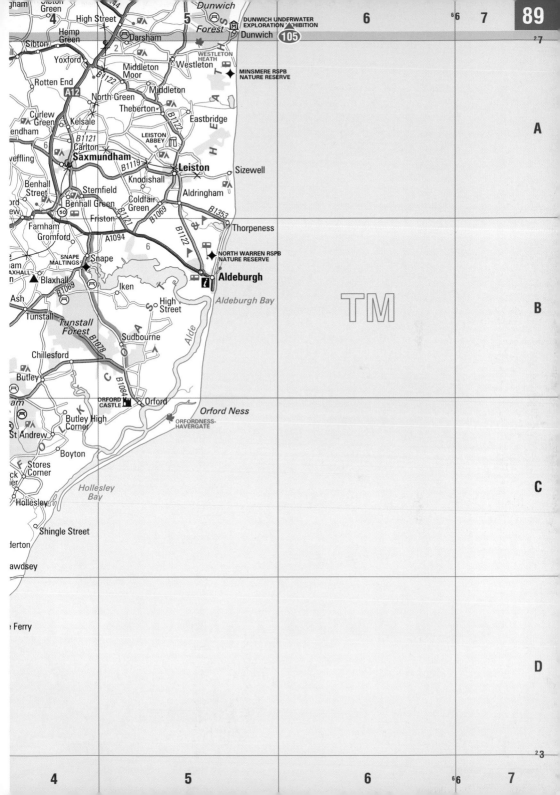

6 ⁶6 7

7 ²7

Dunwich

DUNWICH UNDERWATER EXPLORATION EXHIBITION

Dunwich (105)

Forest

High Street

Hemp Green

Darsham

4

Sibton

Yoxford

Westleton

WESTLETON HEATH

Westleton

MINSMERE RSPB NATURE RESERVE

Rotten End

A12

North Green

Middleton

Middleton Moor

Curlew Green

Kelsale

Theberton

Eastbridge

endham

B1121

Carlton

LEISTON ABBEY

Saxmundham

B1119

Leiston

Sizewell

A

veffling

6

Knodishall

Benhall Street

Sternfield

Coldfair Green

Aldringham

Sibton

Benhall Green

Friston

B1069

B1353

Farnham

50

B1121

Thorpeness

Gromford

A1094

B1122

NORTH WARREN RSPB NATURE RESERVE

Blaxhall

SNAPE MALTINGS

Snape

6

BLAXHALL

Iken

Aldeburgh

B

Ash

Tunstall

High Street

Aldeburgh Bay

TM

Tunstall Forest

Sudbourne

B1078

Alde

Chillesford

Butley

B1084

ORFORD CASTLE

Orford

St Andrew

Butley High Corner

Orford Ness

ORFORDNESS-HAVERGATE

Boyton

Stores Corner

Hollesley Bay

C

Hollesley

Shingle Street

erton

awdsey

Ferry

D

²3

4 5 6 ⁶6 7

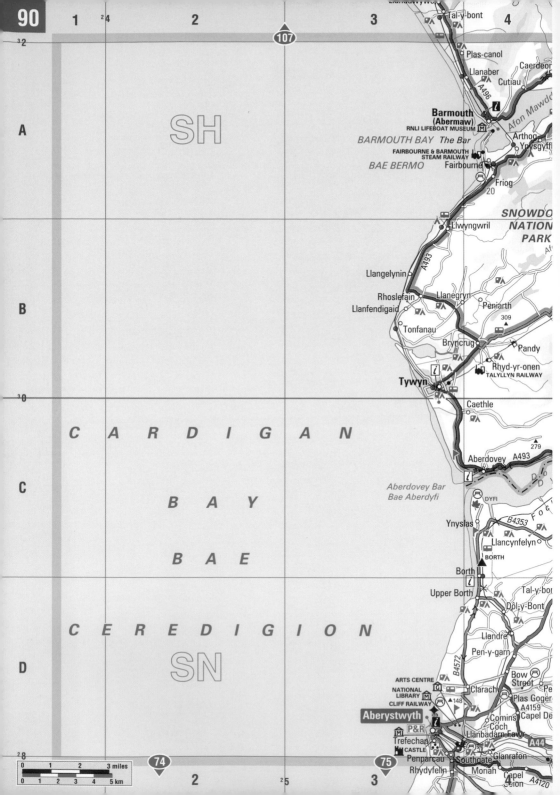

SH

A

SN

B

C A R D I G A N

B A Y

B A E

C

C E R E D I G I O N

D

Llandanwg
Tal-y-bont
Plas-canol
Caerdeon
Llanaber
Cutiau
Barmouth
(Abermaw)
RNLI LIFEBOAT MUSEUM
Arthog
Ynysgyffylog
BARMOUTH BAY The Bar
FAIRBOURNE & BARMOUTH
STEAM RAILWAY
BAE BERMO
Fairbourne
Friog
20

SNOWDO
NATION
PARK

Llwyngwril

Llangelynin
Rhoslefain
Llanegryn
Peniarth
Llanfendigaid
309
Tonfanau
Bryncrug
Pandy
Rhyd-yr-onen
TALYLLYN RAILWAY
Tywyn
Caethle

279
Aberdovey A493
Aberdovey Bar
Bae Aberdyfi
DYFI
Ynyslas
B4353
Llancynfelyn
BORTH
Borth
Upper Borth
Tal-y-bont
Dôl-y-Bont
Llandre
Pen-y-garn
ARTS CENTRE
NATIONAL
LIBRARY
CLIFF RAILWAY
B4572
Bow
Street
Clarach
148
Plas Goger
A4159
Comins
Coch
Capel De
Aberystwyth
P&R
Llanbadarn Fawr
CASTLE
Trefechan
Penparcau
Glanrafon
Southgate
A44
Rhydyfelin
Moriah
Capel
Seion
A4120

107

74

75

0   1   2   3 miles
0   1   2   3   4   5 km

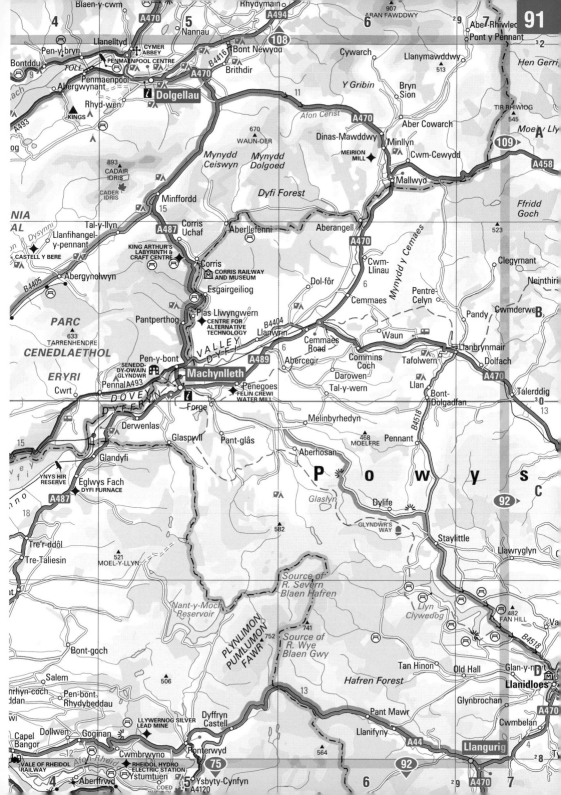

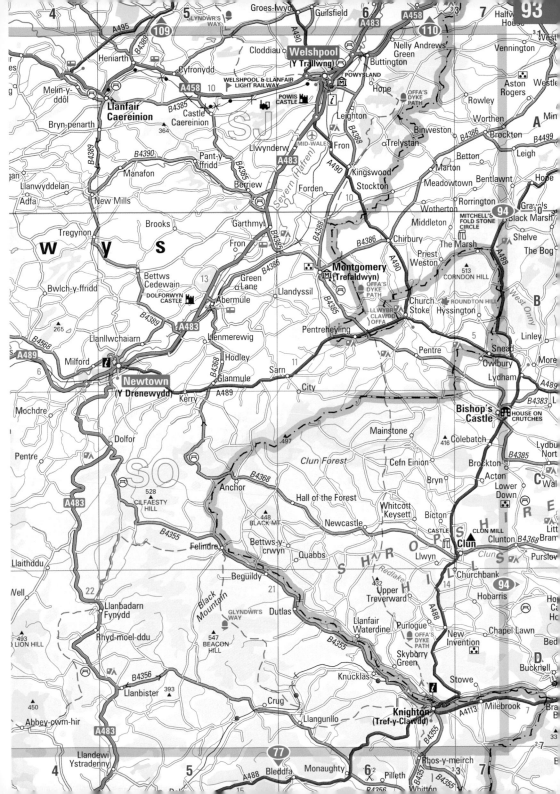

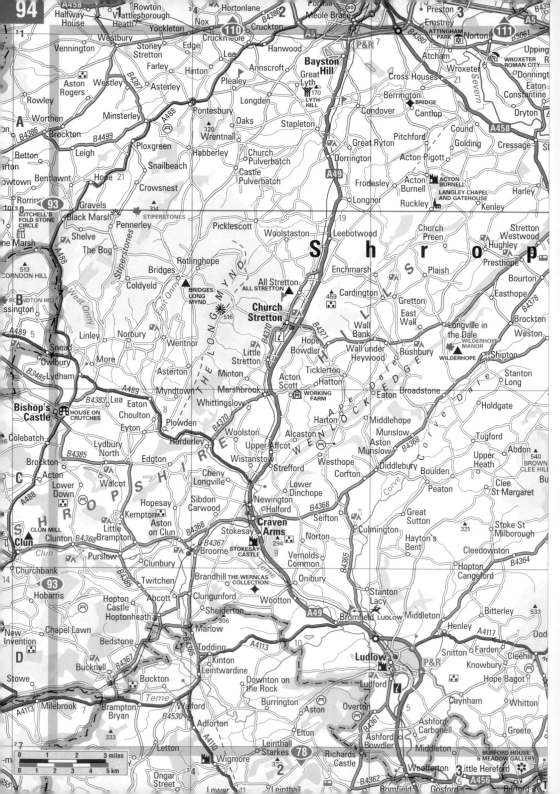

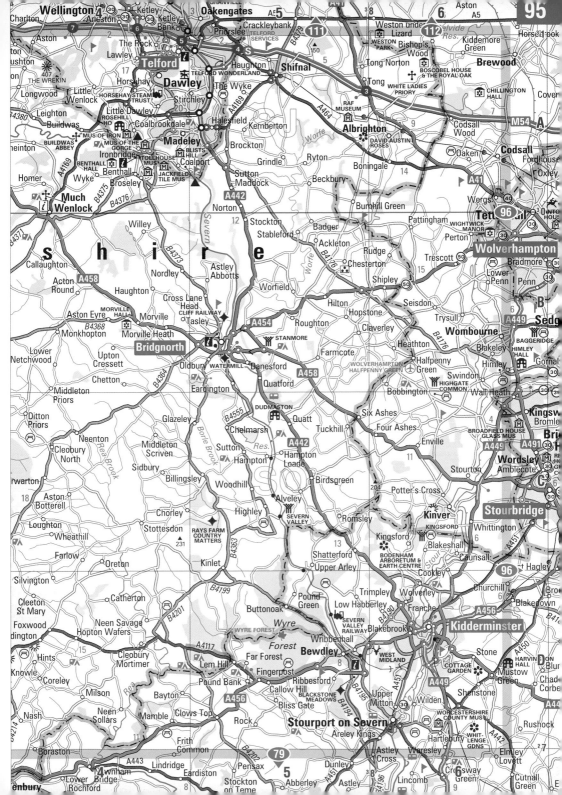

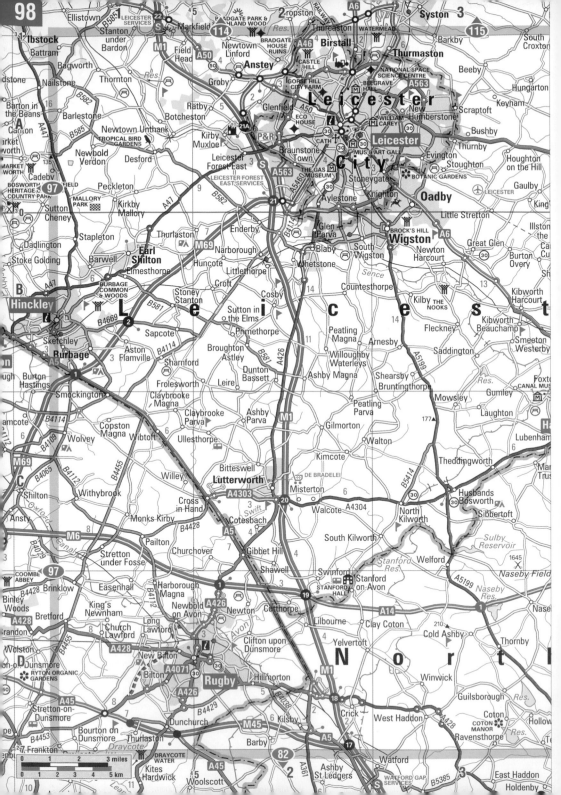

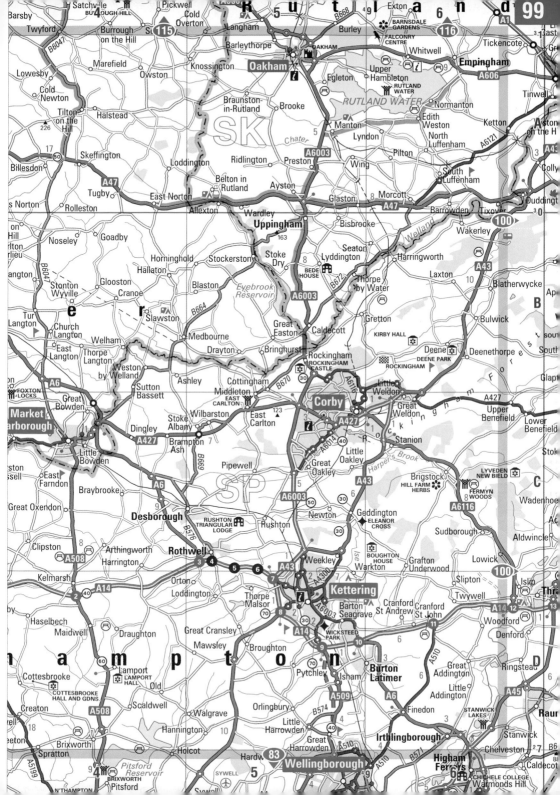

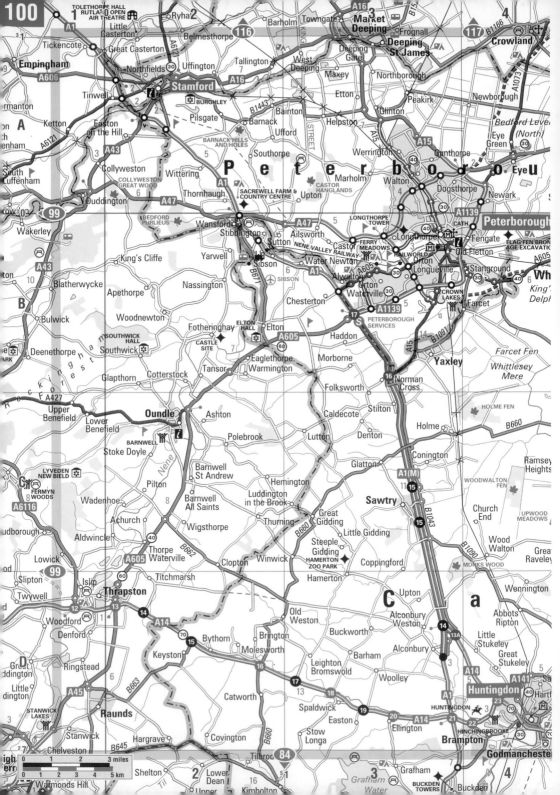

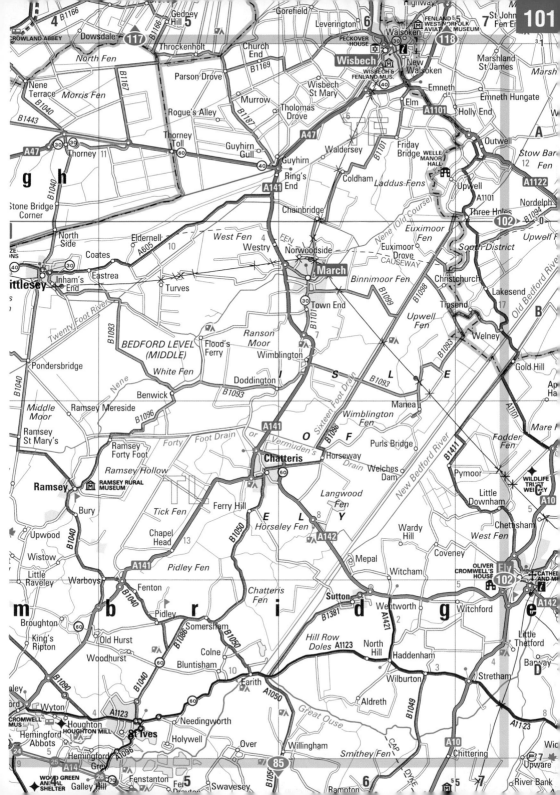

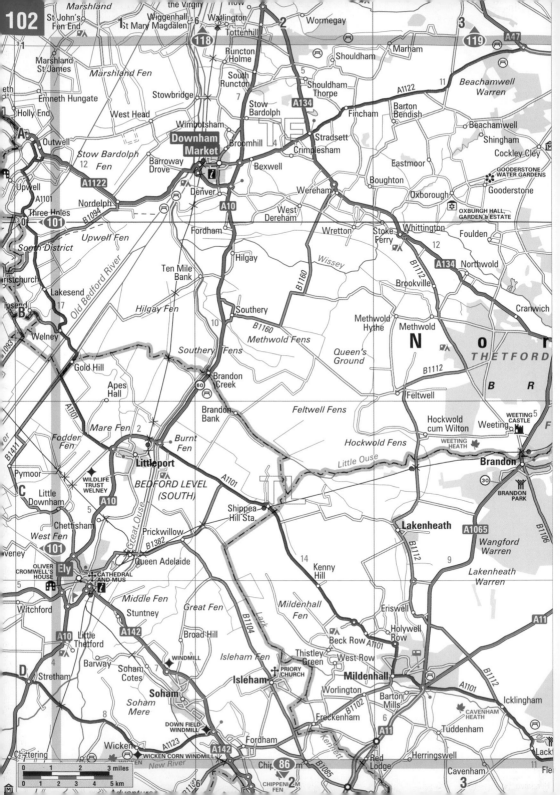

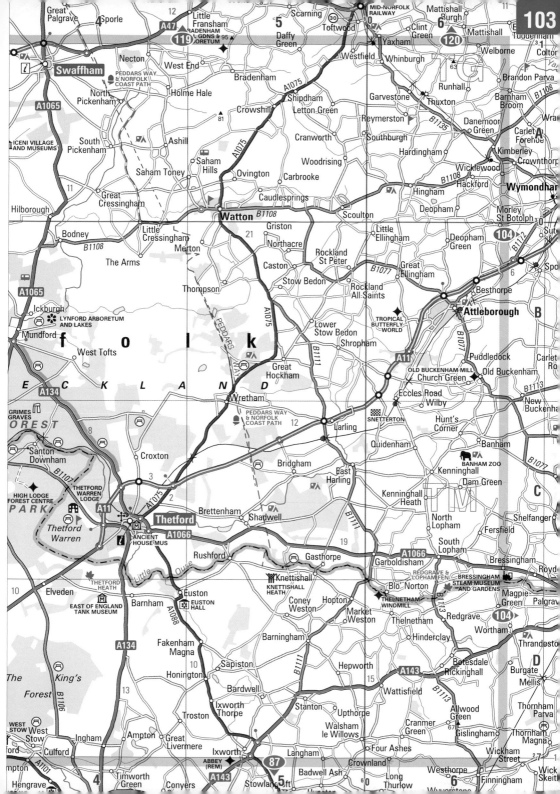

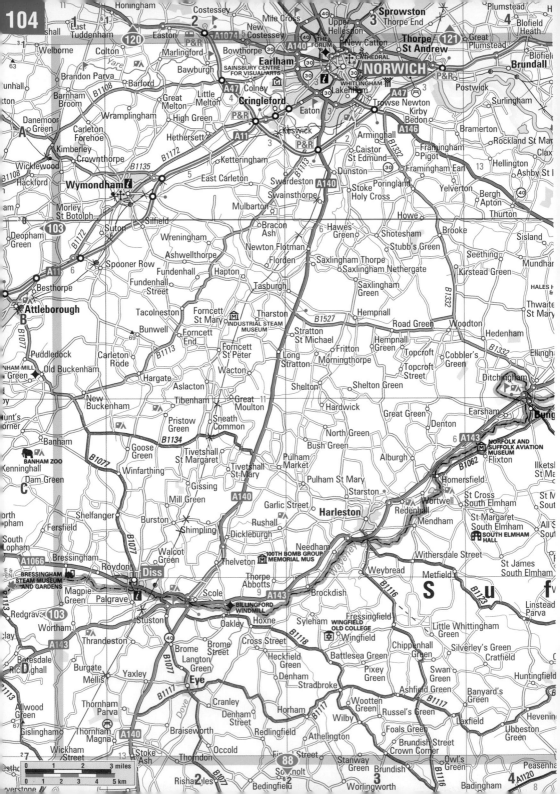

122

C A E R N A R F O N

B A Y

B A E

C A E R N A R F O N

A

SH

L L E Y N

L L E Y N

Clynne

Gyrn-goc

Bryn-yr-eryr

Trefor

564
YR EIFL

Llana

GYR

B

B4417

6

Llithfaen

Carreg Ddu

Porth
Dinllaen

Pistyll

Llwyndyrys

7

Morfa Nefyn

Nefyn

LLEYN HISTORICAL
MARITIME MUSEUM

Fron

B4354

Rhos-fawr

A499

Edern

Tan-y-graig

Porth Ysgadan

B4417

Glanrhyd

Boduan

Llannor

Rhos-y-llan

CORS
GEIRCH

BODVEL HALL
ADVENTURE PARK

A497

Efailnewydd

Denio

Tudweiliog

Rhyd-y-clafdy

Dinas

A499

Pwllheli

C

Porth Golmon

14

Bryn-mawr

Garnfadryn

Llaniestyn

B4415

Penrhos

Carr

South Beach

PENRHYN LLEYN

Rhedyn

7

Pen-y-graig

Llangwnnadl

Sarn
Meyllteyrn

Llanbedrog

Penrhyn Mawr

Pen-y-
groeslon

Bryncroes

Botwnnog

Nanhoron

Mynytho

Trwyn Llanbedrog

Ty-hen

Methlem

Rhydlios

Landegwning

St Tudwal's
Road

A499

Rhoshirwaun

304
MYNYDD
RHIW

PLAS-YN-
RHIW

Llawr
Dref

Llangian

Angorfa St Tudwal

Capel Carmel

B4413

Rhiw

Abersoch

191

Porth Neigwl or
Hell's Mouth

Llanengan

Sarn Bach

St Tudwal's Island East
Ynys St Tudwal Dwyrain

Uwchmynydd

Aberdaron

Llanfaelrhys

Bwlchtocyn

Marchroes

St Tudwal's Island West
Ynys St Tudwal Gorllewin

Bodermid

Cilan Uchaf

D

Pen-y-cil

Bardsey Sound
Swnt Enlli

Trwyn Cilan

L L E Y N

YNYS ENLLI

167

Bardsey
Island
Ynys Enlli

L L E Y N

2

2

3

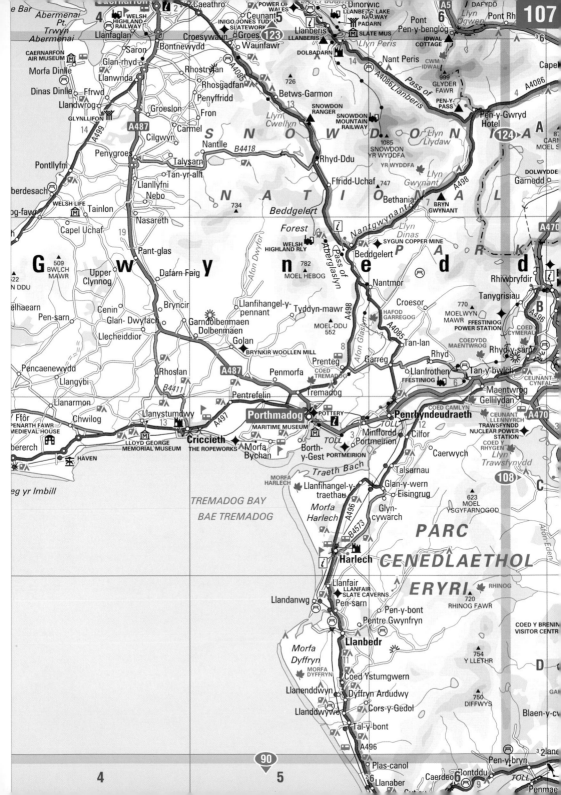

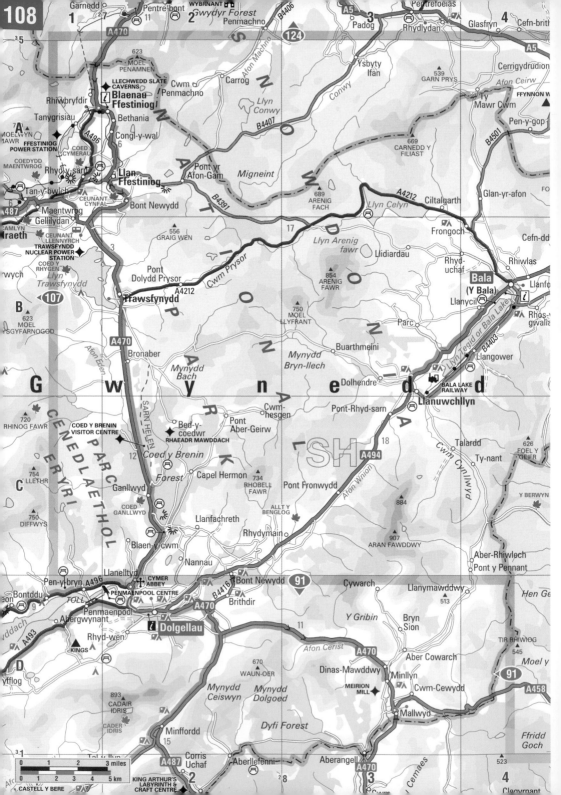

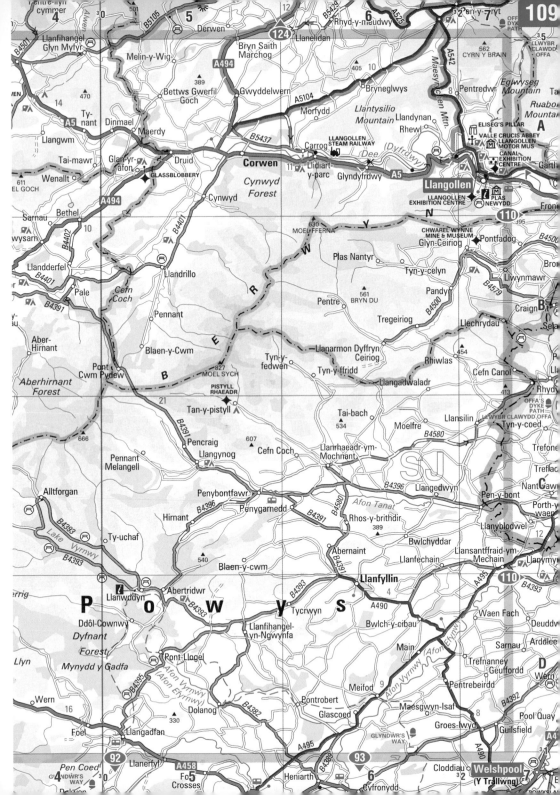

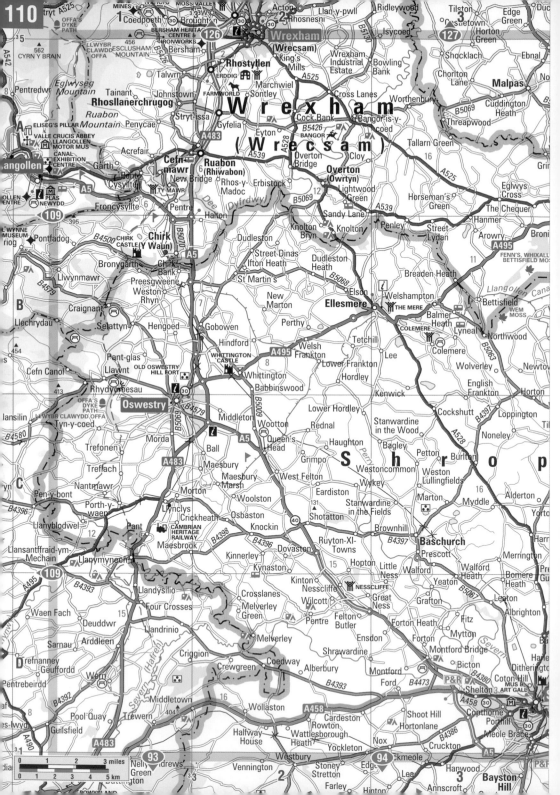

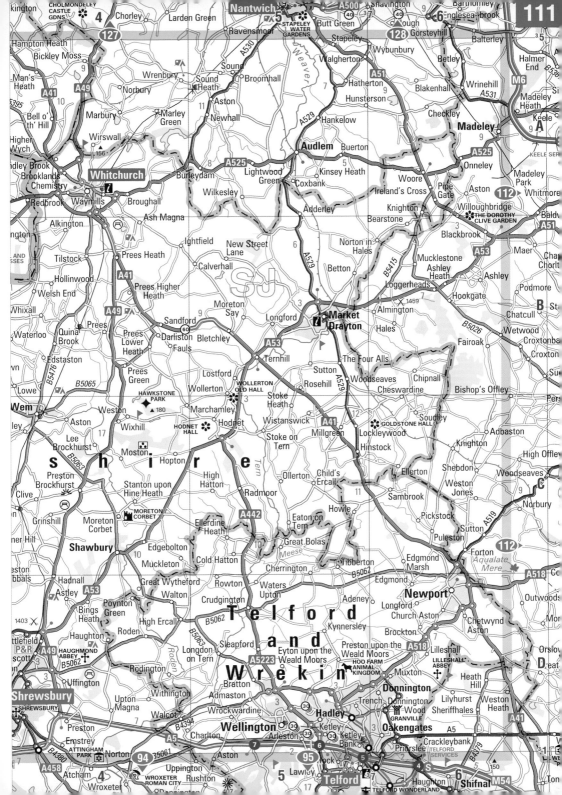

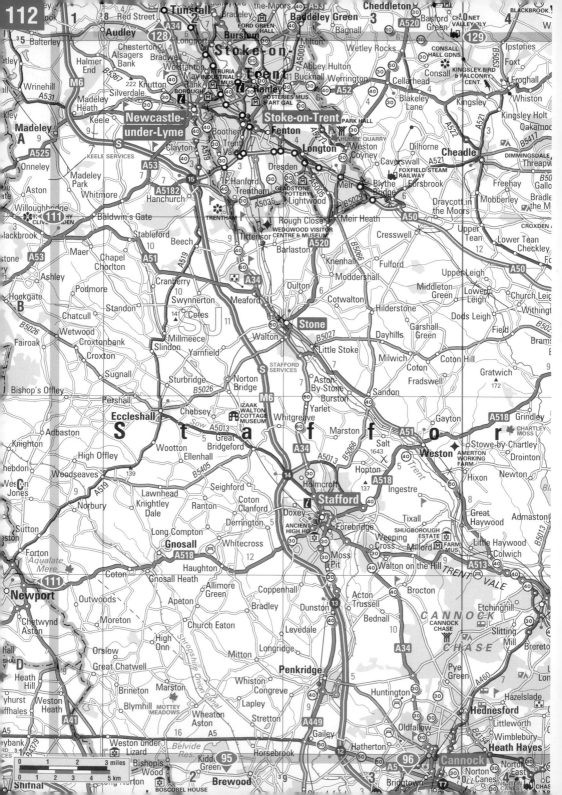

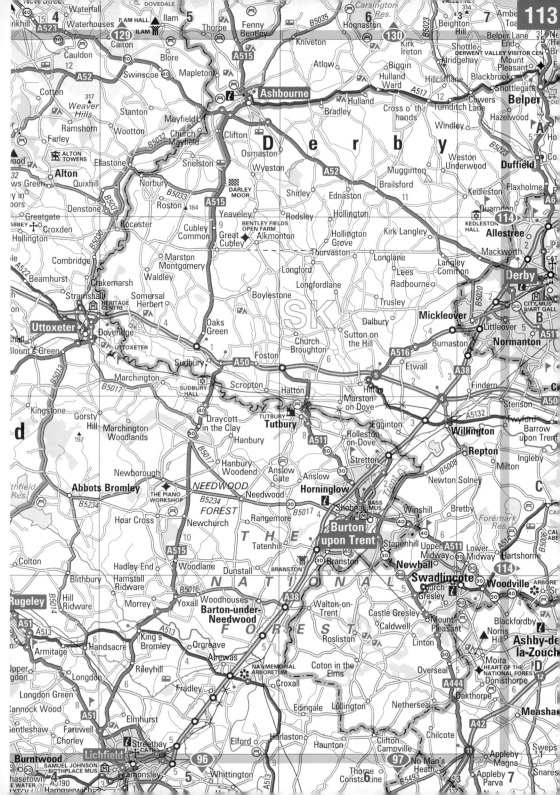

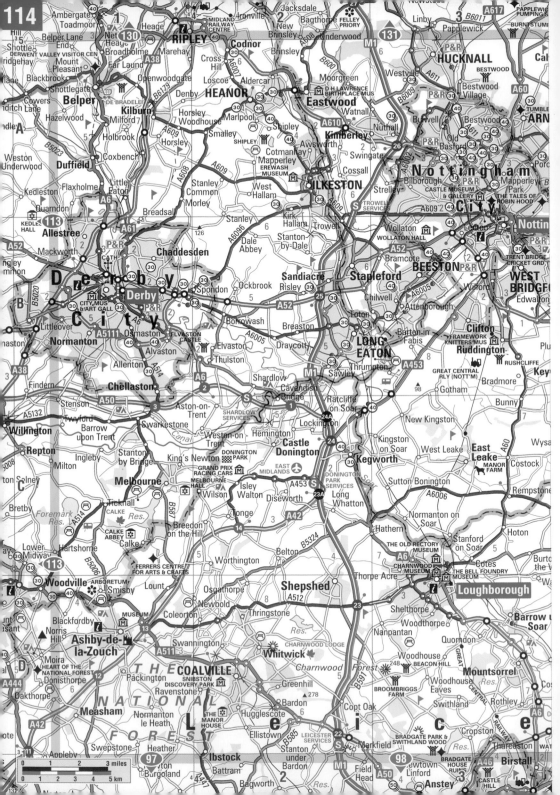

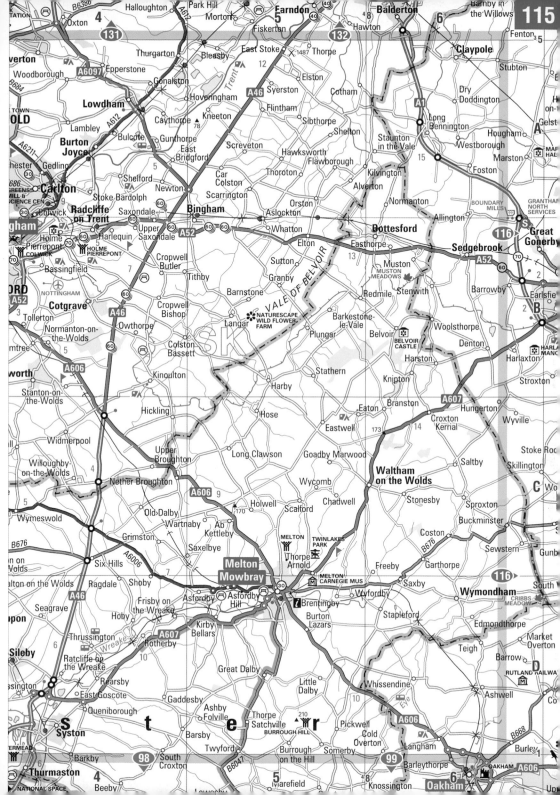

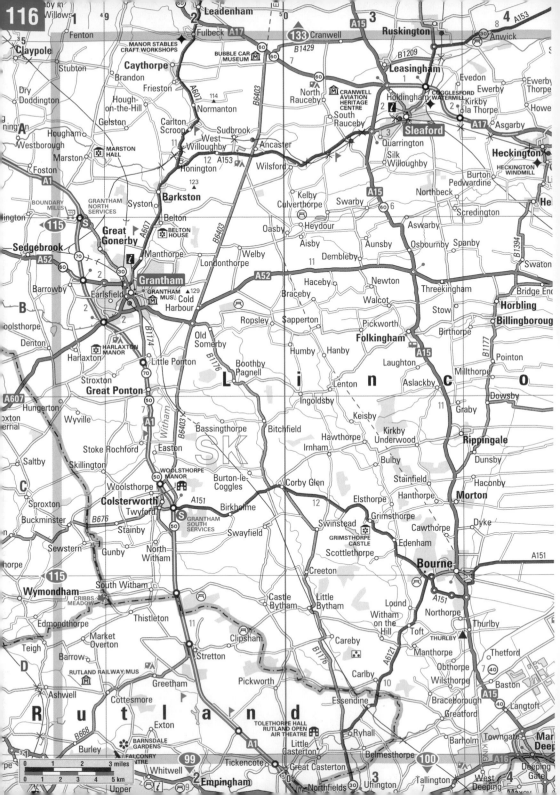

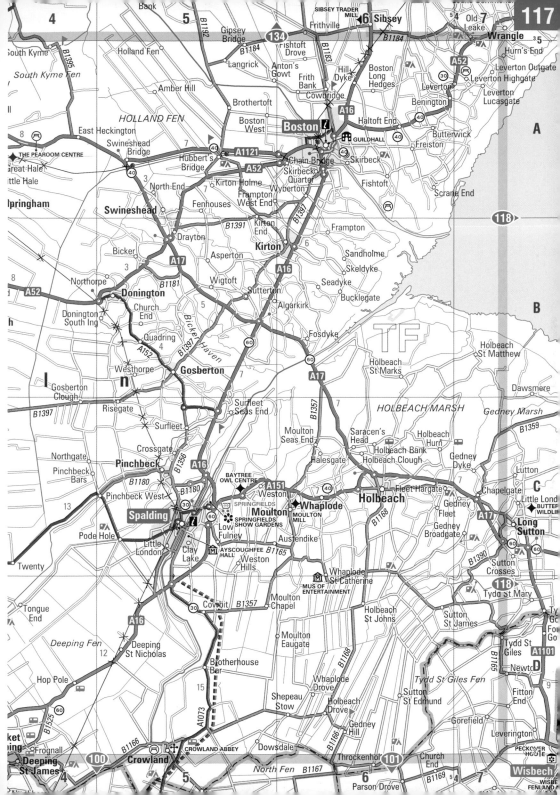

4   5   SIBSEY TRADER MILL   6 Sibsey   5 4 Old 7   118

Bank
B1192
Gipsey Bridge
134   Frithville   B1184   Wrangle   3 5
South Kyme Fen   B1184   Fishtoft Drove   B1183   Hurn's End
Holland Fen   Langrick   Anton's Gowt   Frith Bank   Hill Dyke   Boston Long Hedges   Leverton Outgate
A52
South Kyme   Amber Hill   Cowbridge   30   Leverton Highgate
B1395   Brothertoft   A16   Leverton   Leverton Lucasgate
HOLLAND FEN   Boston West   Boston   i   Benington   40
8   East Heckington   GUILDHALL   Butterwick
THE PEAROOM CENTRE   Swineshead Bridge   40   A1121   Chain Bridge   49   Skirbeck   Freiston   A
Great Hale   Hubbert's Bridge   A52   Skirbeck Quarter   Fishtoft   Scrane End
ttle Hale   3   North End   Kirton Holme   Wyberton   118
pringham   7   Frampton West End   Fenhouses   B1397   Frampton
Swineshead   Drayton   Kirton End   Sandholme   Skeldyke
B1391   6   Bicker   Kirton   A16   Seadyke   Bucklegate   B
8   Northorpe   A17   Asperton   Sutterton   Algarkirk   Fosdyke
A52   Donington   B1181   Wigtoft   60   Holbeach St Matthew
h   Donington South Ing   Church End   5   60   Holbeach St Marks   TF   Dawsmere
Quadring   4   A17   Gedney Marsh
Westhorpe   A152   Gosberton   HOLBEACH MARSH   B1359
l   Gosberton Clough   B1397 Haven   Risegate   Surfleet Seas End   B1357   7   Saracen's Head   Holbeach Hurn   Gedney Dyke   Lutton
n   Surfleet   Moulton Seas End   Halesgate   Holbeach Bank   Holbeach Clough   Gedney   C
Northgate   B1356   Crossgate   A16   BAYTREE OWL CENTRE   Fleet Hargate   Gedney   Chapelgate   Little Lond
Pinchbeck Bars   Pinchbeck   B1180   A151   Weston   7 40   Holbeach   Fleet   BUTTER WILDLI
13   Pinchbeck West   B1180   SPRINGFIELDS   Moulton   MOULTON MILL   Whaplode   A17   Long Sutton
Spalding   i   60   SPRINGFIELDS SHOW GARDENS   Low Fulney   Austendike   B1168   Gedney Broadgate   60   118
Pode Hole   Little London   AYSCOUGHFEE HALL   Weston Hills   B1165   Sutton Crosses   Tydd St Mary
Twenty   Clay Lake   Whaplode St Catherine   B1390   Tydd St Giles   A1101
Tongue End   30   Cowbit   B1357   MUS OF ENTERTAINMENT   Moulton Chapel   Holbeach St Johns   Sutton St James   Tydd St Giles   Newto   D
Deeping Fen   A16   Deeping St Nicholas   12   Moulton Eaugate   B1168   Sutton St Edmund   Fitton End
Hop Pole   Brotherhouse Bar   15   Whaplode Drove   Holbeach Drove   Tydd St Giles Fen   Gorefield   B1165
ket   60   B1525   Shepeau Stow   Gedney Hill   Leverington   PECKOVER HOUSE
ng   Frognall   100   Crowland   CROWLAND ABBEY   Dowsdale   101   B1166   Throckenholt   Church End   Wisbech
Deeping St James   4   5   North Fen B1167   6   Parson Drove   B1169   5 4   7   WISBE FENLAND
A1073

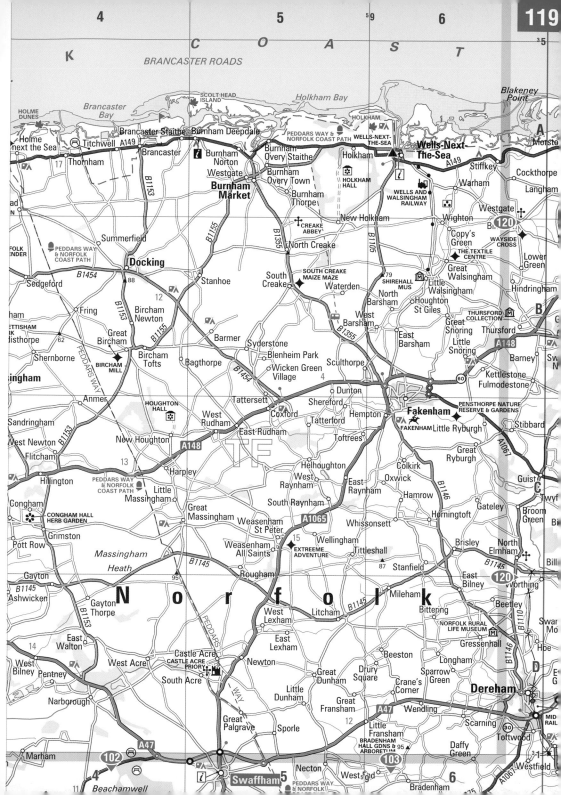

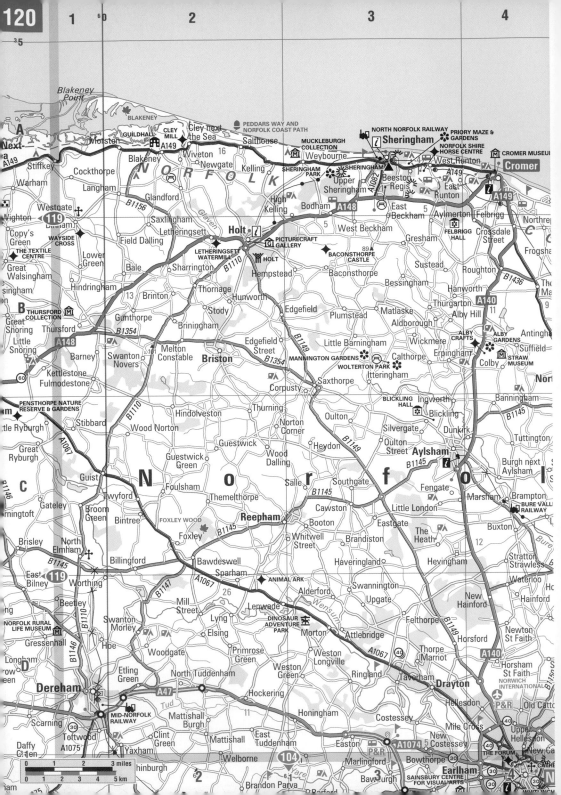

Blakeney Point

Next-a

Stiffkey

Warham

Westgate

Wighton

Copy's Green

THE TEXTILE CENTRE

Great Walsingham

-singham

Great Snoring

Little Snoring

Thursford

THURSFORD COLLECTION

Barney

Kettlestone

Fulmodestone

PENSTHORPE NATURE RESERVE & GARDENS

le Ryburgh

Great Ryburgh

Guist

Gateley

Broom Green

Bintree

Brisley

North Elmham

East Bilney

Worthing

Beetley

NORFOLK RURAL LIFE MUSEUM

Gressenhall

Longham

Dereham

Scarning

Daffy Green

Toftwood

A1075

MID-NORFOLK RAILWAY

Mattishall Burgh

Clint Green

Mattishall

Yaxham

BLAKENEY

GUILDHALL

Morston

CLEY MILL

Cley next the Sea

Cley next the Sea

Salthouse

Weybourne

PEDDARS WAY AND NORFOLK COAST PATH

MUCKLEBURGH COLLECTION

NORTH NORFOLK RAILWAY

Sheringham

PRIORY MAZE & GARDENS

NORFOLK SHIRE HORSE CENTRE

CROMER MUSEUM

Cromer

NORFOLK

Cockthorpe

Langham

Blakeney

Wiveton

Newgate

Kelling

SHERINGHAM PARK

SHERINGHAM

Upper Sheringham

Beeston Regis

West Runton

A149

East Runton

Glandford

Saxlingham

Letheringsett

High Kelling

Bodham

A148

East Beckham

Aylmerton

Felbrigg

FELBRIGG HALL

Crossdale Street

Northrep

Field Dalling

Holt

PICTURECRAFT GALLERY

LETHERINGSETT WATERMILL

HOLT

West Beckham

Gresham

Sustead

Roughton

B1436

Lower Green

Bale

Sharrington

Hempstead

BACONSTHORPE CASTLE

Baconsthorpe

Bessingham

Hanworth

Thurgarton

A140

Hindringham

Brinton

Thornage

Stody

Hunworth

Edgefield

Plumstead

Matlaske

Aldborough

Alby Hill

Gunthorpe

Briningham

Little Barningham

Wickmere

Erpingham

ALBY CRAFTS

ALBY GARDENS

Suffield

STRAW MUSEUM

Colby

Antingh

Swanton Novers

Melton Constable

Edgefield Street

Briston

MANNINGTON GARDENS

WOLTERTON PARK

Calthorpe

Itteringham

Corpusty

Saxthorpe

BLICKLING HALL

Ingworth

Banningham

Stibbard

Hindolveston

Thurning

Norton Corner

Oulton

Silvergate

Blickling

Dunkirk

Tuttington

Wood Norton

Guestwick

Heydon

Oulton Street

Aylsham

B1145

Burgh next Aylsham

Brampton

BURE VALLEY RAILWAY

Guestwick Green

Wood Dalling

Salle

Southgate

Fengate

Marsham

Foulsham

Themelthorpe

Cawston

Little London

Eastgate

The Heath

Buxton

FOXLEY WOOD

Reepham

Booton

Brandiston

Haveringland

Hevingham

Foxley

Whitwell Street

Twyford

Bawdeswell

Sparham

ANIMAL ARK

Alderford

Swannington

Upgate

Felthorpe

New Hainford

Hainford

Waterloo

Mill Street

Lyng

Elsing

Lenwade

DINOSAUR ADVENTURE PARK

Morton

Attlebridge

Thorpe Marriot

Horsford

Newton St Faith

Swanton Morley

Hoe

Woodgate

Primrose Green

Weston Longville

Ringland

Taverham

Drayton

Horsham St Faith

NORWICH INTERNATIONAL

Etling Green

North Tuddenham

Weston Green

A47

Hockering

Honingham

Costessey

Mile Cross

New Costessey

Upper Hellesdon

New Cath

Welborne

Marlingford

Bowthorpe

SAINSBURY CENTRE FOR VISUAL ARTS

Earlham

Easton

East Tuddenham

0   1   2   3 miles
0 1 2 3 4 5km

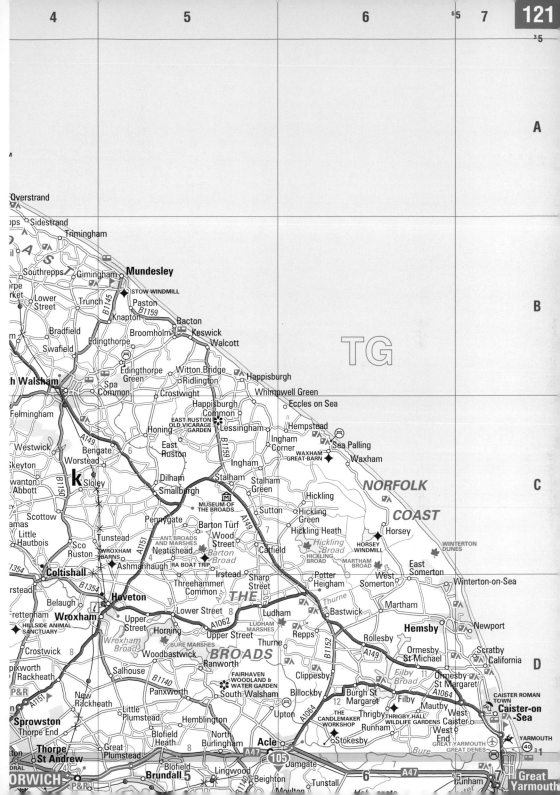

A

B

C

D

Overstrand
Sidestrand
Trimingham
COAST
Mundesley
Southrepps
Gimingham
STOW WINDMILL
Lower Street
Trunch
Paston
B1145
B1159
Knapton
Bacton
Bradfield
Broomholm
Keswick
Edingthorpe
Walcott
Swafield
Edingthorpe Green
Witton Bridge
Happisburgh
h Walsham
Spa Common
Ridlington
Felmingham
Crostwight
Whimpwell Green
Happisburgh Common
Eccles on Sea
TG
East Ruston
EAST RUSTON OLD VICARAGE GARDEN
Lessingham
Hempstead
Honing
Ingham Corner
Sea Palling
Westwick
A149
Bengate
Waxham
WAXHAM GREAT BARN
Skeyton
Worstead
Ingham
Waxham
wanton Abbott
B1150
K
Sloley
Dilham
Stalham
Stalham Green
NORFOLK
Scottow
Smallburgh
Hickling
amas
Little Hautbois
Tunstead
MUSEUM OF THE BROADS
Sutton
Hickling Green
COAST
Sco Ruston
Pennygate
Barton Turf
Wood Street
Hickling Heath
Horsey
B1354
WROXHAM BARNS
ANT, BROADS AND MARSHES
Hickling Broad
HORSEY WINDMILL
WINTERTON DUNES
Coltishall
Neatishead
Barton Broad
Catfield
HICKLING BROAD
MARTHAM BROAD
East Somerton
B1354
Ashmanhaugh
RA BOAT TRIP
Irstead
Sharp Street
Potter Heigham
West Somerton
Winterton-on-Sea
rstead
Threehammer Common
THE
Martham
Belaugh
Hoveton
Lower Street
Ludham
Bastwick
Frettenham
Wroxham
Upper Street
A1062
Thurne
Hemsby
Newport
HILLSIDE ANIMAL SANCTUARY
Horning
Upper Street
Thurne
Repps
Rollesby
Ormesby St Michael
Scratby
Crostwick
Wroxham Broad
BURE MARSHES
Woodbastwick
BROADS
Ranworth
Clippesby
A149
California
P&R
A1151
Salhouse
B1140
Filby Broad
Ormesby St Margaret
CAISTER ROMAN TOWN
New Rackheath
Panxworth
FAIRHAVEN WOODLAND & WATER GARDEN
South Walsham
Billockby
Filby
Mautby
Caister-on-Sea
pxworth Rackheath
Little Plumstead
Hemblington
North Burlingham
Upton
Burgh St Margaret
THE CANDLEMAKER WORKSHOP
THRIGBY HALL WILDLIFE GARDENS
Thrigby
Runham
West Caister
West End
Sprowston
Thorpe End
Blofield Heath
Acle
A1064
Stokesby
GREAT YARMOUTH GREAT DENES
YARMOUTH
Thorpe St Andrew
Great Plumstead
A47
105
Damgate
Bure
Great Yarmouth
ORWICH
Blofield
Brundall   5
Lingwood
Beighton
Tunstall
A47
Runham

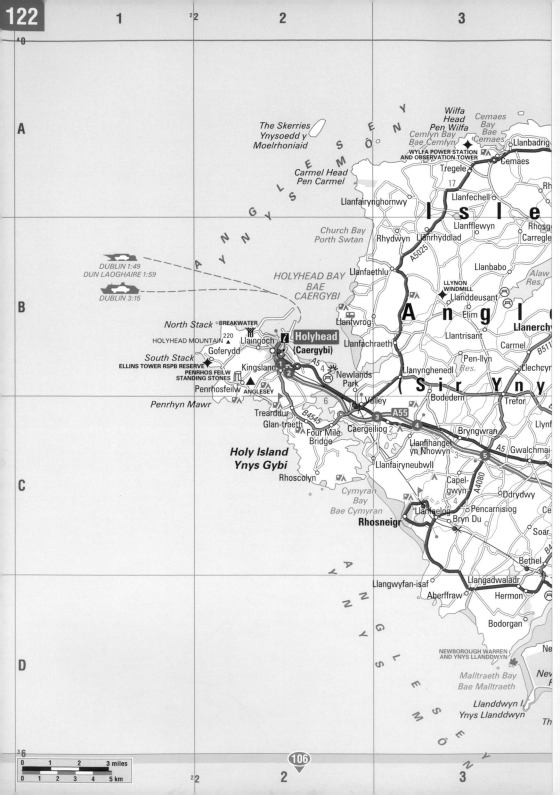

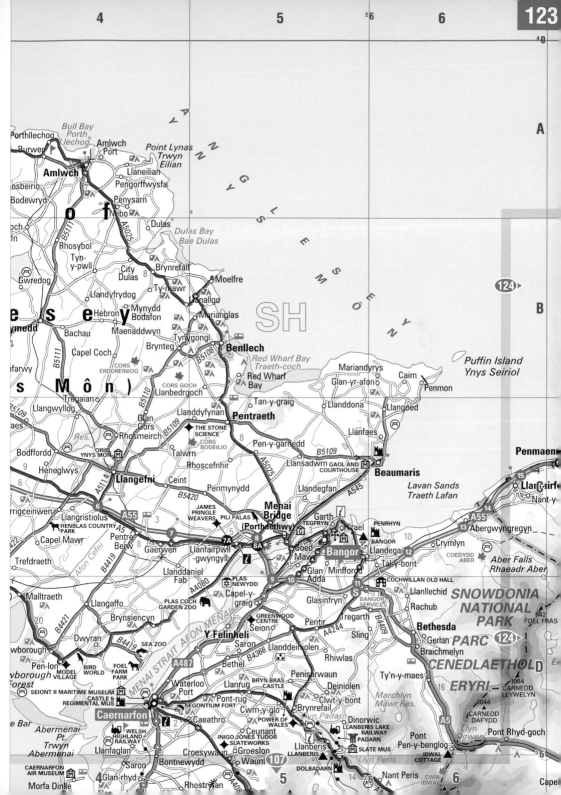

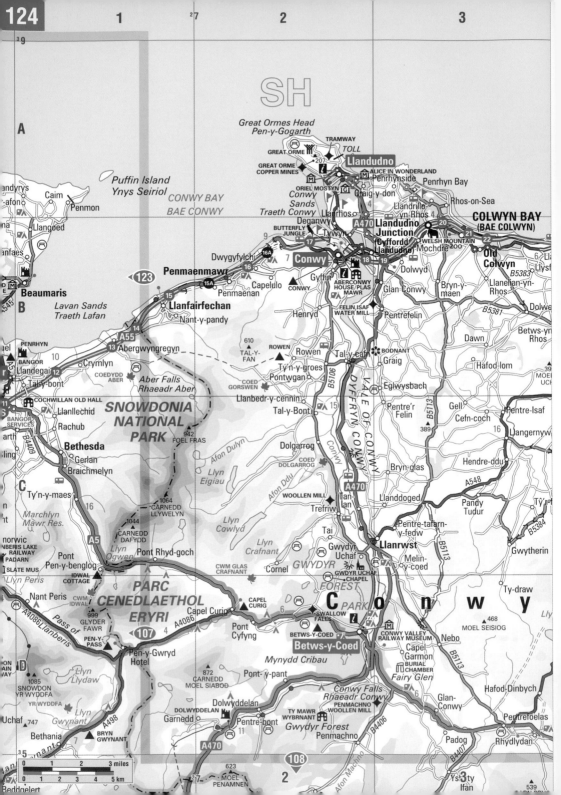

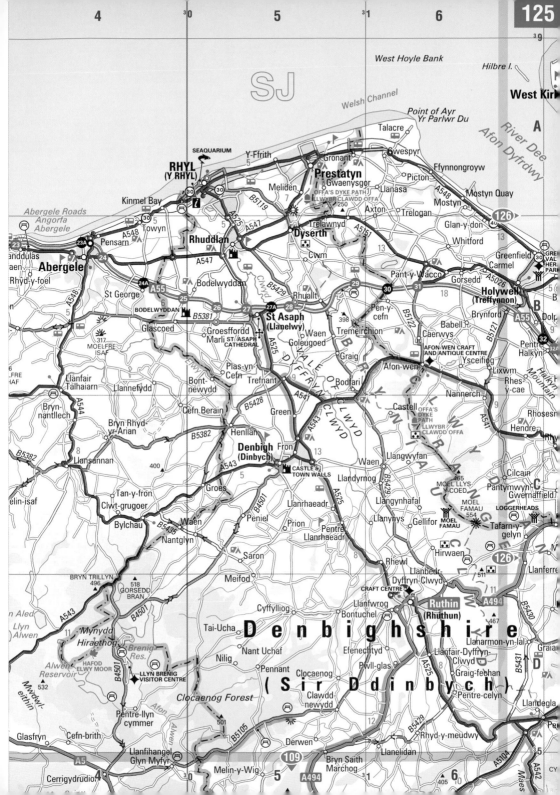

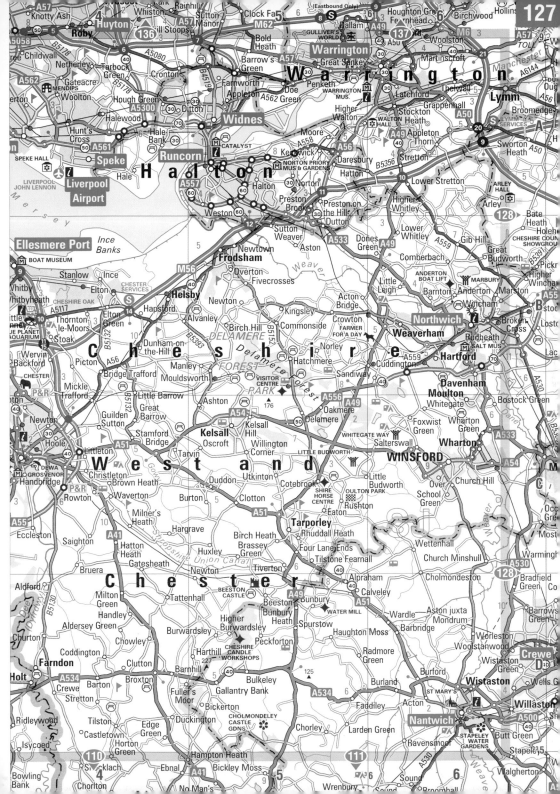

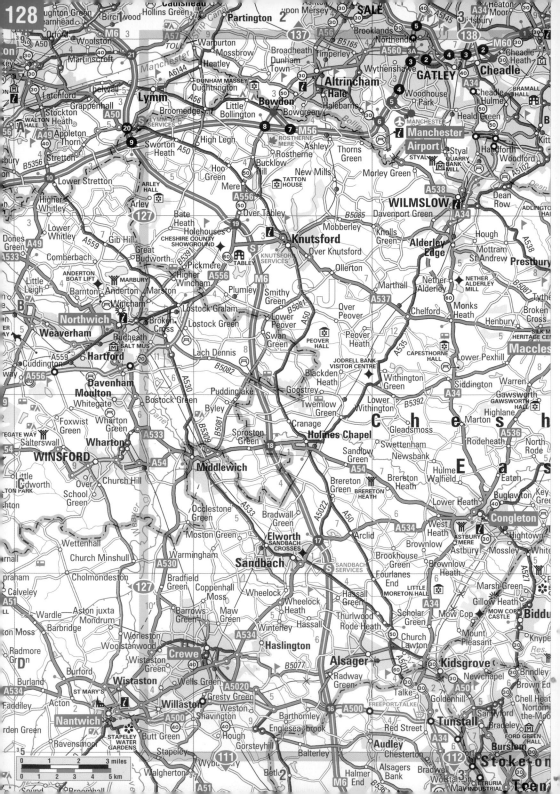

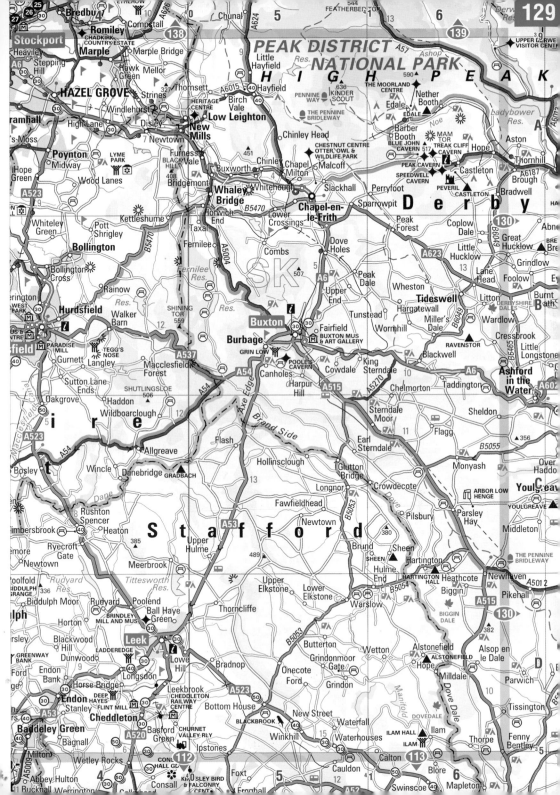

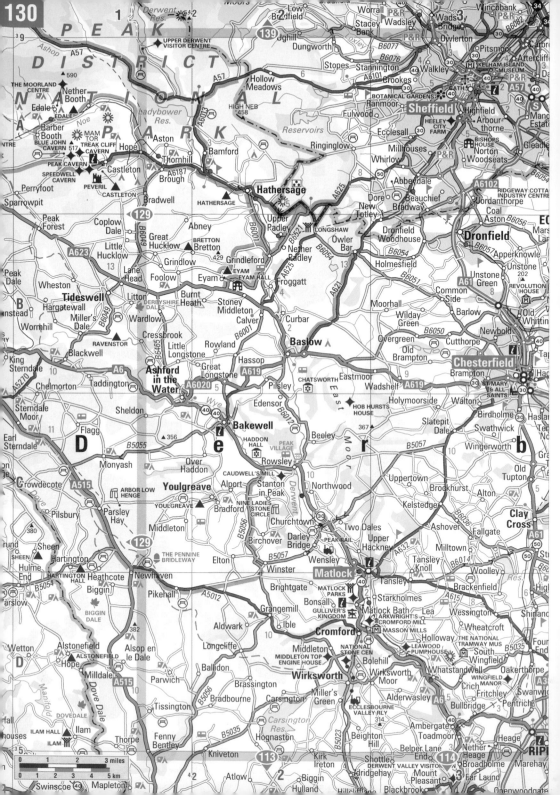

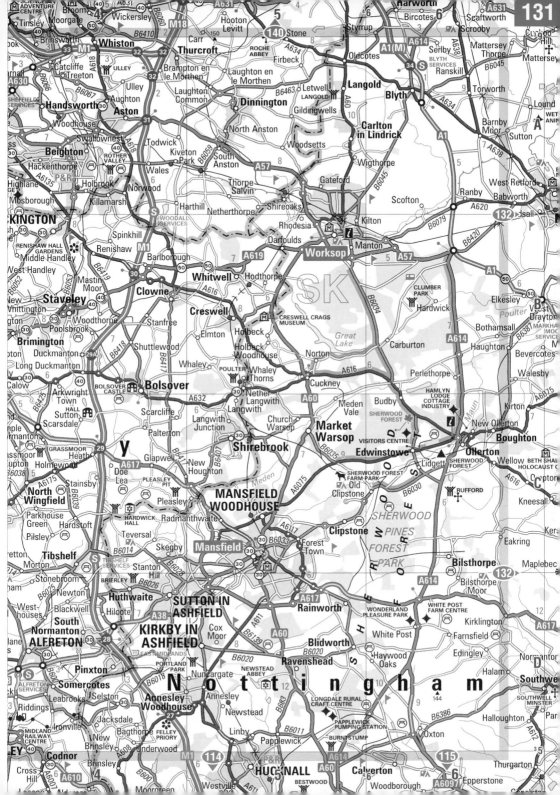

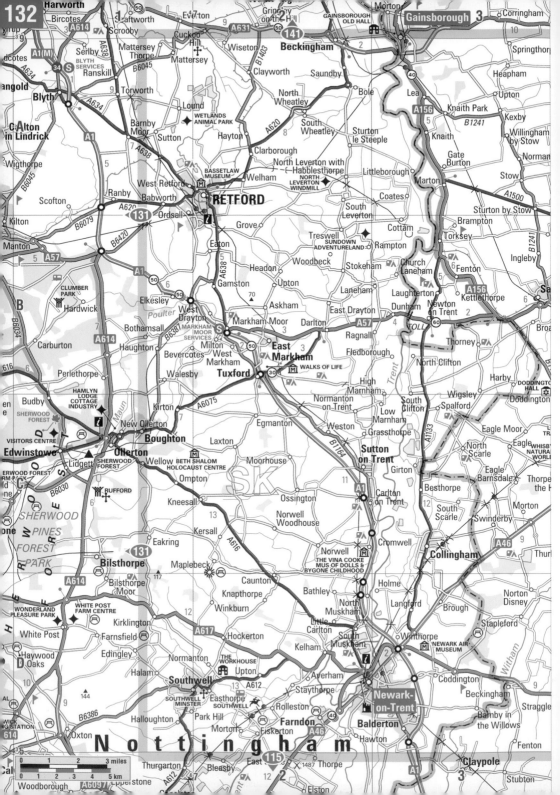

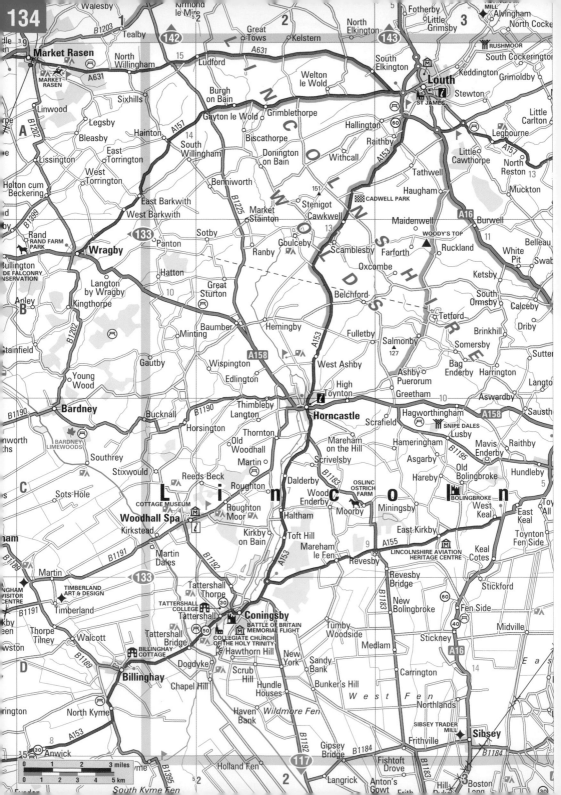

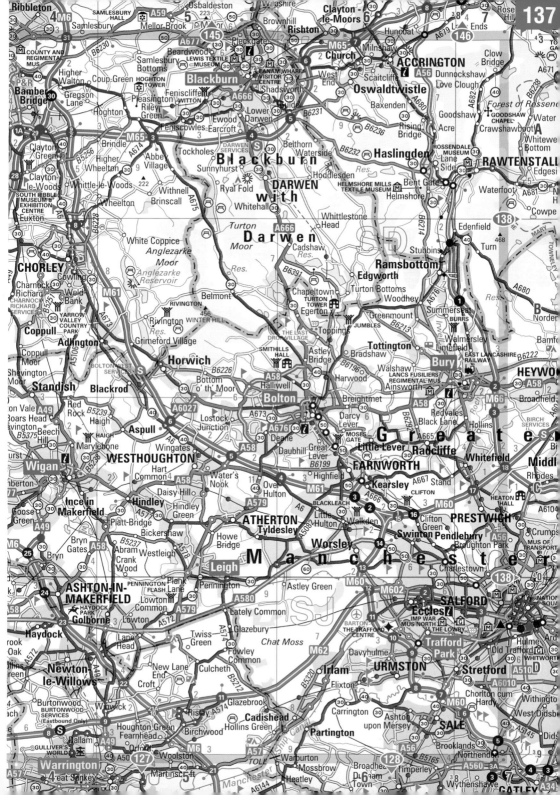

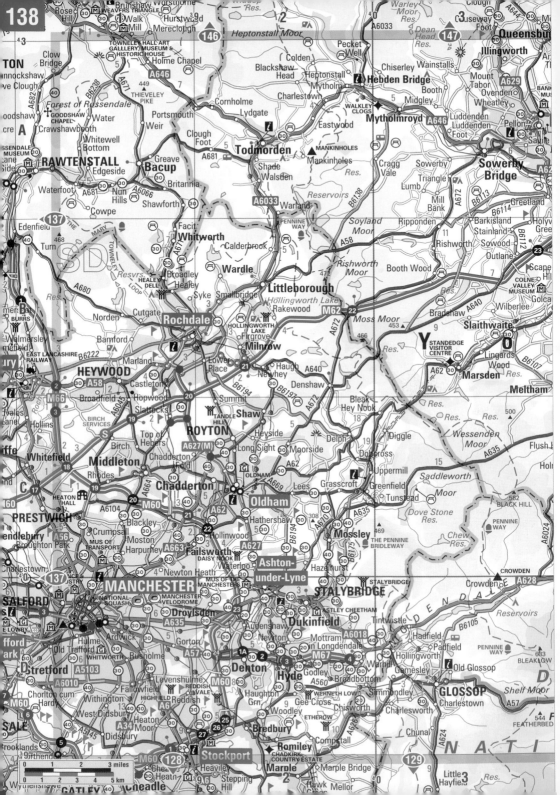

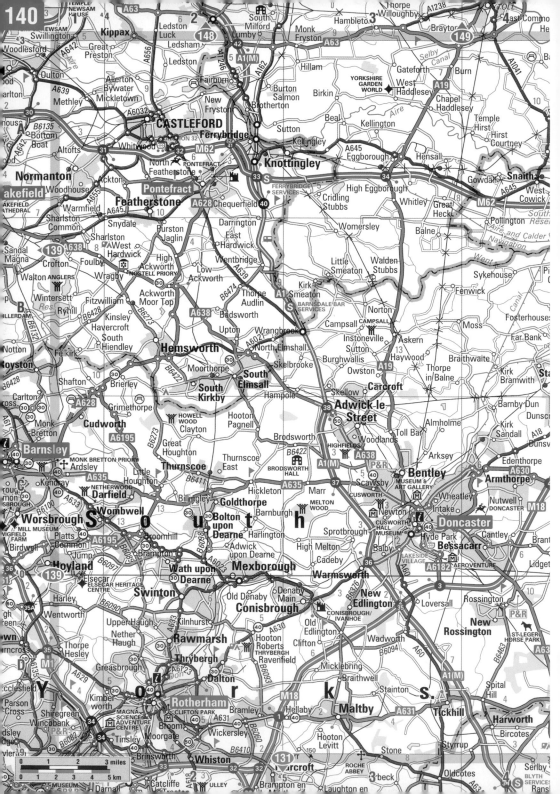

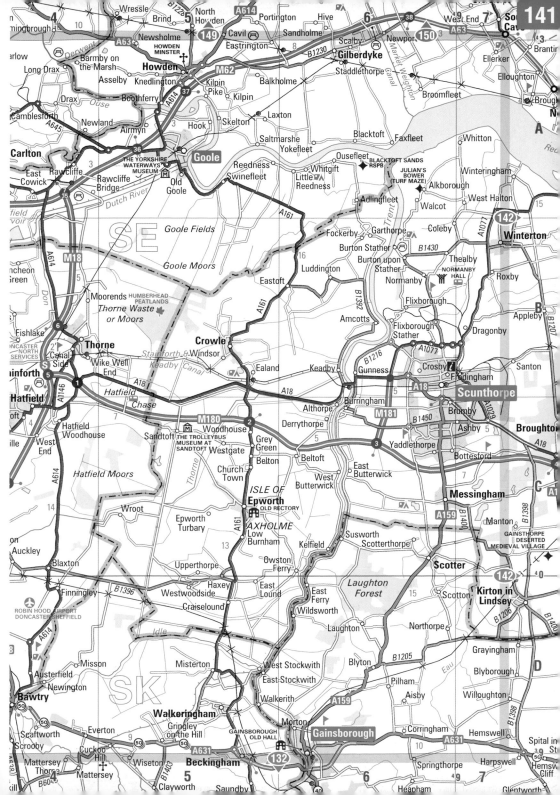

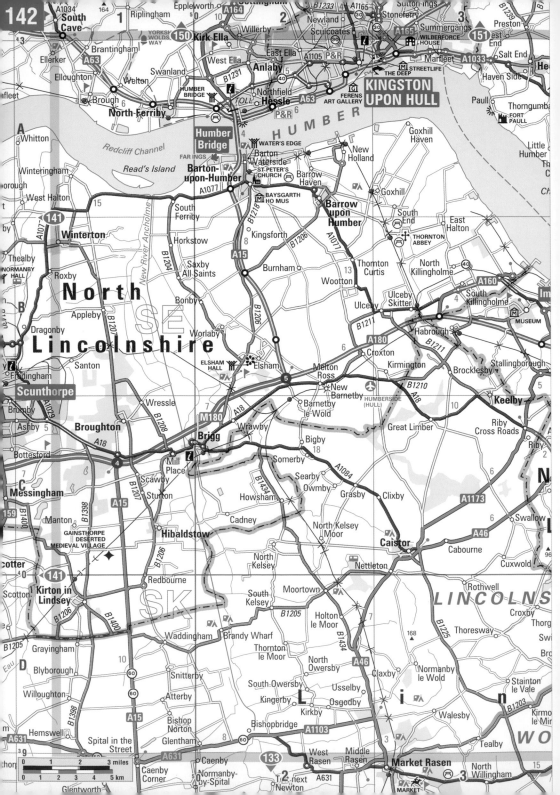

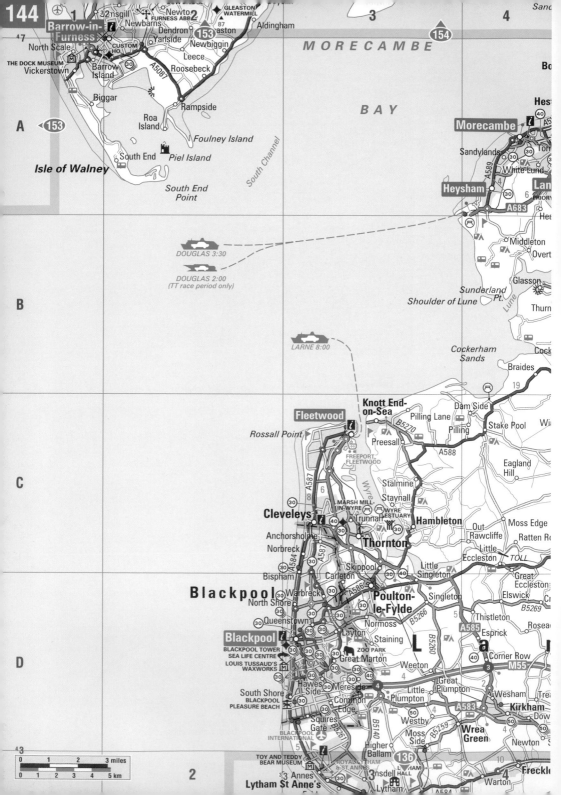

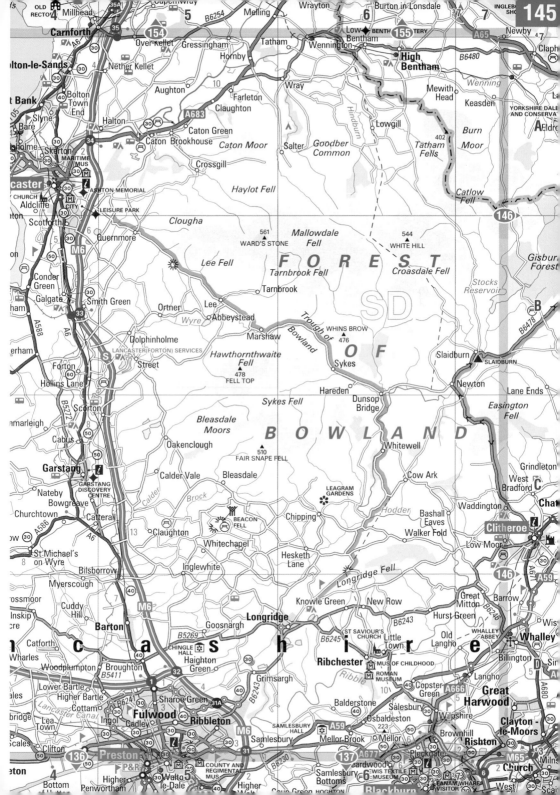

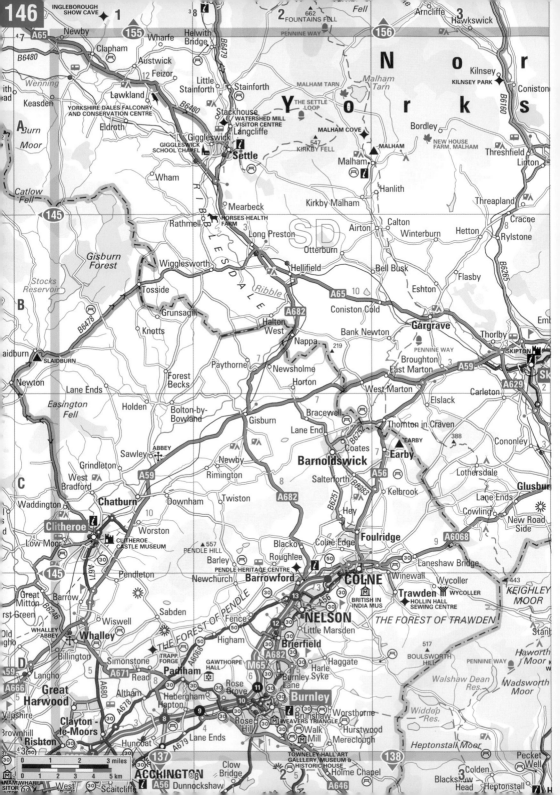

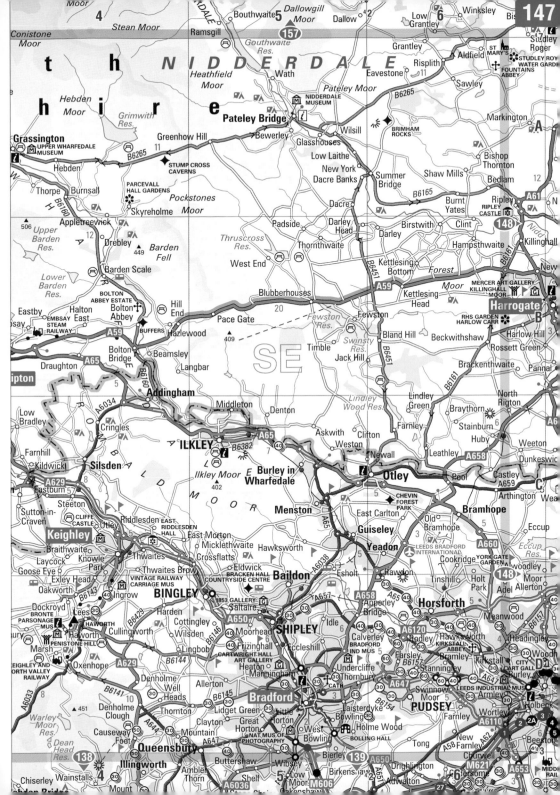

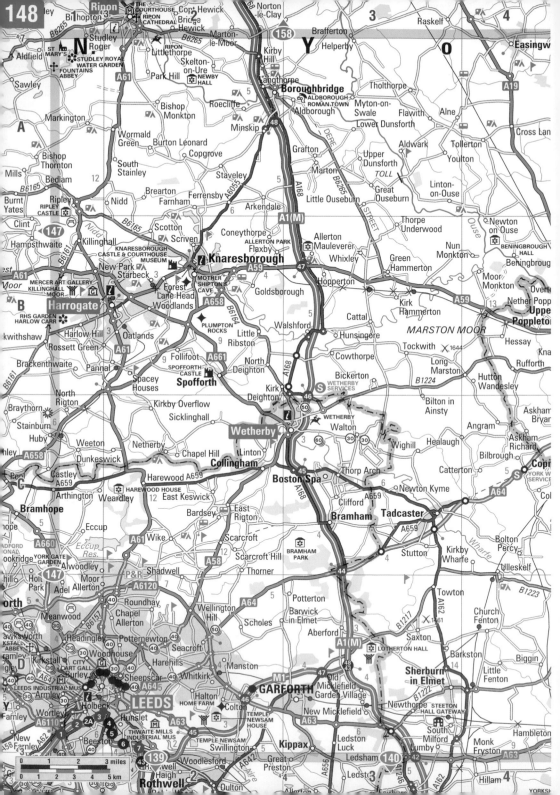

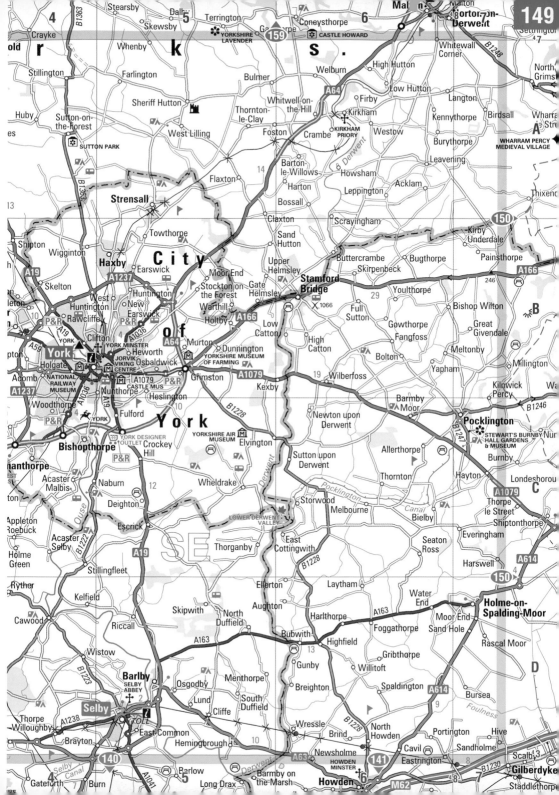

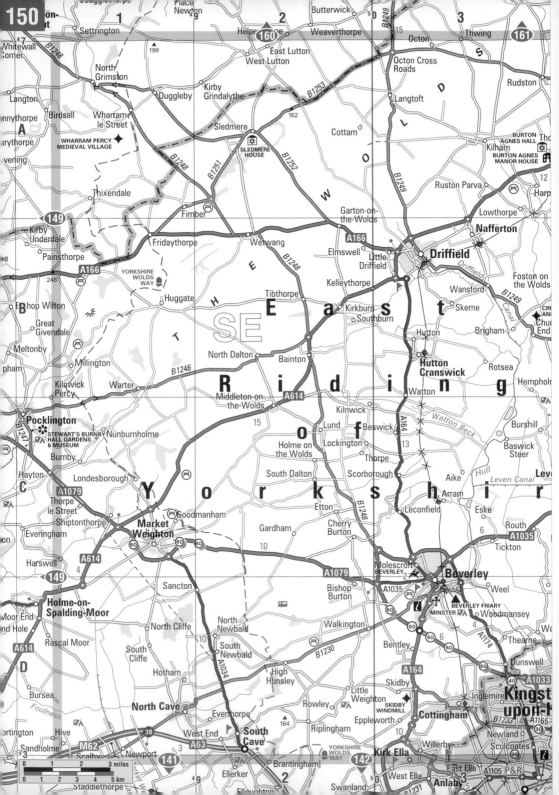

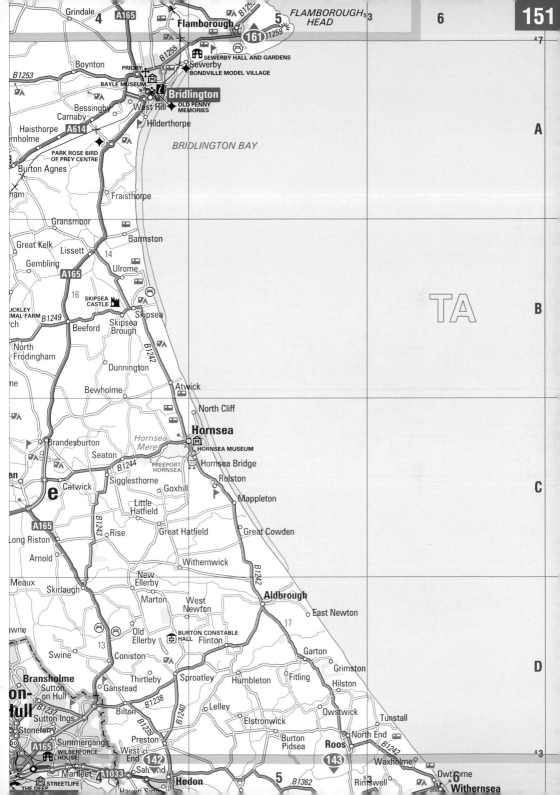

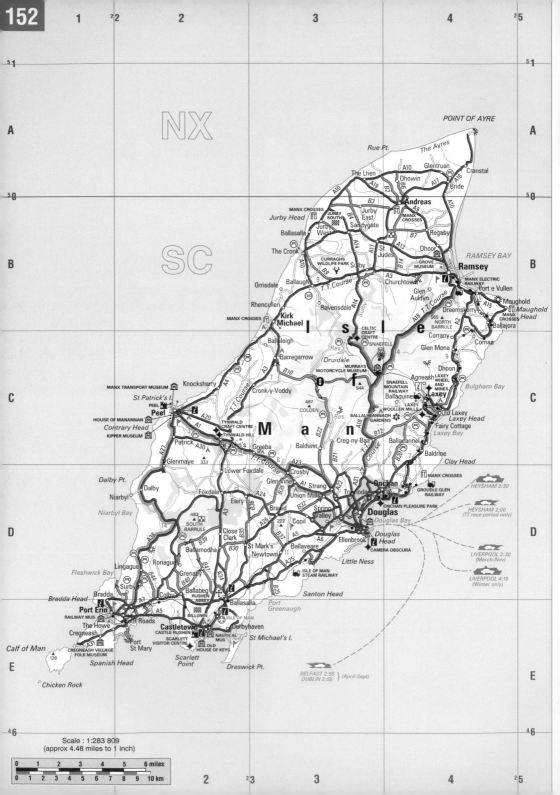

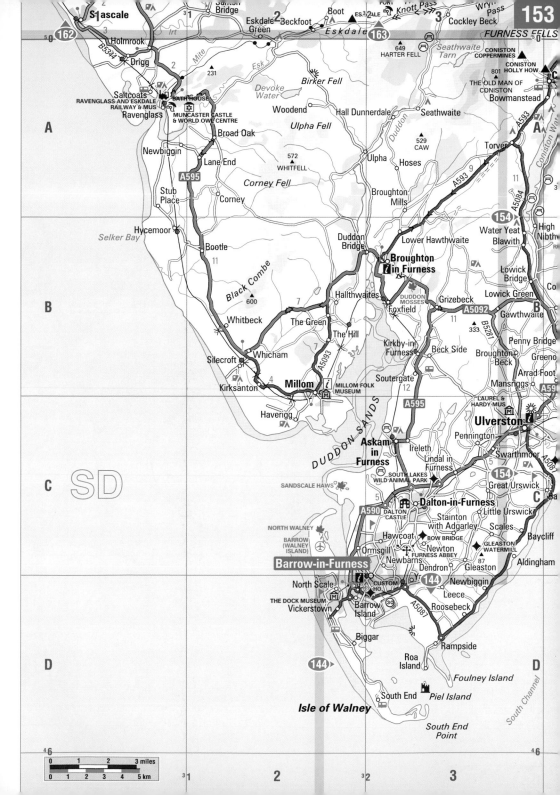

FURNESS FELLS

A

B

C

SD

D

Siscale
Holmrook
Drigg
B5344

Santon
Bridge
Eskdale
Green
Beckfoot
Boot
ES.3
DALE
Knott Pass
Wry'
Pass
Cockley Beck
Eskdale
163
HARTER FELL
Seathwaite
Tarn
CONISTON
COPPERMINES
CONISTON
HOLLY HOW
801
THE OLD MAN OF
CONISTON
Bowmanstead
162
5 0
Saltcoats
RAVENGLASS AND ESKDALE
RAILWAY & MUS
Ravenglass
BATHHOUSE
MUNCASTER CASTLE
& WORLD OWL CENTRE
231
Devoke
Water
Birker Fell
Woodend
Hall Dunnerdale
Seathwaite
Duddon
Birker Fell
Torver
A593
9
A5084
11
A593
Broad Oak
Ulpha Fell
529
CAW
Newbiggin
Lane End
A595
Stub
Place
Corney
WHITFELL
572
Corney Fell
Ulpha
Hoses
Broughton
Mills
154
Water Yeat
Blawith
High
Nibthw
Coniston Water
Hycemoor
Bootle
11
Selker Bay
Black Combe
600
7
Whitbeck
The Green
Silecroft
Whicham
Kirksanton
4
Millom
Haverigg
A5093
7
Duddon
Bridge
Lower Hawthwaite
Broughton
in Furness
Hallthwaites
DUDDON
MOSSES
Foxfield
Grizebeck
A5092
11
Lowick
Bridge
Lowick Green
Gawthwaite
Co
High
Nibthw
The Hill
Kirkby-in-
Furness
Beck Side
333
B5281
Penny Bridge
Broughton
Beck
Greeno
Arrad Foot
Mansriggs
A59
Soutergate
12
MILLOM FOLK
MUSEUM
DUDDON SANDS
A595
LAUREL &
HARDY MUS
Ulverston
Pennington
Swarthmoor
A5087
Askam
in
Furness
Ireleth
Lindal in
Furness
SOUTH LAKES
WILD ANIMAL PARK
154
Great Urswick
SANDSCALE HAWS
5
A590
DALTON
CASTLE
Dalton-in-Furness
Stainton
with Adgarley
Scales
Little Urswick
Baycliff
NORTH WALNEY
BARROW
(WALNEY
ISLAND)
Hawcoat
Ormsgill
BOW BRIDGE
Newton
FURNESS ABBEY
Newbarns
Dendron
Gleaston
GLEASTON
WATERMILL
87
Aldingham
Barrow-in-Furness
North Scale
CUSTOM
HO
39
Newbiggin
Leece
Roosebeck
144
THE DOCK MUSEUM
Vickerstown
Barrow
Island
A5087
Biggar
Rampside
144
Roa
Island
Isle of Walney
South End
Piel Island
Foulney Island
South Channel
South End
Point

4 6

0   1   2   3 miles
0   1   2   3   4   5 km

3 1

2

3 2

3

4 6

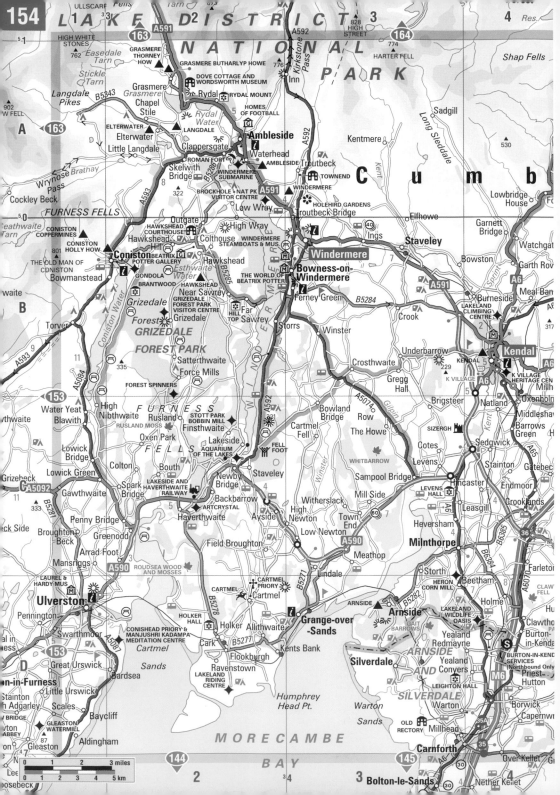

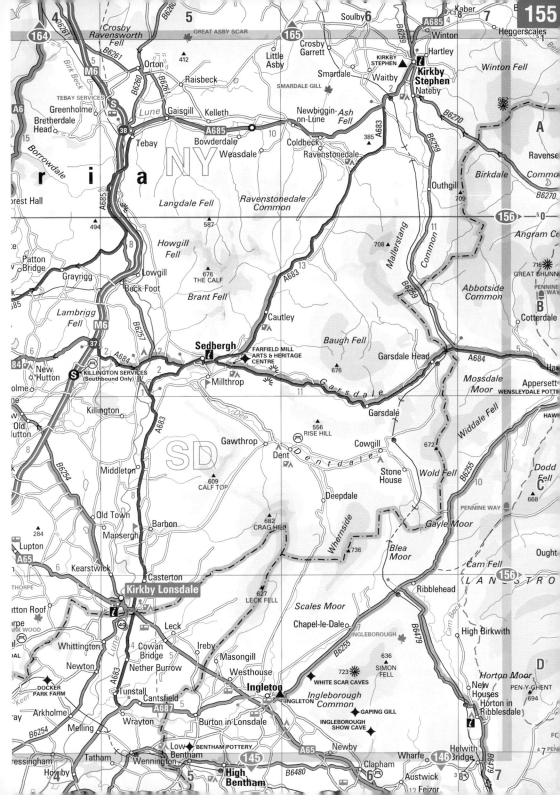

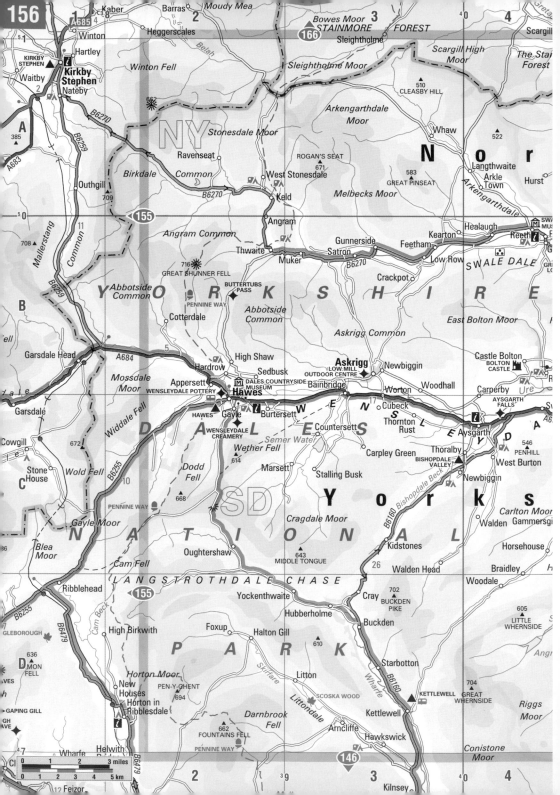

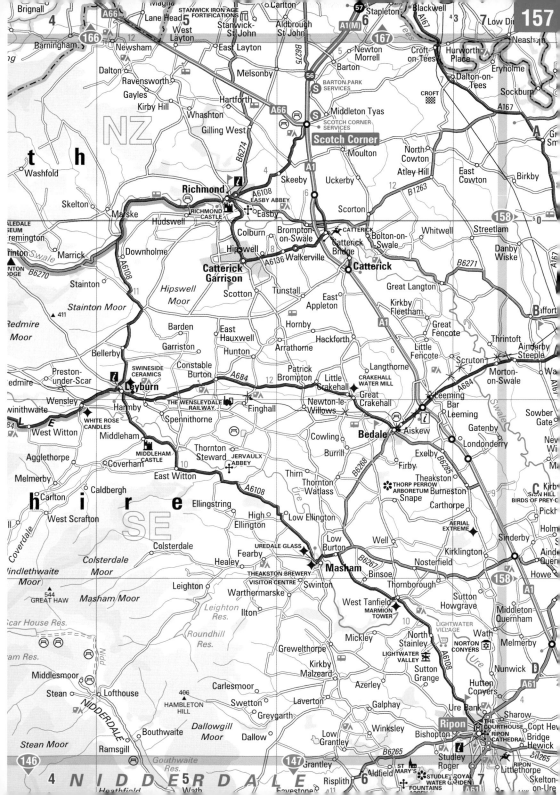

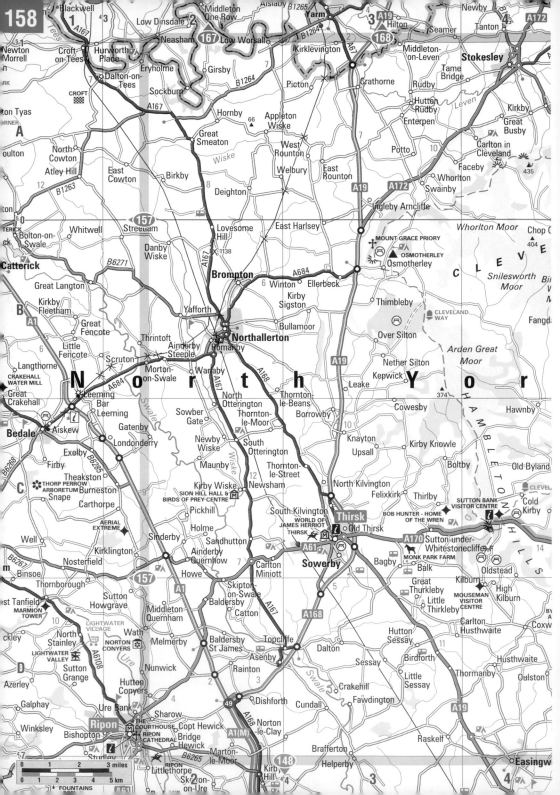

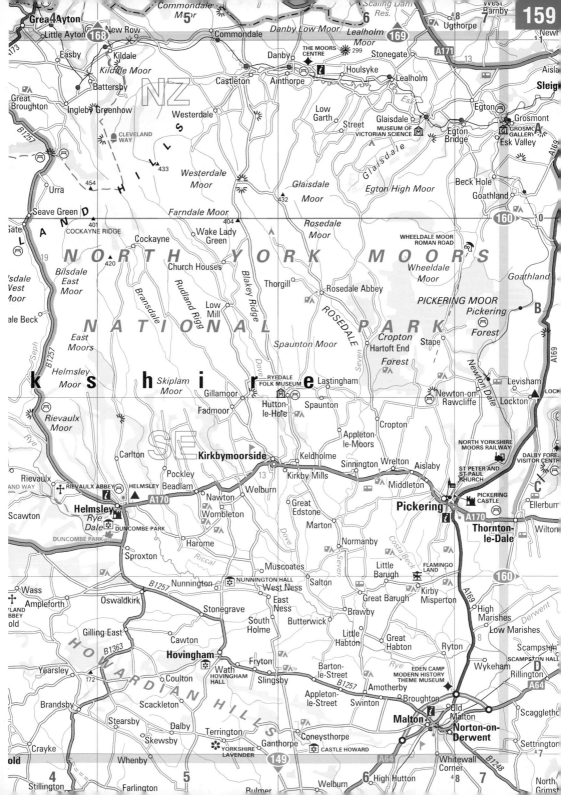

Whitby
Saltwick Bay
East Row
West Barnby
Dunsley
Ugthorpe
Newholm
WHITBY ABBEY
WHITBY
CAPTAIN COOK MEMORIAL MUSEUM
Ruswarp
Stonegate
Lealholm
Aislaby
Stainsacre
Briggswath
Sleights
Sneaton
High Hawsker
Ugglebarnby
Egton
Ness Pt.
CLEVELAND WAY
Sneatonthorpe
Raw
Robin Hood's Bay
OLD COASTGUARD STATION
BOGGLE HOLE
Glaisdale
Grosmont
GROSMONT GALLERY
MUSEUM OF VICTORIAN SCIENCE
Egton Bridge
Esk Valley
Littlebeck
Fylingthorpe
Glaisdale
Old Peak
Egton High Moor
Beck Hole
Goathland
Ravenscar
NZ
Flask Inn
Fylingdales Moor
WHEELDALE MOOR ROMAN ROAD
Staintondale
STAINTONDALE SHIRE HORSE
CLEVELAND WAY
NORTH YORK MOORS NATIONAL PARK
Wheeldale Moor
Goathland Moor
Harwood Dale Forest
Harwood Dale
Cloughton Newlands
Cloughton
PICKERING MOOR
Pickering Forest
Saltergate
Langdale Forest
Broxa Forest
Cropton Hartoft End Forest
Stape
Burniston
Cromer
MOORLAND EXPERIENCE
TOLL
Silpho
Broxa
Suffield
Langdale End
Hackness
Scalby
SCARBOROUGH
SEA LIFE
Newton Dale
Levisham
LOCKTON
Newton-on-Rawcliffe
Lockton
Staindale Forest
Wrench Green
Everley
Barrowcliff
Newby
NORTH RIDING FOREST PARK
Trouts Dale
Wykeham Forest
Cropton
NORTH YORKSHIRE MOORS RAILWAY
Low Dalby
DALBY FOREST VISITOR CENTRE
Dalby Forest
FORGE VALLEY WOODLANDS
Falsgrave
Wrelton
Aislaby
ST PETER AND ST PAUL CHURCH
East Ayton
West Ayton
THE HONEY FARM
Middleton
SE
PICKERING CASTLE
Sawdon
Hutton Buscel
WORDSWORTH GALLERY
Osgodby
Irton
Pickering
Ellerburn
Ruston
Seamer
Thornton-le-Dale
Wilton
Ebberston
Snainton
Wykeham
Allerston
Brompton
Costa Beck
Little Barugh
FLAMINGO LAND
Kirby Misperton
Great Barugh
THE CARRS
Yedingham
Willerby
Flixton
Staxton
High Marishes
Derwent
East Heslerton
Sherburn
Ganton
YORKSHIRE WOLDS WAY
Low Marishes
Great Habton
Ryton
West Knapton
East Knapton
Scampston
SCAMPSTON HALL
Potter Brompton
West Heslerton
Fordon
Rye
EDEN CAMP MODERN HISTORY THEME MUSEUM
Wykeham
Rillington
WOLDS WAY LAVENDER
Amotherby
Broughton
Thorpe Bassett
Wintringham
Foxholes
Swinton
Old Malton
Malton
Norton-on-Derwent
Scagglethorpe
Place Newton
Butterwick
Settrington
Helperthorpe
Weaverthorpe
Octon
East Lutton
West Lutton
North Grimston
Octon Cross Roads
A171 A174 A169 A170 A165 A64 B1410 B1416 B1447 B1415 B1258 B1257 B1248 B1249 B1253 B1261
169 159 150
0 1 2 3 miles
0 1 2 3 4 5 km

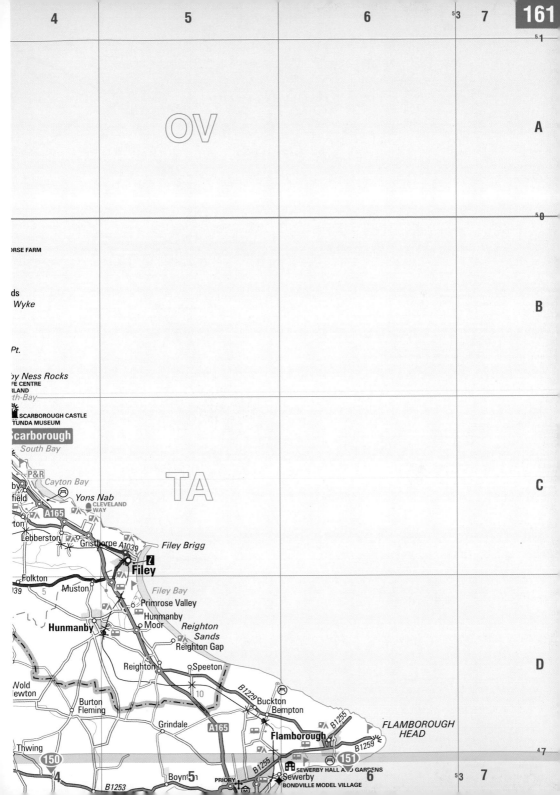

OV

⁵0

A

B

ORSE FARM

ds
Wyke

Pt.

by Ness Rocks
FE CENTRE
RLAND
th-Bay

■ SCARBOROUGH CASTLE
TUNDA MUSEUM

carborough
South Bay

P&R

Cayton Bay

TA

Yons Nab
CLEVELAND
WAY

field

A165

ton

Lebberston   Gristhorpe A1039   *Filey Brigg*

Folkton

Filey

39   5   Muston

Filey Bay

Primrose Valley

Hunmanby
Moor

*Reighton
Sands*

Hunmanby

Reighton Gap

Reighton   Speeton

Wold
ewton

B1229

10   Buckton

Burton
Fleming   Bempton

**FLAMBOROUGH
HEAD**

Grindale   A165

B1255

Thwing

Flamborough

B1259

⁴7

150

SEWERBY HALL AND GARDENS

151

4   Boynt **5**   PRIORY   Sewerby
BONDVILLE MODEL VILLAGE

6   ⁵3   **7**

B1253

C

D

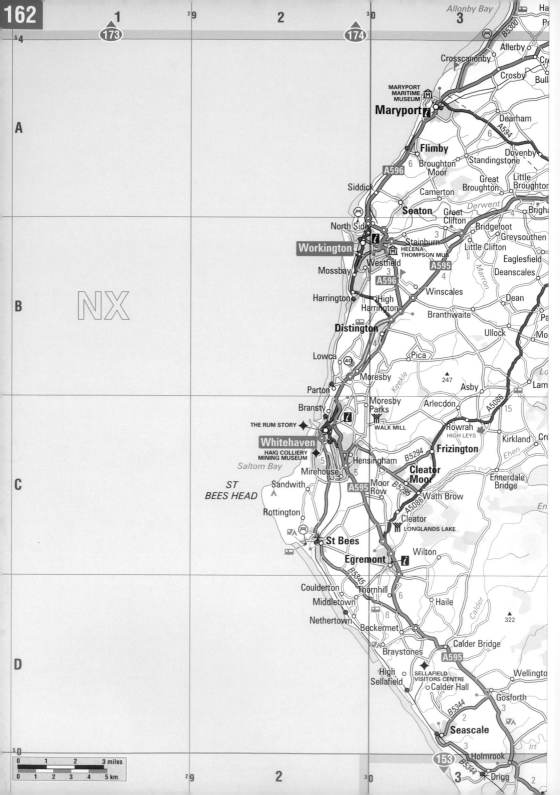

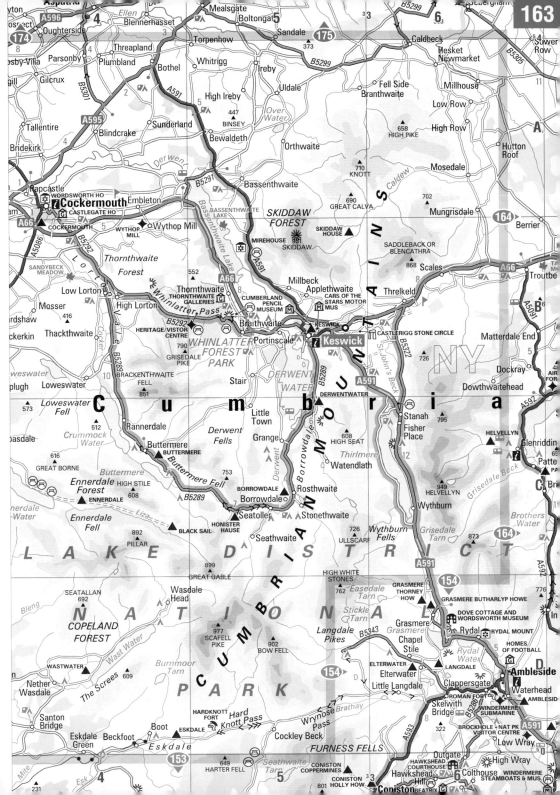

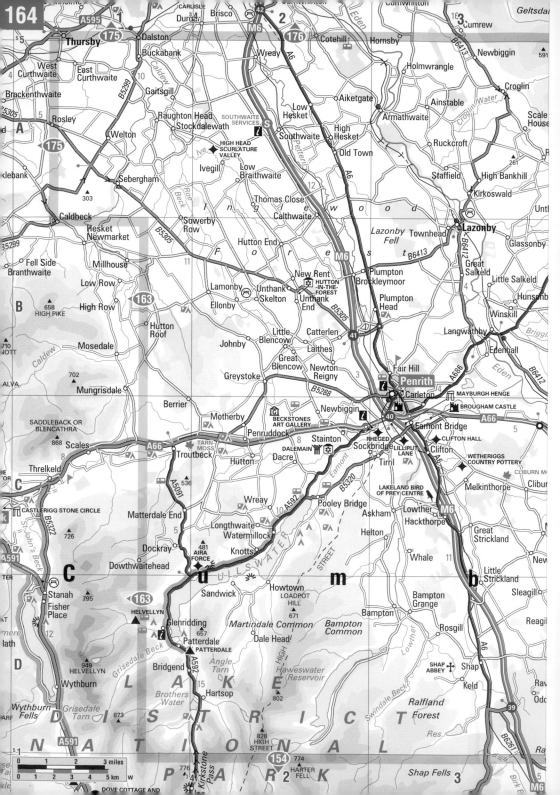

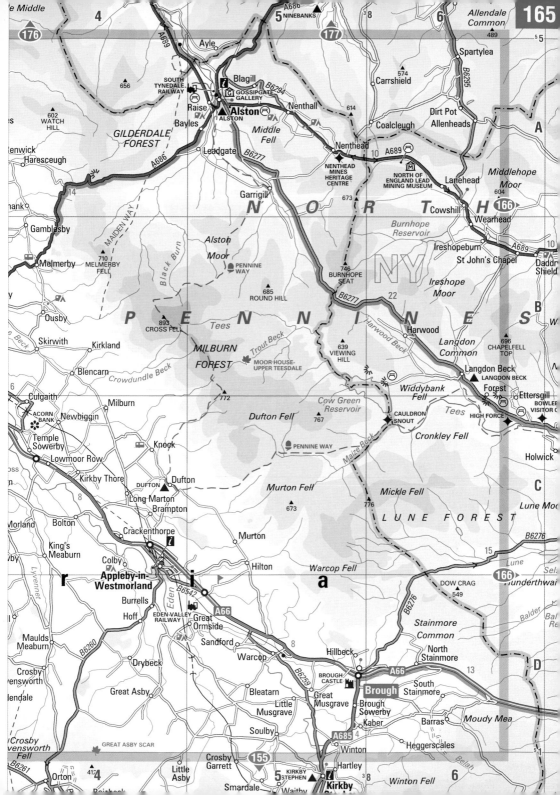

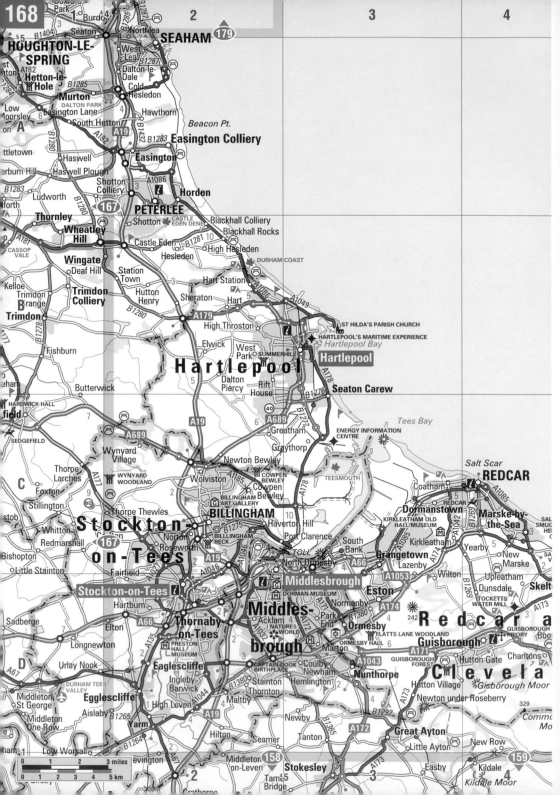

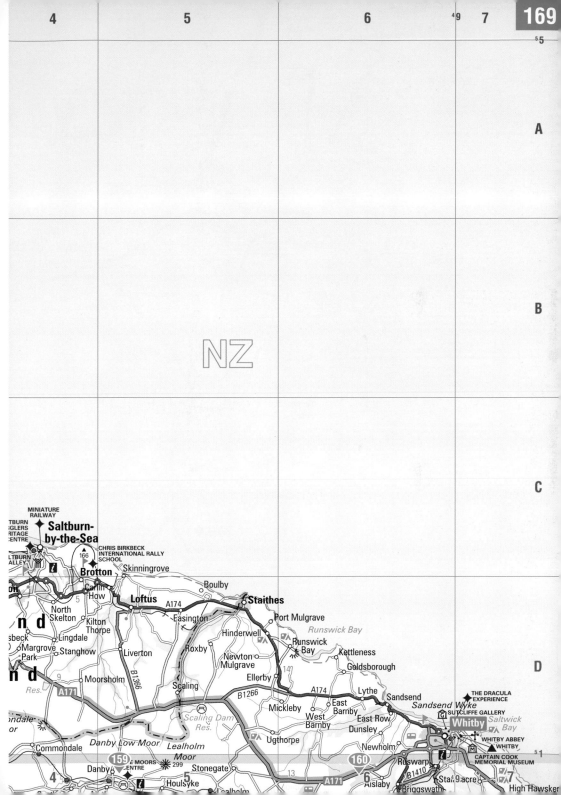

⁵5

A

B

NZ

C

MINIATURE
RAILWAY

TBURN
GLERS
RITAGE
ENTRE

◆ **Saltburn-
by-the-Sea**

LTBURN
ALLEY

CHRIS BIRKBECK
INTERNATIONAL RALLY
SCHOOL

166

Brotton　Skinningrove

on

Carlin
How

Loftus　　Boulby

5

North
Skelton

A174　**Staithes**

Loftus

Kilton
Thorpe

Easington　Port Mulgrave

sbeck　Lingdale

Hinderwell　*Runswick Bay*

Margrove
Park　Stanghow　Liverton　Roxby　Runswick
Bay

n d　Newton
Mulgrave　Kettleness

Moorsholm　Ellerby　Goldsborough

D

Res.　**A171**

9

B1366　Scaling

14

Sandsend Wyke

THE DRACULA
EXPERIENCE

B1266　Lythe

East
Barnby　Sandsend

SUTCLIFFE GALLERY

*Scaling Dam
Res.*

Mickleby　West
Barnby　East Row

Whitby　*Saltwick
Bay*

ondale
or

Ugthorpe　Dunsley

Danby Low Moor　*Lealholm*

Newholm

Commondale　*Moor*　299　Stonegate

159
E MOORS
ENTRE

Ruswarp

WHITBY ABBEY
WHITBY

CAPTAIN COOK
MEMORIAL MUSEUM

⁵1

Danby　Houlsyke　13　**A171**

160

Aislaby　B1410

acre

Briggswath　High Hawsker

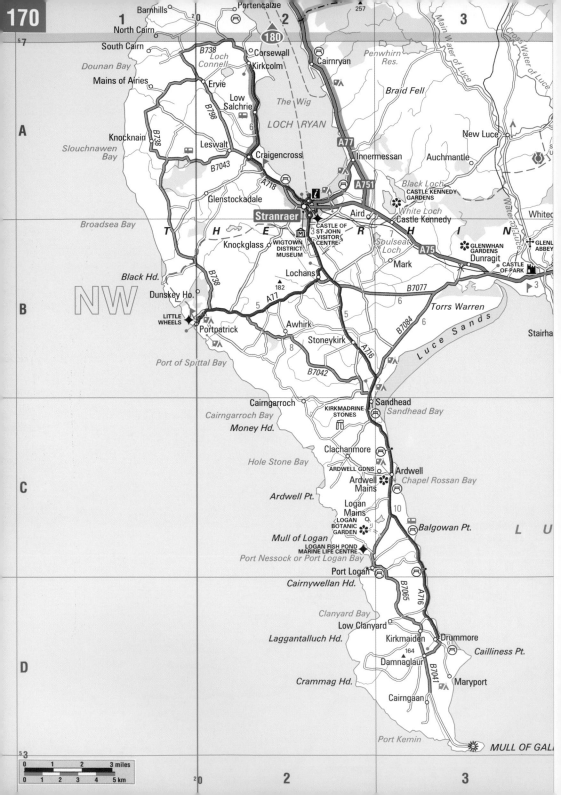

Barnhills
Portencalzie
North Cairn
257
Main Water of Luce
Cross Water of Luce

South Cairn
180
Corsewall
B738
Loch
Connell
Kirkcolm
Cairnryan
Penwhirn
Res.

Dounan Bay
Ervie
Braid Fell

Mains of Airies
Low
Salchrie
B798
The Wig
New Luce

A
LOCH RYAN
A77

Knocknain
B738
Leswalt
Craigencross
Innermessan
Auchmantle
New Luce

Slouchnawen
Bay
B7043
A718
A751
Black Loch

Glenstockadale
CASTLE KENNEDY
GARDENS
White Loch

Broadsea Bay
Stranraer
Aird
Castle Kennedy

T H E
CASTLE OF
ST JOHN
VISITOR
CENTRE
R H I N

Knockglass
WIGTOWN
DISTRICT
MUSEUM
Soulseat
Loch
GLENWHAN
GARDENS
GLEN
ABBEY

Black Hd.
B738
Lochans
Mark
A75
Dunragit
CASTLE
OF PARK
Whited

NW
A77
182
B7077
3

Dunskey Ho.
5
Torrs Warren
Stairha

LITTLE
WHEELS
Awhirk
5
B7084
Luce Sands

Portpatrick
Stoneykirk
A716
6

Port of Spittal Bay
8
B7042

Cairngarroch
Sandhead

KIRKMADRINE
STONES
Sandhead Bay

Cairngarroch Bay

Money Hd.

Clachanmore

C
Hole Stone Bay
ARDWELL GDNS
Ardwell

Ardwell
Mains
Chapel Rossan Bay

Ardwell Pt.
Logan
Mains
10

LOGAN
BOTANIC
GARDEN
Balgowan Pt.
L U

Mull of Logan
LOGAN FISH POND
MARINE LIFE CENTRE

Port Nessock or Port Logan Bay
Port Logan

Cairnywellan Hd.
B7065
A716

Clanyard Bay

Laggantalluch Hd.
Low Clanyard
Kirkmaiden
Drummore

164
Cailliness Pt.

D
Damnaglaur
B7041

Crammag Hd.
Maryport

Cairngaan

Port Kemin
MULL OF GAL

0 1 2 3 miles
0 1 2 3 4 5 km

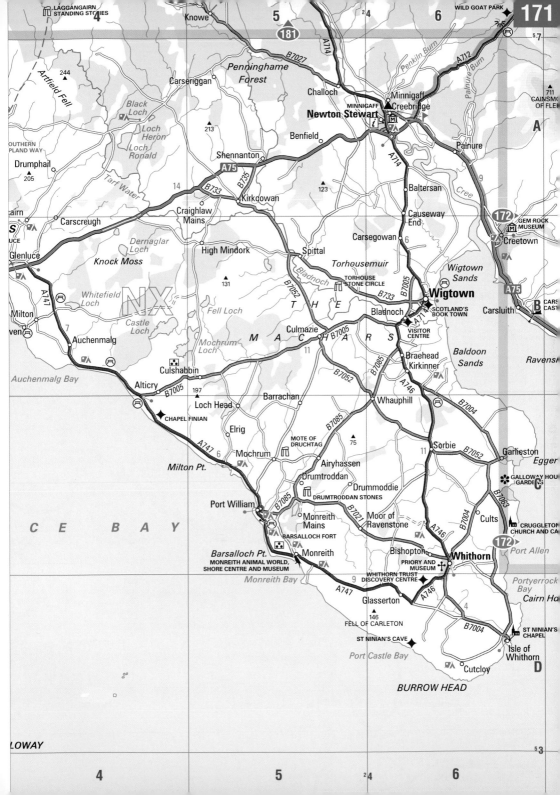

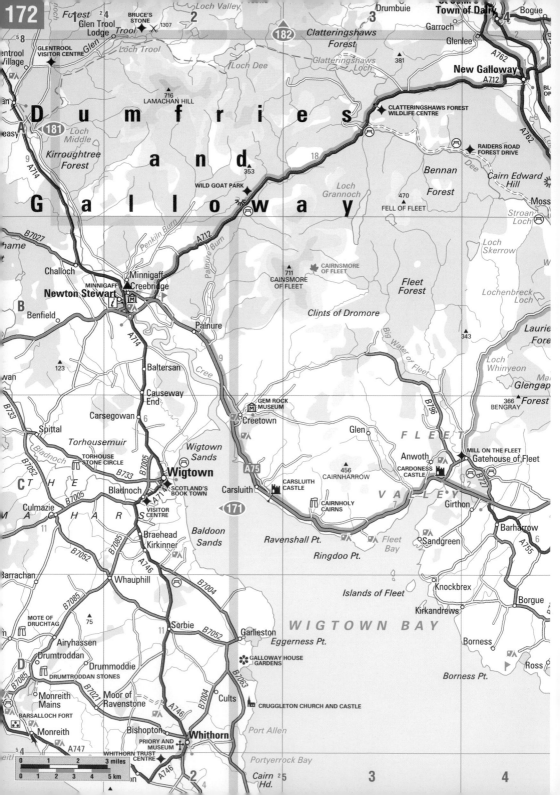

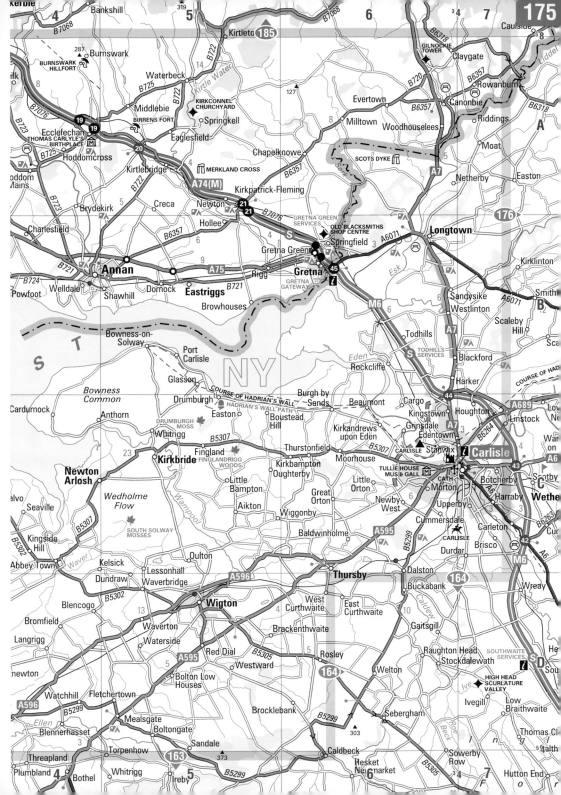

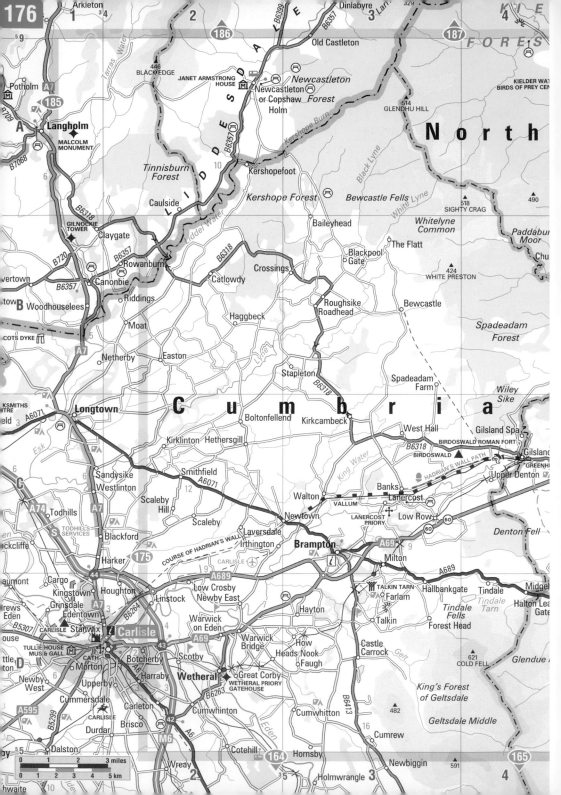

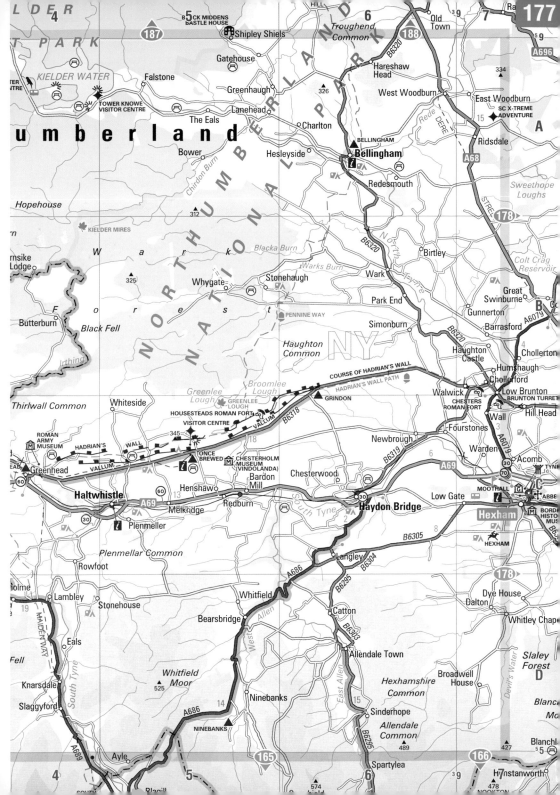

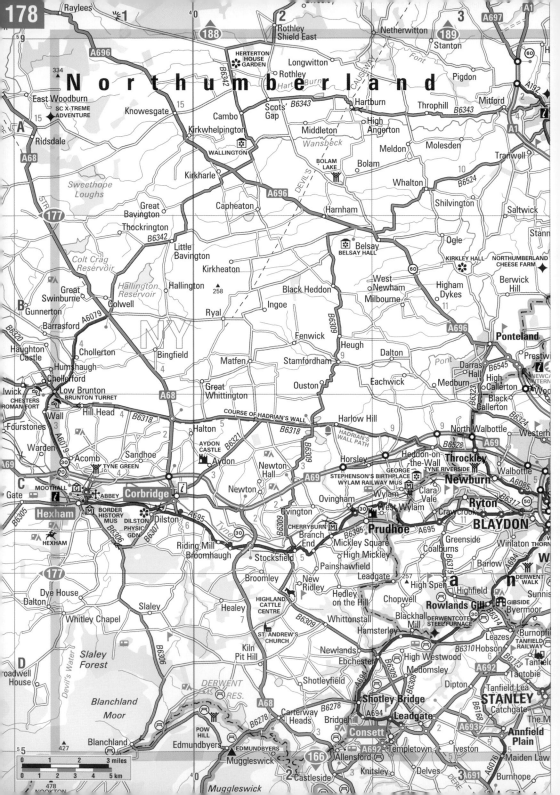

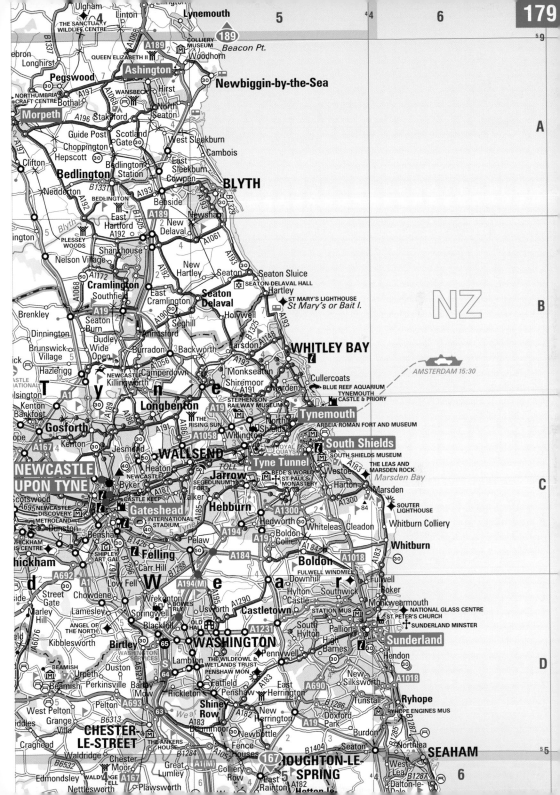

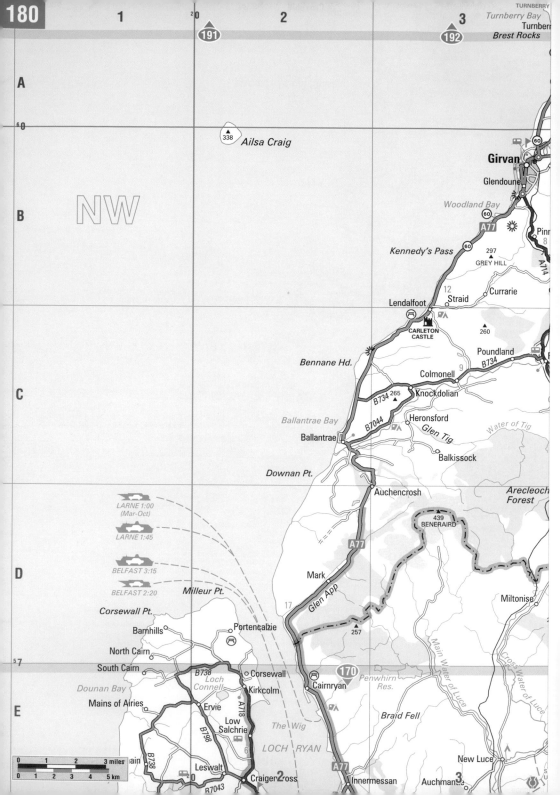

TURNBERRY
Turnberry Bay
Turnberr
Brest Rocks

338 *Ailsa Craig*

Girvan

Glendoune

Woodland Bay

A77

Pinr

Kennedy's Pass

297
GREY HILL

12
Straid

Currarie

Lendalfoot

CARLETON
CASTLE

260

Poundland

Bennane Hd.

Colmonell

B734

9

B734 265
Knockdolian

Heronsford

Ballantrae Bay

B7044

Glen Tig

Water of Tig

Ballantrae

Balkissock

Downan Pt.

Auchencrosh

*Arecleoch
Forest*

LARNE 1:00
(Mar-Oct)

439
BENERAIRD

LARNE 1:45

BELFAST 3:15

Mark

Miltonise

BELFAST 2:20   *Milleur Pt.*

A77

Corsewall Pt.

Glen App

257

Barnhills

Portencalzie

17

North Cairn

South Cairn

Corsewall

B738

170

Penwhirn
Res.

Dounan Bay

*Loch
Connell*

Cairnryan

Mains of Airies

Kirkcolm

Ervie

A718

Braid Fell

Low
Salchrie

The Wig

LOCH RYAN

0   1   2   3 miles
0 1 2 3 4 5 km

ain

B798

B738

New Luce

Leswalt

Craiger2ross

A77

Innermessan

Auchmant

B7043

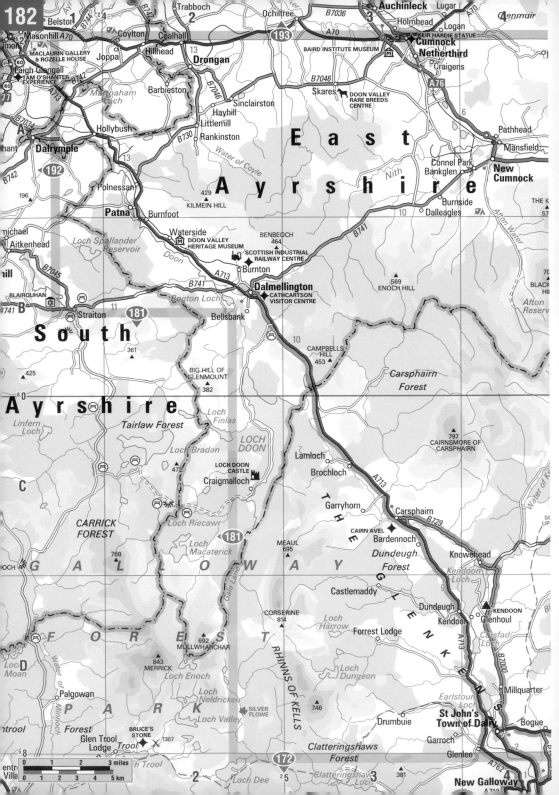

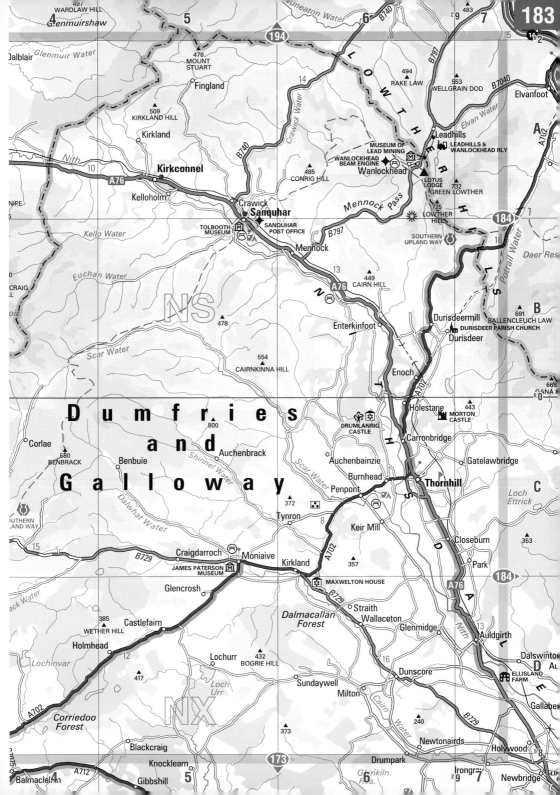

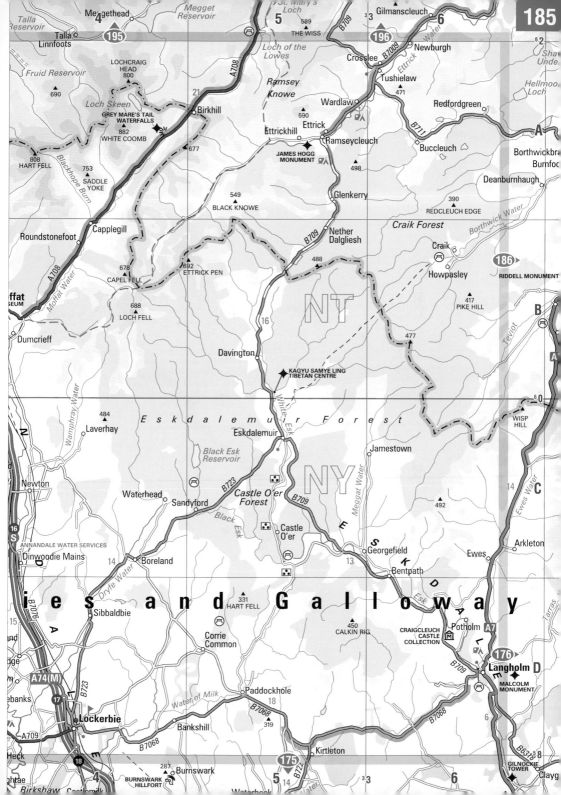

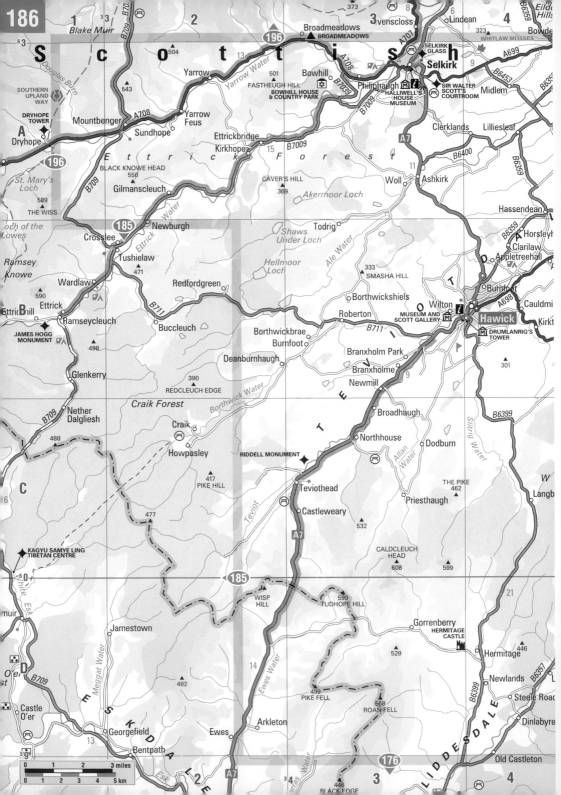

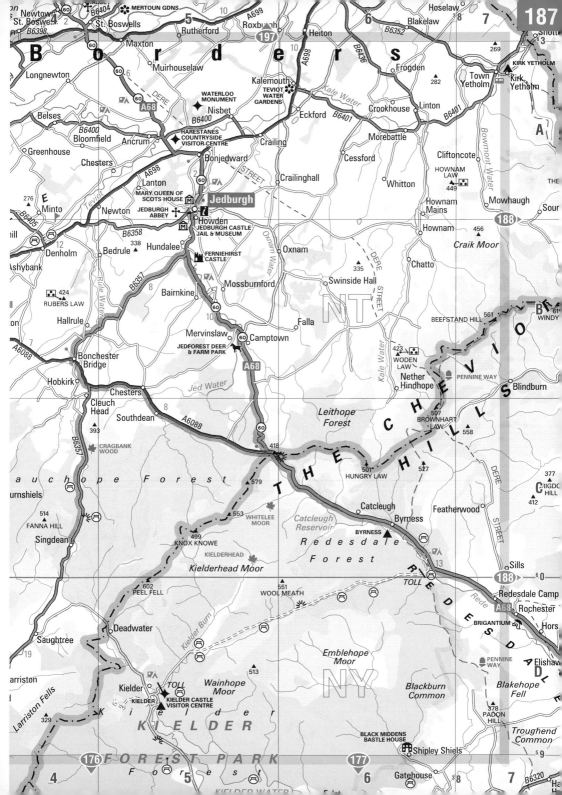

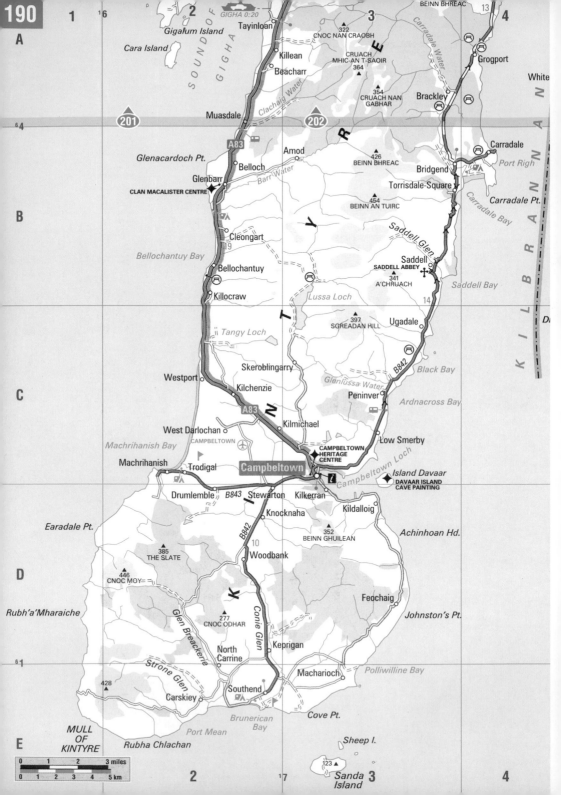

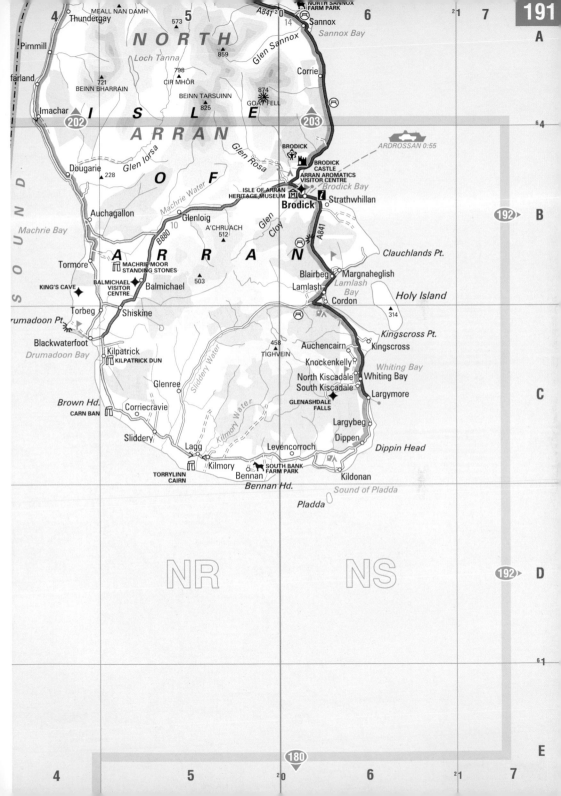

NORTH

Thundergay
MEALL NAN DAMH
573
859
Loch Tanna
798
CIR MHÒR
721
BEINN BHARRAIN
874
BEINN TARSUINN
825
GOAT FELL

ISLE

Pirnmill

Imachar
202

Dougarie

228

Glen Iorsa

Auchagallon

Tormore

MACHRIE MOOR
STANDING STONES
503

KING'S CAVE
BALMICHAEL
VISITOR
CENTRE
Balmichael

Torbeg
Shiskine
Kilpatrick
KILPATRICK DUN

Drumadoon Pt.

Blackwaterfoot
Drumadoon Bay

Brown Hd.
CARN BAN
Corriecravie

Glenree

Sliddery

Lagg
Kilmory
TORRYLINN
CAIRN
Bennan
SOUTH BANK
FARM PARK
Bennan Hd.

ARRAN

Machrie Bay
MACHRIE Water

B880
10
Glenloig
A'CHRUACH
512

ARRAN

Glen Cloy

Glen Rosa

OF

BRODICK
BRODICK
CASTLE
ARRAN AROMATICS
VISITOR CENTRE
ISLE OF ARRAN
HERITAGE MUSEUM
Brodick
Strathwhillan
Brodick Bay

ARDROSSAN 0:55

ARRAN

A841

Blairbeg
Lamlash
Cordon

Clauchlands Pt.

Margnaheglish
Lamlash
Bay
Holy Island

458
TIGHVEIN

Sliddery Water

Kilmory Water

Auchencairn
Knockenkelly
North Kiscadale
South Kiscadale
GLENASHDALE
FALLS
Largybeg
Dippen
Levencorroch

Kingscross Pt.
Kingscross

Whiting Bay
Whiting Bay
Largymore

314

Largybeg
Dippin Head

Kildonan
Sound of Pladda
Pladda

NR

NS

A841

203

Sannox
SANNOX
A841

NORTH SANNOX
FARM PARK
Sannox Bay

Corrie

192

192

192

180

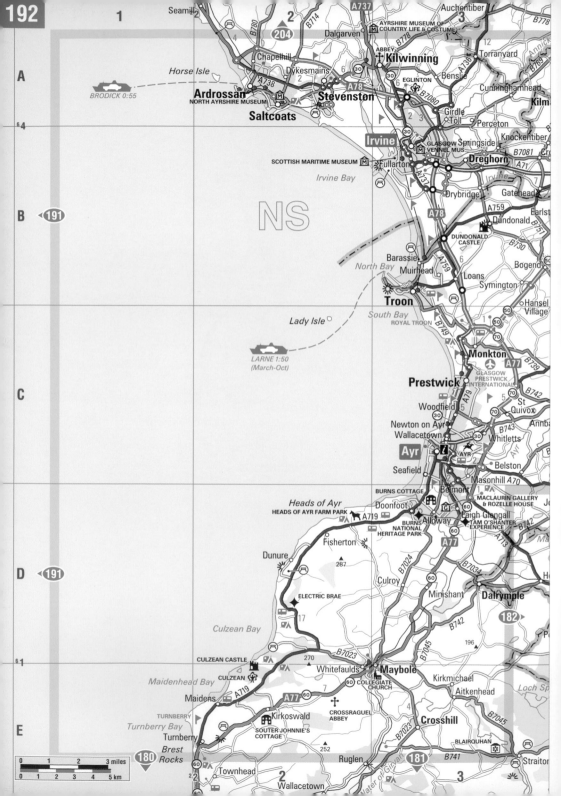

1 **2** **3**

Seamill

A737 Auchentiber

B714 B778

B80 204 B714 Dalgarven A778

AYRSHIRE MUSEUM OF
COUNTRY LIFE & COSTUME

Chapelhill B778 Torranyard

Dykesmains **Kilwinning**

A Horse Isle ABBEY 30 A738 Benslie Cunninghamhead **Kilm**

BRODICK 0:55 EGLINTON

Ardrossan Girdle Kilm

NORTH AYRSHIRE MUSEUM A738 B7080 Toll Perceton

Stevenston

Saltcoats Knockentiber

Irvine GLASGOW Springside Knockentiber

SCOTTISH MARITIME MUSEUM VENNEL MUS B7081 Cro

Dreghorn A71

Fullarton

Irvine Bay A737 Drybridge Gatehead

B 191 Irvine

NS A78 Dundonald B751

DUNDONALD
CASTLE B730

Barassie A759 6 Bogend

North Bay Muirhead Loans

Lady Isle Symington

South Bay **Troon** Hansel
Village

LARNE 1:50 ROYAL TROON

(March-Oct) B749

Monkton A77 B739

C GLASGOW
PRESTWICK
INTERNATIONAL A77

Prestwick A79 5 St
Quivox

Woodfield 30 70 B743 Annba

Newton on Ayr Whitletts

Wallacetown AYR Belston

Ayr 7

Seafield Masonhill A70

Belmont

BURNS COTTAGE MACLAURIN GALLERY
& ROZELLE HOUSE Je

Heads of Ayr Doonfoot

HEADS OF AYR FARM PARK A719 Alloway TAM O'SHANTER
EXPERIENCE Laigh Glengall

BURNS A77 A713

Fisherton NATIONAL
HERITAGE PARK

287 B7024

D 191 Dunure Culroy

ELECTRIC BRAE Minishant **Dalrymple**

17 B742 196 **182**

Culzean Bay B7023

B7045

E₁ CULZEAN CASTLE 270 B7034 He

CULZEAN Whitefaulds **Maybole** Kirkmichael Loch Sp

Maidenhead Bay COLLEGIATE
CHURCH

Maidens A719 A77 Aitkenhead

TURNBERRY CROSSRAGUEL
ABBEY **Crosshill**

E Turnberry Bay Kirkoswald B7023 B7045

Turnberry SOUTER JOHNNIE'S
COTTAGE BLAIRQUHAN

Brest **180** 252 **181** Straiton

Rocks Townhead Ruglen B741

2 **Wallacetown** **3**

0 1 2 3 miles
0 1 2 3 4 5 km

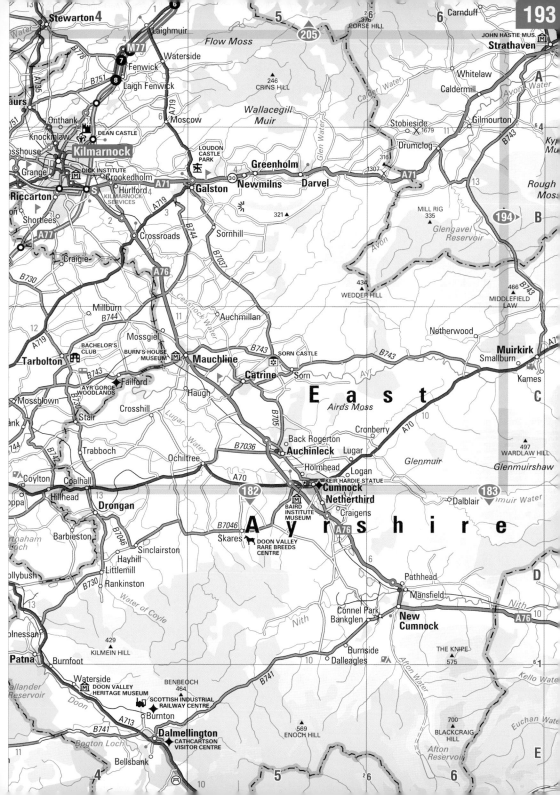

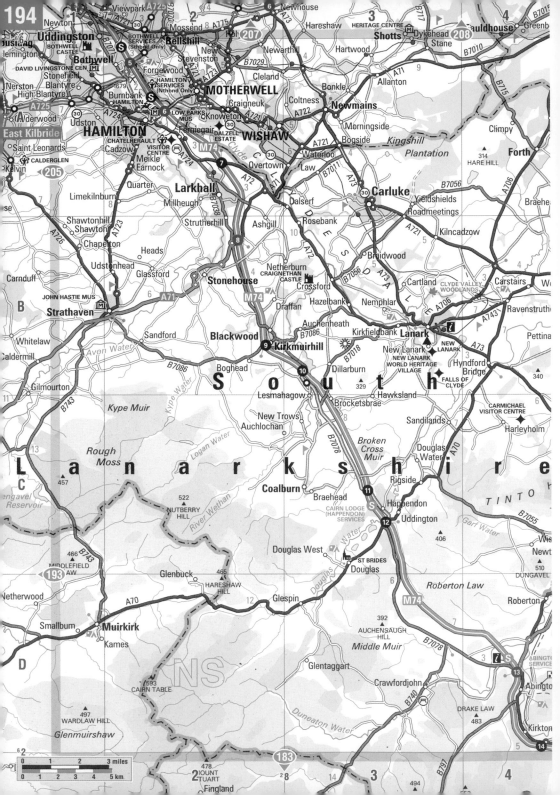

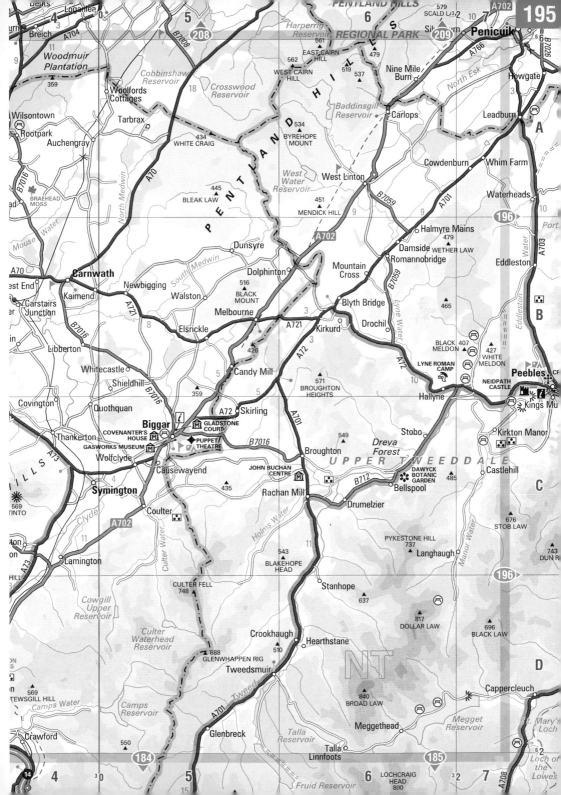

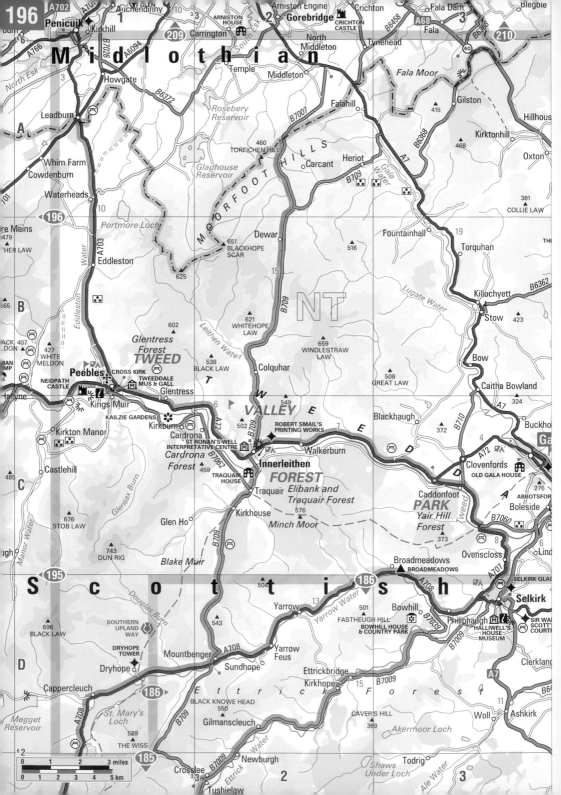

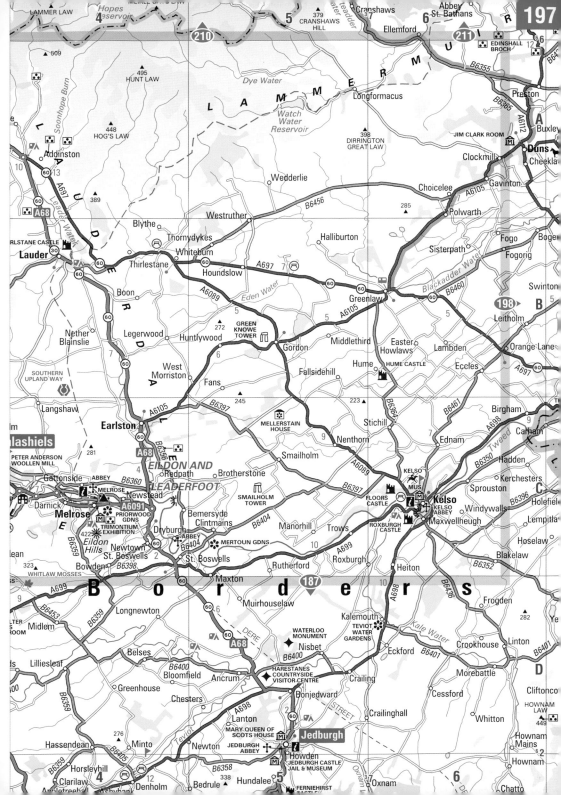

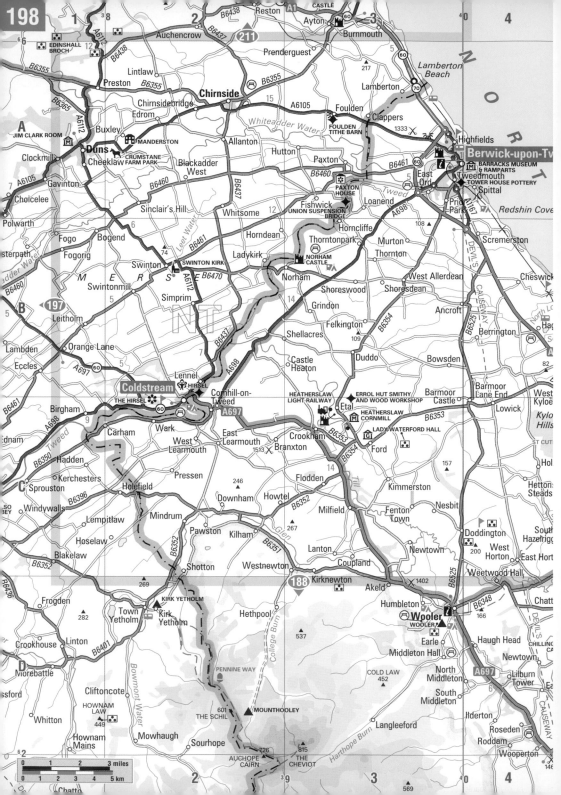

4 5 6 7

A

B

C

D

NU

HUMBERLAND

COAST

Goswick

Tweed

South Low

Beal

60

12

B6353

Fenwick

East
Kyloe

Buckton

HBERTS
WAY

Detchant

Middleton

North Hazelrigg

Belford

B6349

Mousen

Warenton

10

Bellshill

B6348

Greendikes

Chillingham
CASTLE

WILD CATTLE OF
CHILLINGHAM

315

Hepburn

Old Bewick

B6346

New
Bewick

Eglingham

Beanley

Harehope

LINDISFARNE

Causeway
Holy
Island
Sands

Fenham

Guile
Pt.

Emmanuel Hd.

Holy Island
(Lindisfarne)

Holy
Island

LINDISFARNE CASTLE

Castle Pt.

HERITAGE
CENTRE

LINDISFARNE
PRIORY

Elwick

Ross

Budle
Bay

Budle

BAMBURGH
CASTLE

Bamburgh

B1340

Easington

B1342

Waren Mill

Spindlestone

Glororum

Burton

Bradford

B1341

Elford

North
Sunderland

Adderstone

Lucker

60

Newham
Hall

Seahouses

189

Beadnell

Benthall

Farne
Islands

Staple Sound

FARNE ISLANDS

Inner Sound

211

Warenford

Swinhoe

Newham

Fleetham

A1

Newstead

Rosebrough

Chathill

Ellingham

Preston

B1340

Brunton

Beadnell
Bay

High Newton-
by-the-Sea

Brockdam

PRESTON TOWER

Chiston
Bank

Low Newton-
by-the-Sea

15

Brownyside

North Charlton

Doxford

B6347

Embleton Bay

Embleton

Dunstan Steads

Castle Point

DUNSTANBURGH
CASTLE

West
Ditchburn

South
Charlton

Rock

B6341

B1339

Dunstan

Craster

60

B6347

Rennington

Littlemill

Howick

4 5 6 7

169

101

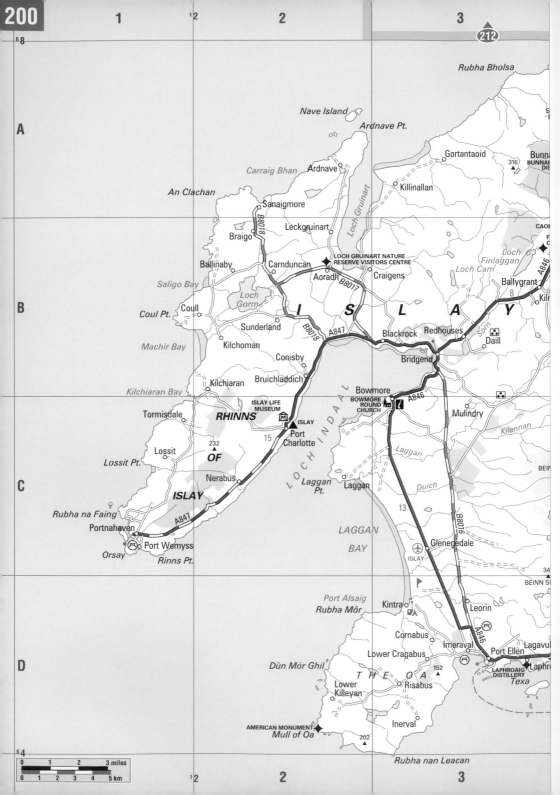

1   ¹2   2   3

212

Rubha Bholsa

A

Nave Island
Ardnave Pt.

Gortantaoid

316

BUNNA...
DIS...

Carraig Bhan   Ardnave

Killinallan

CAO...

An Clachan

Sanaigmore

Loch Gruinart

F...

Loch
Finlaggan

Loch

Leckgruinart

B8018

Braigo

LOCH GRUINART NATURE
RESERVE VISITORS CENTRE

Loch Cam

Ballygrant

A846

Ballinaby   Carnduncan

Aoradh   B8017   Craigens

8   Kil...

Saligo Bay

Loch
Gorm

B   I   S   L   A   Y

Coul Pt.   Coull

Blackrock   Redhouses

Sorn

Daill

Sunderland

B8018   A847

Machir Bay   Kilchoman

Bridgend

Conisby

Bruichladdich

Kilchiaran Bay   Kilchiaran

Bowmore
BOWMORE
ROUND
CHURCH   A846

Mulindry

ISLAY LIFE
MUSEUM   M

Kilennan

Tormisdale   **RHINNS**

ISLAY   Laggan

Port
Charlotte   15

Lossit   232

Laggan
Pt.   Laggan   Duich

C   Lossit Pt.   **OF**

Nerabus

B8016   13

Rubha na Faing   **ISLAY**

A847

LAGGAN

Glenegedale

Portnahaven   Port Wemyss

ISLAY

Orsay   Rinns Pt.   **BAY**

34...

BEINN S...

Port Alsaig
Rubha Mór   Kintra

Leorin

Cornabus   A846

Lagavul...

Imeraval   Port Ellen   Laphr...

D   Dùn Mór Ghil   T H E   O A   Lower Cragabus

LAPHROAIG
DISTILLERY   Texa

Lower
Killeyan   152
Risabus

Dùn Mór Ghil

Inerval

AMERICAN MONUMENT
Mull of Oa

202

Rubha nan Leacan

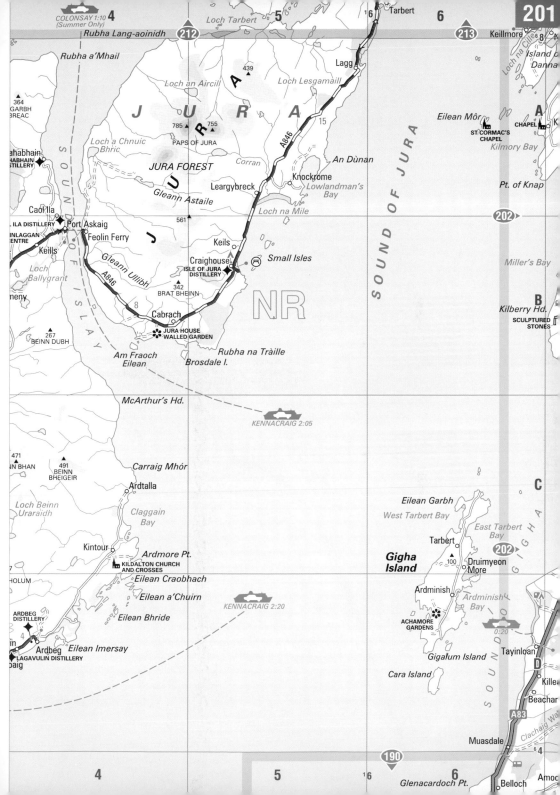

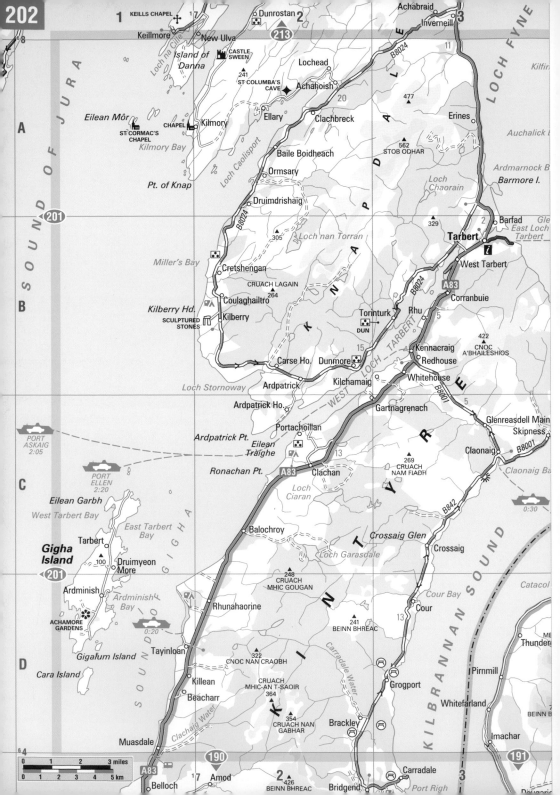

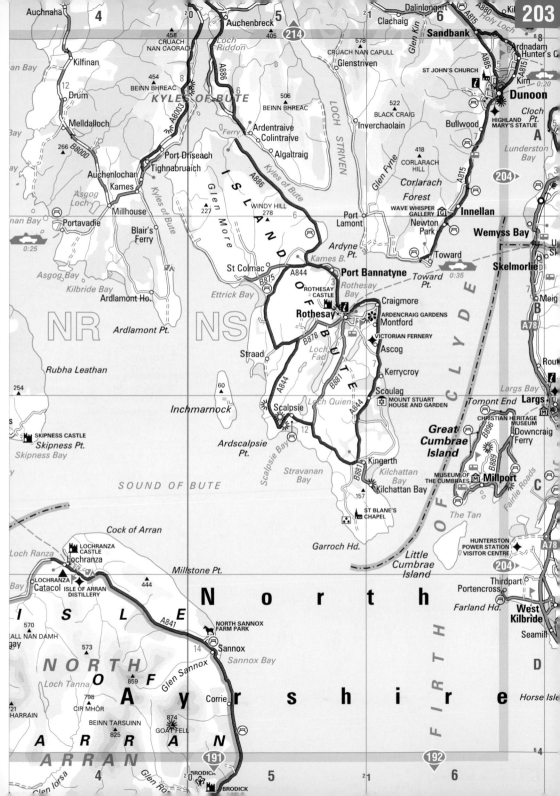

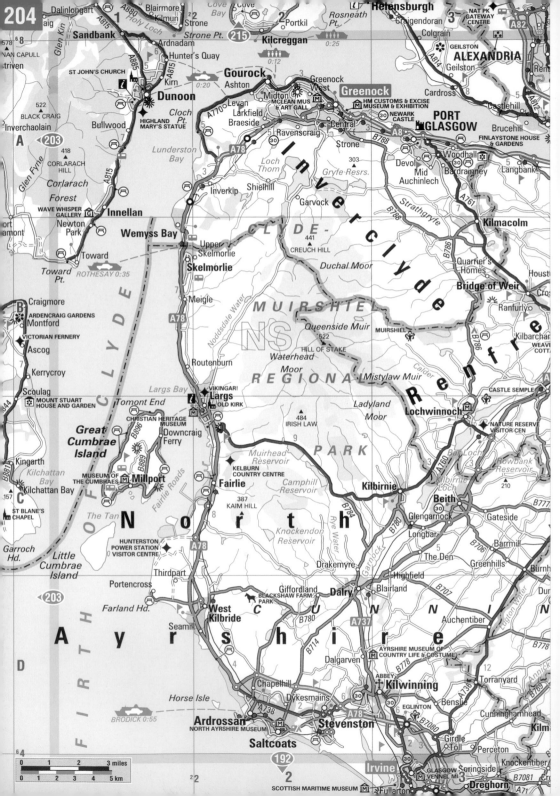

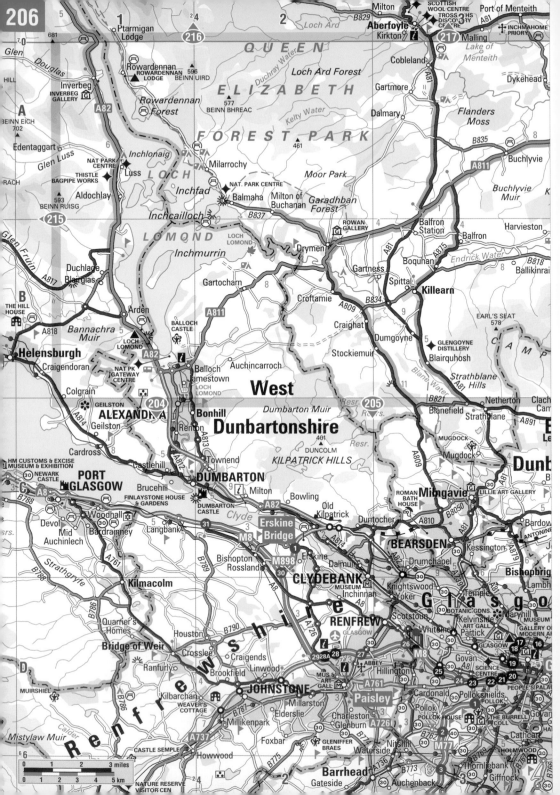

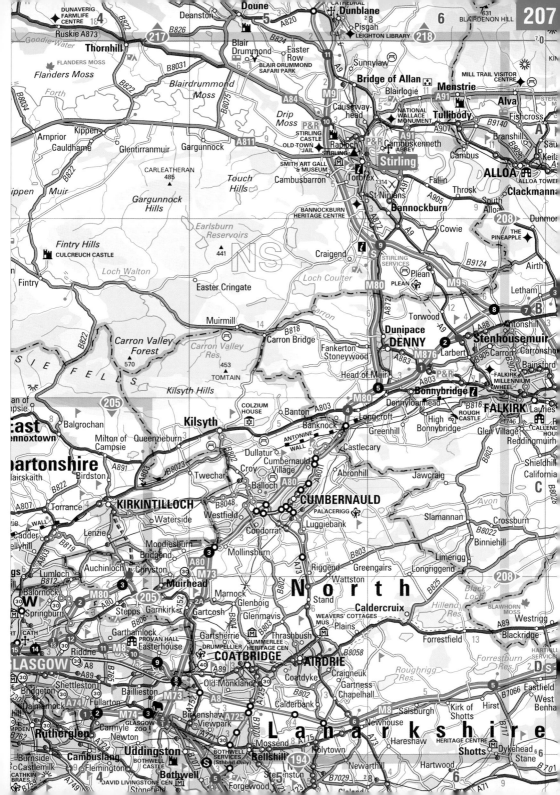

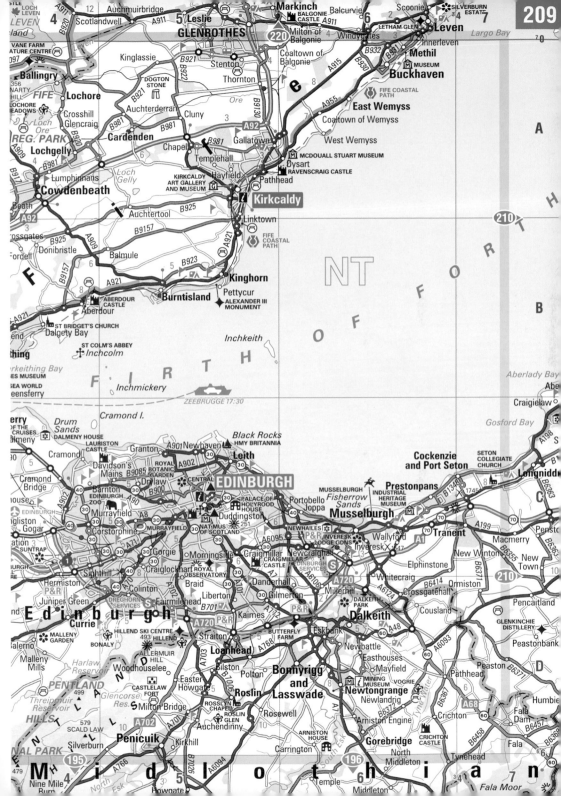

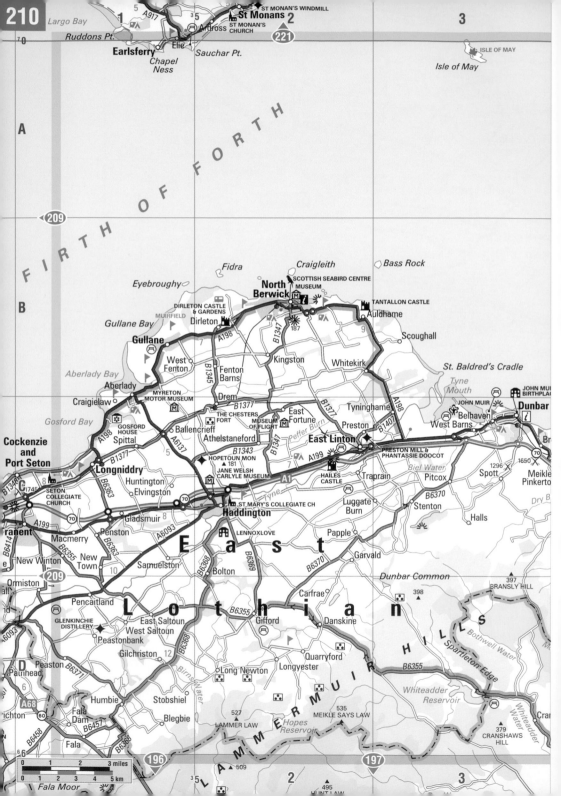

Largo Bay

1

A917

3 5

St Monan's Windmill

St Monans

2

3

Ruddons Pt.

221

Ardross

ST MONAN'S CHURCH

Earlsferry

Elie

Sauchar Pt.

Chapel Ness

ISLE OF MAY

Isle of May

A

F I R T H   O F   F O R T H

209

B

Craigleith

Bass Rock

Fidra

SCOTTISH SEABIRD CENTRE

Eyebroughy

North Berwick

MUSEUM

TANTALLON CASTLE

DIRLETON CASTLE & GARDENS

Dirleton

Auldhame

MUIRFIELD

187

Scoughall

Gullane Bay

B1347

9

Gullane

A198

7

Kingston

Whitekirk

St. Baldred's Cradle

West Fenton

B1345

Fenton Barns

Tyne Mouth

Aberlady Bay

Drem

JOHN MUIR BIRTHPLACE

Aberlady

B1377

THE CHESTERS FORT

MUSEUM OF FLIGHT

East Fortune

B1377

Tyninghame

A198

Dunbar

MYRETON MOTOR MUSEUM

i

Craigielaw

Preston

B1407

JOHN MUIR

Belhaven

Gosford Bay

GOSFORD HOUSE

Ballencrieff

Peffer Burn

B1347

West Barns

Cockenzie and Port Seton

A198

Spittal

A6137

Athelstaneford

East Linton

PRESTON MILL & PHANTASSIE DOOCOT

Br

B1377

5

B1343

A199

1296

1650

70

Biel Water

Longniddry

Huntington

HOPETOUN MON

HAILES CASTLE

Spott

Meikle Pinkerto

B1348

Elvingston

181

JANE WELSH CARLYLE MUSEUM

Traprain

Pitcox

SETON COLLEGIATE CHURCH

A1

Stenton

Dry B

745

B6363

70

Tyne

Halls

Gladsmuir

8

ST MARY'S COLLEGIATE CH

Luggate Burn

B6370

ranent

A199

Haddington

Macmerry

Penston

B6093

LENNOXLOVE

Papple

Garvald

397 BRANSLY HILL

New Winton

B6355

B6363

E a s t

Dunbar Common

398

New Town

10

Samuelston

B6368

Bolton

B6370

Carfrae

Ormiston

209

B6369

L o t h i a n

Pencaitland

GLENKINCHIE DISTILLERY

East Saltoun

Gifford

Danskine

Sparfleton Edge

Bothwell Water

d

West Saltoun

B6355

Peastonbank

B6368

Longyester

Quarryford

B6355

Whiteadder Reservoir

Cran

6093

Gilchriston

12

Long Newton

Whiteadder Water

D

Peaston

B6371

379 CRANSHAWS HILL

Humbie

Stobshiel

Birnswater

Fala Dam

Blegbie

A68

60

B6457

527 LAMMER LAW

535 MEIKLE SAYS LAW

Fala

Hopes Reservoir

L A M M E R M U I R   H I L L S

ch

B6458

B6368

196

197

0   1   2   3 miles
0   1   2   3   4   5 km

Fala Moor

3 5

2

509

495

3

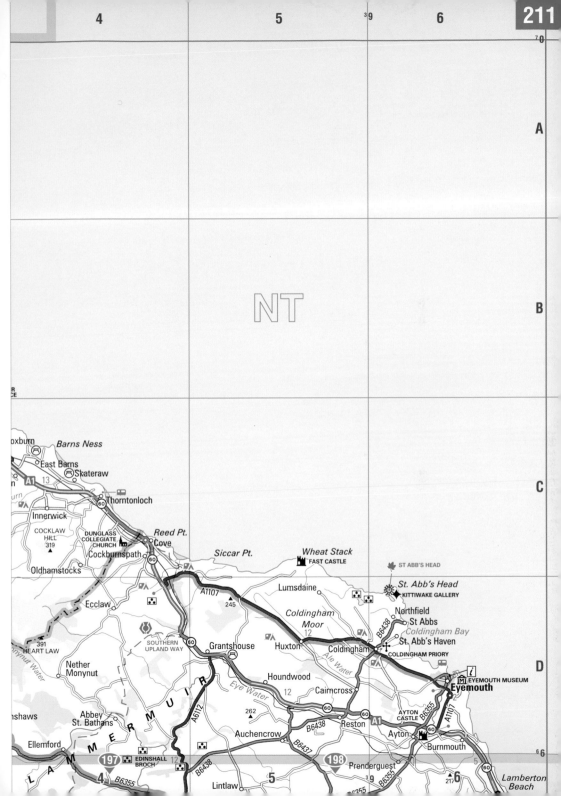

4 5 ³9 6

A

B

NT

C

Barns Ness

ᵒxburn

East Barns
Skateraw
A1 13
Thorntonloch
Innerwick
COCKLAW HILL
319
DUNGLASS COLLEGIATE CHURCH
Reed Pt.
Cove
Cockburnspath
Oldhamstocks
Siccar Pt.
Wheat Stack
FAST CASTLE
ST ABB'S HEAD
St. Abb's Head
KITTIWAKE GALLERY
Lumsdaine
A1107
245
Ecclaw
Coldingham Moor
12
Northfield
St Abbs
Coldingham Bay
B6438
St. Abb's Haven
391
HEART LAW
SOUTHERN UPLAND WAY
Grantshouse
Huxton
Coldingham
COLDINGHAM PRIORY
Nether Monynut
Houndwood
Ale Water
EYEMOUTH MUSEUM
i
Eyemouth
LAMMERMUIR
Eye Water
12
Cairncross
262
A6112
Abbey St. Bathans
Auchencrow
Reston
A1
AYTON CASTLE
B6355
A1107
ᵃshaws
Ellemford
197
EDINSHALL BROCH
12
B6438
198
Ayton
Burnmouth
60
Lamberton Beach
B6355
4
Lintlaw
5
³9
6
217

D

6

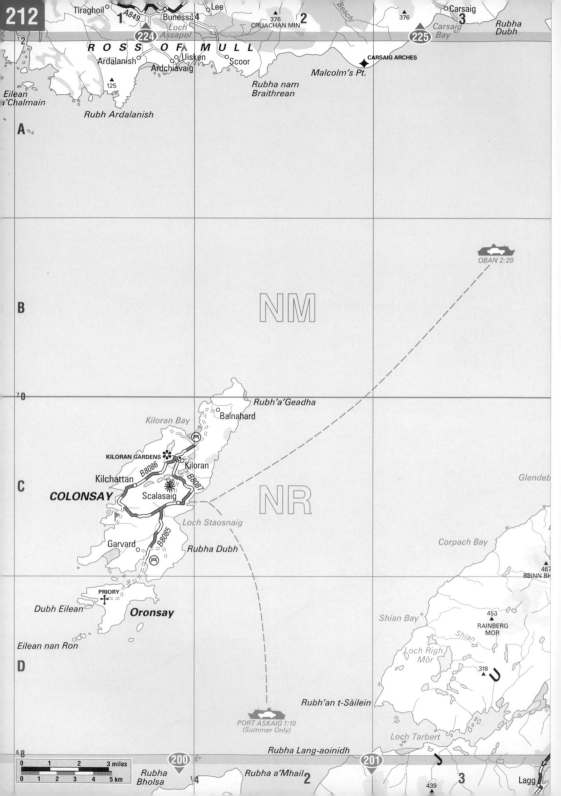

ROSS OF MULL

Tiraghoil
A849
Bunessan
Lee
376
CRUACHAN MIN
Carsaig
376
Carsaig
Bay
Rubha
Dubh
224
Loch
Assapol
225

Ardalanish
Uisken
Scoor
Ardchiavaig
CARSAIG ARCHES
Malcolm's Pt.
Eilean
a'Chalmain
125
Rubha nam
Braithrean
Rubh Ardalanish

A

B

NM

OBAN 2:20

7 0

Rubh'a'Geadha
Kiloran Bay
Balnahard
KILORAN GARDENS
Kiloran
Kilchattan
B8086
B8087
COLONSAY
Scalasaig
Glendeb

C

NR

Loch Staosnaig

Garvard
B8085
Rubha Dubh
Corpach Bay

467
BEINN BH

PRIORY
Dubh Eilean
Oronsay
Shian Bay
453
RAINBERG
MOR
Shian

Eilean nan Ron
Loch Righ
Môr
318

D

Rubh'an t-Sàilein
Corpach Bay

6 8

0 1 2 3 miles
0 1 2 3 4 5 km

200

PORT ASKAIG 1:10
(Summer Only)
Rubh'an t-Sàilein

Loch Tarbert

Rubha
Bholsa
1 4
Rubha a'Mhail 2
Rubha Lang-aoinidh
201
439
3
Lagg

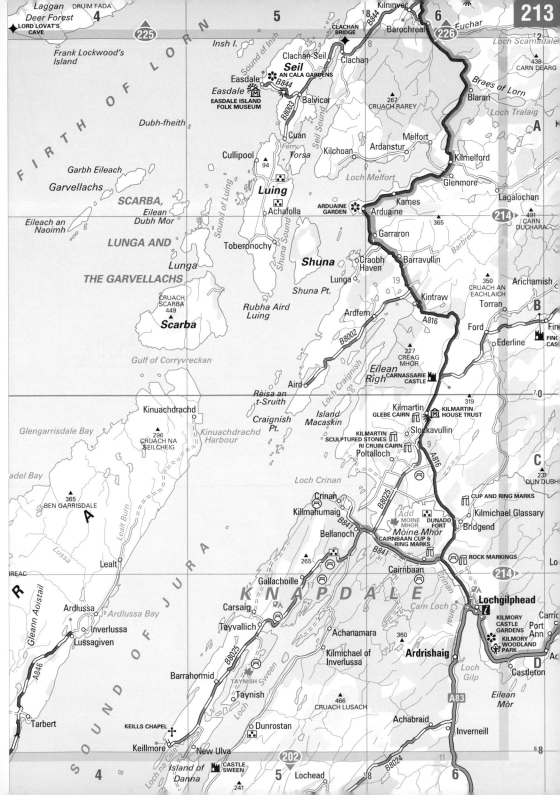

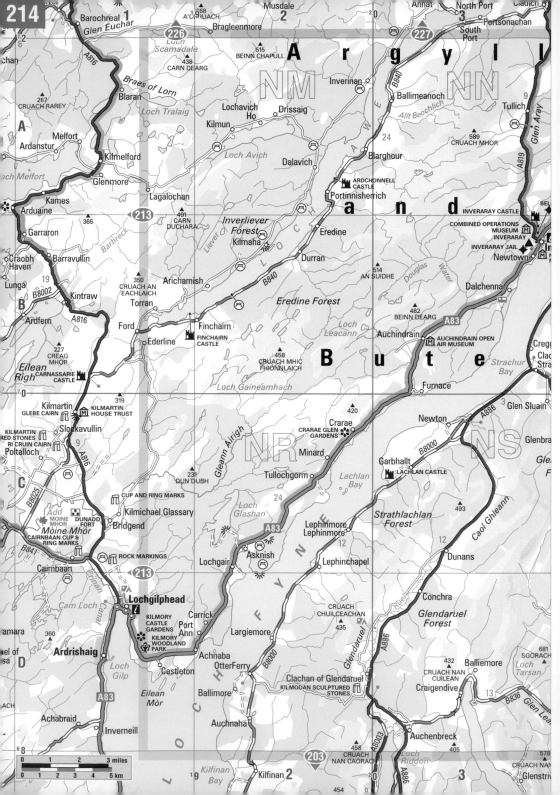

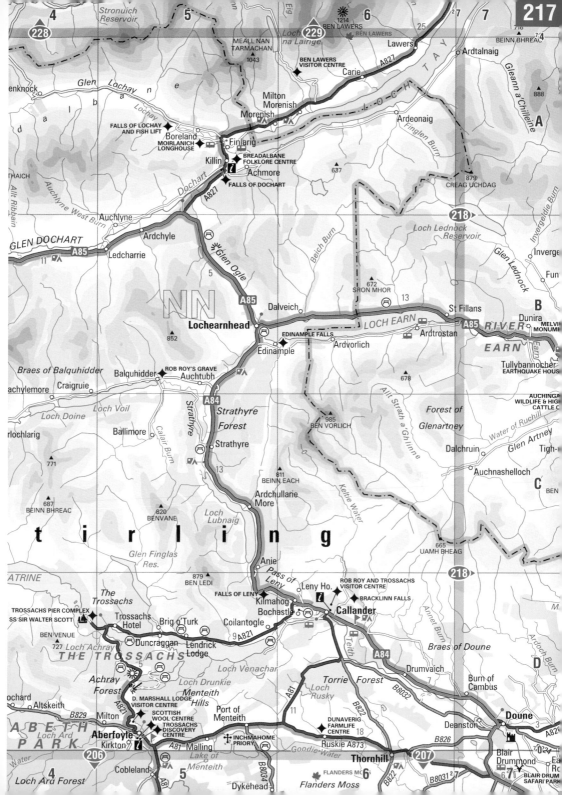

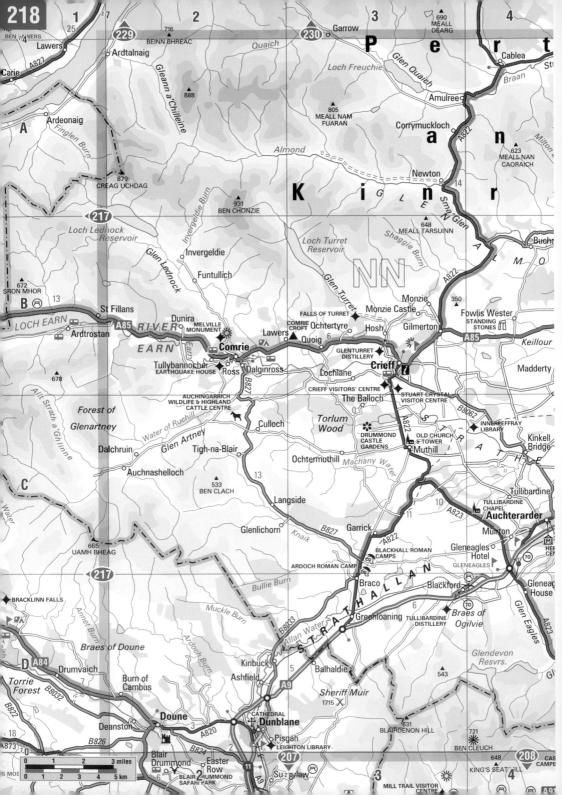

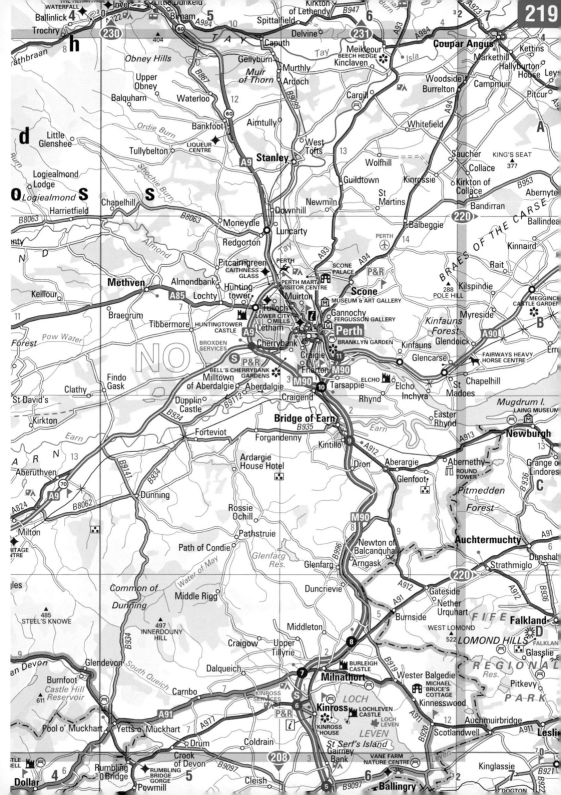

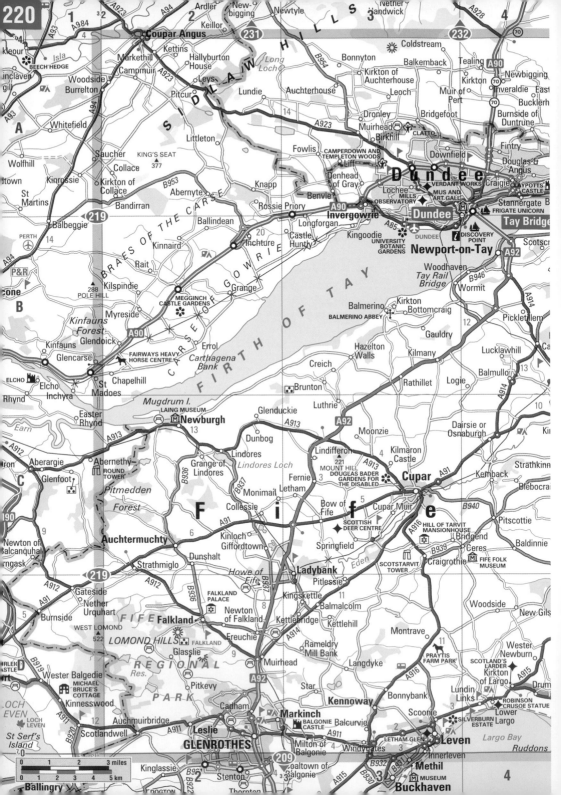

⁷7

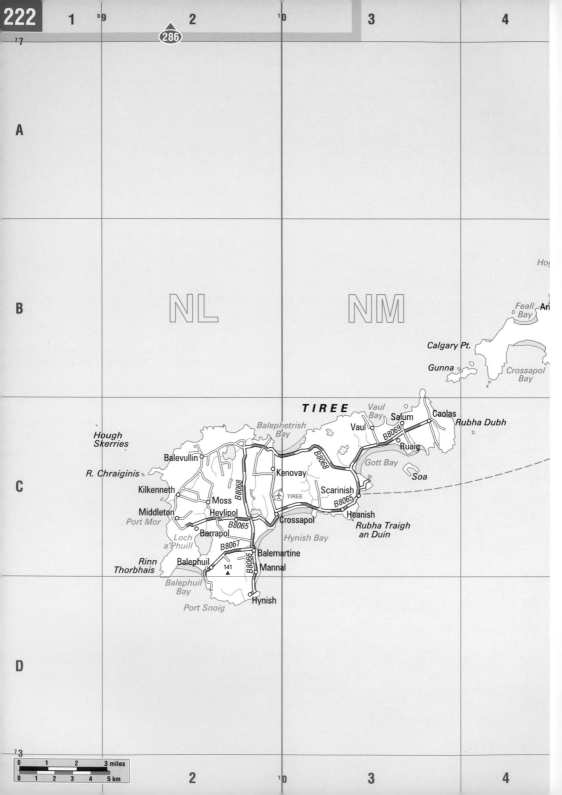

286

A

B

NL NM

Ho⸱

Feall
Bay An⸱

Calgary Pt.

Gunna Crossapol
Bay

TIREE

Vaul
Bay Salum Caolas
Vaul Rubha Dubh
Balephetrish B8069
Bay
Hough Ruaig
Skerries Balevullin B8068 Gott Bay
R. Chraiginis Kenovay Soa
C Kilkenneth B8068 Scarinish
Moss TIREE B8065
Middleton Heylipol Heanish
Port Mor Crossapol Rubha Traigh
Loch B8065 an Duin
a'Phuill Barrapol Hynish Bay
B8067 Balemartine
Rinn Balephuil 141 Mannal
Thorbhais B8066
Balephuil
Bay Hynish
Port Snoig

D

⁷3

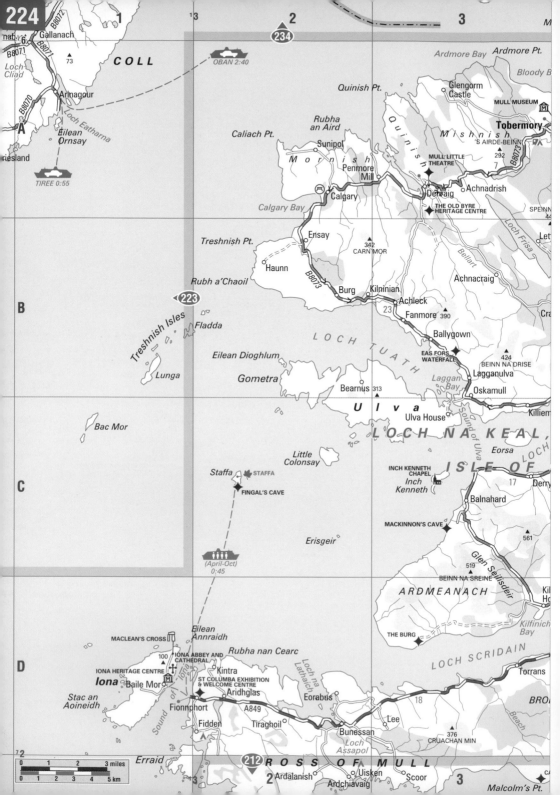

COLL

B8072
B8071
nab 6
Gallanach
B8071
B8070
B8070
Loch Cliad
73

Arinagour

Eilean Ornsay
Loch Eatharna

riesland

TIREE 0:55

OBAN 2:40
234

Ardmore Bay   Ardmore Pt.
Glengorm Castle   Bloody B
MULL MUSEUM

Quinish Pt.

Quinish
Mishnish

Tobermory
'S AIRDE-BEINN
292
7

Caliach Pt.
Rubha an Aird

Sunipol

MULL LITTLE THEATRE

Mornish
Penmore Mill

Calgary
Dervaig
Achnadrish
Calgary Bay

THE OLD BYRE HERITAGE CENTRE
SPEINN

Loch Frisa
Let

Treshnish Pt.
Ensay
342
CARN MOR

Achnacraig

Bellart
Cra

Haunn
B8073
Burg
Kilninian
Achleck
23
Fanmore
390

Ballygown

424
BEINN NA DRISE

Rubh a'Chaoil
223

Fladda

EAS FORS WATERFALL
Lagganulva

Treshnish Isles

Eilean Dioghlum

Gometra

Loch Tuath

Laggan Bay
Oskamull
Killiem

Lunga

Bearnus
313

Ulva
Ulva House

Sound of Ulva

LOCH NA KEAL

Bac Mor

Little Colonsay

Eorsa

ISLE OF

INCH KENNETH CHAPEL
Inch Kenneth
17
Derry

Staffa
STAFFA
FINGAL'S CAVE

Balnahard

MACKINNON'S CAVE

561

Erisgeir

(April-Oct)
0:45

BEINN NA SREINE
519
Glen Seilisdeir

ARDMEANACH

Eilean Annraidh
Rubha nan Cearc

THE BURG

Kilfinichen Bay

Kil
Ho

MACLEAN'S CROSS
IONA ABBEY AND CATHEDRAL
100
IONA HERITAGE CENTRE
Iona
Baile Mor
ST COLUMBA EXHIBITION & WELCOME CENTRE
Kintra

Loch na Lathaich

LOCH SCRIDAIN

Torrans

Stac an Aoineadh

Fionnphort
Aridhglas
Eorabus
Lee
18
BRO

Fidden
Tiraghoil
A849
Bunessan
376
CRUACHAN MIN

Errai d
212
ROSS OF MULL
Loch Assapol

Malcolm's Pt.

Ardalanish
Uisken
Scoor
Ardchiavaig

0   1   3 miles
0 1 2 3 4 5 km

Maclean's Nose
Ardslignish
Glenborrodale
BEN LAGA
B800
235
5
GLENCRIPESDALE
6
11
16

Eilean Mor
Laga
Camuschoirk

Oronsay
Carna
Glencripesdale
516
MEALL AN
DAMHAIN
Liddesdale

KILCHOAN 0:35
Auliston Pt.
0:50
169
582
BEINN NAM
BEATHRACH
Lochuisg
A884
B8043
18
Loch Uisge

ay
MORVERN
Gleann Dubh
Beach
A

TOBERMORY
Calve I.
0:20
Loch
Teacuis
571
BEINN IADAIN
516

TOBERMORY
DISTILLERY
Drimnin
Bonnavoulin
739
BEINN MHEAD

Upper
Druimfin
451
BEINN BHUIDHE
Loch Arienas
Acharn

HE MOR
Rhemore
550
STITHEAN NA
RAPLAICH
Gleann Geal

4
A848
AROS
Ardnacross
Killundine
B849
Claggan
437
BEINN A'
CHAISIL

termore
NM
Larachbeg
KINLOCHALINE
CASTLE
ARDTORNISH
GARDENS
Loch
Tearnait
Loch nan
Clach
B

10
Fiunary
Savary
Achranich
Rannoch
AN
SLEAGHACH
513

SOUND
Aros Mains
Rubha Mor
Lochaline
226
GLAIS BHEINN
479
Eigna

Salen
2
Pennygown
6
Fishnish
Bay
0:15
ARDTORNISH
CASTLE
Ardtornish
Pt.
Inninmore
Bay

Killiechronan
B8035
Killbeg
Corrynachenchy
A849
Garmony
5
Rubha an
Ridire
Bernera I.
Achi

Kellan
B8073
Gruline
412
Scallastle
Bay
Java
Craignure
Bay
OBAN 0:45

ISLAND
Knock
Loch Bà
Scallastle
Craignure
MULL AND WEST HIGHLAND
NARROW GAUGE RAILWAY
Duart
Bay
Duart Pt.
C

MULL
591
BEINN
A'GHRAIG
Glen
Cannel
766
DUN DA
GHAOITHE
TOROSAY
CASTLE &
GARDENS
DUART
CASTLE
Eilean
Musdile

OF
761
BEINN TALAIDH
Lochdon

guaig
NA KEAL
MULL
966
BEN MORE
704
CORRA-BHEINN
Glen
More
Lussa
17
Strathcoil
226
Loch Don
Grass Pt.
KERRER

Aird of
Kinloch
B8035
Coladoir
A849
Loch
Airdeglais
248
Ardmore
Bach I.

Pennycross
BEN BUIE
717
698
CREACH BEINN
Kinlochspelve
Loch
Spelve
Croggan
Rubha nan
Sailthean
Rubha
Seanach
D

Lochbuie
503
BEINN NA CROISE
Leidle
Loch Uisg
Barachandroman

LASS
Carsaig
376
Loch Buie
Laggan
Deer Forest
405
DRUIM FADA
Insh I.
CLACHAN
BRIDGE

Carsaig
Bay
Rubha
Dubh
LORD LOVAT'S
CAVE
Clachan-Seil
Clachan

CARSAIG ARCHES
212
4
Frank Lockwood's
Island
5
213
7
6
Seil
AN CALA GARDENS

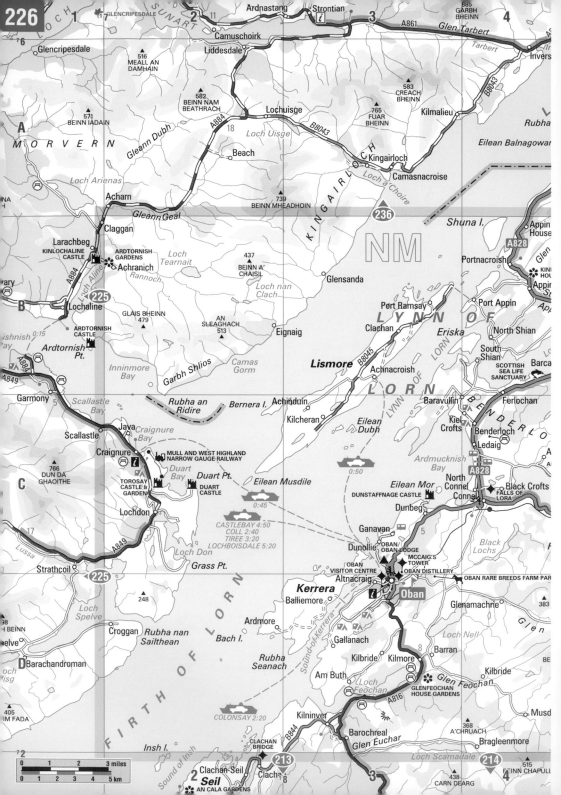

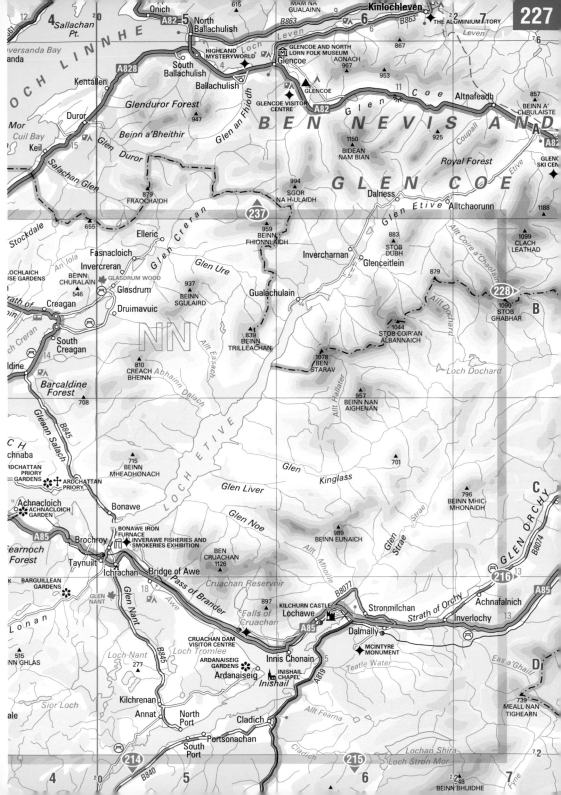

Killiechonate
Inverroy Roybridge
Achluachrach Murlaggan Roughburn
Bri Lochaber
MONESSIE FALLS
239
Spean
A86
Ardverikie Forest
GEA
GLEN SPEAN
240

Leanachan Forest

The Cour

724 BEINN CHLIANAIG

Fersit

Allt Lorach

1087 BEINN A'CHLACHAIR

A

Allt Làire

Loch Ghuilbinn

1046 CHNO DEARG

1114 AONACH BEAG

1177 STOB CHOIRE CLAURIGH
1106

Lairig Leacach

Allt na Lairige

1115 STOB COIRE EASAIN

Uisge Labhair

1148 BEN ALD

1234 AONACH BEAG
1094

LOCH TREIG

Creaguaineach Lodge

237

937 BEINN NA LAP

Corrour Shooting Lodge

Prince Cha Cave

Amhainn Rath

LOCH OSSIAN

Loch Ossian

Corrour Forest

952 SGOR GAIBHRE

B

1130 BINNEIN MOR

630

Ossian

583

MAMORE FOREST

Loch Eilde Beag

Allt na Caim

Rannoch Forest

789 Loch Eilde Mor

906 LEUM UILLEIM

Kinlochmore

Ciaran Water

THE ALUMINIUM STORY

BLACKWATER RESERVOIR

Black Water

Leven

BEN NEVIS

Rannoch Station

B846

Altnafeadh

857 BEINN A' CHRULAISTE

Black Corries Lodge

739 STOB NA CRUAICHE

Loch Eigheach

Gaur

Coupall

Kingshouse Hotel

Loch Gaineamhach

Loch Laidon

C

Royal Forest

AND

GLENCOE SKI CENTRE

Etive

A82

R A N N O C H   M O O R

Alltchaorunn

MUSEUM OF SCOTTISH SKIING AND MOUNTAINEERING
1188

547

Allt

25

GLEN COE

1099 CLACH LEATHAD

Bà

Loch na h-Achlaise
14

Water of Tulla

Loch an Daimh

MEALL E

B L A C K   M O U N T

Loch Bà

Eas Daimh

Loch

Allt Coire a 'Chaolain

D

1090 STOB GHABHAR

WEST HIGHLAND WAY

Loch Tulla

907 MEALL BUIDHE

960 STUCHD AN LOCHAIN

227

Black Mount

1081 BEINN A' CHREACHAIN

Pubil

Cashlie

G

Forest Lodge

Achallader

Inveroran Hotel

Loch Lyon

Loch Dochard

1004 BIENN AN DOTHAIDH

953 BEINN MHANACH

Bridge of Orchy

216

217

BEINN HEASGARNICH

0 1 2 3 miles
0 1 2 3 4 5 km

1076

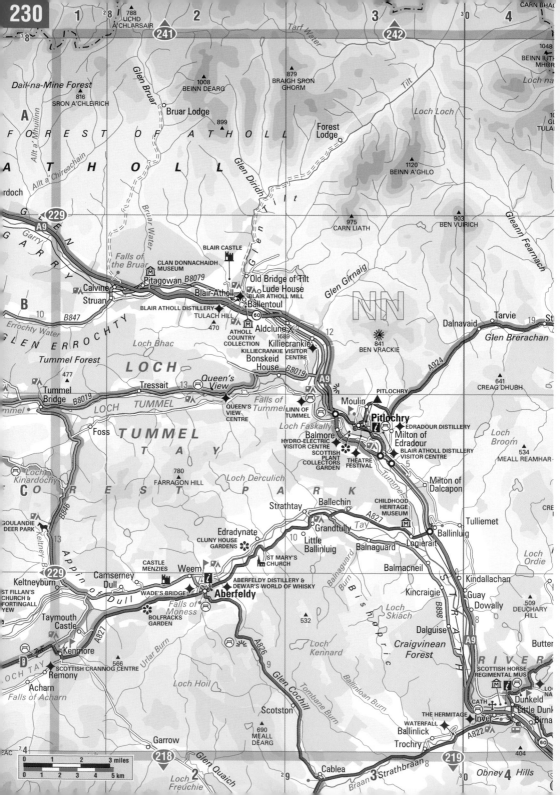

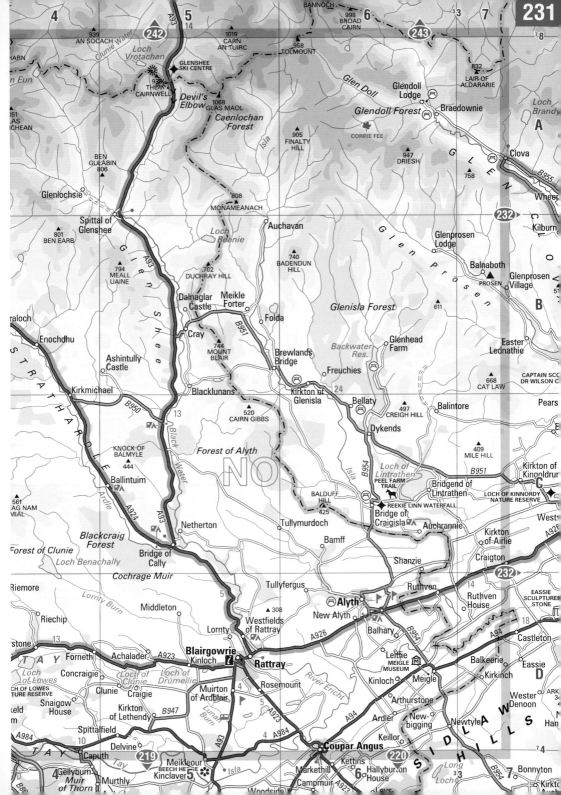

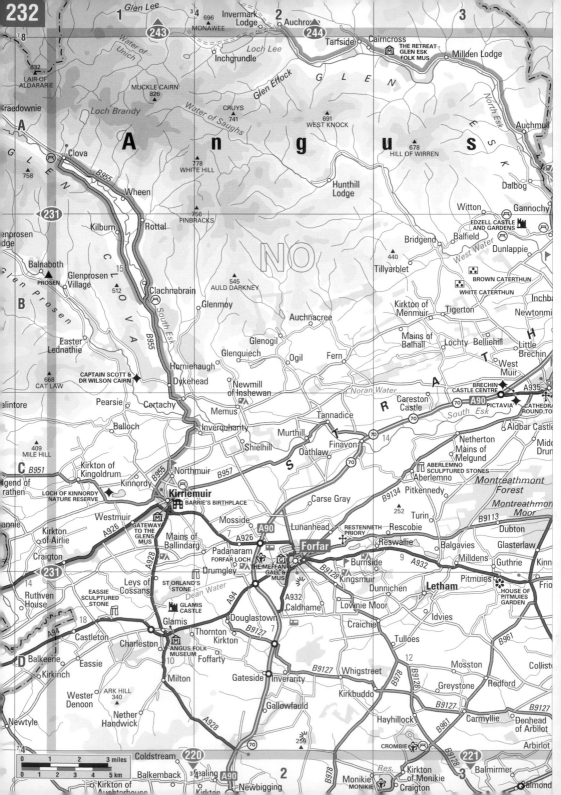

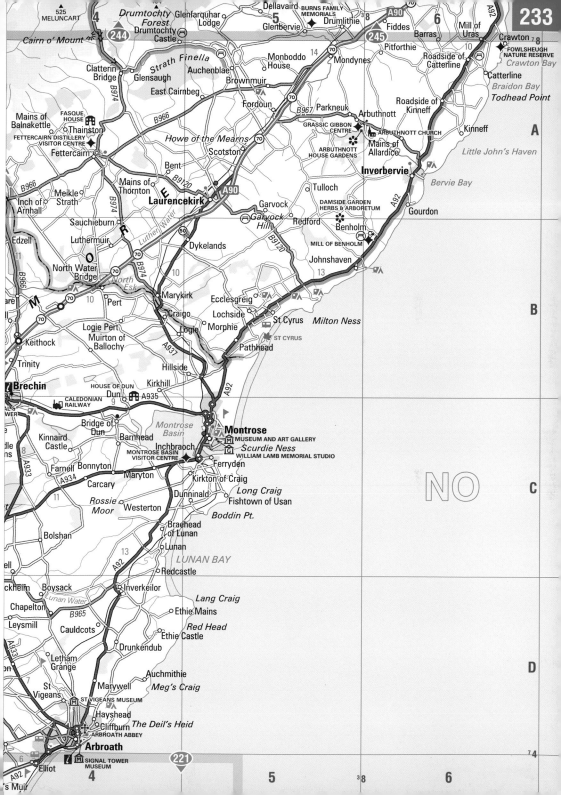

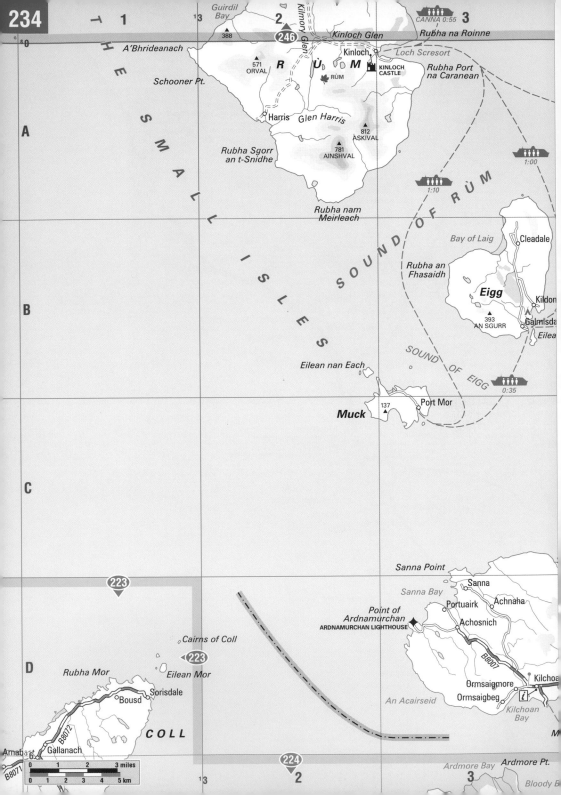

THE SMALL ISLES

Guirdil Bay

Kilmory Glen

246

Kinloch Glen

CANNA 0:55

Rubha na Roinne

388

A'Bhrideanach

571
ORVAL

R   Ù   M

RÙM

Kinloch

Loch Scresort

KINLOCH
CASTLE

Rubha Port
na Caranean

Schooner Pt.

Harris

Glen Harris

812
ASKIVAL

Rubha Sgorr
an t-Snidhe

781
AINSHVAL

1:00

Rubha nam
Meirleach

SOUND OF RÙM

1:10

Bay of Laig

Cleadale

Rubha an
Fhasaidh

Eigg

Kildon

393
AN SGURR

Galmisda

Eilea

SOUND OF EIGG

Eilean nan Each

0:35

Muck

137

Port Mor

Sanna Point

Sanna

Sanna Bay

Portuairk

Achnaha

Point of
Ardnamurchan
ARDNAMURCHAN LIGHTHOUSE

Achosnich

223

B8007

Kilchoa

Cairns of Coll

Rubha Mor

223

Eilean Mor

Ormsaigmore

Ormsaigbeg

Kilchoan
Bay

Sorisdale

Bousd

An Acairseid

COLL

B8072

Arnab

Gallanach

B8071

Kilchoan

224

Ardmore Bay

Ardmore Pt.

Bloody B

0 1 2 3 miles
0 1 2 3 4 5 km

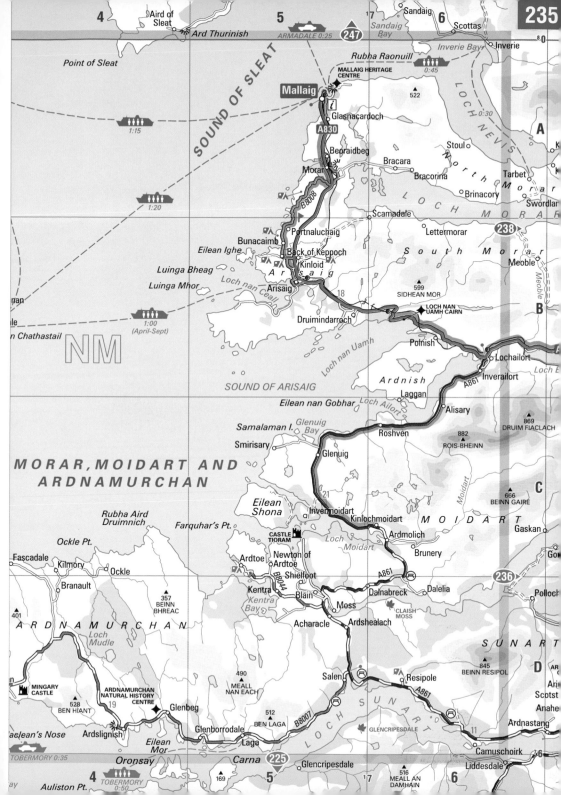

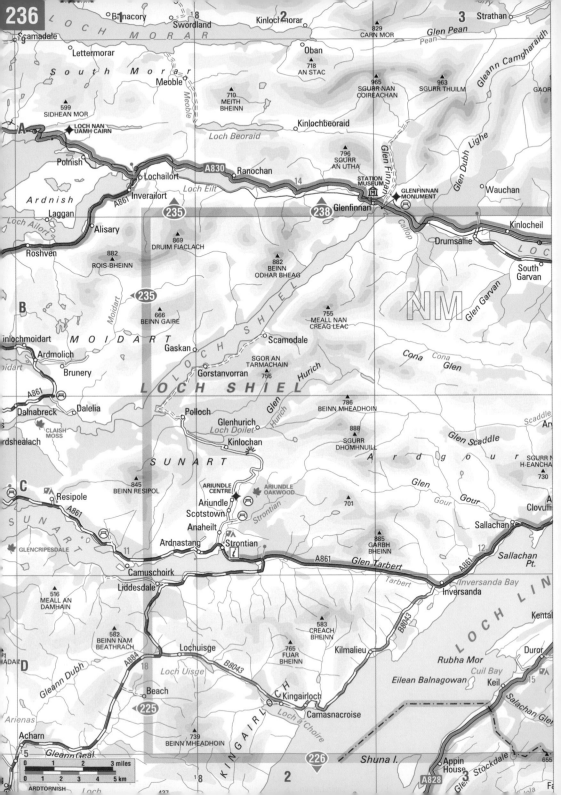

LOCH MORAR

1
Binacory
Swordland
Scamadale
Lettermorar

2
Kinloch Morar

3
Strathan

Glen Pean

South Morar

Oban
718
AN STAC

829
CARN MOR

Meoble

710
MEITH
BHEINN

965
SGURR NAN
COIREACHAN

963
SGURR THUILM

GAOR

599
SIDHEAN MOR

Meoble

Kinlochbeoraid

Gleann Camgharaidh

A
LOCH NAN
UAMH CAIRN
Polnish
A830
Ranochan
Loch Beoraid

796
SGURR
AN UTHA

Glen Finnan

Glen Dubh Lighe

Lochailort
14
STATION
MUSEUM
GLENFINNAN
MONUMENT
Wauchan

Inverailort
A861
235
238
Glenfinnan
Callop
Kinlocheil

Laggan

Alisary

235
Drumsallie
LOCH

Roshven
882
ROIS-BHEINN
869
DRUIM FIACLACH

882
BEINN
ODHAR BHEAG

South
Garvan

Ardnish

Loch Ailort

Moidart

B
inlochmoidart
Ardmolich
MOIDART
666
BEINN GAIRE
Gaskan
LOCH SHIEL
Scamodale
755
MEALL NAN
CREAG LEAC

NM

Glen Garvan

Cona
Glen
Cona

Brunery

A861
Dalelia

LOCH SHIEL
Gorstanvorran
SGOR AN
TARMACHAIN
756

786
BEINN MHEADHOIN

Glen
Hurich

Glen Scaddle

Scaddle

Dalnabreck
CLAISH
MOSS
rdshealach

Polloch
Glenhurich
Loch Doilet
Kinlochan

Hurich

888
SGURR
DHOMHNUILL

Ardgour

SGURR
H-EANCHA
730

C
Resipole
A861
SUNART
845
BEINN RESIPOL

ARIUNDLE
CENTRE
Ariundle
Scotstown
Anaheilt

ARIUNDLE
OAKWOOD

Strontian

701

Glen
Gour

Sallachan
Clovull

GLENCRIPESDALE

Ardnastang
11
Camuschoirk

i
Strontian

A861
Glen Tarbert

885
GARBH
BHEINN

Tarbert

12
Sallachan
Pt.

A861

Inversanda Bay
Inversanda

LOCH LIN

Liddesdale
516
MEALL AN
DAMHAIN

583
CREACH
BHEINN

B8043

Kental

D
Gleann Dubh
582
BEINN NAM
BEATHRACH
A884
Lochuisge
18
Loch Uisge
B8043
765
FUAR
BHEINN
Kilmalieu

Rubha Mor
Cuil Bay

Durot

Keil

15

Arienas

Beach

225
Kingairloch
Loch a'Choire
Eilean Balnagowan

Acharn

739
BEINN MHEADHOIN

Camasnacroise

226

Shuna I.

Appin
House

A828

655

Gleann Geal

0 1 2 3 miles
0 1 2 3 4 5 km

ARDTORNISH
Loch
427

5
8
2
3
Glen Stockdale
Fa

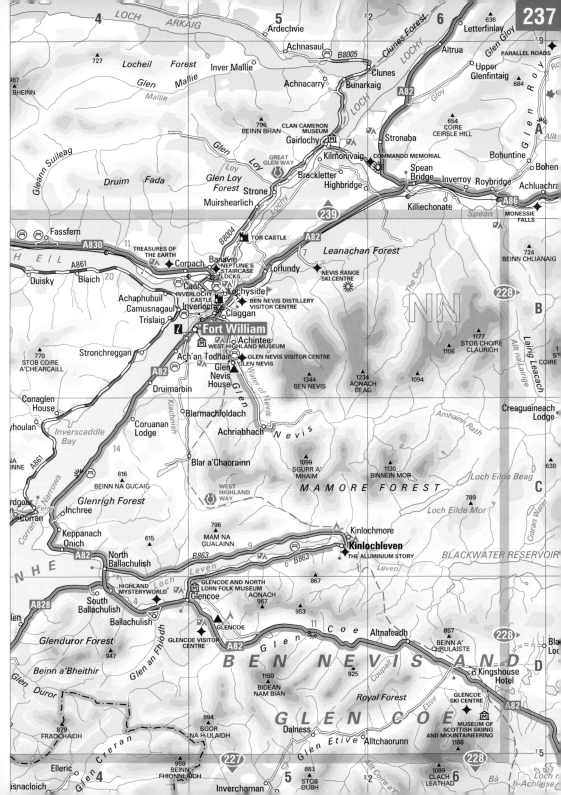

4 LOCH ARKAIG **5** CLUNES FOREST **6**

Ardechvie
Achnasaul
B8005
Letterfinlay
636
Glen Gloy
9
PARALLEL ROADS

Loch Cheil Forest
727
Inver Mallie
Achnacarry
Clunes
Altrua
Upper Glenfintaig
684
A

987 BHEINN
Glen Mallie
Bunarkaig
CLAN CAMERON MUSEUM
796 BEINN BHAN
Gairlochy
Stronaba
654 COIRE CEIRSLE HILL
Bohuntine
Bohen

Gleann Suileag
Glen Loy
GREAT GLEN WAY
Kilmonivaig
COMMANDO MEMORIAL
Spean Bridge
Inverroy
Roybridge
Achluachra
A86

Druim Fada
Glen Loy Forest
Strone
Brackletter
Highbridge
Killiechonate
MONESSIE FALLS

Muirshearlich
239
Spean

Fassfern
B8004
TOR CASTLE
A82
Leanachan Forest
724 BEINN CHLIANAIG

HEIL
A830
11
TREASURES OF THE EARTH
7
228

Duisky A861 Blaich 20
Corpach
Banavie
NEPTUNE'S STAIRCASE LOCKS
Torlundy
NEVIS RANGE SKI CENTRE
NN
B

Achaphubuil
Caol
INVERLOCHY CASTLE
Lochyside
BEN NEVIS DISTILLERY VISITOR CENTRE
1177 STOB CHOIRE CLAURIGH
1106

Camusnagaul
Trislaig
Inverlochy
Claggan
Laing Leachd
Allt na Lairige

770 STOB COIRE A'CHEARCAILL
Stronchreggan
Fort William
Achintee
WEST HIGHLAND MUSEUM
GLEN NEVIS VISITOR CENTRE
1344 BEN NEVIS
1234 AONACH BEAG
1094

Ach'an Todhair
Glen Nevis House
Creaguaineach Lodge

Conaglen House
Druimarbin
Blarmachfoldach
Amhainn Rath

789

Inverscaddle Bay
14
Coruanan Lodge
Achriabhach
N e v i s
Loch Eilde Beag

630

A861 NINNE
Narrows
616 BEINN NA GUCAIG
Blar a'Chaorainn
1099 SGURR A' MHAIM
1130 BINNEIN MOR
Loch Eilde Mor
C

Glenrigh Forest
WEST HIGHLAND WAY
M A M O R E   F O R E S T

rdgour Corran
Inchree
796 MAM NA GUALAINN
Kinlochmore
BLACKWATER RESERVOIR

Keppanach Onich
615
9
Kinlochleven
THE ALUMINIUM STORY

A82
North Ballachulish
B863
Leven
6 B863
867

NHE
Loch Leven
HIGHLAND MYSTERYWORLD
GLENCOE AND NORTH LORN FOLK MUSEUM
AONACH
967

South Ballachulish
Glencoe
953

A828
Ballachulish
GLENCOE VISITOR CENTRE
GLENCOE
A82
11
Glen Coe
Altnafeadh
857 BEINN A' CHRULAISTE
228
Bla Loc
D

Glenduror Forest
947
Glen an Fhiodh
B E N   N E V I S   A N D
Kingshouse Hotel

Beinn a'Bheithir
1150 BIDEAN NAM BIAN
925
Royal Forest
GLENCOE SKI CENTRE
A82

Glen Duror
994 SGOR NA H-ULAIDH
Dalness
G L E N   C O E
MUSEUM OF SCOTTISH SKIING AND MOUNTAINEERING
1188

879 FRAOCHAIDH
Glen Creran
Glen Etive
Alltchaorunn

Elleric
959 BEINN FHIONNLAIDH
227
883 STOB DUBH
228
1099 CLACH LEATHAD

snacloich **4**
Invercharnan
5
6

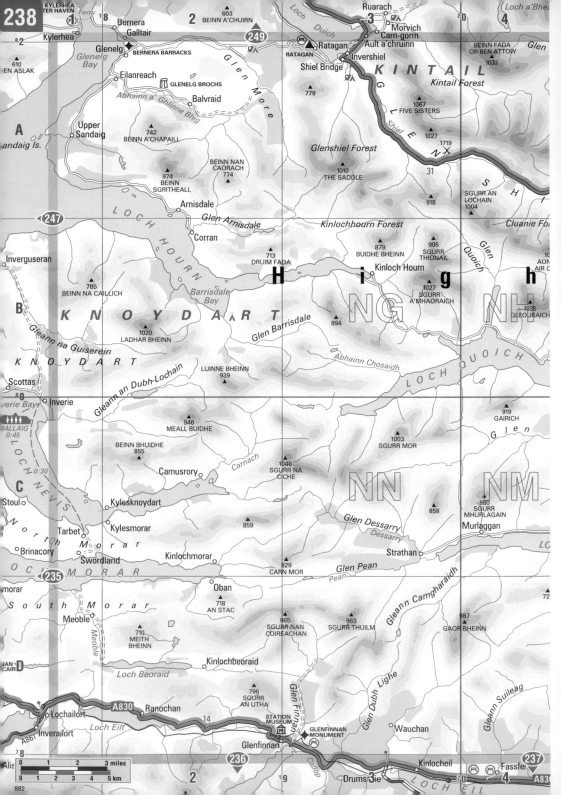

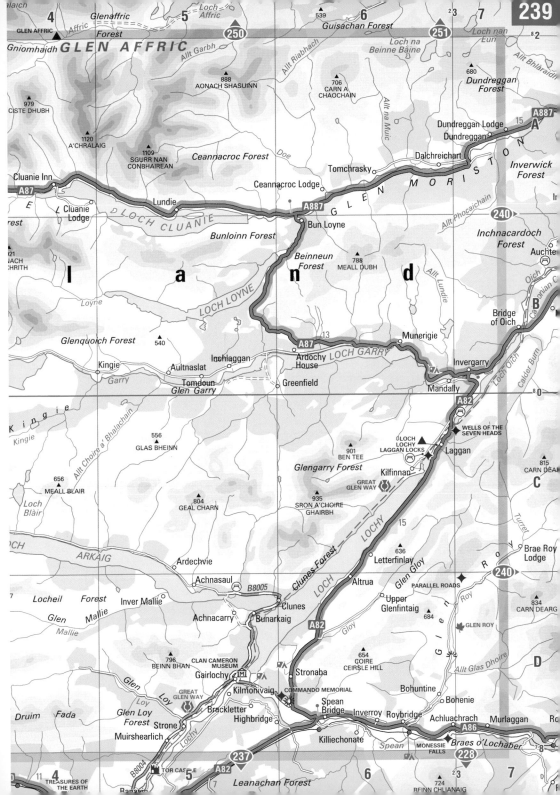

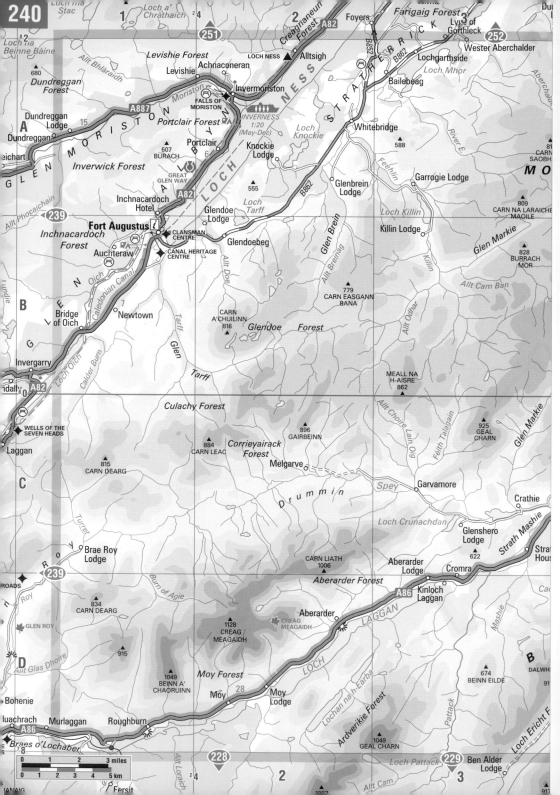

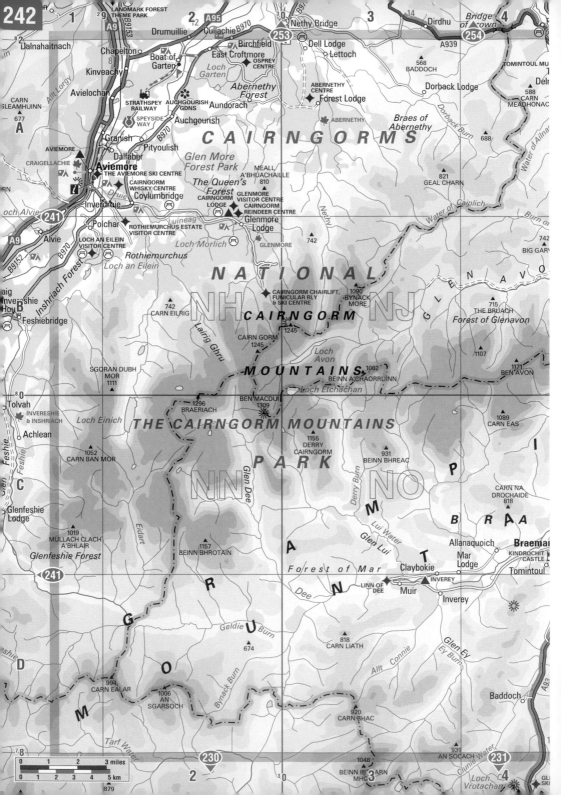

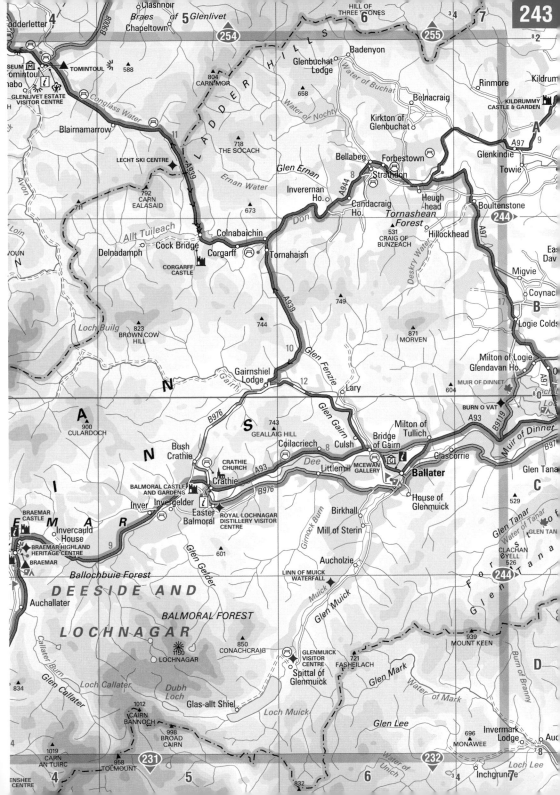

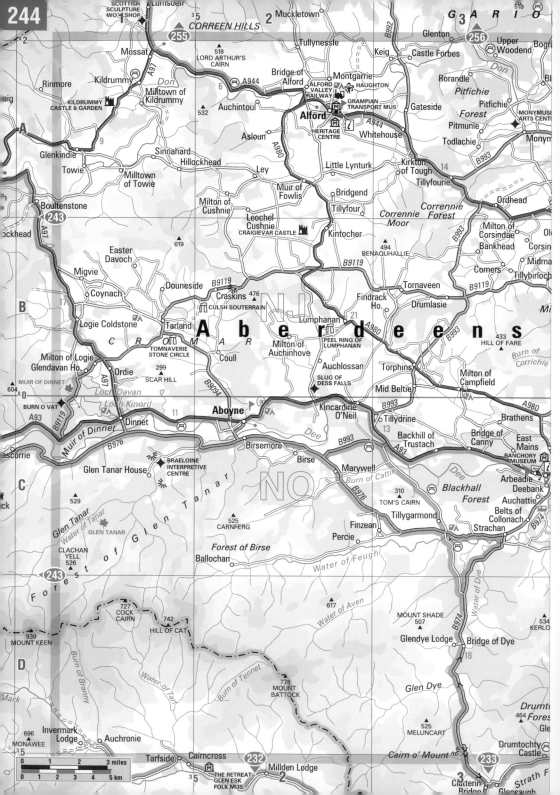

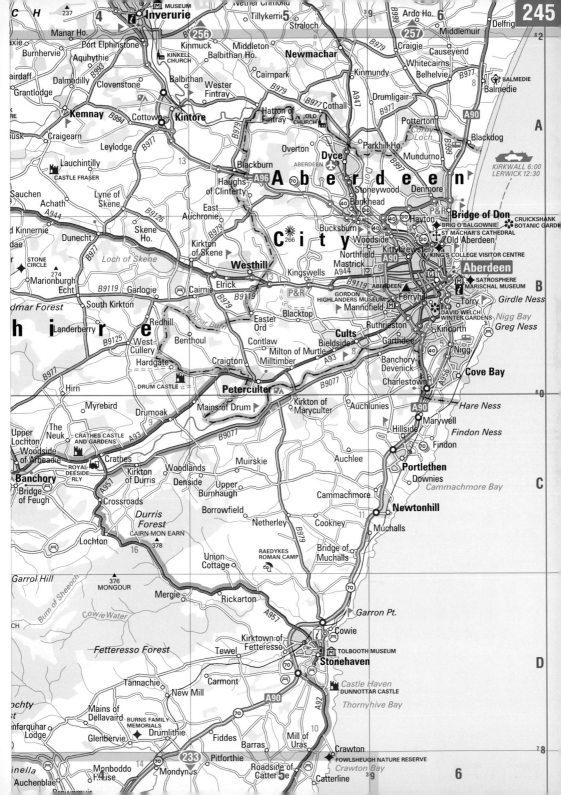

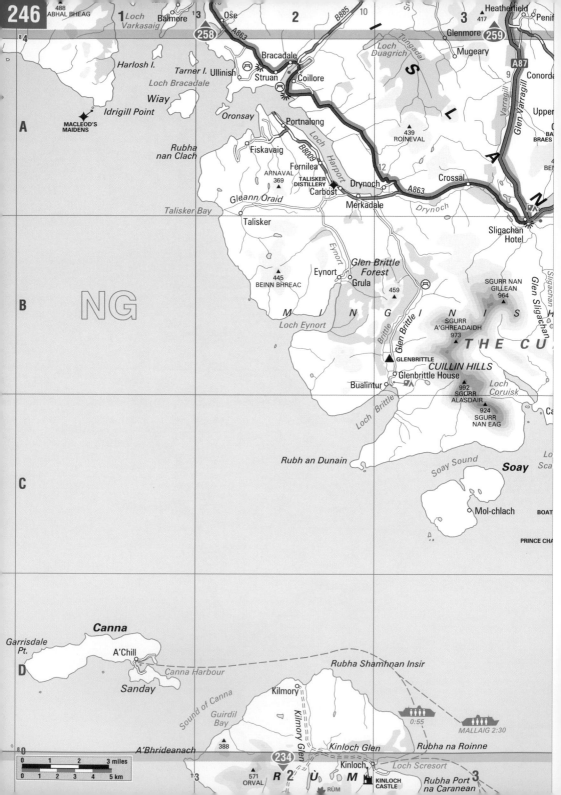

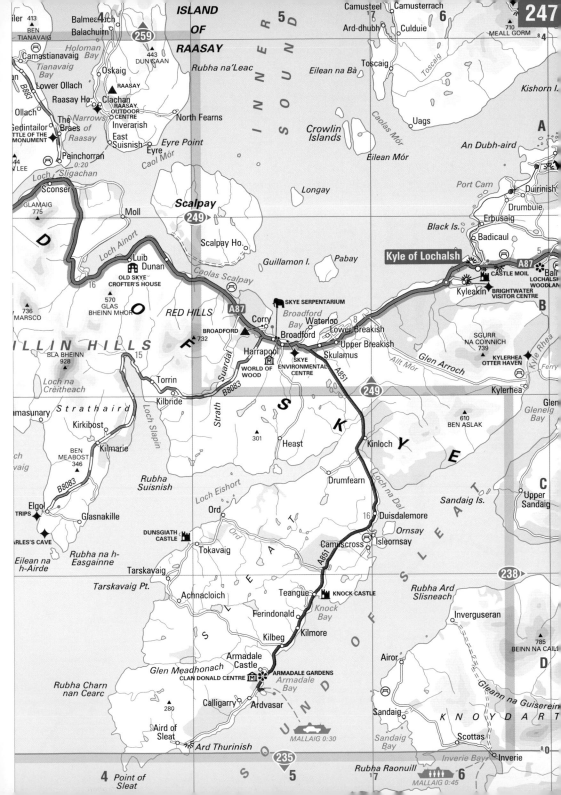

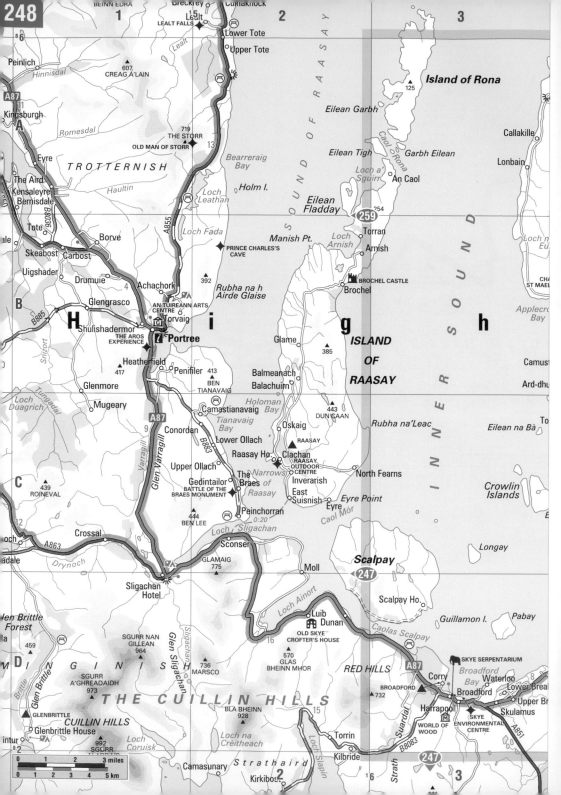

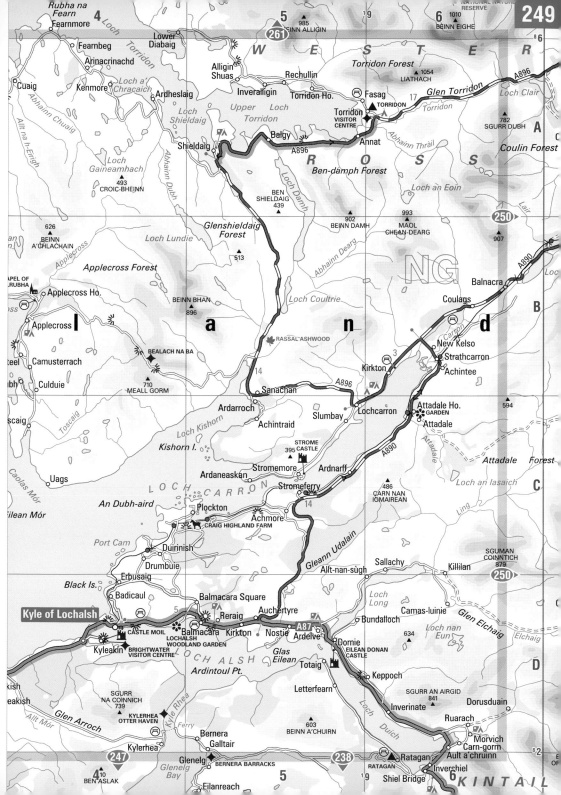

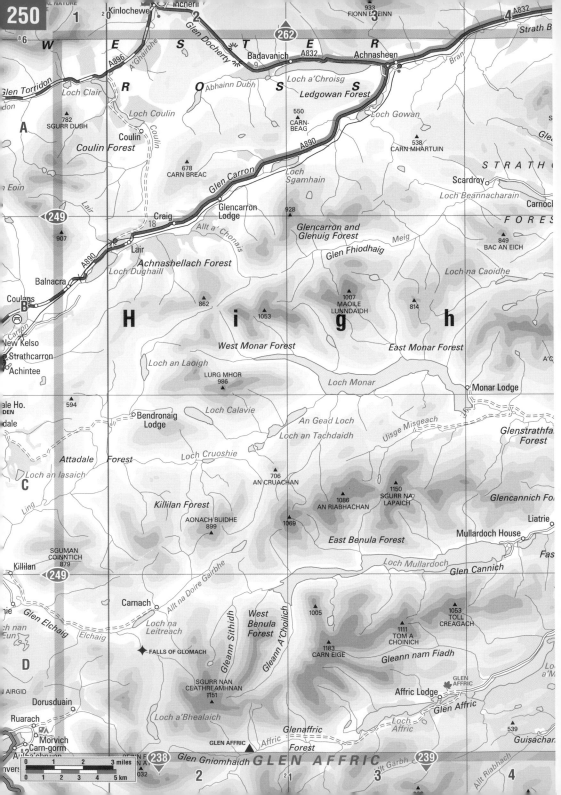

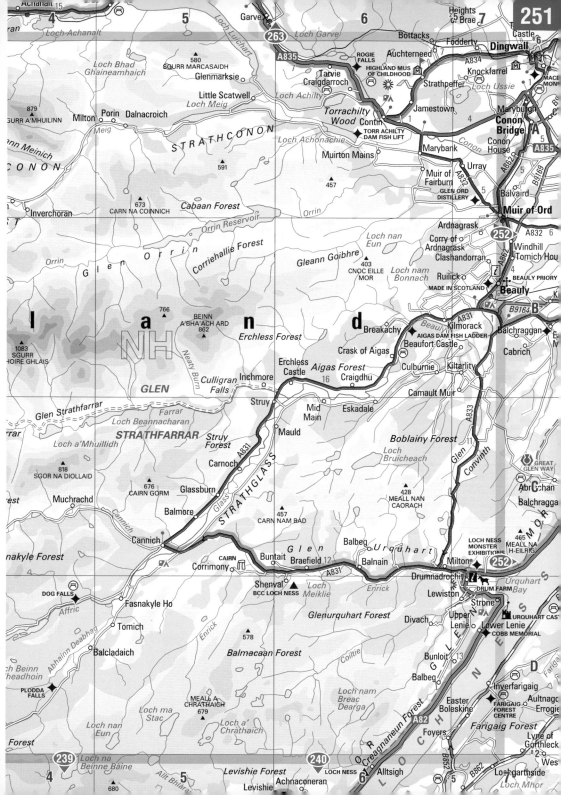

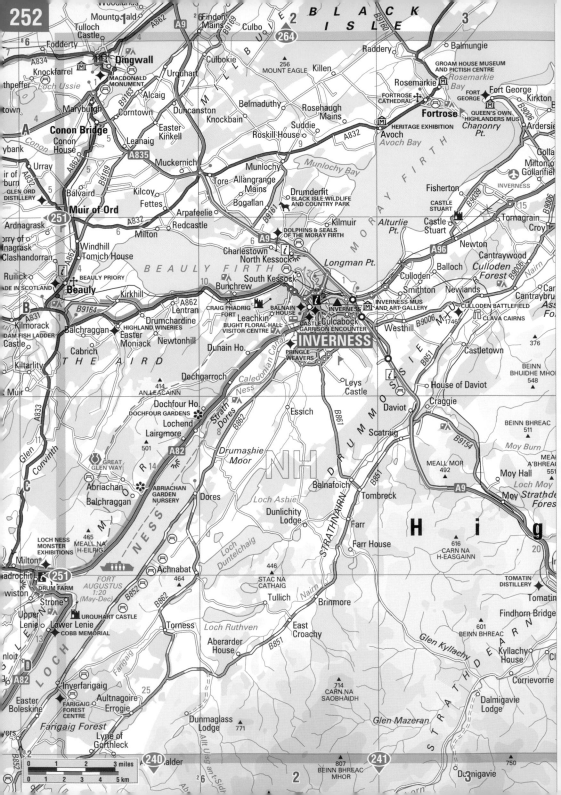

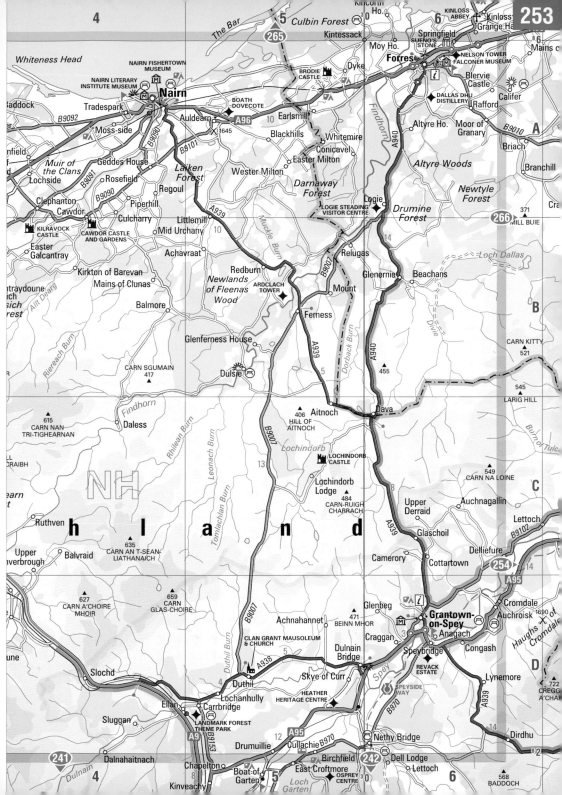

Whiteness Head

NAIRN FISHERTOWN MUSEUM
NAIRN LITERARY INSTITUTE MUSEUM
Nairn
Tradespark
B9092
Moss-side
Baddock
nfield
ich
B9090
B9091
Lochside
Muir of the Clans
Clephanton
Cawdor
Geddes House
Rosefield
Regoul
Piperhill
Culcharry
KILRAVOCK CASTLE
CAWDOR CASTLE AND GARDENS
Easter Galcantray
Kirkton of Barevan
Mains of Clunas
Achavraat
traydoune
ich
sich
rest
Allt Dearg
Balmore
Littlemill
Mid Urchany
Redburn
Newlands of Fleenas Wood
ARDCLACH TOWER

The Bar
265
Culbin Forest
Kincorth Ho.
KINLOSS ABBEY
Kinloss
Grange Ha.

Kintessack
Moy Ho.
SUENO'S STONE
Springfield
6

Dyke
Forres
NELSON TOWER
FALCONER MUSEUM
Mains o
A96
BRODIE CASTLE
Earlsmill
Auldearn
1645
Blackhills
Whitemire
Conicavel
Easter Milton
Wester Milton
Darnaway Forest
Logie
LOGIE STEADING VISITOR CENTRE
Drumine Forest
Blervie Castle
Califer
DALLAS DHU DISTILLERY
Rafford
Altyre Ho.
Moor of Granary
Altyre Woods
Branchill
Newtyle Forest
B9010
Briach
A

266
MILL BUIE
371
Cra

Laiken Forest
A939
10
A940
14

Muckle Burn
B9007
Relugas
Glenernie
Beachans
Loch Dallas
Mount
Ferness
Glenferness House
CARN SGUMAIN
417
Dulsie
Findhorn
615
CARN NAN TRI-TIGHEARNAN
Daless
CRAIBH
Rhilean Burn
NH
Leonach Burn
Tomlachan Burn
B9007
406
HILL OF AITNOCH
Aitnoch
Lochindorb
LOCHINDORB CASTLE
Lochindorb Lodge
484
CARN-RUIGH CHARRACH
Dava
455
5
Dorback Burn
Divie
CARN KITTY
521
545
LARIG HILL
B
549
CARN NA LOINE
C
8
Upper Derraid
Glaschoil
Auchnagallin
Lettoch
B9102
Delliefure
Ruthven
h   l   a   n   d
627
CARN A'CHOIRE MHOIR
659
CARN GLAS-CHOIRE
635
CARN AN T-SEAN-LIATHANAICH
Upper
nverbrough
Balvraid
B9007
Duthil Burn
Cottartown
Camerory
254
A95
A939

Slochd
Ellan
Carrbridge
Sluggan
Achnahannet
471
BEINN MHOR
Glenbeg
Craggan
CLAN GRANT MAUSOLEUM & CHURCH
Dulnain Bridge
A938
5
Duthil
Lochanhully
LANDMARK FOREST THEME PARK
Skye of Curr
HEATHER HERITAGE CENTRE
Speybridge
REVACK ESTATE
SPEYSIDE WAY
B970
Spey
Grantown-on-Spey
Anagach
Congash
Cromdale
Auchroisk
1690
Haughs of Cromdale
Lynemore
722
CREGG A'CHAI
A939
Dirdhu
D

241
Dalnahaitnach
Chapelton
Kinveachy
B9153
8
Drumuillie
12
A95
Boat-of-Garten
5
Loch Garten
Cullachie
B970
242
Nethy Bridge
Birchfield
East Croftmore
OSPREY CENTRE
Dell Lodge
Lettoch
568
BADDOCH
2
4   5   6

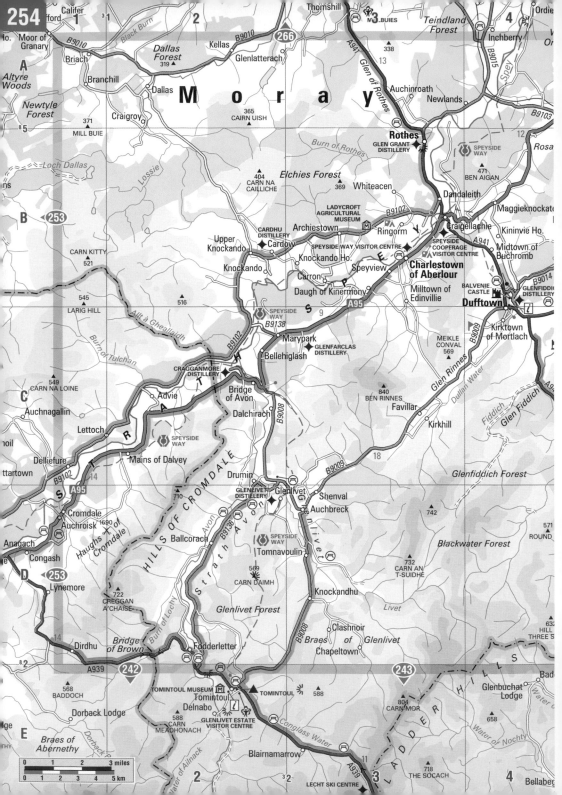

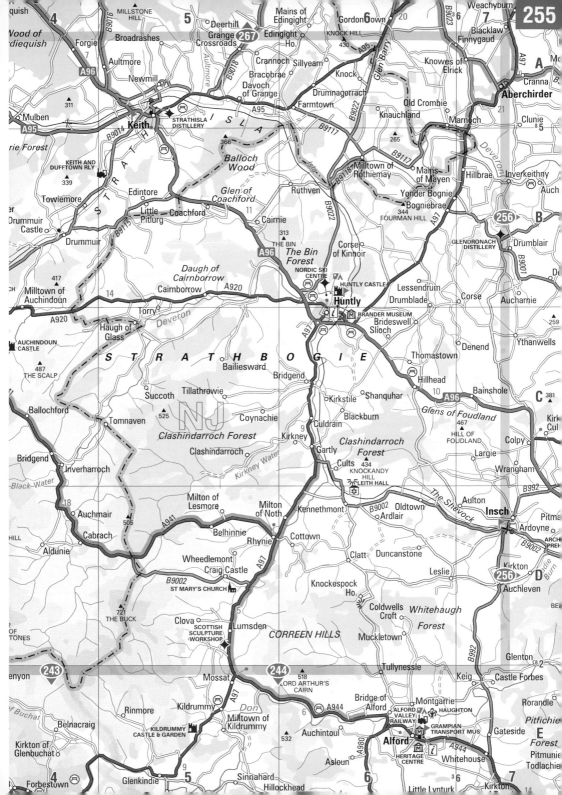

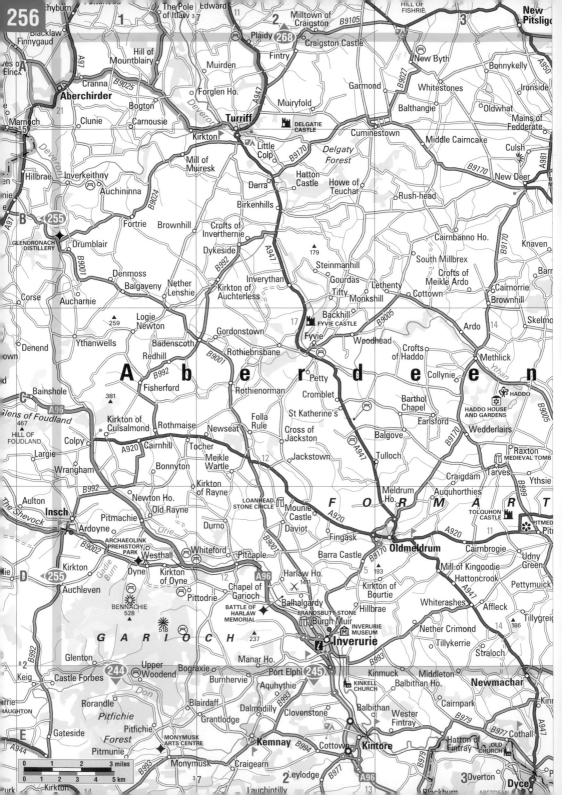

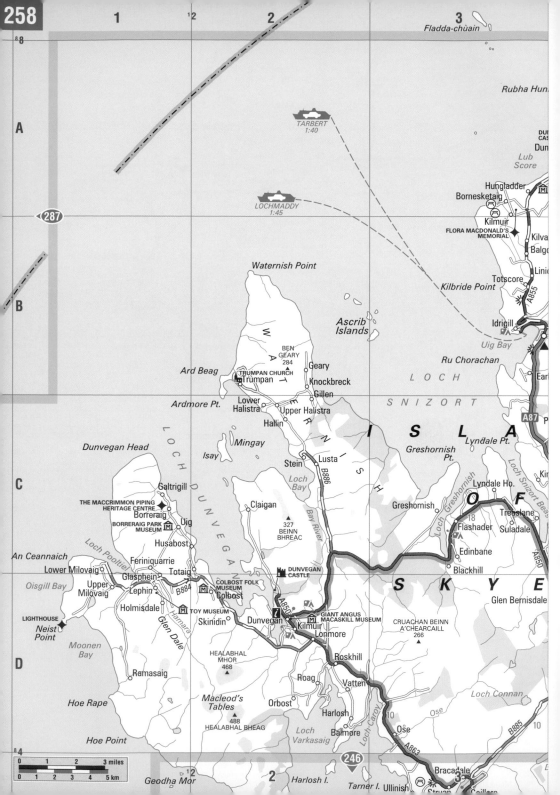

287

246

Fladda-chùain

Rubha Hun...

Lub Score

TARBERT
1:40

LOCHMADDY
1:45

Hungladder
Bornesketaig

Kilmuir
FLORA MACDONALD'S
MEMORIAL

Kilva...
Balgo...

Linic...

Totscore

Waternish Point

Ascrib
Islands

Kilbride Point

Uig Bay

BEN
GEARY
284

Geary

Ard Beag

TRUMPAN CHURCH
Trumpan

Knockbreck

Gillen

Ru Chorachan

LOCH

Ardmore Pt.

Lower
Halistra

Upper Halistra

SNIZORT

Hallin

Earl...

A87

Dunvegan Head

Mingay

Isay

Lusta

Stein

Loch
Bay

Greshornish
Pt.

Lyndale Pt.

ISLA

Galtrigill

THE MACCRIMMON PIPING
HERITAGE CENTRE

Borreraig
BORRERAIG PARK
MUSEUM

Uig

Husabost

Claigan

327
BEINN
BHREAC

Bay River

Greshornish

Lyndale Ho.

Flashader

Treaslane

Suladale

OF

An Ceannaich

Lower Milovaig

Feriniquarrie

Totaig

B884

Edinbane

Blackhill

Loch Snizort Bea...

Kir...

Oisgill Bay

Upper
Milovaig

Glasphein

Lephin

Holmisdale

COLBOST FOLK
MUSEUM
Colbost

DUNVEGAN
CASTLE

SKYE

A850

Glen Bernisdale

LIGHTHOUSE
Neist
Point

Moonen
Bay

Hamara

Glen Dale

TOY MUSEUM

Skinidin

Dunvegan

GIANT ANGUS
MACASKILL MUSEUM
Kilmuir

Lonmore

CRUACHAN BEINN
A'CHEARCAILL
266

Ramasaig

HEALABHAL
MHOR
468

Roag

Vatten

Roskhill

Loch Connan

B885

Hoe Rape

Macleod's
Tables

488
HEALABHAL BHEAG

Orbost

Harlosh

Balmore

Loch
Varkasaig

Ose

Loch Caroy

A863

Ose

Bracadale

Hoe Point

Geodha Mor

Harlosh I.

Tarner I. Ullinish

Struan

4 **5** ⁶ **6** ⁸⁸

A

B

C

D

Eilean Trodday

Rubha na h-Aiseig

DUNTULM
CASTLE
tulm
20 · Balmacqueen
Kilmaluag
MUSEUM OF
ISLAND LIFE

Eilean
Flodigarry
Flodigarry

MEALL NA
SUIRAMACH
543

Staffin I.
Digg
THE QUIRAING Glashvin
Brogaig
Stenscholl Staffin
TROTTERNISH Kilt Rock
466 KILT ROCK & MEALT FALLS
BIOD BUIDHE Elishader
Maligar
Marishader Garros Valtos
611 Rubha nam
BEINN EDRA Breckrey Brathairean
Balnaknock Culnaknock
Lealt
LEALT FALLS Lower Tote
Upper Tote

N Hinnisdal **D**
607
CREAG A'LAIN

11 125 **Island of Rona**
igsburgh
Romesdal Eilean Garbh Callakille
719
THE STORR Eilean Tigh Garbh Eilean Lonbain
Eyre OLD MAN OF STORR 13 Loch a' An Caol
TROTTERNISH Bearreraig Sguirr
The Aird Bay
Kensaleyre Haultin Holm I. Eilean
Bernisdale Loch Fladday
Leathan Torran
Tote Borve Loch Fada Manish Pt. Loch Arnish
Skeabost Carbost Arnish
Uigshader Drumuie PRINCE CHARLES'S
4 CAVE BROCHEL CASTLE CHAPEL
392 Brochel ST MAELRU
Glengrasco Rubha na h
AN TUIREANN ARTS Airde Glaise Applecross
Shulishadermor CENTRE Bay
THE AROS Torvaig
EXPERIENCE **Portree** Glame **ISLAND**
Heatherfield Penifiler 413 385 **OF** Camustee
417 BEN **RAASAY** Ard-dhubh
Glenmore TIANAVAIG Balmeanach
Loch Balachuirn
Quagrich Mugeary Camastianavaig Holoman 443 ⁸⁴
Tianavaig Bay DUN CAAN Rubha na'Leac
Conordan Uskaig Eilean na Bà
Tosca

260
261
249
248
A87 **B883** **B8036**

Uig
UIG

Rha
Conon
Snizort
Tungadal

SOUND OF RAASAY
Caol Rona
INNER SOUND
Loch nan
Eun

NG

Garbh
Eilean

Eilean Mhuire

Eilean an Tighe

Na h-Eileanan Mòra
(Shiant Islands)

A

◁288

288

NG

B

259

Eilean Trodday

Rubha
unish

Rubha na h-Aiseig

259▷

C

DUN LM
CASTLE

Balmacqueen

untulm

Kilmaluag

20

MUSEUM OF
ISLAND LIFE

Eilean
Flodigarry

Flodigarry

MEALL NA
SUIRAMACH
543

Digg

Staffin I.

vaxter

THE QUIRAING

Glashvin

Staffin
Bay

Brogaig

lgown

Stenscholl

Staffin

inicro

TROTTERNISH

466
BIOD BUIDHE

Kilt Rock

KILT ROCK & MEALT FALLS

D

Maligar

Elishader

Loch Mealt

Uig

Marishader

Valtos

UIG

Balnaknock

Garros

611
BEINN EDRA

Breckrey

Culnaknock

*Rubha nam
Brathairean*

Island of Rona

Earlish

Lealt

LEALT FALLS

Conon

Lealt

Lower Tote

Upper Tote

Hinnisdal

0   1   2   3 miles
0 1 2 3 4 5 km

607
CREAG A'LAIN

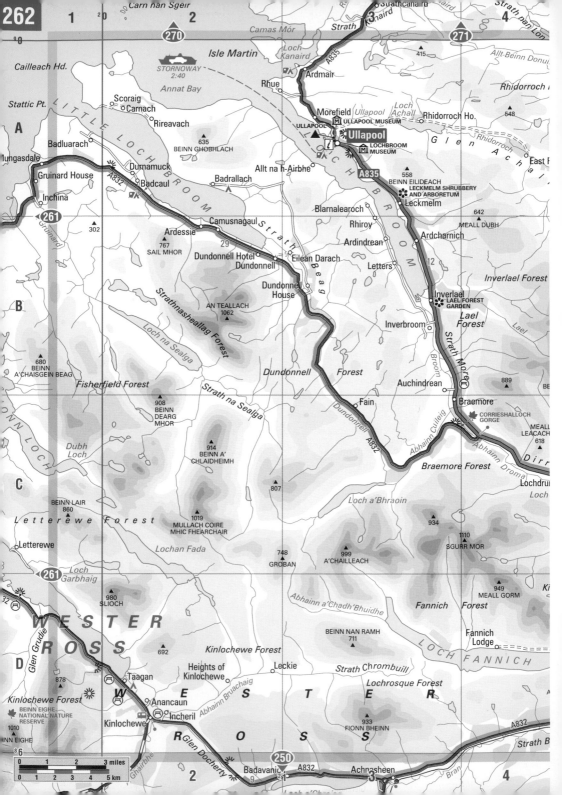

Map labels

Top row: 1 2 0 3 4

Carn nan Sgeir
Strath na Caird
Strath nan Lon
Camas Mór
270
271
Isle Martin
Loch Kanaird
Allt-Beinn Donui
STORNOWAY 2:40
Annat Bay
Rhue
Ardmair
415
Rhidorroch
Cailleach Hd.
Scoraig
Carnach
Rireavach
Morefield Ullapool
Loch Achall
Rhidorroch Ho.
548
Stattic Pt.
635
BEINN GHOBHLACH
ULLAPOOL
ULLAPOOL MUSEUM
Ullapool
Glen Achall
East F
A
Badluarach
Iungasdale
Allt na h-Airbhe
LOCHBROOM MUSEUM
Durnamuck
Badralloch
558
BEINN EILIDEACH
Gruinard House
Badcaul
A832
A835
LECKMELM SHRUBBERY AND ARBORETUM
Leckmelm
642
Inchina
261
302
Camusnagaul
Blarnalearoch
MEALL DUBH
Ardessie
29
Rhiroy
Ardcharnich
767
SAIL MHOR
Dundonnell Hotel
Dundonnell
Eilean Darach
Ardindrean
12
Inverlael Forest
B
Dundonnell House
Letters
Inverlael
LAEL FOREST GARDEN
AN TEALLACH 1062
Lael Forest
680
BEINN A'CHAISGEIN BEAG
Loch na Sealga
Dundonnell Forest
Inverbroom
889
Fisherfield Forest
Strath na Sealga
Auchindrean
Dubh Loch
908
BEINN DEARG MHOR
Fain
Braemore
C
914
BEINN A'CHLAIDHEIMH
CORRIESHALLOCH GORGE
MEALL LEACACH
618
BEINN LAIR 860
807
Braemore Forest
Lochdru
Letterewe
1019
MULLACH COIRE MHIC FHEARCHAIR
Loch a'Bhraoin
Letterewe Forest
Lochan Fada
748
GROBAN
999
A'CHAILLEACH
934
1110
SGURR MOR
261
Loch Garbhaig
980
SLIOCH
949
MEALL GORM
D
WESTER
Abhainn a'Chadh'Bhuidhe
Fannich Forest
692
Kinlochewe Forest
BEINN NAN RAMH 711
Fannich Lodge
ROSS
Heights of Kinlochewe
Leckie
Strath Chrombuill
878
Taagan
Lochrosque Forest
Kinlochewe Forest
Anancaun
933
FIONN BHEINN
1010
INN EIGHE
BEINN EIGHE NATIONAL NATURE RESERVE
Incheril
Kinlochewe
Glen Docherty
250
Badavanich
A832
Achnasheen
Strath B

0 1 2 3 miles
0 1 2 3 4 5 km

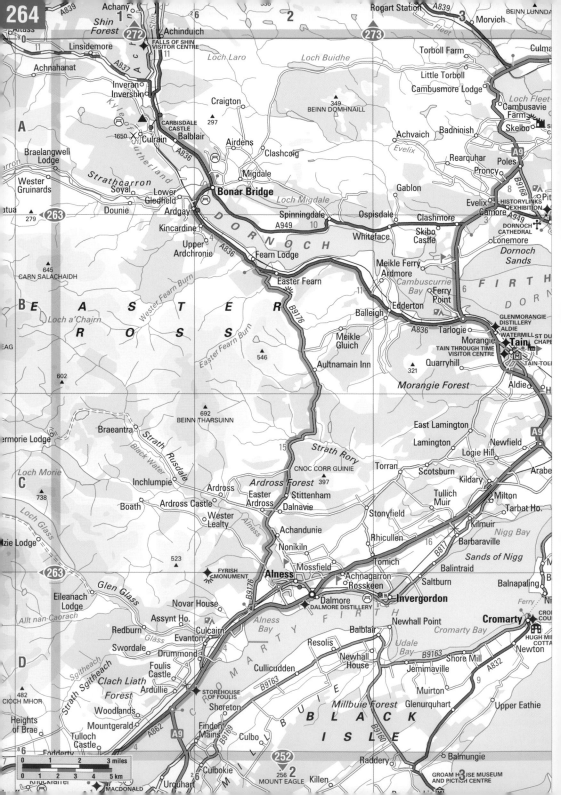

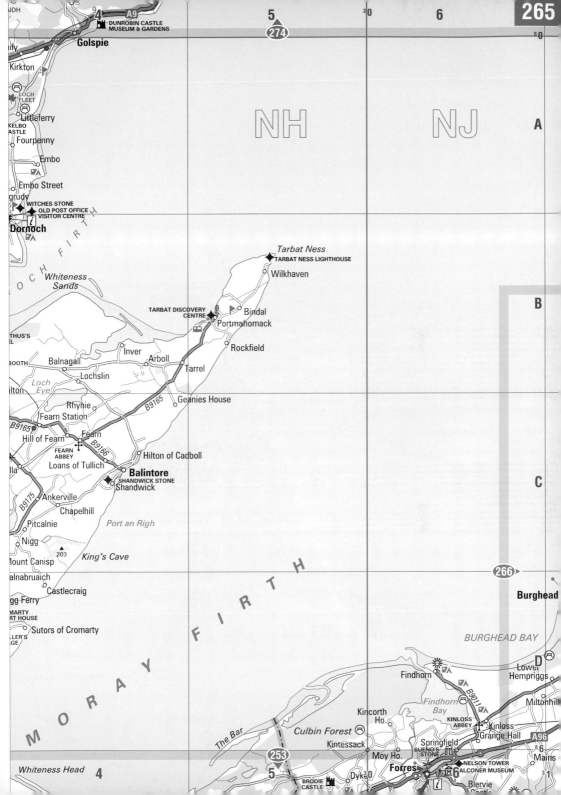

5 **6**

274

NH

NJ

A

B

C

266

Burghead

BURGHEAD BAY

D

A96

4

5

Golspie
Kirkton
DUNROBIN CASTLE
MUSEUM & GARDENS
A9

LOCH
FLEET
Littleferry
KELBO
ASTLE
Fourpenny
Embo
Embo Street
grudy
WITCHES STONE
OLD POST OFFICE
VISITOR CENTRE
Dornoch

LOCH FIRTH

*Whiteness
Sands*

THUS'S
EL

BOOTH
Balnagall
Inver
Arboll
Lochslin
Tarrel
Loch
Eye
ilton
Rhynie
Fearn Station
B9165
B9165
Fearn
Hill of Fearn
B9166
FEARN
ABBEY
Loans of Tullich
Hilton of Cadboll
lla
Balintore
SHANDWICK STONE
Shandwick
B9175
Ankerville
Chapelhill
Pitcalnie
Nigg
203
Port an Righ
King's Cave
ount Canisp
alnabruaich
Castlecraig
MARTY
RT HOUSE
Sutors of Cromarty
LER'S
GE
gg Ferry

Tarbat Ness
TARBAT NESS LIGHTHOUSE
Wilkhaven

TARBAT DISCOVERY
CENTRE
Bindal
Portmahomack
Rockfield

Geanies House

M O R A Y   F I R T H

Findhorn
Lower
Hempriggs
Miltonhill
B9011
*Findhorn
Bay*
Kincorth
Ho.
KINLOSS
ABBEY
Kinloss
Springfield
Grange Hall
Mains
Whiteness Head
4
5
253
Culbin Forest
Kintessack
The Bar
Moy Ho.
Dyke
SUENO'S
STONE
NELSON TOWER
ALCONER MUSEUM
Forres
BRODIE
CASTLE
Blervie
6
1
8
9
0
0
3
0
9

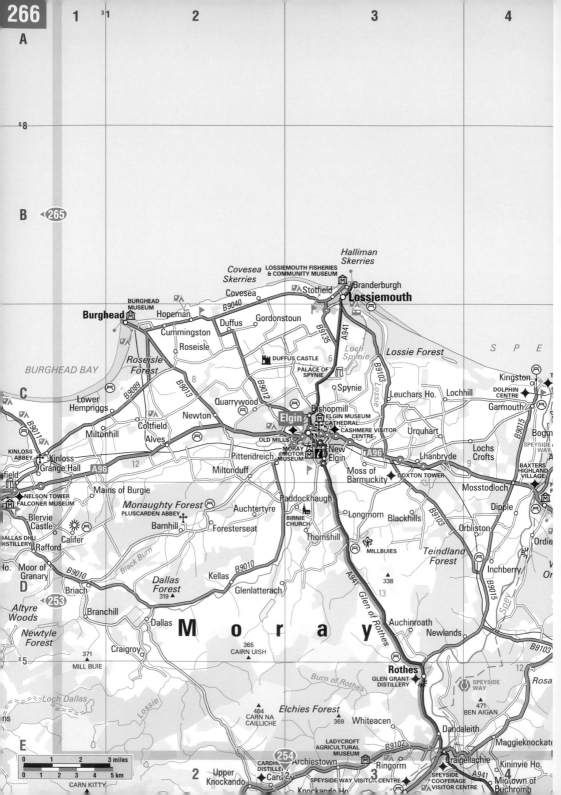

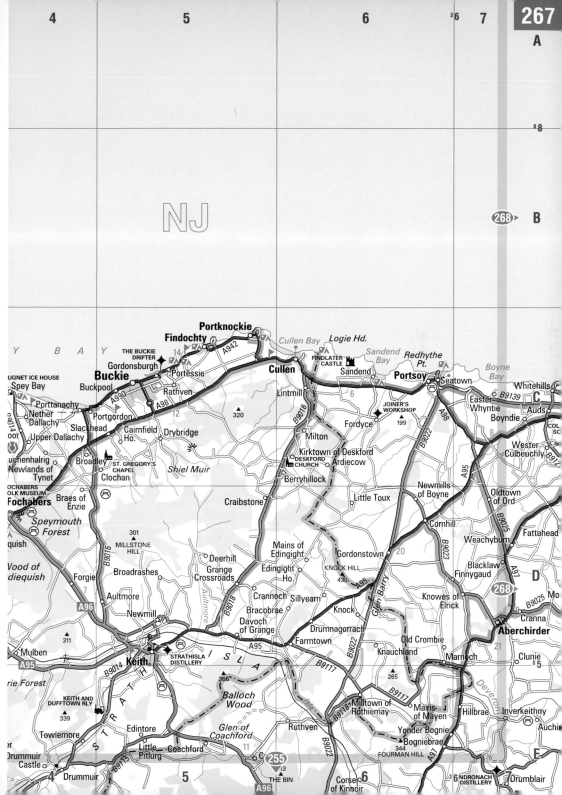

A

B

◄267

C Seatown

Boyne Bay   Knock Hd.   *Boyndie Bay*   Macduff   MACDUFF MARINE AQUARIUM   *Head of Garness*   *Gamrie Bay*   *Troup Hd.*   Crovie   *Pennan Hd.*   Pennan   *Quarry H*

Whitehills   Inverboyndie   BANFF MUSEUM   Easter Silverford   B9031   Gardenstown   Towie

Easter Whyntie   B9139   Auds   Banff   West Greenskares   Dubford   B9031   New Aberdo

Boyndie   COLLEONARD SCULPTURE GARDEN & GALLERY   DUFF HOUSE   Doune Park   Longmanhill   Cushnie   231 WINDYHEADS HILL   Ladysfor

A98   Wester Culbeuchly   B9121   Montcoffer Ho.   15   Minnonie   Nether Glasslaw

A95   Oldtown of Ord   Kirktown of Alva   Keilhill   A947   Netherbrae   Craigmaud

B9025   Greenlaw   King Edward   Gorrachie   Mid Cloch Forbie   227 HILL OF FISHRIE   New Pitslig

hill   Weachyburn   Fattahead   B9121   The Pole of Itlaw   11   Milltown of Craigston   B9105

B9023   Blacklaw   Finnygaud   Hill of Mountblairy   Plâidy   Craigston Castle   Fintry   New Byth   Bonnykelly   A950

D ◄267   A97   Cranna   B9025   Muirden   Garmond   Whitestones   Ironside

ves of Elrick   Aberchirder   Bogton   Forglen Ho.   Muiryfold   Balthangie   Oldwhat   Mains of Fedderate

Marnoch   21   Clunie   Carnousie   A947   Turriff   DELGATIE CASTLE   Cuminestown   Middle Cairncake   Culsh

5   Kirkton   Little Colp   B9170   *Delgaty Forest*   A981

Hillbrae   Inverkeithny   Mill of Muiresk   Darra   Hatton Castle   Howe of Teuchar   Rush-head   New Deer   B9170

Fortrie   B9024   Birkenhills   256   Cairnba o Ho.

E   Auchininna   Brownhill   Crofts of Inverthernie   A947   179   Knaven

Dykeside

0   1   2   3 miles
0   1   2   3   4   5 km

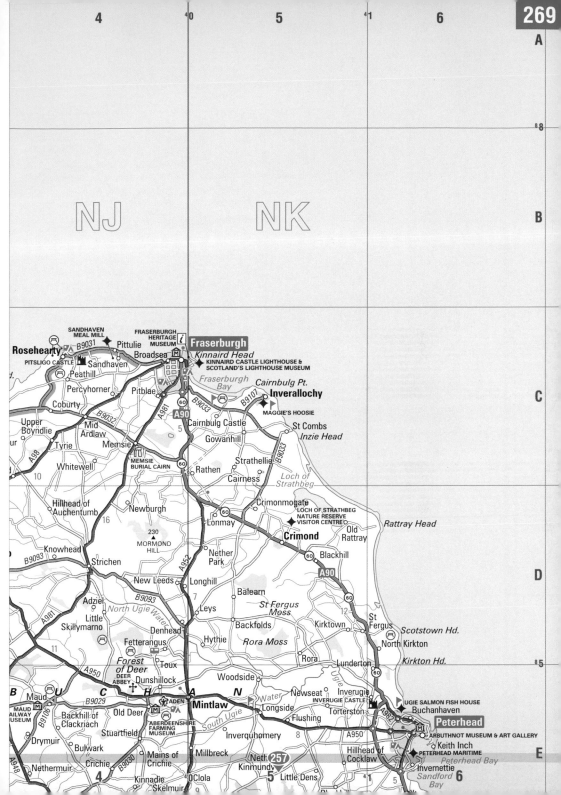

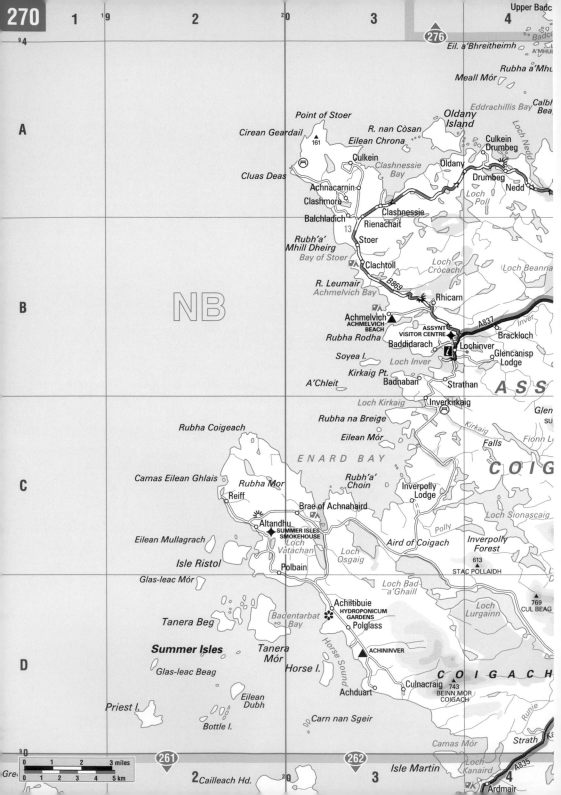

⁹4

A837 276

Upper Badc

Eil. a'Bhreitheimh

A'MHU

Rubha a'Mhu

Meall Mór

Eddrachillis Bay

Calbh
Bea

A

NB

Point of Stoer

Cirean Geardail

▲161

Culkein

R. nan Còsan

Eilean Chrona

Oldany
Island

Culkein
Drumbeg

Loch Nedd

Cluas Deas

Clashnessie
Bay

Achnacarnin

Clashmore

Oldany

Drumbeg

Nedd

Loch
Poll

Balchladich

Clashnessie

13

Rienachait

Stoer

Loch Beanna

Rubh 'a'
Mhill Dheirg

Bay of Stoer

B869

Clachtoll

Loch
Cròcach

Loch Beanna

B

R. Leumair

Achmelvich Bay

Rhicarn

A837

Inver

Achmelvich
ACHMELVICH
BEACH

ASSYNT
VISITOR CENTRE

Brackloch

Rubha Rodha

Baddidarach

Lochinver

Glencanisp
Lodge

Soyea I.

Loch Inver

A SS

Kirkaig Pt.

A'Chleit

Badnaban

Strathan

Loch Kirkaig

Inverkirkaig

Glen
SU

Rubha na Breige

Kirkaig

Glen

Rubha Coigeach

Eilean Mór

Falls

Fionn L

C OI G

C

Camas Eilean Ghlais

Rubha Mór

Reiff

ENARD BAY

Rubh 'a'
Choin

Inverpolly
Lodge

Brae of Achnahaird

Loch Sionascaig

Altandhu

SUMMER ISLES
SMOKEHOUSE

Loch
Vatachan

Polly

Aird of Coigach

Inverpolly
Forest

Eilean Mullagrach

Isle Ristol

Polbain

Loch
Osgaig

▲613
STAC POLLAIDH

Glas-leac Mór

Loch Bad
a'Ghaill

Loch
Lurgainn

▲769
CUL BEAG

Tanera Beg

*Badentarbat
Bay*

Achiltibuie

HYDROPONICUM
GARDENS

Polglass

Summer Isles

Tanera
Mór

Horse I.

Horse Sound

ACHININVER

D

Glas-leac Beag

Eilean
Dubh

Culnacraig

▲743
BEINN MOR
COIGACH

C O I G A C H

Priest I.

Achduart

Runie

Bottle I.

Carn nan Sgeir

Camas Mór

Strath

Loch
Kanaird

A835

⁹0

| 0 | 1 | 2 | | 3 miles |
| 0 | 1 | 2 | 3 | 4 | 5 km |

Gre

261

²2 Cailleach Hd. ²0

262

3 Isle Martin

Ardmair

4

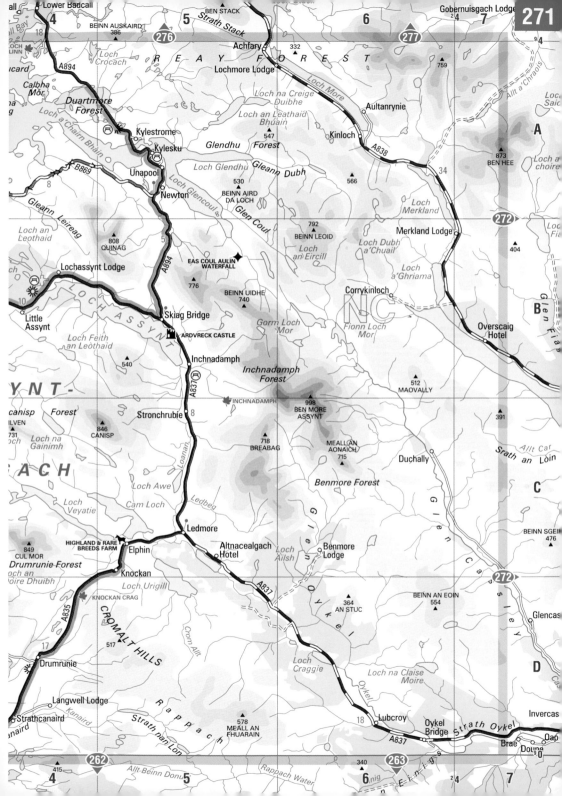

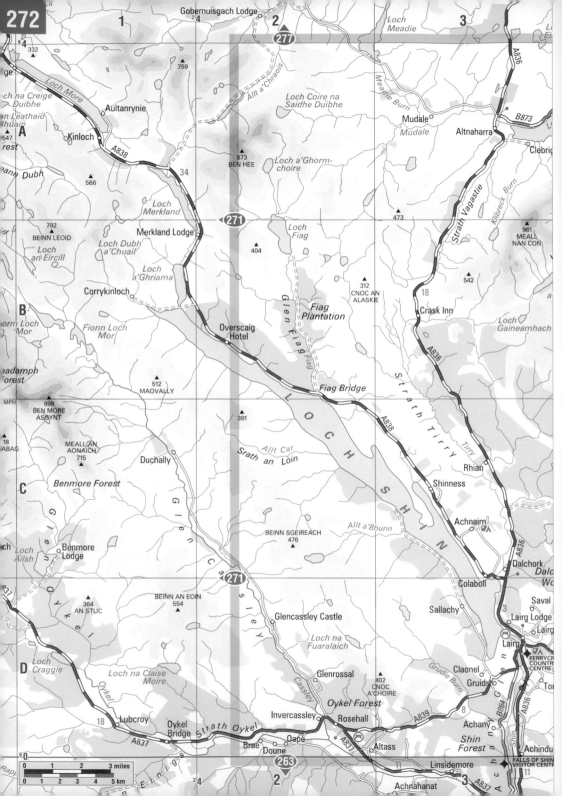

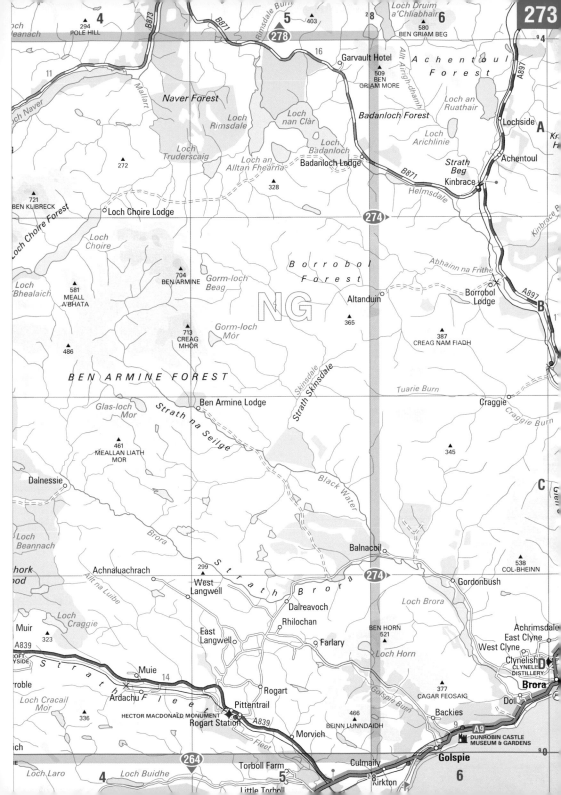

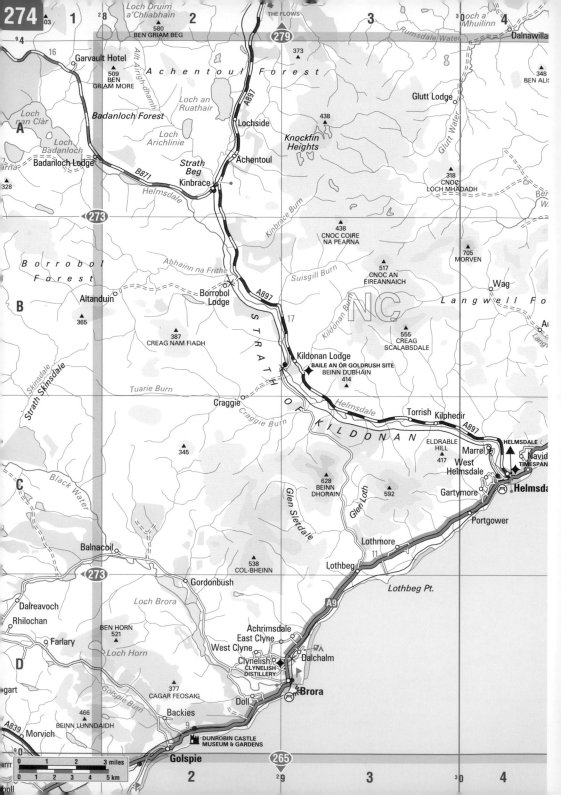

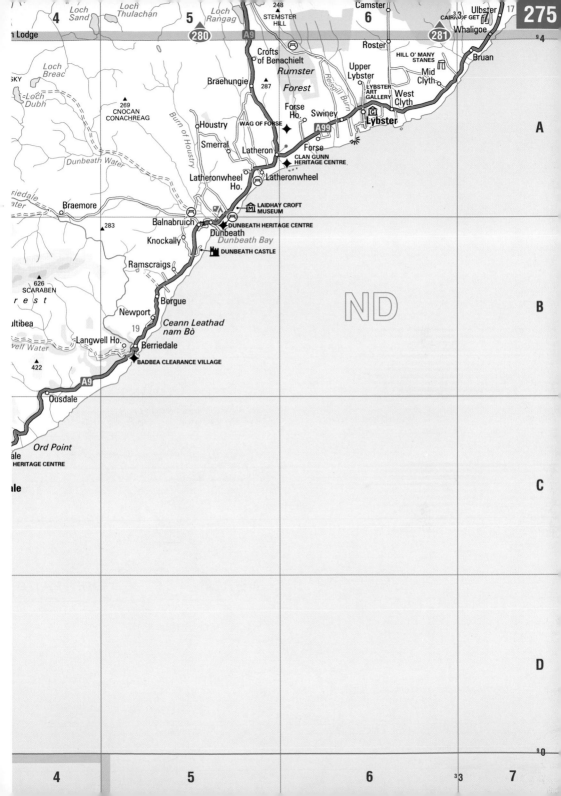

Loch Sand
Loch Thulachan
Loch Rangag
Loch Breac
Loch Dubh
-SKY
n Lodge
248 STEMSTER HILL
Camster
Ulbster 17
CAIRN OF GET
Whaligoe
280
A9
281
9 4
Roster
Crofts of Benachielt
HILL O' MANY STANES
Bruan
Braehungie
Rumster Forest
Upper Lybster
Mid Clyth
287
LYBSTER ART GALLERY
West Clyth
269 CNOCAN CONACHREAG
Forse Ho.
Swiney
Houstry
WAG OF FORSE
A99
Lybster
Smerral
Latheron
Forse
CLAN GUNN HERITAGE CENTRE
Latheronwheel Ho.
Latheronwheel
Dunbeath Water
A
LAIDHAY CROFT MUSEUM
Braemore
Balnabruich
DUNBEATH HERITAGE CENTRE
283
Dunbeath
Knockally
Dunbeath Bay
DUNBEATH CASTLE
Ramscraigs
626 SCARABEN
Borgue
ND
B
Newport
Ceann Leathad nam Bò
ultibea
19
Langwell Ho.
Berriedale
ell Water
422
BADBEA CLEARANCE VILLAGE
A9
Ousdale
Ord Point
ale
HERITAGE CENTRE
C
dale

D

9 0

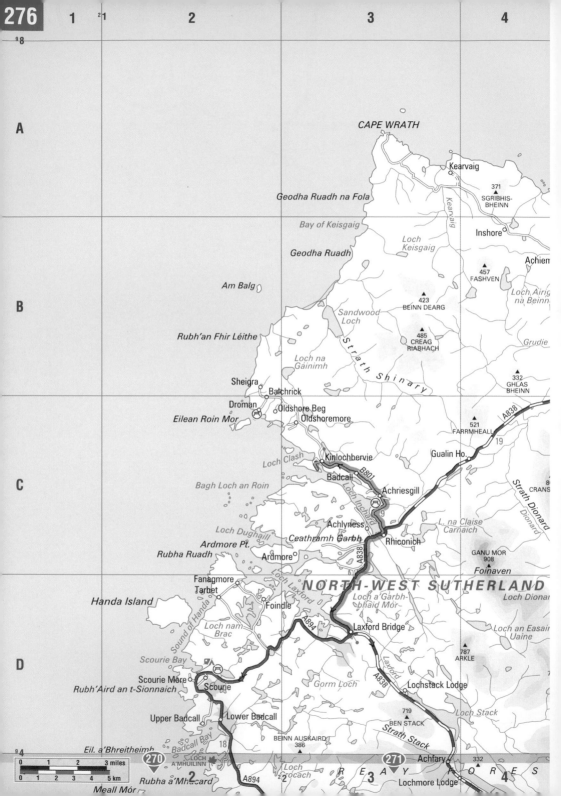

1 ²¹ 2 3 4

A

CAPE WRATH

Kearvaig

371
SGRIBHIS-
BHEINN

Geodha Ruadh na Fola

Inshore

Bay of Keisgaig

Loch
Keisgaig

457
FASHVEN

Achiem

Geodha Ruadh

Loch Airig
na Beinn

Am Balg

423
BEINN DEARG

Sandwood
Loch

485
CREAG
RIABHACH

Grudie

B

Rubh'an Fhir Léithe

Strath Shinary

*Loch na
Gàinimh*

332
GHLAS
BHEINN

Sheigra

Balchrick

521
FARRMHEALL

A838

Droman

Oldshore Beg

19

Eilean Roin Mor

Oldshoremore

Loch Clash

Kinlochbervie

Gualin Ho.

Badcall

B801

Strath Dionard

Bagh Loch an Roin

Achriesgill

CRANS

C

Loch Inchard

9

L. na Claise
Carnaich

Loch Dughaill

Achlyness

Ceathramh Garbh

Rhiconich

GANU MOR
908

Ardmore Pt.

Ardmore

Foinaven

Rubha Ruadh

A838

Fanagmore

NORTH-WEST SUTHERLAND

Tarbet

Loch a'Garbh-
bhaid Mór

Loch Dionar

Handa Island

Foindle

Loch Laxford

Sound of Handa

A894

Laxford Bridge

Loch an Easair
Uaine

*Loch nam
Brac*

787
ARKLE

D

Scourie Bay

A838

Laxford

Rubh'Aird an t-Sionnaich

Scourie More

Scourie

Lochstack Lodge

Gorm Loch

Loch Stack

Upper Badcall

Lower Badcall

719
BEN STACK

Strath Stack

⁹4

Eil. a'Bhreitheimh

18

Badcall Bay

270

LOCH
A'MHUILINN

BEINN AUSKAIRD
386

271

Achfary

332

4

R E A Y

F O R E S

Rubha a'Mhucard

A894

Loch
Crocach

2

3

Lochmore Lodge

Meall Mór

0 1 2 3 miles
0 1 2 3 4 5 km

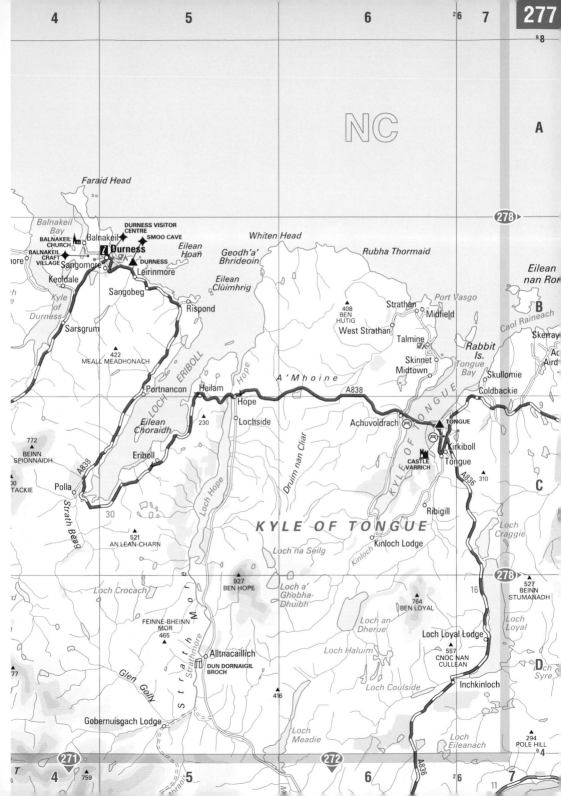

4 **5** **6** **²6 7**

⁹8

NC

A

Faraid Head

Balnakeil
Bay
**BALNAKEIL
CHURCH**
Balnakeil
**DURNESS VISITOR
CENTRE**
**BALNAKEIL
CRAFT
VILLAGE**
Sangomore
Durness
SMOO CAVE
Keoldale
Leirinmore
DURNESS
Eilean
Hoan
Whiten Head
Geodh'a'
Bhrideoin
Rubha Thormaid

Eilean
nan Ron

Sangobeg
Rispond
Eilean
Clùimhrig
Port Vasgo
B
408
BEN
HUTIG
Strathan
Midfield
Caol Raineach
Skerray
Sarsgrum
West Strathan
Talmine
Ac
Aird

Kyle
of
Durness

422
MEALL MEADHONACH

Skinnet
Midtown
Rabbit
Is.
Tongue
Bay
Skullomie
Coldbackie

LOCH ERIBOLL

A'Mhoine

A838

772
BEINN
SPIONNAIDH
TACKIE

Portnancon
Heilam
Hope
Lochside
230
Eilean
Choraidh
Eriboll
Achuvoldrach
Tongue
Kirkiboll
Tongue
**CASTLE
VARRICH**
310
C

Polla
30
Strath Beag
Loch Hope
Drum nan Cliar
KYLE OF TONGUE
Ribigill
Loch
Craggie

521
AN LEAN-CHARN
Kinloch Lodge
278
527
BEINN
STUMANADH
16
Loch Crocach
927
BEN HOPE
Loch a'
Ghobha-
Dhuibh
764
BEN LOYAL
Loch
Loyal

FEINNE-BHEINN
MOR
465
Loch an
Dherue
Loch Loyal Lodge
557
CNOC NAN
CULLEAN
D
Syre

Strath More
Alltnacaillich
**DUN DORNAIGIL
BROCH**
Loch Haluim
Inchkinloch
ch

416
Loch Coulside
294
POLE HILL
9 4
Glen Golly
Gobernuisgach Lodge

Loch
Meadie
Loch
Eileanach
A836

271
759
272
6 ²6 7
11

278

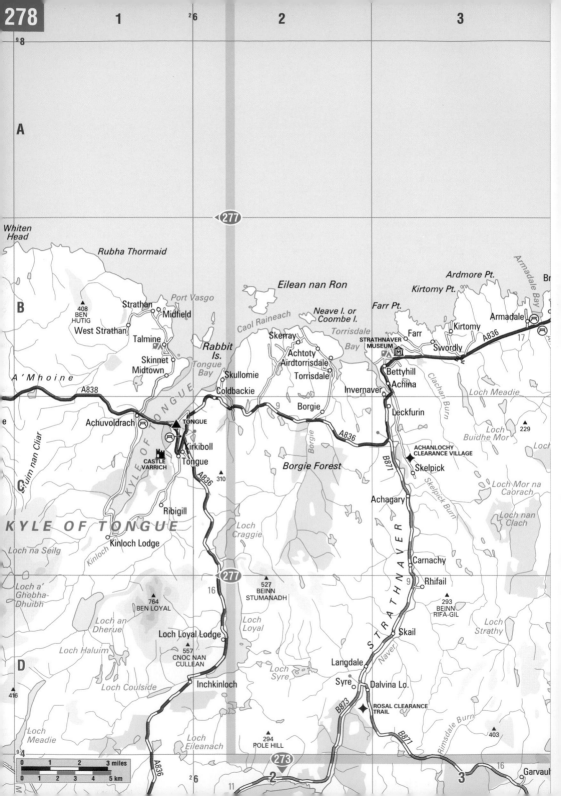

A

Whiten
Head

Rubha Thormaid

Port Vasgo

Eilean nan Ron

Ardmore Pt.

Kirtomy Pt.

Armadale Bay

B

▲ 408
BEN
HUTIG

Strathan
Midfield

West Strathan

Talmine

Skinnet
Midtown

A'Mhoine

Caol Raineach

Rabbit
Is.

Tongue
Bay

Skerray

Achtoty
Airdtorrisdale

Skullomie

Coldbackie

Neave I. or
Coombe I.

Torrisdale
Bay

Torrisdale

Borgie

Farr Pt.

STRATHNAVER
MUSEUM

Bettyhill

Invernaver

Leckfurin

Achina

Farr

Kirtomy

Swordly

A836

Armadale

17

Loch Meadie

A838

Achuvoldrach

KYLE OF TONGUE

Tongue

Kirkiboll

CASTLE
VARRICH

Tongue

▲ 310

A836

Cuim nan Cliar

Ribigill

Kinloch

Kinloch Lodge

Loch na Seilg

KYLE OF TONGUE

A836

Loch
Craggie

Borgie Forest

A836

B871

ACHANLOCHY
CLEARANCE VILLAGE

Skelpick

Achagary

Skelpick Burn

Loch
Buidhe Mor

▲ 229

Loch Mor na
Caorach

Loch nan
Clach

277

Loch a'
Ghobha-
Dhuibh

▲ 764
BEN LOYAL

Loch an
Dherue

Loch Haluim

16

Loch Loyal Lodge

▲ 557
CNOC NAN
CULLEAN

277

▲ 527
BEINN
STUMANADH

Loch
Loyal

S T R A T H N A V E R

Carnachy

Rhifail

9

Skail

Naver

▲ 293
BEINN
RIFA-GIL

Loch
Strathy

D

▲ 416

Inchkinloch

Loch Coulside

Loch
Meadie

Loch
Eileanach

▲ 294
POLE HILL

273

Loch
Syre

Langdale

Syre

B873

Dalvina Lo.

ROSAL CLEARANCE
TRAIL

B871

2

Rimsdale Burn

▲ 403

Garvaul

16

0   1   2   3 miles
0 1 2 3 4 5 km

A836

6

11

2

3

NC

4 | **5** | 30 | **6** | 98 | A

Strathy Point

Totegan

Strathy Bay

Melvich Bay

Baligill

Portskerra

Bighouse

Red Pt.

Fresgoe

Sandside Ho.

Sandside Bay

Dounreay

Buldoo

Achreamie

Brims Ness

ST MARY'S CHAPEL

Crosskirk

Spear Hd.

280

Scrabster

A836

16

Bridge of Forss

144

Thurso

THURSO

Millb

Newlands of Geise

Bu

Aultiphurst

Strathy

Melvich

Isauld

Reay

Achvarasdal

DOUNREAY EXHIBITION CENTRE

CNOC FREKEDAIN CHAMBERED CAIRN

Westfield

B

Lednagullin

A836

Shebster

Forss Water

Lieurary

Golval

Loch Akran

Loch Saorach

Broubster

Loch Calder

Calde Main

Bowside Lodge

254

Strathy Forest

Loch na Seilge

Sandside Burn

Achvarasdal Burn

Loch Thormaid

198

Shurrery

B870

Bu

Meala

A897

Achiemore

Upper Bighouse

Craigtown

Halladale

Dalhalvaig

Shurrery Lodge

Loch Scye

Brawlbin

Dorrery

224

Loch Shurrery

Loch Olginey

Scot Stati

Olgr

The Uair

Trantlemore

Trantlebeg

STRATH HALLADALE

BEINN NAM BAD MOR

290

Loch Tuim Ghlais

Loch Caluim

Torran Water

280

Loch Meadie

Dyke

Forsinain

Loch nam Breac

Loch na Saobhaidhe

Loch-na Saobhaidhe

SLETILL HILL

280

Loch Sletill

Loch Dubh nan Geodh

Loch Gaineimh

Loch Eileanach

Lochmore Cottage

D

21

Forsinard

Loch Crocach

Forsinard Station

221

Altnabreac Station

Lochdhu

Sleach Water

Loch More

Loch Sand

Loch Druim a'Chliabhain

A897

THE FLOWS

580

BEN GRIAM BEG

t Hotel

509 BFN

373

274

Dalnawillan Lodge

Loch a' Mhuilinn

Thurso

94

Achentoul Forest

4 | 5 | 30 | 6

348 BEN ALISKY

Loch Breac

Rumsdale Water

A

B

C

D

1   30   2   3   4

98

DUNNET HEAD
▲127

Briga Hd.   Scarfskerry
Scarfs

STROMNESS   The Thirl   Brough   Ham
1:30   Hunspow
MARY ANN'S   St John's
COTTAGE   Loch
Spear Hd.   Holborn Hd.   Corsback
NATURAL HISTORY DISPLAY   Loch
Brims Ness   Thurso   Clardon Hd.   DUNNET BAY   Heilie
Bay   Dunnet
ST MARY'S   Crosskirk   FLAGSTONE
CHAPEL   Scrabster   THURSO   INTERPRETATIVE
CASTLE   THURSO   TRAIL   Castlehill
279   FOLK MUSEUM   Murkle   Greenland
THURSO   M   Clardon
A836   16   Bridge of Forss   ▲144   Castletown   CASTLETON   Tain
Thurso   Castletown
THURSO   Millbank   Thurso   A836   Haimer   Olrig Ho.
Achreamie   ▲   East   ND   141   Hilliclay
Dounreay   Buldoo   Newlands   Geise   Weydale   Durran   Bow
DOUNREAY   of Geise   6   Achingills   Bowertower
EXHIBITION CENTRE   Westfield   Buckies   Sordale   Stemster   Halcro   Hast
sgoe   Isauld   Achvarasdal   Lieurary   Braal   Knockdee   Stemster Ho.
Ho.   Reay   Shebster   Castle   Roadside   Gillock   No
836   CNOC FREKEDAIN   Calder   Clayock   Wa
CHAMBERED CAIRN   Loch   Mains   Loch
Saorach   Scarmclate   A882   B874
Forss   Broubster   Halkirk   Banniskirk Ho.   Loch Watten
Water   Loch   Brawlbin   Scotscalder   Harpsdale
Loch   Thormaid   Station   Watten
Shurrery   ▲198   Olgrimmore   ▲176   A9
Loch Calder   Loch   B870
Shurrery Lodge   Olginey   Spittal   Backlass
Loch   Dorrery   Acharole
Scye   ▲224   Westerdale   Mybster   Loch of
Seilge   BEINN NAM   Toftingall
kran   ▲290   BAD MOR   Little   Burn of Acharole
Loch   B870   River   17
Tuim   Loch   279   Loch
Ghlais   Caluim   Meadie   Strathmore Lodge   Rangag
Torran   Loch
Loch   Water   Eileanach   GREY CAIRN
Sletill   Altnabreac Station   Loch   OF CAMSTE
Lochmore   Gaineimh   Achavanich
Cottage   ▲221   Lochdhu   Loch   ▲248
Loch   More   STEMSTER   Can
a'   Loch   HILL
Mhuilinn   Dalnawillan Lodge   Ruard   Crofts
Rumsdale Water   275   of Benachielt   Uppe
Loch   A9   Lybste
0   1   2   3 miles   Breac   Loch   Loch   Rangag
0 1 2 3 4 5 km   ▲348   Sand   Thulachan
BEN ALISKY   31

283

A836
B855
B870
B874
A9
A882
B876

4   **5**   **6**   ³5   **7**

⁹8

Langaton Point

Nethertown
Red Head

**Island of
Stroma**

Muckle
Skerry

Pentland
Skerries

ST. MARGARETS
HOPE
0:50

BURWICK 0:40
(May-Sept)

53

Mell Head
Uppertown

A

Men of Mey
Pt.
skerry

St John's Pt.
East Mey

Boars of Duncansby
Gills Bay

CASTLE
OF MEY

Mey

Gills

Kirkstyle

Huna
ℹ

DUNCANSBY HEAD

283

Rattar

19

Barrock

A836

JOHN
O'GROATS
Canisbay

John o'
Groats

Stacks of Duncansby

Inkstack

124 ▲

Brabster

Skirza

Skirza Head

Lochend

Gill Burn

Tofts

Freswick Bay

Reaster

Slickly

Freswick

Ness Head

ND

B

Alterwall

BUCHOLLY CASTLE

ermadden
Lyth

LYTH ARTS CENTRE
Sortat

Nybster

NORTHLANDS
VIKING CENTRE
Auckengill

16

Brough Head

Barrock Ho.

Howe

Keiss

Mireland

KEISS CASTLE

igrow

Kirk

Loch of
Wester

Myrelandhorn

B870

SINCLAIR'S

Killimster

B876

BAY

Mains of Watten

CASTLE
SINCLAIR

CASTLE
GIRNIGOE

Noss Head

C

15

Wick

Reiss

A99

Winless

60 ▲

Ackergill

Sealky Head

Bilbster

B874

WICK

Staxigoe

Strath

Stirkoke Ho.

Milton

A882

Wick

WICK
HERITAGE
CENTRE

Papigoe

ℹ

Broadhaven

adlipster

Newton

Wick Bay

Old Wick

South Hd.

Whiterow

CASTLE OF OLD WICK
Gote O'Tram

Tannach

Hempriggs House

Loch
Hempriggs

Helman Hd.

141 ▲
HILL OF
OLICLETT

A99

Thrumster

D

Gansclet

Sarclet

Loch of
Yarrows

Sarclet Hd.

212 ▲

Ulbster

17

CAIRN OF GET

Whaligoe

⁹4

275

HILL O' MANY
TANES

Bruan

4   **5**   **6**   ³5   **7**

Mid

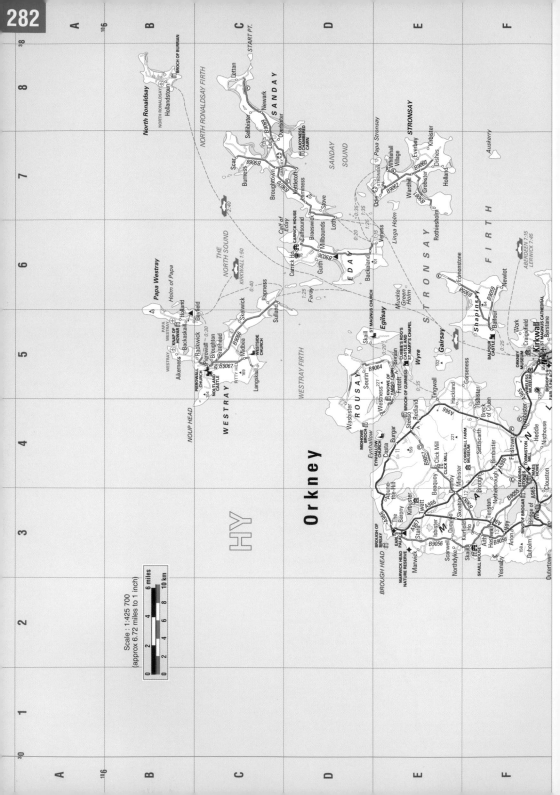

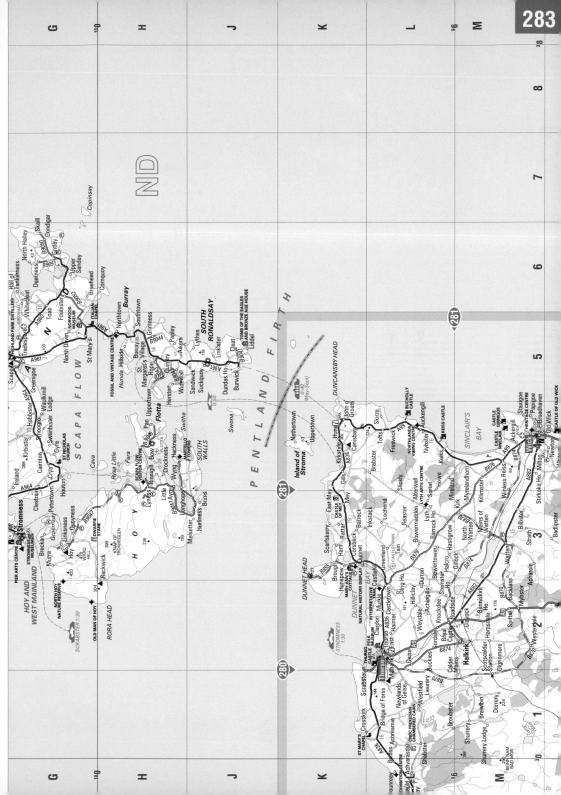

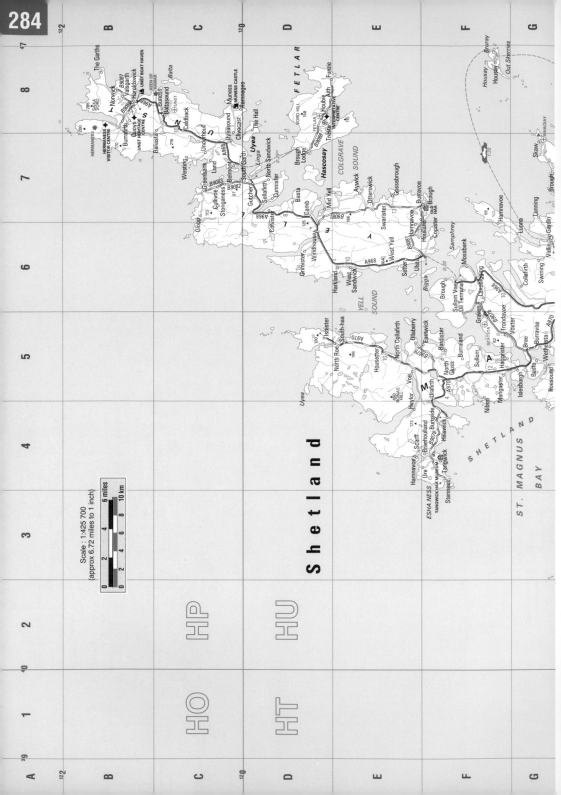

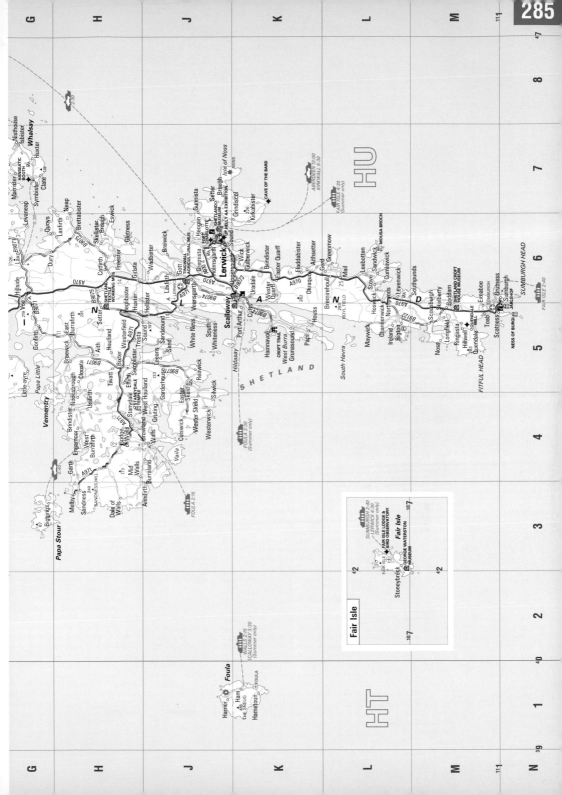

Fair Isle

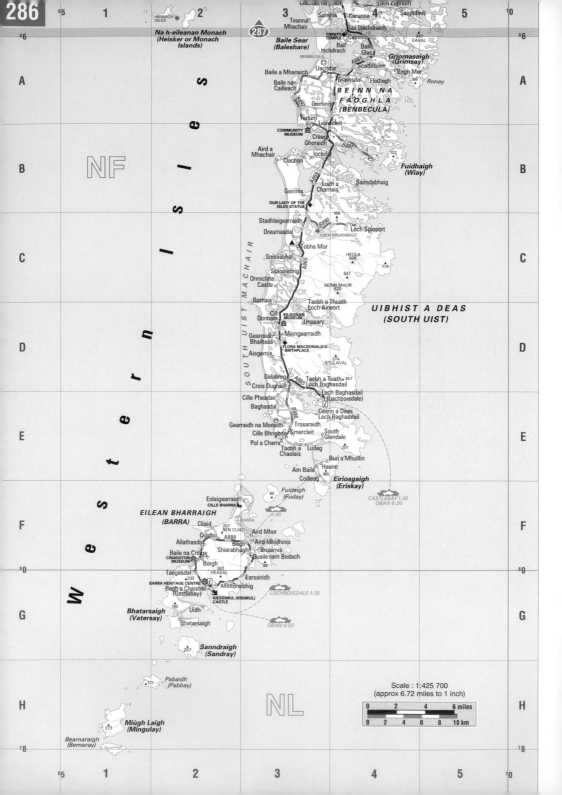

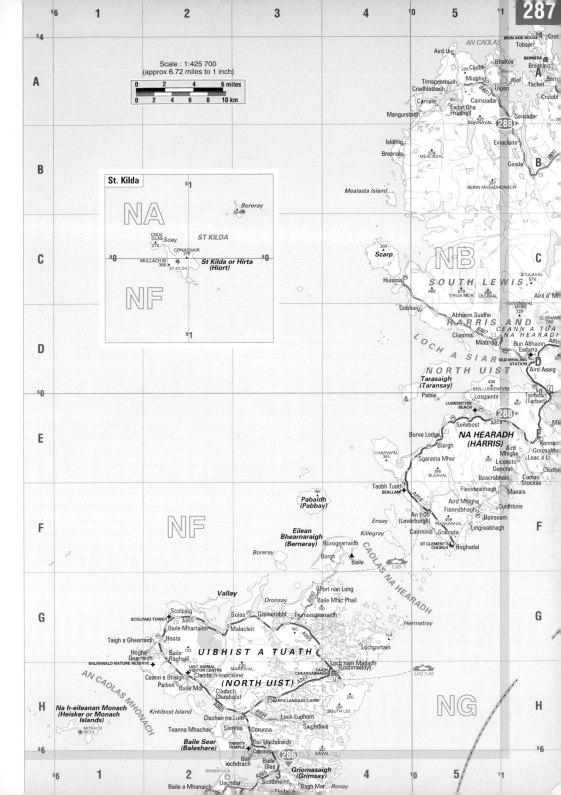

Scale : 1 : 425 700
(approx 6.72 miles to 1 inch)

0   2   4   6 miles
0   2   4   6   8   10 km

St. Kilda

NA

NF

Boreray

CNOC
GLAS   Soay
376
CONACHAIR
MULLACH BI   376
358   ST-KILDA   **St Kilda or Hirta**
(Hiort)
ST KILDA

AN CAOLAS
IRON AGE HOUSE   Crot
Tobson
Aird Uig
BERNERA   Breaclete
Cliobh   Bhaltos
205   Miabhig   Riof
Timsgearraidh   Uigen   Taclet
Cradhlastadh   Cairisiadar
Carnais   Eadar Dha
Fhadhail
Mangurstadh   Geisiadar
SUAINAVAL   288

Islibhig   Einacleite
Breanais   574
MEALISVAL   Giosla
19
BEINN MHEADHONACH

Mealasta Island   397

Scarp   308   NB
SOUTH LEWIS
STULAVAL
Huisinis   579
489   679 MOR   Aird a' Mh
TIRGA MOR   ULLAVAL   CLISHAM
UISGNAVAL   799
Abhainn Suidhe   MORE
729
HARRIS AND
CEANN A TUA
Gobhaig   NA HEARADH
Cliasmol   13   Bun Abhainn   A85
B887   Eadarra
Miabhig   OLD WHALING   Aird Asaig
STATION
NORTH UIST
Tarasaigh   436   BEN LUSKENTYRE
(Taransay)   Tairbeart
Paible   Losgaintir   467   (Tarbert)
LUSKENTYRE   288
BEACH   A859
Seileabost   NA HEARADH
Borve Lodge   23   (HARRIS)
Buirgh   Aird   Kennac
CHAIPAVAL   Mhighe   Greosabh
365   Sgarsta Mhor   386   Leac a' Li
Liceasto
BLEAVAL   Geocrab
398   Beacrabhaic
Taobh Tuath   Fleoideabhagh   Caolas
SEALLAM   A859   Stocinis
Aird Mhighe   Manais
Pabaidh   Fionnsbhagh
(Pabay)   An t-Ob   459   Cuidhtinis
(Leverburgh)   ROINEABHAL   Boirseam
Ensay   Cairminis   Srahnda   Lingreabhagh
Eilean   Killegray   ST CLEMENT'S
Bhearnaraigh   CHURCH   Roghadal
(Berneray)   Ruisigearraidh
Boreray   Borgh   CAOLAS NA HEARADH
Baile   1:00

Valley   Port nan Long
Scolpaig   Oronsay   Baile Mhic Phail
SCOLPAIG TOWER   A865   Solas   Greinetobht   Trumaisgearraidh
Baile Mhartainn   Malacleit   Hermetray
Taigh a Ghearraidh   Hosta   180
Hogha   Baile   133   UIBHIST A TUATH   Lochportain   UIG 1:45
Gearraidh   Raghaill   154
BALRANALD NATURE RESERVE   MARRIVAL   Loch nam Madadh
Ceann a Bhaigh   Claddach-knockline   (Lochmaddy)
Paibeil   Baile Mor   CHEARSABHAGH   NG
Cladach   TAIGH
Chireboist   (NORTH UIST)   A867
Na h-eileanan Monach   Clachan na Luib   BARPA LANGASS CAIRN
(Heisker or Monach   250
Islands)   Teanna Mhachair   Samhla   281   SOUTH LEE
MONACH   Corunna   Saighdinis
ISLES   Kirkibost Island   Loch Euphoirt
Baile Sear   Bail Uachdraich
(Baleshare)   TRINITY   347
Cairinis   TEMPLE   EAVAL
286
BENBECULA   Baile   Baile Glas   Griomasaigh
Iochdrach   (Grimsay)
Baile a Mhanaich   Uachdar   A865   Scotbheinn   Ronay
Flodai   Bagh Mor

NF

AN CAOLAS MHONACH

NG

Index to road maps

How to use the index

Example

Thistleton Rutland   **116** D2

└─ grid square

└─ page number

└─ county or unitary authority
(only shown for duplicate
names)

W Isles

Moray

Highland

Aberds

Aberdeen

Perth
and
Kinross

Angus

Dundee

Argyll
and Bute

Stirling

Fife

Glasgow

Edin

E Loth

N Ayrs

S Lanark

Midloth

E Ayrs

Borders

S Ayrs

Dumfries
and Galloway

Northumberland

Tyne and Wear

IoM

Cumbria

Durham

Hartlepool
Redcar and Cleveland
Middlesbrough
Darlington
Stockton-on-Tees

North Yorkshire

York

E Yorks

Blackpool

Lancs

W Yorks

N Lincs

Anglesey

Mers

Gtr Man

S Yorks

NE Lincs

Conwy

Flint

Ches

Derbys

Lincolnshire

Denb

Notts

Gwyn

Wrex

Staffs

Telford

Shrops

W Mid

Leics

Rutland

Norfolk

Ceredigion

Powys

Worcs

Warks

Northants

Cambs

Hereford

Bedford

Suffolk

Pembs

Carms

Mon

Glos

Oxon

Bucks

Herts

C Beds

Essex

Swansea

Cardiff

Bristol

W Berks

London

Southend

Medway

Wilts

Surrey

Kent

Somerset

Hants

Soton

W Sus

E Sus

Devon

Dorset

IoW

Ptsmth

Brighton

Cornwall

Torbay

Bmouth

Poole

Scilly

Plymouth

Glos	**Gloucestershire**	
Gtr Man	**Greater Manchester**	
Guern	**Guernsey**	
Gwyn	**Gwynedd**	
Halton	**Halton**	
Hants	**Hampshire**	
Hereford	**Herefordshire**	
Herts	**Hertfordshire**	
Highld	**Highland**	
Hrtlpl	**Hartlepool**	
Hull	**Hull**	
IoM	**Isle of Man**	
IoW	**Isle of Wight**	
Invclyd	**Inverclyde**	
Jersey	**Jersey**	
Kent	**Kent**	
Lancs	**Lancashire**	
Leicester	**City of Leicester**	
Leics	**Leicestershire**	
Lincs	**Lincolnshire**	
London	**Greater London**	
Luton	**Luton**	
M Keynes	**Milton Keynes**	
M Tydf	**Merthyr Tydfil**	
Mbro	**Middlesbrough**	
Medway	**Medway**	
Mers	**Merseyside**	
Midloth	**Midlothian**	
Mon	**Monmouthshire**	
Moray	**Moray**	
N Ayrs	**North Ayrshire**	
N Lincs	**North Lincolnshire**	
N Lanark	**North Lanarkshire**	
N Som	**North Somerset**	
N Yorks	**North Yorkshire**	
NE Lincs	**North East Lincolnshire**	
Neath	**Neath Port Talbot**	
Newport	**City and County of Newport**	
Norf	**Norfolk**	
Northants	**Northamptonshire**	
Northumb	**Northumberland**	
Nottingham	**City of Nottingham**	
Notts	**Nottinghamshire**	
Orkney	**Orkney**	
Oxon	**Oxfordshire**	
Pboro	**Peterborough**	
Pembs	**Pembrokeshire**	
Perth	**Perth and Kinross**	
Plym	**Plymouth**	
Poole	**Poole**	

Powys	**Powys**
Ptsmth	**Portsmouth**
Reading	**Reading**
Redcar	**Redcar and Cleveland**
Renfs	**Renfrewshire**
Rhondda	**Rhondda Cynon Taff**
Rutland	**Rutland**
S Ayrs	**South Ayrshire**
S Glos	**South Gloucestershire**
S Lanark	**South Lanarkshire**
S Yorks	**South Yorkshire**
Scilly	**Scilly**
Shetland	**Shetland**
Shrops	**Shropshire**
Slough	**Slough**
Som	**Somerset**
Soton	**Southampton**
Staffs	**Staffordshire**
Southend	**Southend-on-Sea**
Stirling	**Stirling**
Stockton	**Stockton-on-Tees**
Stoke	**Stoke-on-Trent**
Suff	**Suffolk**
Sur	**Surrey**
Swansea	**Swansea**
Swindon	**Swindon**
T&W	**Tyne and Wear**
Telford	**Telford and Wrekin**
Thurrock	**Thurrock**
Torbay	**Torbay**
Torf	**Torfaen**
V Glam	**The Vale of Glamorgan**
W Berks	**West Berkshire**
W Dunb	**West Dunbartonshire**
W Isles	**Western Isles**
W Loth	**West Lothian**
W Mid	**West Midlands**
W Sus	**West Sussex**
W Yorks	**West Yorkshire**
Warks	**Warwickshire**
Warr	**Warrington**
Wilts	**Wiltshire**
Windsor	**Windsor and Maidenhead**
Wokingham	**Wokingham**
Worcs	**Worcestershire**
Wrex	**Wrexham**
York	**City of York**

Abbreviations used in the index

Aberdeen	**Aberdeen City**	Ches W	**Cheshire West and Chester**
Aberds	**Aberdeenshire**	Clack	**Clackmannanshire**
Ald	**Alderney**	Conwy	**Conwy**
Anglesey	**Isle of Anglesey**	Corn	**Cornwall**
Angus	**Angus**	Cumb	**Cumbria**
Argyll	**Argyll and Bute**	Darl	**Darlington**
Bath	**Bath and North East Somerset**	Denb	**Denbighshire**
		Derby	**City of Derby**
Bedford	**Bedford**	Derbys	**Derbyshire**
Bl Gwent	**Blaenau Gwent**	Devon	**Devon**
Blackburn	**Blackburn with Darwen**	Dorset	**Dorset**
		Dumfries	**Dumfries and Galloway**
Blackpool	**Blackpool**	Dundee	**Dundee City**
Bmouth	**Bournemouth**	Durham	**Durham**
Borders	**Scottish Borders**	E Ayrs	**East Ayrshire**
Brack	**Bracknell**	E Dunb	**East Dunbartonshire**
Bridgend	**Bridgend**		
Brighton	**City of Brighton and Hove**	E Loth	**East Lothian**
		E Renf	**East Renfrewshire**
Bristol	**City and County of Bristol**	E Sus	**East Sussex**
		E Yorks	**East Riding of Yorkshire**
Bucks	**Buckinghamshire**		
C Beds	**Central Bedfordshire**	Edin	**City of Edinburgh**
		Essex	**Essex**
Caerph	**Caerphilly**	Falk	**Falkirk**
Cambs	**Cambridgeshire**	Fife	**Fife**
Cardiff	**Cardiff**	Flint	**Flintshire**
Carms	**Carmarthenshire**	Glasgow	**City of Glasgow**
Ceredig	**Ceredigion**		
Ches E	**Cheshire East**		

A

Abbas Combe ... 29 C7
Abberley ... 79 A5
Abberton Essex .. 71 B4
  Worcs. ... 80 B2
Abberwick ... 189 B4
Abbess Roding .. 69 B5
Abbey ... 27 D6
Abbey-cwm-hir .. 93 D4
Abbeydale ... 130 A3
Abbey Dore ... 78 D1
Abbey Field ... 70 A3
Abbey Hulton .. 112 A3
Abbey St.
  Bathans ... 211 D4
Abbeystead ... 145 B5
Abbey Town ... 175 C4
Abbey Village .. 137 A5
Abbey Wood 50 B1
Abbots
  Bickington ... 25 D4
Abbots Bromley .113 C4
Abbotsbury ... 15 C5
Abbotsham ... 25 C5
Abbotskerswell .. 8 A2
Abbots Langley .. 67 C6
Abbots Leigh ... 43 B4
Abbotsley ... 84 B4
Abbots Morton .. 80 B3
Abbots Ripton ..100 D4
Abbots Salford .. 80 B3
Abbotswood ... 32 C2
Abbotts Ann ... 32 A2
Abcott ... 94 D1
Abdon ... 94 C3
Aber ... 74 D3
Aberaeron ... 74 B3
Aberaman ... 41 A5
Aberangell ... 91 A6
Aber-Arad ... 73 C6
Aberarder ... 240 D2
Aberarder
  House ... 252 D2
Aberarder
  Lodge ... 240 D3
Aberargie ... 219 C6
Aberarth ... 74 B3
Aberavon ... 40 B2
Aber-banc ... 73 B6
Aberbeeg ... 41 A7
Abercanaid ... 41 A5
Abercarn ... 41 B7
Abercastle ... 55 A4
Abercegir ... 91 B6
Aberchirder ... 268 D1
Aber Cowarch ... 91 A6
Abercraf ... 59 D5
Abercrombie ... 221 D5
Abercych ... 73 B5
Abercynafon ... 60 B2
Abercynon ... 41 B5
Aberdalgie ... 219 B5
Aberdare
  (Aberdâr) ... 41 A4
Aberdaron ... 106 D1
Aberdeen ... 245 B6
Aberdesach ... 107 A4
Aberdour ... 209 B4
Aberdovey ... 90 C4
Aberdulais ... 40 A2
Aberedw ... 77 C4
Abereiddy ... 54 A3
Abererch ... 106 C3
Aberfan ... 41 A5
Aberfeldy ... 230 D2
Aberffraw ... 122 D3
Aberffrwd ... 75 A5
Aberford ... 148 D3
Aberfoyle ... 217 D5
Abergavenny (Y
  Fenni) ... 61 B4
Abergele ... 125 B4
Aber-Giâr ... 58 A2
Abergorlech ... 58 B2
Abergwesyn ... 76 B2
Abergwili ... 58 C1

Abergwynant ... 91 A4
Aber-gwynfi ... 40 B3
Abergwyngregyn ... 123 C6
Abergynolwyn ... 91 B4
Aber-Hirnant ... 109 B4
Aberhosan ... 91 C6
Aberkenfig ... 40 C3
Aberlady ... 210 B1
Aberlemno ... 232 C3
Aberllefenni ... 91 B5
Abermagwr ... 75 A5
Abermeurig ... 75 C4
Abermule ... 93 B5
Abernaint ... 109 C6
Abernant ... 73 D6
Aber-nant ... 41 A5
Abernethy ... 219 C6
Abernyte ... 220 A2
Aberporth ... 73 A5
Aber-Rhiwlech .. 108 C4
Abersoch ... 106 D3
Abersychan ... 61 C4
Aberthin ... 41 D5
Abertillery
  (Abertyleri) ... 41 A7
Abertridwr Caerph 41 C6
  Powys ... 109 D5
Abertysswg ... 60 C3
Aberuthven ... 219 C4
Aber-Village ... 60 A3
Aberyscir ... 60 A1
Aberystwyth ... 90 D3
Abhainn Suidhe .287 D5
Abingdon ... 65 D5
Abinger Common. 35 B4
Abinger Hammer . 34 B3
Abington ... 194 D4
Abington Pigotts . 85 C5
Ab Kettleby ... 115 C5
Ab Lench ... 80 B3
Ablington Glos... 64 C2
  Wilts. ... 31 A5
Abney ... 130 B1
Aboyne ... 244 C2
Abram ... 137 C5
Abriachan ... 252 C1
Abridge ... 69 D4
Abronhill ... 207 C5
Abson ... 43 B6
Abthorpe ... 82 C3
Abune-the-Hill. .282 E3
Aby ... 135 B4
Acaster Malbis ..149 C4
Acaster Selby ...149 C4
Accrington ... 137 A6
Acha ... 223 B4
Achabraid ... 213 D6
Achachork ... 259 D4
Achafolla ... 213 A5
Achagary ... 278 C3
Achalader ... 231 D5
Achallader ... 228 D2
Acha Mor ... 288 E4
Achanalt ... 263 D4
Achanamara ... 213 D5
Achandunie ... 264 C2
Ach'an Todhair . 237 B4
Achany ... 272 D3
Achaphubuil ... 237 B4
Acharacle ... 235 D5
Acharn Highld....236 D1
  Perth ... 229 D6
Acharole ... 280 C4
Achath ... 245 A4
Achavanich ... 280 D3
Achavraat ... 253 B5
Achddu ... 57 B4
Achduart ... 270 D3
Achentoul ... 274 A2
Achfary ... 271 A5
Achgarve ... 261 A5
Achiemore
  Highld. ... 277 B4
  Highld. ... 279 C4
A'Chill ... 246 D1
Achiltibuie ... 270 D3
Achina ... 278 B3
Achinduich ... 272 D3
Achinduin ... 226 C3
Achingills ... 280 B3

Achintee Highld ..237 B5
  Highld. ... 249 B6
Achintraid ... 249 C5
Achlean ... 241 C6
Achleck ... 224 B3
Achluachrach ...239 D6
Achlyness ... 276 C3
Achmelvich ... 270 B3
Achmore Highld...249 C5
  Stirling ... 217 A5
Achnaba Argyll...214 D2
  Argyll ... 226 C4
Achnabat ... 252 C1
Achnacarnin ... 270 A3
Achnacarry ... 239 D5
Achnacloich
  Argyll ... 227 C4
  Highld. ... 247 D4
Achnaconeran ...240 A2
Achnacraig ... 224 B3
Achnacroish ... 226 B3
Achnadrish ... 224 A3
Achnafalnich ...227 D7
Achnagarron ... 264 D2
Achnaha ... 234 D3
Achnahanat ... 263 A7
Achnahannet ... 253 D5
Achnairn ... 272 C3
Achnaluachrach 273 D4
Achnasaul ... 239 D5
Achnasheen ... 250 A3
Achosnich ... 234 D3
Achranich ... 226 B2
Achreamie ... 279 B6
Achriabhach ... 237 C5
Achriesgill ... 276 C3
Achrimsdale ... 274 D3
Achtoty ... 278 B2
Achurch ... 100 C2
Achuvoldrach ...277 C6
Achvaich ... 264 A3
Achvarasdale ... 279 B5
Ackergill ... 281 C5
Acklam Mbro 168 D2
  N Yorks. ... 149 A6
Ackleton ... 95 B5
Acklington ... 189 C5
Ackton ... 140 A2
Ackworth Moor
  Top ... 140 B2
Acle ... 121 D6
Acock's Green ... 96 C4
Acol ... 53 C5
Acomb Northumb 178 C1
  York ... 149 B4
Aconbury ... 78 D3
Acre ... 137 A6
Acrefair ... 110 A1
Acre Street ... 19 B6
Acton Ches E. ...127 D6
  Dorset ... 16 D3
  London ... 49 A5
  Shrops ... 93 C7
  Suff ... 87 C4
  Wrex ... 126 D3
Acton
  Beauchamp ... 79 B4
Acton Bridge ...127 B5
Acton Burnell ... 94 A3
Acton Green ... 79 B4
Acton Pigott ... 94 A3
Acton Round ... 95 B4
Acton Scott ... 94 C2
Acton Trussell ..112 D3
Acton Turville ... 44 A2
Adbaston ... 111 C6
Adber ... 29 C5
Adderley ... 111 A5
Adderstone ... 199 C5
Addiewell ... 208 D2
Addingham ... 147 C4
Addington Bucks.. 66 A3
  Kent ... 37 A4
  London ... 49 C6
Addinston ... 197 A4
Addiscombe ... 49 C6
Addlestone ... 48 C3
Addlethorpe ... 135 C5
Adel ... 148 D1
Adeney ... 111 D6
Adfa ... 93 A4
Adforton ... 94 D2

Adisham ... 53 D4
Adlestrop ... 64 A3
Adlingfleet ... 141 A6
Adlington ... 137 B5
Admaston Staffs .112 C4
  Telford ... 111 D5
Admington ... 81 C5
Adstock ... 83 D4
Adstone ... 82 B2
Adversane ... 34 D3
Advie ... 254 C2
Adwalton ... 139 A5
Adwell ... 66 D2
Adwick le
  Street ... 140 C3
Adwick upon
  Dearne ... 140 C2
Adziel ... 269 D4
Ae Village ... 184 D2
Affleck ... 256 D3
Affpuddle ... 16 B2
Affric Lodge ... 250 D3
Afon-wen ... 125 B6
Afton ... 18 C2
Agglethorpe ... 157 C4
Agneash ... 152 C4
Aigburth ... 126 A3
Aiginis ... 288 D5
Aike ... 150 C3
Aikerness ... 282 B5
Aikers ... 283 H5
Aiketgate ... 164 A2
Aikton ... 175 C5
Ailey ... 78 C1
Ailstone ... 81 B5
Ailsworth ... 100 B3
Ainderby
  Quernhow ... 158 C2
Ainderby
  Steeple ... 158 B2
Aingers Green... 71 A5
Ainsdale ... 136 B2
Ainsdale-on-
  Sea ... 136 B2
Ainstable ... 164 A3
Ainsworth ... 137 B6
Ainthorpe ... 159 A6
Aintree ... 136 D2
Aird Argyll ... 213 B5
  Dumfries ... 170 A2
  Highld. ... 261 C4
  W Isles ... 288 D6
Aird a Mhachair 286 B3
Aird a' Mhulaidh 288 F2
Aird Asaig ... 288 G2
Aird Dhail ... 288 A5
Airdens ... 264 A2
Aird Mhidhinis . 286 F3
Aird Mhighe
  W Isles ... 287 F5
  W Isles ... 288 H2
Aird Mhor ... 286 F3
Aird of Sleat ... 247 D4
Airdrie ... 207 D5
Aird Thunga ... 288 D5
Airdtorrisdale ...278 B2
Aird Uig ... 287 A5
Airidh a
  Bhruaich ... 288 F3
Airieland ... 173 C5
Airmyn ... 141 A5
Airntully ... 219 A5
Airor ... 247 D6
Airth ... 208 B1
Airton ... 146 B3
Airyhassen ... 171 C5
Aisby Lincs ... 116 B3
  Lincs. ... 141 D6
Aisgernis ... 286 D3
Aiskew ... 157 C6
Aislaby N Yorks. .159 C6
  N Yorks. ... 160 A2
  Stockton ... 168 D2
Aisthorpe ... 133 A4
Aith Orkney ... 282 F3
  Shetland ... 284 D8
  Shetland ... 285 H5
Aithsetter ... 285 K6
Aitkenhead ... 192 E3
Aitnoch ... 253 C5
Akeld ... 188 A2
Akeley ... 83 D4

Akenham ... 88 C2
Albaston ... 11 D5
Alberbury ... 110 D2
Albourne ... 21 A5
Albrighton Shrops 95 A6
  Shrops ... 110 D3
Alburgh ... 104 C3
Albury Herts ... 68 A4
  Sur ... 34 B3
Albury End ... 68 A4
Alby Hill ... 120 B3
Alcaig ... 252 A1
Alcaston ... 94 C2
Alcester ... 80 B3
Alciston ... 22 B3
Alcombe Som. ... 27 A4
  Wilts. ... 44 C2
Alconbury ... 100 D3
Alconbury
  Weston ... 100 D3
Aldbar Castle ...232 C3
Aldborough Norf 120 B3
  N Yorks. ... 148 A3
Aldbourne ... 45 B6
Aldbrough ... 151 D5
Aldbrough St
  John ... 167 D5
Aldbury ... 67 B5
Aldcliffe ... 145 A4
Aldclune ... 230 B3
Aldeburgh ... 89 B5
Aldeby ... 105 B5
Aldenham ... 67 D7
Alderbury ... 31 C5
Aldercar ... 114 A2
Alderford ... 120 D3
Alderholt ... 31 D5
Alderley ... 62 D3
Alderley Edge ..128 B3
Aldermaston ... 46 C3
Aldermaston
  Wharf ... 47 C4
Alderminster ... 81 C5
Alder's End ... 79 C4
Aldersey Green..127 D4
Aldershot ... 34 A1
Alderton Glos...80 D3
  Northants ... 83 C4
  Shrops ... 110 C3
  Suff ... 88 C4
  Wilts. ... 44 A2
Alderwasley ... 130 D3
Aldfield ... 147 A6
Aldford ... 127 D4
Aldham Essex ... 70 A3
  Suff ... 87 C6
Aldie ... 264 B3
Aldingbourne ... 20 B2
Aldingham ... 154 D1
Aldington Kent... 38 B2
  Worcs. ... 80 C3
Aldington Frith... 38 B2
Aldochlay ... 206 A1
Aldreth ... 101 D6
Aldridge ... 96 A3
Aldringham ... 89 A5
Aldsworth ... 64 B2
Aldunie ... 255 D4
Aldwark Derbys ..130 D2
  N Yorks. ... 148 A3
Aldwick ... 20 C2
Aldwincle ... 100 C2
Aldworth ... 46 B3
Alexandria ... 206 C1
Alfardisworthy .. 24 D3
Alfington ... 13 B6
Alfold ... 34 C3
Alfold Bars ... 34 C3
Alfold Crossways 34 C3
Alford Aberds ...244 A2
  Lincs. ... 135 B4
  Som ... 29 B6
Alfreton ... 131 D4
Alfrick ... 79 B5
Alfrick Pound ... 79 B5
Alfriston ... 22 B3
Algaltraig ... 203 A5
Algarkirk ... 117 B5
Alhampton ... 29 B6
Aline Lodge ... 288 F2
Alisary ... 235 C6
Alkborough ... 141 A6

Alkerton ... 81 C6
Alkham ... 39 A4
Alkington ... 111 B4
Alkmonton ... 113 B5
Alladale Lodge . 263 B6
Allaleigh ... 8 B2
Allanaquoich. ...242 C4
Allangrange
  Mains ... 252 A2
Allanton Borders .198 A2
  N Lanark ... 194 A3
Allathasdal ... 286 F2
All Cannings ... 45 C4
Allendale Town .177 D6
Allenheads ... 165 A6
Allensford ... 178 D2
Allens Green ... 69 B4
Allensmore ... 78 D2
Allenton ... 114 B1
Aller ... 28 C4
Allerby ... 162 A3
Allerford ... 27 A4
Allerston ... 160 C2
Allerthorpe ... 149 C6
Allerton Mers....127 A4
  W Yorks ... 147 D5
Allerton
  Bywater ... 140 A2
Allerton
  Mauleverer .. 148 B3
Allesley ... 97 C6
Allestree ... 114 B1
Allet ... 4 C2
Allexton ... 99 A5
Allgreave ... 129 C4
Allhallows ... 51 B5
Allhallows-on-
  Sea ... 51 B5
Alligin Shuas... 249 A5
Allimore Green ..112 D2
Allington Lincs ..115 A6
  Wilts. ... 31 B6
  Wilts. ... 45 C4
Allithwaite ... 154 D2
Alloa ... 208 A1
Allonby ... 174 D3
Alloway ... 192 D3
All Saints South
  Elmham ... 104 C4
All Stretton ... 94 B2
Allt ... 57 B5
Alltchaorunn ...237 D5
Alltforgan ... 109 C4
Alltmawr ... 77 C4
Alltnacaillich... 277 D5
Allt na h-Airbhe 262 A3
Allt-nan-sùgh.. 249 D6
Alltsigh ... 240 A2
Alltwalis ... 58 B1
Alltwen ... 40 A2
Alltyblaca ... 75 D4
Allwood Green ..103 D6
Almeley ... 78 B1
Almer ... 16 B3
Almholme ... 140 C3
Almington ... 111 B6
Alminstone Cross 24 C4
Almondbank ... 219 B5
Almondbury ... 139 B4
Almondsbury... 43 A5
Alne ... 148 A3
Alness ... 264 D2
Alnham ... 188 B2
Alnmouth ... 189 B5
Alnwick ... 189 B4
Alperton ... 49 A4
Alphamstone ... 87 D4
Alpheton ... 87 B4
Alphington ... 13 B4
Alport ... 130 C2
Alpraham ... 127 D5
Alresford ... 71 A4
Alrewas ... 113 D5
Alsager ... 128 D2
Alsagers Bank...112 A2
Alsop en le
  Dale ... 129 D6
Alston Cumb 165 A5
  Devon. ... 14 A3
Alstone ... 80 D2
Alstonefield ... 129 D6
Alswear ... 26 C2

Altandhu. 270 C2
Altanduin 274 B2
Altarnun 10 C3
Altass 272 D2
Alterwall. 281 B4
Altham 146 D1
Althorne 70 D3
Althorpe 141 C6
Alticry 171 B4
Altnabreac
  Station 279 D6
Altnacealgach
  Hotel. 271 C5
Altnacraig 226 D3
Altnafeadh 237 D6
Altnaharra 272 A3
Altofts 139 A6
Alton Derbys. 130 C3
  Hants. 33 B6
  Staffs. 113 A4
Alton Pancras. . .15 A7
Alton Priors. 45 C5
Altrincham. 128 A2
Altrua 239 D6
Altskeith. 217 D4
Altyre Ho. 253 A6
Alva 208 A1
Alvanley 127 B4
Alvaston 114 B1
Alvechurch 96 D3
Alvecote. 97 A5
Alvediston 30 C3
Alveley 95 C5
Alverdiscott. 25 C6
Alverstoke 19 B5
Alverstone 19 C4
Alverton 115 A5
Alves 266 C2
Alvescot 64 C3
Alveston S Glos . . .43 A5
  Warks. 81 B5
Alvie 241 B6
Alvingham 143 D5
Alvington 62 C2
Alwalton 100 B3
Alweston 29 D6
Alwinton 188 C2
Alwoodley 148 C1
Alyth 231 D6
Amatnatua. 263 A6
Am Baile 286 E3
Ambergate. 130 D2
Amber Hill 117 A5
Amberley Glos 63 C4
  W Sus. 20 A3
Amble 189 C5
Amblecote. 96 C1
Ambler Thorn . . .138 A3
Ambleside 154 A2
Ambleston 55 B6
Ambrosden 65 B7
Am Buth 226 D3
Amcotts 141 B6
Amersham. 67 D5
Amesbury. 31 A5
Amington 97 A5
Amisfield 184 D2
Amlwch 123 A4
Amlwch Port. . . .123 A4
Ammanford
  (Rhydaman) 57 A6
Amod. 190 B3
Amotherby. 159 D6
Ampfield 32 C3
Ampleforth 159 D4
Ampney Crucis . .63 C6
Ampney St Mary. .64 C1
Ampney St Peter .64 C1
Amport 32 A1
Ampthill 84 D2
Ampton. 103 D4
Amroth 56 B1
Amulree 218 A3
Anagach 253 D6
Anaheilt 236 C2
Anancaun 262 D2
An Caol 248 A3
An Cnoc 288 D5
Ancroft 198 B3

Ancrum 187 A5
Anderby 135 B5
Anderson 16 B2
Anderton 127 B6
Andover 32 A2
Andover Down . . .32 A2
Andoversford 63 B6
Andreas 152 B4
Anfield 136 D2
Angersleigh 28 D1
Angle. 55 D4
Angram N Yorks . .148 C4
  N Yorks. 156 B2
Anie 217 C5
Ankerville 265 C4
Anlaby 142 A2
Anmer 119 C4
Annan 175 B4
Annat Argyll. 227 D5
  Highld. 249 A5
Anna Valley 32 A2
Annbank 193 C4
Annesley. 131 D5
Annesley
  Woodhouse 131 D4
Annfield Plain. . . .178 D3
Annifirth 285 J3
Annitsford 179 B4
Annscroft 94 A2
Ansdell 136 A2
Ansford. 29 B6
Ansley 97 B5
Anslow 113 C6
Anslow Gate 113 C5
Anstey Herts. 85 D6
  Leics. 98 A2
Anstruther
  Easter. 221 D5
Anstruther
  Wester. 221 D5
Ansty Hants. 33 A6
  Warks. 97 C6
  Wilts. 30 C3
  W Sus. 35 D5
Anthill Common. . .33 D5
Anthorn 175 C4
Antingham 121 B4
An t-Ob
  (Leverburgh) . .287 F5
Anton's Gowt 117 A5
Antonshill 208 B1
Antony 6 B3
Anwick 133 D6
Anwoth 172 C3
Aoradh 200 B2
Apes Hall 102 B1
Apethorpe 100 B2
Apeton 112 D2
Apley 133 B6
Apperknowle. 130 B3
Apperley. 63 A4
Apperley Bridge 147 D5
Appersett. 156 B2
Appin. 226 B4
Appin House 226 B4
Appleby 142 B1
Appleby-in-
  Westmorland . .165 C4
Appleby Magna . .97 A6
Appleby Parva. . . .97 A6
Applecross 249 B4
Applecross Ho. . .249 B4
Appledore Devon. . .25 B6
  Devon. 27 D5
  Kent 38 C1
Appledore Heath .38 B1
Appleford. 65 D6
Applegarthtown 185 D4
Appleshaw. 32 A2
Applethwaite. 163 B5
Appleton Halton. .127 A5
  Oxon. 65 C5
Appleton
  Roebuck 149 C4
Appleton Thorn .127 A6
Appleton Wiske .158 A2

Appletreehall . . .186 B4
Appletreewick . . .147 A4
Appley. 27 C5
Appley Bridge . .136 C4
Apse Heath 19 C4
Apsley End. 84 D3
Apuldram. 20 B1
Aquhythie 245 A4
Arabella 265 C4
Arbeadie. 244 C3
Arbirlot. 233 D4
Arboll 265 B4
Arborfield 47 C5
Arborfield Cross. .47 C5
Arborfield
  Garrison 47 C5
Arbour-thorne . .130 A3
Arbroath. 233 D4
Arbuthnott. 233 A5
Archiestown 254 B3
Arclid 128 C2
Ardachu 273 D4
Ardalanish 224 E2
Ardanaiseig 227 D5
Ardaneaskan. 249 C5
Ardanstur. 213 A6
Ardargie House
  Hotel. 219 C5
Ardarroch 249 C5
Ardbeg Argyll 201 D4
  Argyll. 215 D4
Ardcharnich 262 B3
Ardchiavaig. 224 E2
Ardchullarie
  More. 217 C5
Ardchyle. 217 B5
Ard-dhubh. 249 B4
Arddleen 110 D1
Ardechvie. 239 C5
Ardeley. 68 A3
Ardelve. 249 D5
Arden 206 B1
Ardens Grafton . . .80 B4
Ardentinny 215 D4
Ardentraive 203 A5
Ardeonaig 217 A6
Ardersier 252 A3
Ardessie 262 B2
Ardfern 213 B6
Ardgartan. 215 B5
Ardgay 264 A1
Ardgour 237 C4
Ardheslaig 249 A4
Ardiecow 267 C6
Ardindrean 262 B3
Ardingly 35 D6
Ardington 46 A2
Ardlair. 255 D6
Ardlamont Ho. . .203 B4
Ardleigh 71 A4
Ardler 231 D6
Ardley 65 A6
Ardlui 215 A6
Ardlussa 213 D4
Ardmair 262 A3
Ardmay 215 B5
Ardminish 202 D1
Ardmolich. 235 C6
Ardmore Argyll. . .226 D2
  Highld. 264 B3
  Highld. 276 B3
Ardnacross 225 B4
Ardnadam 203 A6
Ardnagrask 251 B7
Ardnarff 249 C5
Ardnastang 236 C2
Ardnave 200 A2
Ardno 215 B4
Ardo 256 C3
Ardoch 219 A5
Ardochy House . .239 B6
Ardo Ho. 257 D4
Ardoyne 256 D1
Ardpatrick 202 B2
Ardpatrick Ho. . .202 C2
Ardpeaton 215 D5
Ardrishaig 213 D6
Ardross Fife 221 D5
  Highld. 264 C2
Ardrossan 204 D2
Ardross Castle . . .264 C2
Ardshealach 235 D5

Ardsley 140 C1
Ardslignish 235 D4
Ardtalla. 201 C4
Ardtalnaig 218 A2
Ardtoe. 235 C5
Ardtrostan 217 B6
Arduaine 213 A5
Ardullie. 264 D1
Ardvasar. 247 D5
Ardvorlich 217 B6
Ardwell. 170 C3
Ardwell Mains. . .170 C3
Ardwick 138 D1
Areley Kings 95 D6
Arford 34 C1
Argoed 41 B6
Argoed Mill 76 A3
Arichamish 214 B2
Arichastlich. 216 A2
Aridhglas 224 D2
Arileod 223 B4
Arinacrinachd . . .249 A4
Arinagour. 223 B5
Arion 282 F3
Arisaig 235 B5
Ariundle 236 C2
Arkendale 148 A2
Arkesden 85 D6
Arkholme 155 D4
Arkleton 186 D2
Arkle Town 156 A4
Arkley 68 D2
Arksey 140 C3
Arkwright Town 131 B4
Arle 63 A5
Arlecdon 162 C3
Arlesey 84 D3
Arleston 111 D5
Arley 128 A1
Arlingham 62 B3
Arlington Devon. . .25 A7
  E Sus 22 B3
  Glos 64 C2
Armadale Highld . .278 B3
  W Loth 208 D2
Armadale
  Castle 247 D5
Armathwaite. 164 A3
Arminghall. 104 A3
Armitage 113 D4
Armley 148 D1
Armscote 81 C5
Armthorpe. 140 C4
Arnabost. 223 B5
Arncliffe 156 D3
Arncroach 221 D5
Arne. 16 C3
Arnesby 98 B3
Arngask 219 C6
Arnisdale 238 A2
Arnish 248 B2
Arniston Engine 209 D6
Arnol 288 C4
Arnold E Yorks . . .151 C4
  Notts 114 A3
Arnprior 207 A4
Arnside 154 D3
Aros Mains. 225 B4
Arowry 110 B3
Arpafeelie 252 A2
Arrad Foot 154 C2
Arram 150 C3
Arrathorne. 157 B6
Arreton 18 C4
Arrington 85 B5
Arrivain 216 A2
Arrochar 215 B5
Arrow 80 B3
Arthington 147 C6
Arthingworth 99 C4
Arthog. 90 A4
Arthrath 257 C4
Arthurstone 231 D6
Artrochie 257 C5
Arundel 20 B3
Aryhoulan 237 C4
Asby. 162 B3
Ascog 203 B6
Ascot 48 C2
Ascott 81 D6
Ascott-under-
  Wychwood 64 B4

Asenby 158 D2
Asfordby. 115 D5
Asfordby Hill. . . .115 D5
Asgarby Lincs 116 A4
  Lincs. 134 C3
Ash Kent 50 C2
  Kent 53 D4
  Som 29 C4
  Sur 34 A1
Ashampstead 46 B3
Ashbocking. 88 B2
Ashbourne. 113 A5
Ashbrittle. 27 C5
Ash Bullayne. 12 A2
Ashburton 7 A6
Ashbury Devon. . . .11 B6
  Oxon. 45 A6
Ashby 141 C7
Ashby by
  Partney 135 C4
Ashby cum
  Fenby 143 C4
Ashby de la
  Launde. 133 D5
Ashby-de-la-
  Zouch 114 D1
Ashby Folville. . . .115 D5
Ashby Magna 98 B2
Ashby Parva 98 C2
Ashby
  Puerorum 134 B3
Ashby St Ledgers 82 A2
Ashby St Mary. . .104 A4
Ashchurch 80 D2
Ashcombe 13 D4
Ashcott 28 B4
Ashdon 86 C1
Ashe 32 A4
Asheldham. 70 C3
Ashen 86 C3
Ashendon 66 B3
Ashfield Carms. . . .58 C3
  Stirling 218 D2
  Suff 88 A3
Ashfield Green . .104 D3
Ashfield
  Crossways 35 D5
Ashford Devon . . .25 B6
  Hants 31 D5
  Kent 38 A2
  Sur 48 B3
Ashford Bowdler . 94 D3
Ashford
  Carbonell 94 D3
Ashford Hill 46 C3
Ashford in the
  Water 130 C2
Ashgill. 194 B2
Ash Green 97 C6
Ashill Devon 27 D5
  Norf 103 A4
  Som 28 D3
Ashingdon 70 D2
Ashington
  Northumb. 179 A4
  Som 29 C5
  W Sus. 21 A4
Ashintully
  Castle 231 B5
Ashkirk 186 A3
Ashlett 18 A3
Ashleworth 63 A4
Ashley Cambs 86 A2
  Ches E 128 A2
  Devon. 26 D1
  Dorset 17 A5
  Glos 63 D5
  Hants 17 B6
  Hants 32 B2
  Northants. 99 B4
  Staffs 111 B6
Ashley Green 67 C5
Ashley Heath
  Dorset 17 A5
  Staffs 111 B6
Ash Magna 111 B4
Ashmanhaugh. . . .121 C5
Ashmansworth . . .46 D2
Ashmansworthy . .24 D4
Ashmore 30 D3
Ashorne 81 B6

Ashover 130 C3
Ashow 97 D6
Ashprington 8 B2
Ash Priors 27 C6
Ashreigney 26 D1
Ash Street 87 C6
Ashtead 35 A4
Ash Thomas. 27 D5
Ashton Ches W . .127 C5
  Corn 3 C4
  Hants 33 D4
  Hereford 78 A3
  Invclyd. 204 A2
  Northants. 83 C4
  Northants. 100 C2
Ashton Common .44 D2
Ashton-In-
  Makerfield 137 D4
Ashton Keynes . . .63 D6
Ashton under
  Hill 80 D2
Ashton-under-
  Lyne 138 D2
Ashton upon
  Mersey. 137 D6
Ashurst Hants. 32 D2
  Kent 36 C3
  W Sus. 21 A4
Ashurstwood. 36 C2
Ash Vale 34 A1
Ashwater 11 B4
Ashwell Herts. 85 D4
  Rutland. 115 D6
  Som 28 D3
Ashwellthorpe . . .104 B2
Ashwick 29 A6
Ashwicken 119 D4
Ashybank 186 B4
Askam in
  Furness 153 C3
Askern 140 B3
Askerswell 15 B5
Askett 66 C4
Askham Cumb. . . .164 C3
  Notts 132 B2
Askham Bryan. . .149 C4
Askham Richard 148 C4
Asknish. 214 C2
Askrigg 156 B3
Askwith. 147 C5
Aslackby 116 B3
Aslacton 104 B2
Aslockton. 115 B5
Asloun 244 A2
Aspatria 174 D4
Aspenden. 68 A3
Asperton 117 B5
Aspley Guise 83 D6
Aspley Heath. 83 D6
Aspull 137 C5
Asselby 141 A5
Asserby 135 B4
Assington 87 D5
Assynt Ho. 264 C1
Astbury. 128 C3
Astcote 82 B3
Asterley 94 A1
Asterton 94 B1
Asthall. 64 B3
Asthall Leigh. 64 B4
Astley Shrops 111 D4
  Warks. 97 C6
  Worcs. 79 A5
Astley Abbotts . . .95 B5
Astley Bridge . . .137 B6
Astley Cross. 79 A6
Astley Green 137 D6
Aston Ches E. . . .111 A5
  Ches W. 127 B5
  Derbys. 130 A1
  Hereford 94 D2
  Herts. 68 A2
  Oxon. 64 C4
  Shrops 111 C4
  Staffs 111 A6
  S Yorks. 131 A4
  Telford 95 A4
  W Mid 96 C3
  Wokingham 47 A5

292 Ast–Ban

Aston Abbotts.... 66 A4
Aston Botterell... 95 C4
Aston-By-Stone 112 B3
Aston Cantlow ... 80 B4
Aston Clinton ... 66 B4
Aston Crews 62 A2
Aston Cross 80 D2
Aston End...... 68 A2
Aston Eyre 95 B4
Aston Fields 80 A2
Aston Flamville.. 98 B1
Aston Ingham ... 62 A2
Aston juxta
  Mondrum 127 D6
Aston le Walls.... 82 B1
Aston Magna....81 D4
Aston Munslow.. 94 C3
Aston on Clun ... 94 C1
Aston-on-Trent 114 C2
Aston Rogers 94 A1
Aston Rowant ... 66 D3
Aston Sandford ..66 C3
Aston Somerville 80 D3
Aston Subedge...80 C4
Aston Tirrold.... 46 A3
Aston Upthorpe .. 46 A3
Astrop........82 D2
Astwick.........84 D4
Astwood M Keynes 83 C6
  Worcs.........79 B6
Astwood Bank... 80 A3
Aswarby 116 B3
Aswardby 134 B3
Atcham 94 A3
Atch Lench.... 80 B3
Athelhampton ... 16 B1
Athelington 104 D3
Athelney.......28 C3
Athelstaneford .210 C2
Atherington.... 25 C6
Atherstone.... 97 B6
Atherstone on
  Stour 81 B5
Atherton........137 C5
Atley Hill.......157 A6
Atlow.........113 A6
Attadale......249 C6
Attadale Ho.... 249 C6
Attenborough ...114 B3
Atterby 142 D1
Attercliffe 130 A3
Attleborough
  Norf.........103 B6
  Warks........ 97 B6
Attlebridge 120 D3
Atwick.........151 B4
Atworth 44 C2
Aubourn.......133 C4
Auchagallon ... 191 B4
Auchallater 243 D4
Aucharnie 256 B1
Auchattie 244 C3
Auchavan 231 B5
Auchbreck 254 D3
Auchenback ... 205 C5
Auchenbainzie.. 183 C6
Auchenblae.....233 A5
Auchenbrack... 183 C5
Auchenheath... 214 D3
Auchencairn
  Dumfries 173 C5
  Dumfries 184 D2
  N Ayrs 191 C6
Auchencrosh... 180 D3
Auchendinny... 209 D5
Auchengray... 195 A4
Auchenhalrig ...267 C4
Auchenheath... 194 B3
Auchenlochan.. 203 A4
Auchenmalg ... 171 B4
Auchensoul 181 B4
Auchentiber... 204 D3
Auchertyre.... 249 D5
Auchgourish .. 242 A2
Auchincarroch .206 B2
Auchindrain.... 214 B3
Auchindrean... 262 B3
Auchininna ... 256 B1

Auchinleck......193 C5
Auchinloch 205 A6
Auchinroath 266 D3
Auchintoul ...244 A2
Auchiries 257 C5
Auchlee 245 C5
Auchleven 256 D1
Auchlochan 194 C3
Auchlossan 244 B2
Auchlunies......245 C5
Auchlyne 217 B5
Auchmacoy 257 C4
Auchmair.....255 D4
Auchmantle.....170 A3
Auchmillan 193 C5
Auchmithie 233 D4
Auchmuirbridge
  ....220 D2
Auchmull.......232 A3
Auchnacree 232 B2
Auchnagallin..253 C6
Auchnagatt ... 257 B4
Auchnaha......214 D2
Auchnashelloch 218 C2
Aucholzie......243 C6
Auchrannie 231 C6
Auchroisk.......253 D6
Auchronie 244 D1
Auchterarder ...218 C4
Auchteraw 240 B1
Auchterderran ..209 A5
Auchterhouse ..220 A3
Auchtermuchty ..220 C2
Auchterneed ...251 A6
Auchtertool 209 A5
Auchtertyre....266 D2
Auchtubh 217 B5
Auckengill 281 B5
Auckley.......140 C4
Audenshaw 138 D2
Audlem 111 A5
Audley.......128 D2
Audley End 87 D4
Auds 268 C1
Aughton E Yorks.149 D6
  Lancs........136 C2
  Lancs........145 A5
  S Yorks.......131 A4
  Wilts..........45 D6
Aughton Park ..136 C3
Auldearn 253 A5
Aulden 78 B2
Auldgirth 183 D7
Auldhame 210 B2
Auldhouse 205 C6
Ault a'chruinn.. 249 D6
Aultanrynie 271 A6
Aultbea 261 B5
Aultdearg.......263 D4
Aultgrishan....261 B4
Aultguish Inn... 263 C5
Aultibea 274 A4
Aultiphurst.....279 B4
Aultmore 267 D5
Aultnagoire 252 D1
Aultnamain Inn..264 B2
Aultnaslat......239 B5
Aulton.......255 D7
Aundorach.....242 A2
Aunsby 116 B3
Auquhorthies ..256 D3
Aust 43 A4
Austendike 117 C5
Austerfield 141 D4
Austrey........97 A5
Austwick 146 A1
Authorpe.......135 A4
Authorpe Row...135 B5
Avebury 45 C5
Aveley........50 A2
Avening 63 D4
Averham.......132 D2
Aveton Gifford .. 7 C5
Avielochan.....242 A2
Aviemore 242 A1
Avington Hants .. 32 B4
  W Berks.......46 C1
Avoch 252 A3
Avon 17 B5
Avonbridge 208 C2
Avon Dassett...81 C7
Avonmouth.... 43 B4

Avonwick........ 7 B6
Awbridge 32 C2
Awhirk 170 B2
Awkley 43 A4
Awliscombe...... 13 A6
Awre 62 C3
Awsworth.......114 A2
Axbridge........ 42 D3
Axford Hants.... 33 A5
  Wilts..........45 C6
Axminster 14 B2
Axmouth........ 14 B2
Axton........125 A6
Aycliff 39 A5
Aycliffe.......167 C5
Aydon 178 C2
Aylburton...... 62 C2
Ayle 165 A5
Aylesbeare 13 B5
Aylesbury 66 B4
Aylesby.......143 C4
Aylesford 37 A5
Aylesham 53 D4
Aylestone 98 A2
Aylmerton 120 B3
Aylsham 120 C3
Aylton 79 D4
Aymestrey 78 A2
Aynho 82 D2
Ayot St Lawrence. 68 B1
Ayot St Peter... 68 B2
Ayr 192 C3
Aysgarth 156 C4
Ayside 154 C2
Ayston........ 99 A5
Aythorpe Roding . 69 B5
Ayton 211 D6
Aywick 284 E7
Azerley 157 D6

B

Babbacombe.... 8 A3
Babbinswood ...110 B2
Babcary 29 C5
Babel 59 B5
Babraham 85 B7
Babworth......132 A1
Bac 288 C5
Bachau 123 B4
Backaland 282 D6
Backaskaill 282 B5
Backbarrow 154 C2
Backe 56 A2
Backfolds 269 D5
Backford 127 B4
Backford Cross..126 B3
Backhill Aberds .256 C2
  Aberds.......257 C5
Backhill of
  Clackriach....257 B4
Backhill of
  Fortree......257 B4
Backhill of
  Trustach 244 C3
Backies 274 D2
Backlass 280 C4
Back of
  Keppoch 235 B5
Back Rogerton ..193 C5
Backwell....... 42 C3
Backworth 179 B5
Bacon End 69 B6
Baconsthorpe ..120 B3
Bacton Hereford..78 D1
  Norf.........121 B5
  Suff..........87 A6
Bacton Green .. 87 A6
Bacup 138 A1
Badachro 261 C4
Badanloch
  Lodge.......273 A5
Badavanich.....250 A3
Badbury 45 A5
Badby 82 B2
Badcall 276 C4
Badcaul 262 A2
Baddeley Green.129 D4
Baddesley
  Clinton.......97 D5

Baddesley Ensor . 97 B5
Baddidarach....270 B3
Baddoch.......242 D4
Baddock.......252 A3
Badenscoth 256 C2
Badenyon......243 A6
Badger 95 B5
Badger's Mount.. 50 C1
Badgeworth.... 63 B5
Badgworth...... 42 D2
Badicaul 249 D4
Badingham 88 A4
Badlesmere 52 D2
Badlipster 280 D4
Badluarach 262 A1
Badminton..... 44 A2
Badnaban......270 B3
Badninish.......264 A3
Badrallach 262 A2
Badsey 80 C3
Badshot Lea ... 34 B1
Badsworth 140 B2
Badwell Ash ... 87 A5
Bagby 158 C3
Bag Enderby ...134 B3
Bagendon 63 C6
Bagh a Chaisteil
  (Castlebay)....286 G2
Baghasdal 286 E3
Bagh Mor......286 A4
Bagh
  Shiarabhagh...286 F3
Bagillt 126 B2
Baginton 97 D6
Baglan 40 B2
Bagley 110 C3
Bagnall 129 D4
Bagnor 46 C2
Bagshot Sur ... 48 C2
  Wilts..........45 C7
Bagthorpe Norf..119 B4
  Notts........131 D4
Bagworth...... 98 A1
Bagwy Llydiart .. 61 A6
Bail Àrd
  Bhuirgh 288 B5
Baildon.......147 D5
Baile 287 F4
Baile Ailein 288 E3
Baile a
  Mhanaich 288 A3
Baile an Truiseil 288 B4
Bailebeag......244 A3
Baile Boidheach 202 A2
Baile Glas......286 A4
Baile Mhartainn 287 G2
Baile Mhic
  Phail........287 G3
Baile Mor Argyll..224 D1
  W Isles.......287 H2
Baile na Creige. 286 F2
Baile nan
  Cailleach.....288 A3
Baile Raghaill ..287 G2
Baileyhead.....176 B3
Bailiesward 255 C5
Baillieston 205 B6
Bail' lochdrach. 286 A4
Bail Uachdraich.287 H3
Bail' Ur
  Tholastaidh...288 C6
Bainbridge.....156 B3
Bainsford 208 B1
Bainshole......255 C7
Bainton E Yorks ..150 B2
  Pboro.......100 A2
Bairnkine......187 B5
Baker's End.... 68 B3
Baker Street ... 50 A3
Bakewell 130 C2
Bala (Y Bala) ..108 B4
Balachuirn.....248 B2
Balavil........241 B5
Balbeg Highld ..251 D6
  Highld........251 D6
Balbeggie......219 B6
Balbithan 245 A4
Balbithan Ho.. 245 A5
Balblair Highld...264 C1
  Highld........264 B3
Balby 140 C3
Balchladich 270 A3

Balchraggan
  Highld........252 B1
  Highld........252 C1
Balchrick 276 C2
Balchrystie.....221 D4
Balcladaich....251 D4
Balcombe...... 35 C6
Balcombe Lane.. 35 C6
Balcomie 221 C6
Balcurvie 220 D3
Baldersby......158 D2
Baldersby St
  James........158 D2
Balderstone....145 D6
Balderton
  Ches W.......126 C3
  Notts........132 D3
Baldhu 4 C2
Baldinnie 220 C4
Baldock 84 D4
Baldovie 221 A4
Baldrine 152 C4
Baldslow 23 A5
Baldwin 152 C3
Baldwinholme..175 C6
Baldwin's Gate.112 A1
Bale 120 B2
Balearn 269 D5
Balemartine ...222 C2
Balephuil 222 C2
Balerno.......209 D4
Balevullin......222 C2
Balfield 232 B3
Balfour 282 F5
Balfron 206 B3
Balfron Station.206 B3
Balgaveny.....256 B1
Balgavies......232 C3
Balgonar 208 A3
Balgove 256 C3
Balgowan......241 C4
Balgown 258 B3
Balgrochan 205 A6
Balgy 249 A5
Balhaldie 218 D3
Balhalgardy...256 D2
Balham 49 B5
Balhary 231 D6
Baliasta 284 C8
Baligill 279 B4
Balintore Angus ..231 C6
  Highld........265 C4
Balintraid......264 C3
Balk 158 C3
Balkeerie 232 D1
Balkemback ...220 A4
Balkholme 141 A5
Balkissock 180 C3
Ball 110 C2
Ballabeg 152 D2
Ballacannell ...152 C4
Ballachulish ...237 D4
Ballajora......152 B4
Ballaleigh 152 C3
Ballamodha ...152 D2
Ballantrae 180 C2
Ballaquine 152 C4
Ballards Gore .. 70 D3
Ballasalla IoM ..152 B3
  IoM..........152 D2
Ballater 243 C6
Ballaugh......152 B3
Ballaveare 152 D2
Ballcorach 254 D2
Ballechin 230 C3
Balleigh 264 B3
Ballencrieff 210 C1
Ballentoul 230 B2
Ball Haye Green 129 D4
Ball Hill...... 46 C2
Ballidon 130 D2
Ballimeanoch ..214 A3
Ballimore Argyll..214 D2
  Argyll........226 C3
Ballinaby......214 A2
Ballindean 220 B2
Ballingdon 87 C4

Ballinger
  Common 67 C2
Ballingham 78 D3
Ballingry.......209 A4
Ballinlick 230 D3
Ballinluig 230 C3
Ballintuim 231 C5
Balloch Angus ..232 C1
  Highld........252 B3
  N Lanark 207 C5
  W Dunb......206 B1
Ballochan......244 C2
Ballochford 255 C4
Ballochmorrie...181 C4
Balls Cross.... 34 D2
Balls Green 71 A4
Ballygown 224 B3
Ballygrant 200 B3
Ballyhaugh.....223 B4
Balmacara.....249 D5
Balmacara
  Square.......249 D5
Balmaclellan...173 A4
Balmacneil.....230 C3
Balmacqueen ..259 A4
Balmae 173 D4
Balmaha 206 A2
Balmalcolm ...220 D3
Balmeanach ...248 B2
Balmedie 245 A6
Balmer Heath ..110 B3
Balmerino 220 B3
Balmerlawn ... 18 A2
Balmichael 191 B5
Balmirmer 221 A5
Balmore Highld .251 C5
  Highld........253 B4
  Highld........258 D2
  Perth........230 C3
Balmule 209 B5
Balmullo 220 B4
Balmungie 252 A3
Balnaboth 231 B7
Balnabruaich ..264 D2
Balnabruich ...275 B5
Balnacoil 274 C2
Balnacra......250 B1
Balnafoich 252 C2
Balnagall 265 B4
Balnaguard 230 C3
Balnahard Argyll..212 C2
  Argyll........224 C3
Balnain 251 C6
Balnakeil 277 B4
Balnaknock 259 B4
Balnapaling ...264 D3
Balne.........140 B3
Balochroy......202 C2
Balone 221 C4
Balornock 205 B6
Balquharn 219 A5
Balquhidder ...217 B5
Balsall........97 D5
Balsall Common. 97 D5
Balsall Hth..... 96 C3
Balscott 81 C6
Balsham 86 B1
Baltasound 284 C8
Balterley......128 D2
Baltersan 171 A6
Balthangie 268 D3
Baltonsborough . 29 B5
Balvaird 252 A1
Balvicar 213 A5
Balvraid Highld...238 A2
  Highld........253 C4
Bamber Bridge..137 A4
Bambers Green .69 A5
Bamburgh 199 C5
Bamff 231 C6
Bamford Derbys .130 A2
  Gtr Man 138 B1
Bampton Cumb .164 D3
  Devon........27 C4
  Oxon.........64 C4
Bampton
  Grange.......164 D3
Banavie 237 B5
Banbury...... 82 C1
Bancffosfelen .. 57 A4
Banchory 244 C3

Banchory-
Devenick......245 B6
Bancycapel......57 A4
Bancyfelin......56 A3
Bancyffordd....73 C7
Bandirran......220 A2
Banff..........268 C1
Bangor.........123 C5
Bangor-is-y-
coed..........110 A2
Banham.........103 C6
Bank...........18 A1
Bankend........174 B3
Bankglen.......182 A4
Bankhead
Aberdeen.....245 A5
Aberds.......244 B3
Bank Newton....146 B3
Banknock.......207 C5
Banks Cumb.....176 C3
Lancs.........136 A2
Bankshill......185 D4
Bank Street....79 A4
Banningham.....120 C4
Banniskirk Ho..280 C3
Bannister Green..69 A6
Bannockburn....207 A6
Banstead.......35 A5
Bantham........7 C5
Banton.........207 C5
Banwell........42 D2
Banyard's Green 104 C3
Bapchild.......51 C6
Barabhas.......288 C3
Barabhas Iarach 288 C4
Barabhas
Uarach........288 B4
Barachandroman
..............225 D5
Barassie.......192 B3
Baravullin.....226 C3
Barbaraville...264 C3
Barber Booth...129 A6
Barbieston.....182 A2
Barbon.........155 C5
Barbridge......127 D6
Barbrook.......26 A2
Barby..........98 D2
Barcaldine.....227 B4
Barcheston.....81 D5
Barcombe.......22 A2
Barcombe Cross..22 A2
Barden.........157 B5
Bardennoch.....182 C3
Barden Scale...147 B4
Bardfield Saling..69 A6
Bardister......284 F5
Bardney........133 C6
Bardon.........114 D2
Bardon Mill....177 C5
Bardowie.......205 A5
Bardrainney....204 A3
Bardsea........154 D2
Bardsey........148 C2
Bardwell.......103 D5
Bare...........145 A4
Barfad.........202 B3
Barford Norf...104 A2
Warks.........81 A5
Barford St John..82 D1
Barford St Martin. 31 B4
Barford St
Michael.......82 D1
Barfrestone....53 D4
Bargoed
(Bargod)......41 B6
Bargrennan.....181 C5
Barham Cambs..100 D3
Kent..........53 D4
Suff..........88 B2
Barharrow......172 C4
Barhill........173 B6
Bar Hill.......85 A5
Barholm........116 D3
Barkby.........98 A3
Barkestone-le-
Vale..........115 B5
Barkham........47 C5
Barking London..50 A1
Suff..........87 B6
Barkingside....50 A1

Barking Tye....87 B6
Barkisland.....138 B3
Barkston Lincs..116 A2
N Yorks.......148 D3
Barkway........85 D5
Barlaston......112 B2
Barlavington...20 A2
Barlborough....131 B4
Barlby.........149 D5
Barlestone.....98 A1
Barley Herts...85 D5
Lancs.........146 C2
Barley Mow.....179 D4
Barleythorpe...99 A5
Barling........51 A6
Barlow Derbys..130 B3
N Yorks.......140 A4
T&W...........178 C3
Barmby Moor....149 C6
Barmby on the
Marsh.........141 A4
Barmer.........119 B5
Barmoor Castle.198 C3
Barmoor Lane
End...........198 C4
Barmouth
(Abermaw).....90 A4
Barmpton.......167 D6
Barmston.......151 B4
Barnack........100 A2
Barnacle.......97 C6
Barnard Castle.166 D3
Barnard Gate...65 B5
Barnardiston...86 C3
Barnbarroch....173 C6
Barnburgh......140 C2
Barnby.........105 C5
Barnby Dun.....140 C4
Barnby in the
Willows.......132 D3
Barnby Moor....131 A6
Barnes Street..36 B4
Barnet.........68 D2
Barnetby le
Wold..........142 C2
Barney.........120 B1
Barnham Suff...103 D4
W Sus.........20 B2
Barnham
Broom.........104 A1
Barnhead.......233 C4
Barnhill Ches W. 127 C4
Dundee........221 A4
Moray.........266 D2
Barnhills......180 D1
Barningham
Durham........166 D3
Suff..........103 D5
Barnoldby le
Beck..........143 C4
Barnoldswick...146 C2
Barns Green....35 D4
Barnsley Glos..64 C1
S Yorks.......139 C6
Barnstaple.....25 B6
Barnston Essex..69 B6
Mers..........126 A2
Barnstone.....115 B5
Barnt Green....96 D3
Barnton Ches W. 127 B6
Edin..........209 C4
Barnwell All
Saints........100 C2
Barnwell St
Andrew........100 C2
Barnwood.......63 B4
Barochreal.....226 D3
Barons Cross...78 B2
Barr...........181 B4
Barra Castle...256 D2
Barrachan......171 C5
Barrack........256 B3
Barraglom......288 D2
Barrahormid....213 D5
Barran.........226 D3
Barrapol.......222 C2
Barras Aberds..245 D5
Cumb..........165 D6
Barrasford.....177 B7
Barravullin....213 B6
Barregarrow....152 C3
Barrhead.......205 C4

Barrhill.......181 C4
Barrington Cambs 85 C5
Som...........28 D3
Barripper......3 B4
Barmill........204 C3
Barrock........281 A4
Barrock Ho.....281 B4
Barrow Lancs...146 D1
Rutland.......116 D1
Suff..........86 A3
Barroway Drove 102 A1
Barrowburn.....188 B1
Barrowby.......116 B1
Barrowcliff....160 C4
Barrowden......99 A6
Barrowford.....146 D2
Barrow Green...51 C6
Barrow Gurney..43 C4
Barrow Haven...142 A2
Barrow-in-
Furness.......153 D3
Barrow Island..153 D2
Barrow Nook....136 C3
Barrows Green
Ches E........128 D1
Cumb..........154 C4
Barrow's Green.127 A5
Barrow Street..30 B2
Barrow upon
Humber........142 A2
Barrow upon
Soar..........114 D3
Barrow upon
Trent.........114 C1
Barry (Y Barri).41 E6
Barry Island...41 E6
Barsby.........115 D4
Barsham........105 C4
Barston........97 D5
Bartestree.....78 C3
Barthol Chapel.256 C3
Barthomley.....128 D2
Bartley........32 D2
Bartley Green..96 C3
Bartlow........86 C1
Barton Cambs...85 B6
Ches W........127 D4
Glos..........64 A2
Lancs.........136 C2
Lancs.........145 D5
N Yorks.......157 A6
Oxon..........65 C6
Torbay........8 A3
Warks.........80 B4
Barton Bendish.102 A3
Barton Hartshorn 82 D3
Barton in Fabis.114 B3
Barton in the
Beans.........97 A6
Barton-le-Clay..84 D2
Barton-le-
Street........159 D6
Barton-le-
Willows.......149 A6
Barton Mills...102 D3
Barton on Sea..17 B6
Barton on the
Heath.........81 D5
Barton St David.29 B5
Barton Seagrave.99 D5
Barton Stacey..32 A3
Barton Turf....121 C5
Barton-under-
Needwood......113 D5
Barton-upon-
Humber........142 A2
Barton
Waterside.....142 A2
Barugh.........139 C6
Barway.........102 D1
Barwell........98 B1
Barwick Herts..68 B3
Som...........29 D5
Barwick in
Elmet.........148 D2
Baschurch......110 C3
Bascote........81 A7
Basford Green..129 D4
Bashall Eaves..145 C6
Bashley........17 B6
Basildon.......51 A4

Basingstoke....47 D4
Baslow.........130 B2
Bason Bridge...28 A3
Bassaleg.......42 A1
Bassenthwaite..163 A5
Bassett........32 D3
Bassingbourn...85 C5
Bassingfield...115 B4
Bassingham.....133 C4
Bassingthorpe..116 C2
Basta..........284 D7
Baston.........116 D4
Bastwick.......121 D6
Batchworth
Heath.........67 D6
Batcombe Dorset..15 A7
Som...........29 B6
Bate Heath.....128 B1
Batford........67 B7
Bath...........43 C6
Bathampton.....44 C1
Bathealton.....27 C5
Batheaston.....44 C1
Bathford.......44 C1
Bathgate.......208 D2
Bathley........132 D2
Bathpool Corn..10 D3
Som...........28 C2
Bathville......208 D2
Batley.........139 A5
Batsford.......81 D4
Battersby......159 A4
Battersea......49 B5
Battisborough
Cross.........7 C4
Battisford.....87 B6
Battisford Tye..87 B6
Battle E Sus...23 A5
Powys.........76 D4
Battledown.....63 A5
Battlefield....111 D4
Battlesbridge..70 D1
Battlesden.....67 A5
Battlesea Green.104 C3
Battleton......27 C4
Battram........98 A1
Battramsley....18 B2
Baughton.......80 C1
Baughurst......46 D3
Baulking.......64 D4
Baumber........134 B2
Baunton.......63 C6
Baverstock.....31 B4
Bawburgh.......104 A2
Bawdeswell.....120 C2
Bawdrip.......28 B3
Bawdsey........88 C4
Bawtry.........141 D4
Baxenden......137 A6
Baxterley......97 B5
Baybridge......32 C4
Baycliff.......154 D1
Baydon.........45 B6
Bayford Herts..68 C3
Som...........30 C1
Bayles.........165 A5
Baylham........88 B2
Baynard's Green.65 A6
Bayston Hill...94 A2
Baythorn End...86 C3
Bayton.........95 D4
Beach.........236 D1
Beachampton...83 D4
Beachamwell...102 A3
Beachans.......253 B6
Beacharr......202 D1
Beachborough..38 B3
Beachley.......62 D1
Beacon.........14 A1
Beacon End.....70 A3
Beacon Hill....34 C1
Beacon's Bottom.66 D3
Beaconsfield...67 E5
Beacrabhaic...288 H2
Beadlam.......159 C5
Beadlow........84 D3
Beadnell.......189 A5
Beaford........25 D6
Beal Northumb..199 B4
N Yorks.......140 A3
Beamhurst.....113 B4

Beaminster.....15 A4
Beamish........179 D4
Beamsley.......147 B4
Bean...........50 B2
Beanacre......44 C3
Beanley........188 B3
Beaquoy........282 E4
Bear Cross.....17 B4
Beardwood......137 A5
Beare Green....35 B4
Bearley........81 A4
Bearnus........224 B2
Bearpark.......167 A5
Bearsbridge....177 D5
Bearsden.......205 A5
Bearsted.......37 A5
Bearstone......111 B6
Bearwood
Hereford......78 B1
Poole.........17 B4
W Mid.........96 C3
Beattock.......184 B3
Beauchamp
Roding........69 B5
Beauchief.....130 A3
Beaufort......60 C3
Beaufort Castle.251 B7
Beaulieu......18 A2
Beauly........252 B1
Beaumaris.....123 C6
Beaumont Cumb..175 C6
Essex.........71 A5
Beaumont Hill..167 D5
Beausale......97 D5
Beauworth.....33 C4
Beaworthy.....11 B5
Beazley End....70 A1
Bebington.....126 A3
Bebside.......179 A4
Beccles.......105 B5
Becconsall....136 A3
Beckbury......95 A5
Beckenham....49 C6
Beckermet.....162 D3
Beckfoot Cumb..163 D4
Cumb..........174 D4
Beck Foot.....155 B5
Beckford......80 D2
Beckhampton...45 C4
Beck Hole.....159 A7
Beckingham
Lincs.........132 D3
Notts.........141 E5
Beckington....44 D2
Beckley E Sus...37 D6
Hants.........17 B6
Oxon..........65 B6
Beck Row......102 D2
Beck Side.....153 B3
Beckton.......50 A1
Beckwithshaw..147 B6
Becontree.....50 A1
Bedale........157 C6
Bedburn.......166 B4
Bedchester....30 D2
Beddau........41 C5
Beddgelert....107 B5
Beddingham....22 B2
Beddington....49 C6
Bedfield......88 A3
Bedford.......84 B2
Bedham........34 D3
Bedhampton....19 A6
Bedingfield...88 A2
Bedingham....147 A6
Bedlam........147 A6
Bedlington....179 A4
Bedlington
Station.......179 A4
Bedlinog......41 A5
Bedminster....43 B4
Bedmond......67 C6
Bednall......112 D3
Bedrule.......187 B5
Bedstone......94 D1
Bedwas........41 C6
Bedworth......97 C6
Bedworth Heath. 97 C6
Bed-y-coedwr..108 C2
Beeby.........98 A3
Beech Hants...33 B5
Staffs........112 B2

Beech Hill
Gtr Man......137 C4
W Berks.......47 C4
Beechingstoke..45 D4
Beedon........46 B2
Beeford.......151 B4
Beeley........130 C2
Beelsby.......143 C4
Beenham.......46 C3
Beeny.........10 B2
Beer..........14 C2
Beercrocombe..28 C3
Beer Hackett..29 D6
Beesands......8 C2
Beesby........135 A4
Beeson........8 C2
Beeston C Beds..84 C3
Ches W........127 D5
Norf..........119 D6
Notts.........114 B3
W Yorks.......148 D1
Beeston Regis..120 A3
Beeswing......173 B6
Beetham.......154 D3
Beetley.......119 D6
Begbroke......65 B5
Begelly.......55 D7
Beggar's Bush..77 A6
Beguildy......93 D5
Beighton Norf..105 A4
S Yorks.......131 A4
Beighton Hill..130 D2
Beith.........204 C3
Bekesbourne...52 D3
Belaugh.......121 D4
Belbroughton..96 D2
Belchamp Otten..87 C4
Belchamp St
Paul..........86 C3
Belchamp Walter 87 C4
Belchford.....134 B2
Belford.......199 C5
Belhaven......210 C3
Belhelvie.....245 A6
Belhinnie.....255 D5
Bellabeg......243 A6
Bellamore.....181 C4
Bellanoch.....213 C5
Bellaty.......231 C6
Bell Bar......68 C2
Bell Busk.....146 B3
Belleau.......135 B4
Bellehiglash..254 C2
Bell End......96 D2
Bellerby......157 B5
Bellever......12 D1
Belliehill....232 B3
Bellingdon....67 C5
Bellingham....177 A6
Belloch.......190 B2
Bellochantuy..190 B2
Bell o' th' Hill.111 A4
Bellsbank.....182 B2
Bellshill N Lanark 207 D5
Northumb......199 C5
Bellspool.....195 C6
Bellsquarry...208 D3
Bells Yew Green. 36 C4
Belmaduthy...252 B2
Belmesthorpe..116 D3
Belmont
Blackburn.....137 B5
London........49 C5
S Ayrs........192 C3
Shetland......284 C7
Belnacraig....243 A6
Belowda.......5 A4
Belper........114 A1
Belper Lane
End...........114 A1
Belsay........178 B3
Belses........187 A4
Belsford......7 B6
Belstead......88 C2
Belston.......11 B7
Belstone.......11 B7
Belthorn......137 A6
Beltinge......52 C3
Beltoft.......141 C6

Belton Leics 114 C2
Lincs. 116 B2
N Lincs. 141 C5
Norf 105 A5
Belton in Rutland 99 A5
Beltring 37 B4
Belts of
Collonach 244 C3
Belvedere. 50 B1
Belvoir 115 B6
Bembridge. 19 C5
Bemersyde. 197 C4
Bemerton 31 B5
Bempton 161 D5
Benacre 105 C6
Ben Alder
Lodge. 229 A4
Ben Armine
Lodge. 273 C5
Benbuie 183 C5
Ben Casgro 288 E5
Benderloch 226 C4
Bendronaig
Lodge. 250 C2
Benenden. 37 C6
Benfield 171 A5
Bengate 121 C5
Bengeworth. . . . 80 C3
Benhall Green. . . 89 A4
Benhall Street. . . 89 A4
Benholm. 233 B6
Beningbrough. . . 148 B4
Benington Herts . . 68 A2
Lincs. 117 A6
Benllech. 123 B5
Benmore Argyll . . 215 D4
Stirling 216 B4
Benmore Lodge . 271 C6
Bennacott 10 B3
Bennan 191 C5
Benniworth 134 A2
Benover 37 B5
Bensham 179 C4
Benslie 204 D3
Benson 65 D7
Bent. 233 A4
Bent Gate 137 A6
Benthall
Northumb. 189 A5
Shrops 95 A4
Bentham 63 B5
Benthoul 245 B5
Bentlawnt 94 A1
Bentley E Yorks . . 150 D3
Hants 33 A6
Suff 88 D2
S Yorks. 140 C3
Warks. 97 B5
Worcs. 80 A2
Bentley Heath . . . 97 D4
Benton 26 B1
Bentpath 185 C6
Bents 208 D2
Bentworth 33 A5
Benvie 220 A3
Benwick 101 B5
Beoley 80 A3
Beoraidbeg 235 A5
Bepton 20 A1
Berden 69 A4
Bere Alston 6 A3
Bere Ferrers . . . 6 A3
Berepper 3 C4
Bere Regis 16 B2
Bergh Apton . . . 104 A4
Berinsfield 65 D6
Berkeley 62 D2
Berkhamsted . . . 67 C5
Berkley 30 A2
Berkswell 97 D5
Bermondsey . . . 49 B6
Bernera 249 D5
Bernice 215 C4
Bernisdale 259 C4
Berrick Salome . . 65 D7
Berriedale 275 B5
Berrier 164 C1
Berriew. 93 A5

Berrington
Northumb. 198 B4
Shrops 94 A3
Berrow 42 D2
Berrow Green. . . 79 B5
Berry Down
Cross 25 A6
Berry Hill Glos . . . 62 B1
Pembs 72 B3
Berryhillock 267 C6
Berrynarbor. . . . 25 A6
Berry Pomeroy . . 8 A2
Bersham. 110 A2
Berstane. 282 F5
Berwick 22 B3
Berwick Bassett . 45 B4
Berwick Hill. . . . 178 B3
Berwick St
James. 31 B4
Berwick St John. . 30 C3
Berwick St
Leonard 30 B3
Berwick-upon-
Tweed 198 A3
Bescar. 136 B2
Besford. 80 C2
Bessacarr. 140 C4
Bessels Leigh . . . 65 C5
Bessingby 151 A4
Bessingham. . . . 120 B3
Bestbeech Hill . . 36 C4
Besthorpe Norf . . 103 B6
Notts 132 C3
Bestwood 114 A3
Bestwood
Village 114 A3
Beswick 150 C3
Betchworth 35 B5
Bethania Ceredig. . 75 B4
Gwyn 107 A6
Gwyn 108 A2
Bethel Anglesey . . 122 C3
Gwyn 109 B4
Gwyn 123 D5
Bethersden 38 A1
Bethesda Gwyn . . 123 D6
Pembs 55 C6
Bethlehem. 58 C3
Bethnal Green. . . 49 A6
Betley 111 A6
Betsham. 50 B3
Betteshanger . . . 53 D5
Bettiscombe . . . 14 B3
Bettisfield 110 B3
Betton Shrops. . . 93 A7
Shrops 111 B5
Bettws Bridgend . . 40 C4
Mon 61 B4
Newport. 61 D4
Bettws Cedewain 93 B5
Bettws Gwerfil
Goch. 109 A5
Bettws Ifan 73 B6
Bettws Newydd. . 61 C5
Bettws-y-crwyn . 93 C6
Bettyhill 278 B3
Betws 57 A6
Betws Bledrws . . 75 C4
Betws-Garmon. . 107 A5
Betws-y-Coed . . 124 D2
Betws-yn-Rhos . 125 B4
Beulah Ceredig. . . 73 B5
Powys 76 B3
Bevendean. 21 B6
Bevercotes 132 B1
Beverley 150 D3
Beverston 63 D4
Bevington 62 D2
Bewaldeth 163 A5
Bewcastle 176 B3
Bewdley 95 D5
Bewerley 147 A5
Bewholme 151 B4
Bexhill. 23 B5
Bexley 50 B1
Bexleyheath . . . 50 B1
Bexwell 102 A2
Beyton 87 A5
Bhaltos 287 A5
Bhatarsaigh 286 G2
Bibury 64 C2
Bicester 65 A6

Bickenhall 28 D2
Bickenhill. 97 C4
Bicker 117 B5
Bickershaw 137 C5
Bickerstaffe. . . . 136 C3
Bickerton Ches E 127 D5
N Yorks. 148 B3
Bickington Devon . 12 D2
Devon. 25 B6
Bickleigh Devon. . . 7 A4
Devon. 13 A4
Bickleton 25 B6
Bickley 49 C7
Bickley Moss . . . 111 A4
Bicknacre. 70 C1
Bicknoller 27 B6
Bicknor 37 A6
Bickton 31 D5
Bicton Shrops . . . 93 C6
Shrops 110 D3
Bidborough 36 B3
Biddenden 37 C6
Biddenham 84 C2
Biddestone 44 B2
Biddisham 42 D2
Biddlesden 82 C3
Biddlestone 188 C2
Biddulph. 128 D3
Biddulph Moor . . 129 D4
Bideford 25 C5
Bidford-on-Avon. 80 B4
Bidston 136 D1
Bielby 149 C6
Bieldside 245 B5
Bierley IoW 18 D4
W Yorks 147 D5
Bierton 66 B4
Bigbury 7 C5
Bigbury on Sea . . 7 C5
Bigby 142 C2
Biggar Cumb. . . . 153 D2
S Lanark. 195 C5
Biggin Derbys. . . 113 A6
Derbys 129 D6
N Yorks. 148 D4
Biggings 285 G3
Biggin Hill 36 A2
Biggleswade . . . 84 C3
Bighouse 279 B4
Bighton 33 B5
Bignor. 20 A2
Big Sand 261 C4
Bigton 285 L5
Bilberry. 5 A5
Bilborough 114 A3
Bilbrook 27 A5
Bilbrough. 148 C4
Bilbster 281 C4
Bildershaw. 167 C5
Bildeston 87 C5
Billericay 69 D6
Billesdon 99 A4
Billesley 80 B4
Billingborough . . 116 B4
Billinge 136 C4
Billingford 120 C2
Billingham 168 C2
Billinghay 133 D6
Billingley 140 C2
Billingshurst . . . 34 D3
Billingsley 95 C5
Billington C Beds . . 67 A5
Lancs 145 D7
Billockby 121 D6
Billy Row 167 B4
Bilsborrow. 145 D5
Bilsby 135 B4
Bilsham 20 B2
Bilsington 38 B2
Bilson Green . . . 62 B2
Bilsthorpe 131 C6
Bilsthorpe
Moor. 131 D6
Bilston Midloth . . 209 D5
W Mid 96 B2
Bilstone 97 A6
Bilting 38 A2
Bilton E Yorks . . . 151 D4
Northumb. 189 B5
Warks. 98 D1
Bilton in Ainsty . 148 C3
Bimbister 282 F4

Binbrook 143 D4
Binchester
Blocks 167 B5
Bincombe. 15 C6
Bindal 265 B5
Binegar. 29 A6
Binfield. 47 B6
Binfield Hth. . . . 47 B5
Bingfield 178 B1
Bingham. 115 B5
Bingley 147 D5
Bings Heath. . . . 111 D4
Binham. 120 B1
Binley Hants 46 D2
W Mid 97 D6
Binley Woods . . . 97 D6
Binniehill 207 C6
Binsoe. 157 D6
Binstead 19 B4
Binsted 33 A6
Binton 80 B4
Bintree 120 C2
Binweston 93 A7
Birch Essex 70 B3
Gtr Man 138 C1
Bircham
Newton 119 B4
Bircham Tofts . . 119 B4
Birchanger. 69 A5
Birchencliffe. . . . 139 B4
Bircher 78 A2
Birch Green. . . . 70 B3
Birchgrove Cardiff 41 D6
Swansea 40 B2
Birch Heath. . . . 127 C5
Birch Hill 127 B5
Birchington 53 C4
Birchmoor 97 A5
Birchover 130 C2
Birch Vale 129 A5
Birchwood Lincs . 133 C4
Warr. 137 D5
Bircotes 140 D4
Birdbrook 86 C3
Birdforth 158 D3
Birdham 20 C1
Birdholme 130 C3
Birdingbury 82 A1
Birdlip. 63 B5
Birdsall 149 A7
Birds Edge 139 C5
Birdsgreen. 95 C5
Birdsmoor Gate . 14 A3
Birdston 205 A6
Birdwell 139 C6
Birdwood 62 B3
Birgham 198 C1
Birkby 158 A2
Birkdale 136 B2
Birkenhead 126 A3
Birkenhills 256 B2
Birkenshaw
N Lanark 207 D4
W Yorks 139 A5
Birkhall 243 C6
Birkhill Angus. . . 220 A3
Borders 185 A5
Birkholme 116 C2
Birkin 140 A3
Birley 78 B2
Birling Kent. 50 C3
Northumb. 189 C5
Birling Gap 22 C3
Birlingham. 80 C2
Birmingham 96 C3
Birnam 230 D4
Birse 244 C2
Birsemore 244 C2
Birstall Leics. . . . 98 A2
W Yorks 139 A5
Birstwith 147 B6
Birthorpe 116 B4
Birtley Hereford . . 78 A1
Northumb. 177 B6
T&W. 179 D4
Birts Street 79 D5
Bisbrooke 99 B5
Biscathorpe. . . . 134 A2
Biscot 67 A6
Bisham 47 A6
Bishampton . . . 80 B2
Bish Mill 26 C2

Bishop
Auckland 167 C5
Bishopbridge . . . 142 D2
Bishopbriggs . . . 205 B6
Bishop Burton. . . 150 D2
Bishop
Middleham . . . 167 B6
Bishopmill 266 C3
Bishop
Monkton 148 A2
Bishop Norton . . 142 D1
Bishopsbourne . . 52 D3
Bishops
Cannings 44 C4
Bishop's Castle . . 93 C7
Bishop's Caundle 29 D6
Bishop's Cleeve . 63 A5
Bishops Frome . . 79 C4
Bishop's Green. . 69 B6
Bishop's Hull. . . 28 C2
Bishop's
Itchington . . . 81 B6
Bishops Lydeard . 27 C6
Bishops Nympton 26 C2
Bishop's Offley . 112 C1
Bishop'S
Stortford 69 A4
Bishop's Sutton . 33 B5
Bishop's
Tachbrook . . . 81 A6
Bishops Tawton . 25 B6
Bishopsteignton . 13 D4
Bishopstoke . . . 32 D3
Bishopston. . . . 57 D5
Bishopstone
Bucks 66 B4
E Sus 22 B2
Hereford 78 C2
Swindon 45 A6
Wilts. 31 C4
Bishopstrow . . . 30 A2
Bishop Sutton . . 43 D4
Bishop's
Waltham 33 D4
Bishopswood . . . 28 D2
Bishop's Wood . . 95 A6
Bishopsworth . . 43 C4
Bishop
Thornton 147 A6
Bishopthorpe . . 149 C4
Bishopton Darl. . . 167 C6
N Yorks. 157 D7
Renfs 205 A4
Warks. 81 B4
Bishop Wilton . . 149 B6
Bishton 42 A2
Bisley Glos 63 C5
Sur 34 A2
Bispham 144 C3
Bispham Green. . 136 B3
Bissoe 4 D2
Bisterne Close . . 17 A6
Bitchfield 116 C2
Bittadon 25 A6
Bittaford 7 B5
Bittering 119 D6
Bitterley 94 D3
Bitterne 32 D3
Bitteswell 98 C2
Bitton 43 C5
Bix 47 A5
Bixter 285 H5
Blaby 98 B2
Blackacre. 184 C3
Blackadder
West. 198 A2
Blackawton 8 B2
Blackborough
End 118 D3
Blackborough . . 13 A5
Black Bourton . . 64 C3
Blackboys 36 D3
Blackbrook
Derbys 114 A1
Mers. 136 D4
Staffs 111 B6
Blackburn
Aberds 245 A5
Aberds 255 C6
Blackburn. 137 A5
W Loth 208 D2

Black Callerton. . 178 C3
Black Clauchrie . 181 C4
Black Corries
Lodge. 228 C1
Blackcraig 183 D5
Black Crofts. . . . 226 C4
Blackden Heath . 128 B2
Blackdog 245 A6
Black Dog 12 A3
Blackfell. 179 D4
Blackfield. 18 A3
Blackford Cumb . 175 B6
Perth 218 D3
Som 28 A4
Som 29 C6
Blackfordby . . . 114 D1
Blackgang 18 D3
Blackhall
Colliery 168 B2
Blackhall Mill . . 178 D3
Blackhall Rocks . 168 B2
Blackham 36 C2
Blackhaugh 196 C3
Blackheath Essex . 71 A4
Suff 105 D5
Sur 34 B3
W Mid 96 C2
Black Heddon . . 178 B2
Blackhill Aberds. . 257 B5
Aberds 269 D5
Highld. 258 C3
Blackhills Highld . 253 A5
Moray. 266 D3
Blackhorse. . . . 43 B5
Blackland. 44 C4
Black Lane. . . . 137 C6
Blacklaw. 268 D1
Blackley 138 C1
Blacklunans . . . 231 B5
Black Marsh . . . 94 B1
Blackmill 40 C4
Blackmoor. . . . 33 B6
Blackmoor Gate . 26 A1
Blackmore 69 C6
Blackmore End
Essex 86 D3
Herts 67 B7
Black Mount . . . 228 D1
Blackness. 208 C3
Blacknest. 33 A6
Black Notley . . . 70 A1
Blacko. 146 C2
Black Pill 57 C6
Blackpool
Blackpool 144 D3
Devon. 8 C2
Pembs 55 C6
Blackpool Gate . 176 B3
Blackridge 208 D1
Blackrock Argyll . 200 B3
Mon 60 B4
Blackrod. 137 B5
Blackshaw 174 B3
Blackshaw
Head 138 A2
Blacksmith's
Green. 88 A2
Blackstone. . . . 21 A5
Black Tar 55 D5
Blackthorn. . . . 65 B7
Blackthorpe. . . . 87 A5
Blacktoft 141 A6
Blacktop. 245 B5
Black Torrington . 11 A5
Blacktown 42 A1
Blackwall Tunnel 49 A6
Blackwater Corn . 4 C2
Hants 34 A1
IoW 18 C4
Blackwaterfoot. . 191 C4
Blackwell Darl . . 167 D5
Derbys 129 B6
Derbys 131 D4
Warks. 81 C5
Worcs. 96 D2
W Sus. 36 C1
Blackwood 194 B2
Blackwood (Coed
Duon) 41 B6
Blackwood Hill . 129 D4
Blacon. 126 C3
Bladnoch 171 B6

Bladon 65 B5
Blaenannerch . . . 73 B5
Blaenau
 Ffestiniog 108 A2
Blaenavon 61 C4
Blaencelyn. 73 A6
Blaendyryn 59 B6
Blaenffos 73 C4
Blaengarw 40 B4
Blaengwrach. . . . 59 E5
Blaen-gwynfi . . . 40 B3
Blaenpennal 75 B5
Blaenplwyf. 75 A4
Blaenporth. 73 B5
Blaenrhondda. . . 40 A4
Blaen-waun. 73 D5
Blaen-y-coed . . . 73 D6
Blaenycwm 92 D2
Blaen-y-Cwm
 Denb. 109 B5
 Gwyn 108 C2
 Powys 109 C5
Blagdon N Som. . 43 D4
 Torbay 8 A2
Blagdon Hill. . . . 28 D2
Blagill 165 A5
Blaguegate 136 C3
Blaich 237 B4
Blain 235 D5
Blaina 60 C4
Blair Atholl 230 B2
Blairbeg 191 B6
Blairdaff 244 A3
Blair
 Drummond . . . 207 A5
Blairglas 206 B1
Blairgowrie 231 D5
Blairhall 208 B3
Blairingone 208 A2
Blairland 204 D3
Blairlogie 207 A6
Blairmore. 215 D4
Blairnamarrow . . 243 A5
Blairquhosh . . . 206 B3
Blair's Ferry. . . . 203 B4
Blairskaith 205 A5
Blaisdon 62 B3
Blakebrook 95 D6
Blakedown. 96 D1
Blakelaw 197 C6
Blakeley 95 B6
Blakeley Lane . . 112 A3
Blakemere. 78 C1
Blakeney Glos . . 62 C2
 Norf. 120 A2
Blakenhall
 Ches E 111 A6
 W Mid 96 B2
Blakeshall 95 C6
Blakesley 82 B3
Blanchland 178 D2
Blandford Forum 16 A2
Blandford St
 Mary. 16 A2
Bland Hill 147 B6
Blanefield 205 A5
Blankney 133 C5
Blantyre 194 A1
Blar
 a'Chaorainn . . 237 C5
Blaran 214 A1
Blarghour. 214 A2
Blarmachfoldach
 . . . . 237 C4
Blarnalearoch. . 262 A3
Blashford. 17 A5
Blaston 99 B5
Blatherwycke . . . 99 B6
Blawith 154 C1
Blaxhall. 89 B4
Blaxton 141 C4
Blaydon 178 C3
Bleadon 42 D2
Bleak Hey Nook . 138 C3
Blean. 52 C3
Bleasby Lincs . . 133 A6
 Notts 115 A5
Bleasdale 145 C5
Bleatarn 165 D5
Blebocraigs. . . . 220 C4
Bleddfa 77 A6

Bledington. 64 A3
Bledlow 66 C3
Bledlow Ridge . . 66 D3
Blegbie 210 D1
Blencarn. 165 B4
Blencogo 175 D4
Blendworth 33 D6
Blenheim Park . . 119 B5
Blennerhasset. . 175 D4
Blervie Castle . . 253 A6
Bletchingdon . . . 65 B6
Bletchingley 35 A6
Bletchley
 M Keynes 83 D5
 Shrops 111 B5
Bletherston 55 B6
Bletsoe 84 B2
Blewbury 46 A3
Blickling 120 C3
Blidworth 131 D5
Blindburn. 188 B1
Blindcrake. 163 A4
Blindley Heath . . 35 B6
Blisland 10 D2
Blissford. 31 D5
Bliss Gate. 95 D5
Blisworth 83 B4
Blithbury 113 C4
Blitterlees 174 C4
Blockley 81 D4
Blofield. 104 A4
Blofield Heath. . 121 D5
Blo' Norton 103 D6
Bloomfield. 187 A4
Blore 113 A5
Blount's Green . . 113 B4
Blowick. 136 B2
Bloxham. 82 D1
Bloxholm 133 D5
Bloxwich 96 A2
Bloxworth 16 B2
Blubberhouses. . 147 B5
Blue Anchor Som . 27 A5
 Swansea 57 C5
Blue Row 71 B4
Blundeston 105 B6
Blunham 84 B3
Blunsdon St
 Andrew 45 A5
Bluntington 96 D1
Bluntisham 101 D5
Blunts 6 A2
Blyborough 142 D1
Blyford 105 D5
Blymhill 112 D2
Blyth Northumb . 179 A5
 Notts 131 A6
Blyth Bridge . . . 195 B6
Blythburgh. 105 D5
Blythe 197 B4
Blythe Bridge . . 112 A3
Blyton 141 D6
Boarhills 221 C5
Boarhunt 19 A5
Boars Head 137 C4
Boars Hill 65 C5
Boarstall. 66 B2
Boasley Cross . . 11 B5
Boath. 264 C1
Boat of Garten . 242 A2
Bobbing 51 C5
Bobbington 95 B6
Bobbingworth. . . 69 C5
Bocaddon 5 B6
Bochastle 217 D6
Bocking 70 A1
Bocking
 Churchstreet. . 70 A1
Boddam Aberds . 257 B6
 Shetland. 285 M5
Boddington 63 A4
Bodedern 122 B3
Bodelwyddan . . 125 B5
Bodenham
 Hereford 78 B3
 Wilts. 31 C5
Bodenham Moor . 78 B3
Bodermid. 106 D1
Bodewryd. 122 A3
Bodfari 125 B5
Bodffordd 123 C4

Bodham 120 A3
Bodiam 37 D5
Bodicote. 82 D1
Bodieve 9 D5
Bodinnick. 5 B6
Bodle Street
 Green 23 A4
Bodmin. 5 A5
Bodney 103 B4
Bodorgan 122 D3
Bodsham 38 A3
Bodymoor Heath . 97 B4
Bogallan 252 A2
Bogbrae 257 C5
Bogend Borders . 198 B1
 S Ayrs. 192 B3
Boghall 208 D2
Boghead 194 B2
Bogmoor 267 C4
Bogniebrae 255 B6
Bognor Regis . . . 20 C2
Bograxie. 256 E2
Bogside 194 A3
Bogton 268 D1
Bogue 182 D4
Bohenie 239 D6
Bohortha 4 D3
Bohuntine 239 D6
Boirseam 287 F5
Bojewyan 2 B1
Bolam Durham . . 167 C4
 Northumb 178 A2
Boldon 179 C5
Boldon Colliery . 179 C5
Boldre 18 B2
Boldron 166 D3
Bole 132 A2
Bolehill 130 D2
Boleside 196 C3
Bolham 27 D4
Bolham Water . . 27 D6
Bolingey 4 B2
Bollington 129 B4
Bollington
 Cross 129 B4
Bolney 35 D5
Bolnhurst 84 B2
Bolshan 233 C4
Bolsover 131 B4
Bolsterstone . . . 139 D5
Bolstone. 78 D3
Boltby 158 C3
Bolter End 66 D3
Bolton Cumb . . . 165 C4
 E Loth. 210 C2
 E Yorks. 149 B6
 Gtr Man 137 C6
 Northumb 189 B4
Bolton Abbey . . 147 B4
Bolton Bridge . . 147 B4
Bolton-by-
 Bowland 146 C1
Boltonfellend . . 176 C2
Boltongate 175 D5
Bolton-le-
 Sands 145 A4
Bolton Low
 Houses. 175 D5
Bolton-on-
 Swale 157 B6
Bolton Percy . . . 148 C4
Bolton Town
 End 145 A4
Bolton upon
 Dearne. 140 C2
Bolventor 10 D2
Bomere Heath . . 110 D3
Bonar Bridge. . . 264 A2
Bonawe 227 D5
Bonby 142 B2
Boncath 73 C5
Bonchester
 Bridge 187 B4
Bonchurch 19 D4
Bondleigh 12 A1
Bonehill Devon . 12 D2
Bo'ness. 208 B2
Bonhill 206 C1

Boningale 95 A6
Bonjedward. . . . 187 A5
Bonkle 194 A3
Bonnavoulin . . . 225 A4
Bonnington Edin 208 D4
 Kent. 38 B2
Bonnybank. 220 D3
Bonnybridge . . . 207 B6
Bonnykelly 268 D3
Bonnyrigg and
 Lasswade . . . 209 D6
Bonnyton Aberds 220 A3
 Angus. 233 C4
Bonsall 130 D2
Bonskeid House 230 B2
Bont. 61 B5
Bontddu 91 A4
Bont-Dolgadfan. 91 B6
Bont-goch. 91 D4
Bonthorpe 135 B4
Bontnewydd
 Ceredig 75 B5
 Gwyn 107 A4
Bont-newydd . . 125 B5
Bont Newydd
 Gwyn 108 A2
 Gwyn 108 C2
Bontuchel 125 D5
Bonvilston 41 D5
Bon-y-maen 57 C6
Booker 66 D4
Boon 197 B4
Boosbeck 169 D4
Boot. 163 D4
Booth 138 A3
Boothby
 Graffoe. 133 D4
Boothby Pagnell 116 B2
Boothen 112 A2
Boothferry 141 A5
Boothville 83 A4
Booth Wood . . . 138 B3
Bootle Cumb . . . 153 B2
 Mers. 136 D2
Booton 120 C3
Boquhan 206 B3
Boraston 95 D4
Borden Kent . . . 51 C5
 W Sus. 34 D1
Bordley 146 A3
Bordon 33 B7
Bordon Camp . . . 33 B6
Boreham Essex . 70 C1
 Wilts. 30 A2
Boreham Street . 23 A4
Borehamwood . . 68 D1
Boreland
 Dumfries 185 C4
 Stirling 217 A5
Borgh W Isles . . 286 F2
 W Isles 287 F4
Borghastan 288 C3
Borgie. 278 C2
Borgue Dumfries 172 D4
 Highld. 275 B5
Borley 87 C4
Bornais. 286 D3
Borness 172 D4
Boroughbridge. . 148 A2
Borough Green. . 36 A4
Borras Head . . . 126 D3
Borreraig 258 C1
Borrobol Lodge . 274 B2
Borrowash 114 B2
Borrowby. 158 C3
Borrowdale 163 C5
Borrowfield 245 C5
Borth. 90 C4
Borthwickbrae . 186 B3
Borthwickshiels 186 B3
Borth-y-Gest . . . 107 C5
Borve 259 D4
Borve Lodge . . . 287 E5
Borwick 154 D4
Bosavern 2 B1
Bosbury 79 C4
Boscastle 10 B2
Boscombe Bmouth. 17 B5
 Wilts. 31 B5

Boscoppa. 5 B5
Bosham 19 A7
Bosherston 55 E5
Boskenna 2 C2
Bosley 129 C4
Bossall 149 A6
Bossiney 9 C6
Bossingham. . . . 38 A3
Bossington 26 A3
Bostock Green . 127 C6
Boston 117 A6
Boston Long
 Hedges. 117 A6
Boston Spa 148 C3
Boston West . . . 117 A5
Boswinger 5 C4
Botallack 2 B1
Botany Bay 68 D2
Botcherby 175 C7
Botcheston 98 A1
Botesdale. 103 D6
Bothal 179 A4
Bothamsall 131 B6
Bothel 163 A4
Bothenhampton . 15 B4
Bothwell. 194 A2
Botley Bucks . . . 67 C5
 Hants. 32 D4
 Oxon. 65 C5
Botolph Claydon . 66 A3
Botolphs. 21 B4
Bottacks 263 D6
Bottesford Leics . 115 B6
 N Lincs. 141 C6
Bottisham 86 A1
Bottlesford. 45 D5
Bottom Boat . . . 139 A6
Bottomcraig . . . 220 B3
Bottom House. . 129 D5
Bottom of
 Hutton 136 A3
Bottom o' th'
 Moor. 137 B5
Botusfleming 6 A3
Botwnnog 106 C2
Bough Beech. . . 36 B2
Boughrood 77 D5
Boughspring . . . 62 D1
Boughton Norf . . 102 A2
 Northants. 83 A4
 Notts 131 C6
Boughton Aluph. 38 A2
Boughton Lees . 38 A2
Boughton
 Malherbe. . . . 37 B6
Boughton
 Monchelsea . . 37 A5
Boughton Street . 52 D2
Boulby 169 D5
Boulden 94 C3
Boulmer 189 B5
Boulston 55 C5
Boultenstone . . 243 A2
Boultham 133 C4
Bourn 85 B5
Bourne 116 C3
Bourne End Bucks 48 A1
 C Beds 83 C6
 Herts 67 C6
Bournemouth . . . 17 B4
Bournes Green
 Glos 63 C5
 Southend. 51 A6
Bournheath 96 D2
Bournmoor 179 D5
Bournville 96 C3
Bourton Dorset . 30 B1
 N Som 42 C2
 Oxon. 45 A6
 Shrops 94 B3
Bourton on
 Dunsmore . . . 98 D1
Bourton on the
 Hill 81 D4
Bourton-on-the-
 Water 64 A2
Bousd 223 A5
Boustead Hill . . 175 C5
Bouth 154 C2
Bouthwaite 157 D5
Boveney 48 B2

Bovey Tracey. . . . 12 D3
Bovingdon 67 C6
Bovingdon Green
 Bucks. 47 A6
 Herts 67 C6
Bovinger. 69 C5
Bovington Camp 16 C2
Bow Borders . . . 196 B3
 Devon. 12 A2
 Orkney 283 H4
Bowbank 166 C2
Bow Brickhill . . . 83 D6
Bowburn. 167 B6
Bowcombe. 18 C3
Bowd 13 B6
Bowden Borders . 197 C4
 Devon. 8 C2
Bowden Hill. . . . 44 C3
Bowderdale. . . . 155 A5
Bowdon 128 A2
Bower 177 A5
Bowerchalke. . . 31 C4
Bowerhill 44 C3
Bower Hinton . . 29 D7
Bowermadden . . 280 B4
Bowers Gifford. . 51 A4
Bowershall 208 A3
Bowertower . . . 280 B4
Bowes 166 D2
Bowgreave 145 C4
Bowgreen 128 A2
Bowhill 186 A3
Bowhouse 174 B3
Bowland Bridge 154 C3
Bowley 78 B3
Bowlhead Green . 34 C2
Bowling W Dunb. 205 A4
 W Yorks. 147 D5
Bowling Bank . . 110 A2
Bowling Green . 79 B6
Bowmanstead. . 154 B2
Bowmore 200 C3
Bowness-on-
 Solway 175 B5
Bowness-on-
 Windermere. . 154 B3
Bow of Fife 220 C3
Bowsden 198 B3
Bowside Lodge. 279 B4
Bowston 154 B3
Bow Street. 90 D4
Bowthorpe. 104 A2
Box Glos 63 C4
 Wilts. 44 C2
Boxbush 62 B3
Box End 84 C2
Boxford Suff. . . . 87 C5
 W Berks. 46 B2
Boxgrove 20 B2
Boxley 37 A5
Boxmoor. 67 C6
Boxted Essex . . 87 D6
 Suff 87 B4
Boxted Cross. . . 87 D6
Boxted Heath . . 87 D6
Boxworth. 85 A5
Boxworth End . . 85 A5
Boyden Gate . . . 53 C4
Boylestone. 113 B5
Boyndie 268 C1
Boynton 151 A4
Boysack 233 D4
Boyton Corn . . . 10 B4
 Suff 89 C4
 Wilts. 30 B3
Boyton Cross. . . 69 C6
Boyton End 86 C3
Bozeat. 83 B6
Braaid 152 D3
Braal Castle. . . . 280 B3
Brabling Green. . 88 A3
Brabourne 38 A2
Brabourne Lees . 38 A2
Brabster 281 B5
Bracadale. 246 A2
Bracara 235 A6
Braceborough. . 116 D3
Bracebridge . . . 133 C4

Bracebridge Heath 133 C4
Bracebridge Low Fields 133 C4
Braceby 116 B3
Bracewell......146 C2
Brackenfield ...130 D3
Brackenthwaite
Cumb 175 D5
N Yorks......148 B1
Bracklesham ...19 B7
Brackletter 239 D5
Brackley Argyll..202 C3
Northants......82 D2
Brackloch......270 B4
Bracknell 47 C6
Braco......218 D3
Bracobrae 267 D6
Bracon Ash ...104 B2
Bracorina.....235 A6
Bradbourne....130 D2
Bradbury 167 C6
Bradda 152 E1
Bradden 82 C3
Braddock........5 A6
Bradeley......128 D3
Bradenham Bucks 66 D4
Norf 103 A6
Bradenstoke ...44 B4
Bradfield Essex ..88 D2
Norf 121 B4
W Berks 47 B4
Bradfield Combust ...87 B4
Bradfield Green .128 D1
Bradfield Heath ..71 A5
Bradfield St Clare......87 B5
Bradfield St George.......87 A5
Bradford Corn 10 D2
Derbys 130 C2
Devon.........11 A5
Northumb.....199 C5
W Yorks 147 D5
Bradford Abbas ..29 D5
Bradford Leigh ...44 C2
Bradford-on-Avon 44 C2
Bradford-on-Tone.........28 C1
Bradford Peverell 15 B6
Brading 19 C5
Bradley Derbys...113 A6
Hants 33 A5
NE Lincs......143 C4
Staffs......112 D2
W Mid 96 B2
W Yorks 139 A4
Bradley Green ...80 A2
Bradley in the Moors........113 A4
Bradlow 79 D5
Bradmore Notts..114 B3
W Mid 96 B1
Bradninch 13 A5
Bradnop......129 D5
Bradpole 15 B4
Bradshaw
Gtr Man 137 B6
W Yorks......138 B3
Bradstone 11 C4
Bradwall Green .128 C2
Bradway 130 A3
Bradwell Derbys .129 A6
Essex 70 A2
M Keynes 83 D5
Norf 105 A6
Staffs......112 A2
Bradwell Grove...64 C3
Bradwell on Sea..71 C4
Bradwell Waterside ...70 C2
Bradworthy 24 D4
Bradworthy Cross......24 D4
Brae Dumfries ...173 A6
Highld......261 B5
Highld......272 D2

Brae continued
Shetland........284 G5
Braeantra......264 C1
Braedownie....231 A6
Braefield 251 C6
Braegrum......219 B5
Braehead
Dumfries 171 B6
Orkney........282 C5
Orkney........283 G6
S Lanark......194 C3
S Lanark......195 A4
Braehead of Lunan........233 C4
Braehoulland ...284 F4
Braehungie....275 A5
Braelangwell Lodge........263 A7
Braemar......243 C4
Braemore Highld 262 C3
Highld......275 A4
Brae of Achnahaird...270 C3
Brae Roy Lodge .240 C1
Braeside......204 A2
Braes of Enzie...267 D4
Braeswick......282 D7
Braewick......285 H5
Brafferton Darl ..167 C5
N Yorks......158 D3
Brafield-on-the-Green......83 B5
Bragar......288 C3
Bragbury End ...68 A2
Bragleenmore ..226 D4
Braichmelyn....123 D6
Braid......209 D5
Braides......144 B4
Braidley......156 C4
Braidwood......194 B3
Braigo......200 B2
Brailsford......113 A6
Brainshaugh ...189 C5
Braintree......70 A1
Braiseworth....104 D2
Braishfield......32 C2
Braithwaite
Cumb......163 B5
S Yorks......140 B4
W Yorks......147 C4
Braithwell......140 D3
Bramber......21 A4
Bramcote Notts..114 B2
Warks.........97 C7
Bramdean......33 C5
Bramerton......104 A3
Bramfield Herts...68 B2
Suff......105 D4
Bramford......88 C2
Bramhall......128 A3
Bramham......148 C3
Bramhope......147 C6
Bramley Hants...47 A4
Sur......34 B3
S Yorks......140 D2
W Yorks......147 D6
Bramling......53 D4
Brampford Speke 13 B4
Brampton Cambs 100 D4
Cumb......165 C4
Cumb......176 C3
Derbys......130 B3
Hereford......78 D2
Lincs......132 B3
Norf......120 C3
Suff......105 C5
S Yorks......140 C2
Brampton Abbotts......62 A2
Brampton Ash....99 C4
Brampton Bryan..94 D1
Brampton en le Morthen......131 A4
Bramshall......113 B4
Bramshaw 31 D6
Bramshill 47 C5
Bramshott 34 C1
Branault......235 D4
Brancaster......119 A4
Brancaster Staithe......119 A4
Brancepeth......167 B5

Branch End......178 C2
Branchill......266 D1
Branderburgh...266 B3
Brandesburton..151 C4
Brandeston 88 A3
Brand Green......62 A3
Brandhill 94 D2
Brandis Corner...11 A5
Brandiston......120 C3
Brandon Durham .167 B5
Lincs......116 A2
Northumb......188 B3
Suff......102 C3
Warks.........97 D7
Brandon Bank...102 C2
Brandon Creek..102 B2
Brandon Parva..104 A1
Brandsby......159 D4
Brandy Wharf ..142 D2
Brane......2 C2
Bran End......69 A6
Branksome 17 B4
Branksome Park .17 B4
Bransby......132 B3
Branscombe 14 C1
Bransford......79 B5
Bransgore......17 B5
Branshill......208 A1
Bransholme......151 D4
Branson's Cross ..96 D3
Branston Leics...115 C6
Lincs......133 C5
Staffs......113 C6
Branston Booths......133 C5
Branstone 19 C4
Bransty......162 C2
Brant Broughton......133 D4
Brantham......88 D2
Branthwaite
Cumb......162 B3
Cumb......163 A5
Brantingham ..142 A1
Branton
Northumb......188 B3
S Yorks......140 C4
Branton Green..148 A3
Branxholm......186 B3
Branxholm Park .186 B3
Branxton......198 C2
Brassey Green...127 C5
Brassington......130 D2
Brasted......36 A2
Brasted Chart....36 A2
Brathens......244 C3
Bratoft......135 C4
Brattleby......133 A4
Bratton Telford..111 D5
Wilts.......44 D3
Bratton Clovelly .11 B5
Bratton Fleming .26 B1
Bratton Seymour 29 C6
Braughing......68 A3
Braunston......82 A2
Braunstone Town 98 A2
Braunston-in-Rutland......99 A5
Braunton......25 B5
Brawby......159 D6
Brawl......279 B4
Brawlbin......279 C6
Bray......48 B2
Braybrooke......99 C4
Braye Ald.........7
Brayford......26 B1
Bray Shop 10 D4
Braystones......162 D3
Braythorn......147 C6
Bray Wick......48 B1
Brazacott......10 B3
Breach......51 C5
Breachacha Castle......223 B4
Breachwood Green......67 A7
Breacleit......288 D2
Breaden Heath ..110 B3
Breadsall......114 B1
Breadstone 62 C3
Breage......3 C4
Breakachy 251 B6

Bream......62 C2
Breamore......31 D5
Brean......42 D1
Breanais......287 B4
Brearton......148 A2
Breascleit......288 D3
Breaston......114 B2
Brechfa......58 B2
Brechin......232 B3
Breckan......283 G3
Breck of Cruan ..282 F4
Breckrey......259 B5
Brecon (Aberhonddu)..60 A2
Bredbury......138 D2
Brede......23 A6
Bredenbury 79 B4
Bredfield......88 B3
Bredgar......51 C5
Bredhurst......51 C4
Bredicot......80 B2
Bredon......80 D2
Bredon's Norton .80 D2
Bredwardine....78 C1
Breedon on the Hill......114 C2
Breibhig W Isles .286 G2
W Isles......288 D5
Breich......208 D2
Breightmet......137 C6
Breighton......149 D6
Breinton......78 D2
Breinton Common......78 C2
Breiwick......285 J6
Bremhill......44 B3
Bremirehoull....285 L6
Brenchley......37 B4
Brendon......26 A2
Brenkley......179 B4
Brent Eleigh 87 C5
Brentford......49 B4
Brentingby......115 D5
Brent Knoll......42 D2
Brent Pelham ...85 D6
Brentwood......69 D5
Brenzett......38 C2
Brereton......113 D4
Brereton Green .128 C2
Brereton Heath .128 C3
Bressingham...104 C1
Bretby......113 C6
Bretford......98 D1
Bretforton......80 C3
Bretherdale Head......155 A4
Bretherton......136 A3
Brettabister....285 H6
Brettenham Norf 103 C5
Suff......87 B5
Bretton Derbys..130 B2
Flint......126 C3
Brewer Street ...35 A6
Brewlands Bridge......231 B5
Brewood......96 A1
Briach......266 D1
Briants Puddle ..16 B2
Brick End 69 A5
Brickendon......68 C3
Bricket Wood ...67 C7
Bricklehampton .80 C2
Bride......152 A4
Bridekirk......163 A4
Bridell......73 B4
Bridestowe 11 C6
Brideswell......255 C6
Bridford......12 C3
Bridfordmills....12 C3
Bridge......52 D3
Bridge End......116 B4
Bridgefoot
Angus......220 A4
Cumb......162 B3
Bridge Green 85 D6
Bridgehampton .29 C5
Bridge Hewick ..158 D2
Bridgehill......178 D2
Bridgemary......19 A4
Bridgemont......129 A5
Bridgend Aberds .244 A4
Aberds......255 C6

Bridgend continued
Angus......232 B3
Argyll......190 B3
Argyll......200 B3
Argyll......214 C1
Cumb......164 D1
Fife......220 C3
Moray......255 C4
N Lanark......207 C4
Pembs......73 B4
W Loth 208 C3
Bridgend (Pen-y-bont ar Ogwr)..40 A2
Bridgend of Lintrathen......231 C6
Bridge of Alford 244 A2
Bridge of Allan..207 A5
Bridge of Avon ..254 C2
Bridge of Awe...227 D5
Bridge of Balgie 229 D4
Bridge of Cally .231 C5
Bridge of Canny 244 C3
Bridge of Craigisla......231 C6
Bridge of Dee...173 C5
Bridge of Don...245 A6
Bridge of Dun...233 C4
Bridge of Dye...244 D3
Bridge of Earn..219 C6
Bridge of Ericht 229 C4
Bridge of Feugh 245 C4
Bridge of Forss .279 B6
Bridge of Gairn .243 C6
Bridge of Gaur .229 C4
Bridge of Muchalls......245 C5
Bridge of Oich .240 B1
Bridge of Orchy 216 A2
Bridge of Waith .282 F3
Bridge of Walls .285 H4
Bridge of Weir .204 B3
Bridgerule 10 A3
Bridges 94 B1
Bridge Sollers ...78 C2
Bridge Street 87 C4
Bridgeton......205 B6
Bridgetown Corn..10 C4
Som......27 B4
Bridge Trafford .127 B4
Bridge Yate 43 B5
Bridgham......103 C5
Bridgnorth......95 B5
Bridgtown......96 A2
Bridgwater 28 B3
Bridlington......151 A4
Bridport 15 B4
Bridstow......62 A1
Brierfield......146 D2
Brierley Glos.....62 B2
Hereford......78 B2
S Yorks......140 B2
Brierley Hill......96 C2
Briery Hill......60 C3
Brig......142 C2
Briggswath......160 A2
Brigham Cumb ..162 A3
E Yorks......150 B3
Brighouse......139 A4
Brighstone......18 C3
Brightgate......130 D2
Brighthampton...65 C4
Brightling......37 D4
Brightlingsea ...71 B4
Brighton Brighton 21 B6
Corn......4 B4
Brighton Hill 33 A5
Brightons......208 C2
Brightwalton 46 B2
Brightwell......88 C3
Brightwell cum Sotwell......65 D6
Brignall......166 D3
Brig o'Turk......217 D5
Brigsley......143 C4
Brigsteer......154 C3
Brigstock......99 C6
Brill......66 B2
Brilley......77 C6
Brimaston......55 B5
Brimfield......78 A3

Brimington 131 B4
Brimley......12 D2
Brimpsfield 63 B5
Brimpton......46 C3
Brims......283 J3
Brimscombe 63 C4
Brimstage......126 A3
Brinacory......235 A6
Brind......149 D6
Brindister
Shetland......285 H4
Shetland......285 K6
Brindle......137 A5
Brindley Ford ..128 D3
Brineton......112 D2
Bringhurst 99 B5
Brington......100 D2
Brinian......282 E5
Briningham 120 B2
Brinkhill......134 B3
Brinkley......86 B2
Brinklow......98 D1
Brinkworth 44 A4
Brinmore......252 D2
Brinscall......137 A5
Brinsea......42 C3
Brinsley......114 A2
Brinsop......78 C2
Brinsworth......131 A4
Brinton......120 B2
Brisco......175 C7
Brisley......119 C6
Brislington......43 B5
Bristol......43 B4
Briston......120 B2
Britannia......138 A1
Britford......31 C5
Brithdir......91 A5
British Legion Village......37 A5
Briton Ferry 40 B2
Britwell Salome..66 D2
Brixham........8 B3
Brixton Devon....7 B4
London......49 B6
Brixton Deverill..30 B2
Brixworth......99 D4
Brize Norton 64 C4
Broad Blunsdon ..64 D2
Broadbottom...138 D2
Broadbridge 19 A4
Broadbridge Heath......35 C4
Broad Campden .81 D4
Broad Chalke ...31 C4
Broadclyst......13 B4
Broadfield
Gtr Man......138 B1
Lancs......136 A4
Pembs......56 B1
W Sus......35 C5
Broadford......247 B5
Broadford Bridge 34 D3
Broad Green
C Beds......83 C6
Essex......70 A2
Worcs......79 B5
Broadhaugh....186 C3
Broadhaven....281 C5
Broad Haven 55 C4
Broadheath....128 A2
Broad Heath 79 A4
Broadhembury ..13 A6
Broadhempston...8 A2
Broad Hill......102 D1
Broad Hinton ...45 B5
Broadholme
Derbys......114 A1
Lincs......132 B3
Broadland Row ..23 A6
Broadlay......56 B3
Broad Laying ...46 C2
Broadley Lancs..138 B1
Moray......267 C4
Broadley Common......68 C4
Broad Marston ..80 C4
Broadmayne ...16 C1
Broadmeadows .196 C3
Broadmere 33 A5
Broadmoor 55 D6
Broadoak......52 C3

Broad Oak Carms. . 58 C2
Cumb 153 A2
Dorset 14 B4
Dorset 30 D1
E Sus 23 A6
E Sus 36 D4
Hereford 61 A6
Mers. 136 D4
Broadrashes 267 D5
Broadsea 269 C4
Broadstairs 53 C5
Broadstone Poole . 17 B4
Shrops 94 C3
Broad Street 37 A6
Broad Street
Green 70 C2
Broad Town 45 B4
Broadtown Lane. . 45 B4
Broadwas. 79 B5
Broadwater Herts 68 A2
W Sus. 21 B4
Broadway Carms . 56 B2
Pembs 55 C4
Som 28 D3
Suff 105 D4
Worcs. 80 D3
Broadwell Glos . . 62 B1
Glos 64 A3
Oxon. 64 C3
Warks. 82 A1
Broadwell
House. 177 D7
Broadwey. 15 C6
Broadwindsor. . . . 14 A4
Broadwood Kelly 11 A7
Broadwoodwidger
. . . . 11 C5
Brobury 78 C1
Brochel. 248 B2
Brochloch 182 C3
Brochroy. 227 C5
Brockamin 79 B5
Brockbridge 33 D5
Brockdam 189 A4
Brockdish. 104 D3
Brockenhurst . . . 18 A2
Brocketsbrae . . . 194 C3
Brockford Street . 88 A2
Brockhall 82 A3
Brockham 35 B4
Brockhampton
Glos 63 A6
Hereford 78 D3
Brockholes 139 B4
Brockhurst
Derbys 130 C3
Hants 19 A5
Brocklebank 175 D6
Brocklesby. 142 B3
Brockley. 42 C3
Brockley Green. . . 87 B4
Brockleymoor. . . 164 B2
Brockton Shrops . . 93 A7
Shrops 94 B3
Shrops 94 C1
Shrops 95 A3
Telford 111 D6
Brockweir 62 C1
Brockwood 33 C5
Brockworth 63 B4
Brocton 112 D3
Brodick 191 B6
Brodsworth 140 C3
Brogaig. 259 B4
Brogborough 83 D6
Brokenborough. . 44 A3
Broken Cross
Ches E 128 B3
Ches W. 128 B1
Bromborough . . . 126 A3
Brome. 104 D2
Brome Street 104 D2
Bromeswell 88 B4
Bromfield Cumb. 175 D4
Shrops 94 D2
Bromham Bedford. 84 B2
Wilts. 44 C3
Bromley London . . 49 C7
W Mid 96 C2
Bromley
Common 49 C7
Bromley Green. . . 38 B1

Brompton Medway 51 C4
N Yorks. 158 B2
N Yorks. 160 C3
Brompton-on-
Swale 157 B6
Brompton Ralph. . 27 B5
Brompton Regis. . 27 B4
Bromsash. 62 A2
Bromsberrow
Hth. 79 D5
Bromsgrove. 96 D2
Bromyard. 79 B4
Bromyard Downs. 79 B4
Bronaber 108 B2
Brongest 73 B6
Bronington 110 B3
Bronllys 77 D5
Bronnant 75 B5
Bronwydd Arms . . 73 D7
Bronydd 77 C6
Bronygarth 110 B1
Brook Carms. 56 B2
Hants 32 C2
Hants 32 D1
IoW 18 C2
Kent 38 A2
Sur 34 B3
Sur 34 C2
Brooke Norf 104 B3
Rutland. 99 A5
Brookenby 143 D4
Brookend 62 D1
Brook End 84 A2
Brookfield 205 B4
Brook Hill. 31 D6
Brookhouse 145 A5
Brookhouse
Green 128 C3
Brookland 38 C1
Brooklands
Dumfries 173 A6
Gtr Man 137 D6
Shrops 111 A4
Brookmans Park . 68 C2
Brooks 93 B5
Brooks Green 35 D4
Brook Street Kent. 36 B3
Kent 38 B1
W Sus. 35 D6
Brookthorpe 63 B4
Brookville 102 B3
Brookwood 34 A2
Broom C Beds. . . . 84 C3
S Yorks. 140 D2
Warks. 80 B3
Broome Norf 105 B4
Shrops 94 C2
Broomedge 128 A2
Broome Park. . . . 189 B4
Broomer's
Corner 35 D4
Broomfield
Aberds 257 C4
Essex 69 B7
Kent 37 A6
Kent 52 C3
Som 28 B2
Broomfleet 141 A6
Broom Green . . . 120 C1
Broomhall
Ches E 111 A5
Windsor 48 C2
Broomhaugh. . . . 178 C2
Broomhill Norf. . . 102 A2
Northumb. 189 C5
S Yorks. 140 C2
Broom Hill. 17 A4
Broomholm 121 B5
Broomley 178 C2
Broompark 167 A5
Broom's Green . . . 79 D5
Broomy Lodge . . . 31 D6
Brora 274 D3
Broseley 95 A4
Brotherhouse
Bar 117 D5
Brotherstone 197 C5
Brothertoft 117 A5
Brotherton 140 A2
Brotton 169 D4
Broubster 279 B6

Brough Cumb 165 D5
Derbys 130 A1
E Yorks 142 A1
Highld. 280 A4
Notts 132 D3
Orkney 282 F4
Shetland. 284 F6
Shetland. 284 G7
Shetland. 285 H6
Shetland. 285 J7
Broughall 111 A4
Brough Lodge. . . 284 D7
Brough
Sowerby 165 D5
Broughton
Borders 195 C6
Cambs 101 D4
Flint 126 C3
Hants 32 B2
Lancs 145 D5
M Keynes 83 C5
N Lincs 142 C1
Northants 99 D5
N Yorks 146 B3
N Yorks 159 D6
Orkney 282 C5
Oxon. 81 D7
V Glam 40 D4
Broughton Astley. 98 B2
Broughton Beck 154 C1
Broughton
Common 44 C2
Broughton
Gifford 44 C2
Broughton
Hackett 80 B2
Broughton in
Furness 153 B3
Broughton Mills 153 A3
Broughton
Moor. 162 A3
Broughton Park . 138 C1
Broughton Poggs 64 C3
Broughtown 282 C7
Broughty Ferry . . 221 A4
Browhouses 175 B5
Browland 285 H4
Brown Candover . 33 B4
Brown Edge
Lancs 136 B2
Staffs 129 D4
Brown Heath. . . . 127 C4
Brownhill Aberds 256 B1
Aberds 256 B3
Blackburn. 145 D6
Shrops 110 C3
Brownhills Fife . . 221 C5
W Mid 96 A3
Brownlow. 128 C3
Brownlow
Heath 128 C3
Brownmuir 233 A5
Brown's End 79 D5
Brownshill 63 C4
Brownston 7 B6
Brownyside 189 A4
Broxa. 160 B3
Broxbourne 68 C3
Broxburn E Loth . 210 C3
W Loth 208 C3
Broxholme 133 B4
Broxted. 69 A5
Broxton. 127 D4
Broxwood 78 B1
Broyle Side 22 A2
Brù 288 C4
Bruairnis 286 F3
Bruan 275 A7
Bruar Lodge 230 A2
Brucehill 206 C1
Bruera. 127 C4
Bruern Abbey 64 A3
Bruichladdich. . . 200 B2
Bruisyard 88 A4
Brumby 141 C6
Brund 129 C6
Brundall 104 A4
Brundish. 88 A3
Brundish Street . 104 D3
Brunery. 235 C6
Brunshaw. 146 D2

Brunswick
Village 179 B4
Bruntcliffe 139 A5
Bruntingthorpe . . 98 B3
Brunton Fife. . . . 220 B3
Northumb. 189 A5
Wilts. 45 D6
Brushford Devon . 12 A1
Som 27 C4
Bruton. 29 B6
Bryanston. 16 A2
Brydekirk 175 A4
Bryher Scilly 2 E3
Brymbo. 126 D2
Brympton. 29 D5
Bryn Carms 57 B5
Gtr Man 137 C4
Neath. 40 B3
Shrops 93 C6
Brynamman 59 D4
Brynberian. 72 C4
Brynbryddan. . . . 40 B2
Bryncae 41 C4
Bryncethin. 40 C4
Bryncir. 107 B4
Bryn-coch 40 B2
Bryncroes 106 C2
Bryncrug 90 B4
Bryn Du. 122 C3
Bryneglwys 109 A6
Brynford. 126 B1
Bryn Gates 137 C4
Bryn-glas 124 C3
Bryn Golau. 41 C4
Bryngwran. 122 C3
Bryngwyn Ceredig. 73 B5
Mon 61 C5
Powys 77 C5
Brynhenllan. 72 C3
Brynhoffnant 73 A6
Brynithel. 41 A7
Bryn-Iwan 73 C6
Brynmawr 60 B3
Bryn-mawr 106 C2
Brynmenyn 40 C4
Brynmill 57 C6
Brynna 41 C4
Bryn-nantllech. . 125 C4
Bryn-penarth . . . 93 A5
Brynrefail
Anglesey 123 B4
Gwyn 123 D5
Bryn Rhyd-yr-
Arian. 125 C4
Brynsadler. 41 C5
Bryn Saith
Marchog 125 D5
Brynsiencyn. 123 D4
Bryn Sion 91 A6
Brynteg Anglesey 123 B4
Ceredig 58 A1
Bryn-y-gwenin . . 61 B5
Bryn-y-maen . . . 124 B3
Bryn-yr-eryr . . . 106 B3
Buaile nam
Bodach. 286 F3
Bualintur 246 B3
Buarthmeini 108 B3
Bubbenhall 97 D6
Bubwith 149 D6
Buccleuch 185 A6
Buchanhaven. . . 257 B6
Buchanty 218 B4
Buchlyvie 206 A3
Buckabank. 164 A1
Buckden Cambs. . 84 A3
N Yorks. 156 D3
Buckenham 105 A4
Buckerell 13 A6
Buckfast. 7 A6
Buckfastleigh 7 A6
Buckhaven. 209 A6
Buckholm. 196 C3
Buckholt. 61 B7
Buckhorn
Weston. 30 C1
Buckhurst Hill. . . 68 D4
Buckie. 267 C5
Buckies. 280 B3
Buckingham. . . . 82 D3
Buckland Bucks. 66 B4
Devon. 7 C5

Buckland continued
Glos 80 D3
Hants 18 B2
Herts 85 D5
Kent 39 A5
Oxon. 64 D4
Sur 35 A5
Buckland Brewer 25 C5
Buckland
Common 67 C5
Buckland
Dinham 43 D6
Buckland Filleigh 11 A5
Buckland in the
Moor. 12 D2
Buckland
Monachorum . . . 6 A3
Buckland
Newton 15 A6
Buckland St
Mary 28 D2
Bucklebury 46 B3
Bucklegate 117 B6
Bucklerheads . . . 221 A4
Bucklers Hard. . . 18 B3
Bucklesham. 88 A3
Buckley (Bwcle) 126 C2
Bucklow Hill . . . 128 A2
Buckminster . . . 116 C1
Bucknall Lincs . . 133 C6
Stoke 112 A3
Bucknell Oxon . . 65 A6
Shrops 94 D1
Buckpool 267 C5
Bucksburn 245 B5
Buck's Cross 24 C4
Bucks Green 34 C3
Bucks Horn Oak . 33 A7
Buckskin. 47 D4
Buck's Mills. 25 C4
Buckton E Yorks . 161 D5
Hereford 94 D1
Northumb. 199 C4
Buckworth. 100 D3
Budbrooke 81 A5
Budby 131 C6
Budd's Titson . . . 10 A3
Bude. 10 A3
Budlake 13 B4
Budle. 199 C5
Budleigh
Salterton 13 C5
Budock Water. . . . 4 D2
Buerton 111 A5
Buffler's Holt 82 D3
Bugbrooke. 82 B3
Buglawton 128 C3
Bugle. 5 B5
Bugley. 30 A2
Bugthorpe 149 B6
Buildwas 95 A4
Builth Road 76 B4
Builth Wells (Llanfair-
ym-Muallt) 76 B4
Buirgh. 287 E5
Bulby 116 C3
Bulcote. 115 A4
Buldoo 279 B5
Bulford. 31 A5
Bulford Camp . . . 31 A5
Bulkeley. 127 D5
Bulkington Warks 97 C6
Wilts. 44 D3
Bulkworthy 25 D4
Bullamoor 158 B2
Bullbridge 130 D3
Bullbrook. 48 C1
Bulley. 62 B3
Bullgill. 162 A3
Bull Hill. 18 B2
Bullington Hants . 32 A3
Lincs. 133 B5
Bull's Green. 68 B2
Bullwood 203 A6
Bulmer Essex . . . 87 C4
N Yorks. 149 A5
Bulmer Tye 87 D4
Bulphan 50 A3
Bulverhythe. 23 B5
Bulwark 257 B4
Bulwell 114 A3
Bulwick 99 B6

Bumble's Green . . 68 C4
Bun Abhainn
Eadarra 288 G2
Bunacaimb 235 B5
Bunarkaig 239 D5
Bunbury. 127 D5
Bunbury Heath . . 127 D5
Bunchrew 252 B2
Bundalloch 249 D5
Buness 284 C8
Bunessan 224 D2
Bungay. 104 C4
Bunkers Hill 65 B5
Bunker's Hill
Lincs. 133 B4
Lincs. 134 D2
Bunloit 251 D7
Bun Loyne 239 B6
Bunnahabhain . . 201 A4
Bunny 114 C3
Buntait 251 C5
Buntingford. 68 A3
Bunwell 104 B2
Burbage Derbys. . 129 B5
Leics. 98 B1
Wilts. 45 C6
Burchett's Green . 47 A6
Burcombe 31 B4
Burcot. 65 D6
Burcott. 66 A4
Burdon 179 D5
Bures 87 D5
Bures Green 87 D5
Burford Ches E . . 127 D6
Oxon. 64 B3
Shrops 78 A3
Burg 224 B2
Burgar. 282 E4
Burgate Hants . . . 31 D5
Suff 104 D1
Burgess Hill. 21 A6
Burgh 88 B3
Burgh by Sands 175 C5
Burgh Castle . . . 105 A5
Burghclere 46 C2
Burghead 266 C2
Burghfield 47 C4
Burghfield
Common 47 C4
Burghfield Hill . . . 47 C4
Burgh Heath 35 A5
Burghill 78 C2
Burgh le Marsh. . 135 C5
Burgh Muir 256 D2
Burgh next
Aylsham. 120 C4
Burgh on Bain. . . 134 A2
Burgh St
Margaret 121 D6
Burgh St Peter . . 105 B5
Burghwallis 140 B3
Burham. 51 C4
Buriton 33 C6
Burland. 127 D6
Burlawn 9 D5
Burleigh 48 C1
Burlescombe. . . . 27 D5
Burleston 16 B1
Burley Hants 17 A6
Rutland. 116 D1
W Yorks 148 D1
Burleydam 111 A5
Burley Gate 78 C3
Burley in
Wharfedale. . . 147 C5
Burley Lodge. . . . 17 A6
Burley Street. . . . 17 A6
Burlingjobb 77 B6
Burlow 22 A3
Burlton 110 C3
Burmarsh 38 B2
Burmington 81 D5
Burn 140 A3
Burnaston 113 B6
Burnbank 194 A2
Burnby 150 C1
Burncross 139 D6
Burneside 154 B4

Burness 282 C7
Burneston 157 C7
Burnett 43 C5
Burnfoot Borders 186 B3
Borders 186 B4
E Ayrs. 182 B2
Perth 219 D4
Burnham Bucks . . 48 A2
N Lincs. 142 B2
Burnham
Deepdale. 119 A5
Burnham Green . . 68 B2
Burnham
Market 119 A5
Burnham
Norton 119 A5
Burnham-on-
Crouch 70 D3
Burnham-on-
Sea 28 A3
Burnham Overy
Staithe 119 A5
Burnham Overy
Town 119 A5
Burnham
Thorpe 119 A5
Burnhead
Dumfries 183 C6
S Ayrs. 181 A4
Burnhervie. 245 A4
Burnhill Green . . 95 A5
Burnhope. 167 A4
Burnhouse. 204 C3
Burniston 160 B4
Burnlee. 139 C4
Burnley. 146 D2
Burnley Lane. . . . 146 D2
Burnmouth 211 D6
Burn of Cambus 218 D2
Burnopfield 178 D3
Burnsall 147 A4
Burnside Angus . 232 C3
E Ayrs. 182 A3
Fife. 219 D6
Shetland. 284 F1
S Lanark. 205 B6
W Loth 208 C3
Burnside of
Duntrune. 220 A4
Burnswark 175 A4
Burntcommon. . . 34 A3
Burnt Heath. . . . 130 B2
Burnthouse 4 D2
Burnt Houses . . 166 C4
Burntisland 209 B5
Burnton 182 B2
Burntwood. 96 A3
Burnt Yates 147 A6
Burnwynd. 208 D4
Burpham Sur . . . 34 A3
W Sus. 20 B3
Burradon
Northumb. 188 C2
T&W. 179 B4
Burrafirth. 284 B8
Burraland
Shetland. 284 F5
Shetland. 285 J4
Burras. 3 B4
Burravoe
Shetland. 284 F7
Shetland. 284 G5
Burray Village. . . 283 H5
Burrells. 165 D4
Burrelton 220 A2
Burridge Devon . 25 B6
Hants. 32 D4
Burrill 157 C6
Burringham. . . . 141 C6
Burrington Devon 26 D1
Hereford 94 D2
N Som 42 D3
Burrough Green . 86 B2
Burrough on the
Hill 115 D5
Burrow-bridge . . 28 C3
Burrowhill 48 C2
Burry 57 C4
Burry Green. . . . 57 C4

Burry Port (Porth
Tywyn) 57 B4
Burscough. 136 B3
Burscough
Bridge 136 B3
Bursea. 149 D7
Burshill. 150 C3
Bursledon 18 A3
Burslem 112 A2
Burstall. 88 C1
Burstock. 14 A4
Burston Norf. . . 104 C2
Staffs. 112 B3
Burstow 35 B6
Burstwick 143 A4
Burtersett 156 C2
Burtle 28 A3
Burton Ches W . . 126 B3
Ches W. 127 C5
Dorset 17 B5
Lincs. 133 B4
Northumb. 199 C5
Pembs 55 D5
Som 28 A1
Wilts. 44 B2
Burton Agnes . . . 151 A4
Burton Bradstock 15 C4
Burton Dassett . . 81 B6
Burton Fleming . 161 D4
Burton Green
W Mid 97 D5
Wrex 126 D3
Burton Hastings . 97 B7
Burton-in-
Kendal 154 D4
Burton in
Lonsdale 155 D5
Burton Joyce. . . . 115 A4
Burton Latimer . 99 D6
Burton Lazars . . . 115 D5
Burton-le-
Coggles 116 C2
Burton Leonard . 148 A2
Burton on the
Wolds. 114 C3
Burton Overy. . . 98 B3
Burton
Pedwardine . . 116 A4
Burton Pidsea. . . 151 D5
Burton Salmon . 140 A2
Burton Stather . 141 B6
Burton upon
Stather. 141 B6
Burton upon
Trent. 113 C6
Burtonwood . . . 137 D4
Burwardsley . . . 127 D5
Burwarton 95 C4
Burwash. 37 D4
Burwash
Common 36 D4
Burwash Weald . 36 D4
Burwell Cambs. . . 86 A1
Lincs. 134 B3
Burwen. 123 A4
Burwick 283 J5
Bury Cambs. . . . 101 C4
Gtr Man 137 B7
Som 27 C4
W Sus. 20 A3
Bury Green 68 A4
Bury St Edmunds 87 A4
Burythorpe 149 A6
Busby 205 C5
Buscot. 64 D3
Bush Bank 78 B2
Bushbury. 96 A2
Bushby 98 A3
Bush Crathie . . . 243 C5
Bushey 67 D7
Bushey Heath . . 67 D7
Bush Green 104 C3
Bushley. 80 D1
Bushton 45 B4
Buslingthorpe . . 133 A5
Busta. 284 G5
Butcher's Cross . 36 D3
Butcher's Pasture 69 A6
Butcombe 43 C4
Butetown 41 D6
Butleigh 29 B5
Butleigh Wootton 29 B5

Butler's Cross . . . 66 C4
Butler's End. . . . 97 C5
Butlers Marston . 81 C6
Butley 89 B4
Butley High
Corner 89 C4
Butterburn. 177 B4
Buttercrambe . . 149 B6
Butterknowle . . 166 C4
Butterleigh 13 A4
Buttermere
Cumb 163 C4
Wilts. 46 C1
Buttershaw 139 A4
Butterstone 231 D4
Butterton 129 D5
Butterwick
Durham 167 C6
Lincs. 117 A6
N Yorks. 159 D6
N Yorks. 160 D3
Butt Green 127 D6
Buttington 93 A6
Buttonoak 95 D5
Buttsash. 18 A3
Butt's Green . . . 32 C2
Buxhall 87 B6
Buxhall Fen
Street. 87 B6
Buxley 198 A2
Buxted 36 D2
Buxton Derbys . . 129 B5
Norf 120 C4
Buxworth 129 A5
Bwlch 60 A3
Bwlchgwyn . . . 126 D2
Bwlch-Llan 75 C4
Bwlchnewydd . . 73 D6
Bwlchtocyn . . . 106 D3
Bwlch-y-cibau . . 109 D6
Bwlch-y-ddar . . . 109 C6
Bwlch-y-fadfa . . 74 D3
Bwlch-y-ffridd . . 93 B4
Bwlchygroes . . . 73 C5
Bwlch-y-sarnau . 92 D4
Byermoor. 178 D3
Byers Green. . . . 167 B5
Byfield 82 B2
Byfleet 48 C3
Byford. 78 C1
Bygrave 85 D4
Byker. 179 C4
Bylchau. 125 C4
Byley 128 C2
Bynea 57 C5
Byrness 187 C6
Bythorn. 100 D2
Byton 78 A1
Byworth 34 D2

C

Cabharstadh . . . 288 E4
Cablea. 218 A4
Cabourne 142 C3
Cabrach Argyll . . 201 B4
Moray. 255 D4
Cabrich 252 B1
Cabus 145 C4
Cackle Street . . . 36 D2
Cadbury 13 A4
Cadbury Barton . 26 D1
Cadder 205 A6
Caddington . . . 67 B6
Caddonfoot 196 C3
Cadeby Leics . . . 97 A7
S Yorks. 140 C3
Cadeleigh 13 A4
Cade Street 36 D4
Cadgwith 3 D5
Cadham 220 D2
Cadishead 137 D6
Cadle. 57 C6
Cadley Lancs. . . . 145 D5
Wilts. 45 C6
Wilts. 45 D6
Cadmore End . . 66 D3
Cadnam 32 D1
Cadney 142 C2
Cadole 126 C2
Cadoxton 41 E6

Cadoxton-Juxta-
Neath 40 B2
Cadshaw. 137 B6
Cadzow 194 A2
Caeathro 123 D4
Caehopkin 59 D5
Caenby 133 A5
Caenby Corner . 133 A4
Caerau Bridgend. 40 B3
Cardiff 41 D6
Caér-bryn 57 A5
Caerdeon 90 A4
Caerfarchell . . . 54 B3
Caergeiliog . . . 122 C3
Caergwrle 126 D3
Caerleon
(Caerllon) . . . 61 D5
Caer Llan 61 C6
Caernarfon . . . 123 D4
Caerphilly
(Caerffili) . . . 41 C6
Caersws 92 B4
Caerwedros . . . 73 A6
Caerwent 61 D6
Caerwych 107 C6
Caerwys 125 B6
Caethle 90 C4
Caim 123 B6
Caio 58 B3
Cairinis 287 H3
Cairisiadar. 287 A5
Cairminis 287 F5
Cairnbaan 213 C6
Cairnbrogie . . . 256 D3
Cairnbulg
Castle 269 C5
Cairncross
Angus 232 A2
Borders 211 D5
Cairndow 215 A4
Cairness 269 C5
Cairneyhill 208 B3
Cairnfield Ho. . . 267 C5
Cairngaan 170 D3
Cairngarroch. . . 170 C2
Cairnhill 256 C1
Cairnie Aberds . . 245 B5
Aberds 255 B5
Cairnorrie 256 B3
Cairnpark 245 A5
Cairnryan 170 A2
Cairnton. 283 G4
Caister-on-Sea 121 D7
Caistor 142 C3
Caistor St
Edmund 104 A3
Caistron 188 C2
Caitha Bowland . 196 B3
Calais Street 87 D5
Calanais. 288 D3
Calbost 288 F5
Calbourne 18 C3
Calceby 134 B3
Calcot Row . . . 47 B4
Calcott 52 C3
Caldback 284 C8
Caldbeck 163 A6
Caldbergh 157 C4
Caldecote Cambs. 85 B5
Cambs 100 C3
Herts 84 D4
Northants. 82 B3
Caldecott
Northants. 84 A1
Oxon. 65 D5
Rutland. 99 B5
Calderbank . . . 207 D5
Calder Bridge . . 162 D3
Calderbrook . . 138 B2
Caldercruix . . . 207 D6
Calder Hall. . . . 162 D3
Calder Mains. . . 280 C2
Caldermill 205 D6
Calder Vale . . . 145 C5
Calderwood. . . . 205 C6
Caldhame. 232 D2
Caldicot 42 A3
Caldwell Derbys. 113 D6
N Yorks. 167 D4
Caldy 126 A2

Caledrhydiau. . . . 74 C3
Calfsound. 282 D6
Calgary 224 A2
Califer. 266 D1
California Falk . . 208 C2
Norf 121 D7
Calke 114 C1
Callakille 248 A3
Callander 217 D6
Callaughton. . . . 95 B4
Callestick 4 B2
Calligarry. 247 D5
Callington 6 A2
Callow. 78 D2
Callow End . . . 79 C6
Callow Hill Wilts . 44 A4
Worcs. 95 D5
Callows Grave. . . 78 A3
Calmore 32 D2
Calmsden 63 C6
Calne. 44 B4
Calow 131 B4
Calshot 18 A3
Calstock 6 A3
Calstone
Wellington . . . 44 C4
Calthorpe. 120 B3
Calthwaite 164 A2
Calton N Yorks . . 146 B3
Staffs. 129 D6
Calveley 127 D5
Calver 130 B2
Calverhall. 111 B5
Calver Hill 78 C1
Calverleigh . . . 27 D4
Calverley 147 D6
Calvert 66 A2
Calverton
M Keynes 83 D4
Notts 115 A4
Calvine 230 B2
Calvo 174 C4
Cam 62 D3
Camas-luinie . . 249 D6
Camasnacroise . 236 D2
Camastianavaig . 247 A4
Camasunary . . 247 C4
Camault Muir . . 251 B7
Camb. 284 D7
Camber. 38 D1
Camberley 47 C6
Camberwell. . . . 49 B6
Camblesforth . . 141 A4
Cambo 178 A2
Cambois 179 A5
Camborne 3 A4
Cambourne . . . 85 B5
Cambridge Cambs. 85 B6
Glos 62 C3
Cambridge Town 51 A6
Cambus 207 A6
Cambusavie
Farm. 264 A3
Cambusbarron . 207 A5
Cambuskenneth 207 A6
Cambuslang . . . 205 B6
Cambusmore
Lodge. 264 A3
Camden 49 A5
Camelford 10 C2
Camelsdale . . . 34 C1
Camerory 253 C6
Camer's Green . 79 D5
Camerton Bath. . 43 D5
Cumb 162 A3
E Yorks 143 A4
Camghouran . . 229 C4
Cammachmore. . 245 C6
Cammeringham 133 A4
Camore 264 A3
Campbeltown . . 190 C3
Camperdown . . 179 B4
Camp Hill 97 B6
Campmuir . . . 220 A2
Campsall 140 B3
Campsey Ash. . . 88 B4
Campton 84 D3
Camptown . . . 187 B5
Camrose 55 B5
Camserney . . . 230 D2
Camster 281 D4

Camuschoirk. . . . 235 D6
Camuscross. . . . 247 C5
Camusnagaul
Highld. 237 B4
Highld. 262 B2
Camusrory 238 C2
Camusteel 249 B4
Camusterrach. . . 249 B4
Camusvrachan . 229 D5
Canada 32 D1
Canadia 23 A5
Canal Side 141 B4
Candacraig Ho. . 243 A6
Candlesby 135 C4
Candy Mill 195 B5
Cane End 47 B4
Canewdon . . . 70 D2
Canford Bottom . 17 A4
Canford Cliffs . . 17 C4
Canford Magna. . 17 B4
Canham's Green . 87 A6
Canholes 129 B5
Canisbay. 281 A5
Cann 30 C2
Cannard's Grave . 29 A6
Cann Common . 30 C2
Cannich 251 C5
Cannington . . . 28 B2
Cannock 96 A2
Cannock Wood ..112 D4
Canonbie 175 A6
Canon Bridge . . 78 C2
Canon Frome . . 79 C4
Canon Pyon . . . 78 C2
Canons Ashby . . 82 B2
Canonstown . . 2 B3
Canterbury. . . . 52 D3
Cantley Norf . . . 105 A4
S Yorks 140 C4
Cantlop. 94 A3
Canton 41 D6
Cantraybruich. . . 252 B3
Cantraydoune . . 252 B3
Cantraywood . . 252 B3
Cantsfield 155 D5
Canvey Island . . 51 A4
Canwick 133 C4
Canworthy Water. 10 B3
Caol 237 B5
Caolas 222 C3
Caolas
Scalpaigh 288 H3
Caolas Stocinis . 288 H2
Caol Ila 201 A4
Capel. 35 B4
Capel Bangor . . 91 D4
Capel Betws
Lleucu 75 C5
Capel Carmel . . 106 D1
Capel Coch . . . 123 B4
Capel Curig . . . 124 D2
Capel Cynon . . 73 B6
Capel Dewi Carms 58 C1
Ceredig 58 A1
Ceredig 90 D4
Capel Garmon . 124 D3
Capel-gwyn . . . 122 C3
Capel Gwyn . . . 58 C1
Capel Gwynfe . . 59 C4
Capel Hendre . . 57 A5
Capel Hermon . 108 C2
Capel Isaac . . . 58 C2
Capel Iwan. . . . 73 C5
Capel le Ferne . 39 B4
Capel Llanilltern . 41 C5
Capel Mawr . . . 123 C4
Capel St Andrew 89 C4
Capel St Mary . . 88 D1
Capel Seion . . . 75 A5
Capel Tygwydd . 73 B5
Capel Uchaf. . . . 107 A4
Capelulo. 124 B2
Capel-y-graig. . . 123 D5
Capenhurst . . . 126 B3
Capernwray. . . . 154 D4
Capheaton . . . 178 A2
Cappercleuch . . 196 D1
Capplegill 185 B4
Capton 8 B2
Caputh 219 A5
Carbis Bay . . . 2 B3
Carbost Highld . . 246 A2

Carbost *continued*
Highld. 259 D4
Carbrook 130 A3
Carbrooke 103 A5
Carburton 131 B6
Carcant 196 A2
Carcary 233 C4
Carclaze 5 B5
Car Colston 115 A5
Carcroft 140 B3
Cardenden. 209 A5
Cardeston 110 D2
Cardiff
(Caerdydd) 41 D6
Cardigan
(Aberteifi). 73 B4
Cardington
Bedford 84 C2
Shrops 94 B3
Cardinham. 5 A6
Cardonald 205 B5
Cardow. 254 B2
Cardrona 196 C2
Cardross. 206 C1
Cardurnock 175 C4
Careby 116 D3
Careston Castle .232 C3
Carew 55 D6
Carew Cheriton . .55 D6
Carew Newton . . .55 D6
Carey. 78 D3
Carfrae 210 D2
Cargenbridge . . .174 A2
Cargill 219 A6
Cargo 175 C6
Cargreen 6 A3
Carham. 198 C2
Carhampton 27 A5
Carharrack. 4 C2
Carie Perth 217 A6
Perth 229 C5
Carines 4 B2
Carisbrooke 18 C3
Cark. 154 D2
Carlabhagh 288 C3
Carland Cross 4 B3
Carlby 116 D3
Carlecotes 139 C4
Carlesmoor 157 D5
Carleton Cumb . .164 C3
Cumb 176 D2
Lancs 144 D3
N Yorks 146 C3
Carleton
Forehoe 104 A1
Carleton Rode. . .104 B2
Carlingcott 43 D5
Carlin How. 169 D5
Carlisle 175 C7
Carlops 195 A6
Carlton Bedford . .83 B6
Cambs 86 B2
Leics 97 A6
Notts 115 A4
N Yorks. 140 A4
N Yorks 157 C4
N Yorks. 159 C5
N Yorks 167 D4
Stockton. 167 C6
Suff 89 A4
S Yorks 139 B6
W Yorks 139 A6
Carlton Colville .105 C6
Carlton Curlieu . .98 B3
Carlton
Husthwaite . . .158 D3
Carlton in
Cleveland 158 A4
Carlton in
Lindrick 131 A5
Carlton le
Moorland 133 D4
Carlton Miniott .158 C2
Carlton on
Trent. 132 C2
Carlton Scroop .116 A2
Carluke 194 A3
Carmarthen
(Caerfyrddin) . .73 D7
Carmel Anglesey .122 B3
Carms 57 A5
Flint 125 B6

Carmel *continued*
Guern. 6
Gwyn 107 A4
Carmont 245 D5
Carmunnock 205 C6
Carmyle 205 B6
Carmyllie 232 D3
Carnaby 151 A4
Carnach Highld. . .250 D2
Highld. 262 A2
W Isles 288 H3
Carnachy 278 C3
Càrnais 287 A5
Carnbee 221 D5
Carnbo 219 D5
Carnbrea 3 A4
Carnduff 205 D6
Carnduncan 200 B2
Carne 4 D4
Carnforth 154 D3
Carn-gorm 249 D6
Carnhedryn 54 B4
Carnhell Green 3 B4
Carnkie Corn 3 B4
Corn. 4 D2
Carno 92 B3
Carnoch Highld . .251 A4
Highld. 251 C5
Carnock 208 B3
Carnon Downs 4 C2
Carnousie 268 D1
Carnoustie. 221 A5
Carnwath 195 B4
Carnyorth 2 B1
Carperby 156 C4
Carpley Green . . .156 C3
Carr 140 D3
Carradale. 190 B4
Carragraich 288 H2
Carrbridge. 253 D5
Carrefour Selous
Jersey 6
Carreglefn 122 B3
Carreg-wen 73 B5
Carr Hill 179 C4
Carrick Argyll 214 D2
Fife. 220 B4
Carrick Castle . . .215 C4
Carrick Ho. 282 D6
Carriden 208 B3
Carrington
Gtr Man 137 D6
Lincs. 134 D3
Midloth. 209 D6
Carrog Conwy . . .108 A2
Denb. 109 A6
Carron Falk. 208 B1
Moray. 254 B3
Carronbridge . . .183 C6
Carron Bridge . . .207 B5
Carronshore 208 B1
Carrshield 165 A6
Carrutherstown .174 A4
Carrville 167 A6
Carsaig Argyll . . .213 D5
Argyll 225 D4
Carscreugh 171 B4
Carsegowan 171 B6
Carse Gray. 232 C2
Carse Ho. 202 B2
Carseriggan. 171 A5
Carsethorn. 174 C2
Carshalton. 49 C5
Carsington. 130 D2
Carskiey 190 E2
Carsluith 171 B6
Carsphairn. 182 C3
Carstairs 194 B4
Carstairs
Junction 195 B4
Carswell Marsh . .64 D4
Carter's Clay 32 C2
Carterton 64 C3
Carterway
Heads. 178 D2
Carthew 5 B5
Carthorpe 157 C7
Cartington 188 C3
Cartland 194 B3
Cartmel. 154 D2
Cartmel Fell 154 C3
Carway 57 B4

Cary Fitzpaine. . . .29 C5
Cascob 77 A6
Cashlie 228 D3
Cashmoor 30 D3
Cassey Compton . 63 B6
Cassington 65 B5
Cassop 167 B6
Castell. 125 C6
Castellau 41 C5
Castell-Howell . . .74 D3
Castell-y-bwch . . .61 D4
Casterton. 155 D5
Castle Acre 119 D5
Castle Ashby 83 B5
Castle Bolton . . .156 B4
Castle Bromwich . 96 C4
Castle Bytham. . .116 D2
Castlebythe 55 B6
Castle
Donington. 114 C2
Castle Douglas . .173 B5
Castle Eaton 64 D2
Castle Eden. 168 B2
Castlefairn 183 D5
Castle Forbes . . .244 A3
Castleford 140 A2
Castle Frome 79 C4
Castle Green 48 C2
Castle Gresley. . .113 D6
Castle Heaton . . .198 B3
Castle
Hedingham. 86 D3
Castlehill
Borders 195 C7
Highld. 280 B3
W Dunb 206 C1
Castle Hill 37 B4
Castle Huntly. . . .220 B3
Castle Kennedy . 170 B3
Castlemaddy 182 D3
Castlemartin 55 E5
Castlemilk
Dumfries 174 A4
Glasgow. 205 C6
Castlemorris 55 A5
Castlemorton 79 D5
Castle O'er. 185 C5
Castle
Pulverbatch 94 A2
Castle Rising 118 C3
Castleside 166 A3
Castle Stuart 252 B3
Castlethorpe 83 C5
Castleton Angus. .232 D1
Argyll 214 D1
Derbys 129 A6
Gtr Man 138 B1
Newport. 42 A1
N Yorks 159 A5
Castletown
Ches W. 127 D4
Highld. 252 B3
Highld. 280 B3
IoM 152 E2
T&W 179 D5
Castleweary 186 C3
Castley 147 C6
Caston 103 B5
Castor 100 B3
Catacol 203 D4
Catbrain 43 A4
Catbrook 61 C7
Catchall 2 C2
Catchems Corner . 97 D5
Catchgate 178 D3
Catcleugh 187 C6
Catcliffe 131 A4
Catcott 28 B3
Caterham. 35 A6
Catfield. 121 C5
Catfirth. 285 H6
Catford 49 B6
Catforth 145 D4
Cathays 41 D6

Cathcart 205 B5
Cathedine 60 A3
Catherington. 33 D5
Catherton. 95 D4
Catlodge. 241 C4
Catlowdy 176 B2
Catmore 46 A2
Caton. 145 A5
Caton Green 145 A5
Catrine 193 C5
Cat's Ash 61 D5
Catsfield. 23 A5
Catshill 96 D2
Cattal 148 B3
Cattawade 88 D2
Catterall 145 C4
Catterick 157 B6
Catterick Bridge 157 B6
Catterick
Garrison 157 B5
Catterlen 164 B2
Catterline 233 A6
Catterton 148 C4
Catthorpe 98 D2
Catton Northumb .177 D6
N Yorks 158 D3
Catwick 151 C4
Catworth 100 D2
Caudlesprings. . .103 A5
Caulcott 65 A6
Cauldcots 233 D4
Cauldhame 207 A4
Cauldmill 186 B4
Cauldon 113 A4
Caulkerbush 174 C2
Caulside 176 A2
Caunsall 95 C6
Caunton 132 D2
Causewayend . . .195 C5
Causeway End. . .171 A6
Causeway Foot . .147 D4
Causewayhead . .174 C4
Causeway-head 207 A5
Causeyend. 245 A6
Causey Park
Bridge 189 D4
Cautley 155 B5
Cavendish 87 C4
Cavendish
Bridge 114 C2
Cavenham. 86 A3
Caversfield 65 A6
Caversham. 47 B5
Caverswall 112 A3
Cavil 149 D6
Cawdor 253 B4
Cawkwell 134 B2
Cawood 149 D4
Cawsand. 6 B3
Cawston 120 C3
Cawthorne 139 C5
Cawthorpe 116 C3
Cawton 159 D5
Caxton. 85 B5
Caynham 94 D3
Caythorpe Lincs. .116 A2
Notts 115 A4
Cayton 161 C4
Ceann a Bhaigh .287 H2
Ceannacroc
Lodge 239 A6
Ceann a Deas Loch
Baghas-
dail 286 D2
Ceann Shiphoirt 288 F3
Ceann
Tarabhaigh . . .288 F3
Cearsiadair 288 E4
Cefn Berain 125 C4
Cefn-brith 125 D4
Cefn Canol 110 B1
Cefn-coch 124 C3
Cefn Coch 109 C6
Cefn-coed-y-
cymmer 60 C2
Cefn Cribwr. 40 C3
Cefn Cross 40 C3
Cefn-ddwysarn. .109 B6
Cefn Einion 93 C6
Cefneithin 57 A5
Cefn-gorwydd . . .76 C3

Cefn-mawr 110 A1
Cefn-y-bedd. 126 D3
Cefn-y-pant 73 D7
Cei-bach 73 A7
Ceint 123 C4
Cellan 75 D5
Cellarhead 112 A3
Cemaes. 122 A3
Cemmaes 91 B6
Cemmaes Road . .91 B6
Cenarth. 73 B5
Cenin. 107 B4
Central 204 A2
Ceos 288 E4
Ceres. 220 C4
Cerne Abbas 15 A6
Cerney Wick 63 D6
Cerrigceinwen . .123 C4
Cerrigydrudion. .109 A4
Cessford 187 A6
Ceunant 123 D5
Chaceley 79 D6
Chacewater. 4 C2
Chackmore 82 D3
Chacombe 82 C1
Chadderton 138 C2
Chaddesden 114 B1
Chaddesley
Corbett. 96 D1
Chaddleworth . . .46 B2
Chadlington. 64 A4
Chadshunt 81 B6
Chad Valley 96 C3
Chadwell 115 C5
Chadwell St Mary. 50 B3
Chadwick End. . . .97 D5
Chadwick
Green 136 D4
Chaffcombe. 28 D3
Chagford 12 C2
Chailey 22 A1
Chain Bridge 117 A6
Chainhurst 37 B5
Chalbury 17 A4
Chalbury
Common 17 A4
Chaldon 35 A6
Chaldon Herring
or. 16 C1
Chale. 18 D3
Chale Green 18 D3
Chalfont
Common 67 D6
Chalfont St Giles .67 D5
Chalfont St Peter 67 D6
Chalford 63 C4
Chalgrove 66 D2
Chalk 50 B3
Challacombe. 26 A1
Challoch 171 A5
Challock 52 D2
Chalton C Beds . . .67 A6
Hants 33 D6
Chalvington 22 B3
Chancery 75 A4
Chandler's Ford . .32 C3
Channel Tunnel . .38 B3
Channerwick 285 L6
Chantry Som. 29 A7
Suff 88 C2
Chapel 209 A5
Chapel Allerton
Som 42 D3
W Yorks 148 D2
Chapel Amble 9 D5
Chapel Brampton 83 A4
Chapel Chorlton . 112 B2
Chapel End. 97 B6
Chapel-en-le-
Frith 129 A5
Chapelgate 117 C7
Chapel Green
Warks 82 A1
Warks 97 C5
Chapel
Haddlesey 140 A3
Chapelhall 207 D5
Chapel Head 101 C5

Chapelhill
Dumfries 184 C3
Highld. 265 C4
N Ayrs 204 D2
Perth 219 A5
Perth 220 B2
Chapel Hill
Aberds 257 C5
Lincs. 134 D2
Mon 62 D1
N Yorks. 148 C2
Chapelknowe . . .175 A6
Chapel Lawn 93 D7
Chapel-le-Dale .155 D6
Chapel Milton . . .129 A5
Chapel of
Garioch 256 D2
Chapel Row 46 C3
Chapel St
Leonards 135 B5
Chapel Stile. 154 A2
Chapelton Angus 233 D4
Devon. 25 C6
Highld. 242 A4
S Lanark. 194 B1
Chapeltown
Blackburn. 137 B6
Moray. 254 D3
S Yorks 139 D6
Chapmanslade . . .30 A2
Chapmans Well . .11 B4
Chapmore End . . .68 B3
Chappel 70 A2
Chard 14 A3
Chardstock 14 A3
Charfield 62 D3
Charford. 80 A2
Charing 38 A1
Charing Cross. . . .31 D5
Charing Heath . . .38 A1
Charingworth 81 D5
Charlbury 65 B4
Charlcombe. 43 C6
Charlecote. 81 B5
Charles 26 B1
Charlesfield 175 B4
Charleston
Angus. 232 D1
Renfs 205 B4
Charlestown
Aberdeen 245 B6
Corn 5 B5
Derbys 138 D3
Dorset 15 D6
Fife. 208 B3
Gtr Man 137 C7
Highld. 252 B2
Highld. 261 C5
W Yorks 138 A2
Charlestown of
Aberlour 254 B3
Charles Tye 87 B6
Charlesworth 138 D3
Charleton 7 C6
Charlton Hants. . . .32 A2
Herts 68 A1
London 49 B7
Northants. 82 D2
Northumb. 177 A6
Som 43 D5
Telford 111 D4
Wilts. 30 C3
Wilts. 44 A3
Wilts. 45 D5
Worcs. 80 C3
W Sus. 20 A1
Charlton Abbots. .63 A6
Charlton Adam . . .29 C5
Charlton-All-
Saints 31 C5
Charlton
Horethorne 29 C6
Charlton Kings . . .63 A5
Charlton
Mackerell 29 C5
Charlton
Marshall 16 A2

Charlton
Musgrove.....29 C7
Charlton on
Otmoor.....65 B6
Charltons.....168 D4
Charlwood.....35 B5
Charlynch.....28 B2
Charminster.....15 B6
Charmouth.....14 B3
Charndon.....66 A2
Charney Bassett..65 D4
Charnock
Richard.....137 B4
Charsfield.....88 B3
Chart Corner.....37 A5
Charter Alley.....46 D3
Charterhouse.....42 D3
Charterville
Allotments.....64 B4
Chartham.....52 D3
Chartham Hatch..52 D3
Chartridge.....67 C5
Chart Sutton.....37 B6
Charvil.....47 B5
Charwelton.....82 B2
Chasetown.....96 A3
Chastleton.....64 A3
Chasty.....10 A4
Chatburn.....146 C1
Chatcull.....112 B1
Chatham.....51 C4
Chathill.....189 A4
Chattenden.....51 B4
Chatteris.....101 C5
Chattisham.....88 C1
Chatto.....187 B6
Chatton.....188 A3
Chawleigh.....26 D2
Chawley.....65 C5
Chawston.....84 B3
Chawton.....33 B6
Cheadle Gtr Man .128 A3
Staffs.....112 A4
Cheadle Heath..128 A3
Cheadle Hulme..128 A3
Cheam.....49 C5
Cheapside.....34 A3
Chearsley.....66 B3
Chebsey.....112 C2
Checkendon.....47 A4
Checkley Ches E..111 A6
Hereford.....78 D3
Staffs.....112 B4
Chedburgh.....86 B3
Cheddar.....42 D3
Cheddington.....67 B5
Cheddleton.....129 D4
Cheddon
Fitzpaine.....28 C2
Chedglow.....63 D5
Chedgrave.....105 B4
Chedington.....15 A4
Chediston.....105 D4
Chedworth.....63 B6
Chedzoy.....28 B3
Cheeklaw.....198 A1
Cheeseman's
Green.....38 B2
Cheglinch.....25 A6
Cheldon.....26 D2
Chelford.....128 B3
Chellaston.....114 B1
Chell Heath.....128 D3
Chellington.....83 B6
Chelmarsh.....95 C5
Chelmer Village..70 C1
Chelmondiston...88 D3
Chelmorton.....129 C6
Chelmsford.....69 C7
Chelsea.....49 B5
Chelsfield.....50 C1
Chelsworth.....87 C5
Cheltenham.....63 A5
Chelveston.....84 A1
Chelvey.....42 C3
Chelwood.....43 C5
Chelwood
Common.....36 D2
Chelwood Gate..36 D2

Chelworth.....63 D5
Chelworth Green 64 D1
Chemistry.....111 A4
Chenies.....67 D6
Cheny Longville..94 C2
Chepstow (Cas-
gwent).....62 D1
Chequerfield.....140 A2
Cherhill.....44 B4
Cherington Glos ..63 D5
Warks.....81 D5
Cheriton Devon ..26 A2
Hants.....33 C4
Kent.....38 B3
Swansea.....57 C4
Cheriton Bishop..12 B2
Cheriton
Fitzpaine.....12 A3
Cheriton or
Stackpole
Elidor.....55 E5
Cherrington.....111 C5
Cherrybank.....219 B6
Cherry Burton..150 C2
Cherry Hinton....85 B6
Cherry Orchard ..79 B6
Cherry
Willingham.....133 B5
Chertsey.....48 C3
Cheselbourne....16 B1
Chesham.....67 C5
Chesham Bois....67 D5
Cheshunt.....68 C3
Chesley Hay.....96 A2
Chessington.....49 C4
Chester.....127 C4
Chesterblade.....29 A6
Chesterfield.....130 B3
Chester-Le-
Street.....179 D4
Chester Moor ...167 A5
Chesters Borders .187 A5
Borders.....187 B5
Chesterton Cambs .85 A6
Cambs.....100 B3
Glos.....63 C6
Oxon.....65 A6
Shrops.....95 B5
Staffs.....112 A2
Warks.....81 B6
Chesterwood....177 C6
Chestfield.....52 C3
Cheston.....7 B5
Cheswardine.....111 C6
Cheswick.....198 B4
Chetnole.....15 A6
Chettiscombe....27 D4
Chettisham.....102 C1
Chettle.....30 D3
Chetton.....95 B4
Chetwode.....66 A2
Chetwynd Aston 111 D6
Cheveley.....86 A2
Chevening.....36 A2
Chevington.....86 B3
Chevithorne.....27 D4
Chew Magna....43 C4
Chew Stoke.....43 C4
Chewton
Keynsham.....43 C5
Chewton Mendip 43 D4
Chicheley.....83 C6
Chichester.....20 B1
Chickerell.....15 C6
Chicklade.....30 B3
Chicksgrove.....30 B3
Chidden.....33 D5
Chiddingfold....34 C2
Chiddingly.....22 A3
Chiddingstone....36 B2
Chiddingstone
Causeway.....36 B3
Chiddingstone
Hoath.....36 B2
Chideock.....14 B4
Chidham.....19 A6
Chidswell.....139 A5
Chieveley.....46 B2
Chignall St
James.....69 C6
Chignall Smealy..69 B6
Chigwell.....68 D4

Chigwell Row.....69 D4
Chilbolton.....32 B2
Chilcomb.....32 C4
Chilcombe.....15 B5
Chilcompton.....43 D5
Chilcote.....113 D6
Childer
Thornton.....126 B3
Child Okeford....30 D2
Childrey.....46 A1
Child's Ercall....111 C5
Childswickham...80 D3
Childwall.....127 A4
Childwick Green ..67 B7
Chilfrome.....15 B5
Chilgrove.....20 A1
Chilham.....52 D2
Chilhampton.....31 B4
Chilla.....11 A5
Chillaton.....11 C5
Chillenden.....53 D4
Chillerton.....18 C3
Chillesford.....89 B4
Chillingham.....188 A3
Chillington Devon .. 8 C1
Som.....28 D3
Chilmark.....30 B3
Chilson.....64 B4
Chilsworthy Corn..11 D5
Devon.....10 A4
Chilthorne
Domer.....29 D5
Chiltington.....22 A1
Chilton Bucks.....66 B2
Durham.....167 C5
Oxon.....46 A2
Chilton Cantelo ..29 C5
Chilton Foliat....45 B7
Chilton Lane....167 B6
Chilton Polden....28 B3
Chilton Street....86 C3
Chilton Trinity....28 B2
Chilvers Coton....97 B6
Chilwell.....114 B3
Chilworth Hants...32 D3
Sur.....34 B3
Chimney.....65 C4
Chineham.....47 D4
Chingford.....68 D3
Chinley.....129 A5
Chinley Head....129 A5
Chinnor.....66 C3
Chipnall.....111 B6
Chippenhall
Green.....104 D3
Chippenham
Cambs.....86 A2
Wilts.....44 B3
Chipperfield.....67 C6
Chipping Herts....85 D5
Lancs.....145 C6
Chipping
Campden.....81 D4
Chipping Hill.....70 B2
Chipping Norton ..64 A4
Chipping Ongar ..69 C5
Chipping
Sodbury.....43 A6
Chipping Warden 82 C1
Chipstable.....27 C5
Chipstead Kent ...36 A2
Sur.....35 A5
Chirbury.....93 B6
Chirk (Y Waun)..110 B1
Chirk Bank.....110 B1
Chirmorrie.....181 D4
Chirnside.....198 A2
Chirnsidebridge 198 A2
Chirton.....45 D4
Chisbury.....45 C6
Chiselborough....29 D4
Chiseldon.....45 B5
Chiserley.....138 A3
Chislehampton...65 D6
Chislehurst.....50 B1
Chislet.....53 C4
Chiswell Green....67 C7
Chiswick.....49 B5
Chiswick End....85 C5
Chisworth.....138 D2
Chithurst.....34 D1
Chittering.....101 D6

Chitterne.....30 A3
Chittlehamholt...26 C1
Chittlehampton...26 C1
Chittoe.....44 C3
Chivenor.....25 B6
Chobham.....48 C2
Choicelee.....197 A6
Cholderton.....31 A6
Cholesbury.....67 C5
Chollerford.....177 B7
Chollerton.....178 B1
Cholmondeston.127 C6
Cholsey.....46 A3
Cholstrey.....78 B2
Chop Gate.....159 B4
Choppington.....179 A4
Chopwell.....178 D3
Chorley Ches E...127 D5
Lancs.....137 B4
Shrops.....95 C4
Staffs.....113 D4
Chorleywood.....67 D6
Chorlton cum
Hardy.....137 D7
Chorlton Lane...110 A3
Choulton.....94 C1
Chowdene.....179 D4
Chowley.....127 D4
Chrishall.....85 D6
Christchurch
Cambs.....101 B6
Dorset.....17 B5
Glos.....62 B1
Newport.....42 A2
Christian Malford..44 B3
Christleton.....127 C4
Christmas
Common.....66 D3
Christon.....42 D2
Christon Bank...189 A5
Christow.....12 C3
Chryston.....207 C4
Chudleigh.....12 D3
Chudleigh
Knighton.....12 D3
Chulmleigh.....26 D1
Chunal.....138 D3
Church.....137 A6
Churcham.....62 B3
Church Aston....111 D6
Churchbank.....93 D7
Church
Brampton.....83 A4
Churchbridge....96 A2
Church
Broughton.....113 B6
Church
Crookham.....47 D6
Churchdown.....63 B4
Church Eaton....112 D2
Churchend Essex..69 A6
Essex.....71 A4
S Glos.....62 D3
Church End
Cambs.....100 C4
Cambs.....101 A5
C Beds.....67 A5
C Beds.....84 D1
C Beds.....84 D3
Essex.....69 A7
Essex.....86 C1
E Yorks.....150 B3
Hants.....47 D4
Lincs.....117 B5
Warks.....97 B5
Warks.....97 B5
Wilts.....44 B4
Church Enstone....65 A4
Church Fenton...148 D4
Churchfield.....96 B3
Churchgate
Street.....69 B4
Church Green
Devon.....14 B1
Norf.....103 B6
Church Gresley..113 D6
Church
Hanborough....65 B5
Church Hill.....127 C6
Church Houses..159 B5
Churchill Devon...14 A3
Devon.....25 A6

Churchill continued
N Som.....42 D3
Oxon.....64 A3
Worcs.....80 B2
Worcs.....96 D1
Churchinford.....28 D2
Church Knowle...16 C3
Church
Laneham.....132 B3
Church Langton ..99 B4
Church Lawford...98 D1
Church Lawton..128 D3
Church Leigh....112 B4
Church Lench....80 B3
Church
Mayfield.....113 A5
Church
Minshull.....127 C6
Church Norton....20 C1
Churchover.....98 C2
Church Preen....94 B3
Church
Pulverbatch....94 A2
Churchstanton...28 D1
Churchstow.....7 C6
Church Stowe....82 B3
Church Street....51 B4
Church Stretton ..94 B2
Churchtown
Derbys.....130 C2
IoM.....152 B4
Lancs.....145 C4
Mers.....136 B2
Church Town
N Lincs.....141 C5
Sur.....35 A6
Church Village....41 C5
Church Warsop .131 C5
Churnsike
Lodge.....177 B4
Churston Ferrers.. 8 B3
Churt.....34 C1
Churton.....127 D4
Churwell.....139 A5
Chute Standen....45 D7
Chwilog.....107 C4
Chyandour.....2 B2
Cilan Uchaf....106 D2
Cilcain.....126 C1
Cilcennin.....75 B4
Cilfor.....107 C6
Cilfrew.....40 A2
Cilfynydd.....41 B5
Cilgerran.....73 B4
Cilgwyn Carms....59 C4
Gwyn.....107 A4
Pembs.....72 C3
Ciliau Aeron.....74 C3
Cill Donnain....286 D3
Cille Bhrighde...286 E3
Cille Pheadair...286 E3
Cilmery.....76 B4
Cilsan.....58 C2
Ciltalgarth.....108 A3
Cilwendeg.....73 C5
Cilybebyll.....40 A2
Cilycwm.....59 B4
Cimla.....40 B2
Cinderford.....62 B2
Cippyn.....72 B4
Circebost.....288 D2
Cirencester.....63 C6
Ciribhig.....288 C2
City London.....49 A6
Powys.....93 C6
City Dulas.....123 B4
Clachaig.....215 D4
Clachan Argyll...202 C2
Argyll.....213 A5
Argyll.....215 A4
Argyll.....226 B3
Highld.....248 C2
W Isles.....286 B3
Clachaneasy....181 D5
Clachanmore....170 C2
Clachan na Luib 287 H3
Clachan of
Campsie.....205 A6
Clachan of
Glendaruel.....214 D2
Clachan-Seil....213 A5

Clachan
Strachur.....214 B3
Clachbreck.....202 A2
Clachnabrain....232 B1
Clachtoll.....270 B3
Clackmannan....208 A2
Clacton-on-Sea.. 71 B5
Cladach
Chireboist.....287 H2
Claddach-
knockline.....287 H2
Cladich.....227 D5
Claggan Highld...225 B5
Highld.....237 B5
Claigan.....258 C2
Claines.....79 B6
Clandown.....43 D5
Clanfield Hants ...33 D5
Oxon.....64 C3
Clanville.....32 A2
Claonaig.....202 C3
Claonel.....272 D3
Clapgate Dorset...17 A4
Herts.....68 A4
Clapham Bedford..84 B2
London.....49 B5
N Yorks.....146 A1
W Sus.....20 B3
Clap Hill.....38 B2
Clappers.....198 A3
Clappersgate....154 A2
Clapton.....14 A4
Clapton-in-
Gordano.....42 B3
Clapton-on-the-
Hill.....64 B2
Clapworthy.....26 C1
Clarach.....90 D4
Clarbeston.....55 B6
Clarbeston Road..55 B6
Clarborough....132 A2
Clardon.....280 B3
Clare.....86 C3
Clarebrand.....173 B5
Clarencefield....174 B3
Clarilaw.....186 B4
Clark's Green....35 C4
Clarkston.....205 C5
Clashandorran..251 B7
Clashcoig.....264 A2
Clashindarroch..255 C5
Clashmore
Highld.....264 B3
Highld.....270 A3
Clashnessie.....270 A3
Clashnoir.....254 D3
Clate.....285 G7
Clathy.....219 C4
Clatt.....255 D6
Clatter.....92 B3
Clatterford.....18 C3
Clatterin Bridge 233 A4
Clatworthy.....27 B5
Claughton Lancs .145 A5
Lancs.....145 C5
Mers.....126 A3
Claverdon.....81 A4
Claverham.....42 C3
Clavering.....85 D6
Claverley.....95 B5
Claverton.....44 C1
Clawdd-
newydd.....125 D5
Clawthorpe.....154 D4
Clawton.....11 B4
Claxby Lincs.....135 B4
Lincs.....142 D3
Claxton Norf.....104 A4
N Yorks.....149 A5
Claybokie.....242 D3
Claybrooke
Magna.....98 C1
Claybrooke Parva 98 C1
Clay Common....105 C5
Clay Coton.....98 D2
Clay Cross.....130 C3
Claydon Oxon....82 B1
Suff.....88 B2
Claygate
Dumfries.....175 A6
Kent.....37 B5

Claygate *continued*
Sur 49 C4
Claygate Cross 36 A4
Clayhanger Devon 27 C5
W Mid 96 A3
Clayhidon 27 D6
Clayhill E Sus 37 D6
Hants 18 A2
Clay Hill 46 B3
Clay Lake 117 C5
Clayock 280 C3
Claypole 115 A6
Clayton Staffs 112 A2
S Yorks 140 C2
W Sus 21 A5
W Yorks 147 D5
Clayton Green 137 A4
Clayton-le-Moors 146 D1
Clayton-le-Woods 137 A4
Clayton West 139 B5
Clayworth 132 A2
Cleadale 234 B3
Cleadon 179 C5
Clearbrook 7 A4
Clearwell 62 C1
Cleasby 167 D5
Cleat 283 J5
Cleatlam 166 D4
Cleator 162 C3
Cleator Moor 162 C3
Clebrig 272 A3
Cleckheaton 139 A4
Cleedownton 94 C3
Cleehill 94 D3
Clee St Margaret 94 C3
Cleethorpes 143 C5
Cleeton St Mary 95 D4
Cleeve 42 C3
Cleeve Hill 63 A5
Cleeve Prior 80 C3
Clegyrnant 91 B7
Clehonger 78 D2
Cleish 208 A3
Cleland 194 A3
Clench Common 45 C5
Clenchwarton 118 C2
Clent 96 D2
Cleobury Mortimer 95 D4
Cleobury North 95 C4
Cleongart 190 B2
Clephanton 253 A4
Clerklands 186 A4
Clestrain 283 G4
Cleuch Head 187 B4
Cleughbrae 174 A3
Clevancy 45 B4
Clevedon 42 B3
Cleveley 65 A4
Cleveleys 144 C3
Cleverton 44 A3
Clevis 40 D3
Clewer 42 D3
Cley next the Sea 120 A2
Cliaid 286 F2
Cliasmol 287 D5
Cliburn 164 C3
Click Mill 282 E4
Cliddesden 33 A5
Cliffburn 233 D4
Cliffe Medway 51 B4
N Yorks 149 D5
Cliff End 23 A6
Cliffe Woods 51 B4
Clifford Hereford 77 C6
W Yorks 148 C3
Clifford Chambers 81 B4
Clifford's Mesne 62 A3
Cliffsend 53 C5
Clifton Bristol 43 B4
C Beds 84 D3
Cumb 164 C3
Derbys 113 A5
Lancs 145 D4
Northumb 179 A4
Nottingham 114 B3
N Yorks 147 C5
Oxon 82 D1
Clifton *continued*
Stirling 216 A3
S Yorks 140 D3
Worcs 79 C6
York 149 B4
Clifton Campville 113 D6
Cliftoncote 187 A7
Clifton Green 137 C6
Clifton Hampden 65 D6
Clifton Reynes 83 B6
Clifton upon Dunsmore 98 D2
Clifton upon Teme 79 A5
Cliftonville 53 B5
Climaen gwyn 59 E4
Climping 20 B3
Climpy 194 A4
Clink 30 A1
Clint 147 B6
Clint Green 120 D2
Clintmains 197 C5
Cliobh 287 A5
Clippesby 121 D6
Clipsham 116 D2
Clipston 99 C4
Clipstone 131 C5
Clitheroe 146 C1
Cliuthar 288 H2
Clive 111 C4
Clivocast 284 C8
Clixby 142 C3
Clocaenog 125 D5
Clochan 267 C5
Clock Face 136 D4
Clockmill 197 A6
Cloddiau 93 A6
Clodock 61 A5
Clola 257 B5
Clophill 84 D2
Clopton
Northants 100 C2
Suff 88 B3
Clopton Corner 88 B3
Clopton Green 86 B3
Closeburn 183 C6
Close Clark 152 D2
Closworth 29 D5
Clothall 85 D4
Clotton 127 C5
Clough Foot 138 A2
Cloughton 160 B4
Cloughton Newlands 160 B4
Clousta 285 H5
Clouston 282 F3
Clova Aberds 255 D5
Angus 232 A1
Clovelly 24 C4
Clove Lodge 166 D2
Clovenfords 196 C3
Clovenstone 245 A4
Clovullin 237 C4
Clow Bridge 137 A7
Clowne 131 B4
Clows Top 95 D5
Cloy 110 A2
Cluanie Inn 239 A4
Cluanie Lodge 239 A4
Clun 93 C7
Clunbury 94 C1
Clunderwen 55 C7
Clune 252 D3
Clunes 239 D6
Clungunford 94 D1
Clunie Aberds 268 D1
Perth 231 D5
Clunton 94 C1
Cluny 209 A5
Cluny Castle 241 C4
Clutton Bath 43 D5
Ches W 127 D4
Clwt-grugoer 125 C4
Clwt-y-bont 123 D5
Clydach Mon 60 B4
Swansea 40 A1
Clydach Vale 41 B4
Clydebank 205 A4
Clydey 73 C5
Clyffe Pypard 45 B4
Clynder 215 D5
Clyne 40 A3
Clynelish 274 D2
Clynnog-fawr 107 A4
Clyro 77 C6
Clyst Honiton 13 B4
Clyst Hydon 13 A5
Clyst St George 13 C4
Clyst St Lawrence 13 A5
Clyst St Mary 13 B4
Cnoc Amhlaigh 288 D6
Cnwch-coch 75 A5
Coachford 255 B5
Coad's Green 10 D3
Coal Aston 130 B3
Coalbrookdale 95 A4
Coalbrookvale 60 C3
Coalburn 194 C3
Coalburns 178 C3
Coalcleugh 165 A6
Coaley 62 C3
Coalhall 182 A2
Coalhill 70 D1
Coalpit Heath 43 A5
Coalport 95 A4
Coalsnaughton 208 A2
Coaltown of Balgonie 209 A5
Coaltown of Wemyss 209 A6
Coalville 114 D2
Coalway 62 B1
Coat 29 C4
Coatbridge 207 D5
Coatdyke 207 D5
Coate Swindon 45 A5
Wilts 44 C4
Coates Cambs 101 B5
Glos 63 C5
Lancs 146 C2
Notts 132 A3
W Sus 20 A2
Coatham 168 C3
Coatham Mundeville 167 C5
Coatsgate 184 B3
Cobbaton 25 C7
Cobbler's Green 104 B3
Coberley 63 B5
Cobham Kent 50 C3
Sur 48 C4
Cobholm Island 105 A6
Cobleland 206 A3
Cobnash 78 A2
Coburty 269 C4
Cockayne 159 B5
Cockayne Hatley 85 C4
Cock Bank 110 A2
Cock Bridge 243 B5
Cockburnspath 211 C4
Cock Clarks 70 C2
Cockenzie and Port Seton 209 C7
Cockerham 145 B4
Cockermouth 163 A4
Cockernhoe Green 67 A7
Cockfield
Durham 166 C4
Suff 87 B5
Cockfosters 68 D2
Cocking 20 A1
Cockington 8 A2
Cocklake 28 A4
Cockley Beck 163 D5
Cockley Cley 102 A3
Cockshutt 110 C3
Cockthorpe 120 A1
Cockwood 13 C4
Cockyard 78 D2
Codda 10 D2
Coddenham 88 B2
Coddington
Ches W 127 D4
Hereford 79 C5
Notts 132 D3
Codford St Mary 30 B3
Codford St Peter 30 B3
Codicote 68 B2
Codmore Hill 34 D3
Codnor 114 A2
Codrington 43 B6
Codsall 95 A6
Codsall Wood 95 A6
Coedely 41 C5
Coedkernew 42 A1
Coed Mawr 123 C5
Coed Morgan 61 B5
Coedpoeth 126 D2
Coed-Talon 126 D2
Coedway 110 D2
Coed-y-bryn 73 B6
Coed-y-paen 61 D5
Coed-yr-ynys 60 A3
Coed Ystumgwern 107 D5
Coelbren 59 D5
Coffinswell 8 A2
Cofton Hackett 96 D3
Cogan 41 D6
Cogenhoe 83 A5
Cogges 65 C4
Coggeshall 70 A2
Coggeshall Hamlet 70 A2
Coggins Mill 36 D3
Coignafearn Lodge 241 A4
Coig Peighinnean 288 A6
Coig Peighinnean Bhuirgh 288 B5
Coilacriech 243 C6
Coilantogle 217 D5
Coilleag 286 E3
Coillore 246 A2
Coity 40 C4
Col 288 C5
Colaboll 272 C3
Colan 4 A3
Colaton Raleigh 13 C5
Colbost 258 D2
Colburn 157 B5
Colby Cumb 165 C4
IoM 152 D2
Norf 120 B4
Colchester 71 A4
Colcot 41 E6
Cold Ash 46 C3
Cold Ashby 98 D3
Cold Ashton 43 B6
Cold Aston 64 B2
Coldbackie 277 C7
Coldbeck 155 A6
Coldblow 50 B2
Cold Blow 55 C7
Cold Brayfield 83 B6
Coldean 21 B6
Coldeast 12 D3
Colden 138 A2
Colden Common 32 C3
Coldfair Green 89 A5
Coldham 101 A6
Cold Hanworth 133 A5
Coldharbour Glos 62 C1
Kent 36 A3
Sur 35 B4
Cold Harbour 116 B2
Cold Hatton 111 C5
Cold Hesledon 168 A2
Cold Higham 82 B3
Coldingham 211 D6
Cold Kirby 158 C4
Cold Newton 99 A4
Cold Northcott 10 C3
Cold Norton 70 C2
Cold Overton 115 D6
Coldrain 219 D5
Coldred 39 A4
Coldridge 12 A1
Coldstream
Angus 220 A3
Borders 198 C2
Coldwaltham 20 A3
Coldwells 257 B6
Coldwells Croft 255 D6
Coldyeld 94 B1
Cole 29 B6
Colebatch 93 C7
Colebrook 13 A5
Colebrooke 12 B2
Coleby Lincs 133 C4
N Lincs 141 B6
Coleford Devon 12 A2
Coleford *continued*
Glos 62 B1
Som 29 A6
Cole Green 68 B2
Cole Henley 46 D2
Colehill 17 A4
Coleman's Hatch 36 C2
Colemere 110 B3
Colemore 33 B6
Coleorton 114 D2
Colerne 44 B2
Colesbourne 63 B5
Colesden 84 B3
Coles Green 88 C1
Cole's Green 88 A3
Coleshill Bucks 67 D5
Oxon 64 D3
Warks 97 C5
Colestocks 13 A5
Colgate 35 C5
Colgrain 206 B1
Colinsburgh 221 D4
Colinton 209 D5
Colintraive 203 A5
Colkirk 119 C6
Collace 220 A2
Collafirth 284 G6
Collaton St Mary 8 B2
College Milton 205 C6
Collessie 220 C2
Collier Row 69 D5
Collier's End 68 A3
Collier's Green 37 C5
Collier Street 37 B5
Colliery Row 167 A6
Collieston 257 D5
Collin 174 A3
Collingbourne Ducis 45 D6
Collingbourne Kingston 45 D6
Collingham
Notts 132 C3
W Yorks 148 C2
Collington 79 A4
Collingtree 83 B4
Collins Green 137 D4
Colliston 233 D4
Collycroft 97 C6
Collynie 256 C3
Collyweston 100 A1
Colmonell 180 C3
Colmworth 84 B3
Colnabaichin 243 B5
Colnbrook 48 B3
Colne Cambs 101 D5
Lancs 146 C2
Colne Edge 146 C2
Colne Engaine 87 D4
Colney 104 A2
Colney Heath 68 C2
Colney Street 67 C7
Coln Rogers 64 C1
Coln St Aldwyn's 64 C2
Coln St Dennis 64 B1
Colpy 256 C1
Colquhar 196 B2
Colsterdale 157 C5
Colsterworth 116 C2
Colston Bassett 115 B4
Coltfield 266 C2
Colthouse 154 B2
Coltishall 121 D4
Coltness 194 A3
Colton Cumb 154 C2
Norf 104 A2
N Yorks 148 C4
Staffs 113 C4
W Yorks 148 D2
Col Uarach 288 D5
Colva 77 B6
Colvend 173 C6
Colvister 284 D7
Colwall Green 79 C5
Colwall Stone 79 C5
Colwell 178 B1
Colwich 112 C4
Colwick 115 A4
Colwinston 40 D4
Colworth 20 B2
Colwyn Bay (Bae Colwyn) 124 B3
Colyford 14 B2
Colyton 14 B2
Combe Hereford 78 A1
Oxon 65 B5
W Berks 46 C1
Combe Common 34 C2
Combe Down 43 C6
Combe Florey 27 B6
Combe Hay 43 D6
Combeinteignhead 13 D4
Combe Martin 25 A6
Combe Moor 78 A1
Combe Raleigh 13 A6
Comberbach 127 B6
Comberton Cambs 85 B5
Hereford 78 A2
Combe St Nicholas 28 D3
Combpyne 14 B2
Combridge 113 B4
Combrook 81 B6
Combs Derbys 129 B5
Suff 87 B6
Combs Ford 87 B6
Combwich 28 A2
Comers 244 B3
Comins Coch 90 D4
Commercial End 86 A1
Commins Capel Betws 75 C5
Commins Coch 91 B6
Commondale 169 D4
Common Edge 144 D3
Commonmoor 6 A1
Commonside 127 B5
Common Side 130 B3
Compstall 138 D2
Compton Devon 8 A2
Hants 32 C3
Sur 34 B1
Sur 34 B2
W Berks 46 B3
Wilts 45 D5
W Sus 33 D6
Compton Abbas 30 D2
Compton Abdale 63 B6
Compton Bassett 44 B4
Compton Beauchamp 45 A6
Compton Bishop 42 D2
Compton Chamberlayne 31 C4
Compton Dando 43 C5
Compton Dundon 29 B4
Compton Martin 43 D4
Compton Pauncefoot 29 C6
Compton Valence 15 B5
Comrie Fife 208 B3
Perth 218 B2
Conaglen House 237 C4
Conchra 214 D3
Concraigie 231 D5
Conder Green 145 B4
Conderton 80 D2
Condicote 64 A2
Condorrat 207 C5
Condover 94 A2
Coneyhurst 35 D4
Coneysthorpe 159 D6
Coneythorpe 148 B2
Coney Weston 103 D5
Conford 33 B7
Congash 253 D6
Congdon's Shop 10 D3
Congerstone 97 A6
Congham 119 C4
Congleton 128 C3
Congl-y-wal 108 A2
Congresbury 42 C3
Congreve 112 D3
Conicavel 253 A5
Coningsby 134 D2
Conington Cambs 85 A5
Cambs 100 C3
Conisbrough 140 D3
Conisby 200 B2

Conisholme.....143 D6
Coniston Cumb...154 B2
E Yorks.........151 D4
Coniston Cold...146 B3
Conistone......146 A3
Connah's Quay..126 C2
Connel.........226 C4
Connel Park....182 A4
Connor Downs...2 B3
Conon Bridge...252 A1
Conon House....252 A1
Cononley......146 C2
Conordan......247 A4
Consall.......112 A3
Consett.......178 D3
Constable
Burton.......157 B5
Constantine.....3 C5
Constantine Bay...9 D4
Contin........251 A6
Contlaw.......245 B5
Conwy.........124 B2
Conyer.........51 C6
Conyers Green...87 A4
Cooden.........23 B5
Cooil.........152 D3
Cookbury.......11 A5
Cookham........48 A1
Cookham Dean...47 A6
Cookham Rise...48 A1
Cookhill.......80 B3
Cookley Suff...104 D4
Worcs..........95 C6
Cookley Green...66 D2
Cookney.......245 C5
Cookridge....147 C6
Cooksbridge....22 A2
Cooksmill Green..69 C6
Coolham........35 D4
Cooling........51 B4
Coombe Corn....4 B4
Corn..........24 D3
Hants..........33 C5
Wilts..........45 D5
Coombe Bissett..31 C5
Coombe Hill....63 A4
Coombe Keynes..16 C2
Coombes........21 B4
Coopersale
Common.......69 C4
Cootham........20 A3
Copdock........88 C2
Copford Green...70 A3
Copgrove......148 A2
Copister.......284 F6
Cople..........84 C3
Copley........166 C3
Coplow Dale...129 B6
Copmanthorpe..149 C4
Coppathorne....10 A3
Coppenhall....112 D3
Coppenhall
Moss.........128 D2
Copperhouse....2 B3
Coppingford...100 C3
Copplestone....12 A2
Coppull.......137 B4
Coppull Moor..137 B4
Copsale........35 D4
Copster Green..145 D6
Copston Magna..98 C3
Copt Heath.....97 D4
Copt Hewick...158 D2
Copthorne
Shrops.......110 D3
Sur...........35 C6
Copt Oak......114 D2
Copy's Green..119 B6
Copythorne.....32 D2
Corbets Tey....50 A2
Corbridge....178 C1
Corby..........99 C5
Corby Glen....116 C2
Cordon........191 B6
Coreley........95 D4
Cores End......48 A2
Corfe..........28 D2
Corfe Castle...16 C3
Corfe Mullen...16 B3

Corfton.........94 C2
Corgarff......243 B5
Corhampton.....33 C5
Corlae........183 C4
Corley.........97 C6
Corley Ash.....97 C5
Corley Moor....97 C5
Cornaa........152 C4
Cornabus......200 D3
Cornel.........124 C2
Corner Row....144 D4
Corney........153 A2
Cornforth.....167 B6
Cornhill......267 D6
Cornhill-on-
Tweed........198 C2
Cornholme.....138 A2
Cornish Hall End..86 D2
Cornquoy......283 H6
Cornsay........166 A4
Cornsay
Colliery.....167 A4
Corntown Highld.252 A1
V Glam.........40 D4
Cornwell.......64 A3
Cornwood.......7 B5
Cornworthy......8 B2
Corpach.......237 B4
Corpusty......120 B3
Corran Highld..237 C4
Highld.........238 B2
Corranbuie....202 B3
Corrany.......152 C4
Corrie........203 D3
Corrie Common..185 D5
Corriecravie..191 C5
Corriedoo.....183 D5
Corriemoillie.263 D5
Corriemulzie
Lodge........263 A5
Corrievarkie
Lodge........229 A4
Corrievorrie..252 D3
Corrimony....251 C5
Corringham
Lincs........141 D6
Thurrock......51 A4
Corris.........91 B5
Corris Uchaf...91 B5
Corrour Shooting
Lodge........228 B3
Corrow........215 B4
Corry.........247 B5
Corrykinloch..271 B6
Corrymuckloch..218 A3
Corrynachenchy..225 B5
Corry of
Ardnagrask...251 B7
Corsback......280 A4
Corscombe.....15 A5
Corse Aberds..255 B7
Glos..........62 A3
Corse Lawn.....79 D6
Corse of Kinnoir 255 B6
Corsewall.....170 A2
Corsham........44 B2
Corsindae.....244 B3
Corsley........30 A2
Corsley Heath..30 A2
Corsock.......173 A5
Corston Bath...43 C5
Wilts..........44 A3
Corstorphine..209 C4
Cors-y-Gedol..107 D5
Cortachy......232 C1
Corton Suff...105 B6
Wilts..........30 A3
Corton Denham..29 C6
Coruanan
Lodge........237 B4
Corunna.......287 H3
Corwen........109 A5
Coryton Devon..11 C5
Thurrock......51 A4
Cosby..........98 B2
Coseley........96 B2
Cosgrove.......83 C4
Cosham.........19 A5
Cosheston......55 D6
Cossall.......114 A2
Cossington Leics 115 D4
Som...........28 A3
Costa.........282 E4

Costessey.....120 D3
Costock.......114 C3
Coston........115 C6
Cote...........64 C4
Cotebrook.....127 C5
Cotehill......176 D2
Cotes Cumb....154 C3
Leics.........114 C3
Staffs........112 B2
Cotesbach......98 C2
Cotgrave.....115 B4
Cothall.......245 A5
Cotham.......115 A5
Cothelstone....28 B1
Cotherstone...166 D3
Cothill........65 D5
Cotleigh.......14 A2
Cotmanhay.....114 A2
Cotmaton......13 C6
Coton Cambs....85 B6
Northants......98 D3
S Lanark......195 C4
Staffs........112 B3
Staffs........112 C2
Coton Clanford.112 C2
Coton Hill
Shrops.......110 D3
Staffs........112 B3
Coton in the
Elms.........113 D6
Cott...........8 A1
Cottam E Yorks.150 A2
Lancs........145 D5
Notts........132 B3
Cottartown....253 C6
Cottenham......85 A6
Cotterdale....156 B2
Cottered.......68 A3
Cotterstock...100 B2
Cottesbrooke...99 D4
Cottesmore....116 D2
Cotteylands....27 D4
Cottingham
E Yorks......150 D3
Northants......99 B5
Cottingley....147 D5
Cottisford.....82 D2
Cotton Staffs.113 A4
Suff...........87 A6
Cotton End.....84 C2
Cottown Aberds.245 A4
Aberds.......255 D6
Aberds.......256 B3
Cotwalton.....112 B3
Couch's Mill....5 B6
Coughton
Hereford......62 A1
Warks..........80 A3
Coulaghailtro..202 B2
Coulby Newham.168 D3
Coulderton....162 D2
Coulin........250 A2
Coull Aberds..244 B2
Argyll.......200 B2
Coulport......215 D5
Coulsdon.......35 A5
Coulston.......44 D3
Coulter.......195 C5
Coulton.......159 D5
Cound.........94 A3
Coundon Durham 167 C5
W Mid.........97 C6
Coundon
Grange.......167 C5
Countersett...156 C3
Countess......31 A5
Countess Wear..13 C4
Countesthorpe..98 B2
Countisbury....26 A2
County Oak.....35 C5
Coupar Angus..231 D6
Coup Green....137 A4
Coupland......198 C3
Cour...........202 D3
Courance......184 C3
Court-at-Street..38 B2
Courteenhall...83 B4
Court Henry....58 C2
Courtsend......71 D4
Courtway.......28 B2
Cousland......209 D6

Cousley Wood...37 C4
Cove Argyll...215 D5
Borders......211 C4
Devon..........27 D4
Hants..........34 A1
Highld.......261 A5
Cove Bay.....245 B6
Cove Bottom...105 D5
Covehithe.....105 C6
Coven..........96 A2
Coveney......101 C6
Covenham St
Bartholomew..143 D5
Covenham St
Mary.........143 D5
Coventry.......97 D6
Coverack........3 D5
Coverham......157 C5
Covesea.......266 B2
Covington
Cambs........100 D2
S Lanark.....195 C4
Cowan Bridge..155 D5
Cow Ark.......145 C6
Cowbeech.......22 A4
Cowbit........117 D5
Cowbridge Lincs 117 A6
Som...........27 A4
Cowbridge (Y Bont-
Faen)........41 D4
Cowdale.......129 B5
Cowden.........36 B2
Cowdenbeath...209 A4
Cowdenburn...195 A4
Cowers Lane...113 A7
Cowes..........18 B3
Cowesby.......158 C3
Cowfold........35 D5
Cowgill.......155 C6
Cowie Aberds..245 D5
Stirling.....207 B6
Cowley Devon...13 B4
Glos..........63 B5
London.........48 A3
Oxon...........65 C6
Cowleymoor.....27 D4
Cowling Lancs.137 B4
N Yorks......146 C3
N Yorks......157 C6
Cowlinge.......86 B3
Cowpe.........138 A1
Cowpen.......179 A4
Cowpen Bewley.168 C2
Cowplain.......33 D5
Cowshill......165 A6
Cowslip Green..42 C3
Cowstrandburn.208 A3
Cowthorpe....148 B3
Coxbank......111 A5
Coxbench.....114 A1
Cox Common...105 C4
Coxford Norf..119 C5
Soton.........32 D2
Cox Grn........48 B1
Coxheath.......37 A5
Coxhill........39 A4
Coxhoe.......167 B6
Coxley.........29 A5
Cox Moor......131 D5
Coxwold......158 D4
Coychurch......40 D4
Coylton......193 C4
Coylumbridge..242 A2
Coynach......244 B1
Coynachie....255 C5
Coytrahen......40 C3
Crabadon........7 B6
Crabbs Cross...80 A3
Crabtree.......35 D5
Crackenthorpe.165 C4
Crackington
Haven........10 B2
Crackley.......97 D5
Crackleybank..111 D6
Crackpot.....156 B3
Cracoe.......146 A3
Craddock.......27 D5
Cradhlastadh..287 A5
Cradley........79 C5
Cradley Heath..96 C2
Crafthole.......6 B2
Cragg...........7 A6
Craggan.......253 D6

Craggie Highld..252 C3
Highld.......274 C2
Cragg Vale....138 A3
Craghead.....179 D4
Crai...........59 C5
Craibstone....267 D5
Craichie.....232 D3
Craig Dumfries.173 A4
Dumfries.....173 B4
Highld.......250 B2
Craiganor
Lodge........229 C5
Craig Castle..255 D5
Craig-cefn-parc.40 A1
Craigdam.....256 C3
Craigdarroch
Dumfries.....183 C5
Highld.......251 A6
Craigdhu.....251 B6
Craigearn.....245 A4
Craigellachie.254 B3
Craigencross..170 A2
Craigend Perth.219 B6
Stirling.....207 B5
Craigendive..214 D3
Craigengillan.215 D6
Craigends....205 B4
Craigens Argyll..200 B2
E Ayrs.......182 A3
Craighat.....206 B2
Craighead....221 D6
Craighlaw
Highld.......240 C3
Craighouse...201 B5
Craigie Aberds.245 A6
Dundee.......220 A4
Perth........219 B6
Perth........231 D5
S Ayrs.......193 B4
Craigiefield..282 F5
Craigielaw...210 C1
Craiglockhart.209 C5
Craigmalloch.182 C2
Craigmaud....268 D3
Craigmillar..209 C5
Craigmore....203 B6
Craignant....110 B1
Craigneuk
N Lanark.....194 A2
N Lanark.....207 D5
Craignure....225 C6
Craigo.......233 B4
Craig Penllyn..41 D4
Craigrothie..220 C3
Craigroy.....266 D2
Craigruie....217 B4
Craigston
Castle.......268 D2
Craigton
Aberdeen.....245 B5
Angus........221 A5
Angus........232 C1
Highld.......264 A2
Craigtown....279 C4
Craig-y-don..124 A2
Craig-y-nos...59 D5
Craik........185 B6
Crail........221 D6
Crailing.....187 A5
Crailinghall..187 A5
Craiselound..141 D5
Crakehill....158 D3
Crakemarsh...113 B4
Crambe.......149 A6
Cramlington..179 B4
Cramond.....209 C4
Cramond
Bridge.......209 C4
Cranage......128 C2
Cranberry....112 B2
Cranborne.....31 D4
Cranbourne....48 B2
Cranbrook......37 C5
Cranbrook
Common.......37 C5
Crane Moor...139 C6
Crane's Corner.119 D6
Cranfield.....83 C6
Cranford......48 B4
Cranford St
Andrew.......99 D6

Cranford St John..99 D6
Cranham Glos...63 B4
London.........50 A2
Crank.........136 D4
Crank Wood....137 C5
Cranleigh......34 C3
Cranley......104 D2
Cranmer Green.103 D5
Cranmore......18 C2
Cranna.......268 D1
Crannich.....225 B4
Crannoch.....267 D5
Cranoe.........99 B4
Cransford.....88 A4
Cranshaws....210 D3
Cranstal......152 A4
Crantock.......4 C2
Cranwell.....116 A3
Cranwich.....102 B3
Cranworth....103 A5
Craobh Haven.213 B5
Crapstone......7 A4
Crarae.......214 C2
Crask Inn....272 B3
Craskins.....244 B2
Crask of Aigas.251 B6
Craster......189 B5
Craswall......77 D6
Cratfield....104 D4
Crathes......245 C4
Crathie Aberds.243 C5
Highld.......240 C3
Crathorne....158 A3
Craven Arms...94 C2
Crawcrook....178 C3
Crawford Lancs.136 C3
S Lanark.....195 D4
Crawfordjohn..194 D3
Crawick......183 A5
Crawley Hants..32 B3
Oxon..........64 B4
W Sus.........35 C5
Crawley Down..35 C6
Crawleyside..166 A2
Crawshawbooth 137 A7
Crawton......233 A6
Cray N Yorks..156 D3
Perth........231 B5
Crayford......50 B2
Crayke.......159 D4
Crays Hill.....69 D7
Cray's Pond...47 A4
Creacombe.....26 D3
Creagan......227 B4
Creag Ghoraidh.286 B3
Creaguaineach
Lodge........228 B2
Creaksea......70 D3
Creaton.......99 D4
Creca........175 A5
Credenhill....78 C2
Crediton......12 A3
Creebridge...171 A6
Creech
Heathfield....28 C2
Creech St
Michael......28 C2
Creed..........4 C4
Creekmouth....50 A1
Creeting Bottoms 88 B2
Creeting St Mary.88 B1
Creeton......116 C3
Creetown.....171 B6
Creggans.....214 B3
Cregneash....152 E1
Creg-ny-Baa..152 C3
Cregrina......77 B5
Creich.......220 B3
Creigiau......41 C5
Cremyll........6 B3
Creslow.......66 A4
Cressage......94 A3
Cressbrook...129 B6
Cresselly.....55 D6
Cressing......70 A1
Cresswell
Northumb.....189 D5
Staffs.......112 B3
Cresswell Quay..55 D6
Creswell.....131 B5
Cretingham....88 A3
Cretshengan..202 B2

Crewe Ches E 128 D2
Ches W. 127 D4
Crewgreen. 110 D2
Crewkerne. 14 A4
Crianlarich. 216 B3
Cribyn 75 C4
Criccieth 107 C4
Crich 130 D3
Crichie 257 B4
Crichton 209 D6
Crick Mon 61 D6
Northants. 98 D2
Crickadarn 77 C4
Cricket
Malherbie 28 D3
Cricket St
Thomas 14 A3
Crickheath. 110 C1
Crickhowell. 60 B4
Cricklade 64 D2
Cricklewood 49 A5
Cridling Stubbs . .140 A3
Crieff. 218 B3
Criggion 110 D1
Crigglestone 139 B6
Crimond 269 D5
Crimonmogate. . .269 D5
Crimplesham 102 A2
Crinan. 213 C5
Cringleford 104 A2
Cringles 147 C4
Crinow 56 A1
Cripplesease. 2 B3
Cripplestyle. 31 D4
Cripp's Corner . . .37 D5
Croasdale. 162 C3
Crockenhill 50 C2
Crockernwell 12 B2
Crockerton 30 A2
Crocketford or
Ninemile Bar . .173 A6
Crockey Hill. 149 C5
Crockham Hill. . . .36 A2
Crockleford
Heath. 71 A4
Crockness 283 H4
Crock Street 28 D3
Croeserw 40 B3
Croes-goch. 54 A4
Croes-lan. 73 B6
Croesor. 107 B6
Croesyceiliog
Carms 57 A4
Torf 61 D5
Croes-y-
mwyalch 61 D5
Croesywaun. 107 A5
Croft Leics. 98 B2
Lincs. 135 C5
Pembs 73 B4
Warr. 137 D5
Croftamie. 206 B2
Croftmalloch. . . .208 D2
Crofton Wilts 45 C6
W Yorks. 140 B1
Croft-on-Tees . . .157 A6
Crofts of
Benachielt. . . .275 A5
Crofts of Haddo .256 C3
Crofts of
Inverthernie . . .256 B2
Crofts of Meikle
Ardo 256 B3
Crofty 57 C5
Croggan 225 D6
Croglin 164 A3
Croich 263 A6
Crois Dughaill. . .286 D3
Cromarty 264 D3
Cromblet 256 C2
Cromdale. 253 D6
Cromer Herts 68 A2
Norf 120 A4
Cromford 130 D2
Cromhall 62 D2
Cromhall
Common 43 A5
Cromor 288 E5
Cromra 240 C3
Cromwell 132 C2
Cronberry 193 C6
Crondall 33 A6

Cronk-y-Voddy .152 C3
Cronton 127 A4
Crook Cumb 154 B3
Durham. 167 B4
Crookedholm . . .193 B4
Crookham
Northumb. 198 C3
W Berks. 46 C3
Crookham
Village 47 D5
Crookhaugh 195 D6
Crookhouse. 187 A6
Crooklands 154 C3
Crook of Devon .219 D5
Cropredy 82 C1
Cropston 114 D3
Cropthorne 80 C2
Cropton 159 C6
Cropwell Bishop 115 B4
Cropwell Butler . 115 B4
Cros. 288 A6
Crosbost. 288 E4
Crosby Cumb. . . .162 A3
IoM 152 D3
N Lincs 141 B6
Crosby Garrett . .155 A6
Crosby
Ravensworth .165 D4
Crosby Villa. . . .162 A3
Croscombe 29 A5
Cross. 42 D3
Crossaig. 202 C3
Crossal 246 A3
Crossapol. 222 C2
Cross Ash. 61 B6
Cross-at-Hand . .37 B5
Crossburn 207 C6
Crossbush 20 B3
Crosscanonby . .162 A3
Crossdale
Street. 120 B4
Crossens 136 B2
Crossflatts 147 C5
Crossford Fife . .208 B3
S Lanark. 194 B3
Crossgate. 117 C5
Crossgatehall . .209 D6
Crossgates Fife . . .77 A4
Powys 77 A4
Cross Green
Devon. 11 C4
Suff 87 B4
Suff 87 B5
Warks. 81 B6
Cross Hands 57 A5
Cross-hands 73 D4
Cross Hands 55 C6
Crosshill E Ayrs .193 C4
Fife. 209 A4
S Ayrs. 192 E3
Cross Hill 114 A2
Crosshouse 192 B3
Cross Houses . . .94 A3
Crossings 176 B3
Cross in Hand
E Sus 36 D3
Leics. 98 C2
Cross Inn Ceredig. .73 A6
Ceredig 75 B4
Rhondda. 41 C5
Crosskeys. 41 B7
Crosskirk 279 A6
Cross Lane Head .95 B5
Crosslanes 110 D2
Cross Lanes Corn . .3 C4
N Yorks 148 A4
Wrex 110 A2
Crosslee Borders 185 A6
Renfs 205 B4
Crossmichael . . .173 B5
Crossmoor. 144 D4
Cross Oak 60 A3
Cross of
Jackston 256 C2
Cross o' th'
hands 113 A6
Crossroads
Aberds 245 C4
E Ayrs. 193 B4

Cross Street 104 D2
Cross Trickett's . .17 A4
Crossway Hereford 79 D4
Mon 61 B6
Powys 77 B4
Crossway Green . .79 A6
Crossways 16 C1
Crosswell 72 C4
Crosswood. 75 A5
Crosthwaite. . . .154 B3
Croston. 136 B3
Crostwick. 121 D4
Crostwight. 121 C5
Crothair 288 D2
Crouch 36 A4
Croucheston 31 C4
Crouch Hill 29 D7
Crouch House
Green 36 B2
Croughton 82 D2
Crovie 268 C3
Crowan 3 B4
Crowborough . . .36 C3
Crowcombe 27 B6
Crowdecote 129 C6
Crowden. 138 D3
Crow Edge 139 C4
Crowell 66 D3
Crowfield
Northants. 82 C3
Suff 88 B2
Crow Hill 62 A2
Crowhurst E Sus .23 A5
Sur. 36 B1
Crowhurst Lane
End. 36 B1
Crowland 117 D5
Crowlas 2 B3
Crowle N Lincs . .141 B5
Worcs. 80 B2
Crowmarsh
Gifford 47 A4
Crown Corner . .104 D3
Crownhill 6 B3
Crownland 103 E6
Crownthorpe . . .104 A1
Crowntown 3 B4
Crows-an-wra . . .2 C1
Crowshill 103 A5
Crowsnest 94 A1
Crowthorne 47 C6
Crowton 127 B5
Croxall 113 D5
Croxby 142 D3
Croxdale. 167 B5
Croxden 113 B4
Croxley Green . . .67 D6
Croxton Cambs. .84 A4
N Lincs. 142 B2
Norf 103 C4
Staffs 112 B1
Croxtonbank . . .112 B1
Croxton Kerrial . 115 C6
Croy Highld 252 B3
N Lanark 207 C5
Croydon Cambs . .85 C5
London 49 C6
Crubenmore
Lodge 241 C4
Cruckmeole. . . .94 A2
Cruckton 110 D3
Cruden Bay 257 C5
Crudgington . . .111 D5
Crudwell. 63 D5
Crug 93 D5
Crugmeer 9 D5
Crugybar 58 B3
Crulabhig 288 D2
Crumlin
(Crymlyn) 41 B7
Crumpsall 138 C1
Crundale Kent . . .38 A2
Pembs 55 C5
Cruwys
Morchard 26 D3
Crux Easton 46 D2
Crwbin 57 A4
Cryers Hill 66 D3
Crymlyn 123 C6
Crymych 73 C4

Crynant. 40 A2
Crynfryn 75 B4
Cuaig. 249 A4
Cuan 213 A5
Cubbington 81 A6
Cubeck 156 C3
Cubert. 4 B2
Cubley 139 C5
Cubley Common 113 B5
Cublington Bucks .66 A4
Hereford 78 D2
Cuckfield 35 D6
Cucklington. 30 C1
Cuckney 131 B5
Cuckoo Hill 141 D5
Cuddesdon 65 C7
Cuddington
Bucks 66 B3
Ches W. 127 B6
Cuddington
Heath 110 A3
Cuddy Hill 145 D4
Cudham. 36 A2
Cudliptown 11 D6
Cudworth Som. . .28 D3
S Yorks. 140 C1
Cuffley 68 C3
Cuiashader 288 B6
Cuidhir 286 F2
Cuidhtinis 287 F5
Culbo. 264 D2
Culbokie. 252 A2
Culburnie. 251 B6
Culcabock 252 B2
Culcairn 264 D2
Culcharry 253 A4
Culcheth. 137 D5
Culdrain 255 C6
Culduie 249 B4
Culford 103 D4
Culgaith 165 C4
Culham 65 D6
Culkein 270 A3
Culkein
Drumbeg 270 A4
Culkerton. 63 D5
Cullachie 253 D5
Cullen 267 C6
Cullercoats 179 B5
Cullicudden. . . .264 D2
Cullingworth . . .147 D4
Cullipool. 213 A5
Cullivoe 284 C7
Culloch 218 C2
Culloden. 252 B3
Cullompton 13 A5
Culmaily 265 A4
Culmazie 171 B5
Culmington 94 C2
Culmstock 27 D6
Culnacraig 270 D3
Culnaknock 259 B5
Culpho. 88 C3
Culrain 264 A1
Culross. 208 B2
Culroy 192 D3
Culsh Aberds. . . .243 C6
Aberds. 256 B3
Culshabbin 171 B5
Culswick. 285 J4
Cultercullen. . . .257 D4
Cults Aberdeen . .245 B5
Aberds. 255 C6
Dumfries 171 C6
Culverstone
Green 50 C3
Culverthorpe . . .116 A3
Culworth 82 C2
Culzie Lodge . . .263 C7
Cumberland
Village 207 C5
Cumberworth . .135 B5
Cuminestown . .268 D3
Cumlewick. 285 L6
Cummersdale . .175 C6
Cummertrees . .174 B4
Cummingston . .266 C2
Cumnock 193 C5
Cumnor 65 C5
Cumrew 176 D3
Cumwhinton . . .176 D2
Cumwhitton . . .176 D3

Cundall 158 D3
Cunninghamhead
. . . . .204 D3
Cunister 284 D7
Cupar 220 C3
Cupar Muir 220 C3
Cupernham 32 C2
Curbar. 130 B2
Curbridge Hants .32 D4
Oxon. 64 C4
Curdridge 32 D4
Curdworth 97 B4
Curland. 28 D2
Curlew Green . . .89 A4
Currarie 180 B3
Curridge 46 B2
Currie 209 D4
Curry Mallet . . .28 C3
Curry Rivel. 28 C3
Curtisden Green .37 B5
Curtisknowle. . . .7 B6
Cury. 3 C4
Cushnie 268 C2
Cushuish 28 B1
Cusop 77 C6
Cutcloy 171 D6
Cutcombe 27 B4
Cutgate. 138 B1
Cutiau 90 A4
Cutlers Green . . .86 D1
Cutnall Green . . .80 A1
Cutsdean 80 D3
Cutthorpe 130 B3
Cutts 285 K6
Cuxham 66 D1
Cuxton 51 C4
Cuxwold 142 C3
Cwm Bl Gwent. . .60 C3
Denb. 125 B5
Swansea 40 B1
Cwmafan 40 B2
Cwmaman 41 B5
Cwmann 75 D4
Cwmavon 61 C4
Cwmbach Carms .57 B4
Carms 73 D5
Powys 76 B4
Powys 77 D5
Cwmbelan 92 C3
Cwmbran
(Cwmbrân) . . .61 D4
Cwmbrwyno . . .91 D5
Cwm-byr 58 B3
Cwmcarn 41 B7
Cwmcarvan 61 C6
Cwm-Cewydd . . .91 A6
Cwm-cou 73 B5
Cwmcych 73 C5
Cwmdare 41 A4
Cwmderwen 92 A3
Cwmdu Carms . .58 B3
Powys 60 A3
Swansea 57 C6
Cwmduad 73 C6
Cwm-Dulais 57 B6
Cwmdwr. 59 B4
Cwmfelin Bridgend 40 C3
M Tydf 41 A5
Cwmfelin Boeth .56 A1
Cwm-felin-fach . .41 B6
Cwmfelin
Mynach 73 D5
Cwm Ffrwd-oer . .61 C4
Cwmffrwd 57 A4
Cwmgiedd 59 D4
Cwmgors 59 D4
Cwmgwili. 57 A5
Cwmgwrach 40 A3
Cwm-hesgen . . .108 C2
Cwmhiraeth. 73 C6
Cwm-hwnt. 59 E6
Cwmifor 58 C3
Cwm Irfon 76 C2
Cwmisfael 57 A4
Cwm-Llinau 91 B6
Cwmllynfell 59 D4
Cwm-mawr 57 A5
Cwmorgan 73 C5
Cwm-parc 40 B4
Cwmpengraig . . .73 C6

Cwm
Penmachno . .108 A2
Cwmrhos 60 A3
Cwmsychpant . .74 D3
Cwmtillery 60 C4
Cwmwysg. 59 C5
Cwm-y-glo Carms 57 A5
Gwyn 123 D5
Cwmyoy 61 A4
Cwmystwyth 92 D1
Cwrt. 91 B4
Cwrt-newydd . . .74 D3
Cwrt-y-cadno . . .58 A3
Cwrt-y-gollen. . . .60 B4
Cyffylliog 125 D5
Cyfronydd 93 A5
Cymer 40 B3
Cyncoed 41 C6
Cynghordy 59 A5
Cynheidre 57 B4
Cynwyd 109 A5
Cynwyl Elfed . . .73 D6
Cywarch 91 A6

D

Dacre Cumb 164 C2
N Yorks 147 A5
Dacre Banks 147 A5
Daddry Shield . .166 B1
Dadford 82 D3
Dadlington 97 B7
Dafarn Faig 107 B4
Dafen 57 B5
Daffy Green 103 A5
Dagenham 50 A1
Daglingworth . . .63 C5
Dagnall 67 B5
Dail Beag 288 C3
Dail bho Dheas . 288 A5
Dail bho Thuath 288 A5
Daill. 200 B3
Dailly 181 A4
Dail Mor 288 C3
Dairsie or
Osnaburgh . . .220 C4
Daisy Hill 137 C5
Dalabrog 286 D3
Dalavich 214 A2
Dalbeattie 173 B6
Dalblair. 182 A4
Dalbog 232 A3
Dalbury 113 B6
Dalby IoM 152 D2
N Yorks. 159 D5
Dalchalloch 229 B6
Dalchalm 274 D3
Dalchenna 214 B3
Dalchirach 254 C2
Dalchork. 272 C3
Dalchreichart . . .239 A6
Dalchruin 218 C2
Dalderby 134 C2
Dale. 54 D4
Dale Abbey 114 B2
Dale Head 164 C2
Dalelia 235 D6
Dale of Walls. . .285 H3
Daless 253 C4
Dalfaber 242 A2
Dalgarven 204 D2
Dalgety Bay 209 B4
Dalginross 218 B2
Dalguise 230 D3
Dalhalvaig 279 C4
Dalham 86 A3
Dalinlongart . . .215 D3
Dalkeith 209 D6
Dallam 137 D4
Dallas 266 D2
Dalleagles 182 A3
Dallinghoo 88 B3
Dallington E Sus . .23 A5
Northants. 83 A4
Dalmadilly 245 A4
Dalmally 227 D6
Dalmarnock . . .205 B6

Dalmary......206 A3
Dalmellington..182 B2
Dalmeny.....208 C4
Dalmigavie...241 A5
Dalmigavie
Lodge......252 D3
Dalmore......264 D2
Dalmuir.....205 A4
Dalnabreck...235 D5
Dalnacardoch
Lodge......229 A6
Dalnacroich...251 A5
Dalnaglar
Castle.....231 B5
Dalnahaitnach..253 D4
Dalnaspidal
Lodge......229 A5
Dalnavaid....230 B4
Dalnavie.....264 C2
Dalnawillan
Lodge......279 D6
Dalness......237 D5
Dalnessie....273 C4
Dalqueich....219 D5
Dalreavoch...273 D5
Dalry.......204 D2
Dalrymple....192 D3
Dalserf......194 A3
Dalston.....175 C6
Dalswinton...184 D2
Dalton Dumfries.174 A4
Lancs.....136 C3
Northumb....177 D7
Northumb....178 B3
N Yorks.....157 A5
N Yorks.....158 A3
S Yorks.....140 D2
Dalton-in-
Furness......153 C3
Dalton-le-Dale..168 A2
Dalton-on-Tees 157 A6
Dalton Piercy...168 B2
Dalveich....217 B6
Dalvina Lo....278 D2
Dalwhinnie...241 D4
Dalwood......14 A2
Dalwyne.....181 B5
Damerham.....31 D5
Damgate......105 A5
Dam Green....103 C6
Damnaglaur...170 D3
Damside.....195 B6
Dam Side....144 C4
Danbury......70 C1
Danby.......159 A6
Danby Wiske...158 B2
Dandaleith....254 B3
Danderhall...209 D6
Danebridge...129 C4
Dane End......68 A3
Danehill......36 D2
Danemoor
Green......103 A6
Danesford....95 B5
Daneshill....47 D4
Dangerous
Corner.....136 B4
Danskine....210 D2
Darcy Lever...137 C6
Darenth......50 B2
Daresbury...127 A5
Darfield.....140 C2
Darfoulds....131 B5
Dargate......52 C2
Darite........6 A1
Darlaston....96 B2
Darley......147 B6
Darley Bridge..130 C2
Darley Head...147 B5
Darlingscott...81 C5
Darlington...167 D5
Darliston....111 B4
Darlton.....132 B2
Darnall.....130 A3
Darnick.....197 C4
Darowen......91 B6
Darra.......256 B2
Darracott....25 B5
Darras Hall...178 B3

Darrington......140 A2
Darsham.......89 A5
Dartford.......50 B2
Dartford
Crossing......50 B2
Dartington......8 A1
Dartmeet......12 D1
Dartmouth......8 B2
Darton.......139 C6
Darvel.......193 B5
Darwell Hole....23 A4
Darwen.......137 A5
Datchet......48 B2
Datchworth....68 B2
Datchworth
Green.......68 B2
Daubhill.....137 C6
Daugh of
Kinermony...254 B3
Dauntsey......44 A3
Dava........253 C6
Davenham.....127 B6
Davenport
Green.......128 B3
Daventry......82 A2
Davidson's
Mains......209 C5
Davidstow.....10 C2
David's Well...93 D4
Davington....185 B5
Daviot Aberds...256 D2
Highld.......252 C3
Davoch of
Grange.....267 D5
Davyhulme....137 D6
Dawley.......95 A4
Dawlish.......13 D4
Dawlish Warren..13 D4
Dawn........124 B3
Daws Heath....51 A5
Daw's House....10 C4
Dawsmere....118 B1
Dayhills.....112 B3
Daylesford....64 A3
Ddôl-Cownwy...109 D5
Ddrydwy......122 C3
Deadwater....187 D5
Deaf Hill.....167 B6
Deal........53 D5
Deal Hall.....71 D4
Dean Cumb....162 B3
Devon........7 A6
Devon.......25 A6
Dorset.......30 D3
Hants........33 D4
Som.........29 A6
Deanburnhaugh 186 B2
Deane Gtr Man...137 C5
Hants.......46 D3
Deanich Lodge..263 B6
Deanland......30 D3
Dean Prior.....7 A6
Dean Row.....128 A3
Deans.......208 D3
Deanscales...162 B3
Deanshanger...83 D4
Deanston.....218 D2
Dearham.....162 A3
Debach.......88 B3
Debden Essex...68 D4
Essex.......86 D1
Debden Cross...86 D1
Debenham......88 A2
Dechmont....208 C3
Deddington....82 D1
Dedham.......87 D6
Dedham Heath...87 D6
Deebank.....244 C3
Deene.......99 B6
Deenethorpe...99 B6
Deepcar.....139 D5
Deepcut......34 A2
Deepdale.....155 C6
Deeping Gate...100 A3
Deeping St
James.......100 A3
Deeping St
Nicholas.....117 D5
Deerhill.....267 D5
Deerhurst.....63 A4
Deerness....283 G6
Defford......80 C2

Defynnog......59 C6
Deganwy.....124 B2
Deighton N Yorks 158 A2
W Yorks.....139 B4
York........149 C5
Deiniolen....123 D5
Delabole......9 C6
Delamere....127 C5
Delfrigs.....257 D4
Delliefure....254 C1
Dell Lodge....242 A3
Delnabo.....243 A4
Delnadamph...243 B5
Delph.......138 C2
Delves.......166 A4
Delvine.....231 D5
Dembleby....116 B3
Denaby Main...140 D2
Denbigh
(Dinbych)...125 C5
Denbury.......8 A2
Denby.......114 A1
Denby Dale...139 C5
Denchworth....65 D4
Dendron.....153 C3
Denel End.....84 D2
Denend......255 C7
Denford.....100 D1
Dengie.......70 C3
Denham Bucks...48 A3
Suff........86 A3
Suff........104 D2
Denham Street..104 D2
Denhead Aberds .269 D4
Fife........221 C4
Denhead of
Arbilot.....232 D3
Denhead of
Gray.......220 A3
Denholm.....187 B4
Denholme....147 D4
Denholme
Clough......147 D4
Denio.......106 C3
Denmead......33 D5
Denmore.....245 A6
Denmoss.....256 B1
Dennington....88 A3
Denny.......207 B6
Dennyloanhead..207 B6
Denny Lodge...18 A2
Denshaw.....138 B2
Denside.....245 C5
Densole......39 A4
Denston......86 B3
Denstone.....113 A5
Dent........155 C6
Denton Cambs...100 C3
Darl........167 D5
E Sus........22 B2
Gtr Man.....138 D2
Kent........39 A4
Lincs.......115 B6
Norf........104 C3
Northants.....83 B5
N Yorks......147 C5
Oxon........65 C6
Denton's Green.136 D3
Denver......102 A2
Denwick.....189 B5
Deopham.....103 A6
Deopham Green 103 B6
Depden......86 B3
Depden Green...86 B3
Deptford London..49 B6
Wilts........31 B4
Derby.......114 B1
Derbyhaven...152 E2
Dereham.....120 D1
Deri........41 A6
Derril.......10 A4
Derringstone...39 A4
Derrington....112 C2
Derriton.....10 A4
Derryguaig...224 C3
Derry Hill....44 B3
Derrythorpe...141 C6
Dersingham...118 B3
Derwen......124 D3
Dervaig.....224 A3
Derwen......125 D5
Derwenlas....91 C5
Desborough....99 C5

Desford......98 A1
Detchant....199 C4
Detling......37 A5
Deuddwr.....110 D1
Devauden......61 D6
Devil's Bridge..75 A6
Devizes......44 C4
Devol.......204 A3
Devonport......6 B3
Devonside...208 A2
Devoran......4 D2
Dewar.......196 B2
Dewlish......16 B1
Dewsbury....139 A5
Dewsbury Moor.139 A5
Dewshall Court..78 D2
Dhoon......152 C4
Dhoor.......152 B4
Dhowin......152 A4
Dial Post.....21 A4
Dibden......18 A3
Dibden Purlieu..18 A3
Dickleburgh...104 C2
Didbrook......80 D3
Didcot.......46 A3
Diddington....84 A3
Diddlebury....94 C3
Didley.......78 D2
Didling......20 A1
Didmarton....44 A2
Didsbury....138 D1
Didworthy......7 A5
Digby.......133 D5
Digg........259 B4
Diggle.......138 C3
Digmoor.....136 C3
Digswell Park...68 B2
Dihewyd......74 C3
Dilham.......121 C5
Dilhorne....112 A3
Dillarburn...194 B3
Dillington....84 A3
Dilston.....178 C1
Dilton Marsh...30 A2
Dilwyn......78 B2
Dinas Carms...73 C5
Gwyn.......106 C2
Dinas Cross...72 C3
Dinas Dinlle..107 A4
Dinas-Mawddwy .91 A6
Dinas Powys...41 D6
Dinder.......29 A5
Dinedor......78 D3
Dingestow....61 B6
Dingle......126 A3
Dingleden....37 C6
Dingley......99 C4
Dingwall....252 A1
Dinlabyre...186 D4
Dinmael.....109 A5
Dinnet......244 C1
Dinnington Som..28 D4
S Yorks.....131 A5
T&W........179 B4
Dinorwic....123 D5
Dinton Bucks...66 B3
Wilts........31 B4
Dinwoodie
Mains......185 C4
Dinworthy....24 D4
Dippen......191 C6
Dippenhall....33 A7
Dipple Moray...266 D4
S Ayrs......181 A4
Diptford......7 B6
Dipton......178 D3
Dirdhu......254 D1
Dirleton....210 B2
Dirt Pot.....165 A6
Discoed......77 A6
Diseworth....114 C2
Dishes.......282 E7
Dishforth....158 D2
Disley......129 A4
Diss........104 D2
Disserth......76 B4
Distington...162 B3
Ditcham......31 B4
Ditcheat......29 B6
Ditchingham..104 B4
Ditchling.....21 A6
Ditherington..111 D4

Dittisham......8 B2
Ditton Halton...127 A4
Kent........37 A5
Ditton Green...86 B2
Ditton Priors...95 C4
Divach......251 D6
Divlyn......59 B4
Dixton Glos....80 D2
Mon.........61 B7
Dobcross....138 C2
Dobwalls......5 A7
Doccombe....12 C2
Dochfour Ho...252 C2
Dochgarroch..252 B2
Docking.....119 B4
Docklow......78 B3
Dockray.....164 C1
Dockroyd....147 D4
Dodburn.....186 C3
Doddinghurst...69 D5
Doddington
Cambs......101 B5
Kent........51 D6
Lincs.......133 B4
Northumb.....198 C3
Shrops......94 D3
Doddiscombsleigh
..........12 C3
Dodford Northants 82 A3
Worcs.......96 D2
Dodington....43 A6
Dodleston....126 C3
Dods Leigh...112 B4
Dodworth....139 C6
Doe Green....127 A5
Doe Lea......131 C4
Dogdyke.....134 D2
Dogmersfield...47 D5
Dogridge......45 A4
Dogsthorpe...100 A3
Dog Village...13 B4
Dolanog.....109 D5
Dolau Powys....77 A5
Rhondda......41 C4
Dolbenmaen...107 B5
Dolfach......91 B7
Dolfor.......93 C5
Dol-fôr......91 B6
Dolgarrog....124 C2
Dolgellau....91 A5
Dolgran......58 B1
Dolhendre....108 B3
Doll........274 D2
Dollar......208 A2
Dolley Green...77 A6
Dollwen......91 D4
Dolphin.....126 B1
Dolphinholme..145 B5
Dolphinton...195 B6
Dolton......25 D6
Dolwen Conwy..124 B3
Powys.......92 A3
Dolwyd......124 B3
Dolwyddelan..124 D2
Dôl-y-Bont....90 D4
Dol-y-cannau...77 C6
Dolyhir......77 B6
Doncaster....140 C3
Dones Green...127 B6
Donhead St
Andrew.....30 C3
Donhead St Mary 30 C3
Donibristle...209 B4
Donington....117 B5
Donington on
Bain.......134 A2
Donington South
Ing.........117 B5
Donisthorpe...113 D7
Donkey Town...48 C2
Donnington Glos..64 A2
Hereford.....79 D5
Shrops......94 A3
Telford.....111 D6
W Berks......46 C2
W Sus........20 B1
Donnington
Wood.......111 D6
Donyatt......28 D3
Doonfoot....192 D3
Dorback Lodge..242 A3

Dorchester continued
Oxon.........65 D6
Dordon.......97 A5
Dore........130 A3
Dores.......252 C1
Dorking......35 B4
Dormansland...36 B2
Dormanstown...168 C3
Dormington....78 C3
Dormston......80 B2
Dornal.......181 D4
Dorney.......48 B2
Dornie.......249 D5
Dornoch.....264 B3
Dornock.....175 B5
Dorrery.....279 C6
Dorridge......97 D4
Dorrington Lincs 133 D5
Shrops.......94 A2
Dorsington....80 C4
Dorstone......77 C7
Dorton.......66 B2
Dorusduain...250 D1
Dosthill......97 B5
Dottery......15 B4
Doublebois.....5 A6
Dougarie.....191 B4
Doughton......63 D4
Douglas IoM....152 D3
S Lanark.....194 C3
Douglas &
Angus.......220 A4
Douglastown...232 D2
Douglas Water..194 C3
Douglas West..194 C3
Doulting......29 A6
Dounby......282 E3
Doune Highld...272 D2
Stirling.....218 D2
Doune Park...268 C2
Douneside....244 B1
Dounie......264 A1
Dounreay....279 B5
Dousland......7 A4
Dovaston....110 C2
Dove Holes...129 B5
Dovenby.....162 A3
Dover........39 A5
Dovercourt....88 D3
Doverdale....79 A6
Doveridge....113 B5
Doversgreen...35 B5
Dowally.....230 D4
Dowbridge...144 D4
Dowdeswell...63 B5
Dowlais......60 C2
Dowland......25 D6
Dowlish Wake...28 D3
Down Ampney...64 D2
Downcraig
Ferry.......204 C1
Downderry......6 B2
Downe.......50 C1
Downend IoW....18 C4
S Glos.......43 B5
W Berks......46 B3
Downfield....220 A3
Downgate......11 D4
Downham Essex..70 D1
Lancs.......146 C1
Northumb....198 C2
Downham
Market.....102 A2
Down Hatherley..63 A4
Downhead......29 A6
Downhill Perth..219 A5
T&W........179 D5
Downholland
Cross.......136 C2
Downholme...157 B5
Downies.....245 C6
Downley......66 D4
Down St Mary...12 A2
Downside Som...29 A6
Sur.........35 A4
Down Thomas....7 B4
Downton Hants..17 B6
Wilts........31 C5
Downton on the
Rock........94 D2
Dowsby......116 C4
Dowsdale....117 D5

Dowthwaitehead ...163 B6
Doxey ...112 C3
Doxford ...189 A4
Doxford Park ...179 D5
Doynton ...43 B6
Draffan ...194 B2
Dragonby ...141 B7
Drakeland Corner . 7 B4
Drakemyre ...204 C2
Drake's
  Broughton ...80 C2
Drakes Cross ...96 D3
Drakewalls ...11 D5
Draughton
  Northants ...99 D4
  N Yorks ...147 B4
Drax ...141 A4
Draycote ...98 D1
Draycott Derbys ..114 B2
  Glos ...81 D4
  Som ...42 D3
Draycott in the
  Clay ...113 C5
Draycott in the
  Moors ...112 A3
Drayford ...26 D2
Drayton Leics ...9 B5
  Lincs ...117 B5
  Norf ...120 D3
  Oxon ...65 D5
  Oxon ...82 C1
  Ptsmth ...19 A5
  Som ...28 C4
  Worcs ...96 D2
Drayton Bassett . 97 A4
Drayton
  Beauchamp ...67 B5
Drayton Parslow . 66 A4
Drayton St
  Leonard ...65 D6
Drebley ...147 B4
Dreemskerry ...152 B4
Dreenhill ...55 C5
Drefach Carms ...57 A5
  Carms ...73 C6
Dre-fach Carms ...57 A6
  Ceredig ...75 D4
Drefelin ...73 C6
Dreghorn ...192 B3
Drellingore ...39 A4
Drem ...210 C2
Dresden ...112 A3
Dreumasdal ...286 C3
Drewsteignton ...12 B2
Driby ...134 B3
Driffield E Yorks ..150 B3
  Glos ...63 D6
Drigg ...153 A1
Drighlington ...139 A5
Drimnin ...225 A4
Drimpton ...14 A4
Drimsynie ...215 B4
Drinisiadar ...288 H2
Drinkstone ...87 A5
Drinkstone
  Green ...87 A5
Drishaig ...215 A4
Drissaig ...214 A2
Drochil ...195 B6
Droitton ...112 C4
Droitwich Spa ...80 A1
Droman ...276 C2
Dron ...219 C6
Dronfield ...130 B3
Dronfield
  Woodhouse ...130 B3
Drongan ...182 A2
Dronley ...220 A3
Droxford ...33 D5
Droylsden ...138 D2
Druid ...109 A5
Druidston ...55 C4
Druimarbin ...237 B4
Druimavuic ...227 B5
Druimdrishaig . 202 A2
Druimindarroch 235 B5
Druimyeon
  More ...202 C1
Drum Argyll ...203 A4
  Perth ...219 D5
Drumbeg ...270 A4

Drumblade ...255 B6
Drumblair ...256 B1
Drumbuie
  Dumfries ...182 D3
  Highld ...249 C4
Drumburgh ...175 C5
Drumburn ...174 B2
Drumchapel ...205 A5
Drumchardine . 252 B1
Drumchork ...261 B5
Drumclog ...193 B6
Drumderfit ...252 A2
Drumeldrie ...220 D4
Drumelzier ...195 C6
Drumfearn ...247 C5
Drumgask ...241 C4
Drumgley ...232 C2
Drumguish ...241 C5
Drumin ...254 C2
Drumlasie ...244 B3
Drumlemble ...190 D2
Drumligair ...245 A6
Drumlithie ...245 D4
Drummoddie ...171 C5
Drummond ...264 D2
Drumore ...170 D3
Drummuir ...255 B4
Drummuir
  Castle ...255 B4
Drumnadrochit .251 D1
Drumnagorrach 267 D6
Drumoak ...245 C4
Drumpark ...183 D6
Drumphail ...171 A4
Drumrash ...173 A4
Drumrunie ...271 D4
Drums ...257 D4
Drumsallie ...236 B3
Drumstinchall ...173 C6
Drumsturdy ...221 A4
Drumtochty
  Castle ...244 E3
Drumtroddan ...171 C5
Drumuie ...259 D4
Drumuillie ...253 D5
Drumvaich ...217 D6
Drumwhindle ...257 C4
Drunkendub ...233 D4
Drury ...126 C2
Drury Square ...119 D6
Drybeck ...165 D4
Drybridge Moray 267 C5
  N Ayrs ...192 B3
Drybrook ...62 B2
Dryburgh ...197 C4
Dry Doddington .115 A6
Dry Drayton ...85 A5
Dryhope ...196 D1
Drylaw ...209 C5
Drym ...3 B4
Drymen ...206 B2
Drymuir ...257 B4
Drynoch ...246 A3
Dryslwyn ...58 C2
Dryton ...94 A3
Dubford ...268 C3
Dubton ...232 C3
Duchally ...271 C6
Duchlage ...206 B1
Duck Corner ...89 C4
Duckington ...127 D4
Ducklington ...65 C4
Duckmanton ...131 B4
Duck's Cross ...84 B3
Duddenhoe End ..85 D6
Duddingston ...209 C5
Duddington ...100 A1
Duddleswell ...36 D2
Duddo ...198 B3
Duddon ...127 C5
Duddon Bridge ..153 B3
Dudleston ...110 B2
Dudleston
  Heath ...110 B2
Dudley T&W ...179 D4
  W Mid ...96 B2
Dudley Port ...96 B2
Duffield ...114 A1
Duffryn Neath ...40 B3
  Newport ...42 A1
Dufftown ...254 C4
Duffus ...266 C2

Dufton ...165 C4
Duggleby ...150 A1
Duirinish ...249 C4
Duisdalemore ...247 C6
Duisky ...237 B4
Dukestown ...60 B3
Dukinfield ...138 D2
Dulas ...123 B4
Dulcote ...29 A5
Dulford ...13 A5
Dull ...230 D2
Dullatur ...207 C5
Dullingham ...86 B2
Dulnain Bridge ..253 D5
Duloe Bedford ...84 A3
  Corn ...6 B1
Dulsie ...253 B5
Dulverton ...27 C4
Dulwich ...49 B6
Dumbarton ...205 A3
Dumbleton ...80 D3
Dumcrieff ...185 B4
Dumfries ...174 A2
Dumgoyne ...206 B3
Dummer ...33 A4
Dumpford ...34 D1
Dumpton ...53 C5
Dun ...233 C4
Dunain Ho ...252 B2
Dunalastair ...229 C6
Dunan ...247 B4
Dunans ...214 C3
Dunball ...28 A3
Dunbar ...210 C3
Dunbeath ...275 B5
Dunbeg ...226 C3
Dunblane ...218 D2
Dunbog ...220 C2
Duncanston ...252 A1
Duncanstone ...255 D6
Dun
  Charlabhaigh . 288 C2
Dunchurch ...98 D1
Duncote ...82 B3
Duncow ...184 D2
Duncraggan ...217 D5
Duncrievie ...219 D6
Duncton ...20 A2
Dundas Ho ...283 J5
Dundee ...220 A4
Dundeugh ...182 D3
Dundon ...29 B4
Dundonald ...192 B3
Dundonnell ...262 B2
Dundonnell
  Hotel ...262 B2
Dundonnell
  House ...262 B3
Dundraw ...175 D5
Dundreggan ...239 A7
Dundreggan
  Lodge ...240 A1
Dundrennan ...173 D5
Dundry ...43 C4
Dunecht ...245 B4
Dunfermline ...208 B3
Dunfield ...64 D2
Dunford Bridge .139 C4
Dungworth ...130 A2
Dunham ...132 B3
Dunham-on-the-
  Hill ...127 B4
Dunhampton ...79 A6
Dunham Town ...128 A2
Dunholme ...133 B5
Dunino ...221 C5
Dunipace ...207 B6
Dunira ...218 B2
Dunkeld ...230 D4
Dunkerton ...43 D6
Dunkeswell ...13 A6
Dunkeswick ...148 C2
Dunkirk Kent ...52 D2
  Norf ...120 C4
Dunk's Green ...36 A4
Dunlappie ...232 B3
Dunley Hants ...46 D2
  Worcs ...79 A5
Dunlichity
  Lodge ...252 C2
Dunlop ...205 D4

Dunmaglass
  Lodge ...252 D1
Dunmore Argyll ..202 B2
  Falk ...208 B1
Dunnet ...280 A4
Dunnichen ...232 D3
Dunninald ...233 C5
Dunning ...219 C5
Dunnington
  E Yorks ...151 B4
  Warks ...80 B3
  York ...149 B5
Dunnockshaw ...137 A7
Dunollie ...226 C3
Dunoon ...203 A6
Dunragit ...170 B3
Dunrostan ...213 D5
Duns ...198 A1
Dunsby ...116 C4
Dunscore ...183 D6
Dunscroft ...141 C4
Dunsdale ...168 D4
Dunsden Green .. 47 B5
Dunsfold ...34 C3
Dunsford ...12 C3
Dunshalt ...220 C2
Dunshillock ...257 B4
Dunskey Ho ...170 B2
Dunsley ...169 D6
Dunsmore ...66 C3
Dunsop Bridge ..145 B6
Dunstable ...67 B4
Dunstall ...113 C5
Dunstall
  Common ...80 C1
Dunstall Green ...86 A3
Dunstan ...189 B5
Dunstan Steads .189 A5
Dunster ...27 A4
Duns Tew ...65 A5
Dunston Lincs ...133 C5
  Norf ...104 A3
  Staffs ...112 D3
  T&W ...179 C4
Dunsville ...140 C4
Dunswell ...150 D3
Dunsyre ...195 B5
Dunterton ...11 D4
Duntisbourne
  Abbots ...63 C5
Duntisbourne
  Leer ...63 C5
Duntisbourne
  Rouse ...63 C5
Duntish ...15 A6
Duntocher ...205 A4
Dunton Bucks ...66 A4
  C Beds ...84 C4
  Norf ...119 B5
Dunton Bassett .. 98 B2
Dunton Green ...36 A3
Dunton Wayletts .69 D6
Duntulm ...259 A4
Dunure ...192 D2
Dunvant ...57 C5
Dunvegan ...258 D2
Dunwich ...105 D5
Dunwood ...129 D4
Dupplin Castle ..219 C5
Durdar ...175 C7
Durgates ...36 C4
Durham ...167 A5
Durisdeer ...183 B6
Durisdeermill ...183 B6
Durkar ...139 B6
Durleigh ...28 B2
Durley Hants ...32 D4
  Wilts ...45 C6
Durnamuck ...262 A2
Durness ...277 B5
Durno ...256 D2
Duror ...236 D3
Durran Argyll ...214 B2
  Highld ...280 B3
Durrington Wilts ..31 A5
  W Sus ...21 B4
Dursley ...62 D3
Durston ...28 C2
Durweston ...16 A2
Dury ...285 G6
Duston ...83 A4
Duthil ...253 D5

Dutlas ...93 D6
Duton Hill ...69 A6
Dutson ...10 C4
Dutton ...127 B5
Duxford Cambs ...85 C6
  Oxon ...65 D4
Dwygyfylchi ...124 B2
Dwyran ...123 D4
Dyce ...245 A5
Dye House ...178 D1
Dyffryn Bridgend . 40 B3
  Carms ...73 D6
  Pembs ...72 C2
Dyffryn
  Ardudwy ...107 D5
Dyffryn Castell ...91 D5
Dyffryn Ceidrych .59 C4
Dyffryn Cellwen ..59 E5
Dyke Lincs ...116 C4
  Moray ...253 A5
Dykehead Angus .232 B1
  N Lanark ...207 E6
  Stirling ...206 A3
Dykelands ...233 B5
Dykends ...231 C6
Dykeside ...256 B2
Dykesmains ...204 D2
Dylife ...91 C6
Dymchurch ...38 C2
Dymock ...79 D5
Dyrham ...43 B6
Dysart ...209 A6
Dyserth ...125 B5

E

Eachwick ...178 B3
Eadar Dha
  Fhadhail ...287 A5
Eagland Hill ...144 C4
Eagle ...132 C3
Eagle Barnsdale .132 C3
Eagle Moor ...132 C3
Eaglescliffe ...168 D2
Eaglesfield Cumb .162 B3
  Dumfries ...175 A5
Eaglesham ...205 C5
Eaglethorpe ...100 B2
Eairy ...152 D2
Eakley Lanes ...83 B5
Eakring ...132 C1
Ealand ...141 B5
Ealing ...49 A4
Eals ...177 D4
Eamont Bridge ..164 C3
Earby ...146 C3
Earcroft ...137 A5
Eardington ...95 B5
Eardisland ...78 B2
Eardisley ...77 C7
Eardiston Shrops .110 C2
  Worcs ...79 A4
Earith ...101 D5
Earle ...188 A2
Earley ...47 B5
Earlham ...104 A3
Earlish ...258 B3
Earls Barton ...83 A5
Earls Colne ...70 A2
Earl's Croome ...79 C6
Earlsdon ...97 D6
Earlsferry ...221 E4
Earlsfield ...116 B2
Earlsford ...256 C3
Earl's Green ...87 A6
Earlsheaton ...139 A5
Earl Shilton ...98 B1
Earlsmill ...253 A5
Earl Soham ...88 A3
Earl Sterndale ...129 C5
Earlston Borders .197 B4
  E Ayrs ...193 B4
Earl Stonham ...88 B2
Earlswood Mon ...61 D6
  Sur ...35 B5
  Warks ...96 B4
Earnley ...19 B7
Earsairidh ...286 G3
Earsdon ...179 B5
Earsham ...104 C4
Earswick ...149 B5

Eartham ...20 B2
Easby N Yorks ...157 A5
  N Yorks ...159 A4
Easdale ...213 A5
Easebourne ...34 D1
Easenhall ...98 D1
Eashing ...34 B2
Easington Bucks ..66 B2
  Durham ...168 A2
  E Yorks ...143 B5
  Northumb ...199 C5
  Oxon ...66 D2
  Oxon ...82 D1
  Redcar ...169 D5
Easington
  Colliery ...168 A2
Easington Lane ..167 A6
Easingwold ...148 A4
Easole Street ...53 D4
Eassie ...232 D1
East Aberthaw ...41 E5
East Adderbury ...82 D1
East Allington ...7 C6
East Anstey ...26 C3
East Appleton ...157 B6
East Ardsley ...139 A6
East Ashling ...19 A7
East Auchronie ..245 B5
East Ayton ...160 C3
East Bank ...60 C4
East Barkwith ...133 A6
East Barming ...37 A5
East Barnby ...169 D6
East Barnet ...68 D2
East Barns ...211 C4
East Barsham ...119 B6
East Beckham ...120 B3
East Bedfont ...48 B3
East Bergholt ...87 D6
East Bilney ...119 D6
East Blatchington 22 B2
East Boldre ...18 A2
Eastbourne ...22 C4
East Brent ...42 D2
Eastbridge ...89 A5
East Bridgford ...115 A4
East Buckland ...26 B1
East Budleigh ...13 C5
Eastburn ...147 C4
East Burrafirth ...285 H5
East Burton ...16 C2
Eastbury London ...67 D6
  W Berks ...46 B1
East Butsfield ...166 A4
East Butterwick .141 C6
Eastby ...147 B4
East Cairnbeg ...233 A5
East Calder ...208 D3
East Carleton ...104 A2
East Carlton
  Northants ...99 C5
  W Yorks ...147 C6
East Chaldon ...16 C1
East Challow ...46 A1
East Chiltington .21 A6
East Chinnock ...29 D4
East Chisenbury .45 D5
Eastchurch ...52 B1
East Clandon ...34 A3
East Claydon ...66 A3
East Clyne ...274 D2
East Coker ...29 D5
Eastcombe ...63 C4
East Combe ...27 B6
East Common ...149 D5
East Compton ...29 A6
Eastcote London ...48 A4
  Northants ...82 B3
  W Mid ...97 D4
Eastcott Corn ...24 D3
  Wilts ...44 D4
East
  Cottingwith ...149 C6
Eastcourt Wilts ...63 D5
  Wilts ...45 C7
East Cowes ...18 B4
East Cowick ...141 A4
East Cowton ...157 A7

East
Cramlington...179 B4
East Cranmore...29 A4
East Creech......16 C3
East Croachy...252 D2
East Croftmore..242 A2
East Curthwaite.164 A1
East Dean E Sus...22 C3
Hants...........31 C6
W Sus..........20 A2
East Down......25 A7
East Drayton..132 B2
East Ella.......142 A2
East End Dorset...16 B3
E Yorks.......143 A4
Hants..........18 B2
Hants..........33 C5
Hants..........46 C2
Herts..........69 A4
Kent...........37 C6
N Som..........42 B3
Oxon...........65 B4
Easter Ardross..264 C2
Easter Balmoral 243 C5
Easter
Boleskine.....251 D7
Easter Compton..43 A4
Easter Cringate .207 B5
Easter Davoch..244 B1
Easter Earshaig .184 B3
Easter Fearn...264 B2
Easter
Galcantray...253 B4
Eastergate......20 B2
Easterhouse...207 D4
Easter Howgate.209 D5
Easter Howlaws .197 B6
Easter Kinkell..252 A1
Easter
Lednathie....232 B1
Easter Milton..253 A5
Easter Moniack .252 B1
Eastern Green...97 C5
Easter Ord.....245 B5
Easter Quarff...285 K6
Easter Rhynd..219 C6
Easter Row.....207 A5
Easter
Silverford....268 C2
Easter Skeld..285 J5
Easterton.......44 D4
Eastertown......42 D2
Eastertown of
Auchleuchries.257 C5
Easter Whyntie..267 C7
East Farleigh....37 A5
East Farndon....99 C4
East Ferry.....141 D6
Eastfield
N Lanark......208 D1
N Yorks.......160 C4
Eastfield Hall..189 C5
East Fortune..210 C2
East Garston....46 B1
Eastgate Durham 166 B2
Norf..........120 C3
East Ginge......46 A2
East Goscote..115 D4
East Grafton....45 C6
East Grimstead...31 C6
East Grinstead..36 C1
East Guldeford..38 C1
East Haddon....82 A3
East Hagbourne..46 A3
East Halton...142 B3
Eastham......126 A3
East Ham.......50 A1
Eastham Ferry..126 A3
Easthampstead...47 C6
East Hanney.....65 D5
East
Hanningfield...70 C2
East Hardwick..140 B2
East Harling...103 C5
East Harlsey..158 B3
East Harnham...31 C5
East Harptree...43 D4
East Hartford..179 B4
East Harting....33 D6

East Hatley.......85 B4
East Hauxwell...157 B5
East Haven....221 A5
Eastheath.........47 C6
East Heckington 117 A4
East
Hedleyhope...167 A4
East Hendred...46 A2
East Herrington .179 D5
East Heslerton..160 D3
East Hoathly....22 A3
Easthope........94 B3
Easthorpe Essex..70 A3
Leics.........115 B6
Notts.........132 D2
East Horrington..29 A5
East Horsley....34 A3
East Horton...198 C4
Easthouses....209 D6
East Huntspill..28 A3
East Hyde.......67 B7
East Ilkerton...26 A2
East Ilsley.....46 A2
Eastington Devon.12 A2
Glos...........62 C3
Glos...........64 B2
East Keal......134 C3
East Kennett....45 C5
East Keswick..148 C2
East Kilbride..205 C6
East Kirkby...134 C3
East Knapton..160 D2
East Knighton...16 C2
East Knoyle.....30 B2
East Kyloe....199 C4
East Lambrook...28 D4
East Lamington .264 C3
East Langdon....39 A5
East Langton....99 B4
East Langwell..273 D5
East Lavant.....20 B1
East Lavington...20 A2
East Layton...157 A5
Eastleach Martin .64 C3
Eastleach
Turville.......64 C2
East Leake....114 C3
East Learmouth .198 C2
Eastleigh Devon..25 C5
Hants..........32 D3
East Leigh......12 A1
East Lexham...119 D5
East Lilburn...188 A3
Eastling........51 D6
East Linton...210 C2
East Liss.......33 C6
East Looe.......6 B1
East Lound....141 D5
East Lulworth...16 C2
East Lutton...150 A2
East Lydford....29 B5
East Mains....244 C3
East Malling....37 A5
East March.....220 A4
East Marden....33 D7
East Markham...132 B2
East Marton....146 B3
East Meon.......33 C5
East Mere.......27 C4
East Mersea.....71 B4
East Mey......281 A5
East Molesey....49 C4
Eastmoor Derbys 130 B3
Norf..........102 A3
East Morden....16 B3
East Morton...147 C4
East Ness.....159 D5
East Newton...151 D5
Eastney.........19 B5
Eastnor.........79 D5
East Norton.....99 A4
East Nynehead...27 C6
East Oakley.....46 D3
Eastoft........141 B6
East Ogwell.....12 D3
Eastoke.........19 B6
Easton Cambs...100 D3
Cumb.........175 C5
Cumb.........176 B2
Devon.........12 C2
Dorset........15 D6
Hants..........32 B4

Easton continued
Lincs........116 C2
Norf.........120 D3
Som...........29 A5
Suff..........88 B3
Wilts.........44 B2
Easton Grey....44 A2
Easton-in-
Gordano......43 B4
Easton Maudit...83 B5
Easton on the
Hill.........100 A2
Easton Royal....45 C6
East Orchard...30 D2
East Ord.....198 A3
East Panson....11 B4
Eastpark.....174 B3
East Peckham...37 B4
East Pennard...29 B5
East Perry.....84 A3
East Portlemouth..7 D6
East Prawle......8 D1
East Preston...20 B3
East Putford...25 D4
East
Quantoxhead...27 A6
East Rainton...167 A6
East Ravendale..143 D4
East Raynham..119 C5
Eastrea........101 B4
East Rhidorroch
Lodge........262 A4
Eastriggs.....175 B5
East Rigton...148 C2
Eastrington...141 A5
East Rounton..158 A3
East Row......169 D6
East Rudham...119 C5
East Runton...120 A3
East Ruston...121 C5
Eastry..........53 D5
East Saltoun..210 D1
East Sleekburn .179 A4
East Somerton .121 D6
East Stockwith .141 D5
East Stoke Dorset.16 C2
Notts........115 A5
East Stour.....30 C2
East Stourmouth .53 C4
East Stowford..26 C1
East Stratton...32 B4
East Studdal....39 A5
East Suisnish..248 C2
East Taphouse...5 A6
East-the-Water..25 C5
East Thirston..189 D4
East Tilbury....50 B3
East Tisted....33 B6
East Torrington .133 A6
East
Tuddenham...120 D2
East Tytherley..32 C1
East Tytherton..44 B3
East Village....12 A3
Eastville Bristol..43 B5
Lincs.........135 D4
East Wall.......94 B3
East Walton...119 D4
Eastwell......115 C5
East Wellow....32 C2
East Wemyss..209 A6
East Whitburn .208 D2
Eastwick Herts....85 B6
Shetland......284 F5
East Williamston .55 D6
East Winch....119 D3
East Winterslow..31 B6
East Wittering..19 B6
East Witton...157 C5
Eastwood Notts .114 A2
Southend......51 A5
W Yorks.....138 A2
East Woodburn.177 A7
East Woodhay...46 C2
East Worldham...33 B6
East Worlington..26 D2
East Worthing...21 B4
Eastrop.........81 A6
Eaton Ches E....128 C3
Ches W.......127 C5
Leics........115 C5
Norf.........104 A3

Eaton continued
Notts........132 B2
Oxon..........65 C5
Shrops........94 C1
Shrops........94 C3
Eaton Bishop...78 D2
Eaton Bray.....67 A5
Eaton
Constantine...94 A3
Eaton Green....67 A5
Eaton Hastings..64 D3
Eaton on Tern..111 C5
Eaton Socon....84 B3
Eavestone....147 A6
Ebberston....160 C2
Ebbesbourne
Wake.........30 C3
Ebbw Vale (Glyn
Ebwy).......60 C3
Ebchester....178 D3
Ebford.........13 C4
Ebley..........63 C4
Ebnal.........110 A3
Ebrington......81 D4
Ecchinswell....46 D2
Ecclaw........211 D4
Ecclefechan...175 A4
Eccles Borders..197 B6
Gtr Man......137 D6
Kent...........51 C4
Ecclesall.....130 A3
Ecclesfield...139 D6
Ecclesgreig...233 B5
Eccleshall....112 C2
Eccleshill....147 D5
Ecclesmachan..208 C3
Eccles on Sea..121 C6
Eccles Road...103 B6
Eccleston
Ches W.......127 C4
Lancs........136 B4
Mers.........136 D3
Eccleston Park .136 D3
Eccup.........148 C1
Echt..........245 B4
Eckford.......187 A6
Eckington
Derbys.......131 B4
Worcs.........80 C2
Ecton..........83 A5
Edale.........129 A6
Edburton.......21 A5
Edderside....174 D3
Edderton.....264 B3
Eddistone......24 C3
Eddleston....196 B1
Edenbridge.....36 B2
Edenfield....137 B6
Edenhall.....164 B3
Edenham......116 C3
Eden Park......49 C6
Edensor.......130 C2
Edentaggart..215 C6
Edenthorpe...140 C4
Edentown.....175 C6
Ederline.....214 B1
Edern.........106 C2
Edgarley.......29 B5
Edgbaston......96 C3
Edgcott Bucks...66 A2
Som...........26 B3
Edge..........94 A1
Edgebolton...111 C4
Edge End.......62 B1
Edgefield....120 B2
Edgefield Street 120 B2
Edge Green....127 D4
Edge Hill.....136 D2
Edgeside.....138 A1
Edgeworth......63 C5
Edgmond.....111 D6
Edgmond
Marsh........111 C6
Edgton.........94 C2
Edgware........68 D1
Edgworth.....137 B6
Edinample......57 B6
Edinbane.....258 C3
Edinburgh....209 C5
Edingale.....113 D6
Edingight Ho...267 D6
Edingley.....131 D6

Edingthorpe....121 B5
Edingthorpe
Green........121 B5
Edington Som...28 B3
Wilts..........44 D3
Edintore.....255 B5
Edithmead.....28 A3
Edith Weston...99 A6
Edlesborough...67 B5
Edlingham....189 C4
Edlington....134 B2
Edmondsham....31 D4
Edmondsley...167 A5
Edmondthorpe .115 D6
Edmonstone...282 E6
Edmonton......68 D3
Edmundbyers..178 D2
Ednam........197 C6
Ednaston....113 A6
Edradynate...230 C2
Edrom........198 A2
Edstaston....111 B4
Edstone........81 A4
Edvin Loach....79 B4
Edwalton....114 B3
Edwardstone...87 C5
Edwinsford....58 B3
Edwinstowe...131 C6
Edworth........84 C4
Edwyn Ralph....79 B4
Edzell........232 B3
Efail Isaf......41 C5
Efailnewydd...106 C3
Efailwen.......72 D4
Efenechtyd...125 D6
Effingham......35 A4
Effirth......285 H5
Efford.........12 A3
Egdon..........80 B2
Egerton Gtr Man..137 B6
Kent...........37 B7
Egerton Forstal..37 B6
Eggborough...140 A3
Eggbuckland....7 B4
Eggington......67 A5
Egginton.....113 C6
Egglescliffe..168 D2
Eggleston....166 C2
Egham..........48 B3
Egleton........99 A5
Eglingham....189 B4
Egloshayle......9 D5
Egloskerry....10 C3
Eglwysbach...124 B3
Eglwys-Brewis..41 E5
Eglwys Cross..110 A3
Eglwys Fach....91 C4
Eglwyswen......73 C4
Eglwyswrw......72 C4
Egmanton....132 C2
Egremont Cumb..162 D2
Mers.........136 D2
Egton.........159 A7
Egton Bridge..159 A7
Eight Ash Green..70 A3
Eignaig......226 B2
Eil...........241 A6
Eilanreach...238 A2
Eileanach
Lodge........264 D1
Eilean Darach..262 B3
Einacleite...288 E2
Eisgean......288 F4
Eisingrug....107 C5
Elan Village...76 A3
Elberton.......43 A5
Elburton........7 B4
Elcho.........219 B6
Elcombe........45 A5
Eldernell....101 B5
Eldersfield....79 D6
Elderslie....205 B4
Eldon.........167 C5
Eldrick......181 C4
Eldroth......146 A1
Eldwick......147 C5
Elfhowe......154 B3
Elford Northumb..199 C5
Staffs.......113 D5
Elgin.........266 C3
Elgol.........247 C4
Elham..........38 A3

Elie...........221 D4
Elim..........122 B3
Eling..........32 D2
Elishader....259 B5
Elishaw......188 D1
Elkesley.....132 B1
Elkstone.......63 B5
Ellan.........253 D4
Elland........139 A4
Ellary........202 A2
Ellastone....113 A5
Ellemford....211 D4
Ellenbrook...152 B3
Ellenhall....112 C2
Ellen's Green...34 C3
Ellerbeck....158 B3
Ellerburn....160 C2
Ellerby......169 D5
Ellerdine Heath .111 C5
Ellerhayes.....13 A4
Elleric......227 B5
Ellerker.....141 A7
Ellerton E Yorks .149 D6
Shrops.......111 C4
Ellesborough...66 C4
Ellesmere....110 B3
Ellesmere Port .127 B4
Ellingham Norf .105 B4
Northumb.....189 A4
Ellingstring...157 C5
Ellington Cambs.100 D3
Northumb.....189 D5
Elliot.........221 A6
Ellisfield......33 A5
Ellistown....114 D2
Ellon.........257 C4
Ellonby......164 B2
Ellough......105 C5
Elloughton...142 A1
Ellwood.......62 C1
Elm...........101 A6
Elmbridge......80 A2
Elmdon Essex...85 D6
W Mid.........97 C4
Elmdon Heath...97 C4
Elmers End.....49 C6
Elmesthorpe....98 B1
Elmfield.......19 B5
Elm Hill.......30 C2
Elmhurst.....113 D5
Elmley Castle...80 C2
Elmley Lovett...79 A6
Elmore.........62 B3
Elmore Back....62 B3
Elm Park.......50 A2
Elmscott.......24 C3
Elmsett........87 C6
Elmstead Market .71 A4
Elmsted........38 A3
Elmstone......53 C4
Elmstone
Hardwicke.....63 A5
Elmswell E Yorks .150 B2
Suff..........87 A5
Elmton........131 B5
Elphin........271 C5
Elphinstone..209 C6
Elrick........245 B5
Elrig.........171 C5
Elsdon........188 D2
Elsecar......140 C1
Elsenham......69 A5
Elsfield.......65 B6
Elsham.......142 B2
Elsing........120 D2
Elslack......146 C3
Elson.........110 B2
Elsrickle....195 B5
Elstead........34 B2
Elsted.........33 D7
Elsthorpe....116 C3
Elstob........167 C6
Elston Notts...115 A5
Wilts.........31 A4
Elstone.......26 D1
Elstow........84 C2
Elstree.......68 D1
Elstronwick..151 D5
Elswick......144 D4
Elsworth......85 A5
Elterwater...154 A2
Eltham........50 B1

Eltisley 85 B4
Elton Cambs 100 B2
  Ches W. 127 B4
  Derbys 130 C2
  Glos 62 B3
  Hereford 94 D2
  Notts 115 B5
  Stockton. ... 168 D2
Elton Green 127 B4
Elvanfoot 184 A2
Elvaston 114 B2
Elveden. 103 D4
Elvingston 210 C1
Elvington Kent. .. 31 D7
  York 149 C5
Elwick Hrtlpl... 168 B2
  Northumb. 199 C5
Elworth. 128 C2
Elworthy. 27 B5
Ely Cambs 102 C1
  Cardiff 41 D6
Emberton 83 C5
Embleton Cumb .163 A4
  Northumb. 189 A5
Embo. 265 A4
Emborough 43 D5
Embo Street ...265 A4
Embsay. 147 B4
Emery Down 18 A1
Emley 139 B5
Emmbrook. 47 C5
Emmer Green ... 47 B5
Emmington 66 C3
Emneth........101 A6
Emneth
  Hungate.....101 A7
Empingham 99 A6
Empshott 33 B6
Emstrey 111 D4
Emsworth. 19 A6
Enborne 46 C2
Enchmarsh 94 B3
Enderby 98 B2
Endmoor 154 C4
Endon 129 D4
Endon Bank ...129 D4
Enfield 68 D3
Enfield Wash... 68 D3
Enford........ 45 D5
Engamoor 285 H4
Engine Common . 43 A5
Englefield 47 B4
Englefield Green . 48 B2
Englesea-brook 128 D2
English Bicknor . 62 B1
Englishcombe... 43 C6
English
  Frankton.....110 C3
Enham Alamein . 32 A2
Enmore....... 28 B2
Ennerdale
  Bridge 162 C3
Enoch 183 B6
Enochdhu. 231 B4
Ensay 224 B2
Ensbury 17 B4
Ensdon 110 D3
Ensis 25 C6
Enstone 65 A4
Enterkinfoot ..183 B6
Enterpen 158 A3
Enville....... 95 C6
Eolaigearraidh .286 F3
Eorabus 224 D2
Eòropaidh 288 A6
Epperstone ...115 A4
Epping 69 C4
Epping Green
  Essex 68 C4
  Herts 68 C2
Epping Upland .. 68 C4
Eppleby.......167 D4
Eppleworth ...150 D3
Epsom........ 49 C5
Epwell....... 81 C6
Epworth 141 C5
Epworth
  Turbary 141 C5
Erbistock 110 A2
Erbusaig......249 D4
Erchless Castle .251 B6
Erdington..... 96 B4

Eredine.......214 B2
Eriboll........277 C5
Ericstane 184 A3
Eridge Green.... 36 C3
Erines 202 A3
Eriswell.......102 D3
Erith 50 B2
Erlestoke 44 D3
Ermine 133 B4
Ermington 7 B5
Erpingham 120 B3
Errogie 252 D1
Errol 220 B2
Erskine 205 A4
Erskine Bridge .205 A4
Ervie 170 A2
Erwarton...... 88 D3
Erwood....... 77 C4
Eryholme 157 A7
Eryrys 126 D2
Escomb 167 C4
Escrick 149 C5
Esgairdawe 58 A3
Esgairgeiliog.... 91 B5
Esh 167 A4
Esher 48 C4
Esholt 147 C5
Eshott 189 D5
Eshton........146 B3
Esh Winning ...167 A4
Eskadale.......251 C6
Eskbank 209 D6
Eskdale Green .163 D4
Eskdalemuir ...185 C5
Eske 150 C3
Eskham 143 D5
Esk Valley.....159 A7
Esprick 144 D4
Essendine 116 D3
Essendon 68 C2
Essich 252 C2
Essington 96 A2
Esslemont 257 D4
Eston 168 D3
Eswick 285 H6
Etal 198 C3
Etchilhampton ... 44 C4
Etchingham 37 D5
Etchinghill Kent... 38 B3
  Staffs........112 D4
Ethie Castle ...233 D4
Ethie Mains ...233 D4
Etling Green ...120 D2
Eton 48 B2
Eton Wick 48 B2
Etteridge 241 C4
Ettersgill 166 C1
Ettingshall 96 B2
Ettington 81 C5
Etton E Yorks...150 C2
  Pboro........100 A3
Ettrick 185 A5
Ettrickbridge...186 A2
Ettrickhill.....185 A5
Etwall 113 B6
Euston........103 D4
Euximoor Drove 101 B6
Euxton 137 B4
Evanstown..... 41 C4
Evanton 264 D2
Evedon 116 A3
Evelix........264 A3
Evenjobb...... 77 A6
Evenley....... 82 D2
Evenlode 64 A3
Evenwood 167 C4
Evenwood Gate .167 C4
Everbay.......282 E7
Evercreech 29 B6
Everdon 82 B3
Everingham ...149 C7
Everleigh 45 D6
Everley 160 C3
Eversholt 84 D1
Evershot 15 A5
Eversley 47 C5
Eversley Cross .. 47 C5
Everthorpe 150 D2
Everton C Beds.. 84 B4
  Hants........ 18 B1
  Mers.........136 D2
  Notts........141 D4

Evertown 175 A6
Evesbatch 79 C4
Evesham...... 80 C3
Evington 98 A3
Ewden Village...139 D5
Ewell 49 C5
Ewell Minnis ... 39 A4
Ewelme....... 66 D2
Ewen 63 D6
Ewenny 40 D4
Ewerby 116 A4
Ewerby Thorpe..116 A4
Ewes 185 C6
Ewesley 188 D3
Ewhurst 34 B3
Ewhurst Green
  E Sus 37 D5
  Sur.......... 34 C3
Ewloe 126 C3
Ewloe Grn.....126 C2
Ewood 137 A5
Eworthy 11 B5
Ewshot 33 A7
Ewyas Harold .. 61 A5
Exbourne 11 A7
Exbury 18 B3
Exebridge..... 27 C4
Exelby 157 C6
Exeter 13 B4
Exford 26 B3
Exhall 80 B4
Exley Head 147 D4
Exminster..... 13 C4
Exmouth 13 C5
Exnaboe 285 M5
Exning 86 A2
Exton Devon ... 13 C4
  Hants 33 C5
  Rutland.......116 D2
  Som 27 B4
Exwick 13 B4
Eyam 130 B2
Eydon 82 B2
Eye Hereford ... 78 A2
  Pboro........100 A4
  Suff 104 D2
Eye Green 100 A4
Eyemouth......211 D6
Eyeworth 85 C4
Eyhorne Street .. 37 A6
Eyke 88 B4
Eynesbury 84 B3
Eynort 246 B2
Eynsford...... 50 C2
Eynsham 65 C5
Eype 14 B4
Eyre Highld ...248 C2
  Highld.......259 C4
Eythorne...... 39 A4
Eyton Hereford .. 78 A2
  Shrops....... 94 C1
  Wrex 110 A2
Eyton upon the
  Weald Moors ..111 D5

F

Faccombe 46 D1
Faceby 158 A3
Facit 138 B1
Faddiley 127 D5
Fadmoor 159 C5
Faerdre...... 40 A1
Failand 43 B4
Failford 193 C4
Failsworth 138 C1
Fain 262 C3
Fairbourne.... 90 A4
Fairburn......149 D2
Fairfield Derbys ..129 B5
  Stockton.....168 D2
  Worcs........ 80 A3
  Worcs........ 96 D2
Fairford 64 C2
Fair Green 118 D3
Fairhaven.....136 A2
Fair Hill......164 B3
Fairlie 204 C2
Fairlight 23 A6
Fairlight Cove... 23 A6
Fairmile 13 B5

Fairmilehead...209 D5
Fairoak 111 B6
  Fair Oak 32 D3
Fair Oak Green.. 47 C4
Fairseat 50 C3
Fairstead Essex .. 70 B1
  Norf 118 D3
Fairwarp...... 36 D2
Fairy Cottage ...152 C4
Fairy Cross.... 25 C5
Fakenham 119 C6
Fakenham
  Magna 103 D5
Fala 210 D1
Fala Dam 210 D1
Falahill 196 A2
Falcon........ 79 D4
Faldingworth ..133 A5
Falfield 62 D2
Falkenham 88 D3
Falkirk 208 C1
Falkland 220 D2
Falla 187 B6
Fallgate 130 C3
Fallin 207 A6
Fallowfield....138 D1
Fallsidehill....197 B5
Falmer 21 B6
Falmouth 4 D3
Falsgrave 160 C4
Falstone 177 A5
Fanagmore 276 D2
Fangdale Beck ..159 B4
Fangfoss 149 B6
Fankerton 207 B5
Fanmore 224 B3
Fannich Lodge .262 D4
Fans 197 B5
Far Bank......140 B4
Far Bletchley... 83 D5
Farcet 100 B4
Far Cotton 83 B4
Farden 94 D3
Fareham 19 A4
Farewell 113 D4
Far Forest 95 D5
Farforth 134 B3
Faringdon 64 D3
Farington 136 A4
Farlam 176 D3
Farlary 273 D5
Far Laund.....114 A1
Farleigh N Som... 42 C3
  Sur.......... 49 C6
Farleigh
  Hungerford....44 D2
Farleigh Wallop . 33 A5
Farlesthorpe ...135 B4
Farleton Cumb ..154 C4
  Lancs........145 A5
Farley Shrops ... 94 A1
  Staffs........113 A4
  Wilts......... 31 C6
Farley Green ... 34 B3
Farley Hill Luton . 67 A6
  Wokingham ... 47 C5
Farleys End ... 62 B3
Farlington 149 A5
Farlow........ 95 C4
Farmborough .. 43 C5
Farmcote Glos .. 63 A6
  Shrops....... 95 B5
Farmington.... 64 B2
Farmoor 65 C5
Farmtown 267 D6
Farnborough
  Hants........ 34 A1
  London....... 50 C1
  Warks....... 82 C1
  W Berks...... 46 A2
Farnborough
  Green....... 34 A1
Farncombe 34 B2
Farndish 83 A6
Farndon Ches W..127 D4
  Notts........132 D2
Farnell 233 C4
Farnham Dorset.. 30 D3
  Essex 69 A4
  N Yorks.......148 A2
  Suff......... 89 A4
  Sur.......... 34 B1

Farnham
  Common 48 A2
Farnham Green . 69 A4
Farnham Royal . 48 A2
Farnhill.......147 C4
Farningham.... 50 C2
Farnley N Yorks .147 C6
  W Yorks.......147 D6
Farnley Tyas ..139 B4
Farnsfield.....131 D6
Farnworth
  Gtr Man 137 C6
  Halton 127 A5
Farr Highld 241 B6
  Highld.......252 C2
  Highld.......278 B3
Farr House.....252 C2
Farringdon 13 B5
Farrington
  Gurney 43 D5
Far Sawrey.....154 B2
Farsley 147 D6
Farthinghoe ... 82 D2
Farthingloe ... 39 A4
Farthingstone .. 82 B3
Fartown 139 B4
Farway 14 B1
Fasag.........249 A5
Fascadale 235 C4
Faslane Port ...215 D5
Fasnacloich ...227 B5
Fasnakyle Ho ..251 D5
Fatfield 179 D5
Fattahead 268 D1
Faugh 176 D3
Fauldhouse ...208 D2
Faulkbourne ... 70 B1
Faulkland 43 D6
Fauls 111 B4
Faversham 52 C2
Favillar 254 C3
Fawdington ...158 D3
Fawfieldhead ..129 C5
Fawkham Green.. 50 C2
Fawler........ 65 B4
Fawley Bucks ... 47 A5
  Hants........ 18 A3
  W Berks...... 46 A1
Fawley Chapel .. 62 A1
Faxfleet 141 A6
Faygate 35 C5
Fazakerley 136 D2
Fazeley....... 97 A5
Fearby........157 C5
Fearn.........265 C4
Fearnan 229 D6
Fearnbeg 249 A4
Fearnhead 137 D5
Fearn Lodge ..264 B2
Fearnmore 261 D4
Fearn Station ..265 C4
Featherstone
  Staffs........ 96 A2
  W Yorks.......140 A2
Featherwood ..187 C7
Feckenham 80 A3
Feering 70 A2
Feetham 156 B3
Feizor 146 A1
Felbridge 35 C6
Felbrigg 120 B4
Felcourt 36 B1
Felden....... 67 C6
Felin-Crai 59 C5
Felindre Carms .. 58 B3
  Carms........ 58 C2
  Carms........ 59 C4
  Carms........ 73 C6
  Ceredig...... 75 C4
  Powys....... 93 C5
  Swansea 57 B6
Felindre Farchog 72 C4
Felinfach Ceredig. 75 C4
  Powys....... 77 D4
Felinfoel..... 57 B5
Felingwm isaf .. 58 C2
Felingwm uchaf . 58 C2
Felinwynt..... 73 A5
Felixkirk 158 C3
Felixstowe 88 D3
Felixstowe Ferry . 88 D4

Felkington 198 B3
Felkirk 140 B1
Felling 179 C4
Fell Side......163 A6
Felmersham ... 84 B1
Felmingham ..120 C4
Felpham 20 C2
Felsham 87 B5
Felsted 69 A6
Feltham 48 B4
Felthorpe.....120 D3
Felton Hereford .. 78 C3
  Northumb. ...189 C4
  N Som 43 C4
Felton Butler ..110 D2
Feltwell 102 B3
Fenay Bridge...139 B4
Fence 146 D2
Fence Houses ..179 D5
Fen Ditton 85 A6
Fen Drayton... 85 A5
Fen End 97 D5
Fenham 199 B4
Fenhouses 117 A5
Feniscliffe 137 A5
Feniscowles ...137 A5
Feniton 13 B6
Fenlake...... 84 C2
Fenny Bentley .130 D1
Fenny Bridges .. 13 B6
Fenny Compton . 81 B7
Fenny Drayton . 97 B6
Fenny Stratford . 83 D5
Fenrother.....189 D4
Fen Side 134 D3
Fenstanton ... 85 A5
Fenton Cambs..101 D5
  Lincs........132 B3
  Lincs........132 D3
  Stoke 112 A6
Fenton Barns ..210 B2
Fenton Town ..198 C3
Fenwick E Ayrs..205 D4
  Northumb. ...178 B2
  Northumb. ...199 B4
  S Yorks.......140 B3
Feochaig 190 D3
Feock 4 D3
Feolin Ferry ...201 B4
Ferindonald...247 D5
Feriniquarrie ..258 C1
Ferlochan 226 B4
Fern 232 B2
Ferndale..... 41 B5
Ferndown 17 A4
Ferness.......253 B5
Ferney Green ..154 B3
Fernham...... 64 D3
Fernhill Heath... 79 B6
Fernhurst..... 34 D1
Fernie 220 C3
Ferniegair 194 A2
Fernilea 246 A2
Fernilee 129 B5
Ferrensby 148 A2
Ferring 20 B3
Ferrybridge ...140 A2
Ferryden......233 C5
Ferryhill
  Aberdeen 245 B6
  Durham 167 B5
Ferry Hill.....101 C5
Ferryhill Station 167 B6
Ferry Point....264 B3
Ferryside 56 A3
Fersfield......103 C6
Fersit........228 A2
Ferwig 73 B4
Feshiebridge ..241 B6
Fetcham..... 35 A4
Fetterangus ...269 D4
Fettercairn....233 A4
Fettes 252 A1
Fewcott 65 A6
Fewston 147 B5
Ffairfach..... 58 C3
Ffair-Rhos.... 75 B6

Ffaldybrenin 58 A3
Ffarmers 58 A3
Ffawyddog 60 B4
Fforest 57 B5
Fforest-fâch 57 C6
Ffostrasol 73 B6
Ffos-y-ffin 74 B3
Ffridd-Uchaf 107 A5
Ffrith 126 D2
Ffrwd 107 A4
Ffynnon ddrain . . . 73 D7
Ffynnongroyw 125 A6
Ffynnon-oer 75 C4
Fidden 224 D2
Fiddes 245 D5
Fiddington Glos 80 D2
  Som 28 A2
Fiddleford 30 D2
Fiddlers Hamlet . . . 69 C4
Field 112 B4
Field Broughton 154 C2
Field Dalling . . . 120 B2
Field Head 98 A1
Fifehead
  Magdalen 30 C1
Fifehead Neville . . 30 D1
Fifield Oxon 64 B3
  Wilts 45 D5
  Windsor 48 B2
Fifield Bavant . . . 31 C4
Figheldean 31 A5
Filands 37 C4
Filby 121 D6
Filey 161 C5
Filgrave 83 C5
Filkins 64 C3
Filleigh Devon . . . 26 C1
  Devon 26 D2
Fillingham 133 A4
Fillongley 97 C5
Filton 43 B5
Fimber 150 A1
Finavon 232 C2
Fincham 102 A2
Finchampstead . . . 47 C5
Finchdean 33 D6
Finchingfield . . . 86 D2
Finchley 68 D2
Findern 113 B7
Findhorn 265 D6
Findhorn
  Bridge 253 D4
Findochty 267 C5
Findo Gask 219 B5
Findon Aberds . . 245 C6
  W Sus 21 B4
Findon Mains . . . 264 D2
Findrack Ho 244 B3
Finedon 99 D6
Fingal Street . . . 88 A3
Fingask 256 D2
Fingerpost 95 D5
Fingest 66 D3
Finghall 157 C5
Fingland Cumb . 175 C5
  Dumfries 183 A5
Finglesham . . . 53 D5
Fingringhoe . . . 71 A4
Finlarig 217 A5
Finmere 82 D3
Finnart 229 C4
Finningham . . . 87 A6
Finningley . . . 141 D4
Finnygaud . . . 267 D6
Finsbury 49 A6
Finstall 80 A2
Finsthwaite . . 154 C2
Finstock 65 B4
Finstown . . . 282 F4
Fintry Aberds . 268 D2
  Dundee 220 A4
  Stirling 207 B4
Finzean 244 C3
Fionnphort . . 224 D2
Fionnsbhagh . . 287 F5
Firbeck 131 A5
Firby N Yorks . 149 A6
  N Yorks 157 C6

Firgrove 138 B2
Firsby 135 C4
Firsdown 31 B6
First Coast 261 A6
Fir Tree 166 B4
Fishbourne IoW . . 19 B4
  W Sus 20 B1
Fishburn 167 B6
Fishcross 208 A1
Fisherford 256 C1
Fisher Place . . . 163 C6
Fisher's Pond . . . 32 C3
Fisherstreet . . . 34 C2
Fisherton Highld . 252 A3
  S Ayrs 192 D3
Fishguard
  (Abergwaun) . . 72 C2
Fishlake 141 B4
Fishleigh Barton . 25 C6
Fishponds 43 B5
Fishpool 62 A2
Fishtoft 117 A6
Fishtoft Drove . . 117 A6
Fishtown of
  Usan 233 C5
Fishwick 198 A3
Fiskavaig 246 A2
Fiskerton Lincs . 133 B5
  Notts 132 D2
Fitling 151 D5
Fittleton 31 A5
Fittleworth . . . 20 A3
Fitton End . . . 118 D1
Fitz 110 D3
Fitzhead 27 C6
Fitzwilliam . . . 140 B2
Fiunary 225 B5
Five Acres . . . 62 B1
Five Ashes . . . 36 D3
Fivecrosses . . 127 B5
Fivehead 28 C3
Five Oak Green . 36 B4
Five Oaks Jersey . . 6
  W Sus 34 D3
Five Roads . . . 57 B4
Flack's Green . 70 B1
Flackwell Heath . 48 A1
Fladbury 80 C2
Fladdabister . . 285 K6
Flagg 129 C6
Flamborough . 161 D6
Flamstead . . . 67 B6
Flamstead End . 68 C3
Flansham 20 B2
Flanshaw 139 A6
Flasby 146 B3
Flash 129 C5
Flashader . . . 258 C3
Flask Inn . . . 160 A3
Flaunden . . . 67 C6
Flawborough . 115 A5
Flawith 148 A3
Flax Bourton . 43 C4
Flaxby 148 B2
Flaxholme . . . 114 A1
Flaxley 62 B2
Flaxpool 27 B6
Flaxton 149 A5
Fleckney . . . 98 B3
Flecknoe . . . 82 A2
Fledborough . 132 B3
Fleet Hants . . 19 A6
  Hants 47 D6
  Lincs 117 C6
Fleetham . . . 189 A4
Fleet Hargate . 117 C6
Fleetlands . . . 19 A4
Fleetville . . . 67 C7
Fleetwood . . 144 C3
Flemingston . 41 D5
Flemington . 205 C6
Flempton . . . 87 A4
Fleoideabhagh 287 F5
Fletchertown . 175 D5
Fletching . . . 36 D2
Flexbury 10 A3
Flexford 34 B2
Flimby 162 A3
Flimwell . . . 37 C5
Flint (Y Fflint) . 126 B2
Flintham . . . 115 A5
Flint Mountain . 126 B2

Flinton 151 D5
Flintsham 77 B7
Flitcham 119 C4
Flitton 84 D2
Flitwick 84 D2
Flixborough . . 141 B6
Flixborough
  Stather 141 B6
Flixton Gtr Man . 137 D6
  N Yorks 160 D4
  Suff 104 C4
Flockton . . . 139 B5
Flodaigh . . . 286 A4
Flodden . . . 198 C3
Flodigarry . . 259 A4
Flood's Ferry . 101 B5
Flookburgh . 154 D2
Florden . . . 104 B2
Flore 82 A3
Flotterton . . 188 C2
Flowton . . . 88 C1
Flush House . 139 C4
Flushing Aberds . 257 B5
  Corn 4 D3
Flyford Flavell . 80 B2
Foals Green . . 104 D3
Fobbing 51 A4
Fochabers . . . 266 D4
Fochriw 60 C3
Fockerby . . . 141 B6
Fodderletter . 254 D2
Fodderty . . . 251 A7
Foel 109 D4
Foel-gastell . 57 A5
Foffarty . . . 232 D2
Foggathorpe . 149 D6
Fogo 197 B6
Fogorig . . . 198 B1
Foindle . . . 276 D2
Folda 231 B5
Fole 112 B4
Foleshill . . . 97 C6
Folke 29 D6
Folkestone . . 39 B4
Folkingham . 116 B3
Folkington . . 22 B3
Folksworth . 100 C3
Folkton . . . 161 D4
Folla Rule . . 256 C2
Follifoot . . 148 B2
Folly Gate . . 11 B6
Fonthill Bishop . 30 B3
Fonthill Gifford . 30 B3
Fontmell Magna . 30 D2
Fontwell . . . 20 B2
Foolow . . . 130 B1
Foots Cray . 50 B1
Forbestown . 243 A6
Force Mills . 154 B2
Forcett . . . 167 D4
Ford Argyll . 214 B1
  Bucks 66 C3
  Devon 25 C5
  Glos 64 A1
  Northumb . . 198 C3
  Shrops 110 D3
  Staffs 129 D5
  Wilts 44 B2
  W Sus 20 B2
Fordcombe . . 36 B3
Fordell 209 B4
Forden 93 A6
Ford End . . . 69 B6
Forder Grn . . 8 A1
Fordham Cambs . 102 D2
  Essex 70 A3
  Norf 102 B2
Fordhouses . 96 A2
Fordingbridge . 31 D5
Fordon 160 D4
Fordoun . . . 233 A5
Ford's Green . 87 A6
Fordstreet . . 70 A3
Ford Street . 27 D6
Fordwells . . 64 B4
Fordwich . . . 52 D3
Fordyce . . . 267 C6
Forebridge . . 112 C3
Forest 165 B6
Forest Becks . 146 B1
Forestburn
  Gate 188 D3

Foresterseat . . 266 D2
Forest Gate . . . 49 A7
Forest Green . . 35 B4
Forest Hall . . 154 A4
Forest Head . . 176 D3
Forest Hill . . . 65 C6
Forest Lane
  Head 148 B2
Forest Lodge
  Argyll . . . 228 D1
  Highld . . . 242 A3
  Perth 230 A3
Forest Mill . 208 A2
Forest Row . . 36 C2
Forestside . . 33 D6
Forest Town . 131 C5
Forfar 232 C2
Forgandenny . 219 C5
Forge 91 C5
Forge Side . . 60 C4
Forgewood . 194 A2
Forgie 267 D4
Forglen Ho . . 268 D1
Formby . . . 136 C2
Forncett End . 104 B2
Forncett St
  Mary . . . 104 B2
Forncett St
  Peter . . . 104 B2
Forneth . . . 231 D4
Fornham All
  Saints . . . 87 A4
Fornham St
  Martin . . . 87 A4
Forres . . . 253 A6
Forrestfield . 207 D6
Forrest Lodge . 182 D3
Forsbrook . . 112 A3
Forse 275 A6
Forse Ho . . 275 A6
Forsinain . . 279 D5
Forsinard . . 279 D4
Forsinard
  Station . . 279 D4
Forston . . . 15 B6
Fort Augustus . 240 B1
Forteviot . . 219 C5
Fort George Guern . 6
  Highld . . . 252 A3
Forth 194 A4
Forthampton . 79 D6
Forth Road
  Bridge . . 208 C4
Fortingall . . 229 D6
Forton Hants . 32 A3
  Lancs 145 B4
  Shrops . . . 110 D3
  Som 14 A3
  Staffs . . . 111 C6
Forton Heath . 110 D3
Fortrie . . . 256 B1
Fortrose . . 252 A3
Fortuneswell . 15 D6
Fort William . 237 B5
Forty Green . 67 D5
Forty Hill . . 68 D3
Forward Green . 88 B1
Fosbury . . . 45 D7
Fosdyke . . . 117 B6
Foston Derbys . 113 B5
  Lincs 115 A6
  N Yorks . . 149 A5
Foston on the
  Wolds . . . 151 B4
Fotherby . . 143 D5
Fotheringhay . 100 B2
Foubister . . 283 G6
Foulby 140 B1
Foulden Borders . 198 A3
  Norf 102 B3
Foul Mile . . 22 A4
Foulridge . . 146 C2
Foulsham . . 120 C2
Fountainhall . 196 B3
Four Ashes Staffs . 95 C6
  Suff 103 D6

Four Crosses
  Powys 93 A4
  Powys 110 D1
  Wrex 126 D2
Four Elms . . . 36 B2
Four Forks . . . 28 B2
Four Gotes . . 118 D1
Fourlane Ends . 130 D3
Four Lane Ends . 127 C5
Four Lanes . . . 3 B4
Fourlanes End . 128 D3
Four Marks . . 33 B5
Four Mile
  Bridge . . . 122 C2
Four Oaks E Sus . 37 D6
  W Mid 96 B4
  W Mid 97 C5
Fourpenny . . 265 A4
Four Roads Carms . 57 B4
  IoM 152 E2
Fourstones . 177 C6
Four Throws . 37 D5
Fovant 31 C4
Foveran . . . 257 D4
Fowey 5 B6
Fowley
  Common . . 137 D5
Fowlis 220 A3
Fowlis Wester . 218 B4
Fowlmere . . 85 C6
Fownhope . . 78 D3
Foxbar 205 B4
Foxcombe Hill . 65 C5
Fox Corner . . 34 A2
Foxdale . . . 152 D2
Foxearth . . . 87 C4
Foxfield . . . 153 B3
Foxham . . . 44 B3
Foxhole Corn . . 5 B4
  Swansea . . 57 C6
Foxholes . . . 160 D4
Foxhunt Green . 22 A3
Fox Lane . . . 34 A1
Foxley Norf . . 120 C2
  Wilts 44 A2
Fox Street . . 71 A4
Foxt 112 A4
Foxton Cambs . 85 C6
  Durham . . . 167 C6
  Leics 99 B4
Foxup 156 D2
Foxwist Green . 127 C6
Foxwood . . 95 D4
Foy 62 A1
Foyers 251 D6
Fraddam . . . 2 B3
Fraddon . . . 4 B4
Fradley . . . 113 D5
Fradswell . . 112 B3
Fraisthorpe . 151 A4
Framfield . . 36 D2
Framingham
  Earl 104 A3
Framingham
  Pigot . . . 104 A3
Framlingham . 88 A3
Frampton Dorset . 15 B6
  Lincs 117 B6
Frampton
  Cotterell . 43 A5
Frampton
  Mansell . . 63 C5
Frampton on
  Severn . . 62 C3
Frampton West
  End 117 A5
Framsden . . 88 B2
Framwellgate
  Moor . . . 167 A5
Franche . . . 95 D6
Frankby . . . 126 A2
Frankley . . . 96 C2
Frank's Bridge . 77 B5
Frankton . . . 98 D1
Frant 36 C3
Fraserburgh . 269 C4
Frating Green . 71 A4
Fratton . . . 19 B5
Freathy 6 B3
Freckenham . 102 D2
Freckleton . 136 A3

Freehay 112 A4
Freeland 65 B5
Freester 285 H6
Freethorpe . . . 105 A5
Freiston 117 A6
Fremington Devon 25 B6
  N Yorks 156 B4
Frenchay 43 B5
Frenchbeer . . 12 C1
Frenich . . . 216 D4
Frensham . . . 34 B1
Fresgoe . . . 279 B5
Freshfield . . . 136 C1
Freshford . . . 44 C1
Freshwater . . 18 C2
Freshwater Bay . 18 C2
Freshwater East . 55 E6
Fressingfield . 104 D3
Freston . . . 88 D2
Freswick . . . 281 B5
Fretherne . . 62 C3
Frettenham . . 120 D4
Freuchie . . . 220 D2
Freuchies . . 231 B6
Freystrop . . 55 C5
Friar's Gate . 36 C2
Friarton . . 219 B6
Friday Bridge . 101 A6
Friday Street . 22 B4
Fridaythorpe . 150 B1
Friern Barnet . 68 D2
Friesland . . 223 B4
Friesthorpe . 133 A5
Frieston . . . 116 A2
Frieth 66 D2
Frilford . . . 65 D5
Frilsham . . 46 B3
Frimley . . . 34 A1
Frimley Green . 34 A1
Frindsbury . 51 B4
Fring 119 B4
Fringford . . 65 A7
Frinsted . . . 37 A6
Frinton-on-Sea . 71 A6
Friockheim . 232 D3
Friog 90 A4
Frisby on the
  Wreake . . 115 D4
Friskney . . 135 D4
Friskney
  Eaudike . . 135 D4
Friskney Tofts . 135 D4
Friston E Sus . 22 C3
  Suff 89 A5
Fritchley . . 130 D3
Fritham . . . 31 D6
Frith Bank . 117 A6
Frith Common . 79 A4
Frithelstock . 25 D5
Frithelstock
  Stone . . . 25 D5
Frithville . . 134 D3
Frittenden . . 37 B6
Frittiscombe . 8 C2
Fritton Norf . 104 B3
  Norf 105 A5
Fritwell . . . 65 A6
Frizinghall . 147 D5
Frizington . . 162 C3
Frocester . . 62 C3
Frodesley . . 94 A3
Frodingham . 141 B6
Frodsham . . 127 B5
Frogden . . . 187 A6
Froggatt . . 130 B2
Froghall . . 112 A4
Frogmore Devon . 7 C6
  Hants 34 A1
Frognall . . 117 D4
Frogshall . . 121 B4
Frolesworth . 98 B2
Frome 30 A1
Frome St Quintin 15 A5
Fromes Hill . 79 C4
Fron Denb . 125 C5
  Gwyn . . . 106 C3
  Gwyn . . . 107 A5
  Powys . . . 77 A4
  Powys . . . 93 A6
  Powys . . . 93 B5
Froncysllte . 110 A1
Frongoch . . 108 B4

Frostenden 105 C5
Frosterley 166 B3
Frotoft 282 E5
Froxfield.......45 C6
Froxfield Green ..33 C6
Froyle........33 A6
Fryerning......69 C6
Fryton........159 D5
Fulbeck.......133 D4
Fulbourn.......85 B7
Fulbrook........64 B3
Fulford Som 28 C2
  Staffs........112 B3
  York.........149 C5
Fulham........49 B5
Fulking........21 A5
Fullarton
  Glasgow.....205 B6
  N Ayrs.......192 B3
Fuller's Moor ..127 D4
Fuller Street 70 B1
Fullerton.......32 B2
Fulletby.......134 B2
Full Sutton....149 B6
Fullwood......205 C4
Fulmer........48 A2
Fulmodeston..120 B1
Fulnetby......133 B5
Fulstow.......143 D5
Fulwell.......179 D5
Fulwood Lancs..145 D5
  S Yorks......130 A3
Fundenhall...104 B2
Fundenhall
  Street.......104 B2
Funtington....19 A6
Funtley.......19 A4
Funtullich....218 B2
Funzie.......284 D8
Furley........14 A2
Furnace Argyll ..214 B3
  Carms........57 B5
Furnace End....97 B5
Furneaux Pelham 68 A4
Furness Vale....129 A5
Furzehill......26 A2
Furze Platt.....48 A1
Fyfett........28 D2
Fyfield Essex 69 C5
  Glos.........64 C3
  Hants........32 A1
  Oxon.........65 D5
  Wilts.........45 C5
Fylingthorpe ..160 A3
Fyvie........256 C2

G

Gabhsann bho
  Dheas......288 B5
Gabhsann bho
  Thuath......288 B5
Gablon.......264 A3
Gabroc Hill ...205 C4
Gaddesby....115 D4
Gadebridge....67 C6
Gaer.........60 A3
Gaerllwyd......61 D6
Gaerwen.....123 C4
Gagingwell....65 A5
Gaick Lodge ..241 D5
Gailey........112 D3
Gainford......167 D4
Gainsborough
  Lincs.......141 D6
  Suff..........88 C2
Gainsford End..86 D3
Gairloch......261 C5
Gairlochy.....239 D5
Gairney Bank ..208 A4
Gairnshiel
  Lodge......243 B6
Gaisgill......155 A5
Gaitsgill......164 A1
Galashiels....196 C3
Galgate.......145 B4
Galhampton....29 C6
Gallaberry....184 D2
Gallachoille...213 D5
Gallanach Argyll ..223 A5
  Argyll........226 D3

Gallantry Bank ..127 D5
Gallatown.....209 A5
Galley Common ..97 B6
Galleyend......69 C7
Galley Hill......85 A5
Galleywood.....69 C7
Gallin.........229 D4
Gallowfauld...232 D2
Gallows Green ..113 A4
Galltair.......249 D5
Galmisdale....234 B3
Galmpton Devon ..7 C5
  Torbay.........8 B2
Galphay......157 D6
Galston......193 B5
Galtrigill.....258 C1
Gamblesby....165 B4
Gamesley.....138 D3
Gamlingay.....84 B4
Gammersgill...157 C4
Gamston......132 B2
Ganarew......62 B1
Ganavan.....226 C3
Gang..........6 A2
Ganllwyd.....108 C2
Gannochy Angus ..232 A3
  Perth........219 B6
Gansclet......281 D5
Ganstead.....151 D4
Ganthorpe....159 D5
Ganton.......160 D3
Garbat.......263 D6
Garbhallt.....214 C3
Garboldisham..103 C6
Garden City ...126 C3
Gardenstown...268 C2
Garden Village
  Wrex........126 D3
  W Yorks......148 D3
Garderhouse...285 J5
Gardham.....150 C2
Gardin.......284 G6
Gare Hill.......30 A1
Garelochhead..215 C5
Garford.......65 D5
Garforth......148 D3
Gargrave.....146 B3
Gargunnock...207 A5
Garlic Street...104 C3
Garlieston.....171 C6
Garlinge Green..52 D3
Garlogie.....245 B4
Garmond.....268 D3
Garmony.....225 B5
Garmouth.....266 C4
Garn..........58 D3
Garndiffaith.....61 C4
Garndolbenmaen
  ....107 B4
Garnedd......124 D2
Garnett Bridge ..154 B4
Garnfadryn...106 C2
Garnkirk.....207 D4
Garnlydan.....60 B3
Garnswllt......57 B6
Garn-yr-erw....60 B4
Garrabost....288 D6
Garraron.....213 B6
Garras.........3 C5
Garreg.......107 B6
Garrick......218 C3
Garrigill.....165 A5
Garriston.....157 B5
Garroch.....182 D3
Garrogie Lodge .240 A3
Garros.......259 B4
Garrow.......230 D2
Garryhorn....182 C3
Garsdale.....155 C6
Garsdale Head..155 B6
Garsdon.......44 A3
Garshall Green..112 B3
Garsington.....65 C6
Garstang.....145 C4
Garston......127 A4
Garswood.....137 D4
Gartcosh.....207 D4
Garth Bridgend ..40 B3
  Gwyn........123 C5
  Powys........76 C3
  Shetland....285 H4
  Wrex........110 A1

Garthamlock ...205 B6
Garthbrengy 76 D4
Garthdee.....245 B6
Gartheli.......75 C4
Garthmyl......93 B5
Garthorpe Leics..115 C6
  N Lincs......141 B6
Garth Row....154 B4
Gartly........255 C6
Gartmore....206 A3
Gartnagrenach..202 C2
Gartness
  N Lanark....207 D5
  Stirling......206 B3
Gartocharn...206 B2
Garton.......151 D5
Garton-on-the-
  Wolds.......150 B2
Gartsherrie ...207 D5
Gartymore....274 C4
Garvald......210 C2
Garvamore....240 C3
Garvard......212 C1
Garvault Hotel ..273 A5
Garve........263 D5
Garvestone...103 A6
Garvock Aberds ..233 A5
  Invclyd......204 A2
Garway........61 A6
Garway Hill....61 A6
Gaskan.......236 B1
Gastard.......44 C2
Gasthorpe....103 C5
Gatcombe......18 C3
Gateacre.....127 A4
Gatebeck.....154 C4
Gate Burton...132 A3
Gateford.....131 A5
Gateforth.....140 A3
Gatehead.....192 B3
Gate Helmsley..149 B5
Gatehouse....177 A5
Gatehouse of
  Fleet........172 C4
Gatelawbridge..183 C7
Gateley......119 C6
Gatenby......158 C2
Gateshead....179 C4
Gatesheath...127 C4
Gateside Aberds..244 A3
  Angus.......232 D2
  E Renf......205 C4
  Fife.........219 D6
  N Ayrs......204 C3
Gathurst.....136 C4
Gatley.......128 A3
Gattonside....197 C4
Gatwick Airport ..35 B5
Gaufron.......76 A3
Gaulby........98 A3
Gauldry.....220 B3
Gaunt's Common 17 A4
Gautby.......134 B1
Gavinton.....197 A6
Gawber.......139 C6
Gawcott.......82 D3
Gawsworth...128 C3
Gawthorpe....139 A5
Gawthrop....155 C5
Gawthwaite...153 B3
Gaydon.......81 B6
Gayfield.....282 B5
Gayhurst......83 C5
Gayle........156 C2
Gayles.......157 A5
Gayton Mers...126 A2
  Norf........119 D4
  Northants.....83 B4
  Staffs.......112 C3
Gayton le Marsh 135 A4
Gayton le Wold..134 A2
Gayton Thorpe..119 D4
Gaywood.....118 C3
Gazeley.......86 A3
Geanies House ..265 C4
Gearraidh
  Bhailteas.....286 D3
Gearraidh
  Bhaird.......288 E4
Gearraidh na h-
  Aibhne......288 D3

Gearraidh na
  Monadh......286 E3
Geary........258 B2
Geddes House..253 A4
Gedding.......87 B5
Geddington....99 C5
Gedintailor....247 A4
Gedling......115 A4
Gedney......117 C7
Gedney
  Broadgate...117 C7
Gedney Drove
  End.........118 C1
Gedney Dyke..117 C7
Gedney Hill....117 D6
Gee Cross.....138 D2
Geilston.....206 C1
Geirinis......286 B3
Geise........280 B3
Geisiadar....288 D2
Geldeston....105 B4
Gell.........124 C3
Gelli Pembs....55 C6
  Rhondda.....41 B4
Gellideg.......60 C2
Gellifor......125 C6
Gelligaer......41 B6
Gellilydan....107 C6
Gellinudd......40 A2
Gellyburn....219 A5
Gellywen......73 D5
Gelston Dumfries 173 C5
  Lincs........116 A2
Gembling....151 B4
Gentleshaw...113 D4
Geocrab.....288 H2
Georgefield...185 C5
George Green...48 A3
Georgeham.....25 B5
George Nympton 26 C2
Georgetown....60 C3
Gerlan.......123 D6
Germansweek...11 B5
Germoe........2 C3
Gerrans........4 D3
Gerrards Cross...48 A3
Gestingthorpe..87 D4
Geuffordd....109 D7
Gibbet Hill....98 C2
Gibbshill.....173 A5
Gidea Park.....50 A2
Gidleigh.......12 C1
Gidney.......210 D2
Giffnock.....205 C5
Gifford.......210 D2
Giffordland...204 D2
Giffordtown...220 C2
Giggleswick...146 A2
Gilberdyke...141 A6
Gilchriston...210 D1
Gilcrux......163 A4
Gildersome...139 A5
Gildingwells...131 A5
Gileston......41 E5
Gilfach.......41 B6
Gilfach Goch...41 C4
Gilfachrheda...73 A7
Gillamoor....159 C5
Gillar's Green..136 D3
Gillen.......258 C2
Gilling East...159 D5
Gillingham Dorset 30 C2
  Medway.....51 C4
  Norf........105 B5
Gilling West...157 A5
Gillock......280 C4
Gillow Heath...128 D3
Gills.........281 A5
Gill's Green....37 C5
Gilmanscleuch 196 D2
Gilmerton Edin..209 D5
  Perth.......218 B3
Gilmonby.....166 D2
Gilmorton.....98 C2
Gilmourton....205 D6
Gilsland......176 C4
Gilsland Spa...176 C4
Gilston Borders..196 A3
  Herts.........68 B4
Gilwern.......60 B4
Gimingham...121 B4
Giosla.......288 E2

Gipping........87 A6
Gipsey Bridge..117 A5
Girdle Toll....204 D3
Girlsta.......285 H6
Girsby.......158 A2
Girtford.......84 B3
Girthon......172 C4
Girton Cambs ...85 A6
  Notts.......132 C3
Girvan.......180 B3
Gisburn......146 C2
Gisleham.....105 C6
Gislingham...104 D1
Gissing......104 C2
Gittisham......13 B6
Gladestry......77 B6
Gladsmuir....210 C1
Glais.........40 A2
Glaisdale....159 A6
Glame.......248 B2
Glamis.......232 D1
Glan Adda....123 C5
Glanaman.....57 A6
Glan Conwy...124 B3
Glan-Conwy...124 D3
Glandford....120 A2
Glan-Duar.....58 A2
Glandwr.......73 D4
Glan-Dwyfach..107 B4
Glandy Cross...72 D4
Glandyfi......91 C4
Glan Gors....123 C4
Glangrwyney...60 B4
Glanmule......93 B5
Glanrafon.....90 D4
Glanrhyd Gwyn..106 C2
  Pembs........72 B4
Glan-rhyd....107 A4
Glanton.......188 B3
Glanton Pike..188 B3
Glan-traeth...122 C2
Glanvilles
  Wootton......15 A6
Glan-y-don...125 B6
Glan-y-nant....92 C3
Glan-yr-afon
  Anglesey....123 B6
  Gwyn.......108 A4
  Gwyn.......109 A5
Glan-y-wern...107 C6
Glapthorn....100 B2
Glapwell.....131 C4
Glas-allt Shiel..243 D5
Glasbury......77 D5
Glaschoil.....253 C6
Glascoed Denb..125 B4
  Mon.........61 C5
Glascorrie....243 C6
Glascote......97 A5
Glascwm......77 B5
Glasdrum....227 B5
Glasfryn.....125 D4
Glasgow.....205 B5
Glashvin.....259 B4
Glasinfryn....123 D5
Glasnacardoch 235 A5
Glasnakille...247 C4
Glasphein....258 D1
Glaspwll......91 C5
Glassburn....251 C5
Glasserton...171 D6
Glassford....194 B2
Glasshouse Hill..62 A3
Glasshouses...147 A5
Glasslie.....220 D2
Glasson Cumb..175 B5
  Lancs.......144 B4
Glassonby....164 B3
Glasterlaw....232 C3
Glaston.......99 A5
Glastonbury....29 B5
Glatton......100 C3
Glazebrook...137 D5
Glazebury....137 D5
Glazeley......95 C5
Gleadless....130 A3
Gleadsmoss...128 C3
Gleann
  Tholàstaidh..288 C6
Gleaston.....153 C2
Gleiniant......92 B3

Glemsford 87 C4
Glen Dumfries ..172 C3
  Dumfries.....173 A6
Glenamachrie...226 D4
Glen Auldyn...152 B4
Glenbarr.....190 B2
Glenbeg Highld..235 D4
  Highld.......253 D6
Glen Bernisdale .259 D4
Glenbervie....245 D4
Glenboig.....207 D5
Glenborrodale..235 D5
Glenbranter...215 C4
Glenbreck....195 C5
Glenbrein
  Lodge......240 A2
Glenbrittle
  House.......246 B3
Glenbuchat
  Lodge......243 A6
Glenbuck.....194 D2
Glenburn....205 B4
Glencalvie
  Lodge......263 B6
Glencanisp
  Lodge......270 B4
Glencaple....174 B2
Glencarron
  Lodge......250 A2
Glencarse....219 B6
Glencassley
  Castle......272 C2
Glenceitlin...227 B6
Glencoe......237 D4
Glencraig....209 A4
Glencripesdale 225 A5
Glencrosh....183 D5
Glendavan Ho...244 B1
Glendevon....219 D4
Glendoebeg...240 B2
Glendoe Lodge..240 B2
Glendoick....220 B2
Glendoll Lodge..231 A6
Glendoune....180 B3
Glenduckie...220 C2
Glendye Lodge..244 D3
Gleneagles
  Hotel.......218 C4
Gleneagles
  House.......218 D4
Glenegedale...200 C3
Glenelg......238 A2
Glenernie....253 B6
Glenfarg.....219 C6
Glenfarquhar
  Lodge......245 D4
Glenferness
  House.......253 B5
Glenfeshie
  Lodge......241 C6
Glenfield......98 A2
Glenfinnan...238 D3
Glenfoot.....219 C6
Glenfyne Lodge .215 A5
Glengap......173 C4
Glengarnock...204 C3
Glengorm
  Castle......224 A3
Glengrasco...259 D4
Glenhead Farm..231 B6
Glen Ho......196 C1
Glenhoul.....182 D4
Glenhurich...236 C2
Glenkerry....185 A5
Glenkiln.....173 A6
Glenkindie...244 A1
Glenlatterach..266 D2
Glenlee......182 D4
Glenlichorn...218 C2
Glenlivet.....254 D2
Glenlochsie...231 A4
Glenloig......191 B5
Glenluce.....171 B4
Glenmallan...215 C5
Glenmarksie..251 A5
Glenmassan...215 D4
Glenmavis....207 D5
Glenmaye....152 D2
Glenmidge...183 D6

Glen Mona......152 C4
Glenmore Argyll..213 A6
Highld.........259 D4
Glenmore
Lodge........242 B2
Glenmoy.........232 B2
Glen Nevis
House.........237 B5
Glenogil........232 B2
Glen Parva......98 B2
Glenprosen
Lodge........231 B6
Glenprosen
Village......232 B1
Glenquiech.....232 B2
Glenreasdell
Mains........202 C3
Glenree.........191 C5
Glenridding.....164 D1
Glenrossal......272 D2
Glenrothes......220 D2
Glensanda......226 B3
Glensaugh......233 A4
Glenshero
Lodge........240 C3
Glen Sluain.....214 C3
Glenstockadale..170 A2
Glenstriven.....203 A5
Glentaggart.....194 D3
Glen Tanar
House........244 C1
Glentham.......142 D2
Glentirranmuir..207 A4
Glenton........256 D1
Glentress.......196 C1
Glentromie
Lodge........241 C5
Glen Trool
Lodge........181 C6
Glentrool
Village.......181 D5
Glentruan......152 A4
Glentruim
House........241 C4
Glentworth.....133 A4
Glenuig........235 C5
Glenurquhart...264 D3
Glen Village....208 C1
Glen Vine......152 D3
Glespin........194 D3
Gletness.......285 H6
Glewstone......62 A1
Glinton........100 A3
Glooston........99 B4
Glororum......199 C5
Glossop........138 D3
Gloster Hill....189 C5
Gloucester......63 B4
Gloup.........284 C7
Glusburn......147 C4
Glutt Lodge....274 A3
Glutton Bridge..129 C5
Glympton.......65 A5
Glynarthen......73 B6
Glynbrochan....92 C3
Glyn-Ceiriog...109 B7
Glyncoch.......41 B5
Glyncorrwg.....40 B3
Glyn-cywarch...107 C6
Glynde.........22 B2
Glyndebourne...22 A2
Glyndyfrdwy...109 A6
Glyn-neath
(Glynedd)....59 E5
Glynogwr.......41 C4
Glyntaff.......41 C5
Glyntawe.......59 D5
Gnosall........112 C2
Gnosall Heath..112 C2
Goadby........99 B4
Goadby
Marwood.....115 C5
Goatacre.......44 B4
Goathill........29 D6
Goathland......160 A2
Goathurst.......28 B2
Goat Lees......38 C4
Gobernuisgach
Lodge........277 D5

Gobhaig........287 D5
Gobowen.......110 B2
Godalming......34 B2
Godley.........138 D2
Godmanchester.100 D4
Godmanstone....15 B6
Godmersham....52 D2
Godney.........29 A4
Godolphin Cross..3 B4
Godre'r-graig...59 E4
Godshill Hants...31 D5
IoW...........18 C4
Godstone.......35 A6
Godwinscroft...17 B5
Goetre.........61 C5
Goferydd.......122 B2
Goff's Oak.....68 C3
Gogar.........209 C4
Goginan........91 D4
Golan.........107 B5
Golant..........5 B6
Golberdon......10 D4
Golborne.......137 D5
Golcar.........139 B4
Goldcliff.......42 A2
Golden Cross...22 A3
Golden Green...36 B4
Golden Grove...57 A5
Goldenhill.....128 D3
Golden Hill.....17 B6
Golden Pot.....33 A6
Golden Valley...63 A5
Golders Green...49 A5
Goldhanger.....70 C3
Gold Hill......102 B1
Golding.........94 A3
Goldington.....84 B2
Goldsborough
N Yorks.....148 B2
N Yorks.....169 D6
Goldsithney......2 B3
Goldsworthy....25 C4
Goldthorpe....140 C2
Gollanfield....253 A4
Golspie........274 D2
Golval........279 B4
Gomeldon.......31 B5
Gomersal......139 A5
Gomshall.......34 B3
Gonalston.....115 A4
Gonfirth......285 G5
Good Easter....69 B6
Gooderstone...102 A3
Goodleigh......25 B7
Goodmanham...150 C1
Goodnestone
Kent.........52 C2
Kent.........53 D4
Goodrich.......62 B1
Goodrington.....8 B2
Goodshaw.....137 A7
Goodworth
Clatford......32 A2
Goole.........141 A5
Goonbell........4 C2
Goonhavern.....4 B2
Goose Eye.....147 C4
Goose Green
Gtr Man......137 C4
Norf.........104 C2
W Sus........21 A4
Gooseham......24 D3
Goosey........65 D4
Goosnargh.....145 D5
Goostrey......128 B2
Gorcott Hill....80 A3
Gord.........285 L6
Gordon........197 B5
Gordonbush....274 D2
Gordonsburgh..267 C5
Gordonstoun...266 C2
Gordonstown
Aberds.......256 C2
Aberds.......267 D6
Gore..........53 D5
Gorebridge....209 D6
Gore Cross.....44 D4
Gorefield......117 D7
Gore Pit.......70 B2
Gorey Jersey......6
Gorgie........209 C5

Goring.........47 A4
Goring-by-Sea...21 B4
Goring Heath...47 B4
Gorleston-on-
Sea.........105 A6
Gornalwood....96 B2
Gorrachie.....268 D2
Gorran
Churchtown....5 C4
Gorran Haven....5 C5
Gorrenberry...186 D3
Gors..........75 A5
Gorsedd......125 B6
Gorse Hill.....45 A5
Gorseinon......57 C5
Gorseness.....282 F5
Gorsgoch.......74 C3
Gorslas........57 A5
Gorsley........62 A2
Gorstan.......263 D5
Gorstanvorran..236 B2
Gorsteyhill....128 D2
Gorsty Hill....113 C5
Gortantaoid...200 A3
Gorton........138 D1
Gosbeck........88 B2
Gosberton.....117 B5
Gosberton
Clough......117 C4
Gosfield.......70 A1
Gosford........78 A3
Gosforth Cumb..162 D3
T&W.........179 C4
Gosmore........68 A1
Gosport........19 B5
Gossabrough...284 E7
Gossington.....62 C3
Goswick.......199 B4
Gotham.......114 B3
Gotherington...63 A5
Gott..........285 J6
Goudhurst......37 C5
Goulceby......134 B2
Gourdas.......256 B2
Gourdon.......233 A6
Gourock.......204 A2
Govan........205 B5
Govanhill.....205 B5
Goveton........7 C6
Govilon........61 B4
Gowanhill.....269 C5
Gowdall.......140 A4
Gowerton......57 C5
Gowkhall......208 B3
Gowthorpe.....149 B6
Goxhill E Yorks..151 C4
N Lincs......142 A3
Goxhill Haven..142 A3
Goybre........40 C2
Grabhair......288 F4
Graby.........116 C3
Grade..........3 D5
Graffham......20 A2
Grafham Cambs..84 A3
Sur..........34 B3
Grafton Hereford..78 D2
N Yorks......148 A3
Oxon..........64 C3
Shrops.......110 D3
Worcs.........78 A3
Grafton Flyford..80 B2
Grafton Regis...83 C4
Grafton
Underwood....99 C6
Grafty Green...37 B6
Graianrhyd....126 D2
Graig Conwy...124 B3
Graig-fechan..125 D6
Grain..........51 B5
Grainsby......143 D4
Grainthorpe...143 D5
Grampound......4 C4
Grampound Road..4 B4
Gramsdal......286 A4
Granborough....66 A3
Granby........115 B5
Grandborough...82 A1
Grandtully....230 C3
Grange Cumb...163 C5
E Ayrs.......193 B4
Medway........51 C4

Grange continued
Mers.........126 A2
Perth.........220 B2
Grange
Crossroads...267 D5
Grange Hall...265 D6
Grange Hill....68 D4
Grangemill....130 D2
Grange Moor...139 B5
Grangemouth..208 B2
Grange of
Lindores.....220 C2
Grange-over-
Sands........154 D3
Grangepans...208 B3
Grangetown
Cardiff........41 D6
Redcar.......168 C3
Grange Villa...179 D4
Granish.......242 A2
Gransmoor....151 B4
Granston.......55 A4
Grantchester...85 B6
Grantham.....116 B2
Grantley......147 A6
Grantlodge...245 A4
Granton Dumfries 184 B3
Edin.........209 C5
Grantown-on-
Spey........253 D6
Grantshouse...211 D5
Grappenhall...127 A6
Grasby........142 C2
Grasmere......154 A2
Grasscroft....138 C2
Grassendale...126 A3
Grassholme...166 C2
Grassington...147 A4
Grassmoor.....131 C4
Grassthorpe...132 C2
Grateley.......32 A1
Gratwich......112 B4
Graveley Cambs..84 A4
Herts.........68 A2
Gravelly Hill...96 B4
Gravels........94 A1
Graven.......284 F6
Graveney.......52 C2
Gravesend Herts..68 A4
Kent..........50 B3
Grayingham....142 D1
Grayrigg......155 B4
Grays..........50 B3
Grayshott......34 C1
Grayswood......34 C2
Graythorp....168 C3
Grazeley.......47 C4
Greasbrough...140 D2
Greasby.......126 A2
Great Abington..86 C1
Great Addington..99 D6
Great Alne.....80 B4
Great Altcar...136 C2
Great Amwell...68 B3
Great Asby....165 D4
Great Ashfield..87 A5
Great Ayton...168 D3
Great Baddow...70 C1
Great Bardfield..86 D2
Great Barford...84 B3
Great Barr.....96 B3
Great Barrington 64 B3
Great Barrow...127 C4
Great Barton...87 A4
Great Barugh..159 D6
Great Bavington 178 A1
Great Bealings..88 C3
Great Bedwyn...45 C6
Great Bentley...71 A5
Great Billing...83 A5
Great Bircham..119 B4
Great Blakenham 88 B2
Great Blencow..164 B2
Great Bolas...111 C5
Great Bookham..35 A4
Great Bourton..82 C1
Great Bowden...99 C4
Great Bradley...86 B2
Great Braxted...70 B2
Great Bricett...87 B6
Great Brickhill..83 D1

Great
Bridgeford...112 C2
Great Brington..82 A3
Great Bromley...71 A4
Great Broughton
Cumb.........162 A3
N Yorks......158 A4
Great Budworth 127 B6
Great Burdon..167 D6
Great Burgh....35 A5
Great Burstead..69 D6
Great Busby...158 A4
Great Canfield..69 B5
Great Carlton..135 A4
Great Casterton.100 A2
Great Chart....38 A1
Great Chatwell.112 D1
Great Chesterford..85 C7
Great Cheverell..44 D3
Great Chishill..85 D6
Great Clacton...71 B5
Great Cliff....139 B6
Great Clifton..162 B3
Great Coates...143 C4
Great Comberton 80 C2
Great Corby...176 D2
Great Cornard...87 C4
Great Cowden..151 C5
Great Coxwell...64 D3
Great Crakehall.157 B6
Great Cransley..99 D5
Great
Cressingham..103 A4
Great Crosby..136 D2
Great Cubley...113 B5
Great Dalby...115 D5
Great Denham..84 C2
Great
Doddington...83 A5
Great Dunham..119 D5
Great Dunmow..69 A6
Great Durnford..31 B5
Great Easton
Essex.........69 A6
Leics..........99 B5
Great Eccleston 144 C4
Great Edstone..159 C6
Great Ellingham 103 B6
Great Elm......30 A1
Greater Doward..62 B1
Great Eversden..85 B5
Great Fencote..157 B6
Great
Finborough....87 B6
Greatford.....116 D3
Great Fransham 119 D5
Great Gaddesden..67 B6
Greatgate.....113 A4
Great Gidding..100 C3
Great Givendale 149 B7
Great Glemham..88 A4
Great Glen.....98 B3
Great Gonerby..116 B1
Great Gransden..85 B4
Great Green
Norf.........104 C3
Suff..........87 B5
Great Habton..159 D6
Great Hale....116 A4
Greatham Hants...33 B6
Hrtlpl........168 C2
W Sus.........20 A3
Great Hampden..66 C4
Great Harrowden 99 D5
Great Harwood..146 D1
Great Haseley...66 C2
Great Hatfield.151 C4
Great Haywood.112 C3
Great Heath....97 C6
Great Heck....140 A3
Great Henny....87 D4
Great Hinton...44 D3
Great Hockham.103 B5
Great Holland...71 B6
Great Horkesley..87 D5
Great Hormead..68 A3
Great Horton..147 D5
Great Horwood..83 D4
Great Houghton
Northants....83 B4
S Yorks......140 C2

Great Hucklow..130 B1
Great Kelk....151 B4
Great Kimble....66 C4
Great Kingshill..66 D4
Great Langton..157 B6
Great Leighs...70 B1
Great Lever....137 C6
Great Limber..142 C3
Great Linford...83 C5
Great Livermere 103 D4
Great
Longstone...130 B2
Great Lumley..167 A5
Great Lyth.....94 A2
Great Malvern...79 C5
Great
Maplestead....87 D4
Great Marton..144 D3
Great
Massingham..119 C4
Great Melton..104 A2
Great Milton...66 C2
Great Missenden..66 C4
Great Mitton..145 D7
Great Mongeham 53 D5
Great Moulton..104 B2
Great Munden...68 A3
Great Musgrave.165 D5
Great Ness....110 D2
Great Notley...70 A1
Great Oakley
Essex.........71 A5
Northants.....99 C5
Great Offley....67 A7
Great Ormside..165 D5
Great Orton...175 C5
Great Ouseburn.148 A3
Great Oxendon..99 C4
Great Oxney
Green........69 C6
Great Palgrave..119 D5
Great Paxton...84 A4
Great Plumpton.144 D3
Great
Plumstead...121 D5
Great Ponton..116 B2
Great Preston..140 A2
Great Raveley..101 C4
Great Rissington..64 B2
Great Rollright..81 D6
Great Ryburgh..119 C6
Great Ryle....188 B3
Great Ryton....94 A2
Great Saling....69 A7
Great Salkeld..164 B3
Great Sampford..86 D2
Great Sankey..127 A5
Great Saxham...86 A3
Great Shefford..46 B1
Great Shelford..85 B6
Great Smeaton.158 A2
Great Snoring..119 B6
Great Somerford..44 A3
Great Stainton.167 C6
Great
Stambridge....70 D2
Great Staughton..84 A3
Great Steeping..135 C4
Great Stonar...53 D5
Greatstone on
Sea..........38 C2
Great
Strickland....164 C3
Great Stukeley.100 D4
Great Sturton..134 B2
Great Sutton
Ches W.......126 B3
Shrops........94 C3
Great
Swinburne...178 B1
Great Tew.....65 A4
Great Tey......70 A2
Great Thurkleby 158 D3
Great Thurlow..86 B2
Great Torrington.25 D5
Great Tosson..188 C3
Great Totham
Essex.........70 B2
Essex.........70 B2
Great Tows....143 D4
Great Urswick.153 C3
Great Wakering..51 A6

Great Waldingfield.... 87 C5
Great Walsingham ... 119 B6
Great Waltham.. 69 B6
Great Warley.. 69 D5
Great Washbourne.. 80 D2
Great Weldon.. 99 C6
Great Welnetham 87 B4
Great Wenham.. 87 D6
Great Whittington ... 178 B2
Great Wigborough.... 70 B3
Great Wilbraham. 86 B1
Great Wishford.. 31 B4
Great Witcombe.. 63 B5
Great Witley .. 79 A5
Great Wolford.. 81 D5
Greatworth.. 82 C2
Great Wratting.. 86 C2
Great Wymondley.. 68 A2
Great Wyrley.. 96 A2
Great Wytheford.. 111 D4
Great Yarmouth 105 A6
Great Yeldham.. 86 D3
Greave.. 138 A1
Greeba.. 152 C3
Green.. 125 C5
Greenbank.. 284 C7
Greenburn.. 208 D2
Greendikes.. 188 A3
Green End.. 84 B3
Greenfield C Beds .84 D2
  Flint.. 126 B1
  Gtr Man.. 138 C2
  Highld.. 239 B6
  Oxon.. 66 D3
Greenford.. 48 A4
Greengairs.. 207 C5
Greenham.. 46 C2
Green Hammerton ... 148 B3
Greenhaugh.. 177 A5
Greenhead.. 177 C4
Greenhill Falk.. 207 C6
  Kent.. 52 C3
  Leics.. 114 D2
  London.. 49 A4
Greenhills.. 204 C3
Greenhithe.. 50 B2
Greenholm.. 193 B5
Greenholme.. 155 A4
Greenhouse.. 187 A4
Greenhow Hill.. 147 A5
Greenigoe.. 283 G5
Greenland.. 280 B4
Greenlands.. 47 A5
Green Lane.. 93 B5
Greenlaw Aberds 268 D1
  Borders.. 197 B6
Greenlea.. 174 A3
Greenloaning.. 218 D3
Greenmount.. 137 B6
Greenmow.. 285 L6
Greenock.. 204 A2
Greenock West. 204 A2
Greenodd.. 154 C2
Green Ore.. 43 D4
Greenrow.. 174 C4
Green St Green.. 50 C1
Greenside.. 178 C3
Greensidehill.. 188 B2
Greens Norton.. 82 C3
Greenstead Green.. 70 A2
Greensted.. 69 C5
Green Street.. 68 D1
Greenwich.. 49 B6
Greet.. 80 D3
Greete.. 94 D3
Greetham Lincs .134 B3
  Rutland.. 116 D2
Greetland.. 138 A3
Gregg Hall.. 154 B3
Gregson Lane.. 137 A4
Greinetobht.. 287 G3
Greinton.. 28 B4
Gremista.. 285 J6

Grenaby.. 152 D2
Grendon Northants 83 A5
  Warks.. 97 A5
Grendon Common.. 97 B5
Grendon Green.. 78 B3
Grendon Underwood.. 66 A2
Grenofen.. 11 D5
Grenoside.. 139 D6
Greosabhagh.. 288 H2
Gresford.. 126 D3
Gresham.. 120 B3
Greshornish.. 258 C3
Gressenhall.. 119 D6
Gressingham.. 145 A5
Gresty Green.. 128 D2
Greta Bridge.. 166 D3
Gretna.. 175 B6
Gretna Green.. 175 B6
Gretton Glos.. 80 D3
  Northants.. 99 B5
  Shrops.. 94 B3
Grewelthorpe.. 157 D6
Greygarth.. 157 D5
Grey Green.. 141 C5
Greynor.. 57 B5
Greysouthen.. 162 B3
Greystoke.. 164 B2
Greystone Angus 232 D3
  Dumfries.. 174 A2
Greywell.. 47 D5
Griais.. 288 C5
Grianan.. 288 C5
Gribthorpe.. 149 D6
Gridley Corner.. 11 B4
Griff.. 97 C6
Griffithstown.. 61 D4
Grimbister.. 282 F4
Grimblethorpe.. 134 A2
Grimeford Village.. 137 B5
Grimethorpe.. 140 C2
Griminis.. 286 A3
Grimister.. 284 D6
Grimley.. 79 A6
Grimness.. 283 H5
Grimoldby.. 134 A3
Grimpo.. 110 C2
Grimsargh.. 145 D5
Grimsbury.. 82 C1
Grimsby.. 143 B4
Grimscote.. 82 B3
Grimscott.. 10 A3
Grimsthorpe.. 116 C3
Grimston E Yorks 151 D5
  Leics.. 115 C4
  Norf.. 119 C4
  York.. 149 B5
Grimstone.. 15 B6
Grinacombe Moor.. 11 B5
Grindale.. 161 D5
Grindigar.. 283 G6
Grindiscol.. 285 K6
Grindle.. 95 A5
Grindleford.. 130 B2
Grindleton.. 146 C1
Grindley.. 112 C4
Grindley Brook. 111 A4
Grindlow.. 130 B1
Grindon Northumb.. 198 B3
  Staffs.. 129 D5
Grindonmoor Gate.. 129 D5
Gringley on the Hill.. 141 D5
Grinsdale.. 175 C6
Grinshill.. 111 C4
Grinton.. 156 B4
Griomsidar.. 288 E4
Grishipoll.. 223 B4
Grisling Common 36 D2
Gristhorpe.. 161 C4
Griston.. 103 B5
Gritley.. 283 G6
Grittenham.. 44 A4
Grittleton.. 44 A2
Grizebeck.. 153 B3
Grizedale.. 154 B2
Grobister.. 282 E7

Groby.. 98 A2
Groes Conwy.. 125 C5
  Neath.. 40 C2
Groes-faen.. 41 C5
Groesffordd Marli.. 125 B5
Groeslon Gwyn.. 107 A4
  Gwyn.. 123 D5
Groes-lwyd.. 109 D7
Grogport.. 202 D3
Gromford.. 89 B4
Gronant.. 125 A5
Groombridge.. 36 C3
Grosmont Mon.. 61 A6
  N Yorks.. 160 A2
Groton.. 87 C5
Grougfoot.. 208 C3
Grouville Jersey.. 6
Grove Dorset.. 15 D7
  Kent.. 53 C4
  Notts.. 132 B2
  Oxon.. 65 D5
Grove Park.. 49 B7
Grovesend.. 57 B5
Grove Vale.. 96 B3
Grudie.. 263 D5
Gruids.. 272 D3
Gruinard House .261 A6
Grula.. 246 B2
Gruline.. 225 B4
Grunasound.. 285 K5
Grundisburgh.. 88 B3
Grunsagill.. 146 B1
Gruting.. 285 J4
Grutness.. 285 N6
Gualachulain.. 227 B6
Gualin Ho.. 276 C4
Guardbridge.. 221 C4
Guarlford.. 79 C6
Guay.. 230 D4
Guestling Green.. 23 A6
Guestling Thorn.. 23 A6
Guestwick.. 120 C2
Guestwick Green.. 120 C2
Guide.. 137 A6
Guide Post.. 179 A4
Guilden Morden.. 85 C4
Guilden Sutton.. 127 C4
Guildford.. 34 B2
Guildtown.. 219 A6
Guilsborough.. 98 D3
Guilsfield.. 109 D7
Guilton.. 53 D4
Guineaford.. 25 B6
Guisborough.. 168 D4
Guiseley.. 147 C5
Guist.. 120 C1
Guith.. 282 D6
Guiting Power.. 64 A1
Gulberwick.. 285 K6
Gullane.. 210 B1
Gulval.. 2 B2
Gulworthy.. 11 D5
Gumfreston.. 55 D7
Gumley.. 98 B3
Gummow's Shop.. 4 B3
Gunby E Yorks.. 149 D6
  Lincs.. 116 C2
Gundleton.. 33 B5
Gun Hill.. 22 A3
Gunn.. 26 B1
Gunnerside.. 156 B3
Gunnerton.. 177 B7
Gunness.. 141 B6
Gunnislake.. 11 D5
Gunnista.. 285 J7
Gunthorpe Norf.. 120 B2
  Notts.. 115 A4
  Pboro.. 100 A3
Gunville.. 18 C3
Gunwalloe.. 3 C4
Gurnard.. 18 B3
Gurnett.. 129 B4
Gurney Slade.. 29 A6
Gurnos.. 59 E4
Gussage All Saints.. 31 D4

Gussage St Michael.. 30 D3
Guston.. 39 A5
Gutcher.. 284 D7
Guthrie.. 232 C3
Guyhirn.. 101 A5
Guyhirn Gull.. 101 A5
Guy's Head.. 118 C1
Guy's Marsh.. 30 C2
Guyzance.. 189 C5
Gwaenysgor.. 125 A5
Gwalchmai.. 122 C3
Gwaun-Cae-Gurwen.. 59 D4
Gwaun-Leision.. 59 D4
Gwbert.. 73 B4
Gweek.. 3 C5
Gwehelog.. 61 C5
Gwenddwr.. 77 C4
Gwennap.. 4 D2
Gwenter.. 3 D5
Gwernaffield.. 126 C2
Gwernesney.. 61 C6
Gwernogle.. 58 B2
Gwernymynydd.. 126 C2
Gwersyllt.. 126 D3
Gwespyr.. 125 A6
Gwithian.. 2 A3
Gwredog.. 123 B4
Gwyddelwern.. 109 A5
Gwyddgrug.. 58 B1
Gwydyr Uchaf.. 124 C2
Gwynfryn.. 126 D2
Gwystre.. 77 A4
Gwytherin.. 124 C3
Gyfelia.. 110 A2
Gyffin.. 124 B2
Gyre.. 283 G4
Gyrn-goch.. 107 B4

H

Habberley.. 94 A1
Habergham.. 146 D2
Habrough.. 142 B3
Haceby.. 116 B3
Hacheston.. 88 B4
Hackbridge.. 49 C5
Hackenthorpe.. 131 A4
Hackford.. 103 A6
Hackforth.. 157 B6
Hackland.. 282 E4
Hackleton.. 83 B5
Hackness N Yorks.. 160 B3
  Orkney.. 283 H4
Hackney.. 49 A6
Hackthorn.. 133 A4
Hackthorpe.. 164 C3
Haconby.. 116 C4
Hacton.. 50 A2
Hadden.. 198 C1
Haddenham Bucks 66 C3
  Cambs.. 101 D6
Haddington E Loth.. 210 C2
  Lincs.. 133 C4
Haddiscoe.. 105 B5
Haddon Cambs.. 100 B3
  Ches E.. 129 C4
Hade Edge.. 139 C4
Hademore.. 97 A4
Hadfield.. 138 D3
Hadham Cross.. 68 B4
Hadham Ford.. 68 A4
Hadleigh Essex.. 51 A5
  Suff.. 87 C6
Hadley.. 111 D5
Hadley End.. 113 C5
Hadlow.. 36 B4
Hadlow Down.. 36 D3
Hadnall.. 111 D4
Hadstock.. 86 C1
Hady.. 130 B3
Hadzor.. 80 A2
Haffenden Quarter.. 37 B6
Hafod-Dinbych.. 124 D3
Hafod-lom.. 124 B3
Haggate.. 146 D2
Haggbeck.. 176 B2

Haggerston.. 198 B4
Haggrister.. 284 F5
Hagley Hereford.. 78 C3
  Worcs.. 96 C2
Hagworthingham.. 134 C2
Haigh Gtr Man.. 137 C5
  S Yorks.. 139 B5
Haigh Moor.. 139 A5
Haighton Green .145 D5
Haile.. 162 D3
Hailes.. 80 D3
Hailey Herts.. 68 B3
  Oxon.. 65 B4
Hailsham.. 22 B3
Hail Weston.. 84 A3
Haimer.. 280 B3
Hainault.. 69 D4
Hainford.. 120 D4
Hainton.. 134 A1
Hairmyres.. 205 C6
Haisthorpe.. 151 A4
Hakin.. 55 D4
Halam.. 132 D1
Halbeath.. 208 B4
Halberton.. 27 D5
Halcro.. 280 B4
Hale Gtr Man.. 128 A2
  Halton.. 127 A4
  Hants.. 31 D5
Hale Bank.. 127 A4
Halebarns.. 128 A2
Hales Norf.. 105 B4
  Staffs.. 111 B6
Halesfield.. 95 A5
Halesgate.. 117 C6
Halesowen.. 96 C2
Hales Place.. 52 D3
Hale Street.. 37 B4
Halesworth.. 105 D4
Halewood.. 127 A4
Halford Shrops.. 94 C2
  Warks.. 81 C5
Halfpenny Furze.. 56 A2
Halfpenny Green.. 95 B6
Halfway Carms.. 58 B3
  Carms.. 59 B5
  W Berks.. 46 C2
Halfway Bridge.. 34 D2
Halfway House.. 110 D2
Halfway Houses.. 51 B6
Halifax.. 138 A3
Halket.. 205 C4
Halkirk.. 280 C3
Halkyn.. 126 B2
Halland.. 22 A2
Hallaton.. 99 B4
Hallatrow.. 43 D5
Hallbankgate.. 176 D3
Hall Dunnerdale 153 A3
Hallen.. 43 A4
Hall Green W Mid .96 C4
  W Yorks.. 139 B6
Hall Grove.. 68 B2
Halliburton.. 197 B5
Hallin.. 258 C2
Halling.. 51 C4
Hallington Lincs. 134 A3
  Northumb.. 178 B1
Halliwell.. 137 B6
Hall of Tankerness.. 283 G6
Hall of the Forest 93 C6
Halloughton.. 132 D1
Hallow.. 79 B6
Hallrule.. 187 B4
Halls.. 210 C3
Hallsands.. 8 D2
Hall's Green.. 68 A2
Hallthwaites.. 153 B2
Hallworthy.. 10 C2
Hallyburton House.. 220 A2
Hallyne.. 195 B6
Halmer End.. 112 A1
Halmore.. 62 C2
Halmyre Mains .195 B6
Halnaker.. 20 B2
Halsall.. 136 B2
Halse Northants.. 82 C2
  Som.. 27 C6
Halsetown.. 2 B3

Halsham.. 143 A4
Halsinger.. 25 B6
Halstead Essex.. 87 D4
  Kent.. 50 C1
  Leics.. 99 A4
Halstock.. 15 A5
Haltham.. 134 C2
Haltoft End.. 117 A6
Halton Bucks.. 66 B4
  Halton.. 127 A5
  Lancs.. 145 A5
  Northumb.. 178 C1
  Wrex.. 110 B2
  W Yorks.. 148 D2
Halton East.. 147 B4
Halton Gill.. 156 D2
Halton Holegate 135 C4
Halton Lea Gate 176 D3
Halton West.. 146 B2
Haltwhistle.. 177 C5
Halvergate.. 105 A5
Halwell.. 8 B1
Halwill.. 11 B5
Halwill Junction.. 11 A5
Ham Devon.. 14 A2
  Glos.. 62 D2
  Highld.. 280 A4
  Kent.. 53 D5
  London.. 49 B4
  Shetland.. 285 K1
  Wilts.. 46 C1
Hambleden.. 47 A5
Hambledon Hants 33 D5
  Sur.. 34 C2
Hamble-le-Rice.. 18 A3
Hambleton Lancs 144 C3
  N Yorks.. 149 D4
Hambridge.. 28 C3
Hambrook S Glos.. 43 B5
  W Sus.. 19 A6
Ham Common.. 30 C2
Hameringham.. 134 C3
Hamerton.. 100 D3
Hametoun.. 285 K1
Ham Green Hereford.. 79 C5
  Kent.. 37 D6
  Kent.. 51 C5
  N Som.. 43 B4
  Worcs.. 80 A3
Hamilton.. 194 A2
Hammer.. 34 C1
Hammerpot.. 20 B3
Hammersmith.. 49 B5
Hammerwich.. 96 A3
Hammerwood.. 36 C2
Hammond Street 68 C3
Hammoon.. 30 D2
Hamnavoe Shetland.. 284 E4
  Shetland.. 284 E6
  Shetland.. 284 F6
  Shetland.. 285 K5
Hampden Park.. 22 B4
Hamperden End.. 86 D1
Hampnett.. 64 B1
Hampole.. 140 B3
Hampreston.. 17 B4
Hampstead.. 49 A5
Hampstead Norreys.. 46 B3
Hampsthwaite.. 147 B6
Hampton London.. 48 C4
  Shrops.. 95 C5
  Worcs.. 80 C3
Hampton Bishop .78 D3
Hampton Heath .110 A3
Hampton in Arden.. 97 C5
Hampton Loade.. 95 C5
Hampton Lovett.. 80 A1
Hampton Lucy.. 81 B5
Hampton on the Hill.. 81 A5
Hampton Poyle.. 65 B6
Hamrow.. 119 C6
Hamsey.. 22 A2
Hamsey Green.. 35 A6

Hamstall
  Ridware......113 D5
Hamstead IoW.... 18 B3
  W Mid 96 B3
Hamstead
  Marshall 46 C2
Hamsterley
  Durham 166 B4
  Durham 178 D3
Hamstreet 38 B2
Ham Street 29 B5
Hamworthy 16 B3
Hanbury Staffs ..113 C5
  Worcs........... 80 A2
Hanbury
  Woodend......113 C5
Hanby 116 B3
Hanchurch......112 A2
Handbridge 127 C4
Handcross 35 D5
Handforth 128 A3
Handley 127 D4
Handsacre 113 D4
Handsworth
  S Yorks........131 A4
  W Mid 96 B3
Handy Cross 25 C5
Hanford 112 A2
Hanging
  Langford 31 B4
Hangleton 20 B3
Hanham 43 B5
Hankelow.......111 A5
Hankerton 63 D5
Hankham 22 B4
Hanley 112 A2
Hanley Castle ... 79 C6
Hanley Child ... 79 A4
Hanley Swan 79 C6
Hanley William.. 79 A4
Hanlith 146 A3
Hanmer.........110 B3
Hannah 135 B5
Hannington Hants 46 D3
  Northants........ 99 D5
  Swindon........ 64 D2
Hannington Wick 64 D2
Hansel Village...192 B3
Hanslope 83 C5
Hanthorpe 116 C3
Hanwell London .. 49 A4
  Oxon............ 82 C1
Hanwood 94 A2
Hanworth London . 48 B4
  Norf 120 B3
Happendon 194 C3
Happisburgh ...121 B5
Happisburgh
  Common 121 C5
Hapsford 127 B4
Hapton Lancs ...146 D1
  Norf 104 B2
Harberton 8 B1
Harbertonford ... 8 B1
Harbledown...... 52 D3
Harborne 96 C3
Harborough
  Magna 98 D1
Harbottle 188 C2
Harbury 81 B6
Harby Leics 115 B5
  Notts 132 B3
Harcombe 13 B6
Harden W Mid ... 96 A3
  W Yorks........147 D4
Hardenhuish 44 B3
Hardgate 245 B4
Hardham 20 A3
Hardingham 103 A6
Hardingstone ... 83 B4
Hardington 43 D6
Hardington
  Mandeville 29 D5
Hardington
  Marsh.......... 15 A5
Hardley......... 18 A3
Hardley Street ..105 A4
Hardmead 83 C6
Hardrow 156 B2

Hardstoft 131 C4
Hardway Hants... 19 A5
  Som 29 B7
Hardwick Bucks... 66 B4
  Cambs 85 B5
  Norf 104 C3
  Norf 118 D3
  Northants....... 83 A5
  Notts 131 B6
  Oxon........... 65 A6
  Oxon........... 65 C4
  W Mid 96 B3
Hardwicke Glos... 62 B3
  Glos 63 A5
  Hereford 77 C6
Hardy's Green ... 70 A3
Hareby 134 C3
Hareden 145 B6
Harefield 67 D6
Hare Green 71 A4
Hare Hatch 47 B6
Harehills 148 D2
Harehope 188 A3
Haresceugh 165 A4
Harescombe 63 B4
Haresfield 63 B4
Hareshaw 207 D6
Hareshaw Head .177 A6
Hare Street 68 A3
Harewood 148 C2
Harewood End ... 62 A1
Harford Carms ... 58 A3
  Devon........... 7 B5
Hargate 104 B2
Hargatewall.....129 B6
Hargrave Ches W 127 C4
  Northants.......100 D2
  Suff 86 B3
Harker 175 B6
Harkland 284 E6
Harkstead 88 D2
Harlaston 113 D6
Harlaw Ho......256 D2
Harlaxton 116 B1
Harlech 107 C5
Harlequin 115 B4
Harlescott 111 D4
Harlesden 49 A5
Harleston Devon . 8 C1
  Norf 104 C3
  Suff 87 B6
Harlestone 83 A4
Harle Syke 146 D2
Harley Shrops ... 94 A3
  S Yorks........139 D6
Harleyholm 194 C4
Harlington C Beds 84 D2
  London 48 B3
  S Yorks........140 C2
Harlosh 258 D2
Harlow 69 B4
Harlow Hill
  Northumb.......178 C2
  N Yorks........148 B1
Harlthorpe 149 D6
Harlton 85 B5
Harman's Cross . 16 C3
Harmby 157 C5
Harmer Green .. 68 B2
Harmer Hill 110 C3
Harmondsworth.. 48 B3
Harmston 133 C4
Harnham 178 B2
Harnhill 63 C6
Harold Hill 69 D5
Haroldston West .55 C4
Haroldswick 284 B8
Harold Wood 69 D5
Harome 159 C5
Harpenden...... 67 B7
Harpford 13 B5
Harpham 150 A3
Harpley Norf ...119 C4
  Worcs.......... 79 A4
Harpole........ 82 A3
Harpsdale 280 C3
Harpsden 47 A5
Harpswell 133 A4
Harpurhey 138 C1
Harpur Hill 129 B5
Harraby 175 C7
Harrapool 247 B5

Harrier 285 J1
Harrietfield 219 B4
Harrietsham 37 A6
Harrington Cumb 162 B2
  Lincs..........134 B3
  Northants....... 99 C4
Harringworth .. 99 B6
Harris 234 A2
Harrogate 148 B2
Harrold 83 B6
Harrow 49 A4
Harrowbarrow ... 6 A2
Harrowden 84 C2
Harrowgate Hill.167 D5
Harrow on the
  Hill 49 A4
Harrow Street... 87 D5
Harrow Weald... 67 D7
Harston Cambs... 85 B6
  Leics..........115 B6
Harswell 150 C1
Hart 168 B2
Hartburn
  Northumb.......178 A2
  Stockton.......168 D2
Hart Common ...137 C5
Hartest 87 B4
Hartfield 36 C2
Hartford Cambs .101 D4
  Ches W.........127 B6
Hartfordbridge... 47 D5
Hartford End.... 69 B6
Harthill Ches W .127 D5
  N Lanark 208 D2
  S Yorks........131 A4
Hart Hill 67 A7
Hartington 129 C6
Hartland 24 C3
Hartlebury 95 D6
Hartlepool 168 B3
Hartley Cumb ...155 A6
  Kent 37 C5
  Kent 50 C3
Hartley Westpall .47 D4
Hartley Wintney . 47 D5
Hartlip......... 51 C5
Hartoft End 159 B6
Harton N Yorks ..149 A6
  Shrops......... 94 C2
  T&W 179 C5
Hartpury 62 A3
Hartshead 139 A4
Hartshill 97 B6
Hartshorne 113 C7
Hartsop 164 D2
Hart Station 168 B2
Hartwell 83 B4
Hartwood 194 A3
Harvieston 206 B3
Harvington 80 C3
Harvington Cross 80 C3
Harwell 46 A2
Harwich 88 D3
Harwood Durham 165 B6
  Gtr Man.........137 B6
Harwood Dale...160 B3
Harworth 140 D4
Hasbury 96 C2
Hascombe 34 B2
Haselbech 99 D4
Haselbury
  Plucknett....... 29 D4
Haseley......... 81 A5
Haselor......... 80 B4
Hasfield 63 A4
Hasguard 55 D4
Haskayne 136 C2
Hasketon 88 B3
Hasland 130 C3
Haslemere 34 C2
Haslingden 137 A6
Haslingfield 85 B6
Haslington 128 D2
Hassall 128 D2
Hassall Green ..128 D2
Hassall Street .. 38 A2
Hassendean.....186 A4
Hassingham 105 A4
Hassocks 21 A5
Hassop 130 B2

Hastigrow 281 B4
Hastingleigh 38 A2
Hastings 23 B6
Hastingwood.... 69 C4
Hastoe 67 C5
Haswell 167 A6
Haswell Plough .167 A6
Hatch C Beds 84 C3
  Hants 47 D4
  Wilts.......... 30 C3
Hatch
  Beauchamp 28 C3
Hatch End 67 D7
Hatchet Gate.... 18 A2
Hatch Green 28 D3
Hatching Green .. 67 B7
Hatchmere......127 B5
Hatcliffe 143 C4
Hatfield Hereford.. 78 B3
  Herts.......... 68 C2
  S Yorks........141 C4
  Worcs.......... 80 B1
Hatfield Broad
  Oak 69 B5
Hatfield Garden
  Village 68 C2
Hatfield Heath .. 69 B5
Hatfield Hyde ... 68 B2
Hatfield Peverel . 70 B1
Hatfield
  Woodhouse ...141 C4
Hatford 64 D4
Hatherden 46 D1
Hatherleigh 11 A6
Hathern 114 C2
Hatherop 64 C2
Hathersage 130 A2
Hathershaw 138 C2
Hatherton Ches E 111 A5
  Staffs..........112 D3
Hatley St George .85 B4
Hatt 6 A2
Hattingley 33 B5
Hatton Aberds ..257 C5
  Derbys 113 C6
  Lincs..........134 B1
  Shrops......... 94 B2
  Warks.......... 81 A5
Hatton Castle ..256 B2
Hattoncrook 256 D3
Hatton Heath...127 C4
Hatton of
  Fintray........245 A5
Haugh E Ayrs ...193 C4
  Gtr Man........138 B2
  Lincs..........135 B4
Haugham 134 A3
Haugh Head 188 A3
Haughley 87 A6
Haughley Green . 87 A6
Haugh of Glass .255 C5
Haugh of Urr ...173 B6
Haughs of
  Clinterty.......245 A5
Haughton Notts .132 B1
  Shrops......... 95 A5
  Shrops......... 95 B4
  Shrops.........110 C2
  Shrops.........111 D4
  Staffs..........112 C2
Haughton
  Castle.........177 B7
Haughton Grn...138 D2
Haughton Moss .127 D5
Haultwick...... 68 A3
Haunn Argyll....224 B2
  W Isles 286 E3
Haunton 113 D6
Hauxley........189 C5
Hauxton 85 B6
Havant 19 A6
Haven 78 B2
Haven Bank 134 D2
Haven Side 142 A3
Havenstreet 19 B4
Havercroft 140 B1
Haverfordwest
  (Hwlffordd).... 55 C5
Haverhill 86 C2
Haverigg 153 C2

Havering-atte-
  Bower......... 69 D5
Haveringland ...120 C3
Haversham 83 C5
Haverthwaite ...154 C2
Haverton Hill...168 C2
Hawarden
  (Penarlâg).....126 C3
Hawcoat 153 C3
Hawen 73 B6
Hawes 156 C2
Hawes' Green ...104 B3
Hawes Side 144 D3
Hawford 79 A6
Hawick 186 B4
Hawkchurch 14 A3
Hawkedon 86 B3
Hawkenbury Kent .36 C3
  Kent 37 B6
Hawkeridge 44 D2
Hawkerland 13 C5
Hawkesbury
  S Glos 43 A6
  Warks.......... 97 C6
Hawkesbury
  Upton......... 44 A1
Hawkes End.....97 C6
Hawk Green 129 A4
Hawkhill 189 B5
Hawkhurst 37 C5
Hawkinge 39 B4
Hawkley........ 33 C6
Hawkridge 26 B3
Hawkshead 154 B2
Hawkshead Hill .154 B2
Hawksland 194 C3
Hawkswick 156 D3
Hawksworth
  Notts 115 A5
  W Yorks........147 C5
  W Yorks........147 D6
Hawkwell 70 D2
Hawley Hants ... 34 A1
  Kent 50 B2
Hawling 63 A6
Hawnby 158 C4
Haworth 147 D4
Hawstead 87 B4
Hawthorn
  Durham 168 A2
  Rhondda........ 41 C6
  Wilts.......... 44 C2
Hawthorn Hill
  Brack.......... 48 B1
  Lincs..........134 D2
Hawthorpe 116 C3
Hawton 132 D2
Haxby 149 B5
Haxey 141 C5
Haydock 137 D4
Haydon 29 D6
Haydon Bridge .177 C6
Haydon Wick ... 45 A5
Haye 6 A2
Hayes London ... 48 A4
  London 49 C7
Hayfield Derbys .129 A5
  Fife 209 A5
Hay Green 118 D2
Hayhill 182 A2
Hayhillock 232 D3
Hayle 2 B3
Haynes 84 C2
Haynes Church
  End 84 C2
Hay-on-Wye (Y Gelli
  Gandryll)...... 77 C6
Hayscastle 55 B4
Hayscastle Cross 55 B5
Hayshead 233 D4
Hay Street 68 A3
Hayton Aberdeen 245 B6
  Cumb 174 D4
  Cumb 176 D3
  E Yorks........149 C7
  Notts 132 A2
Hayton's Bent .. 94 C3
Haytor Vale 12 D2
Haywards Heath . 35 D6
Haywood 140 B3
Haywood Oaks .131 D6

Hazelbury Bryan.. 16 A1
Hazeley.......... 47 D5
Hazel Grove....129 A4
Hazelhurst 138 C2
Hazelslade 112 D4
Hazel Street ... 37 C4
Hazelton....... 64 B1
Hazelton Walls .220 B3
Hazelwood.....114 A1
Hazlemere 66 D4
Hazlerigg 179 B4
Hazlewood 147 B4
Hazon 189 C4
Heacham 118 B3
Headbourne
  Worthy........ 32 B3
Headbrook..... 77 B7
Headcorn 37 B6
Headingley 148 D1
Headington 65 C6
Headlam 167 D4
Headless Cross .. 80 A3
Headley Hants .. 33 B7
  Hants.......... 46 C3
  Sur............ 35 A5
Head of Muir...207 B6
Headon 132 B2
Heads 194 B2
Heads Nook 176 D2
Heage 130 D3
Healaugh
  N Yorks........148 C3
  N Yorks........156 B4
Heald Green ...128 A3
Heale Devon 26 A1
  Som 29 A6
Healey Gtr Man..138 B1
  Northumb.......178 D2
  N Yorks........157 C5
Healing 143 B4
Heamoor 2 B2
Heanish 222 C3
Heanor 114 A2
Heanton
  Punchardon ... 25 B6
Heapham 132 A3
Hearthstane ...195 D6
Heasley Mill.... 26 B2
Heast..........247 C5
Heath Cardiff ... 41 D6
  Derbys 131 C4
Heath and Reach 67 A4
Heathcote 129 C6
Heath End Hants . 46 C3
  Sur............ 34 B1
  Warks.......... 81 A5
Heather 114 D1
Heatherfield ...259 D4
Heathfield Devon.. 12 D3
  E Sus.......... 36 D3
  Som 27 C6
Heathhall 174 A2
Heath Hayes ...112 D4
Heath Hill 111 D6
Heath House.... 28 A4
Heathrow Airport.48 B3
Heathstock 14 A2
Heathton 95 B6
Heath Town..... 96 B2
Heatley........128 A2
Heaton Lancs ...144 A4
  Staffs..........129 C4
  T&W 179 C4
  W Yorks........147 D5
Heaton Moor ...138 D1
Heaverham 36 A3
Heaviley.......129 A3
Heavitree 13 B4
Hebburn 179 C5
Hebden 147 A4
Hebden Bridge .138 A2
Hebron Anglesey 123 B4
  Carms......... 73 D4
  Northumb.......178 A3
Heck 184 D3
Heckfield 47 C5
Heckfield Green 104 D2
Heckfordbridge .70 A3
Heckington 116 A4
Heckmondwike .139 A5
Heddington 44 C3
Heddle 282 F4

Heddon-on-the-
Wall 178 C3
Hedenham. 104 B4
Hedge End. 32 D3
Hedgerley. 48 A2
Hedging. 28 C3
Hedley on the
Hill. 178 D2
Hednesford. . . .112 D3
Hedon. 142 A3
Hedsor. 48 A2
Hedworth. 179 C5
Hegdon Hill. 78 B3
Heggerscales. . .165 D6
Heglibister. . . .285 H5
Heighington
Darl. 167 C5
Lincs. 133 C5
Heights of Brae .263 D7
Heights of
Kinlochewe. . .262 D2
Heilam. 277 B5
Heiton. 197 C6
Hele Devon. . . 13 A4
Devon. 25 A6
Helensburgh. .215 D5
Helford. 3 C5
Helford Passage. .3 C5
Helhoughton. .119 C5
Helions
Bumpstead. . . .86 C2
Hellaby. 140 D3
Helland. 10 D1
Hellesdon. . . .120 D4
Hellidon. 82 B2
Hellifield. . . .146 B2
Hellingly. 22 A3
Hellington. . . .104 A4
Hellister. 285 J5
Helm. 189 D4
Helmdon. 82 C2
Helmingham. . .88 B2
Helmington
Row. 167 B4
Helmsdale. . .274 C4
Helmshore. . .137 A6
Helmsley. . . .159 C5
Helperby. . . .148 A3
Helperthorpe. .160 D3
Helpringham. .116 A4
Helpston. 100 A3
Helsby. 127 B4
Helsey. 135 B5
Helston. 3 C4
Helstone. 10 C1
Helton. 164 C3
Helwith Bridge .146 A2
Hemblington. .121 D5
Hemel
Hempstead. 67 C6
Hemingbrough. .149 D5
Hemingby. . . .134 B2
Hemingford
Abbots. 101 D4
Hemingford
Grey. 101 D4
Hemingstone 88 B2
Hemington Leics 114 C2
Northants. 100 C2
Som. 43 D6
Hemley. 88 C3
Hemlington. . .168 D3
Hemp Green. . .89 A4
Hempholme. . .150 B3
Hempnall. . . .142 D1
Hempnall Green 104 B3
Hempriggs
House. 281 D5
Hempstead Essex .86 D2
Medway. . . .51 C4
Norf. 120 B3
Norf. 121 C6
Hempsted. 63 B4
Hempton Norf. .119 C6
Oxon. 82 D1
Hemsby. 121 D6
Hemswell. . . .142 D1
Hemswell Cliff .133 A4
Hemsworth. . .140 B2
Hemyock. 27 D6
Henbury Bristol. .43 B4
Ches E. 128 B3

Hendon London. .49 A5
T&W. 179 D6
Hendre. 126 C1
Hendre-ddu. .124 C3
Hendreforgan. . .41 C4
Hendy. 57 B5
Heneglwys. . . .123 C4
Hen-feddau fawr 73 C5
Henfield. 21 A5
Henford. 11 B4
Henghurst. . . .38 B1
Hengoed Caerph. .41 A6
Powys. 77 B6
Shrops. 110 B3
Hengrave. 87 A4
Henham. 69 A5
Heniarth. 93 A5
Henlade. 28 C2
Henley Shrops. .94 D3
Som. 28 B4
Suff. 88 B2
W Sus. 34 D1
Henley-in-Arden 81 A4
Henley-on-
Thames. 47 A5
Henley's Down. . .23 A5
Henllan Ceredig. .73 B6
Denb. 125 C5
Henllan Amgoed .73 D4
Henllys. 61 D4
Henlow. 84 D3
Hennock. 12 C3
Henny Street. . .87 D4
Henryd. 124 B2
Henry's Moat. . .55 B6
Hensall. 140 A3
Henshaw. . . .177 C5
Hensingham. .162 C2
Henstead. . . .105 C5
Henstridge. . . .30 D1
Henstridge Ash. .29 C7
Henstridge
Marsh. 30 C1
Henton Oxon. . . .66 C3
Som. 29 A4
Henwood. . . .10 D3
Heogan. 285 J6
Heol-las. 40 B1
Heol Senni. . .59 C6
Heol-y-Cyw. . .40 C4
Hepburn. . . .188 A3
Hepple. 188 C2
Hepscott. . . .179 A4
Heptonstall. . .138 A2
Hepworth Suff. .103 D5
W Yorks. 139 C4
Herbrandston. . .55 D4
Hereford. 78 C3
Heriot. 196 A2
Hermiston. . .209 C4
Hermitage
Borders. . . .186 D4
Dorset. 15 A6
W Berks. 46 B3
W Sus. 19 A6
Hermon Anglesey 122 D3
Carms. 58 C3
Carms. 73 C6
Pembs. 73 C5
Herne. 52 C3
Herne Bay. . . .52 C3
Herner. 25 C6
Hernhill. 52 C2
Herodsfoot. . . .5 A7
Heronden. . . .69 D6
Heronsford. . .180 C3
Herriard. 33 A5
Herringfleet. .105 B5
Herringswell. .102 D3
Hersden. 53 C4
Hersham Corn. .10 A3
Sur. 48 C4
Herstmonceux. . .22 A4
Herston. 283 H5
Hertford. 68 B3
Hertford Heath. .68 B3
Hertingfordbury. .68 B3
Hesket Bank. .136 A3
Hesket Lane. .145 C6
Hesket
Newmarket. . .163 A6
Heskin Green. .136 B4

Hesleden 168 B2
Hesleyside. . . .177 A6
Heslington. . . .149 B5
Hessay. 148 B4
Hessenford. 6 B2
Hessett. 87 A5
Hessle. 142 A2
Hest Bank. 145 A4
Heston. 48 B4
Hestwall. 282 F3
Heswall. 126 A2
Hethe. 65 A6
Hethersett. . . .104 A2
Hethersgill. . .176 C2
Hethpool. . . .188 A1
Hett. 167 B5
Hetton. 146 B3
Hetton-le-Hole. .167 A6
Hetton Steads. .198 C4
Heugh. 178 B2
Heugh-head. . .243 A6
Heveningham. .104 D4
Hever. 36 B2
Heversham. . .154 C3
Hevingham. . .120 C3
Hewas Water. . . .5 C4
Hewelsfield. . .62 C1
Hewish N Som. . .42 C3
Som. 14 A4
Heworth. . . .149 B5
Hexham. 178 C1
Hextable. 50 B2
Hexton. 84 D3
Hexworthy. . . .12 D1
Hey. 146 C2
Heybridge Essex. .69 D6
Essex. 70 C2
Heybridge Basin. .70 C2
Heybrook Bay. . . .7 C4
Heydon Cambs. . .85 C6
Norf. 120 C3
Heydour. 116 B3
Heylipol. 222 C2
Heylor. 284 E4
Heysham. 144 A4
Heyshott. 20 A1
Heyside. 138 C2
Heytesbury. . . .30 A3
Heythrop. 64 A4
Heywood
Gtr Man. 138 B1
Wilts. 44 D2
Hibaldstow. . .142 C1
Hickleton. . . .140 C2
Hickling Norf. .121 C6
Notts. 115 C4
Hickling Green. .121 C6
Hickling Heath. .121 C6
Hickstead. 35 D5
Hidcote Boyce . . .81 C4
High Ackworth. .140 B2
Higham Derbys. .130 D3
Kent. 51 B4
Lancs. 146 D2
Suff. 86 A3
Suff. 87 D6
Higham Dykes. .178 B3
Higham Ferrers. .83 A6
Higham Gobion. .84 D3
Higham on the
Hill. 97 B6
Highampton. . . .11 A5
Higham Wood. . .36 B3
High Angerton. .178 A2
High Bankhill. .164 A3
High Barnes. .179 D5
High Beach. . . .68 D4
High Bentham. .145 A6
High Bickington. .25 C7
High Birkwith. .155 D6
High Blantyre. .194 A1
High
Bonnybridge. .207 C6
High Bradfield. .139 D5
High Bray. . . .26 B1
Highbridge
Highld. 239 D5
Som. 28 A3
Highbrook. 35 C6
High Brooms. . .36 B3
High Bullen. . .25 C6
Highburton. . .139 B4

Highbury 29 A6
High Buston. .189 C5
High Callerton. .178 B3
High Catton. .149 B6
Highclere. 46 C2
Highcliffe. 17 B6
High Cogges. . . .65 C4
High Coniscliffe 167 D5
High Cross Hants. .33 C6
Herts. 68 B3
High Easter. . .69 B6
High
Eggborough. . .140 A3
High Ellington. .157 C5
Higher Ansty. . .16 A1
Higher Ashton. . .12 C3
Higher Ballam. .144 D3
Higher Bartle. .145 D5
Higher Boscaswell. 2 B1
Higher
Burwardsley. .127 D5
Higher Clovelly. . .24 C4
Higher End. . .136 C4
Higher
Kinnerton. . .126 C3
Higher
Penwortham. .136 A4
Higher Town
Scilly. P02 E4
Higher
Walreddon. 11 D5
Higher Walton
Lancs. 137 A4
Warr. 127 A5
Higher
Wheelton. 137 A5
Higher Whitley. .127 A6
Higher Wych. . .110 A3
High Etherley. .167 C4
Highfield E Yorks 149 D6
Gtr Man. 137 C6
N Ayrs. 204 C3
Oxon. 65 A6
S Yorks. 130 A3
T&W. 178 D3
Highfields Cambs. .85 B5
Northumb. 198 A3
High Garrett. . .70 A1
Highgate. 49 A5
High Grange. .167 B4
High Green Norf. .104 A2
S Yorks. 139 D6
Worcs. 80 C1
High Halden. . .37 C6
High Halstow. . .51 B4
High Ham. 28 B4
High Harrington 162 B3
High Hatton. . .111 C5
High Hawsker. .160 A3
High Hesket. .164 A2
High Hesleden. .168 B2
High Hoyland. .139 B5
High Hunsley. .150 D2
High Hurstwood. .36 D2
High Hutton. .149 A6
High Ireby. . . .163 A5
High Kelling. .120 A3
High Kilburn. .158 D4
High Lands. . . .166 C4
Highlane Ches E. .128 C3
Derbys. 131 A4
High Lane
Gtr Man. 129 A4
Worcs. 79 A4
High Laver. . . .69 C5
Highlaws. . . .174 D4
Highleadon. . . .62 A3
High Legh. . . .128 A2
Highleigh. . . .20 C1
High Leven. .168 D2
Highley. 95 C5
High Littleton. .43 D5
High Lorton. .163 B4
High Marishes. .159 D7
High Marnham. .132 B3
High Melton. .140 C3
High Mickley. .178 C2
High Mindork. .171 B5
Highmoor Cross. .47 A5

Highmoor Hill. .42 A3
Highnam. 62 B3
Highnam Green. .62 A3
High Newton. .154 C3
High Newton-by-the-
Sea. 189 A5
High Nibthwaite 154 C1
High Offley. . .112 C1
High Ongar. . .69 C5
High Onn. . . .112 D2
High Roding. . .69 B6
High Row. . . .163 A6
High
Salvington. . . .21 B4
High Sellafield . .162 D3
High Shaw. . . .156 B2
High Spen. . . .178 D3
Highstead. 51 C6
High Stoop. . .166 A4
High Street Corn. . .5 B4
Kent. 37 C5
Suff. 87 C4
Suff. 89 B5
Suff. 105 D5
Highstreet Green 86 D3
High Street
Green. 87 B6
Hightae. 174 A3
High Throston. .168 B2
Hightown Ches E 128 C3
Mers. 136 C2
Hightown Green. .87 B5
High Toynton. .134 C2
High Trewhitt. .188 C3
High Valleyfield. .208 B3
Highway. 44 B4
Highweek. . . .12 D3
High Westwood .178 D3
Highworth. . . .64 D3
High Wray. . . .154 B2
High Wych. . . .69 B4
High Wycombe. .66 D4
Hilborough. . .103 A4
Hilcote. 131 D4
Hilcott. 45 D5
Hildenborough. .36 B3
Hilden Park. . .36 B3
Hildersham. . . .86 C1
Hilderstone. .112 B3
Hilderthorpe. .151 A4
Hilfield. 15 A6
Hilgay. 102 B2
Hill Pembs. 55 D7
S Glos. 62 D2
W Mid. 96 B4
Hillam. 140 A3
Hillbeck. 165 D5
Hillborough. . .53 C4
Hillbrae Aberds. .255 B7
Aberds. 256 D2
Hill Brow. . . .33 C6
Hillbutts. 16 A3
Hillclifflane. . .113 A6
Hillcommon. . . .27 C6
Hill Dale. . . .136 B3
Hill Dyke. . . .117 A6
Hillend. 208 B4
Hill End Durham. .166 B3
Fife. 208 A3
N Yorks. 147 B4
Hillerton. 12 B2
Hillesden. . . .66 A2
Hillesley. 43 A6
Hillfarance. . .27 C6
Hillhead Aberds. .255 C6
Devon. 8 B3
S Ayrs. 182 A4
Hill Head Hants. .18 A4
Northumb. 178 C1
Hillhead of
Auchentumb. .269 D4
Hillhead of
Cocklaw. . . .257 B5
Hillhouse. . .197 A4
Hilliclay. . . .280 B3
Hillingdon. . . .48 A3
Hillington
Glasgow. . . .205 B5
Norf. 119 C4
Hillmorton. . . .98 D2
Hill Mountain. .55 D5
Hillockhead
Aberds. 243 B6

Hillockhead continued
Aberds. 244 A1
Hill of Beath. .209 A4
Hill of Fearn. .265 C4
Hill of
Mountblairy. . .268 D1
Hill Ridware. .113 D4
Hillside Aberds. .245 C6
Angus. 233 B5
Mers. 136 B2
Orkney. 283 H5
Shetland. . . .285 G6
Hillswick. . . .284 F4
Hill Top Durham. .166 C2
Hants. 18 A3
W Mid. 96 B2
W Yorks. 139 B6
Hill View. . . .16 B3
Hillway. 19 C5
Hillwell. 285 M5
Hilmarton. . . .44 B4
Hilperton. . . .44 D2
Hilsea. 19 A5
Hilston. 151 D5
Hilton Aberds. .257 C4
Cambs. 85 A4
Cumb. 165 C5
Derbys. 113 B6
Dorset. 16 A1
Durham. 167 C4
Highld. 264 B3
Shrops. 95 B5
Stockton. . . .168 D2
Hilton of
Cadboll. 265 C4
Himbleton. . . .80 B2
Himley. 96 B1
Hincaster. . .154 C4
Hinckley. 98 B1
Hinderclay. . .103 D6
Hinderton. . . .126 B3
Hinderwell. . .169 D5
Hindford. . . .110 B2
Hindhead. 34 C1
Hindley. 137 C5
Hindley Green. .137 C5
Hindlip. 80 B1
Hindolveston. .120 C2
Hindon. 30 B3
Hindringham. .120 B1
Hingham. . . .103 A6
Hinstock. . . .111 C5
Hintlesham. . . .88 C1
Hinton Hants. . .17 B6
Hereford. 78 D1
Northants. 82 B2
S Glos. 43 B6
Shrops. 94 A2
Hinton Ampner. .33 C4
Hinton Blewett. .43 D4
Hinton
Charterhouse. . . 43 D6
Hinton-in-the-
Hedges. 82 D2
Hinton Martell. .17 A4
Hinton on the
Green. 80 C3
Hinton Parva. . . .45 A6
Hinton St George 28 D4
Hinton St Mary. .30 D1
Hinton Waldrist. .65 D4
Hints Shrops. . .95 D4
Staffs. 97 A4
Hinwick. 83 A6
Hinxhill. 38 A2
Hinxton. 85 C6
Hinxworth. . . .84 C4
Hipperholme. .139 A4
Hipswell. . . .157 B5
Hirael. 123 C5
Hiraeth. 73 D4
Hirn. 245 B4
Hirnant. 109 C5
Hirst N Lanark. .207 D6
Northumb. 179 A4
Hirst Courtney. .140 A4
Hirwaen. . . .125 C5
Hirwaun. 59 E6
Hiscott. 25 C6

Histon 85 A6
Hitcham 87 B5
Hitchin 68 A1
Hither Green 49 B6
Hittisleigh 12 B2
Hive 149 D7
Hixon 112 C4
Hoaden 53 D4
Hoaldalbert 61 A5
Hoar Cross 113 C5
Hoarwithy 62 A1
Hoath 53 C4
Hobarris 93 D7
Hobbister 283 G4
Hobkirk 187 B4
Hobson 178 D3
Hoby 115 D4
Hockering 120 D2
Hockerton 132 D2
Hockley 70 D2
Hockley Heath . . . 97 D4
Hockliffe 67 A5
Hockwold cum
Wilton 102 C3
Hockworthy 27 D5
Hoddesdon 68 C3
Hoddlesden 137 A6
Hoddomcross . . . 175 A4
Hoddom Mains . . 175 A4
Hodgeston 55 E6
Hodley 93 B5
Hodnet 111 C5
Hodthorpe 131 B5
Hoe Hants 33 D4
Norf 120 D1
Hoe Gate 33 D5
Hoff 165 D4
Hoggard's Green . 87 B4
Hoggeston 66 A4
Hogha
Gearraidh 287 G2
Hoghton 137 A5
Hognaston 130 D2
Hog Patch 34 B1
Hogsthorpe 135 B5
Holbeach 117 C6
Holbeach Bank . . 117 C6
Holbeach
Clough 117 C6
Holbeach Drove 117 D6
Holbeach Hurn . . 117 C6
Holbeach St
Johns 117 D6
Holbeach St
Marks 117 B6
Holbeach St
Matthew 117 B7
Holbeck Notts . . 131 B5
W Yorks 148 D1
Holbeck
Woodhouse . . 131 B5
Holberrow Green . 80 B3
Holbeton 7 B5
Holborn 49 A6
Holbrook Derbys . 114 A1
Suff 88 D2
S Yorks 131 A4
Holburn 198 C4
Holbury 18 A3
Holcombe Devon . 13 D4
Som 29 A6
Holcombe Rogus . 27 D5
Holcot 83 A4
Holden 146 C1
Holdenby 82 A3
Holdenhurst 17 B5
Holdgate 94 C3
Holdingham 116 A3
Holditch 14 A3
Holefield 198 C2
Holehouses 128 B2
Hole-in-the-
Wall 62 A2
Holemoor 11 A6
Holestane 183 C6
Holford 27 A6
Holgate 148 B4
Holker 154 D2
Holkham 119 A5

Hollacombe 11 A4
Holland Orkney . . 282 B5
Orkney 282 E7
Holland Fen 117 A5
Holland-on-Sea . . 71 B6
Hollandstoun . . . 282 B8
Hollee 175 B5
Hollesley 89 C4
Hollicombe 8 A2
Hollingbourne . . . 37 A6
Hollington
Derbys 113 B6
E Sus 23 A5
Staffs 113 B4
Hollington
Grove 113 B6
Hollingworth . . . 138 D3
Hollins 137 C7
Hollinsclough . . . 129 C5
Hollins Green . . . 137 D5
Hollins Lane . . . 145 B4
Hollinwood
Gtr Man 138 C2
Shrops 111 B4
Hollocombe 26 D1
Holloway 130 D3
Hollowell 98 D3
Hollow
Meadows . . . 130 A2
Hollybush Caerph . 41 A6
E Ayrs 182 A1
Worcs 79 D5
Holly End 101 A6
Holly Grn 79 C6
Hollym 143 A5
Hollywood 96 D3
Holmbridge 139 C4
Holmbury St
Mary 35 B4
Holmbush 5 B5
Holmcroft 112 C3
Holme Cambs . . 100 C3
Cumb 154 D4
Notts 132 D3
N Yorks 158 C2
W Yorks 139 C4
Holme Chapel . . 138 A1
Holme Green . . . 149 C4
Holme Hale 103 A4
Holme Lacy 78 D3
Holme Marsh 78 B1
Holme next the
Sea 119 A4
Holme-on-Spalding-
Moor 149 D7
Holme on the
Wolds 150 C2
Holme
Pierrepont . . . 115 B4
Holmer 78 C3
Holmer Green . . . 67 D5
Holme St
Cuthbert 174 D4
Holmes Chapel . 128 C2
Holmesfield 130 B3
Holmeswood . . . 136 B3
Holmewood 131 C4
Holme Wood . . . 147 D5
Holmfirth 139 C4
Holmhead
Dumfries 183 D5
E Ayrs 193 C5
Holmisdale 258 D1
Holmpton 143 A5
Holmrook 153 A1
Holmsgarth 285 J6
Holmwrangle . . . 164 A3
Holne 7 A6
Holnest 15 A6
Holsworthy 10 A4
Holsworthy
Beacon 11 A4
Holt Dorset 17 A4
Norf 120 B2
Wilts 44 C2
Worcs 79 A6
Wrex 127 D4
Holtby 149 B5
Holt End Hants . . 33 B5
Worcs 80 A3
Holt Fleet 79 A6
Holt Heath 79 A6

Holton Oxon 65 C7
Som 29 C6
Suff 105 D4
Holton cum
Beckering . . . 133 A6
Holton Heath 16 B3
Holton le Clay . . 143 C4
Holton le Moor . 142 D2
Holton St Mary . . 87 D6
Holt Park 147 C6
Holwell Dorset . . . 29 D7
Herts 84 D3
Leics 115 C5
Oxon 64 C3
Holwick 166 C2
Holworth 16 C1
Holybourne 33 A6
Holy Cross 96 D2
Holyhead
(Caergybi) . . . 122 B2
Holy Island 199 B5
Holymoorside . . 130 C3
Holyport 48 B1
Holystone 188 C2
Holytown 207 D5
Holywell Cambs . 101 D5
Corn 4 B2
Dorset 15 A5
E Sus 22 C3
Northumb 179 B5
Holywell
(Treffynnon) . 126 B1
Holywell Green . 138 B3
Holywell Lake . . . 27 C6
Holywell Row . . 102 D3
Holywood 184 D2
Homer 95 A4
Homersfield 104 C3
Hom Green 62 A1
Homington 31 C5
Honeyborough . . 55 D5
Honeybourne . . . 80 C4
Honeychurch 12 A1
Honey Hill 52 C3
Honey Street 45 C5
Honey Tye 87 D5
Honiley 97 D5
Honing 121 C5
Honingham 120 D3
Honington Lincs . 116 A2
Suff 103 D5
Warks 81 C5
Honiton 13 A6
Honley 139 B4
Hood Green 139 C6
Hooe E Sus 23 B4
Plym 7 B4
Hooe Common . . 23 A4
Hoo Green 128 A2
Hook E Yorks . . . 141 A5
Hants 47 D5
London 49 C4
Pembs 55 C5
Wilts 45 A4
Hooke 15 B5
Hookgate 111 B6
Hook Green Kent . 37 C4
Kent 50 C3
Hook Norton . . . 81 D6
Hookway 12 B3
Hookwood 35 B5
Hoole 127 C4
Hooley 35 A5
Hoop 61 C7
Hoo St.Werburgh 51 B4
Hooton 126 B3
Hooton Levitt . . 140 D3
Hooton Pagnell . 140 C2
Hooton Roberts . 140 D2
Hope Derbys . . . 129 A6
Devon 7 D5
Highld 277 C5
Powys 93 A6
Shrops 94 A1
Staffs 129 D6
Hope (Yr Hôb) . . 126 D3
Hope Bagot 94 D3
Hope Bowdler . . . 94 B2
Hope End Green . 69 A5
Hope Green 129 A4
Hopeman 266 C2
Hope Mansell . . . 62 B2

Hopesay 94 C1
Hope's Grn 51 A4
Hope under
Dinmore 78 B3
Hopley's Green . . 78 B1
Hopperton 148 B3
Hop Pole 117 D4
Hopstone 95 B5
Hopton Shrops . 110 C2
Shrops 111 C4
Staffs 112 C3
Suff 103 D5
Hopton
Cangeford 94 C3
Hopton Castle . . . 94 D1
Hoptonheath 94 D1
Hopton on Sea . 105 A6
Hopton Wafers . . 95 D4
Hopwas 97 A4
Hopwood
Gtr Man 138 C1
Worcs 96 D3
Horam 22 A3
Horbling 116 B4
Horbury 139 B5
Horcott 64 C2
Horden 168 A2
Horderley 94 C2
Hordle 17 B6
Hordley 110 B2
Horeb Carms 57 B4
Carms 58 C2
Ceredig 73 B6
Horfield 43 B5
Horham 104 D3
Horkesley Heath . 70 A3
Horkstow 142 B1
Horley Oxon 81 C7
Sur 35 B5
Hornblotton
Green 29 B5
Hornby Lancs . . 145 A5
N Yorks 157 B6
N Yorks 158 A2
Horncastle 134 C2
Hornchurch 50 A2
Horncliffe 198 B3
Horndean
Borders 198 B2
Hants 33 D6
Horndon 11 D6
Horndon on the
Hill 50 A3
Horne 35 B6
Horniehaugh . . . 232 B2
Horning 121 D5
Horninghold 99 B5
Horninglow 113 C6
Horningsea 85 A6
Horningsham . . . 30 A2
Horningtoft 119 C6
Hornsby 176 D3
Horns Corner . . . 37 D5
Horns Cross
Devon 25 C4
E Sus 37 D6
Hornsea 151 C5
Hornsea Bridge . 151 C5
Hornsey 49 A6
Hornton 81 C6
Horrabridge 7 A4
Horringer 87 A4
Horringford 18 C4
Horsebridge
Devon 11 D5
Hants 32 B2
Horsebrook 112 D2
Horsehay 95 A4
Horseheath 86 C2
Horsehouse 156 C4
Horsell 34 A2
Horseman's
Green 110 A3
Horseway 101 C6
Horsey 121 C6
Horsford 120 D3
Horsforth 147 D6
Horsham Worcs . . 79 B5
W Sus 35 C4
Horsham St
Faith 120 D4

Horsington Lincs 134 C1
Som 29 C7
Horsley Derbys . 114 A1
Glos 63 D4
Northumb 178 C2
Northumb 188 D1
Horsley Cross . . . 71 A5
Horsleycross
Street 71 A5
Horsleyhill 186 B4
Horsleyhope . . . 166 A3
Horsley
Woodhouse . . 114 A1
Horsmonden 37 B4
Horspath 65 C6
Horstead 121 D4
Horsted Keynes . . 36 D1
Horton Bucks . . . 67 B5
Dorset 17 A4
Lancs 146 B2
Northants 83 B5
S Glos 43 A6
Shrops 110 C3
Som 28 D3
Staffs 129 D4
Swansea 57 D4
Wilts 45 C4
Windsor 48 B3
Horton-cum-
Studley 65 B6
Horton Green . . . 110 A3
Horton Heath . . . 32 D3
Horton Kirby 50 C2
Hortonlane 110 D3
Horwich 137 B5
Horwich End . . . 129 A5
Horwood 25 C6
Hose 115 C5
Hoselaw 198 C2
Hoses 153 A3
Hosh 218 B3
Hosta 287 G2
Hoswick 285 L6
Hotham 150 D1
Hothfield 38 A1
Hoton 114 C3
Houbie 284 D8
Houdston 181 B3
Hough Ches E . . 128 B3
Ches E 128 D2
Hougham 116 A1
Hough Green . . . 127 A4
Hough-on-the-
Hill 116 A2
Houghton Cambs 101 D4
Cumb 175 C7
Hants 32 B2
Pembs 55 D5
W Sus 20 A3
Houghton
Conquest 84 C2
Houghton Green
E Sus 37 D7
Warr 137 D5
Houghton-le-
Side 167 C5
Houghton-Le-
Spring 167 A6
Houghton on the
Hill 98 A3
Houghton Regis . 67 A4
Houghton St
Giles 119 B6
Houlland
Shetland 284 F7
Shetland 285 H5
Houlsyke 159 A6
Hound 18 A3
Hound Green . . . 47 D5
Houndslow 197 B5
Houndwood . . . 211 D5
Hounslow 48 B4
Hounslow Green . 69 B6
Housay 284 F8
House of Daviot 252 B3
House of
Glenmuick . . . 243 C6
Housetter 284 E5
Houss 285 K5
Houston 205 B4

Houstry 275 A5
Houton 283 G4
Hove 21 B5
Hoveringham . . . 115 A4
Hoveton 121 D5
Hovingham 159 D5
How 176 D3
Howbrook 139 D6
How Caple 79 D4
Howden Borders . 187 A5
E Yorks 141 A5
Howden-le-
Wear 167 B4
Howe Highld . . . 281 B5
Norf 104 A3
N Yorks 158 C2
Howe Bridge . . . 137 C5
Howe Green 70 C1
Howell 116 A4
How End 84 C2
Howe of
Teuchar 256 B2
Howe Street
Essex 69 B6
Essex 86 D2
Howey 77 B4
Howgate 196 A1
How Green 36 B2
Howick 189 B5
Howle Durham . 166 C3
Telford 111 C5
Howlett End 86 D1
Howley 14 A2
Hownam 187 B4
Hownam Mains . 187 A6
Howpasley 185 B6
Howsham
N Lincs 142 C2
N Yorks 149 A6
Howslack 184 B3
Howtel 198 C2
Howton 61 A6
Howtown 164 D2
Howwood 204 B3
Hoxne 104 D2
Hoy 283 G3
Hoylake 126 A2
Hoyland 139 C6
Hoylandswaine . 139 C5
Hubberholme . . 156 D3
Hubbert's
Bridge 117 A5
Huby N Yorks . . 147 C6
N Yorks 149 A4
Hucclecote 63 B4
Hucking 37 A6
Hucknall 114 A3
Huddersfield . . . 139 B4
Huddington 80 B2
Hudswell 157 A5
Huggate 150 B1
Hugglescote . . . 114 D2
Hughenden
Valley 66 D3
Hughley 94 B3
Hugh Town Scilly . . 2 C3
Huish Devon 25 D6
Wilts 45 C5
Huish
Champflower . 27 C5
Huish Episcopi . . 28 C4
Huisinis 287 C4
Hulcott 66 B4
Hulland 113 A6
Hulland Ward . . 113 A6
Hullavington 44 A2
Hullbridge 70 D2
Hulme 138 D1
Hulme End 129 D6
Hulme Walfield . 128 C3
Hulverstone 18 C2
Hulver Street . . 105 C5
Humber 78 B3
Humber Bridge . 142 A2
Humberston . . . 143 C5
Humbie 210 D1
Humbleton
E Yorks 151 D5
Northumb 188 A2
Humby 116 B3
Hume 197 B6
Humshaugh 177 B7

Huna 281 A5
Huncoat 146 D1
Huncote 98 B2
Hundalee 187 B5
Hunderthwaite . . 166 C2
Hundleby 134 C3
Hundle Houses . . 134 D2
Hundleton 55 D5
Hundon 86 C3
Hundred Acres . . . 33 D4
Hundred End 136 A3
Hundred House . . . 77 B5
Hungarton 98 A3
Hungerford Hants . 31 D5
W Berks 46 C1
Hungerford
Newtown 46 B1
Hungerton 116 C1
Hungladder 258 A3
Hunmanby 161 D4
Hunmanby
Moor 161 D5
Hunningham 81 A6
Hunny Hill 18 C3
Hunsdon 68 B4
Hunsingore 148 B3
Hunslet 148 D2
Hunsonby 164 B3
Hunspow 280 A4
Hunstanton 118 A3
Hunstanworth . . . 166 A2
Hunsterson 111 A5
Hunston Suff 87 A5
W Sus. 20 B1
Hunstrete 43 C5
Hunt End 80 A3
Hunter's Quay . . . 203 A6
Hunthill Lodge . . . 232 A2
Huntingdon 100 D4
Huntingfield 104 D4
Huntingford 30 B2
Huntington
E Loth. 210 C1
Hereford 77 B6
Staffs 112 D3
York 149 B5
Hunting-tower . . . 219 B5
Huntley 62 B3
Huntly 255 C6
Huntlywood 197 B5
Hunton Kent 37 B5
N Yorks. 157 B5
Hunt's Corner . . . 103 C6
Hunt's Cross 127 A4
Huntsham 27 C5
Huntspill 28 A3
Huntworth 28 B3
Hunwick 167 B4
Hunworth 120 B2
Hurdsfield 129 B4
Hurley Warks 97 B5
Windsor 47 A6
Hurlford 193 B4
Hurliness 283 J3
Hurn 17 B5
Hurn's End 118 A1
Hursley 32 C3
Hurst N Yorks 156 A4
Som 29 D4
Wokingham 47 B5
Hurstbourne
Priors 32 A4
Hurstbourne
Tarrant 46 D1
Hurst Green E Sus . 37 D5
Lancs 145 D6
Hurstpierpoint . . . 21 A5
Hurst Wickham . . . 21 A5
Hurstwood 146 D2
Hurtmore 34 B2
Hurworth Place . . 157 A6
Hury 166 D2
Husabost 258 C2
Husbands
Bosworth 98 C3
Husborne
Crawley 83 D6
Husthwaite 158 D4
Hutchwns 40 D3
Huthwaite 131 D4
Huttoft 135 B5
Hutton Borders . . 198 A3

Hutton continued
Cumb 164 C2
Essex 69 D6
E Yorks 150 B3
Lancs 136 A3
N Som 42 D2
Hutton Buscel . . . 160 C3
Hutton Conyers . 158 D2
Hutton
Cranswick 150 B3
Hutton End 164 B2
Hutton Gate 168 D3
Hutton Henry . . . 168 B2
Hutton-le-Hole . . 159 B6
Hutton Magna . . . 166 D4
Hutton Roof
Cumb 155 D4
Cumb 163 A6
Hutton Rudby . . . 158 A3
Hutton Sessay . . 158 D3
Hutton Village . . . 168 D3
Hutton
Wandesley 148 B4
Huxley 127 C5
Huxter Shetland . . 285 G7
Shetland 285 H5
Huxton 211 D5
Huyton 136 D3
Hycemoor 153 B1
Hyde Glos 63 C4
Gtr Man 138 D2
Hants 31 D5
Hyde Heath 67 C5
Hyde Park 140 C3
Hydestile 34 B2
Hylton Castle . . . 179 D5
Hyndford
Bridge 194 B4
Hynish 222 D2
Hyssington 93 B7
Hythe Hants 18 A3
Kent 38 B3
Hythe End 48 B3
Hythie 269 D5

I

Ibberton 16 A1
Ible 130 D2
Ibsley 17 A5
Ibstock 114 D2
Ibstone 66 D3
Ibthorpe 46 D1
Ibworth 46 D3
Ichrachan 227 C5
Ickburgh 103 B4
Ickenham 48 A3
Ickford 66 C2
Ickham 53 D4
Ickleford 84 D3
Icklesham 23 A6
Ickleton 85 C6
Icklingham 102 D3
Ickwell Green 84 C3
Icomb 64 A3
Idbury 64 B3
Iddesleigh 11 A6
Ide 12 B3
Ideford 12 D3
Ide Hill 36 A2
Iden 37 D7
Iden Green Kent . . . 37 C5
Kent 37 C6
Idle 147 D5
Idlicote 81 C5
Idmiston 31 B5
Idole 57 A4
Idridgehay 113 A6
Idrigill 258 B3
Idstone 45 A6
Idvies 232 D3
Iffley 65 C6
Ifield 35 C5
Ifold 34 C3
Iford 22 B2
Ifton Heath 110 B2
Ightfield 111 B4
Ightham 36 A3
Iken 89 B5
Ilam 129 D6
Ilchester 29 C5

Ilderton 188 A3
Ilford 50 A1
Ilfracombe 25 A6
Ilkeston 114 A2
Ilketshall St
Andrew 105 C4
Ilketshall St
Lawrence 105 C4
Ilketshall St
Margaret 104 C4
Ilkley 147 C5
Illey 96 C2
Illingworth 138 A3
Illogan 3 A4
Illston on the Hill . 99 B4
Ilmer 66 C3
Ilmington 81 C5
Ilminster 28 D3
Ilsington 12 D2
Ilston 57 C5
Ilton N Yorks 157 D5
Som 28 D3
Imachar 202 D3
Imeraval 200 D3
Immingham 142 B3
Impington 85 A6
Ince 127 B4
Ince Blundell 136 C2
Ince in
Makerfield 137 C4
Inchbare 233 B4
Inchberry 266 D4
Inchbraoch 233 C5
Incheril 262 D2
Inchgrundle 232 A2
Inchina 261 A6
Inchinnan 205 B4
Inchkinloch 277 D6
Inchlaggan 239 B5
Inchlumpie 264 C1
Inchmore 251 B5
Inchnacardoch
Hotel 240 A1
Inchnadamph . . . 271 B5
Inch of Arnhall . . 233 A4
Inchree 237 C4
Inchture 220 B2
Inchyra 219 B6
Indian Queens 4 B4
Inerval 200 D3
Ingatestone 69 D6
Ingbirchworth . . . 139 C5
Ingestre 112 C3
Ingham Lincs 133 A4
Norf 121 C5
Suff 103 D4
Ingham Corner . . 121 C5
Ingleborough . . . 118 D1
Ingleby Derbys . . 114 C1
Lincs 132 B3
Ingleby
Arncliffe 158 A3
Ingleby Barwick . 168 D2
Ingleby
Greenhow 159 A4
Inglemire 150 D3
Inglesbatch 43 C6
Inglesham 64 D3
Ingleton Durham . 167 C4
N Yorks. 155 D5
Inglewhite 145 C5
Ingliston 208 C4
Ingoe 178 B2
Ingol 145 D5
Ingoldisthorpe . . 118 B3
Ingoldmells 135 C5
Ingoldsby 116 B3
Ingon 81 B5
Ingram 188 B3
Ingrow 147 D4
Ings 154 B3
Ingst 43 A4
Ingworth 120 C3
Inham's End 101 B4
Inkberrow 80 B3
Inkpen 46 C1
Inkstack 281 A4
Inn 154 A3
Innellan 203 A6
Innerleithen 196 C1
Innerleven 220 D3
Innermessan 170 A2

Innerwick E Loth . 211 C4
Perth 229 D4
Innis Chonain . . . 227 D6
Insch 256 D1
Insh 241 B6
Inshore 276 B4
Inskip 145 D4
Instoneville 140 B3
Instow 25 B5
Intake 140 C3
Inver Aberds 243 C5
Highld. 265 B4
Perth 230 D4
Inverailort 235 B6
Inveraldie 220 A4
Inveralligin 249 A5
Inverallochy 269 C5
Inveran 264 A1
Inveraray 214 B3
Inverarish 248 C2
Inverarity 232 D2
Inverarnan 215 A6
Inverasdale 261 B5
Inverbeg 206 A1
Inverbervie 233 A6
Inverboyndie 268 C1
Inverbroom 262 B3
Invercassley 272 D2
Invercauld
House 243 C4
Inverchaolain . . . 203 A5
Invercharnan . . . 227 B6
Inverchoran 251 A4
Invercreran 227 B5
Inverdruie 242 A2
Inverebrie 257 C4
Invereck 215 D4
Inverernan Ho. . . 243 A6
Invereshie
House 241 B6
Inveresk 209 C6
Inverey 242 D3
Inverfarigaig 251 D7
Invergarry 239 B7
Invergelder 243 C5
Invergeldie 218 B2
Invergordon 264 D3
Invergowrie 220 A3
Inverguseran 247 D6
Inverhadden 229 C5
Inverharroch 255 C4
Inverherive 216 B3
Inverie 247 E6
Inverinan 214 A2
Inverinate 249 D6
Inverkeilor 233 D4
Inverkeithing 208 B4
Inverkeithny 256 B1
Inverkip 204 A2
Inverkirkaig 270 C3
Inverlael 262 B3
Inverlochlarig . . . 216 C4
Inverlochy Argyll . 227 D6
Highld. 237 B5
Inverlussa 213 D4
Inver Mallie 239 D5
Invermark
Lodge 244 D1
Invermoidart 235 C5
Invermoriston . . . 240 A2
Invernaver 278 B3
Inverneill 213 D6
Inverness 252 B2
Invernettie 257 B6
Invernoaden 215 C4
Inveroran Hotel . . 228 D1
Inverpolly
Lodge 270 C3
Inverquharity . . . 232 C2
Inverquhomery . . 257 B5
Inverroy 239 D6
Inversanda 236 D3
Invershiel 238 A3
Invershin 264 A1
Inversnaid Hotel . 215 B6
Inverugie 257 B6
Inveruglas 215 B6
Inveruglass 241 B6
Inverurie 256 D2
Invervar 229 D5
Inverythan 256 B2
Inwardleigh 11 B6
Inworth 70 B2

Inworth 70 B2
Iochdar 286 B3
Iping 34 D1
Ipplepen 8 A2
Ipsden 47 A4
Ipsley 80 A3
Ipstones 129 D5
Ipswich 88 C2
Irby 126 A2
Irby in the
Marsh 135 C4
Irby upon
Humber 142 C3
Irchester 83 A6
Ireby Cumb 163 A5
Lancs 155 D5
Ireland Orkney . . 283 G4
Shetland 285 L5
Ireland's Cross . . 111 A6
Ireleth 153 C3
Ireshopeburn . . . 165 B6
Irlam 137 D6
Irnham 116 C3
Iron Acton 43 A5
Ironbridge 95 A4
Iron Cross 80 B3
Irongray 173 A7
Ironmacannie . . . 173 A4
Ironside 268 D3
Ironville 131 D4
Irstead 121 C5
Irthington 176 C2
Irthlingborough . . 99 D6
Irton 160 C4
Irvine 192 B3
Isauld 279 B5
Isbister Orkney . . 282 E3
Orkney 282 F4
Shetland 284 D5
Shetland 285 G2
Isfield 22 A2
Isham 99 D5
Isle Abbotts 28 C3
Isle Brewers 28 C3
Isleham 102 D2
Isle of Whithorn . 171 D6
Isleornsay 247 C6
Islesburgh 284 G5
Islesteps 174 A2
Isleworth 49 B4
Isley Walton 114 C2
Islibhig 287 B4
Islington 49 A6
Islip Northants . . 100 D1
Oxon. 65 B6
Istead Rise 50 C3
Isycoed 127 D4
Itchen 32 D3
Itchen Abbas . . . 32 B4
Itchen Stoke 33 B4
Itchingfield 35 D4
Itchington 43 A5
Itteringham 120 B3
Itton 12 B1
Itton Common . . . 61 D6
Ivegill 164 A2
Iver 48 A3
Iver Heath 48 A3
Iveston 178 D3
Ivinghoe 67 B5
Ivinghoe Aston . . 67 B5
Ivington 78 B2
Ivington Green . . 78 B2
Ivybridge 7 B5
Ivy Chimneys . . . 68 C4
Ivychurch 38 C2
Ivy Cross 30 C2
Ivy Hatch 36 A3
Iwade 51 C6
Iwerne Courtney or
Shroton 30 D2
Iwerne Minster . . 30 D2
Ixworth 103 D5
Ixworth Thorpe . . 103 D5

J

Jack Hill 147 B6
Jack in the Green 13 B5
Jacksdale 131 D4
Jackstown 256 C2

Jacobstow 10 B2
Jacobstowe 11 A6
Jameston 55 E6
Jamestown
Dumfries 185 C6
Highld. 251 A6
W Dunb 206 B1
Jarrow 179 C5
Jarvis Brook 36 D3
Jasper's Green . . 69 A7
Java 225 C6
Jawcraig 207 C6
Jaywick 71 B5
Jealott's Hill 47 B6
Jedburgh 187 A5
Jeffreyston 55 D6
Jellyhill 205 A6
Jemimaville 264 D3
Jersey Farm 67 C7
Jesmond 179 C4
Jevington 22 B3
Jockey End 67 B6
Johnby 164 B2
John o' Groats . . 281 A5
John's Cross 37 D5
Johnshaven 233 B6
Johnston 55 C5
Johnstone 205 B4
Johnstonebridge
. . . . 184 C3
Johnstown Carms . 57 A4
Wrex 110 A2
Joppa Edin 209 C6
S Ayrs. 182 A2
Jordans 67 D5
Jordanthorpe . . . 130 A3
Jump 140 C1
Jumpers Green . . 17 B5
Juniper Green . . . 209 D4
Jurby East 152 B3
Jurby West 152 B3

K

Kaber 165 D5
Kaimend 195 B4
Kaimes 209 D5
Kalemouth 187 A6
Kames Argyll 203 A4
Argyll 213 A6
E Ayrs. 194 D1
Kea 4 C3
Keadby 141 B6
Keal Cotes 134 C3
Kearsley 137 C6
Kearstwick 155 C5
Kearton 156 B3
Kearvaig 276 A3
Keasden 145 A7
Keckwick 127 A5
Keddington 134 A3
Kedington 86 C3
Kedleston 113 A7
Keelby 142 B3
Keele 112 A4
Keeley Green . . . 84 C2
Keeston 55 C5
Keevil 44 D3
Kegworth 114 C2
Kehelland 3 A4
Keig 244 A3
Keighley 147 C4
Keil 236 D3
Keilarsbrae 208 A1
Keilhill 268 D2
Keillmore 213 D4
Keillor 231 D6
Keillour 219 B4
Keills 201 B4
Keils 201 B5
Keinton
Mandeville 29 B5
Keir Mill 183 C6
Keisby 116 C3
Keiss 281 B5
Keith 267 D5
Keith Inch 257 B6
Keithock 233 B4

Kelbrook 146 C3
Kelby 116 A3
Keld Cumb......164 D3
  N Yorks........156 A2
Keldholme 159 C6
Kelfield N Lincs 141 C6
  N Yorks........149 D4
Kelham.........132 D2
Kellan 225 B4
Kellas Angus....221 A4
  Moray..........266 D2
Kellaton 8 D2
Kelleth 155 A5
Kelleythorpe ..150 B2
Kelling 120 A2
Kellingley......140 A3
Kellington 140 A3
Kelloe 167 B6
Kelloholm 183 A5
Kelly 11 C4
Kelly Bray.......11 C4
Kelmarsh 99 D4
Kelmscot 64 D3
Kelsale 89 A4
Kelsall 127 C5
Kelshall........85 D5
Kelsick 175 C4
Kelso 197 C6
Kelstedge 130 C3
Kelstern 143 D4
Kelston 43 C6
Keltneyburn....229 D6
Kelton 174 A2
Kelty 208 A4
Kelvedon 70 B2
Kelvedon Hatch .69 D5
Kelvin 205 C6
Kelvinside 205 B5
Kelynack 2 B1
Kemback 220 C4
Kemberton 95 A5
Kemble 63 D5
Kemerton 80 D2
Kemeys
  Commander 61 C5
Kemnay 245 A4
Kempley 62 A2
Kempsey 79 C6
Kempsford 64 D2
Kemps Green ...96 D4
Kempshott 47 D4
Kempston 84 C2
Kempston
  Hardwick.....84 C2
Kempton 94 C1
Kemp Town 21 B6
Kemsing 36 A3
Kemsley 51 C6
Kenardington ..38 B1
Kenchester 78 C2
Kencot 64 C3
Kendal 154 B4
Kendoon 182 D4
Kendray 139 C6
Kenfig 40 C3
Kenfig Hill 40 C3
Kenilworth 97 D5
Kenknock 217 A4
Kenley London ..35 A6
  Shrops........94 A3
Kenmore Highld. 249 A4
  Perth 230 D1
Kenn Devon......13 C4
  N Som 42 C3
Kennacley 288 H2
Kennacraig 202 B3
Kennerleigh ...12 A3
Kennet 208 A2
Kennethmont ..255 D6
Kennett 86 A2
Kennford 13 C4
Kenninghall...103 C6
Kenninghall
  Heath 103 C6
Kennington Kent.38 A2
  Oxon..........65 C6
Kennoway 220 D3
Kenny Hill 102 D2

Kennythorpe ...149 A6
Kenovay 222 C2
Kensaleyre 259 C4
Kensington 49 B5
Kensworth 67 B6
Kensworth
  Common 67 B6
Kentallen 237 D4
Kentchurch 61 A6
Kentford 86 A3
Kentisbeare 13 A5
Kentisbury 25 A7
Kentisbury Ford .25 A7
Kentmere 154 A3
Kenton Devon...13 C4
  Suff..........88 A2
  T&W.........179 C4
Kenton
  Bankfoot 179 C4
Kentra 235 D5
Kents Bank 154 D2
Kent's Green ...62 A3
Kent's Oak 32 C2
Kent Street E Sus. 23 A5
  Kent 37 A4
  W Sus.........35 D5
Kenwick 110 B3
Kenwyn 4 C3
Keoldale 277 B4
Keppanach 237 C4
Keppoch 249 D6
Keresley 97 C6
Kernborough 8 C1
Kerne Bridge ...62 B1
Kerris 2 C2
Kerry 93 C5
Kerrycroy 203 B6
Kerrysdale 261 C5
Kerry's Gate ...78 D1
Kersall 132 C2
Kersey 87 C6
Kershopefoot ..176 A2
Kersoe 80 D2
Kerswell 13 A5
Kerswell Grn....79 C6
Kesgrave 88 C3
Kessingland ...105 C6
Kessingland
  Beach 105 C6
Kessington 205 A5
Kestle 5 C4
Kestle Mill 4 B3
Keston 49 C7
Keswick Cumb..163 B5
  Norf.........104 A3
  Norf.........121 B5
Ketley 111 D5
Ketley Bank ...111 D5
Ketsby 134 B3
Kettering 99 D5
Ketteringham ..104 A2
Kettlebaston ...87 B5
Kettlebridge ..220 D3
Kettleburgh ...88 A3
Kettlehill 220 D3
Kettleholm 174 A4
Kettleness 169 D6
Kettleshume ..129 B4
Kettlesing
  Bottom 147 B6
Kettlesing Head 147 B6
Kettlestone ...119 B6
Kettlethorpe ..132 B3
Kettletoft 282 D7
Kettlewell 156 D3
Ketton 100 A1
Kew 49 B4
Kew Br........49 B4
Kewstoke 42 C2
Kexbrough 139 C6
Kexby Lincs...132 A3
  York 149 B6
Key Green 128 C3
Keyham 98 A3
Keyhaven 18 B2
Keyingham 143 A4
Keymer 21 A6
Keynsham 43 C5

Keysoe 84 A2
Keysoe Row 84 A2
Keyston 100 D2
Keyworth 115 B4
Kibblesworth ..179 D4
Kibworth
  Beauchamp ...98 B3
Kibworth
  Harcourt 98 B3
Kidbrooke 49 B7
Kiddemore
  Green 95 A6
Kidderminster ..95 D6
Kiddington 65 A5
Kidlington 65 B5
Kidmore End ...47 B4
Kidsgrove 128 D3
Kidstones 156 C3
Kidwelly
  (Cydweli)......57 B4
Kiel Crofts ...226 C4
Kielder 187 D5
Kierfield Ho....282 F3
Kilbagie 208 B2
Kilbarchan ...205 B4
Kilberry 202 B2
Kilbirnie 204 C3
Kilbride Argyll..226 D3
  Argyll........226 D4
  Highld.......247 D5
Kilburn Angus..232 B1
  Derbys........114 A1
  London........49 A5
  N Yorks......158 D4
Kilby 98 B3
Kilchamaig ...202 B3
Kilchattan ...212 C1
Kilchattan Bay .203 C6
Kilchenzie 190 C2
Kilcheran 226 C3
Kilchiaran ...200 B2
Kilchoan Argyll..213 A5
  Highld.......234 D3
Kilchoman 200 B2
Kilchrenan ...227 D5
Kilconquhar ..221 D4
Kilcot 62 A2
Kilcoy 252 A1
Kilcreggan ...215 D5
Kildale 159 A5
Kildalloig 190 D3
Kildary 264 C3
Kildermorie
  Lodge 263 C7
Kildonan 191 C6
Kildonan Lodge 274 B3
Kildonnan 234 B3
Kildrummy 244 A1
Kildwick 147 C4
Kilfinan 203 A4
Kilfinnan 239 C6
Kilgetty 56 B1
Kilgwrrwg
  Common 61 D6
Kilham E Yorks..150 A3
  Northumb.....198 C2
Kilkenneth ...222 C2
Kilkerran 190 D3
Kilkhampton ...24 D3
Killamarsh ...131 A4
Killay 57 C6
Killbeg 225 B5
Killean 202 D1
Killearn 206 B3
Killen 252 A2
Killerby 167 D4
Killichonate .239 D6
Killiechronan 225 B4
Killiecrankie 230 B3
Killiemor 224 C3
Killimster 281 C5
Killin 217 A5
Killinallan ...200 A3
Killinghall ...148 B1
Killington ...155 C5
Killingworth ..179 B4
Killin Lodge ..240 B3

Killmahumaig ..213 C5
Killochyett ...196 B3
Killocraw 190 B2
Killundine 225 B4
Kilmacolm 204 B3
Kilmaha 214 B2
Kilmahog 217 D6
Kilmalieu 236 D2
Kilmaluag 259 A4
Kilmany 220 B3
Kilmarie 247 C4
Kilmarnock ...193 B4
Kilmaron Castle 220 C3
Kilmartin 213 C6
Kilmaurs 205 D4
Kilmelford ...213 A6
Kilmeny 200 B3
Kilmersdon 43 D5
Kilmeston 33 C4
Kilmichael
  Glassary 214 C1
Kilmichael of
  Inverlussa ..213 D5
Kilmington Devon.14 B2
  Wilts..........30 B1
Kilmonivaig ..239 D5
Kilmorack 251 B6
Kilmore Argyll..226 D3
  Highld.......247 D5
Kilmory Argyll..235 C4
  Highld.......246 D2
  N Ayrs.......191 C5
Kilmuir Highld..252 B2
  Highld.......258 A3
  Highld.......258 D2
  Highld.......264 C3
Kilmun Argyll..214 A2
  Argyll........215 D4
Kilncadzow ...194 B3
Kilndown 37 C5
Kilnhurst 140 D2
Kilninian 224 B2
Kilninver 226 D3
Kiln Pit Hill ..178 D2
Kilnsea 143 B6
Kilnsey 146 A3
Kilnwick 150 C2
Kilnwick Percy 149 B7
Kiloran 212 C1
Kilpatrick ...191 C5
Kilpeck 78 D2
Kilphedir 274 C3
Kilpin 141 A5
Kilpin Pike ..141 A5
Kilrenny 221 D5
Kilsby 98 D2
Kilspindie ...220 B2
Kilsyth 207 C5
Kiltarlity ...251 B7
Kilton Notts..131 B5
  Som 27 A6
Kilton Thorpe 169 D4
Kilvaxter 258 B3
Kilve 27 A6
Kilvington ...115 A5
Kilwinning ...204 D3
Kimberley Norf.103 A6
  Notts........114 A3
Kimber worth .140 D2
Kimberworth ..167 A5
Kimble Wick ...66 C4
Kimbolton Cambs.84 A2
  Hereford.......78 A3
Kimcote 98 C2
Kimmeridge 16 D3
Kimmerston ...198 C3
Kimpton Hants..32 A1
  Herts..........68 B1
Kinbrace 274 A2
Kinbuck 218 D2
Kincaple 221 C4
Kincardine Fife 208 B2
  Highld.......264 B2
Kincardine
  Bridge 208 B2
Kincardine
  O'Neil 244 C2
Kinclaven 219 A6
Kincorth 245 B6
Kincorth Ho...265 D6

Kincraig 241 B6
Kincraigie ...230 D3
Kindallachan 230 D3
Kineton Glos...64 A1
  Warks.........81 B6
Kinfauns 219 B6
Kingairloch ..236 D2
Kingarth 203 C5
Kingcoed 61 C6
King Edward ..268 D2
Kingerby 142 D2
Kingham 64 A3
Kingholm Quay 174 A2
Kinghorn 209 B5
Kingie 239 B5
Kinglassie ...209 A5
Kingoodie 220 B3
King's Acre ...78 C2
Kingsand 6 B3
Kingsbarns ...221 C5
Kingsbridge Devon.7 C6
  Som 27 B4
King's Bromley 113 D5
Kingsburgh ...258 C3
Kingsbury London.49 A5
  Warks.........97 B5
Kingsbury
  Episcopi.....28 C4
King's Caple ..62 A1
Kingsclere 46 D3
King's Cliffe ..100 B2
Kingscote 63 D4
Kingscott 25 D6
King's Coughton 80 B3
Kingscross ...191 C6
Kingsdon 29 C5
Kingsdown 39 A5
Kingseat 208 A4
Kingsey 66 C3
Kingsfold 35 C4
Kingsford E Ayrs.205 D4
  Worcs.........95 C6
Kingsforth ...142 B2
Kingsgate 53 B5
Kingsheanton ..25 B6
King's Heath ..96 C3
Kings Hedges ..85 A6
King's Hill 37 A4
Kingshouse
  Hotel 237 D6
Kingside Hill .175 C4
Kingskerswell ..8 A2
Kingskettle ..220 D3
Kingsland
  Anglesey 122 B2
  Hereford......78 A2
Kings Langley ..67 C6
Kingsley Ches W.127 B5
  Hants.........33 B6
  Staffs.......112 A4
Kingsley Green .34 C1
Kingsley Holt 112 A4
Kingsley Park ..83 A4
King's Lynn ..118 C3
King's Meaburn 165 C4
King's Mills ..110 A2
Kingsmuir Angus 232 D2
  Fife..........221 D5
Kings Muir ...196 C1
King's Newnham .98 D1
King's Newton 114 C1
Kingsnorth 38 B2
King's Norton
  Leics..........98 A3
  W Mid 96 D3
King's Nympton .26 D1
King's Pyon ...78 B2
King's Ripton .101 D4
King's Somborne 32 B2
King's Stag 30 D1
King's Stanley .63 C4
King's Sutton .82 D1
Kingstanding ..96 B3
Kingsteignton .12 D3
King Sterndale 129 B5
King's Thorn ..78 D3
Kingsthorpe ...83 A4
Kingston Cambs..85 B5

Kingston continued
  Hants.........17 A5
  IoW 18 C3
  Kent 52 D3
  Moray.......266 C4
Kingston
  Bagpuize 65 D5
Kingston Blount 66 D3
Kingston by Sea .21 B5
Kingston Deverill 30 B2
Kingstone
  Hereford......78 D2
  Som 28 D3
  Staffs.......113 C4
Kingston Gorse .20 B3
Kingston Lisle ..45 A7
Kingston
  Maurward 15 B7
Kingston near
  Lewes 22 B1
Kingston on
  Soar 114 C3
Kingston Russell 15 B5
Kingston St Mary 28 C2
Kingston
  Seymour 42 C3
Kingston Upon
  Hull 142 A2
Kingston upon
  Thames 49 C4
Kingston Vale ..49 B5
Kingstown ...175 C6
King's Walden ..67 A7
Kingswear 8 B2
Kingswells ...245 B5
Kingswinford ..96 C1
Kingswood Bucks.66 B2
  Glos..........62 D3
  Hereford......77 B6
  Kent 37 A6
  Powys.........93 A6
  S Glos.........43 B5
  Sur...........35 A5
  Warks.........97 D4
Kings Worthy ..32 B3
Kingthorpe ...133 B6
Kington Hereford..77 B6
  Worcs.........80 B2
Kington Langley .44 B3
Kington Magna .30 C1
Kington St
  Michael 44 B3
Kingussie 241 B5
Kingweston 29 B5
Kininvie Ho...254 B4
Kinkell Bridge 218 C4
Kinknockie ...257 B5
Kinlet 95 C5
Kinloch Fife...220 C2
  Highld.......234 A2
  Highld.......247 C5
  Highld.......271 A6
  Perth 231 D5
  Perth 231 D6
Kinlochan 236 C2
Kinlochard ...217 D4
Kinlochbeoraid 238 D2
Kinlochbervie 276 C3
Kinlocheil ...236 B3
Kinlochewe ...262 D2
Kinloch Hourn 238 B3
Kinloch Laggan 240 D3
Kinlochleven 237 C5
Kinloch Lodge 277 C6
Kinlochmoidart 235 C6
Kinlochmore ..237 C5
Kinloch
  Rannoch 229 C5
Kinlochspelve 225 D5
Kinloid 235 B5
Kinloss 265 D6
Kinmel Bay ..125 A4
Kinmuck 256 E3
Kinmundy 245 A5
Kinnadie 257 B4
Kinnaird 220 B2
Kinnaird Castle 233 C4
Kinneff 233 A6
Kinnelhead ..184 B3
Kinnell 233 C4
Kinnerley 110 C2

Kinnersley
Hereford 78 C1
Worcs. 79 C6
Kinnerton. 77 A6
Kinnesswood . . . 219 D6
Kinninvie 166 C3
Kinnordy. 232 C1
Kinoulton 115 B4
Kinross 219 D6
Kinrossie 219 A6
Kinsbourne
Green 67 B7
Kinsey Heath. . . . 111 A5
Kinsham Hereford . 78 A1
Worcs. 80 D2
Kinsley 140 B2
Kinson 17 B4
Kintbury 46 C1
Kintessack 265 D5
Kintillo 219 C6
Kintocher 244 B2
Kinton Hereford . . . 94 D2
Shrops 110 D2
Kintore 245 A4
Kintour 201 C4
Kintra Argyll . . . 200 D3
Argyll 224 D2
Kintraw 213 B6
Kinuachdrachd .213 C5
Kinveachy 242 A2
Kinver 95 C6
Kippax 148 D3
Kippen 207 A4
Kippford or
Scaur 173 C6
Kirbister Orkney.282 E7
Orkney 283 G4
Kirbuster 282 E3
Kirby Bedon . . . 104 A3
Kirby Bellars . . . 115 D5
Kirby Cane 105 B4
Kirby Cross 71 A6
Kirby
Grindalythe. . . 150 A2
Kirby Hill N Yorks 148 A2
N Yorks. 157 A5
Kirby Knowle. . . 158 C3
Kirby-le-Soken . 71 A6
Kirby Misperton 159 D6
Kirby Muxloe . . . 98 A2
Kirby Row 105 B4
Kirby Sigston . . . 158 B3
Kirby Underdale 149 B7
Kirby Wiske . . . 158 C2
Kirdford 34 D3
Kirk 281 C4
Kirkabister 285 K6
Kirkandrews 172 D4
Kirkandrews upon
Eden 175 C6
Kirkbampton . . . 175 C6
Kirkbean 174 C2
Kirk Bramwith . 140 B4
Kirkbride 175 C5
Kirkbuddo 232 D3
Kirkburn Borders 196 C1
E Yorks 150 B2
Kirkburton 139 B4
Kirkby Lincs . . . 142 D2
Mers. 136 D3
N Yorks. 158 A4
Kirkby Fleetham 157 B6
Kirkby Green. . . . 133 D5
Kirkby In
Ashfield 131 D5
Kirkby-in-
Furness 153 B3
Kirkby la
Thorpe 116 A4
Kirkby Lonsdale 155 D5
Kirkby Malham .146 A2
Kirkby Mallory . . . 98 A1
Kirkby
Malzeard 157 D6
Kirkby Mills . . . 159 C6
Kirkbymoorside.159 C5
Kirkby on Bain . . 134 C2
Kirkby Overflow 148 C2
Kirkby Stephen. 155 A6
Kirkby Thore . . . 165 C4
Kirkby
Underwood. . . 116 C3

Kirkby Wharfe. . 148 C4
Kirkcaldy 209 A5
Kirkcambeck. . . . 176 C3
Kirkcarswell . . . 173 D5
Kirkcolm. 170 A2
Kirkconnel 183 A5
Kirkconnell . . . 174 B2
Kirkcowan 171 A5
Kirkcudbright . . . 173 C4
Kirkdale 136 D2
Kirk Deighton . . . 148 B2
Kirk Ella 142 A2
Kirkfieldbank . . . 194 B3
Kirkgunzeon . . . 173 B6
Kirk Hallam . . . 114 A2
Kirkham Lancs . . 144 D4
N Yorks. 149 A6
Kirkhamgate . . . 139 A5
Kirk
Hammerton . . . 148 B3
Kirkharle 178 A2
Kirkheaton
Northumb. . . . 178 B2
W Yorks 139 B4
Kirkhill Angus. . . 233 B4
Highld. 252 B1
Midloth. 209 D5
Moray. 254 C3
Kirkhope 186 A2
Kirkhouse 196 C2
Kirkiboll 277 C6
Kirkibost 247 C4
Kirkinch 231 D7
Kirkinner 171 B6
Kirkintilloch . . . 205 A6
Kirk Ireton . . . 130 D2
Kirkland Cumb . . . 162 C3
Cumb 165 B4
Dumfries 183 A5
Dumfries 183 C6
Kirk Langley . . . 113 B6
Kirkleatham . . . 168 C3
Kirklevington . . . 158 A3
Kirkley 105 B6
Kirklington
Notts 132 D1
N Yorks 157 C7
Kirklinton . . . 176 C2
Kirkliston 208 C4
Kirkmaiden . . . 170 D3
Kirk Merrington 167 B5
Kirkmichael
Perth 231 C4
S Ayrs. 192 E3
Kirk Michael . . . 152 B3
Kirkmuirhill . . . 194 B2
Kirknewton
Northumb. . . . 198 C3
W Loth 208 D4
Kirkney 255 C6
Kirk of Shotts . . . 207 D6
Kirkoswald
Cumb 164 A3
S Ayrs. 192 E2
Kirkpatrick
Durham 173 A5
Kirkpatrick-
Fleming . . . 175 A5
Kirk Sandall . . . 140 C4
Kirksanton . . . 153 B2
Kirk Smeaton . . . 140 B3
Kirkstall 147 D6
Kirkstead 134 C1
Kirkstile 255 C6
Kirkstyle 281 A5
Kirkton Aberds .256 D1
Aberds 268 E1
Angus 220 A4
Angus 232 D2
Borders 186 B4
Dumfries 184 D2
Fife. 220 B3
Highld. 249 B6
Highld. 249 D5
Highld. 252 A3
Highld. 265 A4
Perth 219 C4
S Lanark. 194 D4
Stirling 217 D5
Kirktonhill . . . 196 A3
Kirkton Manor .195 C7
Kirkton of Airlie 231 C7

Kirkton of
Auchterhouse .220 A3
Kirkton of
Auchterless . . . 256 B2
Kirkton of
Barevan 253 B4
Kirkton of
Bourtie. 256 D3
Kirkton of
Collace. 219 A6
Kirkton of Craig 233 C5
Kirkton of
Culsalmond . . . 256 C1
Kirkton of
Durris 245 C4
Kirkton of
Glenbuchat . . . 243 A6
Kirkton of
Glenisla 231 B6
Kirkton of
Kingoldrum . . . 232 C1
Kirkton of
Largo 220 D4
Kirkton of
Lethendy 231 D5
Kirkton of Logie
Buchan. 257 D4
Kirkton of
Maryculter . . . 245 C6
Kirkton of
Menmuir . . . 232 B3
Kirkton of
Monikie 221 A5
Kirkton of Oyne .256 D1
Kirkton of
Rayne 256 D1
Kirkton of
Skene 245 B5
Kirkton of
Tough. 244 A3
Kirktown 269 D5
Kirktown of
Alvah 268 C1
Kirktown of
Deskford 267 C6
Kirktown of
Fetteresso . . . 245 D5
Kirktown of
Kentenber . . . 192 B3
Kirktown of
Mortlach . . . 254 C4
Kirktown of
Slains 257 D5
Kirkurd 195 B6
Kirkwall 282 F5
Kirkwhelpington
. . . . 178 A1
Kirk Yetholm. . . 188 A1
Kirmington . . . 142 B3
Kirmond le
Mire 142 D3
Kirn 203 A6
Kirriemuir . . . 232 C1
Kirstead Green .104 B3
Kirtlebridge . . . 175 A5
Kirtleton 185 D5
Kirtling 86 B2
Kirtling Green. . 86 B2
Kirtlington . . . 65 B5
Kirtomy 278 B3
Kirton Lincs. . . . 117 B6
Notts 132 C1
Suff 88 D3
Kirton End . . . 117 A5
Kirton Holme . . . 117 A5
Kirton in
Lindsey 142 D1
Kislingbury . . . 82 B3
Kites Hardwick. . 82 A1
Kittisford . . . 27 C5
Kittle 57 D5
Kitt's Green . . . 97 C4
Kitt's Moss. . . 128 A3
Kittybrewster . . . 245 B6
Kivernoll. 78 D2
Kiveton Park . . . 131 A4
Knaith. 132 A3
Knaith Park . . . 132 A3
Knap Corner . . . 30 C2
Knapp Perth . . . 220 A2
Som 28 C3
Knapthorpe . . . 132 D2

Knapton Norf 121 B5
York 149 B4
Knapton Green. . . 78 B2
Knapwell 85 A5
Knaresborough .148 B2
Knarsdale. 177 D4
Knauchland . . . 267 D6
Knaven 256 B3
Knayton 158 C3
Knebworth 68 A2
Knedlington . . . 141 A5
Kneesall 132 C2
Kneesworth. . . 85 C5
Kneeton 115 A5
Knelston 57 D4
Knenhall. 112 B3
Knettishall . . . 103 C5
Knightacott . . . 26 B1
Knightcote. 81 B6
Knightley Dale .112 C2
Knighton Devon . . 7 C4
Leicester 98 A2
Staffs 111 A6
Staffs 111 C6
Knighton (Tref-y-
Clawdd). 93 D6
Knightswood . . . 205 B5
Knightwick . . . 79 B5
Knill. 77 A6
Knipton. 115 B6
Knitsley. 166 A4
Kniveton 130 D2
Knock Argyll . . . 225 C4
Cumb 165 C4
Moray. 267 D6
Knockally 275 B5
Knockan 271 C5
Knockandhu . . . 254 D3
Knockando . . . 254 B2
Knockando Ho. . . 254 B3
Knockbain . . . 252 A2
Knockbreck. . . 258 B2
Knockbrex . . . 172 D3
Knockdee 280 B3
Knockdolian . . . 180 C3
Knockenkelly . . . 191 C6
Knockentiber . . . 192 B3
Knockespock
Ho. 255 D6
Knockfarrel . . . 251 A7
Knockglass . . . 170 B2
Knockholt 36 A2
Knockholt Pound 36 A2
Knockie Lodge ..240 A2
Knockin 110 C2
Knockinlaw . . . 193 B4
Knocklearn . . . 173 A5
Knocknaha. . . 190 D2
Knocknain . . . 170 A1
Knockrome . . . 201 A5
Knocksharry . . . 152 C2
Knodishall . . . 89 A5
Knolls Green . . . 128 B3
Knolton 110 B2
Knolton Bryn . . . 110 B2
Knook 30 A3
Knossington . . . 99 A5
Knott End-on-
Sea 144 C3
Knotting 84 A2
Knotting Green. 84 A2
Knottingley . . . 140 A3
Knotts Cumb . . . 164 C2
Lancs 146 B1
Knotty Ash . . . 136 D3
Knotty Green. . 67 D5
Knowbury. 94 D3
Knowe. 181 D5
Knowehead . . . 182 C4
Knowesgate . . . 178 A1
Knowes of
Elrick 267 D7
Knoweton . . . 194 A2
Knowhead . . . 269 D4
Knowle Bristol . 43 B5
Devon. 12 A2
Devon. 13 C5
Devon. 25 B5
Shrops 94 D3
W Mid 97 D4
Knowle Green ...145 D6
Knowle Park . . . 147 C4

Knowl Hill 47 B6
Knowlton Dorset . 31 D4
Kent 53 D4
Knowsley 136 D3
Knowstone . . . 26 C3
Knox Bridge. . . 37 B5
Knucklas 93 D6
Knuston 83 A6
Knutsford. . . 128 B2
Knutton 112 A2
Knypersley. . . 128 D3
Kuggar 3 D5
Kyleakin 247 B6
Kyle of
Lochalsh . . . 249 D4
Kylerhea. 247 B6
Kylesknoydart...238 C2
Kylesku 271 A5
Kylesmorar . . . 238 C2
Kylestrome . . . 271 A5
Kyllachy House .252 D3
Kynaston 110 C2
Kynnersley . . . 111 D5
Kyre Magna. . . 79 A4

L

Labost. 288 C3
Lacasaidh. 288 E4
Lacasdal. 288 D5
Laceby 143 C4
Lacey Green . . . 66 D4
Lach Dennis. . . 128 B2
Lackford. 102 D3
Lacock 44 C3
Ladbroke 81 B7
Laddingford. . . 37 B4
Lade Bank . . . 134 D3
Ladock 4 B3
Lady. 282 C7
Ladybank 220 C3
Ladykirk 198 B2
Ladysford . . . 269 C4
La Fontenelle Guern .. 6
Laga. 235 D5
Lagalochan . . . 214 A1
Lagavulin . . . 201 D4
Lagg Argyll . . . 201 A5
N Ayrs 191 C5
Laggan Argyll . . . 200 C2
Highld. 235 C6
Highld. 239 C6
Highld. 241 C4
S Ayrs. 181 C4
Lagganulva . . . 224 B3
Laide 261 A5
Laigh Fenwick . . 205 D4
Laigh Glengall . 192 D3
Laighmuir . . . 205 D4
Laindon 50 A3
Lair 250 B2
Lairg 272 D3
Lairg Lodge . . . 272 D3
Lairgmore . . . 252 C1
Laisterdyke . . . 147 D5
Laithes 164 B2
Lake IoW 19 C4
Wilts. 31 B5
Lakenham . . . 104 A3
Lakenheath . . . 102 C3
Lakesend . . . 101 B7
Lakeside. 154 C2
Laleham 48 C3
Laleston 40 D3
Lamarsh 87 D4
Lamas 120 C4
Lamb Corner . . . 87 D6
Lamberhurst
Quarter . . . 37 C4
Lamberton . . . 198 A3
Lambeth 49 B6
Lambhill 205 B5
Lambley
Northumb. . . 177 D4
Notts 115 A4
Langford
Budville 27 C6
Langham Essex ..87 D6
Norf 120 A2
Rutland. 115 D6
Suff 103 E5

Lambston 55 C5
Lambton. 179 D4
Lamerton 11 D5
Lamesley 179 D4
Laminess 282 D7
Lamington
Highld. 264 C3
S Lanark. 195 C4
Lamlash 191 B6
Lamloch 182 C3
Lamonby 164 B2
Lamorna 2 C2
Lamorran 4 C3
Lampardbrook . . . 88 A3
Lampeter (Llanbedr
Pont Steffan) . . . 75 D4
Lampeter Velfrey 56 A1
Lamphey. 55 D6
Lamplugh . . . 162 B3
Lamport . . . 99 D4
Lamyatt 29 B6
Lana. 10 B4
Lanark. 194 B3
Lancaster . . . 145 A4
Lanchester. . . 167 A4
Lancing. 21 B4
Landbeach. . . 85 A6
Landcross . . . 25 C5
Landerberry . . . 245 B4
Landford. 31 D6
Landford Manor . 31 C6
Landimore . . . 57 C4
Landkey . . . 25 B6
Landore 57 C6
Landrake 6 A2
Landscove . . . 8 A1
Landshipping . . . 55 C6
Landshipping
Quay. 55 C6
Landulph . . . 6 A3
Landwade . . . 86 A2
Lane. 4 B3
Laneast 10 C3
Lane End Bucks . 66 D4
Cumb 153 A2
Dorset 16 B2
Hants 33 C4
IoW 19 C5
Lancs 146 C2
Lane Ends Lancs .146 B1
Lancs 146 D1
N Yorks 146 C3
Laneham . . . 132 B3
Lanehead
Durham 165 A6
Northumb.. . . . 177 A5
Lane Head
Derbys 129 B6
Durham 166 D4
Gtr Man 137 D5
W Yorks 139 C4
Lanercost . . . 176 C3
Laneshaw
Bridge 146 C3
Lane Side . . . 137 A6
Lanfach. . . 41 B7
Langar. 115 B5
Langbank . . . 204 A3
Langbar . . . 147 B4
Langburnshields.186 C4
Langcliffe. . . 146 A2
Langdale . . . 278 D2
Langdale End . . . 160 B3
Langdon. . . 10 C4
Langdon Beck. . . 165 B6
Langdon Hills . . . 50 A3
Langdyke . . . 220 D3
Langenhoe. . . 71 B4
Langford C Beds . 84 C3
Devon. 13 A5
Essex 70 C2
Notts 132 D3
Oxon. 64 C3

Langhaugh......195 C7
Langho......145 D7
Langholm......185 D6
Langleeford......188 A2
Langley Ches E...129 B4
Hants...........18 A3
Herts..........68 A2
Kent............37 A6
Northumb......177 C6
Slough.........48 B3
Warks..........81 A4
W Sus..........33 C7
Langley Burrell...44 B3
Langley
Common......113 B6
Langley Heath...37 A6
Langley Lower
Green.........85 D6
Langley Marsh...27 C5
Langley Park...167 A5
Langley Street.105 A4
Langley Upper
Green.........85 D6
Langney.........22 B4
Langold.......131 A5
Langore........10 C4
Langport.......28 C4
Langrick......117 A5
Langridge......43 C6
Langridge Ford..25 C6
Langrigg.......175 D4
Langrish........33 C6
Langsett......139 C5
Langshaw......197 C4
Langside......218 C2
Langskaill.....282 C5
Langstone Hants..19 A6
Newport........61 D5
Langthorne....157 B6
Langthorpe....148 A2
Langthwaite....156 A4
Langtoft E Yorks.150 A3
Lincs..........116 D4
Langton Durham .167 D4
Lincs..........134 B3
Lincs..........134 C2
N Yorks........149 A6
Langton by
Wragby......133 B6
Langton Green
Kent...........36 C3
Suff..........104 D2
Langton Herring.15 C6
Langton
Matravers.....17 D4
Langtree.......25 D5
Langwathby....164 B3
Langwell Ho...275 B5
Langwell Lodge.271 D4
Langwith.....131 C5
Langwith
Junction....131 C5
Langworth....133 B5
Lanivet.........5 A5
Lanlivery.......5 B5
Lanner.........4 D2
Lanreath.......5 B6
Lansallos......5 B6
Lansdown......63 A5
Lanteglos Highway.5 B6
Lanton Borders..187 A5
Northumb......198 C3
Lapford........12 A2
Laphroaig....200 D3
La Planque Guern..6
Lapley........112 D2
Lapworth.......97 D4
Larachbeg....225 B5
Larbert.......207 B6
Larden Green...127 D5
Largie........255 C7
Largiemore....214 D2
Largoward....221 D4
Largs.........204 C2
Largybeg.....191 C6
Largymore....191 C6
Larkfield....204 A2
Larkhall.....194 A2
Larkhill.......31 A5

Larling.......103 C5
Larriston.....186 D4
Lartington....166 D3
Lary..........243 B6
Lasham........33 A5
Lashenden.....37 B6
Lassington....62 A3
Lassodie.....208 A4
Lastingham...159 B6
Latcham.......29 A4
Latchford Herts..68 A3
Warr..........127 A6
Latchingdon....70 C2
Latchley......11 D5
Lately Common.137 D5
Lathbury......83 C5
Latheron.....275 A5
Latheronwheel..275 A5
Latheronwheel
Ho..........275 A5
Lathones.....221 D4
Latimer........67 D6
Latteridge.....43 A5
Lattiford......29 C6
Latton........64 D1
Latton Bush....69 C4
Lauchintilly..245 A4
Lauder........197 B4
Laugharne......56 A3
Laughterton...132 B3
Laughton E Sus..22 A3
Leics..........98 C3
Lincs.........116 B3
Lincs.........141 D6
Laughton
Common....131 A5
Laughton en le
Morthen....131 A5
Launcells......10 A3
Launceston....10 C4
Launton.......65 A7
Laurencekirk..233 A5
Laurieston
Dumfries.....173 B4
Falk.........208 C2
Lavendon......83 B6
Lavenham......87 C5
Laverhay.....185 C4
Laversdale....176 C2
Laverstock.....31 B5
Laverstoke....32 A3
Laverton Glos...80 D3
N Yorks.......157 D6
Som...........44 D1
Lavister......126 D3
Law..........194 A3
Lawers Perth..217 A6
Perth........218 B2
Lawford.......88 D1
Lawhitton.....11 C4
Lawkland.....146 A1
Lawley.........95 A4
Lawnhead.....112 C2
Lawrenny......55 D6
Lawshall.......87 B4
Lawton.........78 B2
Laxey.........152 C4
Laxfield.....104 D3
Laxfirth Shetland.285 H6
Shetland.....285 J6
Laxford Bridge.276 D3
Laxobigging..284 F6
Laxton E Yorks..141 A5
Northants......99 B6
Notts.........132 C2
Laycock......147 C4
Layer Breton...70 B3
Layer de la Haye..70 B3
Layer Marney...70 B3
Layham........87 C6
Laylands Green..46 C1
Laytham......149 D6
Layton........144 D3
Lazenby.......168 C3
Lazonby......164 B3
Lea Derbys....130 D3
Hereford......62 A2
Lincs.........132 A3
Shrops........94 A1
Shrops........94 C1
Wilts..........44 A3

Leabrooks....131 D4
Leac a Li.....288 H2
Leachkin.....252 B2
Leadburn.....196 A1
Leadenham....133 D4
Leaden Roding..69 B5
Leadgate Cumb.165 A5
Durham.......178 D3
T&W.........178 D3
Leadhills....183 A6
Leafield......64 B4
Leagrave......67 A6
Leake.........158 B3
Leake
Commonside..134 D3
Lealholm.....159 A6
Lealt Argyll..213 C4
Highld.......259 B5
Lea Marston...97 B5
Leamington
Hastings.....82 A1
Leamonsley....96 A4
Leamside.....167 A6
Leanaig......252 A1
Leargybreck..201 A5
Leasgill.....154 C3
Leasingham...116 A3
Leasingthorpe.167 C5
Leasowe......136 D1
Leatherhead...35 A4
Leatherhead
Common.....35 A4
Leathley.....147 C6
Leaton.......110 D3
Lea Town.....145 D4
Leaveland.....52 D2
Leavening....149 A6
Leaves Green...49 C7
Leazes.......178 D3
Lebberston...161 C4
Lechlade-on-
Thames......64 D3
Leck.........155 D5
Leckford......32 B2
Leckfurin....278 C3
Leckgruinart..200 B2
Leckhampstead
Bucks........83 D4
W Berks.......46 B2
Leckhampstead
Thicket......46 B2
Leckhampton...63 B5
Leckie.......262 D2
Leckmelm....262 A3
Leckwith......41 D6
Leconfield...150 C3
Ledaig.......226 C4
Ledburn.......67 A5
Ledbury.......79 D5
Ledcharrie...217 B5
Ledgemoor....78 B2
Ledicot.......78 A2
Ledmore......271 C5
Lednagullin..278 B3
Ledsham Ches W.126 B3
W Yorks......140 A2
Ledston......140 A2
Ledston Luck.148 D3
Ledwell.......65 A5
Lee Argyll....224 D3
Devon.........25 A5
Hants.........32 D2
Lancs........145 B5
Shrops.......110 B3
Leeans.......285 J5
Leebotten....285 L6
Leebotwood....94 B2
Lee Brockhurst.111 C4
Leece.........153 D3
Leechpool.....55 C5
Lee Clump.....67 C5
Leeds Kent....37 A6
W Yorks......148 D1
Leedstown.....3 B4
Leek.........129 D4
Leekbrook....129 D4
Leek Wootton...81 A5
Lee Mill.......7 B5
Leeming......157 C6
Leeming Bar..157 B6
Lee Moor.......7 A4

Lee-on-the-
Solent.......19 A4
Lees Derbys..113 B6
Gtr Man......138 C2
W Yorks......147 D4
Leeswood....126 C2
Legbourne....134 A3
Legerwood...197 B4
Legsby.......133 A6
Leicester......98 A2
Leicester Forest
East..........98 A2
Leigh Dorset...15 A6
Glos..........63 A4
Gtr Man......138 C2
Kent..........36 B3
Shrops........94 A1
Sur...........35 B5
Wilts.........63 D6
Worcs.........79 B5
Leigh Beck....51 A5
Leigh Common..30 C1
Leigh Delamere..44 B2
Leigh Green....37 C7
Leigh on Sea...51 A5
Leigh Park....19 A6
Leigh Sinton...79 B5
Leighswood....96 A3
Leighterton....63 D4
Leighton N Yorks.157 D5
Powys.........93 A6
Shrops........95 A4
Som...........29 A7
Leighton
Bromswold...100 D3
Leighton Buzzard.67 A5
Leigh upon
Mendip......29 A6
Leigh Woods...43 B4
Leinthall Earls..78 A2
Leinthall Starkes.78 A2
Leintwardine...94 D2
Leire..........98 B2
Leirinmore...277 B5
Leiston.......89 A5
Leitfie.......231 D6
Leith.........209 C5
Leitholm.....198 B1
Lelant.........2 B3
Lelley.......151 D5
Lem Hill......95 D5
Lemmington
Hall.........189 B4
Lempitlaw....198 C1
Lenchwick.....80 C3
Lendalfoot...180 C3
Lendrick Lodge.217 D5
Lenham........37 A6
Lenham Heath...37 B7
Lennel........198 B2
Lennoxtown...205 A6
Lenton Lincs..116 B3
Nottingham...114 B3
Lentran......252 B1
Lenwade......120 D2
Leny Ho.......217 D6
Lenzie.......205 A6
Leoch.........220 A3
Leochel-
Cushnie....244 A2
Leominster....78 B2
Leonard Stanley..63 C4
Leorin........200 D3
Lepe..........18 B3
Lephin.......258 D1
Lephinchapel.214 C2
Lephinmore...214 C2
Le Planel Guern..6
Leppington...149 A6
Lepton.......139 B5
Lerryn.........5 B6
Lerwick......285 J6
Lesbury......189 B5
Le Skerne
Haughton....167 D6
Leslie Aberds.255 D6
Fife.........220 D2
Lesmahagow...194 C3
Lesnewth......10 B2
Lessendrum...255 B6
Lessingham...121 C5
Lessonhall...175 C5

Leswalt.......170 A2
Letchmore Heath.67 D7
Letchworth....84 D4
Letcombe
Bassett......46 A1
Letcombe Regis..46 A1
Letham Angus...232 D3
Falk.........208 B1
Fife.........220 C3
Perth........219 B5
Letham Grange.233 D4
Lethenty......256 B3
Letheringham...88 B3
Letheringsett..120 B2
Lettaford.....12 C2
Lettan.......282 C8
Letterewe....261 C6
Letterfearn..249 D5
Letterfinlay..239 C6
Lettermorar..235 B6
Lettermore...224 B3
Letters.......262 B3
Letterston.....55 B5
Lettoch Highld..242 A3
Highld.......254 C1
Letton Hereford..78 C1
Hereford......94 D1
Letton Green.103 A5
Letty Green....68 B2
Letwell.......131 A5
Leuchars.....221 B4
Leuchars Ho...266 C3
Leumrabhagh..288 F4
Levan.........204 A2
Levaneap.....285 G6
Levedale.....112 D2
Leven E Yorks..151 C4
Fife.........220 D3
Levencorroch.191 C6
Levens.......154 C3
Levens Green...68 A3
Levenshulme..138 D1
Levenwick....285 L6
Leverburgh...287 F5
Leverington..118 D1
Leverton.....117 A7
Leverton
Highgate....117 A7
Leverton
Lucasgate...117 A7
Leverton
Outgate.....117 A7
Le Villocq Guern...6
Levington.....88 D3
Levisham.....160 B2
Levishie.....240 A2
Lew...........64 C4
Lewannick....10 C3
Lewdown.......11 C5
Lewes.........22 A2
Leweston......55 B5
Lewisham......49 B6
Lewiston.....251 D7
Lewistown....40 C4
Lewknor.......66 D3
Leworthy Devon..10 A4
Devon.........26 B1
Lewtrenchard..11 C5
Lexden........70 A3
Ley Aberds....244 A2
Corn...........5 A6
Leybourne.....37 A4
Leyburn......157 B5
Leyfields.....97 A5
Leyhill........67 C5
Leyland......136 A4
Leylodge.....245 A4
Leymoor......139 B4
Leys Aberds..269 D5
Perth........220 A2
Leys Castle..252 B2
Leysdown-on-
Sea..........52 B2
Leysmill.....233 D4
Leys of Cossans.232 D1
Leysters Pole..78 A3
Leyton........49 A6
Leytonstone...49 A6
Lezant........10 D4
Leziate......118 D3
Lhanbryde....266 C3
Liatrie......250 C4
Libanus.......60 A1

Libberton....195 B4
Liberton.....209 D5
Liceasto.....288 H2
Lichfield.....96 A4
Lickey........96 D2
Lickey End....96 D2
Lickfold......34 D2
Liddel.......283 J5
Liddesdale...236 D1
Liddington....45 A6
Lidgate.......86 B3
Lidget.......141 C4
Lidget Green.147 D5
Lidgett......131 C6
Lidlington....84 D1
Lidstone......65 A4
Lieurary.....279 B6
Liff..........220 A3
Lifton........11 C4
Liftondown....11 C4
Lighthorne....81 B6
Lightwater....48 C2
Lightwood....112 A3
Lightwood Green
Ches E.......111 A5
Wrex.........110 A2
Lilbourne.....98 D2
Lilburn Tower.188 A3
Lilleshall...111 D6
Lilley Herts...67 A7
W Berks.......46 B2
Lilliesleaf..186 A4
Lillingstone
Dayrell......83 D4
Lillingstone
Lovell.......83 C4
Lillington Dorset..29 D6
Warks.........81 A6
Lilliput......17 B4
Lilstock......27 A6
Lilyhurst....111 D6
Limbury.......67 A6
Limebrook.....78 A1
Limefield....137 B7
Limekilnburn.194 A2
Limekilns....208 B3
Limerigg.....207 C6
Limerstone....18 C3
Limington.....29 C5
Limpenhoe....105 A4
Limpley Stoke..44 C1
Limpsfield....36 A2
Limpsfield Chart.36 A2
Linby........131 D5
Linchmere....34 C1
Lincluden....174 A2
Lincoln......133 B4
Lincomb......79 A6
Lincombe.......7 B6
Lindale......154 C3
Lindal in
Furness.....153 C3
Lindean......196 C3
Lindfield.....35 D6
Lindford......33 B7
Lindifferon..220 C3
Lindley......139 B4
Lindley Green.147 C6
Lindores.....220 C2
Lindridge....79 A4
Lindsell......69 A6
Lindsey.......87 C5
Linford Hants..17 A5
Thurrock......50 B3
Lingague.....152 D2
Lingards Wood.138 B3
Lingbob......147 D4
Lingdale.....169 D4
Lingen........78 A1
Lingfield.....36 B1
Lingreabhagh.287 F5
Lingwood.....105 A4
Linicro......258 B3
Linkenholt....46 D1
Linkhill......37 D6
Linkinhorne...10 D4
Linklater....283 J5
Linksness....283 G3
Linktown.....209 A5
Linley........94 B1
Linley Green..79 B4
Linlithgow...208 C3

Linlithgow
Bridge 208 C2
Linshiels 188 C1
Linsiadar 288 D3
Linsidemore 264 A1
Linslade 67 A5
Linstead Parva . 104 D4
Linstock 176 D2
Linthwaite 139 B4
Lintlaw 198 A2
Lintmill 267 C6
Linton Borders . . . 187 A6
 Cambs 86 C1
 Derbys 113 D6
 Hereford 62 A2
 Kent 37 B5
 Northumb 189 D5
 N Yorks 146 A3
 W Yorks 148 C2
Linton-on-Ouse 148 A3
Linwood Hants . . . 17 A5
 Lincs 133 A6
 Renfs 205 B4
Lionacleit 286 B3
Lional 288 A6
Liphook 34 C1
Liscard 136 D2
Liscombe 26 B3
Liskeard 6 A1
L'Islet Guern 6
Liss 33 C6
Lissett 151 B4
Liss Forest 33 C6
Lissington 133 A6
Lisvane 41 C6
Liswerry 42 A2
Litcham 119 D5
Litchborough 82 B3
Litchfield 46 D2
Lit. Hallingbury . . 69 B4
Litherland 136 D2
Litlington Cambs . . 85 C5
 E Sus 22 B3
Little Abington . . 86 C1
Little Addington . 99 D6
Little Alne 80 A4
Little Altcar 136 C2
Little Asby 155 A5
Little Assynt . . . 271 B4
Little Aston 96 A3
Little Atherfield . . 18 C3
Little Ayre 283 H4
Little-ayre 285 G5
Little Ayton 168 D3
Little Baddow . . . 70 C1
Little Badminton . 44 A2
Little Ballinluig . 230 C3
Little Bampton . . 175 C5
Little Bardfield . . 86 D2
Little Barford . . . 84 B3
Little
 Barningham . . 120 B3
Little Barrington . 64 B3
Little Barrow . . . 127 B4
Little Barugh . . . 159 D6
Little Bavington . 178 B1
Little Bealings . . . 88 C3
Littlebeck 160 A2
Little Bedwyn . . . 45 C6
Little Bentley . . . 71 A5
Little
 Berkhamsted . . 68 C2
Little Billing 83 A5
Little Birch 78 D3
Little Blakenham . 88 C2
Little Blencow . . 164 B2
Little Bollington 128 A2
Little Bookham . . 35 A4
Littleborough
 Gtr Man 138 B2
 Notts 132 A3
Littlebourne 53 D4
Little Bowden . . . 99 C4
Little Bradley . . . 86 C2
Little Brampton . . 94 C1
Little Brechin . . 232 B3
Littlebredy 15 C5
Little Brickhill . . . 83 D6
Little Brington . . 82 A3
Little Bromley . . . 71 A4
Little
 Broughton . . . 162 A3

Little Budworth . 127 C5
Little Burstead . . 69 D6
Littlebury 85 D7
Littlebury Green . 85 D6
Little Bytham . . . 116 D3
Little Carlton
 Lincs 134 A3
 Notts 132 D2
Little Casterton . 100 A2
Little
 Cawthorpe . . 134 A3
Little Chalfont . . 67 D5
Little Chart 38 A1
Little
 Chesterford . . 85 C7
Little Cheverell . . 44 D3
Little Chishill . . . 85 D6
Little Clacton . . . 71 B5
Little Clifton . . . 162 B3
Little Colp 256 B2
Little Comberton . 80 C2
Little Compton . . 81 D5
Little Cornard . . . 87 D4
Little Cowarne . . . 79 B4
Little Coxwell . . . 64 D3
Little Crakehall . 157 B6
Little
 Cressingham . 103 B4
Little Crosby . . . 136 C2
Little Dalby 115 D5
Little Dawley 95 A4
Littledean 62 B2
Little Dens 257 B5
Little Dewchurch . 78 D3
Little Downham . 101 C7
Little Driffield . . 150 B3
Little Dunham . . 119 D5
Little Dunkeld . . 230 D4
Little Dunmow . . . 69 A6
Little Easton 69 A6
Little Eaton 114 A1
Little Eccleston . 144 C4
Little Ellingham 103 B6
Little End 69 C5
Little Eversden . . 85 B5
Little Faringdon . 64 C3
Little Fencote . . 157 B6
Little Fenton . . . 148 D4
Littleferry 265 A4
Little Finborough . 87 B6
Little Fransham . 119 D6
Little Gaddesden . 67 B5
Little Gidding . . 100 C3
Little Glemham . . 88 B4
Little Glenshee . 219 A4
Little Gransden . . 85 B4
Little Green 29 A7
Little Grimsby . . 143 D5
Little Gruinard . 261 B6
Little Habton . . . 159 D6
Little Hadham . . . 68 A4
Little Hale 116 A4
Littleham Devon . . 13 C5
 Devon 25 C5
Little Hampden . . 66 C4
Littlehampton . . . 20 B3
Little Harrowden . 99 D5
Little Haseley . . . 66 C2
Little Hatfield . . 151 C4
Little Hautbois . 121 C4
Little Haven 55 C4
Little Hay 96 A4
Little Hayfield . . 129 A5
Little Haywood . . 112 C4
Little Heath 97 C6
Littlehempston . . . 8 A2
Little Hereford . . 78 A3
Little Horkesley . . 87 D5
Little Horsted . . . 22 A2
Little Horton . . . 147 D5
Little Horwood . . 83 D4
Littlehoughton . 189 B5
Little Houghton
 Northants 83 B5
 S Yorks 140 C2
Little Hucklow . 129 B6
Little Hulton . . . 137 C6
Little Humber . . 142 A3
Little Hungerford . 46 B3
Little Irchester . . 83 A6
Little Kimble . . . 66 C4

Little Kineton 81 B6
Little Kingshill . . 66 D4
Little Langdale . . 154 A2
Little Langford . . 31 B4
Little Laver 69 C5
Little Leigh 127 B6
Little Leighs 69 B7
Little Lever 137 C6
Little London
 Bucks 66 B2
 E Sus 22 A3
 Hants 32 A3
 Hants 47 D4
 Lincs 117 C5
 Lincs 118 C1
 Norf 120 C3
 Powys 92 C4
Little Longstone 130 B1
Little Lynturk . . 244 A2
Little Malvern . . . 79 C5
Little Maplestead 87 D4
Little Marcle 79 D4
Little Marlow 47 A6
Little Marsden . . 146 D2
Little
 Massingham . 119 C4
Little Melton . . . 104 A2
Littlemill Aberds . 243 C6
 E Ayrs 182 A2
 Highld 253 A5
 Northumb . . . 189 B5
Little Mill 61 C5
Little Milton 65 C7
Little Missenden . 67 D5
Littlemoor 15 C6
Littlemore 65 C6
Little Musgrave 165 D5
Little Ness 110 D3
Little Neston . . . 126 B2
Little Newcastle . 55 B5
Little Newsham . 166 D4
Little Oakley
 Essex 71 A6
 Northants 99 C5
Little Orton 175 C6
Little Ouseburn . 148 A3
Littleover 114 B1
Little Paxton 84 A3
Little Petherick . . . 9 D5
Little Pitlurg . . . 255 B5
Little Plumpton . 144 D3
Little
 Plumstead . . 121 D5
Little Ponton . . . 116 B2
Littleport 102 C1
Little Raveley . . 101 D4
Little Reedness . 141 A6
Little Ribston . . 148 B2
Little Rissington . 64 B2
Little Ryburgh . . 119 C6
Little Ryle 188 B3
Little Salkeld . . . 164 B3
Little Sampford . . 86 D2
Little Sandhurst . 47 C6
Little Saxham . . . 86 A3
Little Scatwell . . 251 A5
Little Shelford . . . 85 B6
Little Singleton . 144 D3
Little
 Skillymarno . 269 D4
Little Smeaton . 140 B3
Little Snoring . . 119 B6
Little Sodbury . . . 43 A6
Little Somborne . 32 B2
Little Somerford . 44 A3
Little Stainforth . 146 A2
Little Stainton . . 167 C6
Little Stanney . . 127 B4
Little Staughton . 84 A3
Little Steeping . . 135 C4
Littlestone on
 Sea 38 C2
Little Stonham . . 88 A2
Little Stretton
 Leics 98 A3
 Shrops 94 B2
Little Strickland 164 D3
Little Stukeley . . 100 D4
Little Sutton . . . 126 B3
Little Tew 65 A4

Little Thetford . . 102 D1
Little Thirkleby . 158 D3
Littlethorpe Leics . 98 B2
 N Yorks 148 A2
Little Thurlow . . . 86 B2
Little Thurrock . . 50 B3
Littleton Ches W . . 127 C4
 Hants 32 B3
 Perth 220 A2
 Som 29 B4
 Sur 34 B2
 Sur 48 C3
Littleton Drew . . 44 A2
Littleton-on-
 Severn 43 A4
Littleton Pannell . 44 D4
Little Torboll . . . 264 A3
Little Torrington . 25 D5
Little Totham . . . 70 B2
Little Toux 267 D6
Littletown 167 A6
Little Town
 Cumb 163 C5
 Lancs 145 D6
Little Urswick . . 153 C3
Little Wakering . . 51 A6
Little Walden . . . 86 C1
Little
 Waldingfield . 87 C5
Little
 Walsingham . 119 B6
Little Waltham . . 69 B7
Little Warley 69 D6
Little Weighton . 150 D2
Little Weldon . . . 99 C6
Little Welnetham . 87 A4
Little Wenlock . . . 95 A4
Little Whittingham
 Green 104 D3
Littlewick Green . 47 B6
Little Wilbraham . 86 B1
Little Wishford . . 31 B4
Little Witley 79 A5
Little Wittenham . 65 D6
Little Wolford . . . 81 D5
Littleworth
 Bedford 84 C2
 Glos 63 C4
 Oxon 64 D4
 Staffs 112 D4
 Worcs 80 B1
Little Wratting . . 86 C2
Little Wymington 83 A6
Little Wymondley 68 A4
Little Wyrley . . . 96 A3
Little Yeldham . . 86 D3
Litton Derbys . . . 129 B6
 N Yorks 156 D3
 Som 43 D4
Litton Cheney . . 15 B5
Liurbost 288 E4
Liverpool 136 D2
Liverpool
 Airport 127 A4
Liversedge 139 A5
Liverton Devon . . 12 D3
 Redcar 169 D5
Livingston 208 D3
Livingston
 Village 208 D3
Lixwm 125 B6
Lizard 3 D5
Llaingoch 122 B2
Llaithddu 93 C4
Llan 91 B6
Llanaber 90 A4
Llanaelhaearn . . 106 B3
Llanafan 75 A5
Llanafan-fawr . . . 76 B3
Llanallgo 123 B4
Llanarmon 107 C4
Llanarmon Dyffryn
 Ceiriog 109 B6
Llanarmon-yn-
 Ial 126 D1
Llanarth Ceredig . . 73 A7
 Mon 61 B5
Llanarthne 58 C2
Llanasa 125 A6
Llanbabo 122 B3
Llanbadarn Fawr . 90 D4

Llanbadarn
 Fynydd 93 D5
Llanbadarn-y-
 Garreg 77 C5
Llanbadoc 61 C5
Llanbadrig 122 A3
Llanbeder 61 D5
Llanbedr Gwyn . . 107 D5
 Powys 60 A4
 Powys 77 C5
Llanbedr-Dyffryn-
 Clwyd 125 D6
Llanbedrgoch . . 123 B5
Llanbedrog 106 C3
Llanbedr-y-
 cennin 124 C2
Llanberis 123 D5
Llanbethery 41 E5
Llanbister 93 D5
Llanblethian 41 D4
Llanboidy 73 D5
Llanbradach 41 B6
Llanbrynmair . . . 91 B6
Llancarfan 41 D5
Llancayo 61 C5
Llancloudy 61 A6
Llancynfelyn 90 C4
Llandaff 41 D6
Llandanwg 107 D5
Llandarcy 40 B2
Llandawke 56 A2
Llanddaniel Fab . 123 C5
Llanddarog 57 A5
Llanddeiniol 75 A4
Llanddeiniolen . 123 D5
Llandderfel 109 B4
Llanddeusant
 Anglesey 122 B3
 Carms 59 C4
Llanddew 77 D4
Llanddewi 57 D4
Llanddewi-Brefi . 75 C5
Llanddewi'r Cwm 76 C4
Llanddewi
 Rhydderch . . . 61 B5
Llanddewi
 Velfrey 56 A1
Llanddoged . . . 124 C3
Llanddona 123 C5
Llanddowror . . . 56 A2
Llanddulas 125 B4
Llanddwywe . . . 107 D5
Llanddyfnan . . . 123 C5
Llandefaelog
 Fach 76 D4
Llandefaelog-tre'r-
 graig 77 E5
Llandefalle 77 D5
Llandegai 123 C5
Llandegfan 123 C5
Llandegla 126 D1
Llandegley 77 A5
Llandegveth 61 D5
Llandegwning . . 106 C2
Llandeilo 58 C3
Llandeilo Graban . 77 C4
Llandeilo'r Fan . . 59 B5
Llandeloy 55 B4
Llandenny 61 C6
Llandevenny 42 A3
Llandewednock . . 3 D5
Llandewi
 Ystradenny . . . 77 A5
Llandinabo 61 A7
Llandinam 92 C4
Llandissilio 55 B7
Llandogo 62 C1
Llandough V Glam . 41 D4
 V Glam 41 D6
Llandovery
 (Llanymddyfri) . 59 B4
Llandow 40 D4
Llandre Carms . . . 58 A3
 Ceredig 90 D4
Llandrillo 109 B5
Llandrillo-yn-
 Rhos 124 A3
Llandrindod Wells
 (Llandrindod) . . 77 A4
Llandrinio 110 D1
Llandudno 124 A2

Llandudno Junction
 (Cyffordd
 Llandudno) . . . 124 B2
Llandwrog 107 A4
Llandybie 57 A6
Llandyfaelog 57 A4
Llandyfan 57 A6
Llandyfriog 73 B6
Llandyfrydog . . . 123 B4
Llandygwydd 73 B5
Llandynan 109 A6
Llandyrnog 125 C6
Llandysilio 110 D1
Llandyssil 93 B5
Llandysul 73 B7
Llanedeyrn 41 C7
Llanedi 57 B5
Llaneglwys 77 D4
Llanegryn 90 B3
Llanegwad 58 C2
Llaneilian 123 A4
Llanelian-yn-
 Rhos 124 B3
Llanelidan 125 D6
Llanelieu 77 D5
Llanellen 61 B5
Llanelli 57 C5
Llanelltyd 91 A5
Llanelly 60 B4
Llanelly Hill 60 B4
Llanelwedd 76 B4
Llanenddwyn . . . 107 D5
Llanengan 106 D2
Llanerchymedd . 123 B4
Llanerfyl 92 A4
Llanfachraeth . . 122 B3
Llanfachreth . . . 108 C2
Llanfaelog 122 C3
Llanfaelrhys . . . 106 D2
Llanfaenor 61 B6
Llanfaes
 Anglesey 123 C6
 Powys 60 A2
Llanfaethlu 122 B3
Llanfaglan 123 D4
Llanfair 107 D5
Llanfair-ar-y-
 bryn 59 B5
Llanfair
 Caereinion . . . 93 A5
Llanfair Clydogau 75 C5
Llanfair-Dyffryn-
 Clwyd 125 D6
Llanfairfechan . . 124 B1
Llanfair
 Kilgheddin . . . 61 C5
Llanfair-Nant-
 Gwyn 73 C4
Llanfairpwll-
 gwyngyll 123 C5
Llanfair
 Talhaiarn 125 B4
Llanfair
 Waterdine 93 D6
Llanfairyneubwll
 . . . . 122 C3
Llanfairynghornwy
 . . . . 122 A3
Llanfallteg 56 A1
Llanfaredd 77 B4
Llanfarian 75 A4
Llanfechain 109 C6
Llanfechan 76 B3
Llanfechell 122 A3
Llanfendigaid . . . 90 B3
Llanferres 126 C1
Llan Ffestiniog . 108 A2
Llanfflewyn 122 B3
Llanfihangel-ar-
 arth 58 B1
Llanfihangel-
 Crucorney 61 A5
Llanfihangel Glyn
 Myfyr 109 A4
Llanfihangel Nant
 Bran 59 B6
Llanfihangel-nant-
 Melan 77 B5

Llanfihangel
Rhydithon 77 A5
Llanfihangel
Rogiet 42 A3
Llanfihangel Tal-y-
llyn 60 A3
Llanfihangel-uwch-
Gwili 58 C1
Llanfihangel-y-
Creuddyn 75 A5
Llanfihangel-yn-
Ngwynfa 109 D5
Llanfihangel yn
Nhowyn 122 C3
Llanfihangel-y-
pennant
Gwyn 91 B4
Gwyn 107 B5
Llanfihangel-y-
traethau 107 C5
Llanfilo 77 D5
Llanfoist 61 B4
Llanfor 108 B4
Llanfrechfa 61 D5
Llanfrothen 107 B6
Llanfrynach 60 A2
Llanfwrog
Anglesey 122 B3
Denb. 125 D6
Llanfyllin 109 D6
Llanfynydd Carms . 58 C2
Flint 126 D2
Llanfyrnach 73 C5
Llangadfan 109 D5
Llangadog 59 C4
Llangadwaladr
Anglesey 122 D3
Powys 109 B6
Llangaffo 123 D4
Llangain 56 A3
Llangammarch
Wells 76 C3
Llangan 41 D4
Llangarron 62 A1
Llangasty
Talyllyn 60 A3
Llangathen 58 C2
Llangattock 60 B4
Llangattock
Lingoed 61 A5
Llangattock nigh
Usk 61 C5
Llangattock-Vibon-
Avel. 61 B6
Llangedwyn ... 109 C6
Llangefni 123 C4
Llangeinor 40 C4
Llangeitho 75 C5
Llangeler 73 C6
Llangelynin 90 B3
Llangendeirne .. 57 A4
Llangennech ... 57 B5
Llangennith 57 C4
Llangenny 60 B4
Llangernyw ... 124 C3
Llangian 106 D2
Llanglydwen ... 73 D4
Llangoed 123 C6
Llangoedmor ... 73 B4
Llangollen 109 A7
Llangolman 55 B7
Llangors 60 A3
Llangovan 61 C6
Llangower 108 B4
Llangrannog 73 A6
Llangristiolus . 123 C4
Llangrove 62 B1
Llangua 61 A5
Llangunllo 93 D6
Llangunnor 57 A4
Llangurig 92 D3
Llangwm Conwy. 109 A4
Mon 61 C6
Pembs 55 D5
Llangwnnadl ... 106 C2
Llangwyfan ... 125 D6
Llangwyfan-isaf 122 D3
Llangwyllog ... 123 C4
Llangwyryfon .. 75 A4

Llangybi Ceredig .. 75 C5
Gwyn 107 B4
Mon 61 D5
Llangyfelach 57 C6
Llangynhafal .. 125 C6
Llangynidr 60 B3
Llangynin 56 A2
Llangynog Carms. 56 A3
Powys 109 C5
Llangynwyd 40 C3
Llanhamlach 60 A2
Llanharan 41 C5
Llanharry 41 C5
Llanhennock 61 D5
Llanhilleth
(Llanilledd) 41 A7
Llanidloes 92 C3
Llaniestyn 106 C2
Llanifyny 91 D6
Llanigon 77 D6
Llanilar 75 A5
Llanilid 41 C4
Llanishen Cardiff . 41 C6
Mon 61 C6
Llanllawddog ... 58 C1
Llanllechid 123 D6
Llanllowell 61 D5
Llanllugan 93 A4
Llanllwch 56 A3
Llanllwchaiarn .. 93 B5
Llanllwni 58 B1
Llanllyfni 107 A4
Llanmadoc 57 C4
Llanmaes 41 E4
Llanmartin 42 A2
Llanmihangel .. 41 D4
Llanmorlais 57 C5
Llannefydd ... 125 B4
Llannon 57 B5
Llannor 106 C3
Llanon 75 B4
Llanover 61 C5
Llanpumsaint .. 73 D7
Llanreithan 55 B4
Llanrhaeadr .. 125 C5
Llanrhaeadr-ym-
Mochnant 109 C6
Llanrhian 54 A4
Llanrhidian 57 C5
Llanrhos 124 A2
Llanrhyddlad .. 122 B3
Llanrhystud 75 B4
Llanrosser 77 D6
Llanrothal 61 B6
Llanrug 123 D5
Llanrumney 41 C7
Llanrwst 124 C3
Llansadurnen .. 56 A2
Llansadwrn
Anglesey 123 C5
Carms 58 B3
Llansaint 56 B3
Llansamlet 40 B1
Llansannan ... 125 C4
Llansannor 41 D4
Llansantffraed
Ceredig 75 B4
Powys 60 A3
Llansantffraed
Cwmdeuddwr . 76 A3
Llansantffraed-in-
Elvel 77 B4
Llansantffraid-ym-
Mechain 109 C7
Llansawel 58 B3
Llansilin 109 C7
Llansoy 61 C6
Llanspyddid 60 A2
Llanstadwell .. 55 D5
Llansteffan 56 A3
Llanstephan .. 77 C5
Llantarnam ... 61 D5
Llanteg 56 A1
Llanthony 61 A4
Llantilio
Crossenny .. 61 B5
Llantilio
Pertholey 61 B5
Llantood 73 B4
Llantrisant
Anglesey 122 B3
Mon 61 D5

Llantrisant continued
Rhondda. 41 C5
Llantrithyd. 41 D5
Llantwit Fardre.. 41 C5
Llantwit Major
(Llanilltud
Fawr) 41 E4
Llanuwchllyn... 108 B3
Llanvaches. 61 D6
Llanvair Discoed .61 D6
Llanvapley 61 B5
Llanvetherine .. 61 B5
Llanveynoe 77 D7
Llanvihangel
Gobion. 61 C5
Llanvihangel-Ystern-
Llewern 61 B6
Llanwarne 61 A7
Llanwddyn ... 109 D5
Llanwenog 74 D3
Llanwern 42 A2
Llanwinio 73 D5
Llanwnda Gwyn .107 A4
Pembs 72 C2
Llanwnnen..... 75 D4
Llanwnog 92 B4
Llanwrda 59 B4
Llanwrin 91 B5
Llanwrthwl. 76 A3
Llanwrtyd. 76 C2
Llanwrtyd Wells
(Llanwrtyd) ... 76 C2
Llanwyddelan ... 93 A4
Llanyblodwel.. 110 C1
Llanybri 56 A3
Llanybydder. ... 58 A2
Llanycefn 55 B6
Llanychaer. 72 C2
Llanycil 108 B4
Llanycrwys. 75 D5
Llanymawddwy.. 91 A7
Llanymynech ... 110 C1
Llanynghenedl .. 122 B3
Llanynys 125 C6
Llan-y-pwll 126 D3
Llanyre 76 A4
Llanystumdwy... 107 C4
Llanywern 60 A3
Llawhaden 55 C6
Llawnt 110 B1
Llawr Dref ... 106 D2
Llawryglyn. 92 B3
Llay 126 D3
Llechcynfarwy .. 122 B3
Llecheiddior ... 107 B4
Llechfaen. 60 A2
Llechryd Caerph.. 60 C3
Ceredig 73 B5
Llechrydau 110 B1
Lledrod 75 A5
Llenmerewig.... 93 B5
Llethrid. 57 C5
Llidiad Nenog ... 58 B2
Llidiardau. 108 B3
Llidiart-y-parc ..109 A6
Llithfaen 106 B3
Llong 126 C2
Llowes 77 C5
Llundain-fach. .. 75 C4
Llwydcoed 41 A4
Llwyn. 93 C6
Llwyncelyn. 74 C3
Llwyndafydd ... 73 A6
Llwynderw. 93 A6
Llwyn-du 61 B4
Llwyndyrys. ... 106 B3
Llwyngwril. 90 B3
Llwyn-hendy. ... 57 C5
Llwynmawr. ... 110 B1
Llwyn-têg. 57 B5
Llwyn-y-brain.. 56 A1
Llwyn-y-groes .. 75 C4
Llwynypia. 41 B4
Llynclys. 110 C1
Llynfaes 123 C4
Llysfaen 124 B3
Llyswen 77 D5
Llysworney ... 41 D4
Llys-y-frân ... 55 B6
Llywel 59 B5
Loan 208 C2
Loanend 198 A3

Loanhead. 209 D5
Loans. 192 B3
Loans of Tullich 265 C4
Lobb 25 B5
Loch a Charnain 286 B4
Loch a'
Ghainmhich ... 288 E3
Lochailort 235 B6
Lochaline. 225 B5
Lochanhully. ... 253 D5
Lochans 170 B2
Locharbriggs... 184 D2
Lochassynt
Lodge. 271 B4
Lochavich Ho ... 214 A2
Lochawe. 227 D6
Loch Baghasdail
(Lochbois-
dale). 286 E3
Lochbuie 225 D5
Lochcarron 249 C5
Loch Choire
Lodge. 273 A4
Lochdhu 279 D6
Lochdochart
House. 216 B4
Lochdon 225 C6
Lochdrum 263 C4
Lochead 202 A2
Lochearnhead.. 217 B5
Lochee 220 A3
Lochend Highld . 252 C1
Highld. 281 B4
Locherben 184 C2
Loch Euphuirt.. 287 H3
Lochfoot. 173 A6
Lochgair. 214 C1
Lochgarthside.. 240 A3
Lochgelly 209 A4
Lochgilphead .. 214 D1
Lochgoilhead .. 215 B5
Loch Head 171 C5
Lochhill 266 C3
Lochindorb
Lodge. 253 C5
Lochinver. 270 B3
Lochlane 218 B3
Loch Loyal
Lodge. 287 D7
Lochluichart ... 263 D5
Lochmaben 184 D3
Lochmore
Cottage. 280 D2
Lochmore
Lodge. 271 A5
Loch nam Madadh
(Lochmaddy).. 287 H4
Lochore 209 A4
Lochportain. ... 287 G4
Lochranza 203 C4
Lochs Crofts .. 266 C4
Loch Sgioport.. 286 C4
Lochside Aberds .233 B5
Highld. 253 A4
Highld. 274 A2
Highld. 277 C5
Lochslin 265 B4
Lochstack
Lodge. 276 D3
Lochton 245 C4
Lochty Angus ... 232 B3
Fife. 221 D5
Shetland. 285 M5
Lochuisge 236 D1
Lochurr. 183 D5
Lochwinnoch .. 204 C3
Lochwood 184 C3
Lochyside. 237 B5
Lockengate 5 A5
Lockerbie 185 D4
Lockeridge 45 C5
Lockerley 32 C1
Locking. 42 D2
Lockinge 46 A2
Lockington
E Yorks. 150 C2
Leics. 114 C2
Locklywood ... 111 C5
Locks Heath ... 18 A4
Lockton 160 B2
Lockwood 139 B4

Loddington continued
Northants. 99 D5
Loddiswell 7 C6
Loddon 105 B4
Lode 86 A1
Loders. 15 B4
Lodsworth 34 D2
Lofthouse
N Yorks. 157 D5
W Yorks. 139 A6
Loftus 169 D5
Logan 193 C5
Loganlea 208 D2
Logan Mains ... 170 D2
Loggerheads... 111 B6
Logie Angus ... 233 B4
Fife. 220 B4
Moray. 253 A6
Logiealmond
Lodge. 219 A4
Logie Coldstone 244 B1
Logie Hill 264 C3
Logie Newton .. 256 C1
Logie Pert 233 B4
Logierait. 230 C3
Login 73 D4
Lolworth 85 A5
Lonbain 248 A3
Londesborough .150 C1
London Colney .. 68 C1
Londonderry... 157 C7
Londonthorpe.. 116 B2
Londubh 261 B5
Lonemore 264 B3
Long Ashton ... 43 B4
Longbar 204 C3
Long
Bennington ... 115 A6
Longbenton ... 179 C4
Longborough ... 64 A2
Long Bredy 15 B5
Longbridge Warks 81 A5
W Mid 96 D3
Longbridge
Deverill 30 A2
Long Buckby ... 82 A3
Longburton 29 D6
Long Clawson .. 115 C5
Longcliffe. 130 D2
Long Common ... 32 D4
Long Compton
Staffs 112 C2
Warks. 81 D5
Longcot 64 D3
Long Crendon .. 66 C2
Long Crichel ... 30 D3
Longcroft. 207 C5
Longden 94 A2
Long Ditton ... 49 C4
Longdon Staffs.. 113 D4
Worcs. 79 D6
Longdon Green. .113 D4
Longdon on
Tern 111 D5
Longdown 12 B3
Longdowns 4 D2
Long Drax 141 A4
Long
Duckmanton . 131 B4
Long Eaton ... 114 B2
Longfield Kent ... 50 C3
Shetland. 285 M5
Longford Derbys .113 B6
Glos 63 A4
London 48 B3
Shrops 111 B5
Telford 111 D6
W Mid 97 C6
Longfordlane .. 113 B6
Longforgan ... 220 B3
Longformacus .. 197 A5
Longframlington
...... 189 C4
Long Green ... 79 D6
Longham Dorset . 17 B4
Norf 119 D6
Long
Hanborough ... 65 B5
Longhaven. ... 257 C6
Longhill 269 D4
Longhirst 179 A4
Longhope Glos... 62 B2

Longhope continued
Orkney 283 H4
Longhorsley ... 189 D4
Longhoughton .. 189 B5
Long Itchington . 81 A7
Longlane Derbys .113 B6
W Berks. 46 B2
Long Lawford ... 98 D1
Longlevens 63 A4
Longley. 139 C4
Longley Green ... 79 B5
Long Load 29 C4
Longmanhill ... 268 C2
Long Marston
Herts. 66 B4
N Yorks. 148 B4
Warks. 81 C4
Long Marton ... 165 C4
Long Melford ... 87 C4
Longmoor Camp . 33 B6
Longmorn 266 D3
Long Newnton .. 63 D5
Longnewton
Borders 187 A4
Stockton. 167 D6
Long Newton... 210 D2
Longney 62 B3
Longniddry 210 C1
Longnor Shrops .. 94 A2
Staffs 129 C5
Longparish 32 A3
Longport 112 A2
Long Preston ... 146 B2
Longridge Lancs .145 D6
Staffs. 112 D3
W Loth 208 D2
Longriggend ... 207 C6
Long Riston ... 151 C4
Longsdon 129 D4
Longshaw. 136 C4
Longside 257 B5
Long Sight 138 C2
Longstanton ... 85 A5
Longstock 32 B2
Longstone 56 B1
Longstowe 85 B5
Long Stratton . 104 B2
Long Street 83 C4
Long Sutton
Hants. 33 A6
Lincs. 118 C1
Som 29 C4
Longthorpe ... 100 B3
Long Thurlow ... 87 A6
Longthwaite .. 164 C2
Longton Lancs .. 136 A3
Stoke. 112 A3
Longtown Cumb. 175 B6
Hereford 61 A5
Longview. 136 D3
Longville in the
Dale 94 B3
Long Whatton.. 114 C2
Longwick. 66 C3
Long Wittenham . 65 D6
Longwitton ... 178 A2
Longwood 95 A4
Longworth. 65 D4
Longyester. ... 210 D2
Lonmay. 269 D5
Lonmore 258 D2
Looe 6 B1
Loose 37 A5
Loosley Row ... 66 C4
Lopcombe
Corner. 31 B6
Lopen 28 D4
Loppington .. 110 C3
Lopwell 6 A3
Lorbottle 188 C3
Lorbottle Hall .. 188 C3
Lornty 231 D5
Loscoe 114 A2
Losgaintir. ... 287 E5
Lossiemouth .. 266 B3
Lossit. 200 C1
Lostford. 111 B5
Lostock Gralam .128 B1
Lostock Green . 128 B1
Lostock Hall .. 136 A4
Lostock
Junction 137 C5

Lostwithiel........5 B6
Loth............282 D7
Lothbeg......274 C3
Lothersdale.....146 C3
Lothmore......274 C3
Loudwater......67 D5
Loughborough..114 D3
Loughor......57 C5
Loughton Essex...68 D4
  M Keynes.......83 D5
  Shrops.......95 C4
Lound Lincs....116 D3
  Notts.......132 A1
  Suff.......105 B6
Lount......114 D1
Louth........134 A3
Love Clough...137 A7
Lovedean.....33 D5
Lover....31 C6
Loversall....140 D3
Loves Green...69 C6
Lovesome Hill..158 B2
Loveston.....55 D6
Lovington.....29 B5
Low Ackworth..140 B2
Low Barlings..133 B5
Low Bentham..145 A6
Low Bradfield..139 D5
Low Bradley..147 C4
Low Braithwaite 164 A2
Lowbridge
  House.........154 A4
Low Brunton...177 B7
Low Burnham..141 C5
Low Burton...157 C6
Low Buston...189 C5
Lowca.......162 B2
Low Catton...149 B6
Low Clanyard..170 D3
Low Coniscliffe..167 D5
Low Crosby...176 B2
Low Dalby....160 C2
Lowdham.....115 A4
Low Dinsdale..167 D6
Lowe........111 B4
Lowe Hill....129 D4
Low Ellington..157 C6
Lower Aisholt...28 B2
Lower Arncott...65 B7
Lower Ashton...12 C3
Lower Assendon..47 A5
Lower Badcall..276 C2
Lower Bartle...145 D4
Lower Basildon..47 B4
Lower Beeding..35 D5
Lower
  Benefield......100 C1
Lower
  Boddington.....82 B1
Lower Brailes...81 D6
Lower Breakish.247 B5
Lower
  Broadheath.....79 B6
Lower
  Bullingham....78 D3
Lower Cam...62 C3
Lower Chapel..76 D4
Lower Chute...45 D7
Lower Cragabus 200 D3
Lower
  Crossings....129 A5
Lower
  Cumberworth..139 C5
Lower Cwm-
  twrch......59 D4
Lower Darwen..137 A5
Lower Dean....84 A2
Lower Diabaig..261 D4
Lower Dicker...22 A3
Lower Dinchope..94 C1
Lower Down...94 C1
Lower Drift...2 C2
Lower
  Dunsforth....148 A3
Lower Egleton..79 C4
Lower Elkstone.129 D5
Lower End....97 B5
Lower Everleigh..45 D5
Lower
  Farringdon....33 B6
Lower Foxdale..152 D2
Lower Frankton.110 B2

Lower Froyle.....33 A6
Lower Gledfield..264 A1
Lower Green....120 B1
Lower Hacheston..88 B4
Lower Halistra...258 C2
Lower Halstow...51 C5
Lower Hardres...52 D3
Lower
  Hawthwaite...153 B3
Lower Heath...128 C3
Lower
  Hempriggs....266 C2
Lower Hergest...77 B6
Lower Heyford...65 A5
Lower Higham...51 B4
Lower Holbrook..88 D2
Lower Hordley..110 C2
Lower
  Horsebridge...22 A3
Lower Killeyan..200 D2
Lower
  Kingswood.....35 A5
Lower
  Kinnerton....126 C3
Lower Langford..42 C3
Lower Largo...220 D4
Lower Leigh...112 B4
Lower Lemington 81 D5
Lower Lenie....251 D7
Lower Lydbrook..62 B1
Lower Lye....78 A2
Lower Machen...42 A1
Lower Maes-
  coed........78 D1
Lower Mayland..70 C3
Lower Midway..113 C7
Lower Milovaig..258 C1
Lower Moor....80 C2
Lower Nazeing...68 C3
Lower
  Netchwood....95 B4
Lower Ollach...247 A4
Lower Penarth..41 D6
Lower Penn....95 B6
Lower
  Pennington...18 B2
Lower Peover...128 B2
Lower Pexhill..128 B3
Lower Place...138 B2
Lower Quinton...81 C4
Lower Rochford..79 A4
Lower Seagry...44 A3
Lower Shelton...84 C1
Lower Shiplake..47 B5
Lower
  Shuckburgh...82 A1
Lower Slaughter..64 A2
Lower Stanton St
  Quintin......44 A3
Lower Stoke...51 B5
Lower Stondon..84 D3
Lower Stow
  Bedon.......103 B5
Lower Street
  Norf.......121 B4
  Norf.......121 D5
Lower Strensham 80 C2
Lower Stretton..127 A6
Lower Sundon...67 A6
Lower Swanwick..18 A3
Lower Swell....64 A2
Lower Tean...112 B4
Lower Thurlton..105 B5
Lower Tote....259 B5
Lower Town....72 C2
Lower Tysoe...81 C6
Lower Upham...32 D4
Lower Vexford...27 B6
Lower Weare...42 D3
Lower Welson...77 B6
Lower Whitley..127 B6
Lower Wield...33 A5
Lower
  Winchendon...66 B3
Lower
  Withington...128 C3
Lower Woodend..97 B5
Lower Woodford.31 B5
Lower Wyche...79 C5
Lowesby.....99 A4
Lowestoft....105 B6
Loweswater...163 B4

Low Etherley....167 C4
Low Fell....179 D4
Lowford......32 D3
Low Fulney....117 C5
Low Garth....159 A6
Low Gate....177 C7
Lowgill Cumb....155 B5
  Lancs.......145 A6
Low Grantley...157 D6
Low Habberley..95 D6
Low Ham....28 C4
Low Hesket...164 A2
Low
  Hesleyhurst...188 D3
Low Hutton...149 A6
Lowick Northants 100 C1
  Northumb.......198 C4
Lowick Bridge..154 C1
Lowick Green..154 C1
Low Laithe...147 A5
Lowlands....61 D4
Low Leighton..129 A5
Low Lorton...163 B4
Low Marishes..159 D7
Low Marnham..132 C3
Low Mill.....159 B5
Low Moor Lancs..146 C1
  W Yorks.......139 A4
Lowmoor Row..165 C4
Low Moorsley..167 A6
Low Newton...154 C3
Low Newton-by-the-
  Sea.........189 A5
Lownie Moor...232 D2
Low Row Cumb..163 A6
  Cumb.......176 C3
  N Yorks.......156 B3
Low Salchrie..170 A2
Low Smerby...190 C3
Lowsonford....81 A4
Lowther......164 C3
Lowthorpe....150 A3
Lowton......137 D5
Lowton
  Common....137 D5
Low Torry....208 B3
Low Worsall...158 A2
Low Wray....154 A2
Loxbeare....27 D4
Loxhill......34 C3
Loxhore....25 B7
Loxley......81 B5
Loxton......42 D2
Loxwood.....34 C3
Lubcroy....271 D6
Lubenham....99 C4
Luccombe....27 A4
Luccombe
  Village......19 D4
Lucker......199 C5
Luckett....11 D4
Luckington....44 A2
Lucklawhill....220 B4
Luckwell Bridge..27 B4
Lucton......78 A2
Ludag......286 E3
Ludborough....143 D4
Ludchurch....56 A1
Luddenden....138 A3
Luddenden Foot 138 A3
Luddesdown....50 C3
Luddington
  N Lincs.......141 B6
  Warks.......81 B4
Luddington in the
  Brook.......100 C3
Lude House....230 B2
Ludford Lincs...134 A2
  Shrops.......94 D3
Ludgershall Bucks..66 B2
  Wilts.......45 D6
Ludgvan.....2 B3
Ludham......121 D5
Ludlow......94 D3
Ludwell.....30 C3
Ludworth....167 A6
Luffincott....10 B4
Lugar......193 C5
Luggate Burn..210 C3
Lugg Green....78 A2
Luggiebank...207 C5
Lugton......205 C4

Lugwardine.....78 C3
Luib......247 B4
Lulham......78 C2
Lullenden....36 B2
Lullington
  Derbys.......113 D6
  Som.......44 D1
Lulsgate Bottom..43 C4
Lulsley......79 B5
Lumb......138 A3
Lumby......148 D3
Lumloch....205 B6
Lumphanan....244 B2
Lumphinnans..209 A4
Lumsdaine....211 D5
Lumsden....255 D5
Lunan......233 C4
Lunanhead....232 C2
Luncarty....219 B5
Lund E Yorks...150 C2
  N Yorks.......149 D5
  Shetland.......284 C7
Lunderton....269 E6
Lundie Angus...220 A2
  Highld.......239 A5
Lundin Links...220 D4
Lunga......213 B5
Lunna......284 G6
Lunning....284 G7
Lunnon.....57 D5
Lunsford....136 C2
Lunsford's Cross..23 A5
Lunt......136 C2
Luntley.....78 B1
Luppitt......13 A6
Lupset......139 B6
Lupton......155 C4
Lurgashall....34 D2
Lusby......134 C3
Luson......7 C5
Luss......206 A1
Lussagiven....213 D4
Lusta......258 C2
Lustleigh....12 C2
Luston......78 A2
Luthermuir....233 B4
Luthrie....220 C3
Luton Devon...13 D4
Luton.......67 A6
  Medway.......51 C4
Lutterworth....98 C2
Lutton Devon...7 B4
  Lincs.......118 C1
  Northants.......100 C3
Lutworthy....26 D2
Luxborough....27 B4
Luxulyan.....5 B5
Lybster....275 A6
Lydbury North..94 C1
Lydcott....26 B1
Lydd......38 C2
Lydden....39 A4
Lyddington....99 B5
Lydd on Sea...38 C2
Lydeard St
  Lawrence....27 B6
Lyde Green...47 D5
Lydford....11 C6
Lydford-on-
  Fosse......29 B5
Lydgate....138 A2
Lydham.....94 B1
Lydiard Green...45 A4
Lydiard Millicent 45 A4
Lydiate....136 C2
Lydlinch....30 D1
Lydney....62 C2
Lydstep....55 E6
Lye......96 C2
Lye Green Bucks..67 C5
  E Sus.......36 C3
Lyford......65 D4
Lymbridge Green 38 A3
Lyme Regis...14 B3
Lyminge.....38 A3
Lymington....18 B2
Lyminster....20 B3
Lymm......128 A1
Lymore......18 B1
Lympne.....38 B3
Lympsham....42 D2
Lympstone....13 C4
Lynch......241 B5

Lyndale Ho......258 C3
Lyndhurst.......18 A2
Lyndon......99 A6
Lyne......48 C3
Lyneal......110 B3
Lyne Down....79 D4
Lyneham Oxon...64 A3
  Wilts.......44 B4
Lynemore....253 D6
Lynemouth....189 D5
Lyne of
  Gorthleck....252 D1
Lyne of Skene...245 A4
Lyness......283 H4
Lyng Norf.......120 D2
  Som.......28 C3
Lynmouth....26 A2
Lynsted....51 C6
Lynton......26 A2
Lyon's Gate....15 A6
Lyonshall....78 B1
Lytchett
  Matravers...16 B3
Lytchett Minster..16 B3
Lyth......281 B4
Lytham......136 A2
Lytham St
  Anne's.......136 A2
Lythe......169 D6
Lythes......283 J5

M

Mabe Burnthouse . 4 D2
Mabie......174 A2
Mablethorpe..135 A5
Macclesfield..129 B4
Macclesfield
  Forest.......129 B4
Macduff....268 C2
Mace Green...88 C2
Macharioch...190 E3
Machen......41 C7
Machrihanish..190 C2
Machynlleth...91 B5
Machynys....57 C5
Mackerel's
  Common....34 D3
Mackworth....113 B7
Macmerry....210 C1
Madderty....219 B4
Maddiston....208 C2
Madehurst....20 A2
Madeley Staffs..111 A6
  Telford.......95 A4
Madeley Heath..112 A1
Madeley Park...112 A1
Madingley....85 A5
Madley......78 D2
Madresfield....79 C6
Madron......2 B2
Maenaddwyn..123 B4
Maenclochog...55 B6
Maendy....41 D5
Maentwrog...107 B6
Maen-y-groes..73 A6
Maer......112 B1
Maerdy Conwy..109 A5
  Rhondda.......41 B4
Maesbrook...110 C1
Maesbury....110 C2
Maesbury
  Marsh......110 C2
Maesgwyn-Isaf..109 C5
Maesgwynne..73 D5
Maeshafn....126 C2
Maesllyn....73 B6
Maesmynis...76 C4
Maesteg....40 B3
Maestir....75 D4
Maes-Treylow..77 A6
Maesybont....57 A5
Maesycrugiau..58 A1
Maesy cwmmer..41 B6
Maesymeillion..73 B7
Magdalen Laver 69 C5
Maggieknockater
  ....254 B4
Magham Down..22 A4
Maghull....136 C2
Magor......42 A3

Magpie Green...104 D1
Maiden Bradley..30 B2
Maidencombe...8 A3
Maidenhall....88 C2
Maidenhead....48 A1
Maiden Law...167 A4
Maiden Newton..15 B5
Maidens......192 E2
Maidensgrave...88 C3
Maiden's Green..48 B1
Maidenwell Corn..10 D2
  Lincs.......134 B3
Maiden Wells...55 E5
Maidford....82 B3
Maids Moreton..83 D4
Maidstone....37 A5
Maidwell....99 D4
Mail......285 L6
Main......109 D6
Maindee.....42 A2
Mainsforth....167 B6
Mains of Airies..170 A1
Mains of
  Allardice....233 A6
Mains of
  Annochie....257 B4
Mains of
  Ardestie....221 A5
Mains of Balhall 232 B3
Mains of
  Ballindarg....232 C2
Mains of
  Balnakettle..233 A4
Mains of
  Birness....257 C4
Mains of Burgie.266 D1
Mains of Clunas 253 B4
Mains of Crichie 257 B4
Mains of Dalvey.254 C2
Mains of
  Dellavaird...245 D4
Mains of Drum..245 C5
Mains of
  Edingight....267 D6
Mains of
  Fedderate...268 E3
Mains of
  Inkhorn....257 C4
Mains of Mayen..255 B6
Mains of
  Melgund....232 C3
Mains of
  Thornton....233 A4
Mains of
  Watten....281 C4
Mainsriddle...174 C2
Mainstone....93 C6
Maisemore....63 A4
Malacleit....287 G2
Malborough....7 D6
Malcoff....129 A5
Maldon....70 C2
Malham....146 A3
Maligar....259 B4
Mallaig....235 A5
Malleny Mills...209 D4
Malling....217 D5
Malltraeth....123 D4
Mallwyd....91 A6
Malmesbury...44 A3
Malmsmead....26 A2
Malpas Ches W...110 A3
  Corn.......4 C3
  Newport.......61 D5
Malswick....62 A3
Maltby Stockton..168 D2
  S Yorks.......140 D3
Maltby le Marsh 135 A4
Malting Green....37 C6
Maltman's Hill..37 B7
Malton....159 D6
Malvern Link...79 C5
Malvern Wells..79 C5
Mamble....95 D4
Manaccan....3 C5
Manafon....93 A5
Manar Ho....256 D2
Manaton....12 C2
Manby......134 A3

Mancetter 97 B6
Manchester 138 D1
Manchester Airport 128 A3
Mancot 126 C3
Mandally 239 B6
Manea 101 C6
Manfield 167 D5
Mangaster 284 F5
Mangotsfield 43 B5
Mangurstadh 287 A5
Mankinholes 138 A2
Manley 127 B5
Man-moel 41 A6
Mannal 222 C2
Mannerston 208 C3
Manningford Bohune 45 D5
Manningford Bruce 45 D5
Manningham 147 D5
Mannings Heath . . 35 D5
Mannington 17 A4
Manningtree 88 D1
Mannofield 245 B6
Manor 50 A1
Manorbier 55 E6
Manordeilo 58 C3
Manor Estate 130 A3
Manorhill 197 C5
Manorowen 72 C2
Manselfield 57 D5
Mansel Lacy 78 C2
Mansell Gamage . 78 C1
Mansergh 155 C5
Mansfield E Ayrs .182 A4
Notts 131 C5
Mansfield Woodhouse . . .131 C5
Mansriggs 154 C1
Manston Dorset . . 30 D2
Kent 53 C5
W Yorks 148 D2
Manswood 16 A3
Manthorpe Lincs .116 B2
Lincs. 116 D3
Manton N Lincs . .142 C1
Notts 131 B5
Rutland. 99 A5
Wilts. 45 C5
Manuden 69 A4
Maperton 29 C6
Maplebeck 132 C2
Maple Cross 67 D6
Mapledurham . . 47 B4
Mapledurwell . . 47 D5
Maplehurst 35 D4
Maplescombe . . 50 C2
Mapleton 113 A5
Mapperley 114 A2
Mapperley Park .114 A3
Mapperton 15 B5
Mappleborough Green 80 A3
Mappleton 151 C5
Mappowder 16 A1
Maraig 288 G2
Marazanvose 4 B3
Marazion 2 B3
Marbhig 288 F5
Marbury 111 A4
March Cambs . .101 B6
S Lanark. 184 A2
Marcham 65 D5
Marchamley 111 C4
Marchington . . .113 B5
Marchington Woodlands 113 C5
Marchroes 106 D3
Marchwiel 110 A2
Marchwood 32 D2
Marcross 40 E4
Marden Hereford . 78 C3
Kent 37 B5
T&W. 179 B5
Wilts. 45 D4
Marden Beech . . 37 B5
Marden Thorn. . . 37 B5
Mardy 61 B5

Marefield 99 A4
Mareham le Fen 134 C2
Mareham on the Hill 134 C2
Marehay 114 A1
Marehill 20 A3
Maresfield 36 D2
Marfleet 142 A3
Marford 126 D3
Margam 40 C2
Margaret Marsh . 30 D2
Margaret Roding . 69 B5
Margaretting 69 C6
Margate 53 B5
Margnaheglish . .191 B6
Margrove Park . .169 D4
Marham 119 D4
Marhamchurch. . 10 A3
Marholm 100 A3
Mariandyrys . . .123 B6
Marianglas . . .123 B5
Mariansleigh . . . 26 C2
Marionburgh . . .245 B4
Marishader . . .259 B4
Marjoriebanks . .184 D3
Mark Dumfries . .170 B3
S Ayrs. 180 D2
Som 28 A3
Markbeech 36 B2
Markby 135 B4
Mark Causeway . 28 A3
Mark Cross E Sus. . 22 A2
E Sus 36 C3
Market Bosworth 97 A7
Market Deeping 116 E4
Market Drayton . 111 B5
Market Harborough 99 C4
Markethill 220 A2
Market Lavington 44 D4
Market Overton .116 D1
Market Rasen . .133 A6
Market Stainton 134 B2
Market Warsop. . 131 C5
Market Weighton 150 C1
Market Weston . .103 D5
Markfield 114 D2
Markham 41 A6
Markham Moor. .132 B2
Markinch 220 D2
Markington 148 A1
Marksbury 43 C5
Marks Tey 70 A3
Markyate 67 B6
Marland 138 B1
Marlborough. . . 45 C5
Marlbrook Hereford 78 B3
Worcs. 96 D2
Marlcliff 80 B3
Marldon 8 A2
Marlesford. 88 B4
Marley Green . .111 A4
Marley Hill . . .179 D4
Marley Mount . . 17 B6
Marlingford . . .104 A2
Mar Lodge . . .242 C3
Marloes 54 D3
Marlow Bucks. . . 47 A6
Hereford 94 D2
Marlow Bottom . 47 A6
Marlpit Hill 36 B2
Marlpool. 114 A2
Marnhull 30 D1
Marnoch 267 D6
Marnock 207 D5
Marple 129 A4
Marple Bridge. . 129 A4
Marr 140 C3
Marrel 274 C4
Marrick 157 B4
Marrister 285 G7
Marros 56 B2
Marsden T&W . .179 C5
W Yorks 138 B3
Marsett 156 C3
Marsh Devon. . . 28 D2
W Yorks 147 D4
Marshall's Heath . 67 B7
Marshalsea 14 A3

Marshalswick . . 67 C7
Marsham 120 C3
Marshaw 145 B5
Marsh Baldon . . 65 D6
Marshborough . . 53 D5
Marshbrook 94 C2
Marshchapel . . .143 D5
Marshfield Newport. 42 A1
S Glos. 44 B1
Marshgate 10 B2
Marsh Gibbon . . 66 A2
Marsh Green Devon. 13 B5
Kent 36 B2
Staffs 128 D3
Marshland St James. 101 A7
Marsh Lane 131 B4
Marshside 136 B2
Marsh Street . . . 27 A4
Marshwood 14 B3
Marske 157 A5
Marske-by-the-Sea 168 C4
Marston Ches W. .127 B6
Hereford 78 B1
Lincs. 116 A1
Oxon. 65 C6
Staffs 112 C3
Staffs 112 C2
Warks. 97 B5
Wilts. 44 D3
Marston Doles . . 82 B1
Marston Green. . 97 C4
Marston Magna . 29 C5
Marston Meysey. 64 D2
Marston Montgomery. . .113 B5
Marston Moretaine 84 C1
Marston on Dove 113 C6
Marston St Lawrence. 82 C2
Marston Stannett. 78 B3
Marston Trussell . 98 C3
Marstow 62 B1
Marsworth 67 B5
Marten 45 D6
Marthall 128 B3
Martham 121 D6
Martin Hants. . . 31 D4
Kent 39 A5
Lincs. 133 D6
Lincs. 134 C2
Martin Dales . . .134 C1
Martin Drove End 31 C4
Martinhoe 26 A1
Martinhoe Cross . 26 A1
Martin Hussingtree 80 A1
Martin Mill. . . . 39 A5
Martinscroft . . .127 A6
Martinstown . . . 15 C6
Martlesham 88 C3
Martlesham Heath 88 C3
Martletwy. 55 C6
Martley 79 A5
Martock 29 D4
Marton Ches E . .128 C3
E Yorks 151 D4
Lincs. 132 A3
Mbro 168 D3
N Yorks. 148 A3
N Yorks. 159 C6
Shrops 93 A6
Shrops 110 C3
Warks. 81 A7
Marton-le-Moor. 158 D2
Martyr's Green . . 34 A3
Martyr Worthy . . 32 B4
Marwick 282 E3
Marwood 25 B6
Marybank 251 A6
Maryburgh . . .252 A1
Maryhill 205 B5
Marykirk 233 B4
Marylebone . . .137 C4
Marypark 254 C2

Maryport Cumb . .162 A3
Dumfries 170 D3
Mary Tavy 11 B6
Maryton 233 C4
Marywell Aberds .244 C2
Aberds 245 C6
Angus. 233 D4
Masham 157 C6
Mashbury 69 B6
Masongill 155 D5
Masonhill 192 C3
Mastin Moor . . 131 B4
Mastrick 245 B5
Matching 69 B5
Matching Green . 69 B5
Matching Tye . . 69 B5
Matfen 178 B2
Matfield 37 B4
Mathern 62 D1
Mathon 79 C5
Mathry 55 A4
Matlaske. 120 B3
Matlock 130 C2
Matlock Bath. . .130 D2
Matson 63 B4
Matterdale End .164 C1
Mattersey 132 A1
Mattersey Thorpe 132 A1
Mattingley 47 D5
Mattishall 120 D2
Mattishall Burgh. 120 D2
Mauchline 193 C4
Maud 257 B4
Maugersbury. . . 64 A3
Maughold. 152 A4
Mauld 251 C6
Maulden 84 D2
Maulds Meaburn 165 D4
Maunby 158 C2
Maund Bryan. . . 78 B3
Maundown. . . . 27 C5
Mautby 121 D6
Mavis Enderby . .134 C3
Mawbray 174 D3
Mawdesley. . . . 136 B3
Mawdlam 40 C3
Mawgan 3 C5
Maw Green . . .128 D2
Mawla 4 C2
Mawnan 3 C5
Mawnan Smith . . 3 C5
Mawsley. 99 D5
Maxey 100 A3
Maxstoke 97 C5
Maxton Borders .197 C5
Kent 39 A5
Maxwellheugh . .197 C6
Maxwelltown. . .174 A2
Maxworthy 10 B3
Mayals 57 C6
May Bank 112 A2
Maybole 192 E3
Mayfield E Sus . . 36 D3
Midloth. 209 D6
Staffs 113 A5
W Loth 208 D2
Mayford 34 A2
Mayland 70 C3
Maynard's Green 22 A3
Maypole Mon . . 61 B6
Scilly 2 E4
Maypole Green Essex. 70 A3
Norf 105 B5
Suff 88 A3
Maywick 285 L5
Meadle 66 C4
Meadowtown . . 93 A7
Meaford 112 B2
Mealabost 288 D5
Mealabost Bhuirgh 288 B5
Meal Bank 154 B4
Mealsgate 175 D5
Meanwood 148 D1
Mearbeck 146 A2
Meare 29 A4
Meare Green . . 28 C3
Mears Ashby . . . 83 A5

Measham 114 D1
Meath Green . . 35 B5
Meathop. 154 C3
Meaux 150 D3
Meavy 7 A4
Medbourne 99 B4
Medburn 178 B3
Meddon 24 D3
Meden Vale . . .131 C5
Medlam 134 D3
Medmenham . . . 47 A6
Medomsley 178 D3
Medstead. 33 B5
Meerbrook. 129 C4
Meer End 97 D5
Meers Bridge . .135 A4
Meesden 85 D6
Meeth 11 A6
Meggethead . .195 D6
Meidrim 73 D5
Meifod Denb. . .125 D5
Powys 109 D6
Meigle N Ayrs. .204 B1
Perth 231 D6
Meikle Earnock .194 A2
Meikle Ferry . .264 B3
Meikle Forter . .231 B5
Meikle Gluich . .264 B2
Meikleour 219 A6
Meikle Pinkerton 211 C4
Meikle Strath . .233 A4
Meikle Tarty . .257 D4
Meikle Wartle. .256 C2
Meinciau 57 A4
Meir. 112 A3
Meir Heath. . . .112 A3
Melbourn 85 C5
Melbourne Derbys 114 C1
E Yorks 149 C6
S Lanark. 195 B5
Melbury Abbas . . 30 C2
Melbury Bubb. . 15 A5
Melbury Osmond 15 A5
Melbury Sampford 15 A5
Melby. 285 H3
Melchbourne . . 84 A2
Melcombe Bingham 16 A1
Melcombe Regis . 15 C6
Meldon Devon . . 11 B6
Northumb. 178 A3
Meldreth 85 C5
Meldrum Ho.. . .256 D3
Melfort 213 A6
Melgarve 240 C2
Meliden 125 A5
Melin-y-coed . .124 C3
Melin-y-ddôl . . 93 A4
Melin-y-grug . . 93 A4
Melin-y-Wig. . .109 A5
Melkinthorpe . .164 C3
Melkridge 177 C5
Melksham 44 C3
Melldalloch. . . .203 A4
Melling Lancs. . .155 D4
Mers. 136 C2
Melling Mount . .136 C3
Mellis 104 D2
Mellon Charles .261 A5
Mellon Udrigle .261 A5
Mellor Gtr Man . .129 A4
Lancs. 145 D6
Mellor Brook . .145 D6
Mells 30 A1
Melmerby Cumb .165 B4
N Yorks. 157 C4
N Yorks. 158 D2
Melplash 15 B4
Melrose 197 C4
Melsetter 283 J3
Melsonby 157 A5
Meltham 138 B4
Melton 88 B3
Meltonby 149 B6
Melton Constable 120 B2

Melton Mowbray . . .115 D5
Melton Ross . . .142 B2
Melvaig 261 B4
Melverley 110 D2
Melverley Green 110 D2
Melvich 279 B4
Membury 14 A2
Memsie. 269 C4
Memus 232 C2
Menabilly 5 B5
Menai Bridge (Porthaethwy) 123 C5
Mendham. 104 C3
Mendlesham. . . 88 A2
Mendlesham Green 88 A1
Menheniot 6 A1
Mennock 183 B6
Menston 147 C5
Menstrie 207 A6
Menthorpe. . . .149 D5
Mentmore 67 B5
Meoble 238 D1
Meole Brace . .110 D3
Meols 136 D1
Meonstoke. . . . 33 D5
Meopham 50 C3
Meopham Station 50 C3
Mepal 101 C6
Meppershall . . 84 D3
Merbach 77 C7
Mere Ches E . . .128 A2
Wilts. 30 B2
Mere Brow. . . .136 B3
Mereclough. . . .146 D2
Mere Grn. 96 B4
Mereside 144 D3
Mereworth 37 A4
Mergie 245 D4
Meriden 97 C5
Merkadale 246 A2
Merkland Dumfries 173 A5
S Ayrs. 181 A4
Merkland Lodge 271 B7
Merley. 17 B4
Merlin's Bridge . 55 C5
Merrington . . .110 C3
Merrion 55 E5
Merriott 28 D4
Merrivale 11 D6
Merrow 34 A3
Merrymeet. . . . 6 A1
Mersham 38 B2
Merstham 35 A5
Merston 20 B1
Merstone 18 C4
Merther 4 C3
Merthyr. 73 D6
Merthyr Cynog . 76 D3
Merthyr-Dyfan . 41 E6
Merthyr Mawr. . 40 D3
Merthyr Tydfil (Merthyr Tudful). . .60 C2
Merthyr Vale . . 41 B5
Merton Devon. . . 25 D6
London 49 B5
Norf 103 B5
Oxon. 65 B6
Mervinslaw . .187 B5
Meshaw 26 D2
Messing 70 B2
Messingham . .141 C6
Metfield 104 C3
Metheringham . .133 C5
Methil 209 A6
Methlem 106 C1
Methley 140 A1
Methlick 256 C3
Methven 219 B5
Methwold. 102 B3
Methwold Hythe 102 B3
Mettingham . .105 C4
Mevagissey 5 C5
Mewith Head. . .145 A7
Mexborough . .140 C2
Mey 281 A4
Meysey Hampton 64 D2

Miabhag W Isles .287 D5
W Isles 288 H2
Miabhig 287 A5
Michaelchurch ...61 A7
Michaelchurch
Escley.......77 D7
Michaelchurch on
Arrow.......77 B6
Michaelston-le-
Pit 41 D6
Michaelston-y-
Fedw.......42 A1
Michaelstow 10 D1
Michaelston-super-
Ely 41 D6
Micheldever 32 B4
Michelmersh.....32 C2
Mickfield 88 A2
Micklebring......140 D3
Mickleby........169 D6
Mickleham......35 A4
Mickleover......113 B7
Micklethwaite...147 C5
Mickleton
Durham 166 C2
Glos 81 C4
Mickletown......140 A1
Mickle Trafford .127 C4
Mickley........157 D6
Mickley Square .178 C2
Mid Ardlaw......269 C4
Mid Auchinlech .204 A3
Midbea.........282 C5
Mid Beltie 244 B3
Mid Calder......208 D3
Mid Cloch
Forbie 268 D2
Mid Clyth 275 A6
Middle Assendon 47 A5
Middle Aston.....65 A5
Middle Barton....65 A5
Middlebie.......175 A5
Middle
Cairncake 256 B3
Middle Claydon ..66 A3
Middle Drums...232 C3
Middleforth
Green.........136 A4
Middleham 157 C5
Middle Handley .131 B4
Middlehope......94 C2
Middle Littleton ..80 C3
Middle Maes-
coed 78 D1
Middlemarsh.....15 A6
Middle Mill 54 B4
Middlemuir......257 D4
Middle Rasen ...133 A5
Middle Rigg.....219 D5
Middlesbrough..168 C2
Middleshaw
Cumb 155 C4
Dumfries 174 A4
Middlesmoor....157 D4
Middlestone 167 B5
Middlestone
Moor........167 B5
Middlestown ...139 B5
Middlethird 197 B5
Middleton
Aberds 245 A5
Argyll 222 C2
Cumb 155 C5
Derbys.......130 C1
Derbys.......130 D2
Essex.........87 D4
Gtr Man 138 C1
Hants 32 A3
Hereford 78 A3
Lancs 144 B4
Midloth......196 A2
Norf 118 D3
Northants.....99 C5
Northumb....178 A2
Northumb....199 C5
N Yorks......147 C5
N Yorks......159 C6
Perth 219 D6
Perth 231 D5
Shrops 93 B6
Shrops 94 D3
Shrops 110 C2

Middleton continued
Suff 89 A5
Swansea 57 D4
Warks..........97 B4
W Yorks 139 A5
Middleton
Cheney........82 C1
Middleton
Green.......112 B3
Middleton Hall .188 A2
Middleton-in-
Teesdale.....166 C2
Middleton Moor..89 A5
Middleton One
Row........167 D6
Middleton-on-
Leven 158 A3
Middleton-on-
Sea 20 B2
Middleton on the
Hill 78 A3
Middleton-on-the-
Wolds 150 C2
Middleton Priors .95 B4
Middleton
Quernham....158 D2
Middleton St
George.......167 D6
Middleton St
Scriven.......95 C4
Middleton
Stoney 65 A6
Middleton Tyas .157 A6
Middletown
Cumb 162 D2
Powys 110 D2
Middle Tysoe ...81 C6
Middle Wallop ..32 B1
Middlewich 128 C1
Middle
Winterslow ...31 B6
Middle Woodford. 31 B5
Middlewood
Green.........88 A1
Middlezoy 28 B3
Middridge 167 C5
Midfield 277 B6
Midge Hall 136 A4
Midgeholme ...176 D4
Midgham 46 C3
Midgley W Yorks .138 A3
W Yorks 139 B5
Midhopestones...139 D5
Midhurst........34 D1
Mid Lavant......20 B1
Midlem 186 A4
Mid Main 251 C6
Midmar........244 B3
Midsomer
Norton 43 D5
Midton 204 A2
Midtown Highld ..261 B5
Highld.......277 B6
Midtown of
Buchromb 254 B4
Mid Urchany ...253 B4
Midville........134 D3
Mid Walls 285 H4
Midway........129 A4
Mid Yell 284 D7
Migdale 264 A2
Migvie.........244 B1
Milarrochy 206 A2
Milborne Port...29 D6
Milborne St
Andrew 16 B2
Milborne Wick ..32 D5
Milbourne......178 B3
Milburn........165 C4
Milbury Heath...62 D2
Milcombe.......81 D7
Milden.........87 C5
Mildenhall Suff .102 D3
Wilts.........118 A3
Milebrook......93 D7
Milebush 37 B5
Mile Cross 120 D4
Mile Elm.......44 C3
Mile End Essex ...70 A3
Glos 62 B1
Mileham 119 D6
Mile Oak.......21 B5

Milesmark 208 B3
Milfield........198 C3
Milford Derbys....114 A1
Devon.........24 C3
Powys 93 B4
Staffs........112 C3
Sur 34 B2
Wilts..........31 C5
Milford Haven (Aber-
daugled-
dau) 55 D5
Milford on Sea ..18 B1
Milkwall........62 C1
Milkwell 30 C3
Milland 34 D1
Millarston.....205 B4
Highld.......280 B3
Mill Bank 138 A3
Millbeck 163 B5
Millbounds 282 D6
Millbreck 257 B5
Millbridge 34 B1
Millbrook C Beds .84 D2
Corn..........6 B3
Soton 32 D2
Millburn.......193 C4
Millcombe 8 C2
Mill Common ...105 C5
Millcorner 37 D6
Milldale........129 D6
Millden Lodge ..232 A3
Milldens.......232 C3
Mill End Bucks ...47 A5
Herts 85 D5
Millerhill 209 D6
Miller's Dale ...129 B6
Miller's Green...130 D2
Millgreen......111 C5
Mill Green Essex ..69 C6
Norf 104 C2
Suff 87 C5
Millhalf........77 C6
Millhayes 14 A2
Millhead 154 D3
Millheugh 194 A2
Mill Hill.......68 D2
Millholme 155 B4
Millhouse Argyll .203 A4
Cumb 163 A6
Millhousebridge
.......185 D4
Millhouse
Green.......139 C5
Millhouses 130 A3
Millikenpark ...205 B4
Millin Cross 55 C5
Millington 150 B1
Mill Lane 47 D5
Millmeece 112 B2
Mill of
Kingoodie 256 D3
Mill of Muiresk .256 B1
Mill of Sterin ...243 C6
Mill of Uras ...245 D5
Millom 153 B2
Millook 10 B2
Mill Place 142 C1
Millpool........10 D2
Millport 204 C1
Millquarter 182 D4
Mill Side......154 C3
Mill Street 120 D2
Millthorpe 116 B4
Millthrop......155 B5
Milltimber 245 B5
Milltown Corn 5 B6
Derbys.......130 C3
Devon........25 B6
Dumfries 175 A6
Milltown of
Aberdalgie ...219 B5
Milltown of
Auchindoun ..255 B4
Milltown of
Craigston 268 D2
Milltown of
Edinvillie 254 B3
Milltown of
Kildrummy ...244 A1
Milltown of
Rothiemay....255 B6

Milltown of
Towie 244 A1
Milnathort 219 D6
Milner's Heath .127 C4
Milngavie......205 A5
Milnrow........138 B2
Milnshaw......137 A6
Milnthorpe.....154 C3
Milo 57 A5
Milson.........95 D4
Milstead........37 A7
Milston........31 A5
Milton Angus...232 D1
Cambs 85 A6
Derbys.......113 C7
Dumfries 171 B4
Dumfries 173 A6
Dumfries 183 D6
Highld.......251 A5
Highld.......251 C6
Highld.......252 B1
Highld.......264 C3
Highld.......281 C5
Moray........267 C6
N Som 42 C2
Oxon.........65 D5
Oxon.........82 D1
Pembs 55 D6
Perth 219 C4
Ptsmth........19 B5
Stirling 217 D5
Stoke.......129 D4
W Dunb 205 A4
Milton Abbas....16 A2
Milton Abbot....11 D5
Milton Bridge .209 D5
Milton Bryan ...83 D6
Milton Clevedon. 29 B6
Milton
Coldwells 257 C4
Milton Combe ...6 A3
Milton Damerel ..25 D4
Miltonduff.....266 C2
Milton End......64 C2
Milton Ernest ...84 B2
Milton Green...127 D4
Miltonhill 266 C1
Milton Hill......65 D1
Miltonise......180 D3
Milton Keynes ..83 D5
Milton Keynes
Village 83 D5
Milton Lilbourne .45 C5
Milton Malsor ..83 B4
Milton
Morenish 217 A6
Milton of
Auchinhove...244 B2
Milton of
Balgonie 220 D3
Milton of
Buchanan ...206 A4
Milton of
Campfield ...244 B3
Milton of
Campsie.....205 A6
Milton of
Corsindae ...244 B3
Milton of
Cushnie 244 A1
Milton of
Dalcapon 230 C3
Milton of
Edradour 230 C3
Milton of
Gollanfield ...252 A3
Milton of
Lesmore 255 D5
Milton of Logie .244 B1
Milton of Murtle 245 B6
Milton of Noth .255 D6
Milton of
Tullich 243 C6
Milton on Stour .30 C1
Milton Regis ...51 C6
Milton under
Wychwood ...64 B3
Milverton Som ...27 C6
Warks..........81 A6
Milwich.......112 B3

Minard 214 C2
Minchinhampton 63 C4
Mindrum.......198 C2
Minehead......27 A4
Minera 126 D2
Minety.........63 D6
Minffordd Gwyn...91 A5
Gwyn.......107 C5
Gwyn.......123 C5
Miningsby 134 C3
Minions 10 D3
Minishant......192 D3
Minllyn 91 A6
Minnes 257 D4
Minngearraidh .286 D3
Minnigaff......171 A6
Minnonie......268 C2
Minskip........148 A2
Minstead.......32 D1
Minsted........34 D1
Minster Kent.....51 B6
Kent 53 C5
Minsterley 94 A1
Minster Lovell ..64 B4
Minsterworth ...62 B3
Minterne Magna .15 A6
Minting 134 B1
Mintlaw 257 B5
Minto 187 A4
Minton 94 B2
Minwear........55 C6
Minworth 97 B4
Mirbister 282 E4
Mirehouse 162 C2
Mireland.......281 B5
Mirfield.......139 B5
Miserden 63 C5
Miskin 41 C5
Misson 141 D4
Misterton Leics ..98 C2
Notts 141 D5
Som 15 A4
Mistley........88 D2
Mitcham.......49 C5
Mitcheldean ...62 B2
Mitchell 4 B3
Mitchel Troy ...61 B6
Mitcheltroy
Common 61 C6
Mitford........178 A3
Mithian 4 B2
Mitton 112 D2
Mixbury 82 D3
Moat 175 A4
Moats Tye 87 B6
Mobberley
Ches E 128 B2
Staffs........112 A4
Moccas 78 C1
Mochdre Conwy .124 B3
Powys 93 C4
Mochrum 171 C5
Mockbeggar 17 A5
Mockerkin 162 B3
Modbury.........7 C5
Moddershall ...112 B3
Moelfre Anglesey 123 B5
Powys 109 C6
Moffat.........184 B3
Moggerhanger ..84 C3
Moira.........113 D7
Molash 52 D2
Mol-chlach 246 C3
Mold (Yr
Wyddgrug) ..126 C2
Moldgreen 139 B4
Molehill Green ..69 A5
Molescroft.....150 C3
Molesden 178 A3
Molesworth 100 D2
Moll 247 A4
Molland 26 C3
Mollington
Ches W.......126 B3
Oxon.........82 C1
Mollinsburn ...207 C5
Monachty 75 B4
Monachylemore 217 C4
Monar Lodge...250 B4
Monaughty 77 A6
Monboddo
House.......233 A5

Mondynes 233 A5
Monevechadan ..215 B4
Monewden......88 B3
Moneydie 219 B5
Moniaive 183 C5
Monifieth 221 A4
Monikie 221 A4
Monimail 220 C2
Monington 72 B4
Monk Bretton .139 C6
Monken Hadley ..68 D2
Monk Fryston ..140 A3
Monkhopton ...95 B4
Monkland 78 B2
Monkleigh 25 C5
Monknash 40 D4
Monkokehampton
.........11 A6
Monkseaton ...179 B5
Monks Eleigh ..87 C5
Monk's Gate ...35 D5
Monks Heath...128 B3
Monk Sherborne .47 D4
Monkshill 256 B2
Monksilver 27 B5
Monks Kirby ...98 C1
Monk Soham ...88 A3
Monkspath 96 D4
Monks
Risborough ...66 C3
Monk Street 69 A6
Monkswood 61 C5
Monkton Devon ..14 A1
Kent 53 C4
Pembs 55 D5
S Ayrs.......192 C3
Monkton Combe .44 C1
Monkton Deverill. 30 B2
Monkton
Farleigh......44 C2
Monkton
Heathfield ...28 C2
Monkton Up
Wimborne....31 D4
Monkwearmouth
.........179 D5
Monkwood 33 B5
Monmouth
(Trefynwy) ...61 B7
Monmouth Cap. .61 A5
Monnington on
Wye.........78 C1
Monreith 171 C5
Monreith Mains .171 C5
Montacute 29 D4
Montcoffer Ho...268 C2
Montford Argyll .203 B6
Shrops 110 D3
Montford
Bridge 110 D3
Montgarrie 244 A2
Montgomery
(Trefaldwyn) ..93 B6
Montrave 220 D3
Montrose 233 C5
Mont Saint Guern ..6
Montsale 71 D4
Monxton........32 A2
Monyash 129 C6
Monymusk 244 A3
Monzie 218 B3
Monzie Castle ..218 B3
Moodiesburn ..207 C4
Moonzie 220 C3
Moor Allerton .148 D1
Moorby 134 C2
Moor Crichel ...16 A3
Moordown 17 B4
Moore 127 A5
Moorend.......62 C3
Moor End
E Yorks......149 D7
York 149 B5
Moorends.....141 B4
Moorgate......140 D2
Moorgreen 114 A2
Moorhall......130 B3
Moorhampton ..78 C1
Moorhead 147 D5

Moorhouse
Cumb 175 C6
Notts 132 C2
Moorlinch 28 B3
Moor Monkton . 148 B4
Moor of
Granary 253 A6
Moor of
Ravenstone. 171 C5
Moor Row 162 C3
Moorsholm 169 D4
Moorside 138 C2
Moor Street. 51 C5
Moorthorpe. . . .140 B2
Moortown Hants . .17 A5
IoW 18 C3
Lincs. 142 D2
Morangie 264 B3
Morar 235 A5
Morborne. 100 B3
Morchard Bishop 12 A2
Morcombelake. . . 14 B4
Morcott 99 A6
Morda 110 C1
Morden Dorset . . .16 B3
London 49 C5
Mordiford 78 D3
Mordon. 167 C6
More 94 B1
Morebath 27 C4
Morebattle. 187 A6
Morecambe. 144 A4
Morefield 262 A3
Moreleigh 7 B6
Morenish 217 A5
Moresby 162 B2
Moresby Parks . .162 C2
Morestead 32 C4
Moreton Dorset . .16 C2
Essex 69 C5
Mers. 136 D1
Oxon. 66 C2
Staffs 112 D1
Moreton Corbet 111 C4
Moretonhampstead
. . . . .12 C2
Moreton-in-
Marsh. 81 D5
Moreton Jeffries .79 C4
Moreton Morrell . 81 B6
Moreton on Lugg 78 C3
Moreton Pinkney 82 C2
Moreton Say 111 B5
Moreton Valence 62 C5
Morfa Carms. 57 C4
Carms. 57 C5
Morfa Bach 56 A3
Morfa Bychan . . .107 C5
Morfa Dinlle 107 A4
Morfa Glas 59 E5
Morfa Nefyn 106 B2
Morfydd 109 A6
Morgan's Vale . . .31 C5
Moriah 75 A5
Morland 164 C3
Morley Derbys . . .114 A1
Durham 166 C4
W Yorks 139 A5
Morley Green . . .128 A3
Morley St
Botolph 104 B1
Morningside
Edin 209 C5
N Lanark 194 A3
Morningthorpe. .104 B3
Morpeth 179 A4
Morphie 233 B5
Morrey 113 D5
Morris Green. . . .86 B3
Morriston 57 C6
Morston 120 A2
Mortehoe 25 A5
Mortimer 47 C4
Mortimer's Cross 78 A2
Mortimer West
End 47 C4
Mortlake. 49 B5
Morton Cumb . . .175 C6
Derbys 131 C4

Morton continued
Lincs. 116 C3
Lincs. 132 C3
Lincs. 141 D6
Norf 120 D3
Notts 132 D2
S Glos. 62 D2
Shrops 110 C1
Morton Bagot . . .80 A4
Morton-on-
Swale 157 B7
Morvah 2 B2
Morval 6 B1
Morvich Highld . .249 D6
Highld. 273 D5
Morville 95 B4
Morville Heath . . .95 B4
Morwenstow 24 D3
Mosborough 131 A4
Moscow 205 D4
Mosedale 163 A6
Moseley W Mid. . . .96 B2
W Mid 96 C3
Worcs. 79 B6
Moss Argyll 222 C2
Highld. 235 D5
S Yorks 140 B3
Wrex 126 D3
Mossat 244 A1
Mossbank 284 F6
Moss Bank 136 D4
Mossbay 162 B2
Mossblown 193 C4
Mossbrow 128 A2
Mossburnford. . .187 B5
Mossdale 173 A4
Moss Edge 144 C4
Mossend. 207 D5
Moss End 47 B6
Mosser 163 B4
Mossfield 264 C2
Mossgiel 193 C4
Mosside 232 C2
Mossley Ches E. . .128 C3
Gtr Man 138 C2
Mossley Hill. . . .126 A3
Moss of
Barmuckity . . .266 C3
Moss Pit 112 C3
Moss-side 253 A4
Moss Side 144 D3
Mosstodloch . . .266 D4
Mosston 232 D3
Mossy Lea 136 B4
Mosterton 15 A4
Moston Gtr Man . .138 C1
Shrops 111 C4
Moston Green . . .128 C2
Mostyn 125 A6
Mostyn Quay . . .125 A6
Motcombe 30 C2
Mothecombe 7 C5
Motherby 164 C2
Motherwell 194 A2
Mottingham 49 B7
Mottisfont 32 C2
Mottistone 18 C3
Mottram in
Longdendale . .138 D2
Mottram St
Andrew 128 B3
Mouilpied Guern 6
Mouldsworth. . . .127 B5
Moulin 230 C3
Moulsecoomb. . . .21 B6
Moulsford 46 A3
Moulsoe 83 C6
Moulton Ches W. . .127 C6
Lincs. 117 C6
Northants. 83 A4
N Yorks 157 A6
Suff 86 A2
V Glam 41 D5
Moulton Chapel 117 D5
Moulton
Eaugate. 117 D6
Moulton St
Mary 105 A4
Moulton Seas
End 117 C6
Mounie Castle. . .256 D2
Mount Corn. 4 B2

Mount continued
Corn 5 A6
Highld. 253 B6
Mountain 147 D4
Mountain Ash
(Aberpennar) . . .41 B5
Mountain Cross .195 B6
Mountain Water . 55 B5
Mountbenger . . .196 D2
Mount Bures 87 D5
Mount Canisp . . .264 C3
Mountfield. 37 D5
Mountgerald 264 D1
Mount Hawke 4 C2
Mountjoy 4 A3
Mountnessing . . .69 D6
Mounton. 61 D7
Mount Pleasant
Ches E 128 D3
Derbys 113 D6
Derbys 114 A1
Flint 126 B2
Hants 18 B1
W Yorks 139 A5
Mountsorrel 114 D3
Mount Sorrel. 31 C4
Mount Tabor 138 A3
Mousehole. 2 C2
Mousen. 199 C5
Mouswald 174 A3
Mow Cop 128 D3
Mowhaugh. 187 A7
Mowsley 98 C3
Moxley 96 B2
Moy Highld 240 D2
Highld. 252 C3
Moy Hall. 252 C3
Moy Ho. 265 D6
Moyles Court. . . .17 A5
Moylgrove 72 B4
Moy Lodge 240 D2
Muasdale 202 D1
Muchalls. 245 C6
Much Birch 78 D3
Much Cowarne . .79 C4
Much
Dewchurch. 78 D2
Muchelney. 28 C4
Much Hadham . . .68 B4
Much Hoole. 136 A3
Muchlarnick 5 B7
Much Marcle. 79 D4
Much Wenlock . . .95 A4
Muckernich 252 A1
Mucking. 50 A3
Muckleford 15 B6
Mucklestone 111 B6
Muckleton 111 C4
Mucktown 255 D6
Muckley Corner . .96 A3
Muckton. 134 A3
Mudale 272 A3
Muddiford 25 B6
Mudeford 17 B5
Mudford 29 D5
Mudgley 28 A4
Mugdock 205 A5
Mugeary 246 A3
Mugginton 113 A6
Muggleswick. . . .166 A3
Muie 273 D4
Muir. 242 D3
Muirden 268 D2
Muirdrum. 221 A5
Muirhead Angus. .220 A3
Fife. 220 D2
N Lanark 207 D4
S Ayrs. 192 B3
Muirhouselaw. . .187 A5
Muirhouses 208 B3
Muirkirk 194 D1
Muirmill 207 B5
Muir of
Fairburn 251 A6
Muir of Fowlis. .244 A2
Muir of Ord. 252 A1
Muir of Pert. 220 A4
Muirshearlich . . .239 D5
Muirskie 245 C5
Muirtack. 257 C4
Muirton Highld. . .264 D3

Muirton continued
Perth 218 C4
Perth 219 B6
Muirton Mains . .251 A6
Muirton of
Ardblair 231 D5
Muirton of
Ballochy. 233 B4
Muiryfold 268 D2
Muker 156 B3
Mulbarton 104 A2
Mulben 267 D4
Mulindry. 200 C3
Mullardoch
House. 250 C4
Mullion 3 D4
Mullion Cove. 3 D4
Mumby 135 B5
Munderfield Row. 79 B4
Munderfield
Stocks 79 B4
Mundesley 121 B5
Mundford 103 B4
Mundham 104 B4
Mundon 70 C2
Mundurno 245 A6
Munerigie 239 B6
Muness 284 C8
Mungasdale. 261 A6
Mungrisdale 163 A6
Munlochy 252 A2
Munsley 79 C4
Munslow 94 C3
Murchington 12 C1
Murcott 65 B6
Murkle 280 B3
Murlaggan
Highld. 238 C4
Highld. 239 D7
Murra 283 G3
Murrayfield 209 C5
Murrow. 101 A5
Mursley. 66 A4
Murthill 232 C2
Murthly 219 A5
Murton Cumb . . .165 C5
Durham 167 A6
Northumb. 198 B3
York 149 B5
Musbury. 14 B2
Muscoates 159 C5
Musdale 226 D4
Musselburgh. . . .209 C6
Muston Leics 115 B6
N Yorks 161 D4
Mustow Green . . .95 D6
Mutehill 173 D4
Mutford 105 C5
Muthill 218 C3
Mutterton 13 A5
Muxton 111 D6
Mybster 280 C3
Myddfai 59 C4
Myddle 110 C3
Mydroilyn. 74 C3
Myerscough 145 D4
Mylor Bridge 4 D3
Mynachlog-ddu . .72 C4
Myndtown. 94 C1
Mynydd Bach 75 A6
Mynydd-bach. . . .61 D6
Mynydd
Bodafon 123 B4
Mynydd-isa. 126 C2
Mynyddygarreg . .57 B4
Mynytho 106 C2
Myrebird. 245 C4
Myrelandhorn. . .281 C4
Myreside 220 B2
Myrtle Hill 59 B4
Mytchett. 34 A1
Mytholm. 138 A2
Mytholmroyd. . . .138 A3
Myton-on-
Swale. 148 A3
Mytton 110 D3

N

Naast. 261 B5
Naburn 149 C4
Nackington 52 D3
Nacton. 88 C3
Nafferton 150 B3
Na Gearrannan . .288 C2
Nailbridge 62 B2
Nailsbourne. 28 C2
Nailsea 42 B3
Nailstone 97 A7
Nailsworth. 63 D4
Nairn. 253 A4
Nalderswood. 35 B5
Nancegollan 3 B4
Nancledra 2 B2
Nanhoron. 106 C2
Nannau 108 C2
Nannerch. 125 C6
Nanpantan 114 D3
Nanpean. 5 B4
Nanstallon 5 A5
Nant-ddu 60 B2
Nanternis 73 A6
Nantgaredig 58 C1
Nantgarw. 41 C6
Nant-glas. 76 A3
Nantglyn. 125 C5
Nantgwyn 92 D3
Nantlle 107 A5
Nantmawr 110 C1
Nantmel. 76 A4
Nantmor. 107 B6
Nant Peris 107 A6
Nant Uchaf. 125 D5
Nantwich 127 D6
Nant-y-Bai 59 A4
Nant-y-cafn 59 E5
Nantycaws 57 A4
Nant-y-derry 61 C5
Nant-y-ffin 58 B2
Nantyffyllon. 40 B3
Nantyglo. 60 B3
Nant-y-moel. 40 B4
Nant-y-pandy. . . .123 C6
Naphill 66 D4
Nappa 146 B2
Napton on the
Hill 82 A1
Narberth
(Arberth). 55 C7
Narborough Leics . 98 B2
Norf 119 D4
Nasareth. 107 A4
Naseby 98 D3
Nash Bucks 83 D4
Hereford 77 A7
Newport. 42 A2
Shrops 95 D4
Nash Lee 66 C4
Nassington. 100 B2
Nasty. 68 A3
Nateby Cumb 155 A6
Lancs 145 C4
Natland. 154 C4
Naughton. 87 C6
Naunton Glos 64 A2
Worcs. 80 D1
Naunton
Beauchamp 80 B2
Navenby. 133 D4
Navestock Heath . 69 D5
Navestock Side. . .69 D5
Navidale. 274 C4
Nawton. 159 C5
Nayland 87 D5
Nazeing. 68 C4
Neacroft. 17 B5
Neal's Green 97 C6
Neap 285 H7
Near Sawrey 154 B2
Neasham 167 D6
Neath (Castell-
Nedd). 40 B2
Neath Abbey 40 B2
Neatishead 121 C5
Nebo Anglesey . . .123 A4
Ceredig 75 B4
Conwy 124 D3
Gwyn 107 A4

Necton 103 A4
Nedd 270 A4
Nedderton 179 A4
Nedging Tye 87 C6
Needham 104 C3
Needham Market. 88 B1
Needingworth. . . .101 D5
Needwood 113 C5
Neen Savage 95 D4
Neen Sollars 95 D4
Neenton 95 C4
Nefyn. 106 B3
Neilston 205 C4
Neinthirion 92 A3
Neithrop. 82 C1
Nelly Andrews
Green 93 A6
Nelson Caerph 41 B6
Lancs 146 D2
Nelson Village . . .179 B4
Nemphlar 194 B3
Nempnett
Thrubwell 43 C4
Nene Terrace 101 A4
Nenthall 165 A5
Nenthead 165 A5
Nenthorn 197 C5
Nerabus 200 C2
Nercwys. 126 C2
Nerston. 205 C6
Nesbit 198 C3
Ness. 126 B3
Nesscliffe. 110 D2
Neston Ches W. . . .126 B2
Wilts. 44 C2
Nether Alderley . .128 B3
Netheravon 31 A5
Nether Blainslie 197 B4
Nether Booth 129 A6
Netherbrae 268 D2
Netherbrough. . . .282 F4
Nether
Broughton 115 C4
Netherburn 194 B3
Nether Burrow . .155 D5
Netherbury 15 B4
Netherby Cumb . .175 A6
N Yorks 148 C2
Nether Cerne 15 B6
Nether Compton . 29 D5
Nethercote 82 A2
Nethercott 25 B5
Nether Crimond 256 D3
Nether
Dalgliesh 185 B5
Nether Dallachy 267 C4
Netherend 62 C1
Nether Exe 13 A4
Netherfield 23 A5
Nether
Glasslaw 268 D3
Netherhampton . .31 C5
Nether
Handwick 232 D1
Nether Haugh . . .140 D2
Nether Heage . . .130 D3
Nether Heyford . . .82 B3
Nether
Hindhope 187 B6
Nether
Howecleuch . . .184 A3
Nether Kellet. . . .145 A5
Nether
Kinmundy 257 B5
Nether
Langwith 131 B5
Netherlaw 173 D5
Nether Leask. . . .257 C5
Nether Lenshie. . .256 B1
Netherley Aberds .245 C5
Mers. 127 A4
Nethermill 184 D3
Nether Monynut 211 D4
Nethermuir. 257 B4
Nether Padley. . . .130 B2
Nether Park. 269 D5
Netherplace 205 C5
Nether
Poppleton 149 B4
Netherseal. 113 D6
Nether Silton 158 B3
Nether Stowey . . .28 B1

Netherthird.....182 A3
Netherthong....139 C4
Netherthorpe...131 A5
Netherton Angus 232 C3
Devon...........12 D3
Hants...........46 D1
Mers...........136 C2
Northumb......188 C2
Oxon............65 D5
Perth.........231 C5
Stirling......205 A5
W Mid..........96 C2
Worcs..........80 C2
W Yorks.......139 B4
W Yorks.......139 B5
Nethertown
Cumb..........162 D2
Highld........281 A5
Nether
Urquhart......219 D6
Nether Wallop...32 B2
Nether Wasdale 163 D4
Nether Whitacre . 97 B5
Netherwitton...189 D4
Netherwood....193 C6
Nether Worton...82 D1
Nethy Bridge..253 D6
Netley.........18 A3
Netley Marsh...32 D2
Netteswell.....69 B4
Nettlebed......47 A5
Nettlebridge...29 A6
Nettlecombe....15 B5
Nettleden......67 B6
Nettleham.....133 B6
Nettlestead....37 A4
Nettlestead
Green.........37 A4
Nettlestone....19 B5
Nettlesworth..167 A5
Nettleton Lincs.142 C3
Wilts..........44 B2
Neuadd.........58 C3
Nevendon......70 D1
Nevern.........72 B3
New Abbey.....174 B2
New Aberdour..268 C3
New Addington..49 C6
Newall........147 C5
New Alresford..33 B4
New Alyth.....231 D6
Newark Orkney..282 C8
Pboro.........100 A4
Newark-on-
Trent........132 D2
New Arley......97 C5
Newarthill....194 A2
New Ash Green..50 C3
New Barn.......50 C3
New Barnetby..142 B4
Newbarns......153 C3
New Barton.....83 A5
Newbattle.....209 D6
New Bewick....188 A3
Newbiggin Cumb 153 A1
Cumb..........153 D3
Cumb..........164 A3
Cumb..........164 C2
Cumb..........165 C4
Durham........166 C2
N Yorks.......156 B3
N Yorks.......156 C3
Newbiggin-by-the-
Sea..........179 A5
Newbigging
Angus........220 A4
Angus........221 A4
S Lanark.....195 B5
New-bigging...231 D6
Newbiggin-on-
Lune.........155 A6
New Bilton.....98 D1
Newbold Derbys. 130 B3
Leics.........114 D2
Newbold on
Avon..........98 D1
Newbold on
Stour.........81 C5
Newbold Pacey..81 B5
Newbold Verdon . 98 A1
New
Bolingbroke...134 D3

Newborough
Anglesey.....123 D4
Pboro........100 A4
Staffs.......113 C5
Newbottle
Northants.....82 D2
T&W..........179 D5
New Boultham .133 B4
Newbourne.....88 C3
New Bradwell...83 C5
New
Brancepeth...167 A5
Newbridge Caerph 41 B7
Ceredig.......75 C4
Corn...........2 B2
Corn...........6 A2
Dumfries.....174 A2
Edin.........208 C4
Hants.........32 D1
IoW...........18 C3
Pembs.........55 A5
New Bridge....110 A1
Newbridge
Green.........79 D6
Newbridge-on-
Usk..........61 D5
Newbridge on
Wye..........76 B4
New Brighton
Flint........126 C2
Mers.........136 D2
New Brinsley..131 D4
Newbrough....177 C6
New Broughton .126 D3
New
Buckenham...104 B1
Newbuildings...12 A2
Newburgh
Aberds.......257 D4
Aberds.......269 D4
Borders......185 A6
Fife.........220 C2
Lancs........136 B3
Newburn......178 C3
Newbury.......46 C2
Newbury Park..50 A1
Newby Cumb...164 C3
Lancs........146 C2
N Yorks......155 D6
N Yorks......160 B4
N Yorks......168 D3
Newby Bridge..154 C2
Newby East....176 D2
New Byth......268 D3
Newby West....175 C6
Newby Wiske...158 C2
Newcastle Mon...61 B6
Shrops........93 C6
Newcastle Emlyn
(Castell Newydd
Emlyn)......73 B6
Newcastleton or
Copshaw
Holm........176 A2
Newcastle-under-
Lyme........112 A2
Newcastle Upon
Tyne........179 C4
New Catton....120 D4
Newchapel Pembs 73 C5
Powys.........92 C3
Staffs.......128 D3
Sur...........35 B6
New Cheriton...33 C4
Newchurch Carms 73 D6
IoW...........19 C4
Kent..........38 B2
Lancs........146 D2
Mon...........61 D6
Powys.........77 B6
Staffs.......113 C5
New Costessey .120 D3
Newcott.........11 D7
New Cowper....174 D4
Newcraighall..209 C6
New Cross Ceredig 75 A5
London........49 B6
New Cumnock..182 A4
New Deer......256 B3
New Delaval...179 B4
Newdigate......35 B4
New Duston.....83 A4

New Earswick...149 B5
New Edlington .140 D3
New Elgin.....266 C3
New Ellerby...151 D4
Newell Grn.....48 B1
New Eltham.....50 B1
New End........80 B3
Newenden......37 D6
Newent.........62 A3
Newerne........62 C2
New Farnley...147 D6
New Ferry.....126 A3
Newfield Durham 167 B5
Highld.......264 C3
Newford Scilly...2 E4
Newfound......46 D3
New Fryston...140 A2
Newgale........54 B4
New Galloway..172 A4
Newgate.......120 A2
Newgate Street...68 C3
New Gilston...220 D4
New Grimsby Scilly. 2 E3
New Hainford..120 D4
Newhall Ches E..111 A5
Derbys.......113 C6
Newhall House..264 D2
Newhall Point..264 D3
Newham........189 A4
Newham Hall...189 A4
New Hartley...179 B5
Newhaven
Derbys.......129 D6
Edin.........209 C5
E Sus.........22 B2
New Haw........48 C3
New Hedges.....56 B1
New Herrington 179 D5
Newhey........138 B2
New Hinksey....65 C6
New Holkham...119 B5
New Holland...142 A2
Newholm......169 D6
New Houghton
Derbys.......131 C4
Norf.........119 C4
Newhouse.....207 D5
New Houses....155 D7
New
Humberstone..98 A3
New Hutton....155 B4
New Hythe......37 A5
Newick.........36 D2
Newingreen....38 B3
Newington Kent..38 B3
Kent..........51 C5
Kent..........53 C5
Notts........141 D4
Oxon..........65 D7
Shrops........94 C2
New Inn Carms..58 A2
Mon...........61 C6
Pembs.........55 A6
Torf..........61 D5
New Invention
Shrops........93 D6
W Mid.........96 A2
New Kelso.....249 B6
New Kingston..114 C3
New Lanark....194 B3
Newland Glos...62 C1
Hull.........150 D3
N Yorks......141 A4
Worcs.........79 C5
Newlandrig....209 D6
Newlands
Borders......186 D4
Highld.......252 B3
Moray........266 D4
Northumb.....178 D2
Newland's Corner 34 B3
Newlandsmuir..205 C6
Newlands of
Geise.......280 B2
Newlands of
Tynet.......267 C4
Newlands Park...136 B3
New Lane......136 B3
New Lane End...137 D5
New Leake.....135 D4
New Leeds.....269 D4
New Longton...136 A4

Newlot.........282 F6
New Luce......170 A3
Newlyn..........2 C2
Newmachar....245 A5
Newmains.....194 A3
New Malden.....49 C5
Newmarket Suff . 86 A2
W Isles......288 D5
New Marske....168 C4
New Marton....110 B3
New Micklefield 148 D3
Newmill Borders .186 B3
Corn...........2 B2
Moray........267 D5
New Mill Aberds .245 D4
Herts.........67 B5
Wilts.........45 C5
W Yorks......139 C4
Newmill of
Inshewan....232 B2
New Mills Ches E 128 A2
Corn...........4 B3
Derbys.......129 A4
Powys.........93 A4
Newmills of
Boyne.......267 D6
Newmiln......219 A6
Newmilns.....193 B5
New Milton.....17 B6
New Moat.......55 B6
Newnham Cambs..85 B6
Glos..........62 B2
Hants.........47 D5
Herts.........84 D4
Kent..........51 D6
Northants.....82 B2
Newnham Bridge 79 A4
New Ollerton..131 C6
New Oscott.....96 B3
Newpark.......221 C4
New Park......148 B1
New Pitsligo..268 D3
New Polzeath....9 D5
Newport Devon...25 B6
Essex.........85 D7
E Yorks......150 D1
Highld.......275 B5
IoW...........18 C4
Norf.........121 D7
Telford......111 D6
Newport
(Casnewydd)...42 A2
Newport
(Trefdraeth)...72 C3
Newport-on-
Tay.........220 B4
Newport Pagnell . 83 C5
Newpound
Common......34 D3
Newquay.........4 A3
New Quay
(Ceinewydd)...73 A6
New Rackheath .121 D4
New Radnor.....77 A6
New Rent......164 B2
New Ridley....178 D2
New Road Side .146 C3
New Romney.....38 C2
New Rossington 140 D4
New Row Ceredig..75 A6
Lancs........145 D6
N Yorks......168 D4
New Sarum......31 B5
Newsbank.....128 C3
Newseat Aberds. 256 C2
Aberds.......257 B5
Newsham
Northumb.....179 B5
N Yorks......158 C2
N Yorks......166 B4
Newsholme
E Yorks......141 A5
Lancs........146 B2
New Silksworth .179 D5
Newsome......139 B4
Newstead
Borders......197 C6
Northumb.....189 A4
Notts........131 D5
New Stevenston 194 A2
New Street....129 D5

New Street
Lane.........111 B5
New Swanage....17 C4
Newthorpe....148 D3
Newton Argyll..214 C3
Borders......187 B2
Bridgend......40 D3
Cambs.........85 C6
Cambs.......118 D1
Cardiff.......42 B1
Ches W.......127 B5
Ches W.......127 C4
Ches W.......127 D5
Cumb.........153 C3
Derbys.......131 D4
Dorset........30 D1
Dumfries.....175 A5
Dumfries.....185 C4
Gtr Man......138 D2
Hereford......78 B3
Hereford......78 D1
Highld.......252 B3
Highld.......264 D3
Highld.......271 A5
Highld.......281 D5
Lancs........144 D4
Lancs........145 B6
Lancs........155 D4
Lincs........116 B3
Moray........266 C2
Norf.........119 D5
Northants.....99 C5
Northumb.....178 C2
Notts........115 A4
Perth........218 A3
S Lanark.....194 C4
S Lanark.....205 B6
Staffs.......112 C4
Suff..........87 C5
Swansea.......57 D6
S Yorks......140 C3
Warks.........98 D2
Wilts.........31 C6
W Loth......208 C3
Newton Abbot...12 D3
Newtonairds...183 D6
Newton Arlosh .175 C4
Newton Aycliffe .167 C5
Newton Bewley .168 C2
Newton
Blossomville...83 B6
Newton
Bromswold.....84 A1
Newton
Burgoland.....97 A4
Newton by Toft. 133 A5
Newton Ferrers...7 C4
Newton
Flotman.....104 B3
Newtongrange .209 D6
Newton Hall...178 C2
Newton Harcourt .98 B3
Newton Heath. .138 C1
Newtonhill
Aberds.......245 C6
Highld.......252 B1
Newton Ho.....256 D1
Newton Kyme..148 C3
Newton-le-Willows
Mers.........137 D4
N Yorks......157 C6
Newton
Longville.....83 D5
Newton Mearns 205 C5
Newtonmill....233 B4
Newtonmore....241 C5
Newton Morrell .157 A6
Newton
Mulgrave....169 D5
Newton of
Ardtoe......235 C5
Newton of
Balanquhal .219 C6
Newton of
Falkland....220 D2
Newton on Ayr .192 C3
Newton on
Ouse........148 B4

Newton on
Trent........132 B3
Newton Park...203 B6
Newton
Poppleford....13 C5
Newton Purcell...82 D3
Newton Regis...97 A5
Newton Reigny .164 B2
Newton St Cyres. 12 B3
Newton St Faith 120 D4
Newton St Loe...43 C6
Newton St
Petrock......25 D5
Newton Solney .113 C6
Newton Stacey...32 A3
Newton Stewart 171 A6
Newton Tony....31 A6
Newton Tracey...25 C6
Newton under
Roseberry...168 D3
Newton upon
Derwent.....149 C6
Newton Valence. 33 B6
New Totley....130 B3
Newtown Argyll .214 B3
Ches W.......127 B5
Corn...........3 C5
Cumb.........174 D3
Cumb.........176 C3
Derbys.......129 A4
Devon.........26 C2
Glos..........62 C2
Glos..........80 D2
Hants.........18 A3
Hants.........31 D6
Hants.........32 C2
Hants.........32 D4
Hants.........33 D5
Hants.........46 C2
Hereford......79 C4
Highld.......240 B1
IoM..........152 D3
IoW...........18 B3
Northumb.....188 A3
Northumb.....188 A3
Northumb.....198 C3
Poole.........17 B4
Shrops......110 B3
Staffs.......129 C4
Staffs.......129 C5
Wilts.........30 C3
New Town.....210 C1
Newtown (Y
Drenewydd)...93 B5
Newtown Linford 98 A2
Newtown St.
Boswells....197 C4
Newtown
Unthank......98 A1
New Tredegar
(Tredegar
Newydd)......41 A6
New Trows.....194 C3
Newtyle......231 D6
New Ulva.....213 D5
New Walsoken .101 A6
New Waltham..143 C4
New
Whittington .130 B3
New Wimpole....85 C5
New Winton....210 C1
New Yatt.......65 B4
New York Lincs .134 D2
N Yorks......147 A5
Neyland.......55 D5
Niarbyl.......152 D2
Nibley.........43 A5
Nibley Green....62 D3
Nibon.........284 F5
Nicholashayne...27 D6
Nicholaston....57 D5
Nidd..........148 A2
Nigg Aberdeen .245 B6
Highld.......265 C4
Nigg Ferry....264 D3
Nightcott......26 C3
Nilig.........125 D5
Nine Ashes.....69 C5
Ninebanks....177 D5

Nine Mile Burn . .195 A6
Nine Wells 54 B3
Ninfield. 23 A5
Ningwood 18 C2
Nisbet 187 A5
Nisthouse Orkney 282 F4
　Shetland. 285 G7
Niton. 18 D4
Nitshill 205 B5
Noak Hill 69 D5
Noblethorpe . . .139 C5
Nobottle 82 A3
Nocton 133 C5
Noke 65 B6
Nolton. 55 C4
Nolton Haven . . . 55 C4
No Man's Heath
　Ches W. 111 A4
　Warks. 97 A5
Nomansland
　Devon. 26 D3
　Wilts. 31 D6
Noneley 110 C3
Nonikiln 264 C2
Nonington 53 D4
Noonsbrough . . .285 H4
Norbreck 144 C3
Norbridge 79 C5
Norbury Ches E . .111 A4
　Derbys 113 A5
　Shrops 94 B1
　Staffs 112 C1
Nordelph 102 A1
Norden 138 B1
Norden Heath . . . 16 C3
Nordley. 95 B4
Norham 198 B3
Norley 127 B5
Norleywood. 18 B2
Normanby
　N Lincs. 141 B6
　N Yorks. 159 C6
　Redcar 168 D3
Normanby-by-
　Spital 133 A5
Normanby by
　Stow 132 A3
Normanby le
　Wold. 142 D3
Norman Cross . . .100 B3
Nprmandy 34 A2
Norman's Bay . . . 23 B4
Norman's Green. . 13 A5
Normanstone . . .105 B6
Normanton
　Derby 114 B1
　Leics. 115 A6
　Lincs. 116 A2
　Notts 132 D2
　Rutland. 99 A6
　W Yorks 140 A1
Normanton le
　Heath 114 D1
Normanton on
　Soar 114 C2
Normanton-on-the-
　Wolds. 115 B4
Normanton on
　Trent. 132 C2
Normoss. 144 D3
Norney 34 B2
Norrington
　Common 44 C2
Norris Green 136 D2
Norris Hill 114 D1
Northacre 103 B5
Northallerton . . .158 B2
Northam Devon . . 25 C5
　Soton. 32 D3
Northampton . . . 83 A4
North Anston . . .131 A5
North Aston 65 A5
Northaw 68 C2
North Baddesley . 32 D2
North
　Ballachulish . .237 C4
North Barrow . . . 29 C6
North Barsham . .119 B6
Northbeck 116 A3

North Benfleet . . .51 A4
North Bersted. . . .20 B2
North Berwick . . .210 B2
North Boarhunt . . 33 C5
Northborough. . . .100 A3
Northbourne 53 D5
North Bovey 12 C2
North Bradley . . . 44 D2
North Brentor 11 C5
North Brewham . . 29 B7
Northbridge
　Street. 37 D5
North Buckland . . 25 A5
North
　Burlingham. . . .121 D5
North Cadbury . . 29 C6
North Cairn 180 D1
North Carlton . . .133 B4
North Carrine 190 E2
North Cave. 150 D1
North Cerney 63 C6
Northchapel 34 D2
North Charford. . .31 D5
North Charlton . .189 A4
North Cheriton . . 29 C6
Northchurch 67 C5
North Cliff 151 C5
North Cliffe 150 D1
North Clifton 132 B3
North
　Cockerington. .143 D1
North Coker. 29 D5
North Collafirth . .284 E5
North Common. . . 36 D1
North Connel 226 C4
North Cornelly . . . 40 C3
North Cotes 143 C5
Northcott 10 B4
North Cove 105 C5
North Cowton . . .157 A6
North Crawley . . . 83 C6
North Cray 50 B1
North Creake 119 B5
North Curry 28 C3
North Dalton 150 B2
North Dawn 283 G5
North Deighton . .148 B2
Northdown 53 B5
North Duffield . . .149 D5
Northdyke 282 E3
North Elkington . .143 D4
North Elmham . . .120 C1
North Elmshall . .140 B2
Northend Bath . . . 44 C1
North End Bucks . . 66 A4
　Essex 69 B6
　E Yorks 151 D5
　Hants 46 C2
　Lincs. 117 A5
　N Som 42 C3
　Ptsmth. 19 A5
　Som 28 C2
　W Sus. 21 B4
Northenden 137 D7
North Erradale . . .261 B4
North Fambridge 70 D2
North Fearns. . . .248 C2
North
　Featherstone . .140 A2
North Ferriby 142 A1
Northfield
　Aberdeen 245 B6
　Borders 211 D6
　E Yorks 142 A2
　W Mid 96 D3
Northfields 100 A2
Northfleet 50 B3
North
　Frodingham . . .151 B4
Northgate 117 C4
North Gluss 284 F5
North Gorley 31 D5
North Green
　Norf 104 C3
　Suff 89 A4
North Greetwell 133 B5
North Grimston .150 A1
North Halley 283 G6
North Halling 51 C4
North Hayling 19 A6

North Hazelrigg . .199 C4
North Heasley . . . 26 B2
North Heath. 34 D3
North Hill Cambs 101 D6
　Corn. 10 D3
North Hinksey. . . . 65 C5
North Holmwood . 35 B4
Northhouse 186 C3
North Howden . . .149 D6
North Huish. 7 B6
North Hykeham .133 C4
Northiam 37 D6
Northill 84 C3
Northington. 33 B4
North Johnston . . 55 C5
North Kelsey 142 C2
North Kelsey
　Moor. 142 C2
North Kessock . . .252 B2
North
　Killingholme. . .142 B3
North
　Kilvington 158 C3
North Kilworth . . 98 C3
North Kirkton . . .269 D6
North Kiscadale 191 C6
North Kyme 133 D6
North Lancing . . . 21 B4
Northlands 134 D3
Northlea. 179 D6
Northleach. 64 B2
North Lee 66 C4
Northleigh 14 B1
North Leigh 65 B4
North Leverton with
　Habblesthorpe 132 A2
Northlew 11 B6
North Littleton . . 80 C3
North Lopham. . . .103 C6
North Luffenham . 99 A6
North Marden . . . 33 D7
North Marston . . 66 A3
North Middleton
　Midloth. 196 A2
　Northumb. 188 A3
North Molton . . . 26 C2
Northmoor. 65 C5
Northmoor Green or
　Moorland 28 B3
North Moreton . . 46 A3
Northmuir 232 C1
North Mundham. . 20 B1
North Muskham 132 D2
North Newbald . .150 D2
North Newington 81 D7
North Newnton. . . 45 D5
North
　Nibley 62 D3
North Oakley. . . . 46 D3
North Ockendon . 50 A2
Northolt 48 A4
Northop 126 C2
Northop Hall 126 C2
North Ormesby. . .168 C3
North Ormsby . . .143 D4
Northorpe Lincs. .116 D3
　Lincs. 117 B5
　Lincs. 141 D6
North
　Otterington. . . .158 C2
Northover Som. . . 29 B4
　Som 29 C5
North Owersby . .142 D2
Northowram 139 A4
North Perrott . . . 15 A4
North Petherton. . 28 B2
North Petherwin . 10 C3
North
　Pickenham 103 A4
North Piddle 80 B2
North Poorton . . 15 B5
Northport. 16 C3
North Port 227 D5
Northpunds 285 L6
North
　Queensferry . . .208 B4
North Radworthy . 26 B2
North Rauceby . .116 A3
Northrepps 120 B4
North Reston 134 A3

North Rigton. . . .148 C1
North Rode 128 C3
North Roe 284 E5
North Runcton . . .118 D3
North Sandwick 284 D7
North Scale 153 D2
North Scarle 132 C3
North Seaton 179 A4
North Shian 226 B4
North Shields 179 C5
North Shoebury . . 51 A6
North Shore. 144 D3
North Side Cumb 162 B3
　Pboro. 101 B4
North Skelton . . .169 D4
North
　Somercotes . . .143 D6
North Stainley. . .157 D6
North
　Stainmore. 165 D6
North Stifford . . . 50 A3
North Stoke Bath. . 43 C6
　Oxon. 47 A4
　W Sus. 20 A3
North Street
　Hants 33 B5
　Kent 52 D2
　Medway 51 B5
　W Berks. 47 B4
North
　Sunderland. . . .199 C6
North Tamerton . 10 B4
North Tawton . . . 12 A1
North Thoresby .143 D4
North Tidworth . . 31 A6
North Togston . . .189 C5
Northtown. 283 H5
North
　Tuddenham . . .120 D2
North Walbottle 178 C3
North Walsham . .121 B4
North Waltham. . . 33 A4
North
　Warnborough. . .47 D5
North Water
　Bridge 233 B4
North Watten . . .280 C4
Northway 80 D2
North Weald
　Bassett. 69 C4
North Wheatley . .132 A2
North
　Whilborough . . . 8 A2
Northwich 127 B6
Northwick 43 A4
North Wick 43 C4
North
　Willingham 133 A6
North Wingfield 131 C4
North Witham . . .116 C2
Northwold 102 B3
Northwood
　Derbys 130 C2
　IoW 18 B3
　Kent 53 C5
　London. 67 D6
　Shrops 110 B3
Northwood
　Green. 62 B3
North Woolwich . .50 B1
North Wootton
　Dorset 29 D6
　Norf 118 C3
　Som 29 A5
North Wraxall . . . 44 B2
North Wroughton 45 A5
Norton E Sus. . . . 22 B2
　Glos 63 A4
　Halton 127 A5
　Herts 84 D4
　IoW 18 C2
　Mon 61 B6
　Northants. 82 A2
　Notts 131 B5
　Powys 77 A7
　Shrops 94 A3
　Shrops 94 C2
　Shrops 95 A5
　Stockton. 168 C2
　Suff 87 A5
　S Yorks 140 B3
　Wilts. 44 A2

Norton continued
　Worcs. 80 B1
　Worcs. 80 C3
　W Sus. 20 B2
　W Sus. 20 C1
Norton Bavant . . . 30 A3
Norton Bridge. . . .112 B2
Norton Canes . . . 96 A3
Norton Canon . . . 78 C1
Norton Corner . . .120 C2
Norton Disney. . . .132 D3
Norton East. 96 A3
Norton Ferris 30 B1
Norton
　Fitzwarren 28 C1
Norton Green . . . 18 C2
Norton
　Hawkfield 43 C4
Norton Heath . . . 69 C6
Norton in Hales .111 B6
Norton-in-the-
　Moors. 128 D3
Norton-Juxta-
　Twycross 97 A6
Norton-le-Clay . .158 D3
Norton Lindsey . . 81 A5
Norton
　Malreward 43 C5
Norton
　Mandeville 69 C5
Norton-on-
　Derwent. 159 D6
Norton St Philip . 43 D6
Norton sub
　Hamdon. 29 D4
Norton
　Woodseats 130 A3
Norwell. 132 C2
Norwell
　Woodhouse . . .132 C2
Norwich 104 A3
Norwick 284 B8
Norwood 131 A4
Norwood Hill. . . . 35 B5
Norwoodside 101 B6
Noseley. 99 B4
Noss 285 M5
Noss Mayo 7 C4
Nosterfield. 157 C6
Nostie 249 D5
Notgrove 64 A2
Nottage. 40 D3
Nottingham 114 B3
Nottington. 15 C6
Notton Wilts 44 C3
　W Yorks 139 B6
Nounsley 70 B1
Noutard's Green. . 79 A5
Novar House 264 D2
Nox 110 D3
Nuffield 47 A4
Nunburnholme . .150 C1
Nuncargate 131 D5
Nuneaton 97 B6
Nuneham
　Courtenay 65 D6
Nun Hills 138 A1
Nun Monkton . . .148 B4
Nunney 30 A1
Nunnington 159 D5
Nunnykirk 188 D3
Nunsthorpe 143 C4
Nunthorpe Mbro .168 D3
　York 149 B5
Nunton 31 C5
Nunwick 157 D7
Nupend. 62 C3
Nursling 32 D2
Nursted. 33 C6
Nutbourne W Sus .19 A6
　W Sus. 20 A3
Nutfield 35 A6
Nuthall 114 A3
Nuthampstead . . 85 D6
Nuthurst. 35 D4
Nutley E Sus 36 D2
　Hants 33 A5
Nutwell 140 C4
Nybster 281 B5
Nyetimber 20 C1
Nyewood 33 C7
Nymet Rowland . . 12 A2

Nymet Tracey 12 A2
Nympsfield 63 C4
Nynehead. 27 C6
Nyton. 20 B2

O

Oadby 98 A3
Oad Street 51 C5
Oakamoor 113 A4
Oakbank. 208 D3
Oak Cross. 11 B6
Oakdale 41 B6
Oake 27 C6
Oaken 95 A6
Oakenclough. . . .145 C5
Oakengates 111 D6
Oakenholt 126 B2
Oakenshaw
　Durham 167 B5
　W Yorks 139 A4
Oakerthorpe 130 D3
Oakes 139 B4
Oakfield 61 D5
Oakford Ceredig. . 74 C3
　Devon. 27 C4
Oakfordbridge . . . 27 C4
Oakgrove 129 C4
Oakham 99 A5
Oakhanger 33 B6
Oakhill 29 A6
Oakhurst 36 A3
Oakington 85 A6
Oaklands Herts . . 68 B2
　Powys 76 B4
Oakle Street 62 B3
Oakley Bedford . . 84 B2
　Bucks. 66 B2
　Fife. 208 B3
　Hants 46 D3
　Oxon. 66 C3
　Poole 17 B4
　Suff 104 D2
Oakley Green . . . 48 B2
Oakley Park 92 C3
Oakmere 127 C5
Oakridge Glos . . . 63 C5
　Hants 47 D4
Oaks 94 A2
Oaksey 63 D5
Oaks Green 113 B5
Oakthorpe 113 D7
Oakwoodhill 35 C4
Oakworth 147 D4
Oape 272 D2
Oare Kent 52 C2
　Som 26 A3
　W Berks 46 B3
　Wilts. 45 C5
Oasby 116 B3
Oathlaw 232 C2
Oatlands 148 B2
Oban Argyll 226 D3
　Highld. 238 D2
Oborne 29 D6
Obthorpe 116 D3
Occlestone
　Green 128 C1
Occold 104 D2
Ochiltree 193 C5
Ochtermuthill . . .218 C3
Ochtertyre 218 B3
Ockbrook 114 B2
Ockham 34 A3
Ockle. 235 C4
Ockley 35 C4
Ocle Pychard. . . . 78 C3
Octon 150 A3
Octon Cross
　Roads. 150 A3
Odcombe 29 D5
Odd Down 43 C6
Oddendale 164 D3
Odder 133 B4
Oddingley 80 B2
Oddington Glos . . 64 A3
　Oxon. 65 B6
Odell 83 B6
Odie 282 E7
Odiham 47 D5
Odstock 31 C5

Odstone 97 A6
Offchurch. 81 A6
Offenham. 80 C3
Offham E Sus 22 A1
  Kent 37 A4
  W Sus. 20 B3
Offord Cluny 84 A4
Offord Darcy 84 A4
Offton 87 C6
Offwell 14 B1
Ogbourne Maizey. 45 B5
Ogbourne St
  Andrew 45 B5
Ogbourne St
  George. 45 B6
Ogil 232 B2
Ogle. 178 B3
Ogmore 40 D3
Ogmore-by-Sea. . 40 D3
Ogmore Vale 40 B4
Okeford
  Fitzpaine 30 D2
Okehampton 11 B6
Okehampton
  Camp 11 B6
Okraquoy 285 K6
Old. 99 D4
Old Aberdeen . . . 245 B6
Old Alresford . . . 33 B4
Oldany. 270 A4
Old Arley 97 B5
Old Basford 114 A3
Old Basing 47 D4
Oldberrow 80 A4
Old Bewick 188 A3
Old Bolingbroke 134 C3
Oldborough. 12 A2
Old Bramhope . . . 147 C6
Old Brampton . . 130 B3
Old Bridge of
  Tilt. 230 B2
Old Bridge of
  Urr. 173 B5
Old Buckenham . 103 B6
Old Burghclere. . . 46 D2
Oldbury Shrops . . 95 B5
  Warks. 97 B6
  W Mid 96 C2
Oldbury-on-
  Severn 62 D2
Oldbury on the
  Hill 44 A2
Old Cassop. 167 B6
Oldcastle Bridgend 40 D4
  Mon 61 A5
Old Castleton . . . 186 D4
Old Catton 120 D4
Old Clee 143 C4
Old Cleeve 27 A5
Old Clipstone . . . 131 C6
Old Colwyn 124 B3
Oldcotes 131 A5
Old Coulsdon . . . 35 A6
Old Crombie 267 D6
Old Dailly 181 B4
Old Dalby 115 C4
Old Deer 257 B4
Old Denaby 140 D2
Old Edlington . . . 140 D3
Old Eldon 167 C5
Old Ellerby 151 D4
Oldfallow 112 D3
Old Felixstowe . . . 88 D4
Oldfield. 79 A6
Old Fletton 100 B3
Oldford 44 D1
Old Glossop. 138 D3
Old Goole. 141 A5
Old Hall 91 D7
Oldham. 138 C2
Oldhamstocks . . . 211 C4
Old Heath. 71 A4
Old Heathfield . . . 36 D3
Old Hill 96 C2
Old Hunstanton . . 118 A3
Old Hurst 101 D4
Old Hutton 155 C4
Old Kea. 4 D3
Old Kilpatrick . . . 205 A4
Old Kinnernie . . . 245 B4
Old Knebworth . . . 68 A2

Oldland. 43 B5
Old Langho 145 D7
Old Laxey 152 C4
Old Leake. 135 D4
Old Malton. 159 D6
Oldmeldrum 256 D3
Old Micklefield. . 148 D3
Old Milton 17 B6
Old Milverton . . . 81 A5
Old Monkland . . . 207 D5
Old Netley 18 A3
Old Philpstoun . . 208 C3
Old Quarrington 167 B6
Old Radnor 77 B6
Old Rattray 269 D5
Old Rayne. 256 D1
Old Romney 38 C2
Oldshore Beg . . . 276 C2
Oldshoremore. . . 276 C3
Old Sodbury 43 A6
Old Somerby . . . 116 B2
Oldstead. 158 C4
Old Stratford . . . 83 C4
Old Thirsk 158 C3
Oldtown 255 D6
Old Town Cumb . 155 C4
  Cumb. 164 A2
  Northumb. 188 D1
  Scilly 2 E4
Oldtown of Ord. . 267 D7
Old Trafford 137 D7
Old Tupton. 130 C3
Old Warden 84 C3
Oldway 57 D5
Oldways End 26 C3
Old Weston 100 D2
Oldwhat 268 D3
Old Whittington 130 B3
Old Wick. 281 D5
Old Windsor 48 B2
Old Wives Lees . . 52 D2
Old Woking 34 A3
Old Woodhall . . . 134 C2
Olgrinmore 280 C2
Oliver's Battery. . 32 C3
Ollaberry 284 E5
Ollerton Ches E . 128 B2
  Notts 131 C6
  Shrops 111 C5
Olmarch 75 C5
Olney 83 B5
Olrig Ho.. . . . . . 280 B3
Olton 96 C4
Olveston 43 A5
Olwen 75 D4
Ombersley 79 A6
Ompton 132 C1
Onchan 152 D3
Onecote 129 D5
Onen 61 B6
Ongar Hill 118 C2
Ongar Street 78 A1
Onibury. 94 D2
Onich 237 C4
Onllwyn 59 D5
Onneley 111 A6
Onslow Village . . . 34 B2
Onthank 205 D4
Openwoodgate . . 114 A1
Opinan Highld. . . 261 A5
  Highld. 261 C4
Orange Lane . . . 198 B1
Orange Row 118 C2
Orasaigh. 288 F4
Orbliston 266 D4
Orbost. 258 D2
Orby. 135 C4
Orchard Hill 25 C5
Orchard Portman 28 C2
Orcheston 31 A4
Orcop 61 A6
Orcop Hill 61 A6
Ord. 247 C5
Ordhead 244 A3
Ordie 244 B1
Ordiequish. 266 D4
Ordsall 132 A1
Ore. 23 A6
Oreton 95 C4
Orford Suff 89 C5
  Warr. 137 D5
Orgreave 113 D5

Orlestone. 38 B1
Orleton Hereford . 78 A2
  Worcs. 79 A4
Orlingbury 99 D5
Ormesby. 168 D3
Ormesby St
  Margaret 121 D6
Ormesby St
  Michael 121 D6
Ormiclate
  Castle. 286 C3
Ormiscaig 261 A5
Ormiston 209 D7
Ormsaigbeg. . . . 234 D3
Ormsaigmore . . . 234 D3
Ormsary 202 A2
Ormskirk 136 C3
Orpington 50 C1
Orrell Gtr Man. . . 136 C4
  Mers. 136 D2
Orrisdale 152 B3
Orroland 173 D5
Orsett 50 A3
Orslow 112 D2
Orston. 115 A5
Orthwaite 163 A5
Ortner. 145 B5
Orton Cumb.. . . . 155 A5
  Northants. 99 D5
Orton
  Longueville. . . 100 B3
Orton-on-the-
  Hill 97 A6
Orton
  Waterville. . . . 100 B3
Orwell 85 B5
Osbaldeston . . . 145 D6
Osbaldwick 149 B5
Osbaston 110 C2
Osbournby 116 B3
Oscroft 127 C5
Ose. 258 D3
Osgathorpe 114 D2
Osgodby Lincs . . 142 D2
  N Yorks. 149 D5
  N Yorks. 161 C4
Oskaig. 248 C2
Oskamull 224 B3
Osmaston Derby . 114 B1
  Derbys. 113 A6
Osmington. 16 C1
Osmington Mills. . 16 C1
Osmotherley . . . 158 B3
Ospisdale 264 B3
Ospringe 52 C2
Ossett 139 A5
Ossington 132 C2
Ostend 70 D3
Oswaldkirk 159 D5
Oswaldtwistle . . 137 A6
Oswestry 110 C1
Otford 36 A3
Otham 37 A5
Othery 28 B3
Otley Suff 88 B3
  W Yorks 147 C6
Otterbourne 32 C3
Otterburn
  Northumb.. . . . 188 D1
  N Yorks. 146 B3
Otterburn Camp 188 D1
Otter Ferry 214 D2
Otterham 10 B2
Otterhampton . . . 28 A2
Ottershaw 48 C3
Otterswick 284 E7
Otterton 13 C5
Ottery St Mary . . 13 B6
Ottinge 38 A3
Ottringham 143 A4
Oughterby 175 C5
Oughtershaw . . . 156 C2
Oughterside 174 D4
Oughtibridge. . . 139 D6
Oughtrington . . . 128 A1
Oulston. 158 D4
Oulton Cumb.. . . 175 C5
  Norf 120 C3
  Staffs. 112 B3
  Suff 105 B6
  W Yorks 139 A6

Oulton Broad . . . 105 B6
Oulton Street . . . 120 C3
Oundle 100 C2
Ousby 165 B4
Ousdale 275 B4
Ousden 86 B3
Ousefleet 141 A6
Ouston Durham . 179 D4
  Northumb. 178 B2
Outertown 282 F3
Outgate. 154 B2
Outhgill 155 A6
Outlane. 138 B3
Out Newton. . . . 143 A5
Out Rawcliffe . . . 144 C4
Outwell 101 A7
Outwick 31 D5
Outwood Sur 35 B6
  W Yorks 139 A6
Outwoods. 112 D1
Ovenden 138 A3
Ovenscloss. 196 C3
Over Cambs. 101 D5
  Ches W. 127 C6
  S Glos. 43 A4
Overbister 282 C7
Overbury 80 D2
Overcombe 15 C6
Over Compton . . . 29 D5
Overgreen 130 B3
Over Green 97 B4
Over Haddon . . . 130 C2
Over Hulton 137 C5
Over Kellet 154 D4
Over Kiddington. 65 A5
Over Knutsford. 128 B2
Overleigh 29 B4
Overley Green. . . 80 B3
Over Monnow . . . 61 B7
Over Norton. 64 A4
Over Peover 128 B2
Overpool 126 B3
Overscaig Hotel 271 B7
Overseal 113 D6
Over Silton. 158 B3
Oversland. 52 D2
Overstone 83 A5
Over Stowey 28 B1
Overstrand. 120 A4
Over Stratton 28 D2
Over Tabley 128 A2
Overthorpe 82 C1
Overton
  Aberdeen 245 A5
  Ches W. 127 A5
  Dumfries 174 B2
  Hants 32 A4
  Lancs 144 B4
  N Yorks. 149 B4
  Shrops 94 D3
  Swansea 57 D4
  W Yorks 139 A5
Overton
  (Owrtyn) 110 A2
Overton Bridge. . 110 A2
Overtown 194 A3
Over Wallop 32 B1
Over Whitacre . . . 97 B5
Over Worton 65 A5
Ovingdean 21 B6
Ovingham. 178 C2
Ovington Durham 166 D4
  Essex 86 C3
  Hants 33 B4
  Norf 103 A5
  Northumb. 178 C2
Ower 32 D2
Owermoigne 16 C1
Owlbury 93 B7
Owler Bar. 130 B2
Owlerton 130 A3
Owl's Green. 88 A3
Owlswick 66 C2
Owmby 142 C2
Owmby-by-
  Spital 133 A5
Owslebury 32 C4
Owston Leics 99 A4
  S Yorks. 140 B3
Owston Ferry . . . 141 C6

Owstwick 151 D5
Owthorne. 143 A5
Owthorpe. 115 B4
Oxborough. 102 A3
Oxcombe 134 B3
Oxenholme 154 C4
Oxenhope. 147 D4
Oxen Park 154 C2
Oxenton 80 D2
Oxenwood 45 D7
Oxford 65 C6
Oxhey 67 D7
Oxhill. 81 C6
Oxley 96 A2
Oxley Green 70 B3
Oxley's Green . . . 37 D4
Oxnam. 187 B2
Oxshott 48 C4
Oxspring 139 C5
Oxted. 36 A1
Oxton Borders. . . 196 A3
  Notts 131 D6
Oxwich 57 D4
Oxwick 119 C6
Oykel Bridge . . . 271 D6
Oyne 256 D1

P

Pabail Iarach . . . 288 D6
Pabail Uarach . . . 288 D6
Pace Gate 147 B5
Packington 114 D1
Padanaram 232 C2
Padbury 83 D4
Paddington 49 A5
Paddlesworth . . . 38 B3
Paddockhaugh . . 266 D3
Paddockhole. . . . 185 D5
Paddock Wood . . 37 B4
Padfield 138 D3
Padiham 146 D1
Padog 124 D3
Padside. 147 B5
Padstow 9 D5
Padworth 47 C4
Page Bank 167 B5
Pagham 20 C1
Paglesham
  Eastend 70 D3
Paibeil 287 H2
Paible 287 E5
Paignton 8 A2
Pailton 98 C1
Painscastle 77 C5
Painshawfield . . 178 C2
Painsthorpe. . . . 149 B7
Painswick 63 C4
Pairc Shiaboist . 288 C3
Paisley 205 B4
Pakefield 105 B6
Pakenham 87 A5
Pale. 109 B4
Palestine 31 A6
Paley Street. 47 B6
Palfrey 96 B3
Palgowan 181 C5
Palgrave. 104 D2
Pallion 179 D5
Palmarsh 38 B3
Palnackie 173 C6
Palnure 171 A6
Palterton 131 C4
Pamber End. 47 D4
Pamber Green . . . 47 D4
Pamber Heath. . . 47 C4
Pamphill. 16 A3
Pampisford 85 C6
Pan 283 H4
Panbride 221 A5
Pancrasweek 10 A3
Pandy Gwyn 90 B4
  Mon 61 A5
  Powys 91 B7
Pandy Tudur . . . 124 C3
Panfield 70 A1
Pangbourne 47 B4
Pannal. 148 B2

Panshanger 68 B2
Pant. 110 C1
Pant-glas Carms . 58 C2
  Gwyn. 107 B4
Pant-glâs 91 C5
Pant-glas. 110 B1
Pantgwyn Carms . 58 C2
  Ceredig 73 B5
Pant-lasau 57 C6
Pant Mawr 91 D6
Panton 134 B1
Pantperthog 91 B5
Pant-teg. 58 C1
Pant-y-Caws. . . . 73 D4
Pant-y-dwr 92 D3
Pant-y-ffridd . . . 93 A5
Pantyffynnon . . . 57 A6
Pantymwyn 126 C1
Pant-yr-awel 40 C4
Pant-y-Wacco . . 125 B6
Panxworth 121 D5
Papcastle 163 A4
Papigoe 281 C5
Papil 285 K5
Papley. 283 H5
Papple 210 C2
Papplewick 131 D5
Papworth
  Everard 85 A4
Papworth St
  Agnes. 85 A4
Par. 5 B5
Parbold. 136 B3
Parbrook Som . . . 29 B5
  W Sus. 34 D3
Parc. 108 B3
Parcllyn 73 A5
Parc-Seymour . . . 61 D6
Parc-y-rhôs 75 D4
Pardshaw. 162 B3
Parham 88 A4
Park 183 C7
Park Corner Oxon 47 A4
  Windsor 47 A6
Parkend 62 C2
Park End Mbro . . 168 D3
  Northumb. . . . 177 B6
Parkeston 88 D3
Parkgate Ches W 126 B2
  Dumfries 184 D3
  Kent 37 C6
  Sur. 35 B5
Park Gate 18 A4
Parkham 25 C4
Parkham Ash. . . . 25 C4
Park Hill Notts . . 132 D1
  N Yorks. 148 A2
Parkhill Ho.. . . . 245 A5
Parkhouse 61 C6
Parkhouse
  Green. 131 C4
Parkhurst 18 B3
Parkmill 57 D5
Parkneuk 233 A5
Parkstone 17 B4
Park Street 35 C4
Parley Cross 17 B4
Parracombe 26 A1
Parrog. 72 C3
Parsley Hay 129 C6
Parsonage Green 69 C7
Parsonby 163 A4
Parson Cross. . . 139 D6
Parson's Heath.. . 71 A4
Partick 205 B5
Partington 137 D6
Partney 135 C4
Parton Cumb.. . . 162 B2
  Dumfries 173 A4
  Glos 63 A4
Partridge Green. . 21 A4
Parwich 130 D1
Passenham 83 D4
Paston 121 B5
Patchacott 11 B5
Patcham 21 B6
Patching 20 B3
Patchole 25 A7

Pateley Bridge . . 147 A5
Paternoster
Heath 70 B3
Pathe 28 B3
Pathhead Aberds 233 B5
E Ayrs. 182 A4
Fife. 209 A5
Midloth. 209 D6
Path of Condie . . 219 C5
Pathstruie 219 C5
Patna. 182 A2
Patney. 45 D4
Patrick 152 C2
Patrick
Brompton 157 B6
Patrington 143 A5
Patrixbourne. 52 D3
Patterdale 164 D1
Pattingham 95 B6
Pattishall 82 B3
Pattiswick Green . 70 A2
Patton Bridge . . . 155 B4
Paul 2 C2
Paulerspury. 83 C4
Paull 142 A3
Paulton. 43 D5
Pavenham 84 B1
Pawlett. 28 A3
Pawston 198 C2
Paxford. 81 D4
Paxton. 198 A3
Payhembury 13 A5
Paythorne 146 B2
Peacehaven. 22 B2
Peak Dale. 129 B5
Peak Forest. 129 B6
Peakirk. 100 A3
Pearsie 232 C1
Peasedown St
John. 43 D6
Peasemore 46 B2
Peasenhall. 89 A4
Pease Pottage . . . 35 C5
Peaslake. 34 B3
Peasley Cross . . . 136 B4
Peasmarsh. 37 D6
Peaston 210 D1
Peastonbank. . . . 210 D1
Peathill 269 C4
Peatling Magna . . 98 B2
Peatling Parva . . . 98 C2
Peaton 94 C3
Peats Corner. 88 A2
Pebmarsh 87 D4
Pebworth. 80 C4
Pecket Well. 138 A2
Peckforton. 127 D5
Peckham 49 B6
Peckleton. 98 A1
Pedlinge. 38 B3
Pedmore 96 C2
Pedwell 28 B4
Peebles. 196 B1
Peel 152 C2
Peel Common. . . . 19 A4
Peel Park 205 C6
Peening Quarter . 37 D6
Pegsdon. 84 D3
Pegswood 179 A4
Pegwell 53 C5
Peinchorran 247 A4
Peinlich 259 C4
Pelaw 179 C4
Pelcomb Bridge. . 55 C5
Pelcomb Cross . . . 55 C5
Peldon 70 B3
Pellon 138 A3
Pelsall. 96 A3
Pelton 179 D4
Pelutho. 174 D4
Pelynt 5 B7
Pemberton. 137 C4
Pembrey. 57 B4
Pembridge. 78 B1
Pembroke
(Penfro). 55 D5
Pembroke Dock (Doc
Penfro) 55 D5

Pembury. 36 B4
Penallt 61 B7
Penally 55 E7
Penalt 62 A1
Penare 5 C4
Penarth. 41 D6
Pen-bont
Rhydybeddau. . . 91 D4
Penbryn 73 A5
Pencader 58 B1
Pencaenewydd. . 107 B4
Pencaitland. 210 D1
Pencarnisiog. . . . 122 C3
Pencarreg 75 D4
Pencelli 60 A2
Pen-clawdd. 57 C5
Pencoed 41 C4
Pencombe 78 B3
Pencoyd 61 A7
Pencraig Hereford 62 A1
Powys 109 C5
Pendeen 2 B1
Penderyn 59 E6
Pendine 56 B2
Pendlebury 137 C6
Pendleton 146 D1
Pendock 79 D5
Pendoggett 9 D6
Pendomer 29 D5
Pendoylan 41 D5
Pendre 40 C4
Pen-ffordd. 55 B6
Pengam 41 B6
Penge 49 B6
Pengenffordd. . . . 77 D5
Pengorffwysfa. . 123 A4
Pengover Green. . 6 A1
Pen-groes-oped 61 C5
Penhale Corn 3 D4
Corn. 4 B4
Penhalvaen. 4 D2
Penhill 45 A5
Penhow 61 D6
Penhurst 23 A4
Peniarth 90 B4
Penicuik. 209 D5
Peniel Carms 58 C1
Denb. 125 C5
Penifiler 259 D4
Peninver. 190 C3
Penisarwaun 123 D5
Penistone 139 C5
Penjerrick 4 D2
Penketh 127 A5
Penkill 181 B4
Penkridge. 112 D3
Penley 110 B3
Penllergaer 57 C6
Penllyn 41 D4
Pen-llyn 122 B3
Pen-lon 123 D4
Penmachno 124 D2
Penmaen 57 D5
Penmaenan 124 B2
Penmaenmawr . . 124 B2
Penmaenpool 91 A4
Penmark 41 E5
Penmarth. 4 D2
Penmon 123 B6
Penmore Mill . . . 224 A3
Penmorfa Ceredig 73 A6
Gwyn 107 B5
Penmynydd 123 C5
Penn Bucks 67 D5
W Mid 96 B1
Pennal 91 B5
Pennan 268 C2
Pennant Ceredig . 75 B4
Denb. 109 B5
Denb. 125 D5
Powys 91 C6
Pennant
Melangell 109 C5
Pennar 55 D5
Pennard 57 D5
Pennerley 94 B1
Pennington
Cumb 153 C3
Gtr Man 137 D5
Hants 18 B2
Penn Street 67 D5

Penny Bridge . . . 154 C2
Pennycross 225 D4
Pennygate 121 C5
Pennygown 225 B4
Pennymoor 26 D3
Pennywell 179 D5
Penparc Ceredig . 73 B5
Pembs 55 A4
Penparcau. 90 D3
Penperlleni 61 C5
Penpillick. 5 B5
Penpol 4 D3
Penpoll. 5 B6
Penpont
Dumfries 183 C6
Powys 59 C6
Penrherber 73 C5
Penrhiwceiber . . 41 B5
Penrhiw goch . . . 57 A5
Penrhiw-llan. 73 B6
Penrhiw-pâl 73 B6
Penrhos 106 C3
Penrhôs 61 B6
Penrhos 59 D4
Penrhosfeilw. . . . 122 B2
Penrhyn Bay . . . 124 A3
Penrhyn-coch. . . . 90 D4
Penrhyndeudraeth
. . . . 107 C6
Penrhynside 124 A3
Penrice 57 D4
Penrith 164 B3
Penrose 9 D4
Penruddock. 164 C2
Penryn 4 D2
Pensarn Carms . . 57 A4
Conwy 125 B4
Pen-sarn Gwyn . 107 B4
Gwyn 107 D5
Pensax 79 A5
Pensby 126 A2
Penselwood. 30 B1
Pensford 43 C5
Penshaw. 179 D5
Penshurst 36 B3
Pensilva 6 A1
Penston 210 C1
Pentewan 5 C5
Pentir 123 D5
Pentire 4 A2
Pentlow 87 C4
Pentney 119 D4
Penton Mewsey . 32 A2
Pentraeth. 123 C5
Pentre Carms . . . 57 A5
Powys 93 B6
Powys 93 C4
Rhondda 41 B4
Shrops 110 D2
Wrex 109 B6
Wrex 110 A1
Pentrebach
M Tydf 41 A5
Swansea 57 B6
Pentre-bâch 75 D4
Pentre-bach 59 B6
Pentrebeirdd . . . 109 D6
Pentre Berw 123 C4
Pentre-bont 124 D2
Pentrecagal. 73 B6
Pentre-celyn
Denb. 125 D6
Powys 91 B6
Pentre-chwyth. . . 57 C6
Pentre-cwrt 73 C6
Pentre Dolau-
Honddu 76 C3
Pentredwr 109 A6
Pentre-dwr 40 B1
Pentrefelin Carms 58 C2
Ceredig 75 D5
Conwy 124 B3
Gwyn 107 C5
Pentrefoelas. . . . 124 D3
Pentre-galar 73 C4
Pentregat. 73 A6
Pentre-Gwenlais 57 A6
Pentre
Gwynfryn. 107 D5
Pentre Halkyn. . 126 B2
Pentreheyling . . . 93 B6
Pentre-Isaf 124 C3

Pentre
Llanrhaeadr . . 125 C5
Pentre-llwyn-
ll yd 76 B3
Pentre-llyn 75 A5
Pentre-llyn
cymmer 125 D4
Pentre Meyrick. . 41 D4
Pentre-poeth . . . 42 A1
Pentre'r Felin . . 124 C3
Pentre'r-felin . . . 59 B6
Pentre-rhew 75 C5
Pentre-tafarn-y-
fedw 124 C3
Pentre-ty-gwyn . 59 B5
Pentrich 130 D3
Pentridge. 31 D4
Pen-twyn 61 C7
Pentyrch. 41 C6
Penuchadre. 40 D3
Penuwch 75 B4
Penwithick. 5 B5
Penwyllt 59 D5
Penybanc. 57 A6
Pen-y-banc. 58 C3
Penybont 77 A5
Pen-y-bont
Carms 73 D6
Gwyn 91 B5
Gwyn 107 D6
Powys 109 C7
Penybontfawr. . . 109 C5
Pen-y-bryn Gwyn . 91 A4
Pembs 73 B4
Pen-y-cae 59 D5
Pen-y-cae-mawr 61 D6
Pen-y-cefn 125 B6
Pen-y-clawdd . . . 61 C6
Pen-y-coedcae . . 41 C5
Penycwm 54 B4
Pen-y-fai 40 C3
Penyffordd. 126 C3
Penyffridd 107 A5
Pen-y-garn Carms 58 B2
Ceredig 90 D4
Penygarnedd. . . 109 C6
Pen-y-garnedd 123 C5
Pen-y-gop. 108 A4
Penygraig 41 B4
Pen-y-graig 106 C1
Penygroes Gwyn 107 A4
Pembs 73 C4
Pen-y-groes. 57 A5
Pen-y-groeslon 106 C2
Pen-y-Gwryd
Hotel. 107 A6
Penyrheol 41 C6
Pen-yr-heol 61 B6
Pen-yr-
Heolgerrig 60 C2
Penysarn 123 A4
Pen-y-stryt 126 D1
Penywaun 41 A4
Penzance 2 B2
Peopleton 80 B2
Peover Heath . . . 128 B2
Peper Harow. . . . 34 B2
Perceton 204 D3
Percie 244 C2
Percyhorner 269 C4
Periton 27 A4
Perivale 49 A4
Perkinsville 179 D4
Perlethorpe. 131 B6
Perranarworthal . . 4 D2
Perranporth 4 B2
Perranuthnoe 2 C3
Perranzabuloe . . . 4 B2
Perry Barr 96 B3
Perry Green Herts. 68 B4
Wilts. 44 A3
Perry Street. 50 B3
Pershall 112 B2
Pershore 80 C2
Pert 233 B4
Pertenhall 84 A2
Perth 219 B6
Perthy 110 B2
Perton 95 B6
Pertwood 30 B2

Peterborough. . . 100 B3
Peterburn 261 B4
Peterchurch 78 D1
Peterculter 245 B5
Peterhead 257 B6
Peterlee 168 A2
Petersfield. 33 C6
Peter's Green . . . 67 B7
Peters Marland. . 25 D5
Peterstone
Wentlooge 42 A1
Peterston super-
Ely. 41 D5
Peterstow 62 A1
Peter Tavy 11 D6
Petertown 283 G4
Petham 52 D3
Petrockstow 11 A6
Pett 23 A6
Pettaugh 88 B2
Petteridge 37 B4
Pettinain 195 B4
Pettistree. 88 B3
Petton Devon . . . 27 C5
Shrops 110 C3
Petts Wood 50 C1
Petty 256 C2
Pettycur 209 B5
Pettymuick 257 D6
Petworth. 34 D2
Pevensey 22 B4
Pevensey Bay . . . 23 B4
Pewsey. 45 C5
Philham 24 C3
Philiphaugh. . . . 186 A3
Phillack 2 B3
Philleigh. 4 D3
Philpstoun 208 C3
Phocle Green . . . 62 A2
Phoenix Green . . 47 D5
Pica 162 B3
Piccotts End 67 C6
Pickering. 159 C6
Picket Piece 32 A2
Picket Post 17 A5
Pickhill 158 C2
Picklescott. 94 B2
Pickletillem 220 B4
Pickmere 128 B1
Pickney 28 C1
Pickstock. 111 C6
Pickwell Devon . . 25 A5
Leics. 115 D5
Pickworth Lincs. . 116 B3
Rutland. 116 D2
Picton Ches W . 127 B4
Flint 125 A6
N Yorks. 158 A3
Piddinghoe 22 B2
Piddington
Northants. 83 B5
Oxon. 66 B2
Piddlehinton 15 B7
Piddletrenthide . . 15 B7
Pidley 101 D5
Piercebridge. . . . 167 D5
Pierowall 282 C5
Pigdon 178 A3
Pikehall 130 D1
Pilgrims Hatch . . 69 D5
Pilham 141 D6
Pill 43 B4
Pillaton 6 A2
Pillerton Hersey . 81 C6
Pillerton Priors. . 81 C5
Pilleth 77 A6
Pilley Hants. 18 B2
S Yorks. 139 C6
Pilling 144 C4
Pilling Lane. . . . 144 C3
Pillowell 62 C2
Pillwell 30 D1
Pilning 43 A4
Pilsbury 129 C6
Pilsdon 14 B4
Pilsgate 100 A2
Pilsley Derbys. . . 130 B2
Derbys. 131 C4
Pilton Devon 25 B6
Northants. 100 C2
Rutland. 99 A6
Som 29 A5

Pilton Green 57 D4
Pimperne. 16 A3
Pinchbeck 117 C5
Pinchbeck Bars . 117 C4
Pinchbeck West 117 C5
Pincheon Green 141 B4
Pinehurst 45 A5
Pinford 136 B2
Pinged 57 B4
Pinhoe 13 B4
Pinkneys Grn. . . . 47 A6
Pinley 97 D6
Pin Mill 88 D3
Pinminnoch. . . . 180 B3
Pinmore 181 B4
Pinmore Mains. . 181 B4
Pinner 48 A4
Pinvin 80 C2
Pinwherry 180 C3
Pinxton 131 D4
Pipe and Lyde . . 78 C3
Pipe Gate 111 A6
Piperhill 253 A4
Piper's Pool. 10 C3
Pipewell 99 C5
Pippacott 25 B6
Pipton 77 D5
Pirbright. 34 A2
Pirnmill 202 D3
Pirton Herts. 84 D3
Worcs. 80 C1
Pisgah Ceredig . . 75 A5
Stirling. 218 D2
Pishill 47 A5
Pistyll 106 B3
Pitagowan 230 B2
Pitblae 269 C4
Pitcairngreen . . . 219 B5
Pitcalnie 265 C4
Pitcaple 256 D2
Pitchcombe 63 C4
Pitchcott 66 A3
Pitchford 94 A3
Pitch Green 66 C3
Pitch Place 34 A2
Pitcombe 29 B6
Pitcorthie. 221 D5
Pitcox 210 C3
Pitcur 220 A2
Pitfichie 244 A3
Pitforthie 233 A6
Pitgrudy 264 A3
Pitkennedy 232 C3
Pitkevy 220 D2
Pitkierie 221 D5
Pitlessie 220 D3
Pitlochry. 230 C3
Pitmachie 256 D1
Pitmain 241 B5
Pitmedden 256 D3
Pitminster 28 D2
Pitmunie 244 A3
Pitney 29 C4
Pitscottie 220 C4
Pitsea 51 A4
Pitsford 83 A4
Pitsmoor 130 A3
Pitstone 67 B5
Pitstone Green . . 67 B5
Pittendreich . . . 266 C2
Pittentrail 273 D5
Pittenweem. . . . 221 D5
Pittington 167 A6
Pittodrie. 256 D1
Pitton 31 B6
Pittswood. 36 B4
Pittulie 269 C4
Pityme 9 D5
Pity Me 167 A5
Pityoulish 242 A2
Pixey Green. . . . 104 D3
Pixham 35 A4
Pixley 79 D4
Place Newton . . 160 D2
Plaidy 268 D2
Plains 207 D5
Plaish 94 B3
Plaistow 34 C3
Plaitford 32 D1
Plank Lane. 137 D5
Plas-canol 90 A3

Plas Gogerddan . . 90 D4
Plas Llwyngwern . 91 B5
Plas Nantyr 109 B6
Plastow Green . . 46 C3
Plas-yn-Cefn . . . 125 B5
Platt. 36 A4
Platt Bridge 137 C5
Platts Common . 139 C6
Plawsworth 167 A5
Plaxtol. 36 A4
Playden 37 D7
Playford 88 C3
Play Hatch 47 B5
Playing Place 3 C6
Playley Green . . . 79 D5
Pleasley 94 A2
Plean 207 B6
Pleasington 137 A5
Pleasley 131 C5
Pleckgate 145 D6
Plenmeller. 177 C5
Pleshey 69 B6
Plockton. 249 C5
Plocrapol 288 H2
Ploughfield 78 C1
Plowden 94 C1
Ploxgreen 94 A1
Pluckley. 38 A1
Pluckley Thorne. . 37 B7
Plumbland. 163 A4
Plumley 128 B2
Plumpton Cumb. 164 B2
    E Sus 21 A6
Plumpton Green. . 21 A6
Plumpton Head . 164 B3
Plumstead London. 50 B1
    Norf 120 B3
Plumtree 115 B4
Plungar. 115 B5
Plush. 15 A7
Plwmp. 73 A6
Plymouth 6 B3
Plympton 7 B4
Plymstock 7 B4
Plymtree. 13 A5
Pockley. 159 C5
Pocklington. . . . 149 C7
Pode Hole 117 C5
Podimore 29 C5
Podington 83 A6
Podmore 112 B1
Point Clear 71 B4
Pointon. 116 B4
Pokesdown 17 B5
Pol a Charra . . . 286 E3
Polbae 181 D4
Polbain 270 C2
Polbathic 6 B2
Polbeth. 208 D3
Polchar. 242 B1
Polebrook 100 C2
Pole Elm. 79 C6
Polegate 22 B3
Poles 264 A3
Polesworth 97 A5
Polgigga. 2 C1
Polglass 270 D3
Polgooth 5 B4
Poling 20 B3
Polkerris 5 B5
Polla 277 C4
Pollington 140 B4
Polloch 236 C1
Pollok 205 B5
Pollokshields . . . 205 B5
Polmassick 5 C4
Polmont 208 C2
Polnessan 182 A2
Polnish 235 B6
Polperro 5 B6
Polruan 5 B6
Polsham 29 A5
Polstead 87 D5
Poltalloch 213 C6
Poltimore 13 B4
Polton. 209 D5
Polwarth 197 A6
Polyphant. 10 C3
Polzeath. 9 D5
Pondersbridge . . 101 B4
Ponders End 68 D3
Pondtail 34 A1

Ponsanooth. 4 D2
Ponsworthy. 12 D2
Pont Aber. 59 C4
Pont Aber-
    Geirw 108 C2
Pontamman. 57 A6
Pontantwn. 57 A4
Pontardawe. 40 A2
Pontarddulais . . . 57 B5
Pont-ar-gothi . . . 58 C2
Pont ar Hydfer . . 59 C5
Pont-ar-llechau. . 59 C4
Pontarsais 58 C1
Pontblyddyn 126 C2
Pontbren Araeth . 58 C3
Pontbren Llwyd . 59 E6
Pont Cwm
    Pydew 109 B5
Pont Cyfyng. . . . 124 D2
Pont Cysllte. . . . 110 A1
Pont Dolydd
    Prysor. 108 B2
Pontefract 140 A2
Ponteland 178 B3
Ponterwyd 91 D5
Pontesbury 94 A1
Pontfadog 110 B1
Pontfaen 55 A6
Pont-faen 76 D3
Pont Fronwydd . 108 C3
Pont-gareg 72 B4
Pontgarreg 73 A6
Pont-Henri 57 B4
Ponthir. 61 D5
Ponthirwaun 72 B4
Pontllanfraith . . 41 B6
Pontlliw 57 B6
Pont-Llogel 109 D5
Pontllyfni 107 A4
Pontlottyn 60 C3
Pontneddfechan . 59 E6
Pontnewydd . . . 61 D4
Pont Pen-y-
    benglog 123 D6
Pontrhydfendigaid
    . . . . 75 B6
Pont Rhyd-
    goch. 124 C1
Pont-Rhyd-sarn 108 C2
Pont Rhyd-y-cyff 40 C3
Pontrhydyfen . . . 40 B2
Pont-rhyd-y-
    groes 75 A6
Pontrilas 61 A5
Pontrobert 109 D6
Pont-rug 123 D5
Ponts Green 23 A4
Pontshill 62 A2
Pont-siân. 74 D3
Pontsticill 60 B2
Pontwgan. 124 B2
Pontyates. 57 B4
Pontyberem 57 A5
Pontyclun. 41 C5
Pontycymer 40 B4
Pontyglasier . . . 72 C4
Pont-y-gwaith . . 41 B5
Pont-y-pant 124 D2
Pont y Pennant . 108 C4
Pontypool (Pont-Y-
    P l) 61 C4
Pontypridd 41 C5
Pont yr Afon-
    Gam 108 A2
Pont-yr-hafod . . 55 B5
Pontywaun 41 B7
Pooksgreen 32 D2
Pool Corn 3 A4
    W Yorks 147 C6
Poole. 17 B4
Poole Keynes . . 63 D5
Poolend 129 D4
Poolewe 261 B6
Pooley Bridge . . 164 C2
Poolfold 128 D3
Poolhill 62 A3
Pool o'
    Muckhart . . . 219 D5
Pool Quay 110 D1
Poolsbrook 131 B4
Pootings. 36 B2
Pope Hill 55 C5

Popeswood 47 C6
Popham 33 A4
Popley 49 A6
Popley. 47 D1
Porchester. 114 A3
Porchfield 18 B3
Porin 251 A5
Poringland. 104 A3
Porkellis 3 B4
Porlock. 26 A3
Porlock Weir. . . . 26 A3
Port Ann. 214 D2
Port Appin 226 B4
Port Arthur 285 K5
Port Askaig 201 B4
Portavadie. 203 B4
Port Bannatyne . 203 B5
Portbury. 43 B4
Port Carlisle . . . 175 B4
Port Charlotte. . 200 C2
Portchester 19 A5
Portclair. 240 A2
Port Clarence . . 168 C2
Port Driseach . . 203 A4
Port Ellen. 200 D3
Port
    Elphinstone . 256 C2
Portencalzie . . . 180 D2
Portencross. . . . 204 D1
Port Erin. 152 E1
Port Erroll 257 C5
Portesham. 15 C6
Portessie 267 C5
Port e Vullen. . . 152 B4
Port-Eynon 57 D4
Portfield Gate . . 55 C5
Portgate 11 C5
Port Gaverne . . . 9 C6
Port Glasgow . . 204 A3
Portgordon 267 C4
Portgower 274 C4
Porth Corn 4 A3
    Rhondda. . . . 41 B5
Porthallow Corn . . 3 C5
    Corn 6 B1
Porthcawl 40 D3
Porthcothan 9 D4
Porthcurno 2 C1
Port Henderson . 261 C4
Porthgain. 54 A4
Porthill 110 D3
Porthkerry 41 E5
Porthleven. 3 C4
Porthllechog . . . 123 A4
Porthmadog . . . 107 C5
Porthmeor 2 B2
Porth Navas 3 C5
Porthoustock . . . 3 C6
Porthpean. 5 B5
Porthtowan 3 A4
Porthyrhyd Carms 57 A5
    Carms 59 B4
Porth-y-waen. . 110 C1
Portincaple 215 C5
Portington 149 D6
Portinnisherrich
    . . . . 214 A2
Portinscale 163 B5
Port Isaac. 9 C5
Portishead. 42 B3
Portkil. 215 D5
Portknockie. . . . 267 C5
Port Lamont . . . 203 A5
Portlethen 245 C6
Portling 173 C6
Port Lion 55 D5
Portloe 4 D4
Port Logan. . . . 170 C2
Portmahomack . 265 B5
Portmeirion. . . . 107 C5
Portmellon 5 C5
Port Mholair . . . 288 D6
Port Mor. 234 C3
Portmore 18 B2
Port Mulgrave. . 169 D5
Portnacroish . . . 226 B4
Portnahaven . . . 200 C1
Portnalong 246 A2
Portnaluchaig. . 235 B5
Portnancon . . . 277 B5

Port Nan Giùran 288 D6
Port nan Long. . 287 G3
Portnellan 216 B4
Port Nis 288 A6
Portobello 209 C6
Port of
    Menteith . . . 217 D5
Porton. 31 B5
Portpatrick 170 B2
Port Quin 9 C5
Port Ramsay . . . 226 B3
Portreath 3 A4
Portree. 259 D4
Port St Mary . . 152 E2
Portscatho. 4 D3
Portsea. 19 A5
Portskerra 279 B4
Portskewett. . . . 43 A4
Portslade-by-
    Sea 21 B5
Portsmouth 19 A5
    Ptsmth 19 A5
    W Yorks 138 A2
Portsonachan . . 227 D5
Portsoy 267 C6
Port Sunlight . . 126 A3
Portswood 32 D3
Port Talbot 40 B2
Porttanachy. . . . 267 C4
Port Tennant. . . 57 C6
Portuairk 234 D3
Portway Hereford. 78 D2
    Worcs. 96 D3
Port Wemyss . . 200 C1
Port William . . . 171 C5
Portwrinkle 6 B2
Poslingford 86 C3
Postbridge 12 D1
Postcombe 66 D3
Postling 38 B3
Postwick 104 A3
Potholm 185 D6
Potsgrove 67 A5
Potten End 67 C6
Potter
    Brompton . . . 160 D3
Potterhanworth . 133 C5
Potterhanworth
    Booths 133 C5
Potter Heigham . 121 D6
Potterne 44 D3
Potterne Wick. . 44 D4
Potternewton . . 148 D2
Potters Bar 68 C2
Potter's Cross . . 95 C6
Potterspury . . . 83 C4
Potter Street. . . 69 C4
Potterton Aberds 245 A6
    W Yorks 148 D3
Potto 158 A3
Potton. 84 C4
Pott Row 119 C4
Pott Shrigley . . 129 B4
Poughill Corn . . . 10 A3
    Devon. 12 A3
Poulshot. 44 D3
Poulton Glos. . . . 64 C2
    Mers. 136 D2
Poulton-le-
    Fylde. 144 D3
Pound Bank. . . . 95 D5
Poundfield. 36 C3
Pound Green
    E Sus 36 D3
    IoW 18 C2
    Worcs. 95 D5
Pound Hill 35 C5
Poundland 180 C3
Poundon. 66 A2
Poundsgate. . . . 12 D2
Poundstock . . . 10 B3
Pound Street . . . 46 C2
Poundon 188 B3
Powderham. . . . 13 C4
Powerstock. . . . 15 B5
Powfoot 174 B4
Powick 79 B6
Powmill 208 A3
Poxwell. 16 C1
Poyle 48 B3
Poynings 21 A5
Poyntington. . . 29 D6

Poynton 129 A4
Poynton Green . 111 D4
Poystreet Green. . 87 B5
Praa Sands 2 C3
Pratt's Bottom . . 50 C1
Praze. 2 B3
Praze-an-Beeble . 3 B4
Predannack
    Wollas 3 D4
Prees. 111 B4
Preesall 144 C3
Prees Green . . . 111 B4
Preesgweene . . 110 B1
Prees Heath. . . . 111 B4
Prees Higher
    Heath 111 B4
Prees Lower
    Heath 111 B4
Prendergast . . . 198 A3
Prendwick 188 B3
Prengwyn. 73 B7
Prenteg 107 B5
Prenton 126 A3
Prescot 136 D3
Prescott 110 C3
Pressen 198 C2
Prestatyn 125 A5
Prestbury Ches E 129 B4
    Glos 63 A5
Presteigne
    (Llanandras). . 77 A7
Presthope 94 B3
Prestleigh 29 A6
Preston Borders . 198 A1
    Brighton 21 B6
    Devon. 12 D3
    Dorset 15 C7
    E Loth. 210 C2
    E Yorks 151 D4
    Glos 63 C6
    Glos 79 D4
    Herts 68 A1
    Kent 52 C2
    Kent 53 C4
    Lancs 136 A4
    Northumb. . . 189 A4
    Rutland. 99 A5
    Shrops 111 D4
    Wilts. 44 B4
    Wilts. 45 B6
Preston Bagot. . 81 A4
Preston Bissett. . 66 A1
Preston Bowyer . 27 C6
Preston
    Brockhurst . . 111 C4
Preston Brook . 127 A5
Preston
    Candover. . . . 33 A5
Preston Capes . . 82 B2
Preston
    Crowmarsh . . 65 D7
Preston
    Gubbals 110 D3
Prestonmill . . . 174 C2
Preston on Stour 81 C5
Preston on the
    Hill 127 A5
Preston on Wye . 78 C1
Prestonpans . . . 209 C6
Preston
    Plucknett. . . . 29 D5
Preston St Mary . 87 B5
Preston-under-
    Scar 157 B4
Preston upon the
    Weald Moors . 111 D5
Preston Wynne . 78 C3
Prestwich 137 C7
Prestwick
    Northumb. . . 178 B3
    S Ayrs 192 C3
Prestwood 66 C4
Price Town 40 B4
Prickwillow . . . 102 C1
Priddy 43 D4
Priesthaugh . . . 186 C3
Priest Hutton . . 154 D4
Priest Weston . . 93 B6
Primethorpe . . 98 B2
Primrose Green . 120 D2
Primrosehill . . . 67 C6
Primrose Valley . 161 D5

Princes Gate . . . 56 A1
Princes
    Risborough. . 66 C4
Princethorpe. . . 97 D7
Princetown
    Caerph 60 B3
    Devon. 11 D6
Prion 125 C5
Prior Muir 221 C5
Prior Park 198 A3
Priors Frome. . . 78 D3
Priors Hardwick . 82 B1
Priorslee 111 D6
Priors Marston . . 82 B1
Priory Wood . . . 77 C6
Priston 43 C5
Pristow Green. . 104 C2
Prittlewell 51 A5
Privett. 33 C5
Prixford 25 B6
Probus 4 C3
Proncy 264 A3
Prospect. 174 D4
Prudhoe 178 C2
Ptarmigan
    Lodge 215 B6
Pubil 228 D3
Puckeridge 68 A3
Puckington . . . 28 D3
Pucklechurch . . 43 B5
Pucknall 32 C2
Puckrup 80 D1
Puddinglake . . 128 C2
Puddington
    Ches W 126 B3
    Devon. 26 D3
Puddledock . . . 103 B6
Puddletown . . . 16 B1
Pudleston. 78 B3
Pudsey 147 D6
Pulborough . . . 20 A3
Puleston. 111 C6
Pulford 126 D3
Pulham 15 A7
Pulham Market. 104 C2
Pulham St Mary 104 C3
Pulloxhill 84 D2
Pumpherston . . 208 D3
Pumsaint 58 A3
Puncheston . . . 55 B6
Puncknowle . . . 15 C5
Punnett's Town . 36 D4
Purbrook 19 A5
Purewell. 17 B5
Purleigh 70 C2
Purley London. . . 49 C6
    W Berks 47 B4
Purlogue 93 D6
Purls Bridge . . 101 C6
Purse Caundle . 29 D6
Purslow 94 C1
Purston Jaglin . 140 B2
Purton Glos. . . . 62 C2
    Glos 62 C2
    Wilts. 45 A4
Purton Stoke. . . 64 D1
Pury End 83 C4
Pusey 65 D4
Putley 79 D4
Putney 49 B5
Putsborough . . . 25 A5
Puttenham Herts. 66 B4
    Sur 34 B2
Puxton 42 C3
Pwll 57 B4
Pwllcrochan . . . 55 D5
Pwll-glas 125 D6
Pwllgloyw 76 D4
Pwllheli 106 C3
Pwllmeyric. . . . 61 D7
Pwll-trap 56 A2
Pwll-y-glaw . . . 40 B2
Pyecombe 21 A5
Pye Corner. . . . 42 A2
Pye Green 112 D3
Pyewipe 143 B4
Pyle 18 D3

Pyle (Y Pîl)......40 C3
Pylle 29 B6
Pymoor......101 C6
Pyrford 34 A3
Pyrton......66 D2
Pytchley 99 D5
Pyworthy 10 A4

Q

Quabbs.........93 C6
Quadring 117 B5
Quainton 66 B3
Quarley......31 A6
Quarndon......114 A1
Quarrier's
  Homes.......204 B3
Quarrington....116 A3
Quarrington Hill 167 B6
Quarry Bank 96 C2
Quarryford......210 D2
Quarryhill......264 B3
Quarrywood ...266 C2
Quarter......194 A2
Quatford......95 B5
Quatt......95 C5
Quebec......167 A4
Quedgeley......63 B4
Queen Adelaide .102 C1
Queenborough 51 B6
Queen Camel 29 C5
Queen Charlton ..43 C5
Queen Dart 26 D3
Queenhill......79 D6
Queen Oak......30 B1
Queensbury....147 D5
Queensferry
  Edin......208 C4
  Flint......126 C3
Queen's Head ...110 C2
Queen's Park
  Bedford.......84 C2
  Northants......83 A4
Queenstown 144 B3
Queen Street Kent 37 B4
  Wilts......44 A4
Queenzieburn ..207 C4
Quemerford.....44 C4
Quendale......285 M5
Quendon......85 D7
Queniborough .115 D4
Quenington 64 C2
Quernmore 145 B5
Quethiock 6 A2
Quholm......282 F3
Quicks Green 46 B3
Quidenham ...103 C6
Quidhampton
  Hants......46 D3
  Wilts......31 B5
Quilquox......257 C4
Quina Brook 111 B4
Quindry......283 H5
Quinton Northants. 83 B4
  W Mid......96 C2
Quintrell Downs ...4 A3
Quixhill......113 A5
Quoditch 11 B5
Quoig......218 B3
Quorndon......114 D3
Quothquan....195 C4
Quoyloo......282 E3
Quoyness......283 G3
Quoys Shetland...284 B8
  Shetland......285 G6

R

Raasay Ho......248 C2
Rabbit's Cross....37 B5
Raby 126 B3
Rachan Mill ...195 C6
Rachub......123 D6
Rackenford 26 D3
Rackham......20 A3
Rackheath 121 D4
Racks......174 A3

Rackwick Orkney 282 C5
  Orkney.......283 H3
Radbourne.......113 B6
Radcliffe Gtr Man 137 C6
  Northumb......189 C5
Radcliffe on
  Trent......115 B4
Radclive......82 D3
Radcot......64 D3
Raddery......252 A3
Radernie......221 D4
Radford Semele ..81 A6
Radipole......15 C6
Radlett......67 D7
Radley......65 D6
Radmanthwaite .131 C5
Radmoor......111 C5
Radmore Green .127 D5
Radnage......66 D3
Radstock......43 D5
Radstone......82 C2
Radway......81 C6
Radway Green ..128 D2
Radwell Bedford...84 B2
  Herts......84 D4
Radwinter......86 D2
Radyr......41 C6
Rafford......253 A6
Ragdale......115 D4
Raglan......61 C6
Ragnall......132 B3
Rahane......215 D5
Rainford......136 C3
Rainford
  Junction......136 C3
Rainham London ..50 A2
  Medway......51 C5
Rainhill......136 D3
Rainhill Stoops..136 D4
Rainow......129 B4
Rainton......158 D2
Rainworth......131 D5
Raisbeck......155 A5
Raise......165 A5
Rait......220 B2
Raithby Lincs ...134 A3
  Lincs......134 C3
Rake......33 C7
Rakewood......138 B2
Ram......75 D4
Ramasaig......258 D1
Rame Corn 4 D2
  Corn......6 C3
Rameldry Mill
  Bank......220 D3
Ram Lane......38 A1
Rampisham 15 A5
Rampside......153 D3
Rampton Cambs...85 A6
  Notts......132 B2
Ramsbottom ...137 B6
Ramsbury......45 B6
Ramscraigs 275 B5
Ramsdean......33 C6
Ramsdell......46 D3
Ramsden
  Bellhouse 69 D7
Ramsden Heath ..69 D7
Ramsey Cambs...101 C4
  Essex......88 D3
  IoM......152 B4
Ramseycleuch .185 A5
Ramsey Forty
  Foot......101 C5
Ramsey Heights 101 C4
Ramsey Island....70 C3
Ramsey
  Mereside....101 C4
Ramsey St
  Mary's.......101 C4
Ramsgate......53 C5
Ramsgill......157 D5
Ramshorn......113 A4
Ramsnest
  Common......34 C2
Ranais......288 E5
Ranby Lincs......133 A5
  Notts......131 A6
Rand......133 B6
Randwick......63 C4

Ranfurly......204 B3
Rangag......280 D3
Rangemore 113 C5
Rangeworthy......43 A5
Rankinston 182 A2
Ranmoor......130 A3
Ranmore
  Common......35 A4
Rannerdale 163 C4
Rannoch
  Station......228 C3
Ranochan......238 D2
Ranskill......131 A6
Ranton......112 C2
Ranworth......121 D5
Raploch......207 A5
Rapness......282 C6
Rascal Moor ...149 D7
Rascarrel......173 D5
Rashiereive 257 D4
Raskelf......158 D3
Rassau......60 B3
Rastrick......139 A4
Ratagan......238 A3
Ratby......98 A2
Ratcliffe Culey ...97 B6
Ratcliffe on
  Soar......114 C2
Ratcliffe on the
  Wreake......115 D4
Rathen......269 C5
Rathillet......220 B3
Rathmell......146 B2
Ratho......208 C4
Ratho Station ..208 C4
Rathven......267 C5
Ratley......81 C6
Ratlinghope......94 B2
Rattar......281 A4
Ratten Row 144 C4
Rattery......7 A6
Rattlesden......87 B5
Rattray......231 D5
Raughton Head .164 A1
Raunds......100 D1
Ravenfield......140 D2
Ravenglass 153 A1
Raveningham ..105 B4
Ravenscar......160 A3
Ravenscraig....204 A2
Ravensdale 152 B3
Ravensden......84 B2
Ravenseat......156 A2
Ravenshead 131 D5
Ravensmoor ...127 D6
Ravensthorpe
  Northants......98 D3
  W Yorks......139 A5
Ravenstone
  Leics......114 D2
  M Keynes......83 B5
Ravenstonedale 155 A6
Ravenstown....154 D2
Ravenstruther ..194 B4
Ravensworth ...157 A5
Raw......160 A3
Rawcliffe E Yorks 141 A4
  York......149 B4
Rawcliffe
  Bridge......141 A4
Rawdon......147 D6
Rawmarsh......140 D2
Rawreth......70 D1
Rawridge......14 A2
Rawtenstall 137 A7
Raxton......256 C3
Raydon......87 D6
Raylees......188 D2
Rayleigh......70 D2
Rayne......70 A1
Rayners Lane 48 A4
Raynes Park 49 C5
Reach......86 A1
Read......146 D1
Reading......47 B5
Reading Street ...37 C7
Reagill......165 D4
Rearquhar 264 A3
Rearsby......115 D4
Reaster......281 B4
Reawick......285 J5
Reay......279 B5

Rechullin......249 A5
Reculver......53 C4
Redberth 55 D6
Redbourn......67 B7
Redbourne......142 D1
Redbrook Mon....62 B1
  Wrex......111 A4
Redburn Highld ..253 B5
  Highld......264 D1
  Northumb......177 C5
Redcar......168 C4
Redcastle Angus .233 C4
  Highld......252 B1
Redcliff Bay......42 B3
Red Dial......175 D5
Redding......205 B6
Reddingmuirhead
  ......208 C2
Reddish......138 D1
Redditch......80 A3
Rede......87 B4
Redenhall......104 C3
Redesdale
  Camp......187 D7
Redesmouth ...177 A6
Redford Aberds ..233 A5
  Angus......232 D3
  Durham......166 B3
Redfordgreen ..185 A6
Redgorton......219 B5
Redgrave......103 D6
Redhill Aberds ..245 B4
  Aberds......256 C1
  N Som......42 C3
  Sur......35 A5
Red Hill......79 B6
Redhouse......202 B3
Redhouses......200 B3
Red Houses Jersey ..6
Redisham......105 C5
Redland Bristol ...43 B4
  Orkney......282 E4
Redlingfield......104 D2
Red Lodge......102 D2
Redlynch Som....29 B7
  Wilts......31 C6
Redmarley
  D'Abitot......79 D5
Redmarshall ...167 C6
Redmile......115 B5
Redmire......156 B4
Redmoor......5 A5
Rednal......110 C2
Redpath......197 C4
Redpoint......261 D4
Red Rail......62 A1
Red Rock......137 C4
Red Roses......56 A2
Red Row......189 D5
Redruth......3 A4
Red Street......128 D3
Redvales......137 C2
Red Wharf Bay .123 B5
Redwick Newport .42 A3
  S Glos......43 A4
Redworth......167 C5
Reed......85 D5
Reedham......105 A5
Reedness......141 A5
Reeds Beck 134 C2
Reepham Lincs...133 B5
  Norf......120 C2
Reeth......156 B4
Regaby......152 B4
Regoul......253 A4
Reiff......270 C2
Reigate......35 A5
Reighton......161 D5
Reighton Gap ..161 D5
Reinigeadal 288 G3
Reiss......281 C5
Rejerrah......4 B2
Releath......3 B4
Relubbus......2 B3
Relugas......253 B6
Remenham 47 A5
Remenham Hill....47 A5
Remony......229 D6
Rempstone 114 C3
Rendcomb......63 C6
Rendham......88 A4
Rendlesham 88 B4

Renfrew......205 B5
Renhold......84 B2
Renishaw......131 B4
Rennington 189 B5
Renton......206 C1
Renwick......164 A3
Repps......121 D6
Repton......113 C7
Reraig......249 D5
Rescobie......232 C3
Resipole......235 D6
Resolis......264 D2
Resolven......40 A3
Reston......211 D5
Reswallie......232 C3
Retew......4 B4
Retford......132 A2
Rettendon......70 D1
Rettendon Place ..70 D1
Revesby......134 C2
Revesby Bridge .134 C3
Rewe......13 B4
Rew Street......18 B3
Reydon......105 D5
Reydon Smear .105 D5
Reymerston....103 A6
Reynalton......55 D6
Reynoldston 57 C4
Rezare......11 D4
Rhandirmwyn ...59 A4
Rhayader (Rhaeadr
  Gwy)......76 A3
Rhedyn......106 C2
Rhemore......225 A4
Rhencullen 152 B3
Rhes-y-cae 126 B1
Rhewl Denb......109 A6
  Denb......125 C6
Rhian......272 C3
Rhicarn......270 B3
Rhiconich......276 C3
Rhicullen......264 C2
Rhidorroch Ho..262 A3
Rhifail......278 D3
Rhigos......59 E6
Rhilochan......273 D5
Rhiroy......262 B3
Rhiw......106 D2
Rhiwbina......41 C6
Rhiwbryfdir 107 B6
Rhiwderin......42 A1
Rhiwlas Gwyn....108 B4
  Gwyn......123 D5
  Powys......109 B6
Rhodes......138 C1
Rhodesia......131 B5
Rhodes Minnis ...38 A3
Rhodiad......54 B3
Rhondda......41 B4
Rhonehouse or
  Kelton Hill....173 C5
Rhoose (Y Rhws) .41 E5
Rhôs Carms......73 C6
  Neath......40 A2
Rhosaman......59 D4
Rhosbeirio......123 A2
Rhoscefnhir....123 C5
Rhoscolyn......122 C2
Rhoscrowther....55 D5
Rhosesmor 126 C2
Rhos-fawr......106 C3
Rhosgadfan ...107 A5
Rhosgoch......123 B4
Rhos-goch......77 C5
Rhos-hill......73 B4
Rhoshirwaun....106 D1
Rhoslan......107 B4
Rhoslefain......90 B3
Rhosllanerchrugog
  ......110 A1
Rhosmaen......58 C3
Rhosmeirch....123 C4
Rhosneigr......122 C3
Rhosnesni......126 D3
Rhos-on-Sea ..124 A3
Rhosrobin......126 D3
Rhossili......57 D4
Rhosson......54 B3
Rhostryfan......107 A4
Rhostyllen......110 A2
Rhosybol......123 B4
Rhos-y-brithdir 109 C6

Rhos-y-garth 75 A5
Rhos-y-gwaliau 108 B4
Rhos-y-llan......106 C2
Rhos-y-Madoc .110 A2
Rhos-y-meirch....77 A6
Rhu Argyll......202 B3
  Argyll......215 D5
Rhuallt......125 B5
Rhuddall Heath .127 C5
Rhuddlan Ceredig .58 A1
  Denb......125 B5
Rhue......262 A2
Rhulen......77 B5
Rhunahaorine ..202 D2
Rhŷd-y-foel....125 B4
Rhyd
  Gwyn......107 B6
  Powys......92 A3
Rhydargaeau....58 C1
Rhydcymerau 58 B2
Rhydd......79 C6
Rhyd-Ddu......107 A5
Rhydding......40 B2
Rhydfudr......75 B4
Rhydlewis......73 B6
Rhydlios......106 C1
Rhydlydan......124 D3
Rhyd-moel-ddu .93 D4
Rhydness......77 C5
Rhydowen......74 D3
Rhyd-Rosser....75 B4
Rhydspence......77 C6
Rhydtalog......126 D2
Rhyd-uchaf 108 B4
Rhyd-wen......91 A5
Rhydwyn......122 B3
Rhyd-y-clafdy .106 C3
Rhydycroesau ..110 B1
Rhydyfelin Ceredig 75 A4
  Rhondda......41 C5
Rhyd-y-fro 59 E4
Rhyd-y-gwin....57 B6
Rhydymain......108 C3
Rhyd-y-meirch....61 C5
Rhyd-y-
  meudwy......125 D6
Rhydymwyn....126 C2
Rhyd-y-pandy....57 B6
Rhyd-yr-onen....90 B4
Rhyd-y-sarn ...107 B6
Rhyl (Y Rhyl)....125 A5
Rhymney
  (Rhymni)......60 C3
Rhynd Fife......221 B4
  Perth......219 B6
Rhynie Aberds ..255 D5
  Highld......265 C4
Ribbesford......95 D5
Ribblehead 155 D6
Ribbleton......145 D5
Ribchester......145 D6
Ribigill......277 C6
Riby......142 C3
Riby Cross
  Roads......142 C3
Riccall......149 D5
Riccarton......193 B4
Richards Castle ..78 A2
Richings Park 48 B3
Richmond London .49 B4
  N Yorks......157 A5
Rickarton 245 D5
Rickinghall 103 D6
Rickleton......179 D4
Rickling......85 D6
Rickmansworth ..67 D6
Riddings Cumb ..175 A7
  Derbys......131 D4
Riddlecombe....25 D7
Riddlesden 147 C4
Riddrie......205 B6
Ridge Dorset......16 C3
  Hants......32 D2
  Wilts......30 B3
Ridgebourne....77 A4
Ridge Green 35 B6
Ridgehill......43 C4
Ridge Lane......97 B5
Ridgeway Cross .79 C5
Ridgewell......86 C3
Ridgewood......22 A2
Ridgmont......84 D1

Riding Mill......178 C2
Ridleywood....127 D4
Ridlington Norf ..121 B5
 Rutland.......99 A5
Ridsdale......177 A7
Riechip......231 D4
Riemore.......230 D4
Rienachait....270 A3
Rievaulx......159 C4
Rift House 168 B2
Rigg.........175 B5
Riggend......207 C5
Rigsby........135 B4
Rigside.......194 C3
Riley Green....137 A5
Rileyhill......113 D5
Rilla Mill.......10 D3
Rillington......160 D2
Rimington.....146 C2
Rimpton........29 C6
Rimswell......143 A5
Rinaston.......55 B5
Ringasta......285 M5
Ringford......173 C4
Ringinglow....130 A2
Ringland......120 D3
Ringles Cross...36 D2
Ringmer........22 A2
Ringmore........7 C5
Ringorm......254 B3
Ring's End.....101 A5
Ringsfield.....105 C5
Ringsfield
 Corner......105 C5
Ringshall Herts ...67 B5
 Suff..........87 B6
Ringshall Stocks .87 B6
Ringstead Norf...119 A4
 Northants.......100 D1
Ringwood.......17 A5
Ringwould......39 A5
Rinmore......243 A7
Rinnigill......283 H4
Rinsey.........2 C3
Riof..........288 D2
Ripe..........22 A3
Ripley Derbys ..130 D3
 Hants.........17 B5
 N Yorks.......148 A1
 Sur...........34 A3
Riplingham....150 D2
Ripon.........157 D7
Rippingale....116 C3
Ripple Kent......39 A5
 Worcs........79 D6
Ripponden....138 B3
Rireavach.....262 A2
Risabus......200 D3
Risbury.......78 B3
Risby.........86 A3
Risca (Rhisga)...60 D4
Rise..........151 C4
Riseden........36 C4
Risegate......117 C5
Riseholme....133 B4
Riseley Bedford....84 A2
 Wokingham......47 C5
Rishangles......88 A2
Rishton......146 D1
Rishworth....138 B3
Rising Bridge ..137 A6
Risley Derbys ..114 B2
 Warr.........137 D5
Risplith......147 A6
Rispond......277 B5
Rivar..........45 C7
Rivenhall End ...70 B2
River Bank.....86 A1
Riverhead......36 A3
Rivington.....137 B5
Roachill.......26 C3
Roade........83 B4
Road Green....104 B3
Roadhead.....176 B3
Roadmeetings .194 B3
Roadside......280 B3
Roadside of
 Catterline...233 A6
Roadside of
 Kinneff......233 A6
Roadwater.....27 B5
Roag.........258 D2

Roa Island.....153 D3
Roath..........41 D6
Roberton
 Borders......186 B3
 S Lanark......194 D4
Robertsbridge....37 D5
Roberttown....139 A4
Robeston Cross ..55 D4
Robeston
 Wathen......55 C6
Robin Hood....139 A6
Robin Hood's
 Bay.........160 A3
Roborough Devon..7 A4
 Devon........25 D6
Roby..........136 D3
Roby Mill......136 C4
Rocester......113 B5
Roch..........55 B4
Rochdale......138 B1
Roche..........5 A4
Rochester
 Medway.......51 C4
 Northumb......188 D1
Rochford........70 D2
Rock Corn........9 D5
 Northumb......189 A5
 Worcs........95 D5
 W Sus........21 A4
Rockbeare......13 B5
Rockbourne....31 D5
Rockcliffe Cumb .175 B6
 Dumfries......173 C6
Rock Ferry....126 A3
Rockfield Highld .265 B5
 Mon.........61 B6
Rockford......17 A5
Rockhampton....62 D2
Rockingham....99 B5
Rockland All
 Saints.......103 B5
Rockland St
 Mary........104 A4
Rockland St
 Peter.......103 B5
Rockley........45 B5
Rockwell End ...47 A5
Rockwell Green..27 C6
Rodborough....63 C4
Rodbourne
 Swindon......45 A5
 Wilts.........44 A3
Rodbourne
 Cheney.......45 A5
Rodd..........77 A7
Roddam......188 A3
Rodden.......15 C6
Rode..........44 D2
Rodeheath....128 C3
Rode Heath....128 D3
Roden.......111 D4
Rodhuish......27 B5
Rodington....111 D4
Rodley Glos.....62 B3
 W Yorks......147 D6
Rodmarton....63 D5
Rodmell.......22 B2
Rodmersham....51 C6
Rodney Stoke...42 D3
Rodsley......113 A6
Rodway.......28 B2
Rodwell.......15 D6
Roecliffe......148 A2
Roe Green.....85 D5
Roehampton....49 B5
Roesound.....284 G5
Roffey.........35 C4
Rogart......273 D5
Rogart Station ..273 D5
Rogate.......33 C7
Rogerstone....42 A1
Roghadal.....287 F5
Rogiet........42 A3
Rogue's Alley ...101 A5
Roke..........66 D2
Roker.......179 D6
Rollesby.....121 D6
Rolleston Leics...99 A4
 Notts.......132 D2
Rolleston-on-
 Dove.......113 C6

Rolston.......151 C5
Rolvenden......37 C6
Rolvenden Layne .37 C6
Romaldkirk....166 C2
Romanby......158 B2
Romannobridge .195 B6
Romansleigh....26 C2
Romford........50 A2
Romiley......138 D2
Romsey........32 C2
Romsey Town ...85 B6
Romsley Shrops ...95 C5
 Worcs........96 D2
Ronague......152 D2
Rookhope.....166 A2
Rookley........18 C4
Rooks Bridge....42 D2
Roos..........151 D5
Roosebeck.....153 D3
Rootham's Green .84 B3
Rootpark......195 A4
Ropley........33 B5
Ropley Dean....33 B5
Ropsley......116 B2
Rora.........269 D5
Rorandle......244 A3
Rorrington.....93 A7
Roscroggan......3 A4
Rose..........4 B2
Roseacre Kent.....37 A5
 Lancs......144 D4
Rose Ash......26 C2
Rosebank.....194 B3
Rosebrough....189 A4
Rosebush......55 B6
Rosecare......10 B2
Rosedale Abbey .159 B6
Roseden......188 A3
Rosefield.....253 A4
Rose Green....20 C2
Rose Grove....146 D2
Rosehall......272 D2
Rosehaugh
 Mains......252 A2
Rosehearty....269 C4
Rosehill......111 B5
Rose Hill E Sus...22 A2
 Lancs......146 D2
 Suff..........88 C2
Roseisle......266 C2
Roselands......22 B4
Rosemarket.....55 D5
Rosemarkie....252 A3
Rosemary Lane...27 D6
Rosemount....231 D5
Rosenannon.....5 A4
Rosewell......209 D5
Roseworth....168 C2
Roseworthy.....3 B4
Rosgill......164 D3
Roshven......235 C6
Roskhill......258 D2
Roskill House ..252 A2
Roslin......209 D5
Rosliston....113 D6
Rosneath.....215 D5
Ross Dumfries...172 D4
 Northumb......199 C5
 Perth.......218 B2
Rossett......126 D3
Rossett Green ..148 B2
Rossie Ochill...219 C5
Rossie Priory...220 A2
Rossington....140 D4
Rosskeen.....264 D2
Rossland.....205 A4
Ross-on-Wye...62 A2
Roster.......281 E4
Rostherne....128 A2
Rosthwaite....163 C5
Roston.......113 A5
Rosyth......208 B4
Rothbury.....188 C3
Rotherby.....115 D4
Rotherfield....36 D3
Rotherfield Greys 47 A5
Rotherfield
 Peppard......47 A5
Rotherham....140 D2
Rothersthorpe...83 B4
Rotherwick....47 D5

Rothes........254 B3
Rothesay.....203 B5
Rothiebrisbane..256 C2
Rothienorman...256 C2
Rothiesholm....282 E7
Rothley Leics...114 D3
 Northumb......178 A2
Rothley Shield
 East........188 D3
Rothmaise....256 C1
Rothwell Lincs ..142 D3
 Northants.......99 C5
 W Yorks......139 A6
Rothwell Haigh..139 A6
Rotsea.......150 B3
Rottal.......232 B1
Rotten End.....89 A4
Rottingdean....21 B6
Rottington....162 C2
Roud..........18 C4
Rougham Norf...119 C5
 Suff..........87 A5
Rougham Green...87 A5
Roughburn.....240 D1
Rough Close....112 B3
Rough Common ..52 D3
Roughlee.....146 C2
Roughley......96 B4
Roughsike....176 B3
Roughton Lincs .134 C2
 Norf.......120 B4
 Shrops........95 B5
Roughton Moor .134 C2
Roundhay.....148 D2
Roundstreet
 Common......34 D3
Roundway......44 C4
Rousdon.......14 B2
Rous Lench....80 B3
Routenburn....204 B1
Routh.......150 C3
Row Corn.......10 D1
 Cumb.......154 C3
Rowanburn....175 A7
Rowardennan...206 A1
Rowde..........44 C3
Rowen.......124 B2
Rowfoot......177 C4
Row Heath......71 B5
Rowhedge......71 A4
Rowhook.......35 C4
Rowington......81 A5
Rowland......130 B2
Rowlands Castle..33 D6
Rowlands Gill ..178 D3
Rowledge......33 A7
Rowlestone....61 A5
Rowley E Yorks..150 D2
 Shrops........93 A7
Rowley Hill....139 B4
Rowley Regis...96 C2
Rowly..........34 B3
Rowney Green...96 D3
Rownhams......32 D2
Rowrah......162 C3
Rowsham......66 B4
Rowsley......130 C2
Rowstock......46 A2
Rowston.......133 D5
Rowton Ches W...127 C5
 Shrops........110 D2
 Telford.......111 D5
Roxburgh......197 C6
Roxby N Lincs ..141 B7
 N Yorks......169 D5
Roxton........84 B3
Roxwell.......69 C6
Royal Leamington
 Spa........81 A6
Royal Oak Darl...167 C5
 Lancs.......136 C3
Royal Tunbridge
 Wells........36 C3
Roybridge.....239 D6
Roydhouse....139 B5
Roydon Essex...68 C4
 Norf.......104 C1
 Norf.......119 C4
Roydon Hamlet...68 C4
Royston Herts....85 C5
 S Yorks......139 B6

Royton.......138 C2
Rozel Jersey..........6
Ruabon
 (Rhiwabon)....110 A2
Ruaig.......222 C3
Ruan Lanihorne...4 C3
Ruan Minor.....3 D5
Ruarach......249 D6
Ruardean......62 B2
Ruardean
 Woodside.....62 B2
Rubery........96 D2
Ruckcroft....164 A3
Ruckhall......78 D2
Ruckinge......38 B2
Ruckland.....134 B3
Ruckley.......94 A3
Ruckley.......94 A3
Rudbaxton.....55 B5
Rudby.......158 A3
Ruddington....114 B3
Rudford.......62 A3
Rudge Shrops....95 B6
 Som.........44 D2
Rudgeway......43 A5
Rudgwick......34 C3
Rudhall.......62 A2
Rudheath....128 B1
Rudley Green...70 C2
Rudry........41 C6
Rudston......150 A3
Rudyard......129 D4
Rufford......136 B3
Rufforth.....148 B4
Rugby........98 D2
Rugeley......112 D4
Ruglen......181 A4
Ruilick......251 B7
Ruishton......28 C2
Ruisigearraidh...287 F4
Ruislip.......48 A3
Ruislip Common..48 A3
Rumbling
 Bridge......208 A3
Rumburgh....104 C4
Rumford........9 D4
Rumney........41 D7
Runcorn......127 A5
Runcton.......20 B1
Runcton Holme .102 A2
Rundlestone....11 D6
Runfold........34 B1
Runhall......103 A6
Runham Norf...105 A6
 Norf.......121 D6
Runnington....27 C6
Runsell Green...70 C1
Runswick Bay ..169 D6
Runwell.......70 D1
Ruscombe.....47 B5
Rushall Hereford..79 D4
 Norf.......104 C2
 Wilts.........45 D5
 W Mid........96 A3
Rushbrooke....87 A4
Rushbury......94 B3
Rushden Herts...85 D5
 Northants.......83 A6
Rushenden....51 B6
Rushford......103 C5
Rush Green....50 A2
Rush-head.....256 B3
Rushlake Green ..22 A4
Rushmere.....105 C5
Rushmere St
 Andrew......88 C3
Rushmoor......33 B6
Rushock.......96 D1
Rusholme....138 D1
Rushton Ches W..127 C5
 Northants.......99 C5
 Shrops........95 A4
Rushton
 Spencer......129 C4
Rushwick......79 B6
Rushyford....167 C5
Ruskie.......217 D6
Ruskington...133 D5
Rusland......154 C2
Rusper........35 C5
Ruspidge......62 B2
Russell's Water ..47 A5
Russel's Green..104 D3

Rusthall.......36 C3
Rustington......20 B3
Ruston.......160 C3
Ruston Parva...150 A3
Ruswarp......160 A2
Rutherford....197 C5
Rutherglen....205 B6
Ruthernbridge...5 A5
Ruthin
 (Rhuthun)....125 D6
Ruthrieston...245 B6
Ruthven Aberds .255 B6
 Angus.......231 D6
 Highld.......241 C5
 Highld.......253 C4
Ruthven House .231 D7
Ruthvoes.......4 A4
Ruthwell.....174 B3
Ruyton-XI-
 Towns.......110 C2
Ryal.........178 B2
Ryal Fold.....137 A5
Ryall.........14 B4
Ryarsh........37 A4
Rydal........154 A2
Ryde..........19 B4
Rye...........37 D7
Ryecroft Gate ..129 C4
Rye Foreign....37 D6
Rye Harbour....38 D1
Ryehill......143 A4
Rye Park......68 B3
Rye Street.....79 D5
Ryhall......116 D3
Ryhill.......140 B1
Ryhope......179 D6
Rylstone.....146 B3
Ryme Intrinseca..29 D5
Ryther.......149 D4
Ryton Glos......79 D5
 N Yorks......159 D6
 Shrops........95 A5
 T&W........178 C3
Ryton-on-
 Dunsmore.....97 D6

S

Sabden.......146 D1
Sacombe......68 B3
Sacriston.....167 A5
Sadberge.....167 D6
Saddell......190 B3
Saddington....98 B3
Saddle Bow....118 D3
Saddlescombe...21 A5
Sadgill......154 A3
Saffron Walden...86 D1
Sageston......55 D6
Saham Hills...103 A5
Saham Toney...103 A5
Saighdinis....287 H3
Saighton.....127 C4
St Abbs......211 D6
St Agnes Corn.....4 B2
 Scilly..........2 F3
St Albans......67 C7
St Allen........4 B3
St Andrews....221 C5
St Andrew's
 Major........41 D6
St Anne Ald........6
St Annes......136 A2
St Ann's.....184 C3
St Ann's Chapel
 Corn.......11 D5
 Devon.........7 C5
St Anthony-in-
 Meneage......3 C5
St Anthony's Hill..22 B4
St Arvans......61 D7
St Asaph
 (Llanelwy)...125 B5
St Athan......41 E5
St Aubin Jersey......6
St Austell......5 B5
St Bees......162 C2
St Blazey.......5 B5

St Brelade *Jersey* 6
St Breock 9 D5
St Breward 10 D1
St Briavels 62 C1
St Bride's 54 C4
St Brides Major . . 40 D3
St Bride's
  Netherwent 42 A3
St Brides super
  Ely 41 D5
St Brides
  Wentlooge 42 A1
St Budeaux 6 B3
Saintbury 80 D4
St Buryan 2 C2
St Catherine 44 B1
St Catherine's . . 215 B4
St Clears
  (Sanclêr) 56 A2
St Cleer 6 A1
St Clement 4 C3
St Clements *Jersey* . . 6
St Clether 10 C3
St Colmac 203 B5
St Columb Major . . 4 A4
St Columb Minor . . 4 A3
St Columb Road . . 4 B4
St Combs 269 C5
St Cross South
  Elmham 104 C3
St Cyrus 233 B5
St David's 218 B4
St David's
  (Tyddewi) 54 B3
St Day 4 C2
St Dennis 4 B4
St Devereux 78 D2
St Dogmaels 73 B4
St Dogwells 55 B5
St Dominick 6 A3
St Edith's 44 C3
St Endellion 9 D5
St Enoder 4 B3
St Erme 4 B3
St Erney 6 B2
St Erth 2 B3
St Ervan 9 D4
St Eval 4 A3
St Ewe 5 C4
St Fagans 41 D6
St Fergus 269 D5
St Fillans 217 B6
St Florence 55 D6
St Genny's 10 B2
St George 125 B4
St George's 41 D5
St Germans 6 B2
St Giles 133 B4
St Giles in the
  Wood 25 D6
St Giles on the
  Hth 11 B4
St Harmon 92 D3
St Helena 97 A5
St Helen
  Auckland 167 C4
St Helens *IoW* . . 19 C5
  Mers 136 D4
St Helen's 23 A6
St Helier *Jersey* . . . 6
  London 49 C5
St Hilary *Corn* 2 B3
  V Glam 41 D5
Saint Hill 36 C1
St Illtyd 41 A7
St Ippolytts 68 A1
St Ishmael's 54 D4
St Issey 9 D5
St Ive 6 A2
St Ives *Cambs* . . 101 D5
  Corn 2 A3
  Dorset 17 A5
St James South
  Elmham 104 D4
St Jidgey 9 E5
St John 6 B3
St John's *IoM* . . . 152 C2
  Jersey 6

St John's *continued*
  Sur 34 A2
  Worcs 79 B6
St John's
  Chapel 166 B1
St John's Fen
  End 118 D2
St John's
  Highway 118 D2
St John's Town of
  Dalry 182 D4
St Judes 152 B3
St Just 2 B1
St Just in
  Roseland 4 D3
St Katherine's . . 256 C2
St Keverne 3 C5
St Kew 9 D6
St Kew Highway . . 9 D6
St Keyne 6 A1
St Lawrence *Corn* . . 5 A4
  Essex 70 C3
  IoW 18 D4
St Leonards
  Dorset 17 A5
  E Sus 23 B5
St Leonard's . . . 67 C5
Saint Leonards . . 205 C6
St Levan 2 C1
St Lythans 41 D6
St Mabyn 9 D6
St Madoes 219 B6
St Margarets . . . 68 B3
St Margaret's . . . 78 D1
St Margaret's at
  Cliffe 39 A5
St Margaret South
  Elmham 104 C4
St Mark's 152 D2
St Martin 6 B1
St Martins *Corn* . . . 3 C5
  Perth 219 A6
St Martin's *Jersey* . . . 6
  Shrops 110 A2
St Mary Bourne . . 46 D2
St Mary Church . . 41 D5
St Mary Cray . . . 50 C1
St Mary Hill 41 D4
St Mary Hoo 51 B5
St Mary in the
  Marsh 38 C2
St Mary's *Jersey* . . . 6
  Orkney 283 G5
St Mary's Bay . . . 38 C2
St Maughans . . . 61 B6
St Mawes 4 D3
St Mawgan 4 A3
St Mellion 6 A2
St Mellons 42 A1
St Merryn 9 D4
St Mewan 5 B4
St Michael
  Caerhays 5 C4
St Michael
  Penkevil 4 C3
St Michaels 78 A3
St Michael's . . . 37 C6
St Michael's on
  Wyre 145 C4
St Michael South
  Elmham 104 C4
St Minver 9 D5
St Monans 221 D5
St Neot 5 A6
St Neots 84 A3
St Newlyn East . . . 4 B3
St Nicholas *Pembs* 72 C1
  V Glam 41 D5
St Nicholas at
  Wade 53 C4
St Ninians 207 A5
St Osyth 71 B5
St Osyth Heath . . 71 B5
St Ouens *Jersey* . . . 6
St Owens Cross . . 62 A1
St Paul's Cray . . 50 C1
St Paul's Walden . 68 A1
St Peter Port *Guern* . . 6
St Peter's *Jersey* . . . 6
  Kent 53 C5
St Petrox 55 E5
St Pinnock 5 A7

St Quivox 192 C3
St Ruan 3 D5
St Sampson *Guern* . . . 6
St Stephen 4 B4
St Stephens *Corn* . . 6 B3
  Herts 67 C7
St Stephen's . . . 10 C4
St Teath 9 C6
St Thomas 13 B4
St Tudy 9 D6
St Twynnells . . . 55 E5
St Veep 5 B6
St Vigeans 233 D4
St Wenn 5 A4
St Weonards . . . 61 A6
Salcombe 7 D6
Salcombe Regis . 13 C6
Salcott 70 B3
Sale 137 D6
Saleby 135 B4
Sale Green 80 B2
Salehurst 37 D5
Salem *Carms* . . . 58 C3
  Ceredig 91 D4
Salen *Argyll* . . 225 B4
  Highld 235 D5
Salesbury 145 D6
Salford *C Beds* . . 83 D6
  Gtr Man 137 D7
  Oxon 64 A3
Salford Priors . . 80 B3
Salfords 35 B5
Salhouse 121 D5
Saline 208 A3
Salisbury 31 C5
Sallachan 236 C3
Sallachy *Highld* . 249 C6
  Highld 272 D3
Salle 120 C3
Salmonby 134 B3
Salmond's Muir . 221 A5
Salperton 64 A1
Salph End 84 B2
Salsburgh 207 D6
Salt 112 C3
Saltaire 147 D5
Saltash 6 B3
Saltburn 264 D3
Saltburn-by-the-
  Sea 169 C4
Saltby 115 C6
Saltcoats *Cumb* . 153 A1
  N Ayrs 204 D2
Saltdean 22 B1
Salt End 142 A3
Salter 145 A6
Salterforth 146 C2
Salterswall 127 C6
Saltfleet 143 D6
Saltfleetby All
  Saints 143 D6
Saltfleetby St
  Clements . . . 143 D6
Saltfleetby St
  Peter 135 A4
Saltford 43 C5
Salthouse 120 A2
Saltmarshe . . . 141 A5
Saltney 126 C3
Salton 159 D6
Saltwick 178 B3
Saltwood 38 B3
Salum 222 C3
Salvington 21 B4
Salwarpe 80 A1
Salwayash 15 B4
Sambourne 80 A3
Sambrook 111 C6
Samhla 287 H2
Samlesbury . . . 145 D5
Samlesbury
  Bottoms 137 A5
Sampford
  Arundel 27 D6
Sampford Brett . 27 A5
Sampford
  Courtenay . . . 12 A1
Sampford
  Peverell 27 D5
Sampford Spiney 11 D6
Sampool Bridge 154 C3
Samuelston . . . 210 C1

Sanachan 249 B5
Sanaigmore . . . 200 A2
Sancreed 2 C2
Sancton 150 D2
Sand *Highld* . . . 261 A6
  Shetland 285 J5
Sandaig 247 D6
Sandale 175 D5
Sandal Magna . 139 B6
Sandbach 128 C2
Sandbank 215 D4
Sandbanks 17 C4
Sandend 267 C6
Sanderstead . . . 49 C6
Sandfields 63 A5
Sandford *Cumb* 165 D5
  Devon 12 A3
  Dorset 16 C3
  IoW 18 C4
  N Som 42 D3
  Shrops 111 B4
  S Lanark . . . 194 B2
Sandfordhill . . . 257 B6
Sandford on
  Thames 65 C6
Sandford Orcas . 29 C6
Sandford St
  Martin 65 A5
Sandgate 38 B3
Sandgreen 172 C3
Sandhaven 269 C4
Sandhead 170 C2
Sandhills 34 C2
Sandhoe 178 C1
Sand Hole 149 D7
Sandholme
  E Yorks 150 D1
  Lincs 117 B6
Sandhurst *Brack* . 47 C6
  Glos 63 A4
  Kent 37 D5
Sandhurst Cross . 37 D5
Sandhutton . . . 158 C2
Sand Hutton . . . 149 B5
Sandiacre 114 B2
Sandilands *Lincs* 135 A5
  S Lanark . . . 194 C3
Sandiway 127 B6
Sandleheath . . . 31 D5
Sandling 37 A5
Sandlow Green . 128 C2
Sandness 285 H3
Sandon *Essex* . . 70 C1
  Herts 85 D5
  Staffs 112 B3
Sandown 19 C4
Sandplace 6 B1
Sandridge *Herts* 67 B7
  Wilts 44 C3
Sandringham . . 118 C3
Sandsend 169 D6
Sandside Ho . . 279 B5
Sandsound . . . 285 J5
Sandtoft 141 C5
Sandway 37 A6
Sandwell 96 C3
Sandwich 53 D5
Sandwick *Cumb* 164 D2
  Orkney 283 J5
  Shetland 285 L6
Sandwith 162 C2
Sandy *Carms* . . 57 B4
  C Beds 84 C3
Sandy Bank . . . 134 D2
Sandycroft . . . 126 C3
Sandyford
  Dumfries 185 C5
  Stoke 128 C3
Sandygate 152 B3
Sandy Haven . . . 55 D4
Sandhills 173 C6
Sandylands . . . 144 A4
Sandy Lane *Wilts* . 44 C3
Sangobeg 277 B5
Sangomore . . . 277 B5
Sanna 234 D3
Sanndabhaig
  W Isles 286 B4
  W Isles 288 D5

Sannox 203 D5
Sanquhar 183 B5
Santon 142 B1
Santon Bridge . 163 D4
Santon
  Downham . . . 103 C4
Sapcote 98 B1
Sapey Common . 79 A5
Sapiston 103 D5
Sapley 100 D4
Sapperton *Glos* . 63 C5
  Lincs 116 B3
Saracen's Head 117 C6
Sarclet 281 D5
Sardis 57 B5
Sarn *Bridgend* . . 40 C4
  Powys 93 B6
Sarnau *Carms* . . 56 A3
  Ceredig 73 A6
  Gwyn 109 B4
  Powys 76 D4
  Powys 110 D1
Sarn Bach . . . 106 D3
Sarnesfield . . . 78 B1
Sarn Meyllteyrn 106 C2
Saron *Carms* . . 57 A6
  Carms 73 C6
  Denb 125 C5
  Gwyn 107 A4
  Gwyn 123 D5
Sarratt 67 D6
Sarre 53 C4
Sarsden 64 A3
Sarsgrum 277 B4
Satley 166 A4
Satron 156 B3
Satterleigh 26 C1
Satterthwaite . . 154 B2
Satwell 47 A5
Sauchen 244 A3
Saucher 219 A6
Sauchie 208 A1
Sauchieburn . . 233 B4
Saughall 126 B3
Saughtree . . . 187 D4
Saul 62 C3
Saundby 132 A2
Saundersfoot . . 56 B1
Saunderton . . . 66 C3
Saunton 25 B5
Sausthorpe . . 134 C3
Saval 272 D3
Savary 225 B5
Savile Park . . . 138 A3
Sawbridge 82 A2
Sawbridgeworth . 69 B4
Sawdon 160 C3
Sawley *Derbys* . 114 B2
  Lancs 146 C1
  N Yorks 147 A6
Sawston 85 C6
Sawtry 100 C3
Saxby *Leics* . . 115 D6
  Lincs 133 A5
Saxby All Saints 142 B1
Saxelbye 115 C5
Saxham Street . 88 A1
Saxilby 132 B3
Saxlingham . . . 120 B2
Saxlingham
  Green 104 B3
Saxlingham
  Nethergate . . 104 B3
Saxlingham
  Thorpe 104 B3
Saxmundham . . 89 A4
Saxondale . . . 115 B4
Saxon Street . . 86 B2
Saxtead 88 A3
Saxtead Green . 88 A3
Saxthorpe . . . 120 B3
Saxton 148 D3
Sayers Common . 21 A5
Scackleton . . . 159 D5
Scadabhagh . . 288 H2
Scaftworth . . . 141 D4
Scagglethorpe . 160 D2
Scaitcliffe . . . 137 A6
Scalasaig . . . 212 C1
Scalby *E Yorks* . 141 A6
  N Yorks 160 B4
Scaldwell 99 D4

Scaleby 176 C2
Scaleby Hill . . . 176 C2
Scale Houses . . 164 A3
Scales *Cumb* . . 153 C3
  Cumb 163 B6
  Lancs 145 D4
Scalford 115 C5
Scaling 169 D5
Scallastle . . . 225 C5
Scalloway . . . 285 K6
Scalpay 288 H3
Scalpay Ho . . . 247 B5
Scalpsie 203 C5
Scamadale . . . 235 A6
Scamblesby . . 134 B2
Scamodale . . . 236 B2
Scampston . . . 160 D2
Scampton . . . 133 B4
Scapa 283 G5
Scapegoat Hill . 138 B3
Scar 282 C7
Scarborough . . 160 C4
Scarcliffe 131 C4
Scarcroft 148 C2
Scarcroft Hill . . 148 C2
Scardroy 250 A4
Scarff 284 E4
Scarfskerry . . . 281 A4
Scargill 166 D3
Scarinish 222 C3
Scarisbrick . . . 136 B2
Scarning 119 D6
Scarrington . . . 115 A5
Scartho 143 C4
Scarwell 282 E3
Scatness 285 M5
Scatraig 252 C3
Scawby 142 C1
Scawsby 140 C3
Scawton 158 C4
Scayne's Hill . . 35 D6
Scethrog 60 A3
Scholar Green . 128 D3
Scholes *W Yorks* 139 A4
  W Yorks 139 C4
  W Yorks 148 D2
School Green . . 127 C6
Scleddau 55 A5
Scofton 131 A4
Scole 104 D2
Scolpaig 287 G2
Scone 219 B6
Sconser 247 A4
Scoonie 220 D3
Scoor 224 E3
Scopwick 133 D5
Scoraig 262 A2
Scorborough . . 150 C3
Scorrier 4 C2
Scorton *Lancs* . 145 C5
  N Yorks 157 A6
Sco Ruston . . . 121 C4
Scotbheinn . . . 286 A4
Scotby 176 D2
Scotch Corner . 157 A6
Scotforth 145 B4
Scothern 133 B5
Scotland Gate . 179 A4
Scotlandwell . . 219 D6
Scotsburn . . . 264 C3
Scotscalder
  Station 280 C2
Scotscraig . . . 220 B4
Scot's Gap . . . 178 A2
Scotston *Aberds* 233 A5
  Perth 230 D3
Scotstoun . . . 205 B5
Scotstown . . . 236 C2
Scotswood . . . 178 C3
Scottas 247 D6
Scotter 141 C6
Scotterthorpe . 141 C6
Scottlethorpe . 116 C3
Scotton *Lincs* . 141 D6
  N Yorks 148 B2
  N Yorks 157 B5
Scottow 121 C4
Scoughall . . . 210 B3
Scoulag 203 C6
Scoulton 103 A5
Scourie 276 D2
Scourie More . . 276 D2

Scousburgh.... 285 M5
Scrabster...... 280 B2
Scrafield...... 134 C3
Scrainwood.... 188 A2
Scrane End 117 A6
Scraptoft...... 98 A3
Scratby...... 121 D7
Scrayingham.. 149 A6
Scredington... 116 A3
Scremby...... 135 C4
Scremerston.. 198 B4
Screveton..... 115 A5
Scrivelsby.... 134 C2
Scriven...... 148 B2
Scrooby...... 141 D4
Scropton...... 113 B5
Scrub Hill..... 134 D2
Scruton...... 157 B6
Sculcoates.... 150 D3
Sculthorpe... 119 B5
Scunthorpe... 141 B6
Scurlage...... 57 D4
Seaborough... 14 A4
Seacombe..... 136 D2
Seacroft Lincs .135 C5
  W Yorks 148 D2
Seadyke...... 117 B6
Seafield S Ayrs. .192 C3
  W Loth......208 B3
Seaford...... 22 C2
Seaforth...... 136 D2
Seagrave...... 115 D4
Seaham...... 168 A2
Seahouses.... 199 C6
Seal...... 36 A3
Sealand...... 126 C3
Seale...... 34 B1
Seamer N Yorks .160 C4
  N Yorks......168 D2
Seamill...... 204 D2
Sea Palling... 121 C6
Searby...... 142 C2
Seasalter..... 52 C2
Seascale...... 162 D3
Seathorne.... 135 C5
Seathwaite
  Cumb......153 A3
  Cumb......163 C5
Seatoller..... 163 C5
Seaton Corn ... 6 B2
  Cumb......162 A3
  Devon...... 14 B2
  Durham......179 D5
  E Yorks......151 C4
  Northumb....179 B5
  Rutland...... 99 B6
Seaton Burn .. 179 B4
Seaton Carew .168 C3
Seaton Delaval .179 B5
Seaton Ross .. 149 C6
Seaton Sluice .179 B5
Seatown Aberds..267 C6
  Dorset...... 14 B4
Seave Green ..159 A4
Seaview...... 19 B5
Seaville...... 175 C4
Seavington St
  Mary...... 28 D3
Seavington St
  Michael...... 28 D4
Sebergham... 164 A1
Seckington.... 97 A5
Second Coast .261 A6
Sedbergh..... 155 B5
Sedbury...... 62 D1
Sedbusk...... 156 B2
Sedgeberrow... 80 D3
Sedgebrook... 115 B6
Sedgefield.... 167 C6
Sedgeford.... 119 B4
Sedgehill..... 30 C2
Sedgley...... 96 B2
Sedgwick..... 154 C4
Sedlescombe... 23 A5
Sedlescombe
  Street......23 A5
Seend...... 44 C3
Seend Cleeve .. 44 C3
Seer Green.... 67 D5
Seething...... 104 B4
Sefton...... 136 C2
Seghill...... 179 B4

Seifton...... 94 C2
Seighford..... 112 C2
Seilebost..... 287 E5
Seion...... 123 D5
Selattyn...... 110 B1
Selborne..... 33 B6
Selby...... 149 D5
Selham...... 34 D2
Selhurst...... 49 C6
Selkirk...... 186 A3
Sellack...... 62 A1
Sellafirth.... 284 D7
Sellibister... 282 C8
Sellindge..... 38 B2
Sellindge Lees .. 38 B3
Selling...... 52 D2
Sells Green.... 44 C3
Selly Oak..... 96 C3
Selmeston.... 22 B3
Selsdon...... 49 C6
Selsey...... 20 C1
Selsfield
  Common......35 C6
Selsted...... 39 A4
Selston...... 131 D4
Selworthy.... 27 A4
Semblister.... 285 H5
Semer...... 87 C5
Semington.... 44 C2
Semley...... 30 C2
Send...... 34 A3
Send Marsh... 34 A3
Senghenydd... 41 B6
Sennen...... 2 C1
Sennen Cove... 2 C1
Sennybridge (Pont
  Senni)......59 C6
Serlby...... 131 A6
Sessay...... 158 D3
Setchey...... 118 D3
Setley...... 18 A2
Setter Shetland .284 E6
  Shetland......285 H5
  Shetland......285 J7
Settiscarth... 282 F4
Settle...... 146 A2
Settrington... 160 D2
Sevenhampton . 63 A6
Seven Kings... 50 A1
Sevenoaks..... 36 A3
Sevenoaks Weald 36 A3
Seven Sisters .. 59 E5
Severn Beach .. 43 A4
Severnhampton . 64 D3
Severn Stoke... 79 C6
Sevington..... 38 A2
Sewards End... 86 D1
Sewardstone... 68 D3
Sewardstonebury 68 D3
Sewerby...... 151 A4
Seworgan..... 4 D2
Sewstern..... 116 C1
Sezincote..... 81 D4
Sgarasta Mhor . 287 E5
Sgiogarstaigh .288 A6
Shabbington... 66 C2
Shackerstone .. 97 A6
Shackleford... 34 B2
Shade...... 138 A2
Shadforth.... 167 A6
Shadingfield .. 105 C5
Shadoxhurst... 38 B1
Shadsworth... 137 A6
Shadwell Norf .103 C5
  W Yorks......148 C5
Shaftesbury... 30 C2
Shafton...... 140 B1
Shalbourne... 45 C7
Shalcombe.... 18 C2
Shalden...... 33 A5
Shaldon...... 13 D4
Shalfleet..... 18 C3
Shalford Essex .. 69 A7
  Sur......34 B3
Shalford Green .. 69 A7
Shallowford... 26 A2
Shalmsford
  Street......52 D2
Shalstone.... 82 D3
Shamley Green .. 34 B3

Shandon...... 215 D5
Shandwick.... 265 C4
Shangton...... 99 B4
Shankhouse... 179 B4
Shanklin...... 19 C4
Shanquhar.... 255 C6
Shanzie...... 231 C6
Shapwick Dorset .. 16 A3
  Som...... 28 B4
Shardlow..... 114 B2
Shareshill..... 96 A2
Sharlston..... 140 B1
Sharlston
  Common......140 B1
Sharnbrook... 84 B1
Sharnford..... 98 B1
Sharoe Green .. 145 D5
Sharow...... 158 D2
Sharpenhoe... 84 D2
Sharperton... 188 C2
Sharpness..... 62 C2
Sharp Street .. 121 C5
Sharpthorne... 35 C6
Sharrington... 120 B2
Shatterford.... 95 C5
Shaugh Prior... 7 A4
Shavington... 128 D2
Shaw Gtr Man .138 C2
  W Berks......46 C2
  Wilts......44 C2
Shawbury..... 111 C4
Shawdon Hall .188 B3
Shawell...... 98 C2
Shawford..... 32 C3
Shawforth.... 138 A1
Shaw Green... 136 B4
Shawhead..... 173 A6
Shawhill...... 175 B5
Shaw Mills.... 147 A6
Shawton...... 194 B1
Shawtonhill .. 194 B1
Shear Cross... 30 A2
Shearington... 174 B3
Shearsby...... 98 B3
Shebbear..... 11 A5
Shebdon...... 111 C6
Shebster..... 279 B6
Sheddens..... 205 C5
Shedfield..... 33 D4
Sheen...... 129 C6
Sheepscar.... 148 D2
Sheepscombe... 63 B4
Sheepstor..... 7 A4
Sheepwash.... 11 A5
Sheepway..... 42 B3
Sheepy Magna .. 97 A6
Sheepy Parva .. 97 A6
Sheering...... 69 B5
Sheerness..... 51 B6
Sheet...... 33 C6
Sheffield..... 130 A3
Sheffield Bottom 47 C4
Sheffield Green . 36 D2
Shefford..... 84 D3
Shefford
  Woodlands 46 B1
Sheigra...... 276 B2
Sheinton...... 95 A4
Shelderton.... 94 D2
Sheldon Derbys .129 C6
  Devon...... 13 A6
  W Mid......97 C4
Sheldwich..... 52 D2
Shelf...... 139 A4
Shelfanger... 104 C2
Shelfield Warks .. 80 A4
  W Mid......96 A3
Shelford..... 115 A4
Shellacres.... 198 B2
Shelley Essex .. 69 C5
  Suff......87 D6
  W Yorks......139 B5
Shellingford.... 64 D4
Shellow Bowells . 69 C6
Shelsley
  Beauchamp ... 79 A5
Shelsley Walsh .. 79 A5
Shelthorpe.... 114 D3
Shelton Bedford ..84 A2
  Norf......104 B3
  Notts......115 A5

Shelton continued
  Shrops......110 D3
Shelton Green. .104 B3
Shelve...... 94 B1
Shelwick...... 78 C3
Shenfield..... 69 D6
Shenington... 81 C6
Shenley...... 68 C1
Shenley Brook
  End......83 D5
Shenleybury... 68 C1
Shenley Church
  End......83 D5
Shenmore..... 78 D1
Shennanton... 171 A5
Shenstone Staffs. .96 A4
  Worcs......95 D6
Shenton...... 97 A6
Shenval Highld .251 D6
  Moray......254 D3
Shepeau Stow. .117 D6
Shephall..... 68 A2
Shepherd's
  Green......47 A5
Shepherd's Port 118 B3
Shepherdswell . 39 A4
Shepley...... 139 C4
Shepperdine... 62 D2
Shepperton... 48 C3
Shepreth..... 85 C5
Shepshed..... 114 D2
Shepton
  Beauchamp ... 28 D4
Shepton Mallet. 29 A6
Shepton
  Montague 29 B6
Shepway...... 37 A5
Sheraton..... 168 B2
Sherborne Dorset. 29 D6
  Glos......64 B2
Sherborne St
  John......47 D4
Sherbourne.... 81 A5
Sherburn
  Durham......167 A6
  N Yorks......160 D3
Sherburn Hill .. 167 A6
Sherburn in
  Elmet......148 D3
Shere...... 34 B3
Shereford..... 119 C5
Sherfield English 32 C1
Sherfield on
  Loddon......47 D4
Sherford..... 8 C1
Sheriffhales.... 111 D6
Sheriff Hutton .. 149 A5
Sheringham... 120 A3
Sherington... 83 C5
Shernal Green .. 80 A2
Shernborne... 119 B4
Sherrington... 30 B3
Sherston..... 44 A2
Sherwood Green . 25 C6
Shettleston... 205 B6
Shevington... 136 C4
Shevington
  Moor......136 B4
Shevington Vale 136 C4
Sheviock...... 6 B2
Shide...... 18 C3
Shiel Bridge... 238 A3
Shieldaig Highld .249 A5
  Highld......261 C5
Shieldhill
  Dumfries......184 D3
  Falk......208 C1
  S Lanark......195 B5
Shielfoot..... 235 D5
Shielhill Angus .232 C2
  Inverclyd......204 A2
Shifford...... 65 C4
Shifnal...... 95 A5
Shildon...... 167 C5
Shillingford Devon 27 C4
  Oxon......65 D6
Shillingford St
  George......13 C4
Shillingstone... 30 D2
Shillington... 84 D3
Shillmoor..... 188 C1

Shilton Oxon..... 64 C3
  Warks......97 C7
Shilvington... 178 A3
Shimpling Norf .104 C2
  Suff......87 B4
Shimpling Street .87 B4
Shincliffe..... 167 A5
Shiney Row... 179 D5
Shinfield..... 47 C5
Shingham..... 102 A3
Shingle Street. . 89 C4
Shinner's Bridge . 8 A1
Shinness..... 272 C3
Shipbourne... 36 A3
Shipdham..... 103 A5
Shiphay...... 8 A2
Shiplake...... 47 B5
Shipley Derbys .114 A2
  Northumb......189 B4
  Shrops......95 B6
  W Sus......35 D4
  W Yorks......147 D5
Shipley Shiels .. 187 D6
Shipmeadow... 105 C4
Shippea Hill
  Sta......102 C2
Shippon...... 65 D5
Shipston-on-
  Stour......81 C5
Shipton Glos... 63 B6
  N Yorks......149 B4
  Shrops......94 B3
Shipton Bellinger 31 A6
Shipton Gorge .. 15 B4
Shipton Green .. 19 A7
Shipton Moyne .. 44 A2
Shipton on
  Cherwell......65 B5
Shipton Solers .. 63 B6
Shiptonthorpe .150 C1
Shipton-under-
  Wychwood 64 B3
Shirburn...... 66 D2
Shirdley Hill .. 136 B2
Shiregreen.... 139 D6
Shirehampton... 43 B4
Shiremoor.... 179 B5
Shirenewton... 61 D6
Shirkoak...... 38 B1
Shirland...... 130 D3
Shirley Derbys .113 A6
  London......49 C6
  Soton......32 D3
  W Mid......96 D4
Shirl Heath.... 78 B2
Shirrell Heath .. 33 D4
Shirwell...... 25 B6
Shirwell Cross .. 25 B6
Shiskine..... 191 C5
Shobdon..... 78 A2
Shobnall..... 113 C6
Shobrooke.... 12 A3
Shoby...... 115 D4
Shocklach.... 110 A3
Shoeburyness... 51 A6
Sholden...... 53 D5
Sholing...... 32 D3
Shoot Hill..... 110 D3
Shop Corn...... 9 D4
  Corn......24 D3
Shop Corner... 88 D3
Shoreditch.... 49 A6
Shoreham..... 50 C2
Shoreham-By-
  Sea......21 B5
Shore Mill.... 264 D3
Shoresdean... 198 B3
Shoreswood... 198 B3
Shoreton..... 264 D2
Shorncote.... 63 D6
Shorne...... 50 B3
Shortacombe... 11 C6
Shortgate..... 22 A2
Short Heath... 96 A2
Shortlanesend . 4 C3
Shortlees..... 193 B4
Shortstown... 84 C2
Shorwell...... 18 C3
Shoscombe.... 43 D6

Shotatton..... 110 C2
Shotesham.... 104 B3
Shotgate...... 70 D1
Shotley...... 88 D3
Shotley Bridge .178 D2
Shotleyfield... 178 D2
Shotley Gate... 88 D3
Shottenden... 52 D2
Shottermill... 34 C1
Shottery..... 81 B4
Shotteswell... 81 C7
Shottisham... 88 C4
Shottle...... 113 A7
Shottlegate... 113 A7
Shotton Durham .168 B2
  Flint......126 C3
  Northumb......198 C2
Shotton Colliery 167 A6
Shotts...... 207 D6
Shotwick..... 126 B3
Shouldham... 102 A2
Shouldham
  Thorpe......102 A2
Shoulton..... 79 B6
Shover's Green... 37 C4
Shrawardine... 110 D3
Shrawley..... 79 A6
Shrewley
  Common...... 81 A5
Shrewsbury... 110 D3
Shrewton..... 31 A4
Shripney..... 20 B2
Shrivenham... 45 A6
Shropham.... 103 B5
Shrub End.... 70 A3
Shucknall..... 78 C3
Shudy Camps .. 86 C2
Shulishadermor 259 D4
Shurdington... 63 B5
Shurlock Row... 47 B6
Shurrery..... 279 C6
Shurrery Lodge .279 C6
Shurton...... 28 A2
Shustoke..... 97 B5
Shute Devon... 12 A3
  Devon......14 B2
Shutford..... 81 C6
Shuthonger... 80 D1
Shutlanger.... 83 B4
Shuttington... 97 A5
Shuttlewood .. 131 B4
Siabost bho
  Dheas......288 C3
Siabost bho
  Thuath......288 C3
Siadar...... 288 B4
Siadar Iarach .. 288 B4
Siadar Uarach .. 288 B4
Sibbaldbie.... 185 D4
Sibbertoft.... 98 C3
Sibdon Carwood . 94 C2
Sibford Ferris .. 81 D6
Sibford Gower .. 81 D6
Sible Hedingham 86 D3
Sibsey...... 134 D3
Sibson Cambs ..100 B2
  Leics......97 A6
Sibthorpe.... 115 A5
Sibton...... 89 A4
Sibton Green .. 105 D4
Sicklesmere... 87 A4
Sicklinghall .. 148 C2
Sid...... 13 C6
Sidbury Devon .. 13 B6
  Shrops......95 C4
Sidcot...... 42 D3
Sidcup...... 50 B1
Siddick...... 162 A3
Siddington
  Ches E......128 B3
  Glos......63 D6
Sidemoor..... 96 D2
Sidestrand... 121 B4
Sidford...... 13 B6
Sidlesham.... 20 C1
Sidley...... 23 B5
Sidlow...... 35 B5
Sidmouth..... 13 C6
Sigford...... 12 D2

Sigglesthorne...151 C4
Sighthill.........209 C4
Sigingstone......41 D4
Signet...........64 B3
Silchester.......47 C4
Sildinis.........288 F3
Sileby...........114 D3
Silecroft........153 B2
Silfield.........104 B2
Silian...........75 C4
Silkstone........139 C5
Silkstone
  Common........139 C5
Silk Willoughby.116 A3
Silloth..........174 C4
Sills............188 C1
Sillyearn........267 D6
Siloh............59 B4
Silpho...........160 B3
Silsden..........147 C4
Silsoe...........84 D2
Silverburn.......209 D5
Silverdale Lancs.154 D3
  Staffs.........112 A2
Silver End.......70 B2
Silvergate.......120 C3
Silverhill.......23 A5
Silverley's
  Green..........104 D3
Silverstone......82 C3
Silverton........13 A4
Silvington.......95 D4
Silwick..........285 J4
Simmondley.......138 D3
Simonburn........177 B6
Simonsbath.......26 B2
Simonstone.......146 D1
Simprim..........198 B2
Simpson..........83 D5
Simpson Cross....55 C4
Sinclair's Hill..198 A2
Sinclairston.....182 A2
Sinderby.........158 C2
Sinderhope.......177 D6
Sindlesham.......47 C5
Singdean.........187 C4
Singleborough....83 D4
Singleton Lancs..144 D3
  W Sus..........20 A1
Singlewell.......50 B3
Sinkhurst Green..37 B6
Sinnahard........244 A1
Sinnington.......159 C6
Sinton Green.....79 A6
Sipson...........48 B3
Sirhowy..........60 B3
Sisland..........104 B4
Sissinghurst.....37 C5
Sisterpath.......197 B6
Siston...........43 B5
Sithney..........3 C4
Sittingbourne....51 C5
Six Ashes........95 C5
Sixhills.........133 A6
Six Hills........115 C4
Six Mile Bottom..86 B1
Sixpenny
  Handley........30 D3
Sizewell.........89 A5
Skail............278 D3
Skaill Orkney....282 D5
  Orkney.........282 F3
  Orkney.........283 G6
Skares...........182 A3
Skateraw.........211 C4
Skaw.............284 G7
Skeabost.........259 D4
Skeabrae.........282 E3
Skeeby...........157 A6
Skeffington......99 A4
Skeffling........143 B5
Skegby...........131 C4
Skegness.........135 C5
Skelberry........285 M5
Skelbo...........264 A3
Skelbrooke.......140 B3
Skeldyke.........117 B6
Skellingthorpe..133 B4
Skellister.......285 H6

Skellow..........140 B3
Skelmanthorpe....139 B5
Skelmersdale.....136 C3
Skelmonae........256 C3
Skelmorlie.......204 B1
Skelmuir.........257 B4
Skelpick.........278 C3
Skelton Cumb.....164 B2
  E Yorks........141 A5
  N Yorks........157 A4
  Redcar.........169 D4
  York...........149 B4
Skelton-on-Ure...148 A2
Skelwick.........282 C5
Skelwith Bridge..154 A2
Skendleby........135 C4
Skene Ho.........245 B4
Skenfrith........61 A6
Skerne...........150 B3
Skeroblingarry...190 C3
Skerray..........278 B2
Skerton..........145 A4
Sketchley........98 B1
Sketty...........57 C6
Skewen...........40 B2
Skewsby..........159 D5
Skeyton..........120 C4
Skiag Bridge.....271 B5
Skibo Castle.....264 B3
Skidbrooke.......143 D6
Skidbrooke North
  End............143 D6
Skidby...........150 D3
Skilgate.........27 C4
Skillington......116 C1
Skinburness......174 C4
Skinflats........208 B2
Skinidin.........258 D2
Skinnet..........277 B6
Skinningrove.....169 C5
Skipness.........202 C3
Skippool.........144 C3
Skipsea..........151 B4
Skipsea Brough...151 B4
Skipton..........146 B3
Skipton-on-
  Swale..........158 D2
Skipwith.........149 D5
Skirbeck.........117 A6
Skirbeck
  Quarter........117 A6
Skirlaugh........151 D4
Skirling.........195 C5
Skirmett.........47 A5
Skirpenbeck......149 B6
Skirwith.........165 B4
Skirza...........281 B5
Skulamus.........247 B5
Skullomie........277 B7
Skyborry Green...93 D6
Skye of Curr.....253 D5
Skyreholme.......147 A4
Slackhall........129 A5
Slackhead........267 C5
Slad.............63 C4
Slade Devon......25 A6
  Pembs.........55 C5
Slade Green......50 B2
Slaggyford.......177 D4
Slaidburn........145 B7
Slaithwaite......138 B3
Slaley...........178 D1
Slamannan........207 C6
Slapton Bucks....67 A5
  Devon.........8 C2
  Northants.....82 C3
Slatepit Dale....130 C3
Slattocks........138 C1
Slaugham.........35 D5
Slaughterford....44 B2
Slawston.........99 B4
Sleaford Hants...33 B7
  Lincs.........116 A3
Sleagill.........164 D3
Sleapford........111 D5
Sledge Green.....79 D6
Sledmere.........150 A2
Sleightholme.....166 D2
Sleights.........160 A2
Slepe............16 B3
Slickly..........281 B4
Sliddery.........191 C5

Sligachan Hotel..246 B3
Slimbridge.......62 C3
Slindon Staffs...112 B2
  W Sus.........20 B2
Slinfold.........35 C4
Sling............123 D6
Slingsby.........159 D5
Slioch...........255 C6
Slip End C Beds..67 B6
  Herts.........85 B4
Slipton..........99 D6
Slitting Mill....112 D4
Slochd...........253 D4
Slockavullin.....213 C6
Sloley...........121 C4
Sloothby.........135 B4
Slough...........48 B2
Slough Green.....35 D5
Sluggan..........253 D4
Slumbay..........249 C5
Slyfield.........34 A2
Slyne............145 A4
Smailholm........197 C5
Smallbridge......138 B2
Smallburgh.......121 C5
Smallburn
  Aberds........257 B5
  E Ayrs........194 D1
Small Dole.......21 A5
Smalley..........114 A2
Smallfield.......36 B6
Small Hythe......37 C6
Smallridge.......14 A3
Smannell.........32 A2
Smardale.........155 A6
Smarden.........37 B6
Smarden Bell.....37 B6
Smeatharpe.......28 D1
Smeeth...........38 B2
Smeeton
  Westerby......98 B3
Smercleit........286 E3
Smerral..........275 A5
Smethwick........96 C3
Smirisary........235 C5
Smisby...........114 D1
Smithfield.......176 C2
Smith Green......145 B4
Smithincott......27 D5
Smith's Green....69 A5
Smithstown......261 C4
Smithton.........252 B3
Smithy Green.....128 B2
Smockington......98 C1
Smoogro.........283 G4
Smythe's Green...70 B3
Snaigow House....231 D4
Snailbeach.......94 A1
Snailwell........86 A2
Snainton.........160 C3
Snaith...........140 A4
Snape N Yorks....157 C6
  Suff..........89 B4
Snape Green......136 B2
Snarestone.......97 A6
Snarford.........133 A5
Snargate.........38 C1
Snave............38 C2
Snead............93 B7
Sneath
  Common........104 C2
Sneaton..........160 A2
Sneatonthorpe....160 A3
Snelland.........133 A5
Snelston.........113 A5
Snettisham.......118 B3
Sniseabhal.......286 C3
Snitter..........188 C3
Snitterby........142 D1
Snitterfield.....81 B5
Snitton..........94 D3
Snodhill.........77 C7
Snodland.........51 C3
Snowden Hill.....139 C5
Snowdown.........53 D4
Snowshill........80 D3
Snydale..........140 B2
Soar Anglesey....122 C3
  Carms........58 C3
  Devon........7 D6
Soar-y-Mynydd....76 B1
Soberton.........33 D5

Soberton Heath...33 D5
Sockbridge.......164 C3
Sockburn.........158 A2
Soham............102 D1
Soham Cotes......102 D1
Solas............287 G3
Soldon Cross.....24 D4
Soldridge........33 B5
Sole Street Kent..38 A2
  Kent..........50 C3
Solihull.........97 D4
Sollers Dilwyn...78 B2
Sollers Hope.....79 D4
Sollom...........136 B3
Solva............54 B3
Somerby Leics....115 D5
  Lincs.........142 C2
Somercotes.......131 D4
Somerford........17 B5
Somerford
  Keynes........63 D6
Somerley.........19 B7
Somerleyton......105 B5
Somersal
  Herbert.......113 B5
Somersby.........134 B3
Somersham
  Cambs........101 D5
  Suff..........88 C1
Somerton Oxon....65 A5
  Som...........29 C4
Sompting.........21 B4
Sonning..........47 B5
Sonning
  Common........47 A5
Sonning Eye......47 B5
Sontley..........110 A2
Sopley...........17 B5
Sopwell..........67 C7
Sopworth.........44 A2
Sorbie...........171 C6
Sordale..........280 B3
Sorisdale........223 A5
Sorn.............193 C5
Sornhill.........193 B5
Sortat...........281 B4
Sotby............134 B2
Sots Hole........133 C6
Sotterley........105 C5
Soudley..........111 C6
Soughton.........126 C2
Soulbury.........66 A4
Soulby...........165 D5
Souldern.........82 D2
Souldrop.........84 A1
Sound Ches E.....111 A5
  Shetland......285 H5
  Shetland......285 J6
Sound Heath......111 A5
Soundwell........43 B5
Sourhope.........188 A1
Sourin..........282 D5
Sourton..........11 B6
Soutergate.......153 B3
South Acre.......119 D5
Southall.........48 A4
South Allington..8 D1
South Alloa......208 A1
Southam Glos.....63 A5
  Warks.........81 A7
South
  Ambersham....34 D2
Southampton......32 D3
South Anston.....131 A5
South Ascot......48 C2
South
  Ballachulish..237 D4
South Balloch....181 B5
South Bank.......168 C3
South Barrow.....29 C6
South Beach.....106 C3
South Benfleet...51 A4
South Bersted....20 B2
Southborough.....36 B3
Southbourne
  Bmouth.......17 B5
  W Sus.........19 A6
South Brent......7 A5
South Brewham....29 B7
South
  Broomhill....189 D5
Southburgh.......103 A5

South
  Burlingham....105 A4
Southburn........150 B2
South Cadbury....29 C6
South Cairn......170 A1
South Carlton....133 B4
South Cave.......150 D2
South Cerney.....63 D6
South Chard......14 A3
South Charlton...189 A4
South Cheriton...29 C6
Southchurch......51 A6
South Cliffe.....150 D1
South Clifton....132 B3
South
  Cockerington..134 A3
South Cornelly...40 C3
Southcott........45 D5
Southcourt.......66 B4
South Cove.......105 C5
South Creagan....227 B4
South Creake.....119 B5
South Croxton....115 D4
South Croydon....49 C6
South Dalton.....150 C2
South Darenth....50 C2
Southdean........187 C5
Southdene........136 D3
South
  Duffield......149 D5
South Elkington..134 A2
South Elmsall....140 B2
Southend Argyll..190 E2
  W Berks.......46 B3
  Wilts.........45 B5
South End Bucks..66 A4
  Cumb.........153 D3
  N Lincs.......142 A3
Southend-on-
  Sea...........51 A5
Southernden......37 B6
Southerndown.....40 D3
Southerness......174 C2
South Erradale...261 C4
Southery.........102 B2
South Fambridge..70 D2
South Fawley.....46 A1
South Ferriby....142 A1
Southfield.......179 B4
Southfleet.......50 B3
South Garth......284 D7
South Garvan.....236 B3
Southgate Ceredig.75 A4
  London........68 D2
  Norf..........120 C3
  Swansea.......57 D5
South Glendale...286 E3
South Godstone...35 B6
South Gorley.....31 D5
South Green
  Essex.........69 D6
  Kent..........51 C5
South-haa........284 E5
South Ham........47 D4
South
  Hanningfield..70 D1
South Harting....33 D6
South Hatfield...68 C2
South Hayling....19 B6
South Hazelrigg.199 C4
South Heath......34 D2
South Heighton...22 B2
South Hetton.....167 A6
South Hiendley..140 B1
South Hill.......10 D4
South Hinksey....65 C6
South Hole.......24 C3
South Holme......159 D5
South Holmwood..35 B4
South
  Hornchurch....50 A2
South Hykeham..133 C4
South Hylton....179 D5
Southill.........84 C3
South Kelsey....142 D2
South Kessock...252 B2
South
  Killingholme.142 B3
South Kilvington.158 C3
South Kilworth...98 C3
South Kirkby.....140 B2

South Kirkton...245 B4
South Kiscadale.191 C6
South Kyme.......117 A4
South Lancing....21 B4
Southleigh.......14 B2
South Leigh......65 C4
South Leverton..132 A2
South Littleton..80 C3
South Lopham....103 C6
South Luffenham..99 A6
South Malling....22 A2
South Marston....45 A5
South
  Middleton....188 A2
South Milford....148 D3
South Millbrex..256 B3
South Milton.....7 C6
South Mimms.....68 C2
Southminster.....70 D3
South Molton.....26 C2
Southmoor........65 D4
South Moreton....46 A3
South Mundham...20 B1
South Muskham..132 D2
South Newbald...150 D2
South Newington..81 D7
South Newton.....31 B4
South
  Normanton....131 D4
South Norwood...49 C6
South Nutfield...35 B6
South Ockendon..50 A2
Southoe..........84 A3
Southolt.........88 A2
South Ormsby....134 B3
Southorpe.......100 A2
South
  Otterington..158 C2
South Owersby...142 D2
Southowram......139 A4
South Oxhey......67 D7
South Perrott....15 A4
South Petherton..28 D4
South Petherwin..10 C4
South
  Pickenham....103 A4
South Pool.......7 C6
Southport.......136 B2
South Port......227 D5
Southpunds......285 L6
South Radworthy..26 B2
South Rauceby...116 A3
South Raynham..119 C5
Southrepps......121 B4
South Reston....135 A4
Southrey........133 C6
Southrop........64 C2
South Runcton...102 A2
South Scarle....132 C3
Southsea........19 B5
South Shian.....226 B4
South Shields...179 C5
South Shore.....144 D3
South
  Somercotes...143 D6
South Stainley..148 A2
South
  Stainmore....165 D6
South Stifford...50 B3
Southstoke......43 C6
South Stoke Oxon.46 A3
  W Sus.........20 B3
South Street
  E Sus.........22 A1
  Kent..........52 C3
  Kent..........52 D2
  London........36 A2
South Tawton....12 B1
South Thoresby..135 B4
South Tidworth...31 A6
Southtown Norf..105 A6
  Orkney.......283 H5
South Town......33 B5
South View......47 D4
Southwaite......164 A2
Southwark.......49 B6
South
  Warnborough..33 A6
Southwater......35 D4

Southwater
Street 35 D4
Southway 29 A5
South Weald 69 D5
Southwell Dorset. .15 D6
Notts 132 D1
South Weston . . .66 D3
South Wheatley
Corn. 10 B3
Notts 132 A2
South
Whiteness 285 J5
Southwick Hants. .19 A5
Northants. 100 B2
T&W. 179 D5
Wilts. 44 D2
W Sus. 21 B5
South Widcombe .43 D4
South Wigston . .98 B2
South
Willingham. . . .134 A1
South Wingfield 130 D3
South Witham. . .116 D2
Southwold 105 D6
South Wonston . .32 B3
Southwood Norf .105 A4
Som 29 B5
South Woodham
Ferrers. 70 D2
South Wootton .118 C3
South Wraxall 29 C2
South Zeal 12 B1
Soval Lodge. . . .288 E4
Sowber Gate . . .158 C2
Sowerby N Yorks. .158 A3
W Yorks 158 A3
Sowerby Bridge 138 A3
Sowerby Row . .164 B1
Sowood 138 B3
Sowton 13 B4
Soyal 264 A1
Spacey Houses . .148 B2
Spa Common . . .121 B4
Spadeadam
Farm. 176 B3
Spalding. 117 C5
Spaldington. . . .149 D6
Spaldwick 100 D3
Spalford 132 C3
Spanby 116 B3
Sparham 120 D2
Spark Bridge . . .154 C2
Sparkford. 29 C6
Sparkhill. 96 C3
Sparkwell. 7 B4
Sparrow Green . .119 D6
Sparrowpit. 129 A5
Sparsholt Hants. .32 B3
Oxon. 46 A1
Spartylea 165 A6
Spaunton 159 C6
Spaxton 28 B2
Spean Bridge . .239 D6
Spear Hill. 21 A4
Speen Bucks. . . .66 D4
W Berks. 46 C2
Speeton 161 D5
Speke 127 A4
Speldhurst. 36 B3
Spellbrook. 69 B4
Spelsbury 64 A4
Spelter 40 B3
Spencers Wood . .47 C5
Spennithorne . . .157 C5
Spennymoor . . .167 B5
Spetchley. 80 B1
Spetisbury. 16 A3
Spexhall 105 C4
Spey Bay. 267 C4
Speybridge 253 D6
Speyview 254 B3
Spilsby 135 C4
Spindlestone . . .199 C5
Spinkhill 131 B4
Spinningdale. . . .264 B2
Spirthill 44 B3
Spital Hill. 140 D4
Spital in the
Street. 133 A4
Spithurst 17 C8
Spittal Dumfries .171 B5
E Loth. 210 C1

Spittal continued
Highld. 280 C3
Northumb. 198 A4
Pembs 55 B5
Stirling 206 B3
Spittalfield. 231 D5
Spittal of
Glenmuick. 243 D6
Spittal of
Glenshee. 231 A5
Spixworth 120 D4
Splayne's Green. .36 D2
Spofforth 148 B2
Spondon 114 B2
Spon End 97 D6
Spon Green 126 C2
Spooner Row . . .104 B1
Sporle 119 D5
Spott 210 C3
Spratton 99 D4
Spreakley 34 B1
Spreyton. 12 B1
Spridlington . . .133 A5
Springburn 205 B6
Springfield
Dumfries 175 B6
Essex. 69 C7
Fife. 220 C3
Moray. 253 A6
W Mid 96 C3
Springhill. 96 A2
Springholm 173 B6
Springkell 175 A5
Springside 192 B3
Springthorpe . . .132 A3
Spring Vale 139 C5
Spring Valley. . .152 D3
Springwell. 179 D4
Sproatley 151 D4
Sproston Green .128 C2
Sprotbrough . . .140 C3
Sproughton 88 C2
Sprouston 197 C6
Sprowston 120 D4
Sproxton Leics. .115 C6
N Yorks. 159 C5
Spurstow 127 D5
Spynie 266 C3
Squires Gate . . .144 D3
Sranda 287 F5
Sronphadruig
Lodge. 229 A6
St. Abb's Haven .211 D6
Stableford Shrops. .95 B5
Staffs 112 B2
Stacey Bank. . . .139 D5
Stackhouse 146 A1
Stackpole. 55 E5
Staddiscombe. . . .7 B4
Staddlethorpe. . .141 A6
Stadhampton . . .65 D7
Stadhlaigearraidh
. . . . .286 C3
Staffield 164 A3
Staffin 259 B4
Stafford 112 C3
Stagsden 84 C1
Stainburn Cumb. .162 B3
N Yorks. 147 C6
Stainby 116 C2
Staincross 139 B6
Staindrop 166 C4
Staines 48 B3
Stainfield Lincs. .116 C3
Lincs. 133 B6
Stainforth
N Yorks. 146 A2
S Yorks 140 B4
Staining 144 D3
Stainland 138 B3
Stainsacre 160 A3
Stainsby 131 C4
Stainton Cumb. .154 C4
Cumb. 164 C2
Durham 166 D3
Mbro 168 D2
N Yorks. 157 B5
S Yorks 140 D3
Stainton by
Langworth 133 B5
Staintondale . . .160 B3
Stainton le Vale .142 D3

Stainton with
Adgarley 153 C3
Stair Cumb. 163 B5
E Ayrs. 193 C4
Stairhaven 171 B4
Staithes 169 D5
Stakeford 179 A4
Stake Pool 144 C4
Stalbridge 30 D1
Stalbridge
Weston. 29 D7
Stalham 121 C5
Stalham Green . .121 C5
Stalisfield Green .51 D6
Stallingborough 142 B3
Stalling Busk . . .156 C3
Stalmine. 144 C3
Stalybridge 138 D2
Stambourne 86 D3
Stambourne
Green. 86 D3
Stamford 100 A2
Stamford Bridge
Ches W. 127 C4
E Yorks 149 B6
Stamfordham . .178 B2
Stanah 163 C6
Stanborough . . .68 B2
Stanbridge C Beds .67 A5
Dorset. 17 A4
Stanbrook 79 C6
Stanbury. 147 D4
Stand Gtr Man. . .137 C6
N Lanark 207 D5
Standburn 208 C2
Standeford. 96 A2
Standen 37 B6
Standford. 33 B7
Standingstone . .162 A3
Standish 137 B4
Standlake. 65 C4
Standon Hants. . .32 C3
Herts 68 A3
Staffs 112 B2
Stane. 194 A3
Stanfield. 119 C6
Stanford C Beds . .84 C3
Kent. 38 B3
Stanford Bishop .79 B4
Stanford Bridge . .79 A5
Stanford Dingley .46 B3
Stanford in the
Vale 64 D4
Stanford-le-
Hope. 50 A3
Stanford on Avon 98 D2
Stanford on
Soar 114 C3
Stanford on
Teme 79 A5
Stanford Rivers . .69 C5
Stanfree 131 B4
Stanghow. 169 D4
Stanground. . . .100 B4
Stanhoe 119 B5
Stanhope
Borders 195 D6
Durham 166 B2
Stanion 99 C6
Stanley Derbys. .114 A2
Durham 178 D3
Lancs 136 C3
Perth 219 A6
Staffs 129 D4
W Yorks 139 A6
Stanley
Common 114 A2
Stanley Gate . . .136 C3
Stanley Hill 79 C4
Stanlow 127 B4
Stanmer 21 B6
Stanmore Hants. .32 C3
London 67 D7
W Berks. 46 B2
Stannergate . . .220 A4
Stanningfield . . .87 B4
Stanningley 147 D6
Stannington
Northumb. 179 B4
S Yorks 130 A3
Stansbatch. 78 A1
Stansfield 86 B3
Stanstead 87 C4

Stanstead
Abbotts 68 B3
Stansted 50 C3
Stansted Airport. .69 A5
Stansted
Mountfitchet 69 A5
Stanton Glos. 80 D3
Mon 61 A5
Northumb. 178 A3
Staffs 113 A5
Suff 103 D5
Stanton by
Bridge 114 C1
Stanton-by-
Dale 114 B2
Stanton Drew . . .43 C4
Stanton
Fitzwarren 64 D2
Stanton Harcourt .65 C5
Stanton Hill 131 C4
Stanton in Peak .130 C2
Stanton Lacy . . .94 D2
Stanton Long . . .94 B3
Stanton-on-the-
Wolds 115 B4
Stanton Prior . . .43 C5
Stanton St
Bernard 45 C4
Stanton St John .65 C6
Stanton St
Quintin 44 B3
Stanton Street . .87 A5
Stanton under
Bardon 114 D2
Stanton upon Hine
Heath 111 C4
Stanton Wick . . .43 C5
Stanwardine in the
Fields 110 C3
Stanwardine in the
Wood 110 C3
Stanway Essex . . .70 A3
Glos 80 D3
Stanway Green .104 D3
Stanwell 48 B3
Stanwell Moor . .48 B3
Stanwick 100 D1
Stanwick-St-
John. 167 D4
Stanwix 175 C7
Stanydale 285 H4
Staoinebrig 286 C3
Stape. 159 B6
Stapehill. 17 A4
Stapeley 111 A5
Stapenhill 113 C6
Staple Kent. 53 D4
Som 27 A6
Staple Cross 37 D5
Staplefield. 35 D5
Staple Fitzpaine .28 D2
Stapleford Cambs .85 B6
Herts 68 B3
Leics. 115 D6
Lincs. 132 D3
Notts 114 B2
Wilts. 31 B4
Stapleford
Abbotts 69 D5
Stapleford
Tawney 69 D5
Staplegrove. 28 C2
Staplehay 28 C2
Staplehurst 37 B5
Staplers 18 C4
Stapleton Bristol. .43 B5
Cumb. 176 B3
Hereford 78 A1
Leics. 98 B1
N Yorks. 167 D5
Shrops 94 A3
Som 29 C4
Staplow 79 C4
Star Fife. 220 D3
Pembs 73 C5
Som 42 D3
Stara 282 E3
Starbeck 148 B2
Starbotton 156 D3
Starcross 13 C4

Stareton 97 D6
Starkholmes 130 D3
Starlings Green . .85 D6
Starston 104 C3
Startforth 166 D3
Startley 44 A3
Stathe 28 C3
Stathern 115 B5
Station Town . . .168 B2
Staughton Green 84 A3
Staughton
Highway. 84 A3
Staunton Glos . . .62 A3
Glos 62 B1
Staunton in the
Vale 115 A6
Staunton on
Arrow 78 A1
Staunton on Wye 78 C1
Staveley Cumb. .154 B3
Cumb 154 C2
Derbys 131 B4
N Yorks. 148 A2
Staverton Devon . .8 A1
Glos 63 A4
Northants. 82 A2
Wilts. 44 C2
Staverton Bridge .63 A4
Stawell 28 B3
Staxigoe 281 C5
Staxton 160 D4
Staylittle. 91 C6
Staynall 144 C3
Staythorpe. 132 D2
St. Boswells 197 C4
Stean. 157 D4
Stearsby 159 D5
Steart 28 A2
Stebbing 69 A6
Stebbing Green . .69 A6
Stedham. 34 D1
Steele Road 186 D4
Steen's Bridge . .78 B3
Steep. 33 C6
Steeple Dorset . . .16 C3
Essex 70 C3
Steeple Ashton . .44 D3
Steeple Aston . .65 A5
Steeple Barton .65 A5
Steeple
Bumpstead 86 C2
Steeple Claydon .66 A1
Steeple Gidding 100 C3
Steeple Langford .31 B4
Steeple Morden . .85 C4
Steep Marsh 33 C6
Steeton 147 C4
Stein 258 C2
Steinmanhill . . .256 B2
Stelling Minnis . .38 A3
Stemster 280 B3
Stemster Ho. . . .280 B3
Stenalees. 5 B5
Stenhousemuir. .207 B6
Stenigot 134 A2
Stenness 284 F4
Stenscholl 259 B4
Stenso 282 E4
Stenson 114 C1
Stenton E Loth. .210 C3
Fife. 209 A5
Stenwith. 115 B6
Stepaside. 56 B1
Stepping Hill. . . .129 A4
Steppingley 84 D2
Stepps 205 B6
Sterndale Moor .129 C6
Sternfield. 89 A4
Sterridge 25 A6
Stert 44 D4
Stetchworth 86 B2
Stevenage 68 A2
Stevenston. 204 D2
Steventon Hants. .32 A4
Oxon. 65 D5
Stevington 84 B1
Stewartby 84 C2
Stewarton Argyll .190 D2
E Ayrs. 205 D4
Stewkley. 66 A3
Stewton 134 A3
Steyne Cross 19 C5

Steyning. 21 A4
Steynton. 55 D5
Stibb 24 D3
Stibbard 120 C1
Stibb Cross 25 D5
Stibb Green 45 C6
Stibbington 100 B2
Stichill 197 C6
Sticker 5 B4
Stickford. 134 D3
Sticklepath 12 B1
Stickney. 134 D3
Stiffkey 119 A6
Stifford's Bridge .79 C5
Stillingfleet 149 C4
Stillington
N Yorks. 149 A4
Stockton 167 C6
Stilton 100 C3
Stinchcombe. . . .62 D3
Stinsford 15 B7
Stirchley. 95 A5
Stirkoke Ho. 281 C5
Stirling Aberds. .257 B6
Stirling 207 A5
Stisted 70 A1
Stithians. 4 D2
Stittenham 264 C2
Stivichall 97 D6
Stixwould 134 C1
St. Margaret's
Hope. 283 H5
Stoak. 127 B4
Stobieside 193 B6
Stobo. 195 C6
Stoborough 16 C3
Stoborough
Green 16 C3
Stobshiel 210 D1
Stobswood. 189 D5
Stock. 69 D6
Stockbridge. 32 B2
Stockbury 51 C5
Stockcross. 46 C2
Stockdalewath .164 A1
Stockerston 99 B5
Stock Green 80 B2
Stockheath 19 A6
Stockiemuir. . . .206 B3
Stockingford. . . .97 B6
Stocking Pelham .69 A4
Stockland. 14 A2
Stockland Bristol .28 A2
Stockleigh
English. 12 A3
Stockleigh
Pomeroy 12 A3
Stockley. 44 C4
Stocklinch 28 D3
Stockport. 138 D1
Stocksbridge. . .139 D5
Stocksfield. 178 C2
Stockton Hereford .78 A3
Norf 105 B4
Shrops. 93 A6
Shrops. 95 B5
Warks. 82 A1
Wilts. 30 B3
Stockton Heath .127 A6
Stockton-on-
Tees 168 D2
Stockton on
Teme 79 A5
Stockton on the
Forest. 149 B5
Stock Wood 80 B3
Stodmarsh 53 C4
Stody. 120 B2
Stoer 270 B3
Stoford Som 29 D5
Wilts. 31 B4
Stogumber 27 B5
Stogursey. 28 A2
Stoke Devon 24 C3
Hants 19 A6
Hants 46 B1
Medway. 51 B5
Suff 88 C2
Stoke Abbott. . . .15 A4

Stoke Albany.....99 C5
Stoke Ash.....104 D2
Stoke Bardolph .115 A4
Stoke Bliss.....79 A4
Stoke Bruerne ...83 C4
Stoke by Clare ...86 C3
Stoke-by-
Nayland.......87 D5
Stoke Canon ...13 B4
Stoke Charity ...32 B3
Stoke Climsland..11 D4
Stoke D'Abernon 35 A4
Stoke Doyle....100 C2
Stoke Dry.....99 B5
Stoke Farthing ..31 C4
Stoke Ferry.....102 B3
Stoke Fleming ...8 C2
Stokeford......16 C2
Stoke Gabriel ...8 B2
Stoke Gifford ...43 B5
Stoke Golding ..97 B6
Stoke Goldington 83 C5
Stoke Green 48 A2
Stokeham.......132 B2
Stoke Hammond ..66 A4
Stoke Heath....111 C5
Stoke Holy
Cross......104 A3
Stokeinteignhead
.......13 D4
Stoke Lacy.....79 C4
Stoke Lyne.....65 A6
Stoke Mandeville..66 B4
Stokenchurch....66 D3
Stoke Newington 49 A6
Stokenham 8 C2
Stoke on Tern ...111 C5
Stoke-on-Trent 112 A2
Stoke Orchard ...63 A5
Stoke Poges 48 A2
Stoke Prior
Hereford.......78 B3
Worcs..........80 A2
Stoke Rivers ...26 B1
Stoke Rochford ..116 C2
Stoke Row......47 A4
Stoke St Gregory 28 C3
Stoke St Mary ...28 C2
Stoke St Michael .29 A6
Stoke St
Milborough....94 C3
Stokesay......94 C2
Stokesby.......121 D6
Stokesley.......158 A4
Stoke sub
Hamdon.......29 D4
Stoke Talmage ..66 D2
Stoke Trister ...30 C1
Stoke Wake 16 A1
Stolford 28 A2
Stondon Massey..69 C5
Stone Bucks 66 B3
Glos...........62 D2
Kent...........38 C1
Kent...........50 B2
Staffs.........112 B3
S Yorks.........131 A5
Worcs..........95 D6
Stone Allerton ..42 D3
Ston Easton....43 D5
Stone Bridge
Corner......101 A4
Stonebroom ...131 D4
Stone Chair....139 A4
Stone Cross E Sus..22 B4
Kent..........53 D5
Stone-edge
Batch......42 B3
Stoneferry....151 D4
Stonefield....194 A1
Stonegate E Sus..37 D4
N Yorks.......159 A6
Stonegrave....159 D5
Stonehaugh...177 B5
Stonehaven...245 D6
Stonehouse Glos..63 C4
Northumb......177 D4
S Lanark.......194 B2
Stone House ..155 C6

Stoneleigh.....97 D6
Stonely.........84 A3
Stoner Hill.....33 C6
Stonesby......115 C6
Stonesfield ...65 B4
Stone's Green..71 A5
Stone Street Kent..36 A3
Suff..........87 D5
Suff..........105 C4
Stonethwaite ..163 C5
Stoneybreck...285 R4
Stoneyburn ...208 D2
Stoney Cross...31 D6
Stoneygate
Aberds......257 C5
Leicester 98 A3
Stoneyhills....70 D3
Stoneykirk....170 B2
Stoney
Middleton...130 B2
Stoney Stanton..98 B1
Stoney Stoke...29 B7
Stoney Stratton ..29 B6
Stoney Stretton ..94 A1
Stoneywood
Aberdeen....245 A5
Falk..........207 B5
Stonganess ...284 C7
Stonham Aspal ..88 B2
Stonnall 96 A3
Stonor.......47 A5
Stonton Wyville ..99 B4
Stony Cross ...79 C5
Stonyfield....264 C2
Stony Stratford..83 C4
Stoodleigh....27 D4
Stopes.........130 A2
Stopham......20 A3
Stopsley.......67 A7
Stores Corner...89 C4
Storeton......126 A3
Stornoway....288 D5
Storridge.....79 C5
Storrington....20 A3
Storrs.......154 B2
Storth.......154 C3
Storwood....149 C6
Stotfield.....266 B3
Stotfold.......84 D4
Stottesdon....95 C4
Stoughton Leics..98 A3
Sur..........34 A2
W Sus.........33 D7
Stoul........235 A6
Stoulton......80 C2
Stourbridge....96 C2
Stourpaine...16 A2
Stourport on
Severn......95 D6
Stour Provost ..30 C1
Stour Row 30 C2
Stourton Staffs..95 C6
Warks.........81 D5
Wilts.........30 B1
Stourton
Caundle......29 D7
Stove Orkney....282 D7
Shetland.....285 L6
Stoven......105 C5
Stow Borders ..196 B3
Lincs.........116 B3
Lincs.........132 A3
Stow Bardolph..102 A2
Stow Bedon....103 B5
Stowbridge....102 A2
Stow cum Quy...85 A7
Stowe.........93 D7
Stowe-by-
Chartley....112 C4
Stowe Green ...62 C1
Stowell.......29 C6
Stowford.....11 C5
Stowlangtoft ...87 A5
Stow Longa....100 D3
Stow Maries ...70 D2
Stowmarket....87 B6
Stow-on-the-
Wold.......64 A2
Stowting.......38 A3
Stowupland ...87 B6
Straad.......203 B5
Strachan......244 C3

Stradbroke 104 D3
Stradishall.....86 B3
Stradsett 102 A2
Stragglethorpe .133 D4
Straid.......180 B3
Straith.......183 D6
Straiton Edin ...209 D5
S Ayrs.........181 A5
Straloch Aberds..256 D3
Stramshall 113 B4
Strang.......152 D3
Stranraer....170 A2
Stratfield
Mortimer.....47 C4
Stratfield Saye ..47 C4
Stratfield Turgis. 47 C4
Stratford 49 A6
Stratford St
Andrew.....89 A4
Stratford St Mary 87 D6
Stratford Sub
Castle.......31 B5
Stratford Tony ..31 C4
Stratford-upon-
Avon.......81 B4
Strath Highld....261 C4
Highld.........281 C4
Strathan Highld..238 C3
Highld.........270 B3
Highld.........277 B6
Strathaven....194 B2
Strathblane ...205 A5
Strathcanaird ..271 D4
Strathcarron ..249 B6
Strathcoil 225 C5
Strathdon.....243 A6
Strathellie 269 C5
Strathkinness ..221 C4
Strathmashie
House.......240 C3
Strathmiglo ...220 C2
Strathmore
Lodge......280 D3
Strathpeffer ...251 A6
Strathrannoch ..263 C5
Strathtay 230 C3
Strathvaich
Lodge.......263 C5
Strathwhillan ..191 B6
Strathy.......279 B4
Strathyre.....217 C5
Stratton Corn ...10 A3
Dorset.......15 B6
Glos...........63 C6
Stratton Audley ..65 A7
Stratton on the
Fosse.......43 D5
Stratton St
Margaret.....45 A5
Stratton St
Michael......104 B3
Stratton
Strawless ...120 C4
Stravithie.....221 C5
Streat 21 A6
Streatham 49 B6
Streatley C Beds..67 A6
W Berks......46 A3
Street Lancs 145 B5
N Yorks.......159 A6
Som...........29 B4
Street Dinas ...110 B2
Street End Kent...52 D3
W Sus.........20 C1
Street Gate ...179 D4
Streethay.....113 D5
Streetlam.....157 B7
Streetly......96 B3
Street Lydan ...110 B3
Streetly End....86 C2
Strefford.....94 C2
Strelley......114 A3
Strensall 149 A5
Stretcholt....28 A2
Strete.......8 C2
Stretford....137 D7
Strethall......85 D6
Stretham.....101 D7
Strettington....20 B1
Stretton Ches W..127 D4
Derbys........130 C3

Stretton continued
Rutland.......116 D2
Staffs.........112 D2
Staffs.........113 C6
Warr..........127 A6
Stretton
Grandison....79 C4
Stretton-on-
Dunsmore.....97 D7
Stretton-on-
Fosse.......81 D5
Stretton Sugwas .78 C2
Stretton under
Fosse.......98 C1
Stretton
Westwood.....94 B3
Strichen......269 D4
Strines.......129 A4
Stringston 28 A1
Strixton......83 A6
Stroat.......62 D1
Stromeferry...249 C5
Stromemore...249 C5
Stromness....283 G3
Stronaba.....239 D6
Stronachlachar..216 C4
Stronchreggan .237 B4
Stronchrubie...271 C5
Strone Argyll...215 D4
Highld.........239 D5
Highld.........252 D1
Invclyd.......204 A2
Stronmilchan ..227 D6
Strontian 236 C2
Strood......51 C4
Strood Green Sur .35 B5
W Sus.........34 D3
W Sus.........35 C4
Stroud Glos....63 C4
Hants.........33 C6
Stroud Green ...70 D2
Stroxton.....116 B2
Struan Highld ...230 B2
Perth.........230 B2
Strubby......135 A4
Strumpshaw ..104 A4
Strutherhill ...194 B2
Struy.......251 C5
Stryt-issa 110 A1
Stuartfield ...257 B4
Stubbington ...19 A4
Stubbins......137 B6
Stubbs Cross ...38 B1
Stubbs Green ..105 B4
Stubb's Green ..104 B3
Stubhampton ...30 D3
Stub Place 153 A1
Stubton......115 A6
Stuckgowan ...215 B6
Stuckton.......31 D5
Studham......67 B6
Studland......17 C4
Studley Warks ...80 A3
Wilts.........44 B3
Studley Roger ..157 D6
Stump Cross ...85 C7
Stuntney......102 D1
Sturbridge 112 B2
Sturmer......86 C2
Sturminster
Marshall.....16 A3
Sturminster
Newton......30 D1
Sturry.......52 C3
Sturton......122 C1
Sturton by Stow 132 A3
Sturton le
Steeple.....132 A2
Stuston......104 D2
Stutton N Yorks..148 C3
Suff..........88 D2
Styal.......128 A3
Styrrup......140 D4
Suainebost....288 A6
Suardail.....288 D5
Succoth Aberds ..255 C5
Argyll.........215 B5
Suckley......79 B5
Suckquoy.....283 J5
Sudborough 99 C6
Sudbourne 89 B5

Sudbrook Lincs ..116 A2
Mon..........43 A4
Sudbrooke.....133 B5
Sudbury Derbys ..113 B5
London........49 A4
Suff..........87 C4
Suddie.......252 A2
Sudgrove.....63 C5
Suffield Norf....120 B4
N Yorks.......160 B3
Sugnall......112 B1
Sugwas Pool ...78 C2
Suladale.....258 C3
Sulaisiadar...288 D6
Sulby.......152 B3
Sulgrave......82 C2
Sulham......47 B4
Sulhamstead ...47 C4
Sulland......282 C6
Sullington 20 A3
Sullom......284 F5
Sullom Voe Oil
Terminal....284 F5
Sully.......41 E6
Sumburgh 285 N6
Summer Bridge .147 A6
Summercourt....4 B3
Summerfield ...119 B4
Summergangs .151 D4
Summer-house .167 D5
Summerleaze ...42 A3
Summersdale ...20 B1
Summerseat ...137 B6
Summertown ...65 C6
Summit.......138 C2
Sunbury-on-
Thames.....48 C4
Sundaywell ...183 D6
Sunderland
Argyll.........200 B2
Cumb.........163 A4
T&W..........179 D5
Sunderland
Bridge......167 B5
Sundhope 196 D2
Sundon Park ...67 A6
Sundridge 36 A2
Sunipol......224 A2
Sunk Island ...143 B4
Sunningdale ...48 C2
Sunninghill ...48 C2
Sunningwell ...65 C5
Sunniside
Durham......166 B4
T&W..........179 D4
Sunnyhurst ...137 A5
Sunnylaw 207 A5
Sunnyside 36 C1
Sunton......45 D6
Surbiton......49 C4
Surby.......152 D2
Surfleet......117 C5
Surfleet Seas
End.......117 C5
Surlingham ...104 A4
Sustead......120 B3
Susworth.....141 C6
Sutcombe 24 D4
Suton.......104 B1
Sutors of
Cromarty....265 D4
Sutterby.....134 B3
Sutterton....117 B5
Sutton Cambs ...101 D6
C Beds........84 C4
Kent..........39 A5
London........49 C5
Mers..........136 D4
Norf..........121 C5
Notts.........115 B5
Notts.........132 A1
N Yorks.......140 A4
Oxon..........65 C5
Pboro.........100 B2
Shrops........95 C5
Shrops........111 B5
Som...........29 B6
Staffs.........111 C6
Suff..........88 C4
Sur..........34 B4
S Yorks.......140 B3
W Sus.........20 A2
Sutton at Hone..50 B2

Sutton Bassett ...99 B4
Sutton Benger ...44 B3
Sutton
Bonington....114 C3
Sutton Bridge ..118 C1
Sutton Cheney ..97 A7
Sutton Coldfield..96 B4
Sutton Courtenay 65 D6
Sutton Crosses ..118 C1
Sutton Grange .157 D6
Sutton Green....34 A3
Sutton
Howgrave....157 D7
Sutton In
Ashfield.....131 D4
Sutton-in-
Craven.....147 C4
Sutton Ings ...151 D4
Sutton in the
Elms.......98 B2
Sutton Lane
Ends.......129 B4
Sutton Leach...136 D4
Sutton Maddock..95 A5
Sutton Mallet ...28 B3
Sutton
Mandeville....30 C4
Sutton Manor ..136 D4
Sutton Montis ...29 C6
Sutton on Hull .151 D4
Sutton on Sea..135 A5
Sutton-on-the-
Forest......149 A4
Sutton on the
Hill.........113 B6
Sutton on Trent .132 C2
Sutton St
Edmund......117 D6
Sutton St
James.......117 D6
Sutton St
Nicholas......78 C3
Sutton
Scarsdale ...131 C4
Sutton Scotney ..32 B3
Sutton under
Brailes......81 D6
Sutton-under-White-
stonecliffe.....158 C3
Sutton upon
Derwent.....149 C6
Sutton Valence ..37 B6
Sutton Veny....30 A2
Sutton Waldron .30 D2
Sutton Weaver .127 B5
Sutton Wick....43 D4
Swaby.......134 B3
Swadlincote ...113 D7
Swaffham.....103 A4
Swaffham
Bulbeck.....86 A1
Swaffham Prior ..86 A1
Swafield.....121 B4
Swainby.....158 A3
Swainshill 78 C2
Swainsthorpe ..104 A3
Swainswick 43 C6
Swalcliffe.....81 D6
Swalecliffe....52 C3
Swallow......142 C3
Swallowcliffe ...30 C3
Swallowfield ...47 C5
Swallownest ...131 A4
Swallows Cross ..69 D6
Swanage......17 D4
Swanbister ...283 G4
Swanbourne ...66 A4
Swan Green
Ches W........128 B2
Suff..........104 D3
Swanland....142 A1
Swanley......50 C2
Swanley Village ..50 C2
Swanmore....33 D4
Swannington
Leics.........114 D2
Norf..........120 D3
Swanscombe...50 B3
Swansea
(Abertawe)....57 C6
Swanton Abbott 121 C4

Swanton Morley.......120 D2
Swanton Novers 120 B2
Swanton Street...37 A6
Swanwick
  Derbys.........131 D4
  Hants..........18 A4
Swarby..........116 A3
Swardeston......104 A3
Swarister.......284 E7
Swarkestone.....114 C1
Swarland........189 C4
Swarland Estate 189 C4
Swarthmoor......153 C3
Swathwick.......130 C3
Swaton..........116 B4
Swavesey........85 A5
Sway............18 B1
Swayfield.......116 C2
Swaythling......32 D3
Sweet Green.....79 A4
Sweetham........12 B3
Sweethouse......5 A5
Sweffling.......88 A4
Swepstone.......114 D1
Swerford........81 D6
Swettenham......128 C3
Swetton.........157 D5
Swffryd.........60 D4
Swiftsden.......37 D5
Swilland........88 B2
Swillington.....148 D2
Swimbridge......25 C7
Swimbridge Newland.......25 B7
Swinbrook.......64 B3
Swinderby.......132 C3
Swindon Glos....63 A5
  Staffs........95 B6
  Swindon.......45 A5
Swine...........151 D4
Swinefleet......141 A5
Swineshead
  Bedford.......84 A2
  Lincs.........117 A5
Swineshead Bridge........117 A5
Swiney..........275 A6
Swinford Leics..98 D2
  Oxon..........65 C5
Swingate........114 A3
Swingfield Minnis........39 A4
Swingfield Street 39 A4
Swinhoe.........189 A5
Swinhope........143 D4
Swining.........284 G6
Swinithwaite....156 C4
Swinnow Moor...147 D6
Swinscoe........113 A5
Swinside Hall...187 B6
Swinstead.......116 C3
Swinton Borders 198 B2
  Gtr Man.......137 C6
  N Yorks.......157 D6
  N Yorks.......159 D6
  S Yorks.......140 D2
Swintonmill.....198 B2
Swithland.......114 D3
Swordale........264 D1
Swordland.......238 C1
Swordly.........278 B3
Sworton Heath..128 A1
Swydd-ffynnon...75 B5
Swynnerton.....112 B2
Swyre...........15 C5
Sychtyn.........92 A3
Syde............63 B5
Sydenham London 49 B6
  Oxon..........66 C3
Sydenham Damerel.......11 D5
Syderstone......119 B5
Sydling St Nicholas......15 A5
Sydmonton......46 D2
Syerston.......115 A5
Syke............138 B1
Sykehouse......140 B4
Sykes...........145 B6
Syleham.........104 D3
Sylen...........57 B5

Symbister.......285 G7
Symington
  S Ayrs........192 B3
  S Lanark......195 C4
Symondsbury.....14 B4
Symonds Yat.....62 B1
Synod Inn.......73 A7
Syre............278 D2
Syreford........63 A6
Syresham........82 C3
Syston Leics....115 D4
  Lincs.........116 A2
Sytchampton.....79 A6
Sywell..........83 A5

T

Taagan..........262 D2
Tàbost..........288 A6
Tabost..........288 F4
Tackley.........65 A5
Tacleit.........288 D2
Tacolneston....104 B2
Tadcaster......148 C3
Taddington.....129 B6
Taddiport.......25 D5
Tadley..........47 C4
Tadlow..........85 C4
Tadmarton.......81 D6
Tadworth........35 A5
Tafarnau-bach...60 B3
Tafarn-y-gelyn..126 C1
Taff's Well.....41 C6
Tafolwern.......91 B6
Tai.............124 C2
Taibach.........40 C2
Tai-bach........109 C6
Taigh a Ghearraidh...287 G2
Tai-mawr........109 A4
Tain Highld....264 B3
  Highld........280 B4
Tainant........110 A1
Tainlon........107 A4
Tairbeart (Tarbert)....288 G2
Tai'r-Bull......60 A1
Tairgwaith......59 D4
Tai-Ucha.......125 D5
Takeley.........69 A5
Takeley Street..69 A5
Talachddu.......77 D4
Talacre........125 A6
Talardd.........108 C3
Talaton.........13 B5
Talbenny........54 C4
Talbot Green....41 C5
Talbot Village..17 B4
Tale............13 A5
Talerddig.......92 A3
Talgarreg.......74 C3
Talgarth........77 D5
Talisker.......246 A2
Talke...........128 D3
Talkin.........176 D3
Talladale......261 C6
Talla Linnfoots 195 D6
Tallarn Green...110 A3
Tallentire.....163 A4
Talley..........58 B3
Tallington.....100 A2
Talmine........277 B6
Talog...........73 D6
Talsarn.........59 C4
Tal-sarn........75 C4
Talsarnau......107 C6
Talskiddy.......4 A4
Talwrn Anglesey 123 C4
  Wrex.........110 A1
Tal-y-bont
  Ceredig.......91 D4
  Conwy........124 C2
  Gwyn.........107 D5
Talybont-on-Usk 60 A3
Tal-y-cafn.....124 B2
Talygarn........41 C5
Talyllyn........60 A3
Tal-y-llyn......91 B5
Talysarn.......107 A4
Talywain........61 C4

Tal-y-wern......91 B6
Tame Bridge....158 A4
Tamerton Foliot..6 A3
Tamworth........97 A5
Tandem.........139 B4
Tanden..........37 C7
Tanerdy.........73 D7
Tanfield.......178 D3
Tanfield Lea...178 D3
Tangasdal......286 G2
Tangiers........55 C5
Tangley.........46 D1
Tanglwst........73 C6
Tangmere........20 B2
Tangwick.......284 F4
Tan Hinon.......91 D6
Tankersley.....139 C6
Tankerton.......52 C3
Tan-lan Conwy..124 C2
  Gwyn.........107 B6
Tannach........281 D5
Tannachie......245 D4
Tannadice......232 C2
Tannington......88 A3
Tansley........130 D3
Tansley Knoll..130 C3
Tansor.........100 B2
Tantobie.......178 D3
Tanton.........168 D3
Tanworth-in-Arden........96 D4
Tan-y-bwlch....107 B6
Tan-y-fron.....125 C4
Tan-y-graig
  Anglesey.....123 C5
  Gwyn.........106 C3
Tan-y-groes.....73 B5
Tan-y-pistyll..109 C5
Tan-yr-allt....107 A4
Tanyrhydiau.....75 B6
Taobh a Chaolais.....286 E3
Taobh a' Ghlinne.....288 F4
Taobh a Thuath Loch Aineort......286 D3
Taobh a Tuath Loch Baghasdail......286 D3
Taobh Tuath....287 F4
Taplow..........48 A2
Tapton.........130 B3
Tarbat Ho......264 C3
Tarbert Argyll.202 B3
  Argyll.......202 C1
  Argyll.......213 D4
Tarbet Argyll..215 B6
  Highld.......238 C1
  Highld.......276 D2
Tarbock Green..127 A4
Tarbolton......193 C4
Tarbrax........195 A5
Tardebigge......80 A3
Tarfside.......232 A2
Tarland........244 B1
Tarleton.......136 A3
Tarlogie.......264 B3
Tarlscough.....136 B3
Tarlton.........63 D5
Tarnbrook......145 B5
Tarporley......127 C5
Tarr............27 B6
Tarrant Crawford 16 A3
Tarrant Gunville..30 D3
Tarrant Hinton..30 D3
Tarrant Keyneston....16 A3
Tarrant Launceston...16 A3
Tarrant Monkton 16 A3
Tarrant Rawston 16 A3
Tarrant Rushton 16 A3
Tarrel.........265 B4
Tarring Neville..22 B2
Tarrington......79 C4
Tarsappie......219 B6
Tarskavaig.....247 D4
Tarves.........256 C3
Tarvie Highld..251 A6
  Perth........230 B4

Tarvin.........127 C4
Tasburgh.......104 B3
Tasley..........95 B4
Taston..........65 A4
Tatenhill......113 C6
Tathall End.....83 C5
Tatham.........145 A6
Tathwell.......134 A3
Tatling End.....48 A3
Tatsfield.......36 A2
Tattenhall.....127 D4
Tattenhoe.......83 D5
Tatterford.....119 C5
Tattersett.....119 B5
Tattershall....134 D2
Tattershall Bridge.......134 D1
Tattershall Thorpe.......134 D2
Tattingstone....88 D2
Tatworth........14 A3
Taunton.........28 C2
Taverham.......120 D3
Tavernspite.....56 A1
Tavistock.......11 D5
Taw Green.......12 B1
Tawstock........25 C6
Taxal..........129 B5
Tay Bridge.....220 B4
Tayinloan......202 D1
Taymouth Castle.......230 D1
Taynish........213 D5
Taynton Glos....62 A3
  Oxon..........64 B3
Taynuilt.......227 C5
Tayport........221 B4
Tayvallich.....213 D5
Tealby.........142 D3
Tealing........220 A4
Teangue........247 D5
Teanna Mhachair....287 H2
Tebay..........155 A5
Tedburn St Mary.12 B3
Teddington Glos.80 D2
  London........49 B4
Tedstone Delamere.....79 B4
Tedstone Wafre..79 B4
Teeton..........98 D3
Teffont Evias...30 B3
Teffont Magna...30 B3
Tegryn..........73 C5
Teigh.........115 D6
Teigncombe......12 C1
Teigngrace......12 D3
Teignmouth......13 D4
Telford.........95 A4
Telham..........23 A5
Tellisford......44 D2
Telscombe......22 B2
Telscombe Cliffs 22 B2
Templand.......184 D3
Temple Corn.....10 D2
  Glasgow......205 B5
  Midloth......196 A2
Temple Balsall..97 D5
Temple Bar Carms 57 A5
  Ceredig.......75 C4
Temple Cloud....43 D5
Temple Combe....29 C7
Temple Ewell....39 A4
Temple Grafton..80 B4
Temple Guiting..64 A1
Templehall.....209 A5
Temple Herdewyke....81 B6
Temple Hirst...140 A4
Temple Normanton....131 C4
Temple Sowerby......165 C4
Templeton Devon 26 D3
  Pembs........55 C7
Templeton Bridge........26 D3
Templetown.....178 D3
Tempsford.......84 B3
Tenbury Wells...78 A3

Tenby (Dinbych-y-Pysgod).......56 B1
Tendring........71 A5
Tendring Green..71 A5
Ten Mile Bank..102 B2
Tenston........282 F3
Tenterden.......37 C6
Terling.........70 B1
Ternhill.......111 B5
Terregles Banks 174 A2
Terrick.........66 C4
Terrington.....159 D5
Terrington St Clement......118 D2
Terrington St John.........118 D2
Teston..........37 A5
Testwood........32 D2
Tetbury.........63 D4
Tetbury Upton...63 D4
Tetchill.......110 B2
Tetcott.........10 B4
Tetford........134 B3
Tetney.........143 C5
Tetney Lock....143 C5
Tetsworth.......66 C2
Tettenhall......96 B1
Teuchan........257 C5
Teversal.......131 C4
Teversham.......85 B6
Teviothead.....186 C3
Tewel..........245 D5
Tewin...........68 B2
Tewkesbury......80 D1
Teynham.........51 C6
Thackthwaite...163 B4
Thainstone.....233 A4
Thakeham........21 A4
Thame...........66 C3
Thames Ditton...49 C4
Thames Haven....51 A4
Thamesmead......50 A1
Thanington......52 D3
Thankerton.....195 C4
Tharston.......104 B2
Thatcham........46 C3
Thatto Heath...136 D4
Thaxted.........86 D2
The Aird.......259 C4
Theakston......157 C7
Thealby........141 B6
Theale Som......29 A4
  W Berks.......47 B4
The Arms.......103 B4
The Bage........77 C6
The Balloch....218 C3
The Barony.....282 E3
Theberton.......89 A5
The Bog.........94 B1
The Bourne......33 A7
The Braes......247 A4
The Broad.......78 A2
The Butts.......30 A1
The Camp Glos...63 C5
  Herts.........67 C7
The Chequer....110 A3
The City........66 D3
The Common......31 B6
The Craigs.....263 A6
The Cronk......152 B3
Theddingworth...98 C3
Theddlethorpe All Saints......135 A4
Theddlethorpe St Helen........135 A4
The Dell.......105 B5
The Den........204 C3
The Eals.......177 A5
The Eaves.......62 C2
The Flatt......176 B3
The Four Alls..111 B5
The Garths.....284 B8
The Green Cumb 153 B2
  Wilts.........30 B2
The Grove.....174 A2
The Hall.......284 D8
The Haven.......34 C3
The Heath Norf 120 C3
  Suff..........88 D2
The Hill.......153 B2
The Howe Cumb 154 C3

The Howe continued
  IoM...........152 E1
The Hundred.....78 A3
Thelbridge Barton........26 D2
The Lee.........67 C5
The Lhen.......152 A3
Thelnetham.....103 D6
Thelveton......104 C2
Thelwall.......127 A6
The Marsh Powys 93 B7
  Wilts.........45 A4
Themelthorpe...120 C2
The Middles....179 D4
The Moor........37 D5
The Mumbles (Y Mwmbwls).....57 D6
The Murray.....205 C6
The Neuk.......245 C4
Thenford........82 C2
The Oval........43 C6
The Pole of Itlaw........268 D1
The Quarry......62 D3
Therfield.......85 D5
The Rhos........55 C6
The Rock........95 A4
The Ryde........68 C2
The Sands.......34 B1
The Stocks......37 D7
The Vauld.......78 C3
The Wyke........95 A5
Theydon Bois....68 D4
Thickwood.......44 B2
Thimbleby Lincs 134 C2
  N Yorks......158 B3
Thingwall......126 A2
Thirdpart......204 D1
Thirlby........158 C3
Thirlestane....197 B4
Thirn..........157 C6
Thirsk.........158 C3
Thirtleby......151 D4
Thistleton Lancs 144 D4
  Rutland......116 D2
Thixendale.....150 A1
Thockrington...178 B1
Tholomas Drove 101 A5
Tholthorpe.....148 A3
Thomas Chapel..55 D7
Thomas Close...164 A2
Thomastown.....255 C6
Thompson.......103 B5
Thomshill......266 D3
Thong...........50 B3
Thongsbridge...139 C4
Thoralby.......156 C4
Thoresway......142 D3
Thorganby Lincs 143 C4
  N Yorks......149 C5
Thorgill.......159 B6
Thorington.....105 D5
Thorington Street........87 D6
Thorlby........146 B3
Thorley.........69 B4
Thorley Street
  Herts.........69 B4
  IoW...........18 C2
Thormanby.....158 D3
Thornaby-on-Tees........168 D2
Thornage.......120 B2
Thornborough
  Bucks.........83 D4
  N Yorks......157 D6
Thornbury Devon..11 A5
  Hereford......79 B4
  S Glos........62 D2
  W Yorks......147 D5
Thornby.........98 D3
Thorncliffe....129 D5
Thorncombe
  Dorset........14 A3
  Dorset........16 A2

Thorncombe
  Street. 34 B3
Thorncote Green 84 C3
Thorncross 18 C3
Thorndon. 88 A2
Thorndon Cross . 11 B6
Thorne 141 B4
Thorner 148 C2
Thorne St
  Margaret. 27 C5
Thorney Notts . . 132 B3
  Pboro 101 A4
Thorney Crofts .143 A4
Thorney Green . . 87 A6
Thorney Hill. . . . 17 B5
Thorney Toll . . . 101 A5
Thornfalcon. . . . 28 C2
Thornford 29 D6
Thorngumbald . .143 A4
Thornham 119 A4
Thornham
  Magna 104 D2
Thornham
  Parva 104 D2
Thornhaugh. . . . 100 A2
Thornhill Cardiff . 41 C6
  Cumb 162 D3
  Derbys 130 A1
  Dumfries 183 C6
  Soton 32 D3
  Stirling 207 A4
  W Yorks 139 B5
Thornhill Edge . 139 B5
Thornhill Lees. . 139 B5
Thornholme . . . 151 A4
Thornley Durham 166 B4
  Durham 167 B6
Thornliebank . . 205 C5
Thorns 86 B3
Thornsett 129 A5
Thorns Green . . 128 A2
Thornthwaite
  Cumb 163 B5
  N Yorks. 147 B5
Thornton Angus .232 D1
  Bucks 83 D4
  E Yorks 149 C6
  Fife. 209 A5
  Lancs 144 C3
  Leics. 98 A1
  Lincs. 134 C2
  Mbro 168 D2
  Mers. 136 C2
  Northumb. . . . 198 B3
  Pembs 55 D5
  W Yorks 147 D5
Thornton Curtis .142 B2
Thorntonhall . . 205 C5
Thornton Heath . 49 C6
Thornton
  Hough 126 A3
Thornton in
  Craven 146 C3
Thornton-le-
  Beans 158 B2
Thornton-le-
  Clay. 149 A5
Thornton-le-
  Dale 160 C2
Thornton le
  Moor. 142 D2
Thornton-le-
  Moor. 158 C2
Thornton-le-
  Moors. 127 B4
Thornton-le-
  Street 158 C3
Thorntonloch . . 211 C4
Thorntonpark . .198 B3
Thornton Rust. .156 C3
Thornton
  Steward 157 C5
Thornton
  Watlass 157 C6
Thornwood
  Common 69 C4
Thornydykes . . 197 B5
Thoroton 115 A5
Thorp Arch . . . 148 C3

Thorpe Derbys . .129 D6
  E Yorks 150 C2
  Lincs. 135 A4
  Norf 105 B5
  Notts 115 A5
  N Yorks. 147 A4
  Sur. 48 C3
Thorpe Abbotts .104 D2
Thorpe Acre . . . 114 C3
Thorpe Arnold . 115 C5
Thorpe Audlin . 140 B2
Thorpe Bassett .160 D2
Thorpe Bay 51 A6
Thorpe by Water . 99 B5
Thorpe Common . 88 D3
Thorpe
  Constantine . . . 97 A5
Thorpe Culvert .135 C4
Thorpe End . . . 121 D4
Thorpe
  Fendykes. . . . 135 C4
Thorpe Green
  Essex 71 A5
  Suff 87 B5
Thorpe Hesley .140 D1
Thorpe in Balne 140 B3
Thorpe in the
  Fallows 133 A4
Thorpe Langton . 99 B4
Thorpe Larches .167 C6
Thorpe-le-Soken 71 A5
Thorpe le
  Street. 150 C1
Thorpe Malsor . . 99 D5
Thorpe
  Mandeville 82 C2
Thorpe Market . 120 B4
Thorpe Marriot .120 D3
Thorpe Morieux . 87 B5
Thorpeness 89 B5
Thorpe on the
  Hill 133 C4
Thorpe St
  Andrew 104 A3
Thorpe St Peter .135 C4
Thorpe Salvin . 131 A5
Thorpe
  Satchville . . . 115 D5
Thorpe Thewles 168 C2
Thorpe Tilney .133 D6
Thorpe
  Underwood . . 148 B3
Thorpe
  Waterville . . . 100 C2
Thorpe
  Willoughby . . 149 D4
Thorrington . . . 71 A4
Thorverton 13 A4
Thrandeston . . 104 D2
Thrapston 100 D1
Thrashbush . . . 207 D5
Threapland
  Cumb 163 A4
  N Yorks. 146 A3
Threapwood
  Ches W. 110 A3
  Staffs 112 A4
Three Ashes . . . 61 A7
Three Bridges . . 35 C5
Three Burrows . 4 C2
Three Chimneys . 37 C6
Three Cocks . . . 77 D5
Three Crosses . . 57 C5
Three Cups
  Corner 36 D4
Threehammer
  Common 121 D5
Three Holes. . . 101 A7
Threekingham . 116 B3
Three Leg Cross . 37 C4
Three Legged
  Cross 17 A4
Threemile Cross. 47 C5
Threemilestone . 4 C2
Threemiletown .208 C3
Three Oaks . . . 23 A6
Threlkeld 163 B6
Threshfield . . . 146 A3
Thrigby 121 D6
Thringarth . . . 166 C2
Thringstone . . 114 D2
Thrintoft 157 B7

Thriplow. 85 C6
Throckenholt . .101 A5
Throcking 85 D5
Throckley. 178 C3
Throckmorton . . 80 C2
Throphill 178 A3
Thropton 188 C3
Throsk. 207 A6
Throwleigh 12 B1
Throwley 52 D1
Thrumpton . . . 114 B3
Thrumster . . . 281 D5
Thrunton 188 B3
Thrupp Glos . . . 63 C4
  Oxon. 65 B5
Thrushelton. . . . 11 C5
Thrussington. . 115 D4
Thruxton Hants . 32 A1
  Hereford 78 D2
Thrybergh . . . 140 D2
Thulston 114 B2
Thundergay . . .202 D3
Thundersley . . . 51 A4
Thundridge . . . 68 B3
Thurcaston . . . 114 D3
Thurcroft 131 A4
Thurgarton Norf .120 B3
  Notts 115 A4
Thurgoland . . . 139 C5
Thurlaston Leics . 98 B2
  Warks. 98 D1
Thurlbear 28 C2
Thurlby Lincs . . 116 D4
  Lincs. 133 C4
Thurleigh 84 B2
Thurlestone . . . 7 C5
Thurloxton . . . 28 B2
Thurlstone . . . 139 C5
Thurlton 105 B5
Thurlwood . . . 128 D3
Thurmaston . . . 98 A3
Thurnby 98 A3
Thurne 121 D6
Thurnham Kent . 37 A6
  Lancs 145 B4
Thurning Norf . .120 C2
  Northants. . . . 100 C2
Thurnscoe . . . 140 C2
Thurnscoe East .140 C2
Thursby 175 C6
Thursford 120 B1
Thursley 34 C2
Thurso 280 B3
Thurso East . . .280 B3
Thurstaston . . 126 A2
Thurston 87 A5
Thurstonfield . .175 C6
Thurstonland . . 139 B4
Thurton 104 A4
Thurvaston . . . 113 B6
Thuxton 103 A6
Thwaite N Yorks .156 B2
  Suff 88 A2
Thwaites. 147 C4
Thwaite St Mary 104 B4
Thwaites Brow .147 C4
Thwing 160 D4
Tibbermore . . . 219 B5
Tibberton Glos . . 62 A3
  Telford 111 C5
  Worcs. 80 B2
Tibenham 104 C2
Tibshelf 131 C4
Tibthorpe 150 B2
Ticehurst 37 C4
Tichborne 33 B4
Tickencote . . . 100 A1
Tickenham 42 B3
Tickhill 140 D3
Ticklerton 94 B2
Ticknall 114 C1
Tickton 150 C3
Tidcombe 45 D6
Tiddington Oxon . 66 C2
  Warks. 81 B5
Tidebrook 36 D4
Tideford 6 B2
Tideford Cross . 6 A2
Tidenham 62 D1
Tideswell 129 B6
Tidmarsh 47 B4
Tidmington . . . 81 D5

Tidpit. 31 D4
Tidworth. 31 A6
Tiers Cross. . . . 55 C5
Tiffield 82 B3
Tifty 256 B2
Tigerton 232 B3
Tigh-na-Blair . .218 C2
Tighnabruaich . 203 A4
Tighnafiline. . . 261 B5
Tigley 7 A6
Tilbrook 84 A2
Tilbury 50 B3
Tilbury Juxta
  Clare. 86 C3
Tile Cross. 97 C4
Tile Hill. 97 D5
Tilehurst 47 B4
Tilford. 34 B1
Tilgate 35 C5
Tilgate Forest
  Row. 35 C5
Tillathrowie. . . 255 C5
Tillers Green . . 62 A3 (not present?)
Tilley 111 C4
Tillicoultry . . . 208 A2
Tillingham 70 C3
Tillington
  Hereford 78 C2
  W Sus. 34 D2
Tillington
  Common 78 C2
Tillyarblet . . . 232 B3
Tillybirloch . . . 244 B3
Tillycorthie . . . 257 D4
Tillydrine 244 C3
Tillyfour 244 A2
Tillyfourie 244 A3
Tillygarmond. . 244 C3
Tillygreig 256 D3
Tillykerrie 256 D3
Tilmanstone . . . 53 D5
Tilney All Saints 118 D2
Tilney High End .118 D2
Tilney St
  Lawrence . . . 118 D2
Tilshead 31 A4
Tilstock 111 B4
Tilston 127 D4
Tilstone
  Fearnall. 127 C5
Tilsworth 67 A5
Tilton on the Hill . 99 A4
Timberland . . . 133 D6
Timbersbrook . . 128 C3
Timberscombe . . 27 A4
Timble. 147 B5
Timperley 128 A2
Timsbury Bath . . 43 D5
  Hants 32 C2
Timsgearraidh .287 A5
Timworth Green . 87 A4
Tincleton 16 B1
Tindale 176 D4
Tingewick 82 D3
Tingley 139 A5
Tingrith 84 D2
Tingwall 282 E4
Tinhay 11 C4
Tinshill 147 D6
Tinsley 140 D2
Tintagel 9 C6
Tintern Parva . . 62 C1
Tintinhull 29 D5
Tintwistle 138 D3
Tinwald 184 D3
Tinwell 100 A2
Tipperty 257 D4
Tipsend. 101 B7
Tipton 96 B2
Tipton St John . 13 B5
Tiptree 70 B2
Tirabad 59 A5
Tiraghoil 224 D2
Tirley 63 A4
Tirphil 41 A6
Tirril 164 C3
Tir-y-dail. 57 A6
Tisbury 30 C3
Tisman's
  Common 34 C3
Tissington . . . 130 D1
Titchberry 24 C3
Titchfield 18 A4

Titchmarsh . . . 100 D2
Titchwell 119 A4
Tithby 115 B4
Titley. 78 A1
Titlington 189 B4
Titsey 36 A2
Tittensor 112 B2
Tittleshall. . . . 119 C5
Tiverton Ches W. 127 C5
  Devon. 27 D4
Tivetshall St
  Margaret. . . . 104 C2
Tivetshall St
  Mary 104 C2
Tividale 96 B2
Tivy Dale 139 C5
Tixall 112 C3
Tixover 99 A6
Toab Orkney . . .283 G6
  Shetland. . . . 285 M5
Toadmoor 130 D3
Tobermory . . . 225 A4
Toberonochy . . 213 B5
Tobha Mor. . . . 286 C3
Tobhtarol 288 D2
Tobson 288 D2
Tocher 256 C1
Tockenham . . . 44 B4
Tockenham Wick 44 A4
Tockholes 137 A5
Tockington . . . 43 A5
Tockwith 148 B3
Todber 30 C2
Todding 94 D2
Toddington
  C Beds 67 A6
  Glos 80 D3
Todenham 81 D5
Todhills 175 B6
Todlachie 244 A3
Todmorden . . . 138 A2
Todrig 186 B3
Todwick 131 A4
Toft Cambs . . . 85 B5
  Lincs. 116 D3
Toft Hill Durham .167 C4
  Lincs. 134 C2
Toft Monks . . . 105 B5
Toft next
  Newton 133 A5
Toftrees 119 C5
Tofts 281 B5
Toftwood 120 D1
Togston 189 C5
Tokavaig. 247 C5
Tokers Green . . 47 B5
Tolastadh a
  Chaolais. . . . 288 D2
Tolastadh bho
  Thuath 288 C6
Toll Bar. 140 C3
Tollard Royal. . . 30 D3
Toll End 96 B2
Toller Fratrum . 15 B5
Toller Porcorum . 15 B5
Tollerton Notts . 115 B4
  N Yorks. 148 A4
Tollesbury 70 B3
Tolleshunt D'Arcy 70 B3
Tolleshunt Major . 70 B3
Toll of Birness . 257 C5
Tolm 288 D5
Tolpuddle 16 B1
Tolvah 241 C6
Tolworth 49 C4
Tomatin 253 D4
Tombreck 252 C2
Tomchrasky . . 239 A6
Tomdoun 239 B5
Tomich Highld .251 D5
  Highld. 264 C2
Tomich House. .252 B1
Tomintoul
  Aberds 242 C4
  Moray. 243 A4
Tomnaven 255 C5
Tomnavoulin . .254 D3
Tonbridge 36 B3
Tondu 40 C3
Tonfanau 90 B3

Tong Shrops . . . 95 A5
  W Yorks 147 D6
Tonge 114 C2
Tongham 34 B1
Tongland 173 C4
Tong Norton . . 95 A5
Tongue 277 C6
Tongue End. . . 117 D4
Tongwynlais . . 41 C6
Tonna 40 B2
Ton-Pentre . . . 41 B4
Tonwell. 68 B3
Tonypandy . . . 41 B4
Tonyrefail 41 C5
Toot Baldon. . . 65 C6
Toothill 32 D2
Toot Hill 69 C5
Topcliffe. 158 D3
Topcroft. 104 B3
Topcroft Street. 104 B3
Top of Hebers .138 C1
Toppesfield . . . 86 D3
Toppings 137 B6
Topsham 13 C4
Torbay. 8 B3
Torbeg 191 C5
Torboll Farm. . .264 A3
Torbrex. 207 A5
Torbryan 8 A2
Torcross. 8 C2
Tore. 252 A2
Torinturk 202 B3
Torksey. 132 B3
Torlum 286 A3
Torlundy. 237 B5
Tormarton 43 B6
Tormisdale . . . 200 C1
Tormitchell . . . 181 B4
Tormore 191 B4
Tornagrain. . . . 252 B3
Tornahaish . . . 243 B5
Tornaveen 244 B3
Torness. 252 D1
Toronto 167 B4
Torpenhow . . . 163 A5
Torphichen . . . 208 C2
Torphins 244 B3
Torpoint 6 B3
Torquay 8 A3
Torquhan 196 B3
Torran Argyll. . .214 B1
  Highld. 248 B2
  Highld. 264 C3
Torrance 205 A6
Torrans. 224 D3
Torranyard. . . . 204 D3
Torre 8 A3
Torridon 249 A6
Torridon Ho.. . . 249 A5
Torrin 247 B4
Torrisdale 278 B2
Torrisdale-
  Square 190 B3
Torrish 274 C3
Torrisholme . . . 145 A4
Torroble 272 D3
Torry Aberdeen .245 B6
  Aberds 255 C5
Torryburn. 208 B3
Torterston . . . 257 B5
Torthorwald . . .174 A3
Tortington 20 B3
Tortworth. 62 D3
Torvaig 259 D4
Torver 154 B1
Torwood 207 B6
Torworth 131 A6
Tosberry. 24 C3
Toscaig. 249 C4
Toseland 84 A4
Tosside. 146 B1
Tostock. 87 A5
Totaig Highld . .249 D5
  Highld. 258 C2
Tote. 259 D4
Totegan 279 B4
Tothill 135 A4
Totland 18 C2
Totnes 8 A2
Toton. 114 B3
Totronald 223 B4
Totscore 258 B3

Tottenham.......68 D3
Tottenhill......118 D3
Tottenhill Row....118 D3
Totteridge......68 D2
Totternhoe......67 A5
Tottington.....137 B6
Totton.........32 D2
Touchen End.....48 B1
Tournaig......261 B5
Toux.........269 D4
Tovil.........37 A5
Toward........203 B6
Towcester......82 C3
Towednack......2 B2
Tower End.....118 D3
Towersey......66 C3
Towie Aberds...244 A1
 Aberds......268 C3
Towiemore.....255 B6
Tow Law......166 B4
Townend......205 A4
Town End Cambs 101 B6
 Cumb......154 C3
Towngate......116 D4
Townhead Cumb 164 B3
 Dumfries....173 D4
 S Ayrs......181 A4
 S Yorks.....139 C4
Townhead of
 Greenlaw....173 B5
Townhill......208 B4
Town Row......36 C3
Townsend Bucks..66 C3
 Herts.......67 C7
Townshend......2 B3
Town Yetholm..187 A7
Towthorpe....149 B5
Towton......148 D3
Towyn.......125 B4
Toxteth......126 A3
Toynton All
 Saints.....134 C3
Toynton Fen
 Side.......134 C3
Toynton St
 Peter......135 C4
Toy's Hill.....36 A2
Trabboch.....193 C4
Traboe........3 C5
Tradespark
 Highld......253 A4
 Orkney......283 G5
Trafford Park..137 D6
Trallong.......59 C6
Tranent......209 C7
Tranmere.....126 A3
Trantlebeg....279 C4
Trantlemore...279 C4
Tranwell.....178 A3
Trapp.........57 A6
Traprain.....210 C2
Traquair.....196 C2
Trawden.....146 D3
Trawsfynydd...108 B2
Trealaw.......41 B5
Treales......144 D4
Trearddur....122 C2
Treaslane....258 C3
Trebanog......41 B5
Trebanos......40 A2
Trebartha.....10 D3
Trebarwith......9 C6
Trebetherick....9 D5
Treborough.....27 B5
Trebudannon.....4 A3
Trebullett......10 D4
Treburley......10 D4
Trebyan........5 A5
Trecastle......59 C5
Trecenydd......41 C6
Trecwn........55 A5
Tredavoe.......2 C2
Treddiog......55 B4
Tredegar......10 C6
Tredington Glos .63 A5
 Warks.......81 C5
Tredinnick......9 D5
Tredomen......77 D5
Tredunnock.....61 D5
Tredustan......77 D5
Treen.........2 C1

Treeton......131 A4
Trefasser......72 C1
Trefdraeth....123 C4
Trefecca......77 D5
Trefechan......90 D3
Trefeglwys.....92 B3
Trefenter......75 B5
Treffgarne.....55 B5
Treffynnon.....54 B4
Trefgarn Owen..54 B4
Trefil.........60 B3
Trefilan......75 C4
Trefin........54 A4
Treflach.....110 C4
Trefnanney....109 D7
Trefnant.....125 B5
Trefonen.....110 C1
Trefor Anglesey.122 B3
 Gwyn......106 B3
Treforest......41 C5
Trefriw......124 C2
Tregadillett...10 C3
Tregaian.....123 C4
Tregare.......61 B6
Tregarth.....123 D6
Tregeare......10 C3
Tregeiriog....109 B6
Tregele......122 A3
Tre-Gibbon.....60 C1
Tregidden......3 C5
Treglemais.....54 B4
Tregole.......10 B2
Tregonetha......5 A4
Tregony........4 C4
Tregoss........5 A4
Tregoyd.......77 D6
Tregroes......73 B7
Tregurrian......4 A3
Tregynon......93 B4
Trehafod......41 B5
Treharris......41 B5
Treherbert.....40 B4
Trekenner......10 D4
Treknow.......10 C2
Trelan.........3 D5
Trelash.......10 B2
Trelassick......4 B3
Trelawnyd....125 B5
Trelech.......73 C5
Treleddyd-fawr..54 B3
Trelewis......41 B6
Treligga.......9 C6
Trelights.......9 D5
Trelill.........9 D6
Trelissick......4 D3
Trellech......61 C7
Trelleck Grange..61 C6
Trelogan.....125 A6
Trelystan.....93 A6
Tremadog.....107 B5
Tremail.......10 C2
Tremain......73 B5
Tremaine......10 C3
Tremar........6 A1
Trematon.......6 B3
Tremeirchion..125 B5
Trenance.......4 A3
Trenarren......5 C5
Trench.......111 D5
Treneglos......10 C3
Trenewan.......5 B6
Trent.........29 D5
Trentham.....112 A2
Trentishoe.....26 A1
Trent Vale....112 A2
Treoes........40 D4
Treorchy
 (Treorci)....41 B4
Tre'r-ddôl......91 C4
Trerule Foot.....6 B2
Tresaith......73 A5
Tresawle.......4 B3
Trescott......95 B6
Trescowe.......2 C3
Tresham......62 D3
Tresillian......4 C3
Tresinwen......72 B1
Treskinnick
 Cross.......10 B3
Tresmeer......10 C3
Tresparrett.....10 B2

Tresparrett Posts. 10 B2
Tressait......230 B2
Tresta Shetland....284 D8
 Shetland....285 H5
Treswell......132 B2
Tre-Taliesin....91 C4
Trethosa........4 B4
Trethurgy.......5 B5
Tretio.........54 B3
Tretire.........62 A1
Tretower.......60 A3
Treuddyn.....126 D2
Trevalga.......10 C1
Trevanson.......9 D5
Trevarren.......4 A4
Trevarrian......4 A3
Trevarrick......5 C4
Trevaughan....56 A1
Tre-vaughan...73 D7
Treveighan......9 D6
Trevellas.......4 B2
Treverva........4 D2
Trevethin......61 C4
Trevigro........6 A2
Treviscoe.......4 B4
Trevone.........9 D4
Trewarmett......9 C6
Trewassa......10 C2
Trewellard......2 B1
Trewen........10 C3
Trewennack......3 C4
Trewern......110 D1
Trewethern......9 D6
Trewidland......6 B1
Trewint Corn...10 B2
 Corn.......10 C3
Trewithian......4 D3
Trewoofe........2 C2
Trewoon........5 B4
Treworga........4 C3
Treworlas.......4 D3
Tre-wyn........61 A5
Treyarnon.......9 D4
Treyford W Sus.....20 A1
 W Sus......33 D7
Trezaise........5 B4
Triangle.....138 A3
Triffleton.....55 B5
Trimdon......167 B6
Trimdon
 Colliery....167 B6
Trimdon Grange 167 B6
Trimingham...121 B4
Trimley Lower
 Street.......88 D3
Trimley St Martin 88 D3
Trimley St Mary .88 D3
Trimpley......95 D5
Trimsaran......57 B4
Trimstone......25 A5
Trinafour....229 B6
Trinant.......41 A7
Tring.........67 B5
Tring Wharf....67 B5
Trinity Angus...233 B4
 Jersey......P06
Trisant.......75 A6
Trislaig......237 B4
Trispen.........4 B3
Tritlington...189 D5
Trochry......230 D3
Trodigal......190 C2
Troed-rhiwdalar .76 B3
Troedyraur....73 B6
Troedyrhiw.....41 A5
Tromode......152 D3
Trondavoe....284 F5
Troon Corn......3 B4
 S Ayrs......192 B3
Trosaraidh....286 E3
Trossachs Hotel 217 D5
Troston......103 D4
Trottiscliffe...50 C3
Trotton.......34 D1
Troutbeck Cumb .154 A3
 Cumb......164 C1
Troutbeck
 Bridge......154 A3
Trowbridge....44 D2
Trowell......114 B2
Trow Green....62 C1

Trowle Common ..44 D2
Trowley Bottom...67 B6
Trows.......197 C5
Trowse Newton..104 A3
Trudoxhill......30 A1
Trull.........28 C2
Trumaisgear-
 raidh......287 G3
Trumpan......258 B2
Trumpet.......79 D4
Trumpington...85 B6
Trunch......121 B4
Trunnah......144 C3
Truro...........4 C3
Trusham.......12 C3
Trusley......113 B6
Trusthorpe....135 A5
Trysull.......95 B6
Tubney........65 D5
Tuckenhay.......8 B2
Tuckhill.......95 C5
Tuckingmill.....3 A4
Tuddenham....102 D3
Tuddenham St
 Martin......88 C2
Tudeley.......36 B4
Tudhoe......167 B5
Tudorville.....62 A1
Tudweiliog...106 C2
Tuesley........34 B2
Tuffley........63 B4
Tufton Hants...32 A3
 Pembs......55 B6
Tugby.........99 A4
Tugford.......94 C3
Tullibardine..218 C4
Tullibody.....207 A6
Tullich Argyll..214 A3
 Highld......252 D2
Tullich Muir...264 C3
Tulliemet.....230 C2
Tulloch Aberds..233 A5
 Aberds......256 C3
 Perth......219 B5
Tulloch Castle..264 A1
Tullochgorm...214 C2
Tulloes......232 D3
Tullybannocher 218 B2
Tullybelton...219 A5
Tullyfergus...231 D6
Tullymurdoch.231 C5
Tullynessle...244 A2
Tumble........57 A5
Tumby
 Woodside...134 D2
Tummel Bridge .229 C6
Tunga.......288 D5
Tunstall E Yorks..151 D6
 Kent.......51 C5
 Lancs......155 D5
 Norf......105 A5
 N Yorks....157 B6
 Stoke......128 D3
 Suff.......89 B4
 T&W.......179 D5
Tunstead Derbys..129 B6
 Gtr Man....138 C3
 Norf......121 C4
Tunworth......33 A5
Tupsley.......78 C3
Tupton......130 C3
Turgis Green....47 D4
Turin.......232 C3
Turkdean.....64 B2
Tur Langton...99 B4
Turleigh......44 C2
Turn........137 B7
Turnastone....78 D1
Turnberry....192 E2
Turnditch....113 A6
Turners Hill....35 C6
Turners Puddle..16 B2
Turnford......68 C3
Turnhouse...209 C4
Turnworth.....16 A2
Turriff......268 D2
Turton Bottoms .137 B6
Turves......101 B5
Turvey........83 B6
Turville......66 D2
Turville Heath..66 D2
Turweston.....82 D3

Tushielaw....185 A6
Tutbury.....113 C6
Tutnall.......96 D2
Tutshill......62 D1
Tuttington...120 C4
Tutts Clump....46 B3
Tuxford.....132 B2
Twatt Orkney...282 E3
 Shetland....285 H5
Twechar.....207 C4
Tweedmouth..198 A3
Tweedsmuir..195 D5
Twelve Heads....4 C2
Twemlow Green 128 C2
Twenty......117 C4
Twerton.......43 C6
Twickenham...49 B4
Twigworth....63 A4
Twineham......21 A5
Twinhoe.......43 D6
Twinstead....87 D4
Twinstead Green .87 D4
Twiss Green...137 D5
Twiston......146 C2
Twitchen Devon...26 B2
 Shrops......94 D1
Two Bridges....11 D7
Two Dales....130 C2
Two Mills....126 B3
Twycross......97 A6
Twyford Bucks...66 A2
 Derbys.....114 C1
 Hants......32 C3
 Leics......115 D5
 Lincs......116 C2
 Norf......120 C2
 Wokingham...47 B5
Twyford
 Common.....78 D3
Twyn-y-Sheriff..61 C6
Twynholm....173 C4
Twyning......80 D1
Twyning Green...80 D1
Twynllanan....59 C4
Twynmynydd...57 A6
Twywell......99 D6
Tyberton......78 D1
Tyburn........96 B4
Ty'r-felin-isaf..124 C3
Tycroes......57 A6
Tycrwyn.....109 D6
Tydd Gote....118 D1
Tydd St Giles..118 D1
Tydd St Mary..118 D1
Tyddyn-mawr...107 B5
Ty-draw.....124 D3
Tye Green
 Essex......69 C4
 Essex......70 A1
 Essex......86 D1
Ty-hen Carms...73 D6
 Gwyn......106 C1
Tyldesley....137 C5
Tyler Hill.....52 C3
Tylers Green....67 D5
Tylorstown....41 B5
Tylwch........92 C3
Ty-mawr.....123 B4
Ty Mawr......58 A2
Ty Mawr Cwm..108 A4
Ty-nant Conwy...109 A4
 Gwyn......108 C4
Tyncelyn......75 B5
Tyndrum.....216 A3
Tyneham......16 C2
Tynehead.....196 A2
Tynemouth...179 C5
Tyne Tunnel...179 C5
Tynewydd......40 B4
Tyninghame..210 C3
Tynron......183 C6
Tyn-y-celyn..109 B6
Tyn-y-coed...110 C1
Tyn-y-fedwen..109 B6
Tyn-y-ffridd..109 B6
Tyn-y-graig...123 B5
Ty'n-y-groes..124 B2
Ty'n-y-maes...123 D6
Tyn-y-pwll...123 B4
Ty'n-yr-eithin...75 B5

Tyrie.......269 C4
Tyringham....83 C5
Tythecott.....25 D5
Tythegston....40 D3
Tytherington
 Ches E.....129 B4
 S Glos......43 A5
 Som.......30 A1
 Wilts......30 A3
Tytherleigh...14 A3
Ty-uchaf.....109 C5
Tywardreath.....5 B5
Tywyn Conwy..124 B2
 Gwyn......90 B3

U

Uachdar.....286 A3
Uags.......249 C4
Ubbeston Green 104 D4
Ubley........43 D4
Uckerby.....157 A6
Uckfield......36 D2
Uckington.....63 A5
Uddingston...207 D4
Uddington...194 C3
Udimore......23 A6
Udny Green...256 D3
Udny Station..257 D4
Udston......194 A1
Udstonhead..194 B2
Uffcott.......45 B5
Uffculme......27 D5
Uffington Lincs..100 A2
 Oxon.......45 A7
 Shrops.....111 D4
Ufford Pboro....100 A2
 Suff.......88 B3
Ufton........81 A6
Ufton Nervet....47 C4
Ugadale......190 C3
Ugborough......7 B5
Uggeshall....105 C5
Ugglebarnby..160 A2
Ughill......139 D5
Ugley........69 A5
Ugley Green....69 A5
Ugthorpe....169 D5
Uidh.......286 G2
Uig Argyll....215 D4
 Highld......258 B3
 Highld......258 C1
Uigen.......287 A5
Uigshader....259 D4
Uisken......224 E2
Ulbster......281 D5
Ulceby Lincs....135 B4
 N Lincs.....142 B3
Ulceby Skitter.142 B3
Ulcombe......37 B6
Uldale......163 A5
Uley........62 D3
Ulgham......189 D5
Ullapool....262 A3
Ullenhall.....80 A4
Ullenwood....63 B5
Ulleskelf....148 C4
Ullesthorpe....98 C2
Ulley.......131 A4
Ullingswick...78 C3
Ullinish.....246 A2
Ullock......162 B3
Ulnes Walton 136 B4
Ulpha.......153 A2
Ulrome......151 B4
Ulsta.......284 E6
Ulva House...224 C3
Ulverston...154 D1
Ulwell........17 C4
Umberleigh...25 C7
Unapool.....271 A5
Unasary.....286 D3
Underbarrow..154 B3
Undercliffe...147 D5
Underhoull...284 C7
Underriver....36 A3
Underwood...131 D4
Undy........42 A3

Unifirth. 285 H4
Union Cottage. . .245 C5
Union Mills 152 D3
Union Street 37 C5
Unstone 130 B3
Unstone Green . .130 B3
Unthank Cumb . .164 B2
Cumb 165 A4
Unthank End 164 B2
Upavon 45 D5
Up Cerne 15 A6
Upchurch 51 C5
Upcott. 78 B1
Upend 86 B2
Up Exe. 13 A4
Upgate 120 D3
Uphall 208 C3
Uphall Station. . .208 C3
Upham Devon 12 A3
Hants. 32 C4
Uphampton 79 A6
Up Hatherley 63 A5
Uphill 42 D2
Up Holland. 136 C4
Uplawmoor 205 C4
Upleadon 62 A3
Upleatham 168 D4
Uplees. 52 C1
Uploders. 15 B5
Uplowman 27 D5
Uplyme 14 B3
Up Marden. 33 D6
Upminster 50 A2
Up Nately 47 D4
Upnor 51 B4
Upottery 14 A2
Upper Affcot 94 C2
Upper
   Ardchronie 264 B2
Upper Arley 95 C5
Upper Arncott . . .65 B7
Upper Astrop 82 D2
Upper Badcall. . . .276 D2
Upper Basildon. . .46 B3
Upper Beeding . . .21 A4
Upper Benefield 100 C1
Upper Bighouse 279 C4
Upper
   Boddington. . . .82 B1
Upper Borth 90 D4
Upper Boyndlie .269 C4
Upper Brailes 81 D6
Upper Breakish .247 B5
Upper Breinton. . .78 C2
Upper
   Broadheath. . . .79 B6
Upper
   Broughton. . . .115 C4
Upper
   Bucklebury . . .46 C3
Upper
   Burnhaugh . . .245 C5
Upperby 175 C7
Upper Caldecote .84 C3
Upper Catesby . . .82 B2
Upper Chapel 76 C4
Upper Church
   Village 41 C5
Upper Chute 45 D6
Upper Clatford . . .32 A2
Upper Clynnog . .107 B4
Upper
   Cumberworth. .139 C5
Upper Cwmbran. .61 D4
Upper Cwm-
   twrch 59 D4
Upper Dallachy .267 C4
Upper Dean. 84 A2
Upper Denby 139 C5
Upper Denton . . .176 C4
Upper Derraid . . .253 C6
Upper Dicker 22 B3
Upper
   Dovercourt 88 D3
Upper Druimfin .225 A4
Upper
   Dunsforth 148 A3
Upper Eathie. . . .264 D3
Upper Elkstone. .129 D5

Upper End 129 B5
Upper
   Farringdon 33 B6
Upper Framilode . .62 B3
Upper
   Glenfintaig . . .239 D6
Upper Gornal 96 B2
Upper
   Gravenhurst. . . .84 D3
Upper Green Mon . .61 B5
W Berks. 46 C1
Upper Grove
   Common 62 A1
Upper Hackney .130 C2
Upper Hale 34 B1
Upper Halistra . .258 C2
Upper Halling . . .50 C3
Upper
   Hambleton 99 A5
Upper Hardres
   Court 52 D3
Upper Hartfield . .36 C2
Upper Haugh. . . .140 D2
Upper Heath 94 C3
Upper
   Hellesdon 120 D4
Upper Helmsley .149 B5
Upper Hergest . . .77 B6
Upper Heyford
   Northants. 82 B3
   Oxon. 65 A5
Upper Hill 78 B2
Upper Hopton . . .139 B4
Upper
   Horsebridge. . . .22 A3
Upper Hulme. . . .129 C5
Upper Inglesham .64 D3
Upper
   Inverbrough . .253 C4
Upper Killay 57 C5
Upper
   Knockando . . .254 B2
Upper Lambourn .45 A7
Upper Leigh. 112 B4
Upper Lenie. 251 D7
Upper Lochton . .244 C3
Upper Longdon .113 D4
Upper Lybster . .275 A6
Upper Lydbrook . .62 B2
Upper Maes-
   coed 78 D1
Upper Midway . .113 C6
Uppermill. 138 C2
Upper Milovaig .258 D1
Upper Minety 63 D6
Upper Mitton 95 D6
Upper North
   Dean. 66 D4
Upper Obney 219 A5
Upper Ollach 247 A4
Upper Padley . . .130 B2
Upper Pollicott. . .66 B3
Upper
   Poppleton 149 B4
Upper Quinton . . .81 C4
Upper Ratley 32 C2
Upper Rissington .64 B3
Upper Rochford . .79 A4
Upper Sandaig . .238 A1
Upper Sanday . .283 G6
Upper Sapey 79 A4
Upper
   Saxondale. . . .115 B4
Upper Seagry 44 A3
Upper Shelton . . .84 C1
Upper
   Sheringham . .120 A3
Upper
   Skelmorlie . . .204 B2
Upper Slaughter . .64 A2
Upper Soudley . . .62 B2
Uppersound. 285 J6
Upper Stondon . . .84 D3
Upper Stowe 82 B3
Upper Stratton . . .45 A5
Upper Street
   Hants 31 D5
   Norf 121 B5
   Norf 121 D5
   Suff 88 D2
Upper Strensham 80 D2
Upper Sundon. . . .67 A6

Upper Swell. 64 A2
Upper Tean 112 B4
Upperthong. 139 C4
Upperthorpe 141 C5
Upper Tillyrie . . .219 D6
Upperton 34 D2
Upper Tooting . . .49 B5
Upper Tote 259 C5
Uppertown
   Derbys. 130 C3
   Highld. 281 A5
   Orkney. 283 H5
Upper Town. 43 C4
Upper
   Treverward. . . .93 D6
Upper Tysoe 81 C6
Upper Upham 45 B6
Upper
   Wardington 82 C1
Upper Weald. 83 D4
Upper Weedon . . .82 B3
Upper Wield 33 B5
Upper
   Winchendon. . .66 B3
Upper Witton 96 B3
Upper Woodend 244 A3
Upper Woodford . .31 B5
Upper Wootton. . .46 D3
Upper Wyche 79 C5
Uppingham 99 B5
Uppington 95 A4
Upsall 158 C3
Upshire. 68 C4
Up Somborne 32 B2
Upstreet 53 C4
Up Sydling 15 A6
Upthorpe 103 D5
Upton Cambs 100 D3
   Ches W. 127 C4
   Corn 10 A3
   Dorset 16 B3
   Dorset 16 C1
   Hants 32 D2
   Hants 46 D1
   Leics. 97 B6
   Lincs. 132 A3
   Mers. 126 A2
   Norf 121 D5
   Northants. 83 A4
   Notts 132 B2
   Notts 132 D2
   Oxon. 46 A3
   Pboro. 100 A3
   Slough 48 B2
   Som 27 C4
   W Yorks 140 B2
Upton Bishop 62 A2
Upton Cheyney . .43 C5
Upton Cressett . . .95 B4
Upton Cross. 10 D3
Upton Grey 33 A5
Upton Hellions . . .12 A3
Upton Lovell 30 A3
Upton Magna . . .111 D4
Upton Noble 29 B7
Upton Pyne 13 B4
Upton St
   Leonard's 63 B4
Upton
   Scudamore. 30 A2
Upton Snodsbury. 80 B2
Upton upon
   Severn 79 C6
Upton Warren 80 A2
Upwaltham 20 A2
Upware 102 D1
Upwell. 101 A6
Upwey. 15 C6
Upwood 101 C4
Uradale 285 K6
Urafirth 284 F5
Urchfont. 44 D4
Urdimarsh 78 C3
Ure. 284 F4
Ure Bank 157 D7
Urgha 288 H2
Urishay Common 77 D7
Urlay Nook. 167 D6
Urmston. 137 D6
Urpeth. 179 D4
Urquhart Highld . .252 A1
   Moray. 266 C3

Urra. 159 A4
Urray 251 A7
Ushaw Moor 167 A5
Usk (Brynbuga) . . .61 C5
Usselby 142 D2
Usworth 179 D5
Utkinton 127 C5
Utley 147 C4
Uton. 12 B3
Utterby 143 D5
Uttoxeter 113 B4
Uwchmynydd . . .106 D1
Uxbridge 48 A3
Uyeasound. 284 C7
Uzmaston. 55 C5

V

Valley 122 C2
Valleyfield 173 C4
Valley Truckle. . . .10 C1
Valsgarth 284 B8
Valtos 259 B5
Van 92 C3
Vange 51 A4
Varteg 61 C4
Vatten 258 D2
Vaul 222 C3
Vaynor 60 B2
Veensgarth 285 J6
Velindre 77 D5
Vellow. 27 B5
Veness 282 E6
Venn Green 25 D4
Vennington 94 A1
Venn Ottery 13 B5
Venny Tedburn . . .12 B3
Ventnor 19 D4
Vernham Dean . . .46 D1
Vernham Street . .46 D1
Vernolds
   Common 94 C2
Verwood 17 A4
Veryan 4 D4
Vicarage 14 C2
Vickerstown 153 D2
Victoria Corn 5 A4
Vidlin. 284 G6
Viewpark 207 D5
Vigo Village. 50 C3
Vinehall Street . . .37 D5
Vine's Cross 22 A3
Viney Hill 62 C2
Virginia Water . . .48 C2
Virginstow 11 B4
Vobster. 29 A7
Voe Shetland 284 E5
   Shetland. 285 G6
Vowchurch 78 D1
Voxter. 284 F5
Voy. 282 F3

W

Wackerfield. 167 C4
Wacton. 104 B2
Wadbister 285 J6
Wadborough. 80 C2
Waddesdon 66 B3
Waddingham. . . .142 D1
Waddington
   Lancs 146 C1
   Lincs. 133 C4
Wadebridge. 9 D5
Wadeford 28 D3
Wadenhoe 100 C2
Wadesmill 68 B3
Wadhurst 36 C4
Wadshelf 130 B3
Wadsley 139 D6
Wadsley Bridge .139 D6
Wadworth 140 D3
Waen Denb 125 C4
   Denb. 125 C6
Waen Fach. 109 D7
Waen
   Goleugoed . . .125 B5
Wag 274 B4

Wainfleet All
   Saints. 135 D4
Wainfleet Bank. .135 D4
Wainfleet St
   Mary. 135 D5
Wainfleet Tofts. .135 D5
Wainhouse
   Corner 10 B2
Wainscott. 51 B4
Wainstalls 138 A3
Waitby. 155 A6
Waithe 143 C4
Wakefield. 139 A6
Wake Lady
   Green 159 B5
Wakerley 99 B6
Wakes Colne 70 A2
Walberswick 105 D5
Walberton 20 B2
Walbottle 178 C3
Walcot Lincs 116 B3
   N Lincs 141 A6
   Shrops 94 C1
   Swindon 45 A5
   Telford 111 D4
Walcote Leics 98 C2
   Warks. 80 B4
Walcot Green . . .104 C2
Walcott Lincs . . .133 D6
   Norf 121 B5
Walden 156 C4
Walden Head . . .156 C3
Walden Stubbs . .140 B3
Waldersey 101 A6
Waldershare 53 C4
Walderslade 51 C4
Walderton 33 D6
Walditch 15 B4
Waldley 113 B5
Waldridge 179 D4
Waldringfield 88 C3
Waldringfield
   Heath 88 C3
Waldron 22 A3
Wales 131 A4
Walesby Lincs . . .142 D3
   Notts 132 B1
Walford Hereford. .62 A1
   Hereford 94 D1
   Shrops 110 C3
Walford Heath . .110 D3
Walgherton 111 A5
Walgrave 99 D5
Walhampton 18 B2
Walkden 137 C6
Walker 179 C4
Walker Barn 129 B4
Walkerburn 196 C2
Walker Fold. 145 C6
Walkeringham . .141 D5
Walkerith 141 D5
Walkern 68 A2
Walker's Green. . .78 C3
Walkerville 157 B6
Walkford 17 B6
Walkhampton 7 A4
Walkington 150 D2
Walkley 130 A3
Walk Mill 146 D2
Wall Northumb . .177 C7
   Staffs 96 A4
Wallacetown
   S Ayrs. 181 A4
   S Ayrs. 192 C3
Wallands Park . . .22 A2
Wallasey 136 D2
Wall Bank 94 B3
Wallcrouch 37 C4
Wall Heath. 96 C1
Wallingford 47 A4
Wallington Hants . .19 A4
   Herts 85 D4
   London 49 C5
Wallis 55 B6
Walliswood 35 C4
Walls 285 J4
Wallsend 179 C4
Wallston 41 D6
Wall under
   Heywood 94 B3
Wallyford 209 C6
Walmer. 53 D5

Walmer Bridge. .136 A3
Walmersley 137 B7
Walmley 96 B4
Walpole 105 D4
Walpole Cross
   Keys. 118 D2
Walpole
   Highway. 118 D2
Walpole Marsh .118 D1
Walpole St
   Andrew 118 D2
Walpole St
   Peter 118 D2
Walsall 96 B3
Walsall Wood 96 A3
Walsden 138 A2
Walsgrave on
   Sowe 97 C6
Walsham le
   Willows 103 D5
Walshaw 137 B6
Walshford 148 B3
Walsoken 118 D1
Walston 195 B5
Walsworth 84 D4
Walters Ash. 66 D4
Walterston. 41 D5
Walterstone. 61 A5
Waltham Kent 38 A3
   NE Lincs 143 C4
Waltham Abbey . .68 C3
Waltham Chase . .33 D4
Waltham Cross. . .68 C3
Waltham on the
   Wolds 115 C6
Waltham St
   Lawrence 47 B6
Walthamstow 49 A6
Walton Cumb . . .176 C3
   Derbys 130 C3
   Leics. 98 C2
   Mers. 136 D2
   M Keynes 83 D5
   Pboro. 100 A3
   Powys 77 B6
   Som 29 B4
   Staffs 112 B2
   Suff 88 D3
   Telford 111 D4
   Warks. 81 B5
   W Yorks 139 B6
   W Yorks 148 C3
Walton Cardiff . . .80 D2
Walton East. 55 B6
Walton-in-
   Gordano 42 B3
Walton-le-Dale .137 A4
Walton-on-
   Thames 48 C4
Walton on the Hill
   Staffs 112 C3
   Sur. 35 A5
Walton-on-the-
   Naze 71 A6
Walton on the
   Wolds 114 D3
Walton-on-
   Trent. 113 D6
Walton West 55 C4
Walwen 126 B2
Walwick 177 B7
Walworth 167 D5
Walworth Gate . .167 C5
Walwyn's Castle. .55 C4
Wambrook. 14 A2
Wanborough Sur. . .34 B2
   Swindon. 45 A6
Wandsworth 49 B5
Wangford 105 D5
Wanlockhead . . .183 A6
Wansford E Yorks 150 B3
   Pboro. 100 B2
Wanstead 49 A7
Wanstrow. 29 A7
Wanswell 62 C2
Wantage 46 A1
Wapley 43 B6
Wappenbury 81 A6
Wappenham. 82 C3
Warbleton 22 A4
Warblington 19 A6
Warborough 65 D6

Warboys........101 C5
Warbreck......144 D3
Warbstow....10 B3
Warburton....128 A2
Warcop......165 D5
Warden Kent....52 B2
  Northumb......177 C7
Ward End......96 C4
Ward Green....87 A6
Wardhill......282 E7
Wardington....82 C1
Wardlaw......185 A5
Wardle Ches E....127 D6
  Gtr Man......138 B2
Wardley......99 A5
Wardlow......130 B1
Wardy Hill....101 C6
Ware Herts......68 B3
  Kent........53 C4
Wareham......16 C3
Warehorne......38 B1
Warenford....189 A4
Waren Mill....199 C5
Warenton......199 C5
Wareside......68 B3
Waresley Cambs..84 B4
  Worcs........95 D6
Warfield......48 B1
Warfleet........8 B2
Wargrave......47 B5
Warham......119 A6
Warhill........138 D2
Wark Northumb...177 B6
  Northumb....198 C2
Warkleigh....26 C1
Warkton......99 D5
Warkworth
  Northants....82 C1
  Northumb....189 C5
Warlaby......158 B2
Warland......138 A2
Warleggan......5 A6
Warlingham....35 A6
Warmfield....140 A1
Warmingham..128 C2
Warmington
  Northants....100 B2
  Warks........81 C7
Warminster....30 A2
Warmlake......37 A6
Warmley......43 B5
Warmley Tower..43 B5
Warmonds Hill..83 A6
Warmsworth..140 C3
Warmwell......16 C1
Warndon......80 B1
Warnford......33 C5
Warnham......35 C4
Warninglid....35 D5
Warren Ches E..128 B3
  Pembs........55 E5
Warren Heath...88 C3
Warren Row....47 A6
Warren Street..51 D6
Warrington
  M Keynes......83 B5
  Warr........127 A6
Warsash......18 A3
Warslow......129 D5
Warter......150 B1
Warthermarske.157 D6
Warthill......149 B5
Wartling......23 B4
Wartnaby....115 C5
Warton Lancs..136 A3
  Lancs......154 D3
  Northumb....188 C3
  Warks........97 A5
Warwick......81 A5
Warwick Bridge 176 D2
Warwick on
  Eden......176 D2
Wasbister......282 D4
Wasdale Head..163 D4
Washaway......5 A5
Washbourne....8 B1
Wash Common..46 C2
Washfield......27 D4
Washfold......157 A4
Washford......27 A5
Washford Pyne..26 D3

Washingborough
........133 B5
Washington
  T&W........179 D5
  W Sus........21 A4
Wasing......46 C3
Waskerley....166 A3
Wasperton......81 B5
Wasps Nest....133 C5
Wass........159 D4
Watchet......27 A5
Watchfield Oxon..64 D3
  Som........28 A3
Watchgate....154 B4
Watchhill....175 D6
Watcombe......8 A3
Watendlath....163 C5
Water Devon....12 C2
  Lancs......138 A1
Waterbeach....85 A6
Waterbeck....175 A5
Waterden....181 B5
Water End
  E Yorks......149 D6
  Herts........67 B6
  Herts........68 C2
Waterfall....129 D5
Waterfoot E Renf 205 C5
  Lancs......138 A1
Waterford Hants..18 B2
  Herts........68 B3
Waterhead Cumb 154 A2
  Dumfries....185 C4
Waterheads...196 A1
Waterhouses
  Durham......167 A4
  Staffs......129 D5
Wateringbury..37 A4
Waterloo
  Gtr Man......138 C2
  Highld......247 D5
  Mers........136 D2
  N Lanark....194 A3
  Norf........120 D4
  Perth......219 A5
  Poole........17 B4
  Shrops......111 B4
Waterloo Port..123 D4
Waterlooville...19 A5
Watermeetings.184 A2
Watermillock..164 C2
Water Newton.100 B3
Water Orton....97 B4
Waterperry....66 C2
Waterrow......27 C5
Watersfield....20 A3
Waterside
  Aberds......257 D5
  Blackburn....137 A6
  Cumb......175 D5
  E Ayrs......182 B2
  E Ayrs......205 D4
  E Dunb......207 C4
  E Renf......205 C5
Water's Nook..137 C5
Waterstock....66 C1
Waterston......55 D5
Water Stratford .82 D3
Waters Upton.111 D5
Water Yeat....154 C1
Watford Herts....67 D7
  Northants......82 A3
Watford Gap....96 A4
Wath N Yorks..147 A5
  N Yorks......157 D7
  N Yorks......159 D5
Wath Brow....162 C3
Wath upon
  Dearne......140 C2
Watley's End....43 A5
Watlington Norf..118 D3
  Oxon........66 D1
Watnall......114 A3
Watten......280 C4
Wattisfield....103 D6
Wattisham......87 B6
Wattlesborough
  Heath......110 D2
Watton E Yorks..150 B3
  Norf........119 D5
Watton at Stone..68 B3
Wattston......207 C5

Wattstown......41 B5
Wauchan......238 D3
Waulkmill
  Lodge......283 G4
Waun........91 B6
Waunarlwydd....57 C6
Waunclunda....58 B3
Waunfawr....107 A5
Waungron......57 B5
Waunlwyd......60 C3
Waun-y-clyn....57 B4
Wavendon......83 D6
Waverbridge..175 D5
Wawne......150 D3
Waxham......121 C6
Waxholme....143 A5
Way........53 C5
Wayfield......51 C4
Wayford......14 A4
Waymills......111 A4
Wayne Green....61 B6
Way Village....26 D3
Weachyburn...268 D1
Weald........64 C4
Wealdstone....49 A4
Weardley......148 C1
Weare........42 D3
Weare Giffard....25 C5
Wearhead......165 B6
Weasdale......155 A5
Weasenham All
  Saints......119 C5
Weasenham St
  Peter......119 C5
Weatherhill....35 B6
Weaverham....127 B6
Weaverthorpe..160 D3
Webheath......80 A3
Wedderlairs...256 C3
Wedderlie....197 A5
Weddington....97 B6
Wedhampton....45 D4
Wedmore......28 A4
Wednesbury....96 B2
Wednesfield....96 A2
Weedon......66 C3
Weedon Bec....82 B3
Weedon Lois....82 C3
Weeford......96 A4
Week......26 D2
Weeke........32 B3
Weekley......99 C5
Week St Mary....10 B3
Weel........150 D3
Weeley......71 A5
Weeley Heath....71 A5
Weem......230 D2
Weeping Cross..112 C3
Weethley Gate....80 B3
Weeting......102 C3
Weeton E Yorks.143 A5
  Lancs......144 D3
  N Yorks......148 C1
Weetwood Hall.188 A3
Weir........138 A1
Weir Quay......6 A3
Welborne....120 E2
Welbourn....133 D4
Welburn N Yorks 149 A6
  N Yorks......159 C5
Welbury......158 A2
Welby......130 B2
Welches Dam..101 C6
Welcombe......24 D3
Weld Bank....137 B4
Weldon......189 D4
Welford Northants 98 C3
  W Berks......46 B2
Welford-on-
  Avon......81 B4
Welham Leics....99 B4
  Notts......132 A2
Welham Green....68 C2
Well Hants......33 A6
  Lincs......135 D4
  N Yorks......157 C6
Welland......79 C5
Wellbank......221 A4

Welldale......175 B4
Well End......48 A1
Wellesbourne....81 B5
Well Heads....147 D4
Well Hill......50 C1
Welling......50 B1
Wellingborough..83 A5
Wellingham...119 C5
Wellingore....133 D4
Wellington Cumb 162 D3
  Hereford......78 C2
  Som........27 C6
  Telford......111 D5
Wellington Heath 79 C5
Wellington Hill..148 D2
Wellow Bath....43 D6
  IoW........18 C2
  Notts......131 C6
Wellpond Green..68 A4
Wells........29 A5
Wellsborough....97 A6
Wells Green...128 D1
Wells-Next-The-
  Sea......119 A6
Wellswood......8 A3
Well Town....13 A4
Wellwood......208 B3
Welney......102 B1
Welshampton..110 B3
Welsh Bicknor....62 B1
Welsh End......111 B4
Welsh Frankton.110 B2
Welsh Hook....55 B5
Welsh Newton....61 B6
Welshpool (Y
  Trallwng)......93 A6
Welsh St Donats..41 D5
Welton Cumb...164 A1
  E Yorks......142 A1
  Lincs......133 B5
  Northants......82 A2
Welton Hill....133 A5
Welton le
  Marsh......135 C4
Welton le Wold..134 A2
Welwick......143 A5
Welwyn......68 B2
Welwyn Garden
  City......68 B2
Wem......111 C4
Wembdon......28 B2
Wembley......49 A4
Wembury......7 C4
Wembworthy....12 A1
Wemyss Bay...204 B1
Wenallt Ceredig...75 A5
  Gwyn......109 A4
Wendens Ambo...85 D7
Wendlebury....65 B6
Wendling......119 D6
Wendover......66 C4
Wendron........3 B4
Wendy......85 C5
Wenfordbridge...10 D1
Wenhaston....105 D5
Wennington
  Cambs......100 D4
  Lancs......155 D5
  London......50 A2
Wensley Derbys.130 C2
  N Yorks......157 C4
Wentbridge...140 B2
Wentnor......94 B1
Wentworth
  Cambs......101 D6
  S Yorks......140 D1
Wenvoe......41 D6
Weobley......78 B2
Weobley Marsh...78 B2
Wereham....102 A2
Wergs......95 A6
Wern Powys....109 D4
  Powys......110 D1
Wernffrwd......57 C5
Wernyrheolydd...61 B5
Werrington Corn..10 C4
  Pboro......100 A3
  Staffs......112 A3
Wervin......127 B4
Wesham......144 D4
Wessington...130 D3
Westacott......25 B6

West Acre....119 D4
West Adderbury..82 D1
West Allerdean..198 B3
West Alvington....7 C6
West Amesbury..31 A5
West Anstey....26 C3
West Ashby....134 B2
West Ashling....19 A7
West Ashton....44 D2
West Auckland.167 C4
West Ayton....160 C3
West
  Bagborough....27 B6
West Barkwith.133 A6
West Barnby....169 D6
West Barns....210 C3
West Barsham..119 B6
West Bay........15 B4
West Beckham.120 B3
West Bedfont....48 B3
West Benhar....208 D1
Westbere......52 C3
West Bergholt....70 A3
West Bexington..15 C5
West Bilney....119 D4
West
  Blatchington....21 B5
Westborough..115 A6
Westbourne
  Bmouth......17 B4
  Suff........88 C2
  W Sus........19 A6
West Bowling..147 D5
West Bradford.146 C1
West Bradley....29 B5
West Bretton...139 B5
West Bridgford.114 B3
West Bromwich...96 B3
Westbrook......46 B2
West Buckland
  Devon......26 B1
  Som........28 C1
West Burrafirth .285 H4
West Burton
  N Yorks......156 C4
  W Sus........20 A2
Westbury Bucks..82 D3
  Shrops......94 A1
  Wilts........44 D2
Westbury Leigh..44 D2
Westbury-on-
  Severn......62 B3
Westbury on
  Trym......43 B4
Westbury-sub-
  Mendip......29 A5
West
  Butterwick...141 C6
Westby......144 D3
West Byfleet....48 C3
West Caister...121 D7
West Calder...208 D3
West Camel....29 C5
West Challow....46 A1
West
  Chelborough...15 A5
West
  Chevington...189 D5
West Chiltington..20 A3
West Chiltington
  Common......20 A3
West Chinnock...29 D4
West Chisenbury..45 D5
West Clandon....34 A3
West Cliffe....39 A5
Westcliff-on-Sea 51 A5
West Clyne....274 D2
West Clyth....275 A6
West Coker....29 D5
Westcombe......29 B6
West Compton
  Dorset......15 B5
  Som........29 A5
Westcote......64 A3
Westcott Bucks...66 B3
  Devon......13 A5
  Sur........35 B4
Westcott Barton..65 A5
West Cowick..140 A4
West Cranmore..29 A6
West Cross......57 D6
West Cullery..245 B4

West Curry......10 B3
West
  Curthwaite ...175 D6
West Darlochan 190 C2
Westdean......22 C3
West Dean Wilts..31 C6
  W Sus........20 A1
West Deeping..100 A3
West Derby....136 D2
West Dereham..102 A2
West Didsbury .138 D1
West Ditchburn.189 A4
West Down....25 A6
West Drayton
  London......48 B3
  Notts......132 B2
West Ella....142 A2
West End Bedford..84 B1
  E Yorks......150 D2
  E Yorks......151 D4
  Hants........32 D3
  Lancs......137 A6
  Norf........103 A5
  Norf........121 D7
  N Som........42 C3
  N Yorks......147 B5
  Oxon........65 C5
  S Lanark....195 B4
  Suff........105 C5
  Sur........48 C2
  S Yorks......141 C4
  Wilts........30 C3
  Wilts........44 B3
West End Green..47 C4
Wester
  Aberchalder ..252 D1
Wester
  Balgedie 219 D6
Wester
  Culbeuchly ..268 C1
Westerdale
  Highld......280 C3
  N Yorks......159 A5
Wester
  Dechmont ...208 D3
Wester Denoon .232 D1
Westerfield
  Shetland....285 H5
  Suff........88 C2
Wester Fintray .245 A5
Westergate......20 B2
Wester
  Gruinards ...263 A7
Westerham....36 A2
Westerhope...178 C3
Wester Lealty .264 C2
Westerleigh....43 B6
Wester Milton .253 A6
Wester
  Newburn.....220 D4
Wester Quarff .285 K6
Wester Skeld...285 J4
Westerton Angus 233 C4
  Durham....167 B5
  W Sus........20 B1
Westerwick...285 J4
West Farleigh....37 A5
West Felton...110 C2
West Fenton..210 B1
West Ferry....221 A4
Westfield Cumb.162 B2
  E Sus........23 A6
  Hereford......79 C5
  Highld......279 B6
  N Lanark....207 C5
  Norf........103 A5
  W Loth......208 C2
Westfields......15 A7
Westfields of
  Rattray 231 D5
West Firle......22 B2
Westgate
  Durham......166 B2
  N Lincs......141 C5
  Norf........119 A5
  Norf........119 A6
Westgate on Sea .53 B5

West Ginge 46 A2
West Grafton. 45 C6
West Green 47 D5
West Greenskares . . 268 C2
West Grimsted . . 31 C6
West Grinstead. . . 35 D4
West Haddlesey 140 A3
West Haddon 98 D3
West Hagbourne . 46 A3
West Hagley 96 C2
Westhall Aberds. . 256 D1
Suff 105 C5
West Hall 176 C3
West Hallam 114 A2
West Halton. . . . 141 A7
Westham Dorset . . 15 D6
E Sus 22 B4
Som 28 A4
West Ham 49 A7
Westhampnett . . . 20 B1
West Handley . . 130 B3
West Hanney 65 D5
West Hanningfield . . 70 D1
West Hardwick . 140 B2
West Harnham . . 31 C5
West Hartree . . . 43 D4
West Hatch 28 C2
Westhay 28 A4
Westhead 136 C3
West Head 102 A1
West Heath
Ches E 128 C3
Hants 34 A1
Hants 46 D3
West Helmsdale 274 C4
West Hendred . . . 46 A2
West Heslerton . 160 D3
Westhide 78 C3
Westhill Aberds . 245 B5
Highld. 252 B3
West Hill Devon . . 13 B5
E Yorks 151 A4
N Som 42 B3
West Hoathly. . . 35 C6
West Holme. . . . 16 C2
Westhope
Hereford 78 B2
Shrops 94 C2
West Horndon. . . 50 A3
Westhorpe Lincs . 117 B5
Suff 87 A6
West Horrington . 29 A5
West Horsley. . . . 34 A3
West Horton . . . 198 C4
West Hougham. . . 39 A4
Westhoughton . . 137 C5
West Houlland . . 285 H4
Westhouse. 155 D5
West-houses. . . . 131 D4
Westhumble 35 A4
West Huntington . . 149 B5
West Hythe 38 B3
West Ilsley 46 A2
Westing 284 C7
West Itchenor . . . 19 A6
West Keal. 134 C3
West Kennett . . . 45 C5
West Kilbride . . 204 D2
West Kingsdown . 50 C2
West Kingston . . 44 B2
West Kinharrachie . 257 C4
West Kirby 126 A2
West Knapton . . 160 D2
West Knighton . . 16 C1
West Knoyle . . . 30 B2
West Kyloe. . . . 199 B4
Westlake 7 B5
West Lambrook . 28 D4
West Langdon . . . 39 A5
West Langwell . 273 D4
West Lavington
Wilts. 44 D4
W Sus. 34 D1
West Layton . . 157 A5
West Lea 168 A2

West Leake 114 C3
West Learmouth . . 198 C2
Westleigh Devon . . 25 C5
Devon. 27 D5
Gtr Man 137 C5
West Leigh. 12 A1
Westleton 89 A5
West Lexham . . 119 D5
Westley Shrops . . 94 A1
Suff 87 A4
Westley Waterless . . . 86 B2
West Lilling 149 A5
Westlington. . . . 66 B3
Westlinton. 175 B6
West Linton . . . 195 A6
West Liss 33 C6
West Littleton . . 43 B6
West Looe 6 B1
West Luccombe . 26 A3
West Lulworth . . 16 C2
West Lutton . . . 150 A2
West Lydford. . . 29 B5
West Lyng 28 C3
West Lynn 118 C3
West Malling . . . 37 A4
West Malvern . . . 79 C5
West Marden . . . 33 D6
West Marina . . . 23 B5
West Markham. 132 B2
Westmarsh 53 C4
West Marsh . . . 143 B4
West Marton . . 146 B2
West Meon 33 C5
West Mersea . . . 71 B4
Westmeston . . . 21 A6
Westmill 68 A3
West Milton . . . 15 B5
Westminster . . . 49 B6
West Minster . . 51 B6
West Molesey . . 48 C4
West Monkton . 28 C2
West Moors. . . . 17 A4
West Morriston . 197 B5
West Muir 232 B3
Westness 282 E4
West Ness 159 D5
West Newham. 178 B2
Westnewton
Cumb 174 D4
Northumb. 198 C4
West Newton
E Yorks 151 D4
Norf 118 C3
West Norwood . . 49 B6
Westoe 179 C5
West Ogwell . . . 12 D3
Weston Bath. . . 43 C6
Ches E 128 D2
Devon. 13 C6
Dorset 15 D6
Halton 127 A5
Hants 33 C6
Herts 85 D4
Lincs. 117 C5
Northants. . . . 82 C2
Notts 132 C2
N Yorks. 147 C5
Shrops 94 B3
Shrops 111 C4
Staffs 112 C3
W Berks. 46 B1
Weston Beggard . 78 C3
Westonbirt. . . . 44 A2
Weston by Welland 99 B4
Weston Colville . 86 B2
Westoncommon 110 C3
Weston Coyney. 112 A3
Weston Favell . . 83 A4
Weston Green
Cambs 86 B2
Norf 120 D3
Weston Heath . 112 D1
Weston Hills . . 117 C5
Westoning 84 D2
Weston-in-Gordano . . . 42 B3
Weston Jones . 111 C6

Weston Longville . . . 120 D3
Weston Lullingfields . . 110 C3
Weston-on-the-Green 65 B6
Weston-on-Trent. 114 C2
Weston Patrick. . 33 A5
Weston Rhyn. . . 110 B1
Weston-Sub-Edge 80 C4
Weston-super-Mare. . . . 42 C2
Weston Turville . 66 B4
Weston under Lizard. 112 D2
Weston under Penyard . . . 62 A2
Weston under Wetherley . . . 81 A6
Weston Underwood
Derbys 113 A6
M Keynes 83 B5
Westonzoyland . 28 B3
West Orchard . . 30 D2
West Overton . . 45 C5
Westow. 149 A6
West Park 168 B2
West Parley . . . 17 B4
West Peckham . 36 A4
West Pelton . . . 179 D4
West Pennard . . 29 B5
West Pentire . . . 4 A2
West Perry 84 A3
Westport Argyll . 190 C2
Som 28 D3
West Putford. . . 25 D4
West Quantoxhead . . . 27 A6
West Rainton . . 167 A6
West Rasen . . . 133 A5
West Raynham . 119 C5
West Retford. . . 132 A1
Westrigg 208 D2
West Rounton . 158 A3
West Row. 102 D2
West Rudham . 119 C5
West Runton . . 120 A3
Westruther . . . 197 B5
Westry 101 B5
West Saltoun . . 210 D1
West Sandwick . 284 E6
West Scrafton . . 157 C4
West Sleekburn . 179 A4
West Somerton . 121 D6
West Stafford . . 16 C1
West Stockwith . 141 D5
West Stoke . . . 20 B1
West Stonesdale . . 156 A2
West Stoughton . 28 A4
West Stour . . . 30 C1
West Stourmouth 53 C4
West Stow . . . 103 D4
West Stowell . . 45 C5
West Strathan . 277 B6
West Stratton . . 32 A4
West Street . . . 37 A7
West Tanfield . 157 D6
West Taphouse . . 5 A6
West Tarbert . . 202 B3
West Thirston . 189 D4
West Thorney . . 19 A6
West Thurrock . 50 B2
West Tilbury . . 50 B3
West Tisted . . . 33 C5
West Tofts Norf . 103 B4
Perth 219 A6
West Torrington . 133 A6
West Town Hants . 19 B6
N Som 42 C3
West Tytherley . 32 C1
West Tytherton . 44 B3
Westville 114 A3
West Walton . . 118 D1
West Walton Highway. . . . 118 D1
Westward. . . . 175 D5
Westward Ho! . . 25 C5
Westwell Kent . . 38 A1

Westwell continued
Oxon. 64 C3
Westwell Leacon . 38 A1
West Wellow 32 D1
West Wemyss . . . 209 A6
Westwick Cambs . . 85 A6
Durham 166 D3
Norf 121 C4
West Wick 42 C2
West Wickham
Cambs 86 C2
London 49 C6
West Williamston . . 55 D6
West Willoughby . 116 A2
West Winch. . . . 118 D3
West Winterslow . 31 B6
West Wittering. . . 19 B6
West Witton . . . 157 C4
Westwood Devon. . 13 B5
Wilts. 44 D2
West Woodburn 177 A6
West Woodhay . . 46 C1
West Woodlands . 30 A1
Westwoodside . .141 D5
West Worldham . . 33 B6
West Worlington . 26 D2
West Worthing . . 21 B4
West Wratting . . 86 B2
West Wycombe . 66 D4
West Wylam . . 178 C3
West Yell 284 E6
Wetheral 176 D2
Wetherby 148 C3
Wetherden. . . . 87 A6
Wetheringsett. . 88 A2
Wethersfield . . 86 D3
Wethersta . . . 284 G5
Wetherup Street . 88 A2
Wetley Rocks . . 112 A3
Wettenhall . . . 127 C6
Wetton 129 D6
Wetwang 150 B2
Wetwood 111 B6
Wexcombe 45 D6
Wexham Street. . 48 A2
Weybourne . . . 120 A3
Weybread. . . . 104 C3
Weybridge. . . . 48 C3
Weycroft 14 B3
Weydale 280 B3
Weyhill 32 A2
Weymouth 15 D6
Whaddon Bucks. . 83 D5
Cambs 85 C5
Glos 63 B4
Wilts. 31 C5
Whale 164 C3
Whaley 131 B5
Whaley Bridge . 129 A5
Whaley Thorns . 131 B5
Whaligoe 281 D5
Whalley 146 D1
Whalton 178 A3
Wham 146 A1
Whaplode . . . 117 C6
Whaplode Drove 117 C6
Whaplode St Catherine . . 117 C6
Wharfe 146 A1
Wharles 144 D4
Wharncliffe Side 139 D5
Wharram le Street 150 A1
Wharton 127 C6
Wharton Green . 127 C6
Whashton. . . . 157 A5
Whatcombe . . . 16 A2
Whatcote 81 C6
Whatfield 87 C6
Whatley Som . . 14 A3
Som 30 A1
Whatlington . . 23 A5
Whatstandwell . 130 D3
Whatton 115 B5
Whauphill . . . 171 C6
Whaw 156 A4
Wheatacre . . . 105 B6
Wheatcroft . . . 130 D3

Wheathampstead. 68 B1
Wheathill 95 C4
Wheatley Devon. . 13 B4
Hants 33 A6
Oxon. 65 C6
S Yorks. 140 C3
W Yorks 138 A3
Wheatley Hill . . 167 B6
Wheaton Aston. . 112 D2
Wheddon Cross . . 27 B4
Wheedlemont . . 255 D5
Wheelerstreet. . . 34 B2
Wheelock. . . . 128 D2
Wheelock Heath . . 128 D2
Wheelton 137 A5
Wheen 232 A1
Wheldrake . . . 149 C5
Whelford 64 D2
Whelpley Hill . . 67 C5
Whempstead. . . 68 A3
Whenby 149 A5
Whepstead . . . 87 B4
Wherstead . . . 88 C2
Wherwell 32 A2
Wheston 129 B6
Whetsted 37 B4
Whetstone . . . 98 B2
Whicham . . . 153 B2
Whichford . . . 81 D6
Whickham . . . 179 C4
Whiddon Down. . 12 B1
Whigstreet. . . 232 D2
Whilton 82 A3
Whimble 11 A4
Whim Farm . . 195 A7
Whimple. . . . 13 B5
Whimpwell Green 121 C5
Whinburgh . . . 103 A6
Whinnieliggate. 173 C5
Whinnyfold . . 257 C5
Whippingham . . 18 B4
Whipsnade. . . . 67 B6
Whipton 13 B4
Whirlow 130 A3
Whisby 133 C4
Whissendine . . 115 D6
Whissonsett . . 119 C6
Whistlefield
Argyll 215 C4
Argyll 215 C5
Whistley Green . . 47 B5
Whiston Mers. . 136 D3
Northants. . . . 83 A5
Staffs 112 A4
Staffs 112 D2
S Yorks 131 A4
Whitbeck . . . 153 B2
Whitbourne . . 79 B5
Whitburn T&W. . 179 C6
W Loth 208 D2
Whitburn
Colliery 179 C6
Whitby Ches W. . 126 B3
N Yorks. . . . 169 D6
Whitbyheath . . 126 B3
Whitchurch Bath. . 43 C5
Bucks 66 A3
Cardiff 41 C6
Devon. 11 D5
Hants 32 A3
Hereford . . . 62 B1
Oxon. 47 B4
Pembs 54 B3
Shrops 111 A4
Whitchurch Canonicorum . 14 B3
Whitchurch Hill . 47 B4
Whitcombe . . . 15 C7
Whitcott Keysett . 93 C6
Whiteacen . . . 254 B3
Whiteacre Heath . 97 B5
Whitebridge . . 240 A2
Whitebrook . . . 62 C1
Whiteburn . . . 197 B4
Whitecairn . . . 171 B4
Whitecairns . . 245 A6
Whitecastle . . 195 B5
Whitechapel . . 145 C5
Whitecleat . . 283 G6
White Coppice . 137 B5

Whitecraig 209 C6
Whitecroft 62 C2
Whitecross Corn . . 9 D5
Falk 208 C2
Staffs 112 C2
Whiteface . . . 264 B3
Whitefarland . 202 D3
Whitefaulds . . 192 E2
Whitefield
Gtr Man 137 C7
Perth 219 A6
Whiteford . . . 256 D2
Whitegate . . . 127 C6
Whitehall
Blackburn . . . 137 A5
W Sus. 35 D4
Whitehall Village . . 282 E7
Whitehaven . . 162 C2
Whitehill 33 B6
Whitehills
Aberds 268 C1
S Lanark. . . . 205 C6
Whitehough . . 129 A5
Whitehouse
Aberds 244 A3
Argyll 202 B3
Whiteinch . . . 205 B5
Whitekirk . . . 210 B2
White Lackington 15 B7
White Ladies Aston 80 B2
Whitelaw . . . 205 D6
Whiteleas . . . 179 C5
Whiteley Bank . . 19 C4
Whiteley Green . 129 B4
Whiteley Village. . 48 C3
White Lund . . 144 A4
Whitemans Green 35 D6
White Mill . . . 58 C1
Whitemire . . . 253 A5
Whitemoor . . . 5 B4
Whitemore . . 128 C3
Whitenap . . . 32 C2
White Ness . . 285 J5
White Notley . . 70 B1
Whiteoak Green . 64 B4
Whiteparish . . . 31 C5
White Pit . . . 134 B3
White Post . . 131 D6
Whiterashes . 256 D3
White Rocks . . 61 A6
White Roding . 69 B5
Whiterow . . . 281 D5
Whiteshill. . . 63 C4
Whiteside
Northumb. . . 177 C5
W Loth 208 D2
Whitesmith . . 22 A3
Whitestaunton . 28 D2
Whitestone Devon. 12 B3
Devon. 25 A5
Warks. 97 C6
Whitestones . 268 D3
Whitestreet Green 87 D5
Whitewall Corner 159 D6
White Waltham . 47 B6
Whiteway Glos. . 63 B5
Glos 63 D4
Whitewell Aberds 269 C4
Lancs 145 C6
Whitewell Bottom 138 A1
Whiteworks . . 11 D7
Whitfield Kent . 39 A5
Northants. . . 82 D3
Northumb. . 177 D5
S Glos. 62 D2
Whitford Devon . . 14 B1
Flint 125 B6
Whitgift . . . 141 A6
Whitgreave . . 112 C2
Whithorn . . . 171 C6
Whiting Bay. . 191 C6
Whitkirk . . . 148 D2
Whitland . . . 56 A1
Whitletts . . . 192 C3
Whitley N Yorks . . 140 A3

Whitley continued
Reading 47 B5
Wilts. 44 C2
Whitley Bay . . .179 B5
Whitley Chapel .178 D1
Whitley Lower. . .139 B5
Whitley Row . . . 36 A2
Whitlock's End . .96 D4
Whitminster 62 C3
Whitmore. 112 A2
Whitnage 27 D5
Whitnash 81 A6
Whitney-on-Wye 77 C6
Whitrigg Cumb. . .163 A5
Cumb 175 C5
Whitsbury 31 D5
Whitsome. 198 A2
Whitson 42 A2
Whitstable 52 C3
Whitstone 10 B3
Whittingham . . .188 B3
Whittingslow. . . .94 C2
Whittington Glos. . 63 A6
Lancs 155 D5
Norf 102 B3
Shrops 110 B2
Staffs. 95 C6
Staffs. 97 A4
Worcs. 80 B1
Whittlebury 82 C3
Whittle-le-
Woods 137 A4
Whittlesey 101 B4
Whittlesford . . .85 C6
Whittlestone
Head 137 B6
Whitton Borders. .187 A6
N Lincs. 141 A7
Northumb. . . .188 C3
Powys. 77 A6
Shrops. 94 D3
Stockton. . . .167 C6
Suff. 88 C2
Whittonditch. . . .45 B6
Whittonstall. . . .178 D2
Whitway. 46 D2
Whitwell Derbys. .131 B5
Herts. 68 A1
IoW. 18 D4
N Yorks. 157 B6
Rutland. 99 A6
Whitwell-on-the-
Hill 149 A6
Whitwell Street .120 C3
Whitwick. 114 D2
Whitwood. 140 A2
Whitworth. 138 B1
Whixall. 111 B4
Whixley. 148 B3
Whoberley. . . .97 D6
Whorlton
Durham 166 D4
N Yorks. 158 A3
Whygate. 177 B5
Whyle. 78 A3
Whyteleafe 35 A6
Wibdon. 62 D1
Wibsey. 147 D5
Wibtoft. 98 C1
Wichenford. . . .79 A5
Wichling. 37 A7
Wick Bmouth. . . .17 B5
Devon. 13 A6
Highld. 281 C5
S Glos. 43 B6
Shetland. 285 K6
V Glam. 40 D4
Wilts. 31 C5
Worcs. 80 C2
W Sus. 20 B3
Wicken Cambs . .102 D1
Northants. 83 D4
Wicken Bonhunt .85 D6
Wickenby. 133 A5
Wicken Green
Village. 119 B5
Wickersley. . . .140 D2
Wickford. 70 D1
Wickham Hants . .33 D4
W Berks. 46 B1
Wickham
Bishops 70 B2

Wickhambreux. . .53 D4
Wickhambrook. . .86 B3
Wickhamford 80 C2
Wickham Market. 88 B4
Wickhampton . . .105 A5
Wickham St Paul 87 D4
Wickham Skeith. . 88 A1
Wickham Street
Suff. 86 B3
Suff. 88 A1
Wick Hill. 47 C5
Wicklewood 104 A1
Wickmere 120 B3
Wick St
Lawrence. . . .42 C2
Wickwar. 43 A6
Widdington. . . .86 D1
Widdrington. . . .189 D5
Widdrington
Station. 189 D5
Widecombe in the
Moor. 12 D2
Widegates 6 B1
Widemouth Bay . .10 A3
Wide Open. 179 B4
Widewall. 283 H5
Widford Essex . . .69 C6
Herts. 68 B4
Widham 45 A4
Widmer End 66 D4
Widmerpool 115 C4
Widnes. 127 A5
Wigan. 137 C4
Wiggaton 13 B6
Wiggenhall St
Germans. 118 D2
Wiggenhall St Mary
Magdalen. . . .118 D2
Wiggenhall St Mary
the Virgin. . . .118 D2
Wigginton Herts . .67 B5
Oxon. 81 D6
Staffs. 97 A5
York. 149 B4
Wigglesworth . . .146 B2
Wiggonby. 175 C5
Wiggonholt 20 A3
Wighill. 148 C3
Wighton. 119 B6
Wigley. 45 D5
Wigmore Hereford 78 A2
Medway. 51 C5
Wigsley. 132 B3
Wigsthorpe 100 C2
Wigston. 98 B3
Wigthorpe. . . .131 A5
Wigtoft. 117 B5
Wigton. 175 D5
Wigtown. 171 B6
Wigtwizzle. . . .139 D5
Wike. 148 C2
Wike Well End . .141 B4
Wilbarston. . . .99 C5
Wilberfoss. . . .149 B6
Wilberlee. 138 B3
Wilburton. . . .101 D6
Wilby Norf. 103 C6
Northants. 83 A5
Suff. 104 D3
Wilcot. 45 C5
Wilcott. 110 D2
Wilcrick. 42 A3
Wilday Green . . .130 B3
Wildboarclough 129 C4
Wilden Bedford. . .84 B2
Worcs. 95 D6
Wildhern. 46 D1
Wildhill. 68 C2
Wildmoor. 96 D2
Wildsworth. . . .141 D6
Wilford. 114 B3
Wilkesley. 111 A5
Wilkhaven. . . .265 B5
Wilkieston. . . .208 D4
Willaston Ches E .128 D1
Ches W. 126 B3
Willen. 83 C5
Willenhall W Mid .96 B2
W Mid. 97 D6
Willerby E Yorks. .150 D3
N Yorks. 160 D4

Willersey 80 D4
Willersley. 77 C7
Willesborough . . .38 A2
Willesborough
Lees. 38 A2
Willesden. 49 A5
Willett. 27 B6
Willey Shrops 95 B4
Warks. 98 C1
Willey Green 34 A2
Williamscott 82 C1
Willian. 84 D4
Willingale. 69 C5
Willingdon. 22 B3
Willingham 101 D6
Willingham by
Stow. 132 A3
Willington Bedford 84 C3
Derbys. 113 C6
Durham. 167 B4
T&W. 179 C5
Warks. 81 D5
Willington
Corner. 127 C5
Willisham Tye . . . 87 B6
Willitoft. 149 D6
Williton. 27 A5
Willoughbridge .111 A6
Willoughby Lincs 135 B4
Warks. 82 A2
Willoughby-on-the-
Wolds. 115 C4
Willoughby
Waterleys 98 B2
Willoughton 142 D1
Willows Grn. 69 B7
Willsbridge. 43 B5
Willsworthy 11 C6
Wilmcote. 81 B4
Wilmington Devon 14 B2
E Sus. 22 B3
Kent. 50 B2
Wilminstone 11 D5
Wilmslow. 128 A3
Wilnecote. 97 A5
Wilpshire. 145 D6
Wilsden. 147 D4
Wilsford Lincs . . .116 A3
Wilts. 31 B5
Wilts. 45 D5
Wilsill. 147 A5
Wilsley Pound. . . .37 C5
Wilsom. 33 B6
Wilson. 114 C2
Wilsontown. . . .195 A4
Wilstead. 84 C2
Wilsthorpe. . . .116 D3
Wilstone. 67 B5
Wilton Borders. . .186 B3
Cumb. 162 C3
N Yorks. 160 C2
Redcar. 168 D3
Wilts. 31 B4
Wilts. 45 C6
Wimbish. 86 D1
Wimbish Green. . .86 D2
Wimblebury 112 D4
Wimbledon 49 B5
Wimblington . . .101 B6
Wimborne
Minster. 17 B4
Wimborne St
Giles. 31 D4
Wimbotsham. . . .102 A2
Wimpson. 32 D2
Wimpstone. . . .81 C5
Wincanton. 29 C7
Wincham. 128 B1
Winchburgh. . . .208 C3
Winchcombe. . . .63 A6
Winchelsea. . . .23 A7
Winchelsea
Beach. 23 A7
Winchester. . . .32 C3
Winchet Hill. 37 B5
Winchfield. 47 D5
Winchmore Hill
Bucks. 67 D5
London. 68 D3
Wincle. 129 C4
Wincobank. . . .140 D1
Windermere 154 B3

Winderton. 81 C6
Windhill. 252 B1
Windhouse. . . .284 D6
Windlehurst 129 A4
Windlesham 48 C2
Windley. 113 A7
Windmill Hill
E Sus. 22 A4
Som. 28 D3
Windrush. 64 B2
Windsor N Lincs . .141 B5
Windsor. 48 B2
Windsoredge 63 C4
Windygates. . . .220 D3
Windyknowe . . .208 D2
Windywalls 197 C6
Wineham. 35 D5
Winestead. 143 A4
Winewall. 146 C3
Winfarthing. . . .104 C2
Winford IoW. 19 C4
N Som. 43 C4
Winforton. 77 C6
Winfrith
Newburgh. 16 C2
Wing Bucks. 66 A4
Rutland. 99 A5
Wingate. 168 B2
Wingates
Gtr Man. 137 C5
Northumb. . . .189 D4
Wingerworth. . . .130 C3
Wingfield C Beds. .67 A5
Suff. 104 D3
Wilts. 44 D2
Wingham 53 D4
Wingmore. 38 A3
Wingrave. 66 B4
Winkburn. 132 D2
Winkfield. 48 B1
Winkfield Row . . .48 B1
Winkhill. 129 D5
Winklebury 47 D4
Winkleigh. 12 A1
Winksley. 157 D6
Winkton. 17 B5
Winlaton. 178 C3
Winless. 281 C5
Winmarleigh. . . .145 C4
Winnal. 78 D2
Winnall. 32 C3
Winnersh. 47 B5
Winscales. 162 B3
Winscombe. . . .42 D3
Winsford Ches W 127 C6
Som. 27 B4
Winsham. 14 A3
Winshill. 113 C6
Winskill. 164 B3
Winslade. 33 A5
Winsley. 44 C2
Winslow. 66 A3
Winson. 64 C1
Winson Grn. 96 C3
Winsor. 32 D2
Winster Cumb. . .154 B3
Derbys. 130 C2
Winston Durham .166 D4
Suff. 88 A2
Winstone. 63 C5
Winston Green. . .88 A2
Winswell. 25 D5
Winterborne
Bassett. 45 B5
Winterborne
Clenston. 16 A2
Winterborne
Herringston . . .15 C6
Winterborne
Houghton 16 A2
Winterborne
Kingston. 16 B2
Winterborne
Monkton
Dorset. 15 C6
Wilts. 45 B5
Winterborne
Stickland. 16 A2
Winterborne
Whitechurch . .16 A2
Winterborne
Zelston. 16 B2

Winterbourne
S Glos. 43 A5
W Berks. 46 B2
Winterbourne
Abbas. 15 B6
Winterbourne
Dauntsey. 31 B5
Winterbourne
Down. 43 B5
Winterbourne
Earls. 31 B5
Winterbourne
Gunner. 31 B5
Winterbourne
Steepleton . . .15 C6
Winterbourne
Stoke. 31 A4
Winterburn. . . .146 B3
Winter Gardens . .51 A4
Winteringham . . .142 A1
Winterley. 128 D2
Wintersett. . . .140 B1
Wintershill. 32 D4
Winterton. 142 B1
Winterton-on-
Sea. 121 D6
Winthorpe Lincs .135 C5
Notts. 132 D3
Winton Bmouth. . .17 B4
Cumb. 165 D5
N Yorks. 158 B3
Wintringham . . .160 D2
Winwick Cambs . .100 C3
Northants. 98 D3
Warr. 137 D5
Wirksworth. . . .130 D2
Wirksworth
Moor. 130 D3
Wirswall. 111 A4
Wisbech. 101 A6
Wisbech St
Mary. 101 A6
Wisborough
Green. 34 D3
Wiseton. 132 A2
Wishaw N Lanark 194 A2
Warks. 97 B4
Wisley. 34 A3
Wispington. . . .134 B2
Wissenden. 37 B7
Wissett. 105 D4
Wistanstow. . . .94 C2
Wistanswick 111 C5
Wistaston. 128 D1
Wistaston
Green. 128 D1
Wiston Pembs. . . .55 C6
S Lanark. 195 C4
W Sus. 21 A4
Wistow Cambs . .101 C4
N Yorks. 149 D4
Wiswell. 146 D1
Witcham. 101 C6
Witchampton 16 A3
Witchford. 101 D7
Witham. 70 B2
Witham Friary. . .30 A1
Witham on the
Hill 116 D3
Withcall. 134 A2
Withdean. 21 B6
Witherenden Hill 36 D4
Witheridge. 26 D3
Witherley. 97 B6
Withern. 135 A4
Withernsea. . . .143 A5
Withernwick 151 C4
Withersdale
Street. 104 C3
Withersfield. . . .86 C2
Witherslack. . . .154 C3
Withiel. 5 A4
Withiel Florey. . . .27 B4
Withington Glos . .63 B6
Gtr Man. 138 D1
Hereford. 78 C3
Shrops. 111 D4
Staffs. 112 B4
Withington
Green. 128 B3
Withleigh. 27 D4
Withnell. 137 A5

Withybrook. . . .98 C1
Withycombe 27 A5
Withycombe
Raleigh. 13 C5
Withyham. 36 C2
Withypool. 26 B3
Witley. 34 C2
Witnesham. . . .88 B2
Witney. 65 B4
Wittering. 100 A2
Wittersham. . . .37 D6
Witton Angus . . .232 A3
Worcs. 80 A1
Witton Bridge. . .121 B5
Witton Gilbert. . .167 A5
Witton-le-Wear 166 B4
Witton Park. . . .167 B4
Wiveliscombe . . .27 C5
Wivelrod. 33 B5
Wivelsfield. . . .35 D6
Wivelsfield
Green. 35 D6
Wivenhoe. 71 A4
Wivenhoe Cross . .71 A4
Wiveton. 120 A2
Wix. 71 A5
Wixford. 80 B3
Wixhill. 111 C4
Wixoe. 86 C3
Woburn. 83 D6
Woburn Sands . .83 D6
Wokefield Park. . .47 C4
Woking. 34 A3
Wokingham. . . .47 C6
Wolborough 12 D3
Woldingham 35 A6
Wold Newton
E Yorks. 160 D4
NE Lincs. 143 D4
Wolfclyde. 195 C5
Wolferton. 118 C3
Wolfhill. 219 A6
Wolf's Castle. . . .55 B5
Wolfsdale. 55 B5
Woll. 186 A3
Wollaston
Northants. 83 A6
Shrops. 110 D2
Wollaton. 114 B3
Wollerton. 111 B5
Wollescote. 96 C2
Wolsingham 166 B3
Wolstanton 112 A2
Wolston. 97 D7
Wolvercote. . . .65 C5
Wolverhampton . 96 B2
Wolverley Shrops 110 B3
Worcs. 95 D6
Wolverton Hants . .46 D3
M Keynes. 83 C5
Warks. 81 A5
Wolverton
Common. 46 D3
Wolvesnewton. . .61 D6
Wolvey. 98 C1
Wolviston. 168 C2
Wombleton. . . .159 C5
Wombourne. . . .95 B6
Wombwell. . . .140 C1
Womenswold . . .53 D4
Womersley. 140 B3
Wonastow. 61 B6
Wonersh. 34 B3
Wonson. 12 C1
Wonston. 32 B3
Wooburn. 48 A2
Wooburn Green . .48 A2
Woodacott. 11 A4
Woodale. 156 D4
Woodbank. . . .190 D2
Woodbastwick .121 D5
Woodbeck. 132 B2
Woodborough
Notts. 115 A4
Wilts. 45 D5
Woodbridge
Dorset. 29 D7
Suff. 88 C3
Woodbury. 13 C5

Woodbury
 Salterton........13 C5
Woodchester 63 C4
Woodchurch Kent. 38 B1
 Mers..........126 A2
Woodcombe 27 A4
Woodcote 47 A4
Woodcott......46 D2
Woodcroft......62 D1
Woodcutts......30 D3
Wood Dalling ..120 C2
Woodditton....86 B2
Woodeaton 65 B6
Woodend Cumb .153 A2
 Northants.......82 C3
 W Sus..........19 A7
Wood End Herts ..68 A3
 Warks..........96 D4
 Warks..........97 B5
Wood Enderby ..134 C2
Woodend Green. 82 C3
Woodfalls......31 C5
Woodfield Oxon...65 A6
 S Ayrs.........192 C3
Wood Field 35 A4
Woodford Corn ..24 D3
 Devon...........8 B1
 Glos...........62 D2
 Gtr Man.......128 A3
 London.........68 D4
 Northants.......99 D6
Woodford Bridge 68 D4
Woodford Halse. 82 B2
Woodgate Norf ..120 D2
 W Mid..........96 C2
 Worcs..........80 A2
 W Sus..........20 B2
Woodgreen......31 D5
Wood Green 68 D3
Woodhall Herts ..68 B2
 Invclyd.......204 A3
 N Yorks.......156 B3
Woodhall Spa ..134 C1
Woodham......48 C3
Woodham
 Ferrers........70 D1
Woodham
 Mortimer....70 D2
Woodham Walter 70 C2
Woodhaven....220 B4
Wood Hayes 96 A2
Woodhead....256 C2
Woodhey......137 B6
Woodhill.......95 C5
Woodhorn....179 A4
Woodhouse
 Leics.........114 D2
 N Lincs.......141 C5
 S Yorks.......131 A4
 W Yorks......140 A1
 W Yorks......148 D1
Woodhouse
 Eaves.........114 D3
Woodhouselee..209 D5
Woodhouselees 175 A6
Woodhouse
 Park.........128 A3
Woodhouses...113 D5
Woodhurst....101 D5
Woodingdean....21 B6
Woodkirk......139 A5
Woodland Devon....8 A1
 Durham.......166 C3
Woodlands
 Aberds.......245 C4
 Dorset.........17 A4
 Hants..........32 D2
 Highld.......264 D1
 N Yorks.......148 B2
 S Yorks.......140 C3
Woodlands Park. 47 B6
Woodlands St
 Mary.........46 B1
Woodlane......113 C5
Wood Lanes....129 A4
Woodleigh......7 C6
Woodlesford...139 A6

Woodley Gtr Man 138 D2
Wokingham......47 B5
Woodmancote
 Glos...........62 D3
 Glos...........63 A5
 Glos...........63 C6
 W Sus..........19 A6
 W Sus..........21 A5
Woodmancott....33 A4
Woodmansey...150 D3
Woodmansterne. 35 A5
Woodminton....31 C4
Woodnesborough
...............53 D5
Woodnewton ...100 B2
Wood Norton ...120 C2
Woodplumpton .145 D5
Woodrising 103 A5
Woodseaves
 Shrops........111 B5
 Staffs.........112 C1
Woodsend 45 B6
Woodsetts....131 A5
Woodsford.....16 B1
Wood's Green ..36 C4
Woodside
 Aberdeen.....245 B6
 Aberds.......257 B5
 Brack..........48 B2
 Fife..........220 D4
 Hants..........18 B2
 Herts..........68 C2
 Perth........220 A2
Woodside of
 Arbeadie.....245 C4
Woodstock Oxon..65 B5
 Pembs.........55 B6
Wood Street
 Norf.........121 C5
 Sur............34 A2
Woodthorpe
 Derbys.......131 B4
 Leics.........114 D3
 York.........149 C4
Woodton......104 B3
Woodtown Devon .25 C5
 Devon.........25 C5
Woodvale......136 B2
Woodville......113 D7
Wood Walton ..100 C4
Woodyates......31 D4
Woofferton 78 A3
Wookey.........29 A5
Wookey Hole....29 A5
Wool..........16 C2
Woolacombe....25 A5
Woolage Green..39 A4
Woolaston......62 D1
Woolavington...28 A3
Woolbeding....34 D1
Wooldale......139 C4
Wooler.........188 A2
Woolfardis-
 worthy
 Devon.........12 A3
 Devon.........24 C4
Woolfords
 Cottages.....195 A5
Woolhampton...46 C3
Woolhope......79 D4
Woolhope
 Cockshoot....79 D4
Woolland......16 A1
Woollaton......25 D5
Woolley Bath 43 C6
 Cambs........100 D3
 Corn...........24 D3
 Derbys.......130 C3
 W Yorks......139 C6
Woolmere Green 80 A2
Woolmer Green..68 B2
Woolpit........87 A5
Woolscott......82 A1
Woolsington...178 C3
Woolstanwood..128 D1
Woolstaston....94 B2
Woolsthorpe
 Lincs.........115 B6
 Lincs.........116 C2

Woolston Devon....7 C6
 Shrops.........94 C2
 Shrops........110 C2
 Soton..........32 D3
 Warr.........127 A6
Woolstone
 M Keynes......83 D5
 Oxon..........45 A6
Woolton......127 A4
Woolton Hill....46 C2
Woolverstone...88 D2
Woolverton....44 D1
Woolwich......50 B1
Woolwich Ferry .50 B1
Woonton........78 B1
Wooperton 188 A3
Woore.........111 A6
Wootten Green..104 D3
Wootton Bedford ..84 C2
 Hants..........17 B6
 Hereford.......78 B1
 Kent...........39 A4
 N Lincs.......142 B2
 Northants......83 B4
 Oxon..........65 B5
 Oxon..........65 C5
 Shrops.........94 D2
 Shrops........110 C2
 Staffs........112 C2
 Staffs........113 A5
Wootton Bassett. 45 A4
Wootton Bridge. 18 B4
Wootton
 Common.....18 B4
Wootton
 Courtenay ...27 A4
Wootton
 Fitzpaine....14 B3
Wootton Rivers. 45 C5
Wootton St
 Lawrence....46 D3
Wootton Wawen. 81 A4
Worcester 79 B6
Worcester Park .49 C5
Wordsley......96 C1
Worfield.......95 B5
Work..........282 F5
Workington....162 B2
Worksop......131 B5
Worlaby......142 B2
World's End.....46 B2
Worle..........42 C2
Worleston....127 D6
Worlingham....105 C5
Worlington....102 D2
Worlingworth...88 A3
Wormald Green.148 A2
Wormbridge....78 D2
Wormegay.....118 D3
Wormelow Tump 78 D2
Wormhill.......129 B6
Wormingford....87 D5
Worminghall....66 C2
Wormington....80 D3
Worminster....29 A5
Wormit........220 B3
Wormleighton..82 B1
Wormley Herts...68 C3
 Sur............34 C2
Wormley West
 End..........68 C3
Wormshill......37 A6
Wormsley......78 C2
Worplesdon....34 A2
Worrall.......139 D6
Worsbrough...139 C6
Worsbrough
 Common.....139 C6
Worsley......137 C6
Worstead......121 C5
Worsthorne....146 D2
Worston......146 C1
Worswell.......7 C4
Worth Kent.....53 D5
 W Sus..........35 C6
Wortham......104 D1
Worthen.......94 A1
Worthenbury...110 A3
Worthing Norf ..120 D1
 W Sus..........21 B4

Worthington....114 C2
Worth Matravers. 16 D3
Worting........47 D4
Wortley S Yorks .139 D6
 W Yorks......147 D6
Worton N Yorks .156 B3
 Wilts..........44 D3
Wortwell......104 C3
Wotherton......93 A6
Wotter..........7 A4
Wotton........35 B4
Wotton-under-
 Edge.........62 D3
Wotton
 Underwood.....66 B2
Woughton on the
 Green.........83 D5
Wouldham......51 C4
Wrabness......88 D2
Wrafton........25 B5
Wragby Lincs ..133 B6
 W Yorks......140 B2
Wragholme....143 D5
Wramplingham.104 A2
Wrangbrook...140 B2
Wrangham....256 C1
Wrangle......135 D4
Wrangle Bank..135 D4
Wrangle
 Lowgate.....135 D4
Wrangway......27 D6
Wrantage......28 C3
Wrawby.......142 C2
Wraxall Dorset ..15 A5
 N Som.........42 B3
 Som...........29 B6
Wray.........145 A6
Wraysbury.....48 B3
Wrayton......155 D5
Wrea Green....144 D3
Wreay Cumb ...164 C2
 Cumb.........164 C2
Wrecclesham ...34 B1
Wrekenton....179 D4
Wrelton......159 C6
Wrenbury.....111 A4
Wrench Green..160 C3
Wreningham...104 B2
Wrentham....105 C5
Wrenthorpe...139 A6
Wrentnall......94 A2
Wressle E Yorks..149 D6
 N Lincs.......142 C1
Wrestlingworth..85 C4
Wretham......103 C5
Wretton......102 B2
Wrexham
 (Wrecsam)....126 D3
Wrexham Industrial
 Estate.......110 A2
Wribbenhall....95 D5
Wrightington
 Bar..........136 B4
Wrinehill......111 A6
Wrington......42 C3
Writhlington....43 D6
Writtle.........69 C6
Wrockwardine .111 D5
Wroot........141 C5
Wrotham......36 A4
Wrotham Heath. 36 A4
Wroughton.....45 A5
Wroxall IoW....19 D4
 Warks..........97 D5
Wroxeter......94 A3
Wroxham......121 D5
Wroxton.......81 C7
Wyaston......113 A5
Wyberton......117 A6
Wyboston......84 B3
Wybunbury....111 A6
Wychbold......80 A2
Wych Cross....36 C2
Wyck..........33 B6
Wyck Rissington .64 A2
Wycoller......146 D3
Wycomb......115 C5
Wycombe Marsh .66 D4
Wyddial.......85 D5
Wye..........38 A2

Wyesham........61 B7
Wyfordby......115 D5
Wyke Dorset 30 C1
 Shrops.........95 A4
 Sur............34 A2
 W Yorks......139 A4
Wykeham
 N Yorks.......159 D7
 N Yorks.......160 C3
Wyken..........97 C6
Wyke Regis.....15 B5
Wykey........110 C2
Wylam........178 C3
Wylde Green....96 B4
Wyllie.........41 B6
Wylye..........31 B4
Wymering......19 A5
Wymeswold....115 C4
Wymington.....83 A6
Wymondham
 Leics.........115 D6
 Norf.........104 A2
Wyndham......40 B4
Wynford Eagle ..15 B5
Wyng.........283 H4
Wynyard Village 168 C2
Wyre Piddle.....80 C2
Wysall........115 C4
Wythall........96 D3
Wytham........65 C5
Wythburn.....163 C6
Wythenshawe..128 A3
Wythop Mill...163 B4
Wyton........101 D4
Wyverstone....87 A6
Wyverstone
 Street.........87 A6
Wyville.......116 C1
Wyvis Lodge...263 C6

Y

Yaddlethorpe...141 C6
Yafford.........18 C3
Yafforth......158 B2
Yalding........37 A4
Yanworth......63 B6
Yapham......149 B6
Yapton.........20 B2
Yarburgh.....143 D5
Yarcombe......14 A2
Yard...........27 B5
Yardley........96 C4
Yardley Gobion.. 83 C4
Yardley Hastings. 83 B5
Yardro.........76 B6
Yarkhill.......79 C4
Yarlet........112 C3
Yarlington.....29 C6
Yarlside......153 D3
Yarm.........168 D2
Yarmouth......18 C2
Yarnbrook......44 D2
Yarnfield.....112 B2
Yarnscombe....25 C6
Yarnton.......65 B5
Yarpole........78 A2
Yarrow......196 D2
Yarrow Feus...196 D2
Yarsop.........78 C2
Yarwell......100 B2
Yate...........43 A6
Yateley........47 C6
Yatesbury.....45 B4
Yattendon.....46 B3
Yatton Hereford ..78 A2
 N Som.........42 C3
Yatton Keynell ..44 B2
Yaverland......19 C5
Yaxham.......120 D2
Yaxley Cambs ..100 B3
 Suff.........104 D2
Yazor..........78 C2
Yeading........48 A4
Yeadon.......147 C6

Yealmpton......7 B4
Yearby.......168 C4
Yearsley......159 D4
Yeaton........110 D3
Yeaveley......113 A5
Yedingham....160 D2
Yeldon.........84 A2
Yelford........65 C4
Yelland........25 B5
Yelling.........85 A4
Yelvertoft......98 D2
Yelverton Devon...7 A4
 Norf.........104 A3
Yenston.........29 C7
Yeoford........12 B2
Yeolmbridge....10 C4
Yeo Mill.......26 C3
Yeovil.........29 D5
Yeovil Marsh...29 D5
Yeovilton......29 C5
Yerbeston......55 D6
Yesnaby......282 F3
Yetlington....188 C3
Yetminster.....29 D5
Yettington.....13 C5
Yetts o'
 Muckhart.....219 D5
Y Felinheli....123 D5
Y Ffôr........106 C3
Y-Ffrith......125 A5
Yieldshields...194 A3
Yiewsley.......48 A3
Ynysboeth.....41 B5
Ynysddu.......41 B6
Ynysgyfflog....90 A4
Ynyshir........41 B5
Ynyslas........90 C4
Ynys-meudwy...59 E4
Ynystawe......40 A1
Ynysybwl......41 B5
Yockenthwaite.156 D3
Yockleton.....110 D2
Yokefleet......141 A6
Yoker........205 B5
Yonder Bognie .255 B6
York.........149 B4
Yorkletts......52 C2
Yorkley........62 C2
York Town.....47 C6
Yorton........111 C4
Youlgreave....130 C2
Youlstone......24 D3
Youlthorpe....149 B6
Youlton.......148 A3
Young's End....70 B1
Young Wood ..133 B6
Yoxall........113 D5
Yoxford........89 A4
Ysbyty-Cynfyn ..75 A6
Ysbyty Ifan...108 A3
Ysbyty Ystwyth..75 A6
Ysceifiog.....125 B6
Yspitty........57 C5
Ystalyfera......59 E4
Ystrad.........41 B4
Ystrad Aeron...75 C4
Ystradfellte.....59 D5
Ystradffin......76 C1
Ystradgynlais...59 D4
Ystradmeurig...75 B6
Ystrad-mynach. 41 B6
Ystradowen
 Carms.........59 D4
 V Glam.........41 D5
Ystumtuen......75 A6
Ythanbank....257 C4
Ythanwells....256 C1
Ythsie........256 C3

Z

Zeal
 Monachorum..12 A2
Zeals..........30 B1
Zelah...........4 B3
Zennor.........2 B2